Bump to baby and beyond

The complete guide from conception to pregnancy and beyond

(a comprehensive parenting guide).

By

Sarah Owen

Part 2 of 2

Content page	
General tips thoughts, observations and comments for life with a baby.	91
Tips to help develop your baby's brain	139
Activities to do with children	149
Through the eyes of a child	163
Terrific toddlers and beyond	165
Pregnant with your second child and toddler in tow	167
Parental Guidance	171
Returning to work and Childcare	197
Education and School	221
Other	227
Dealing with bad behaviour	249
Tips and tools	261
Your baby journal	439
Appendices	451

Bathing Baby;

You don't need to bath your baby every day but you should wash their face, neck, hands and bottom carefully every day. This is often called 'topping and tailing'. It is particularly important to wash their under arms and groin area, especially to get any build up of the Vernix (the protective skin greace) which builds up on their skin and gets in all the creases (especially where their skin is wrinkly). Always wash the face first (top) and then the tail. Or use separate water and bowls for top and tail (you can buy special bowls with a top and tail section although this isn't necessary).

Your babies umbilical cord will fall off in about one or two weeks after they are born (4-12 days). It will dry out and drop off. It will become smelly as it gets gangrene, it will smell more just before it drops off. Keep it dry and roll back the top of the nappy (and tape down if necessary) to get the air to it. Let it drop off naturally (don't pull it off). Until it falls off you should only give your baby sponge baths. If your baby is circumcised, you need to wait until this has healed, as well. Newborns only need to be bathed 2 or 3 times a week (otherwise it will dry their skin). You don't need to clean out the umbilical cord; it will probably look pussy as it naturally clears out and dries up. If you do want to clean it you should use water that has been boiled and then cooled to clean if you think there is an infection (they used to recommend that you clean it with surgical spirit but they don't recommend that you do this now). Clean underneath it, and keep it dry.

You should usually leave it 2 weeks before bathing baby, even if the umbilical cord heals earlier. The reason for this is that when the baby is born s/he is born covered in a greasy coating to protect his/her skin. Therefore if you leave it 2 weeks this coating can sink in and stop the skin drying out, where as if you wash off this protective layer you are more likely for your baby to get skin complaints. Also your baby gets used to smells and bathing too early washes away their familiar smells. Furthermore bathing too early cools baby. When they are first born their body can't control their temperature. As it is very warm in the womb they need to stay warm when they are first born, so they don't get a shock from coming out of a warm environment into a cool one. This is why the labour wards in the hospital are very warm. After 2-3 days, or when you take baby home they don't need it so warm (and you have to be careful that they don't overheat).

The first 48 hours the baby has to be warm s/he has come out of a womb which is warm and can't regulate his/her temperature so needs to be kept warm. In the hospital they will put lots of blankets on baby (its worth double checking but most hospitals supply the blankets), they may also ask you to put a hat on baby. When you get baby home you won't need to keep baby so warm and won't need hat in doors. After about 5 days, if it is particularly warm you may just want to have baby in vest (as you don't want baby to overheat).

When your baby is born s/he inhales and is covered in mucus like liquid, this is why you may need to use a nose aspirator. You will also find that the mucus like liquid gets into baby's eyes. Therefore for the first few days and maybe longer your baby will have sticky gooey eyes (similar to when an adult gets conjunctivitis). Therefore the eyes will need to be cleaned every day. Obviously if the eyes are still sticky after any length of time you need to get the eyes checked out by a doctor.

To wash your baby's eyes get some cotton wool and a bowl of water, slightly dampen the cotton wool and the gently wipe the eye from the inside out (this is better than wiping from the outside in as it takes things out of the eye and stops dirt getting in). Never use the same water that has been used to clean other areas of the baby then on the eyes (especially if you have just cleaned baby's bottom). This is why you could have a top and tail bowl, or you could just start with cleaning the eyes and face and then work around the body, cleaning the bottom area last because poo and traces of poo have bacteria that cause infections so you don't want to be using anything that has wiped the bottom area on any other parts of babies body (to stop infections spreading).

Your newborn baby will be very wrinkly so you gently need to clean inside the wrinkles and also around the genitals (and with a boy gently pull the foreskin back and clean that area). Once you have cleaned the area with damp cotton wool you then need to dry it with dry cotton wool. It is important to dry babies skin as you don't want the skin staying damp, especially not in-between the creases as this may then cause a fungal infection. Traditionally you would then put talc powder on to draw out any excess water, and stop skin rubbing, but it is not recommended now as it can be harmful to baby if inhaled. Instead you can get liquid talc. This goes on as a liquid but soaks up excess moisture as powdered talc would, without the risk of it being inhaled. It is particularly good to put this in the skins creases, as this is where moisture can hold and your baby may develop sore patches (also under the neck and arms). I found as my son got to 6 months and got his baby had that he got chaffing in the creases in his legs and his nappy also rubbed where it hung down (when he was between 2 sizes), nappy rash cream, particularly sudocream helped to heal the sores and liquid talc also helped to prevent it. He also got a sore under his willy from where the nappy was wet, sudocream cleared this up in 2 days.

You should do a top and tail wash of the baby every day and bath baby every 3-4 days or once a week (bathing baby more often may dry skin out), although you may want to bath baby if baby does a messy poo. Although when baby gets older you may want to bath baby as part of the bed time routine, in order to relax baby before bed.

When you start bathing baby it is also important to wash baby's eyes and face first. This is because baby's don't like water being splashed in their face so you need to wash their face before you put them in the bath and then avoid splashing their face with water once they are in the bath. It also stops anything from their skin going into the eyes.

At first baby may not like bath time, but baby will soon come to love bath time. Babies normally like water but don't like excessive splashing or water being splashed in their face.

Cuddle and caress your baby to make baby feel secure. If you don't mind cooler water in your bath you can get in the bath and bath with your baby. Although think about how you will get in and out of bath safely whilst holding baby.

Just plain water and cotton wool is best for new born babies (baby products such as shampoo can be used after 6 weeks). Remember talc powder shouldn't be used (apparently this can cause asthma).

Bathing helps to establish a good bed time routine. Don't bath young babies just before or after a feed. If you try bathing a baby and s/he is hungry this will make the baby cry and if you bath baby after a feed baby maybe sick (you should avoid moving baby too much after s/he has just been fed). Bath baby and then feed him/her.

For newborns you may want to use a baby bath and baby seat. Never leave babies or small children near water unattended, not even for a second. Babies like to be immersed in water i.e. up to their chest, never fully immerse them or put their head under the water (if they are ½ in and ½ out they may feel cold and so baby may cry if you use a bath seat).

Don't run the bath with the baby in it and as baby gets old enough to touch things you may want to wrap a towel around the taps to cover them and avoid baby touching them, although as you will be with baby at all times whilst s/he is in the bath this may not be necessary.

Don't bath your baby straight after a feed or when a feed is due. If baby is hungry or unwell s/he may scream when you bath him/her.

Make sure water isn't too cold and babies tummy is covered to help baby feel warm and secure and not cry in bath.

When your baby becomes a toddler and is playing in mud and dirt you may want to bath every few days, or even every day. You can make bathing part of the bed time routine, to clean and settle your baby before bed. You can use bubble bath with lavender and/or baby lotion with lavender to help settle and calm your toddler before bed (most brands have a soothing bed time range with lavender in). You can use coconut oil on your babies hair, to condition and get rid of cradle cap.

To bath your baby;

Ensure that you have everything you need with you in the bathroom at arms reach.

Fill your baby bath ½ way full (the water should be 36/37 degrees). If you don't have a baby bath and are putting baby straight into the bath you will waste more water and it may be harder to reach in, you may therefore want to use a sink or washing up bowl if you haven't got a bath.

Wash the baby's eyes and face first, with water and cotton wool. Always wash each eye with a separate piece of cotton wool and dry afterwards (wipe the eye from the inside out so you are washing dirt out of and not into the eye). If baby has sticky eye (which is common due to the mucus getting in the eyes, also babies don't have tear ducts), you can use breast milk in the eye or cool water which has been boiled and then cooled. Sticky eye is common and should clear up with no need to worry but if it is bad get it checked by the doctor. Always wash your hands after cleaning baby's eyes and don't wipe your eyes as you don't want to catch an eye infection.

Then wash baby's ears and neck, don't forget to wash behind their ears. Wash your baby's hands regularly as they touch things and then put their hands in their mouth. You may want to leave baby's nappy on whilst you wash baby and then take nappy off, at the last minute just before putting baby in the bath.

Lower your baby into the bath, with your arm underneath baby support babies head. With the same arm hold the baby securely (ideally with your hand around the fleshy part of the top of his/her arm). With the other hand hold babies legs whilst you lower him/her into the bath. Slowly lower baby into the bath, perhaps in a sitting position with feet first (if baby finds the bath a shock).and then once in, use that hand to gently wash/ splash water onto baby and wash (avoiding splashing the face).

Wash the baby from the head and work down. Use a cup or cup your hands to pour water over the back of baby's head to wash baby's hair. You can use a small amount of shampoo, be careful of the soft spot on baby's head.

Thoroughly wash the neck, ears, buttocks and groin area and any crease (if not circumcised boys will need their foreskin pulling back and washing).

Dry your baby well and wrap up and cuddle (ensure that baby doesn't get too cold whilst being dried).

If babies skin is dry you can put pure virgin oil on your baby.

Don't bath after feed (leave it approx. 1 hour) so that baby isn't sick, but not when due a feed as baby will be hungry and grumpy.

Give 2-3 baths a week.

It is a good idea to cut babies nails after a bath as they will be softer.

When bathing and changing nappies on a girl always clean front to back to avoid germs from faeces entering the vagina or uretha. Keep clear of the vagina and never clean inside the lips of the vulva.

With a boy hold his penis up to clean underneath and wipe the testicles, never pull the foreskin back. Rememeber boys wee when you lift the nappy off so hold it over the penis for a few seconds after removing the nappy. Sometimes they get a stiffy, don't be alarmed this is normal, or it may mean he is about to do a wee (over you if you are nearby), in my experience.

N.B. Be careful of your back. You can get change stations that have a bath built in but you still have to empty the water out. You could use a jug to empty some of the water out so it isn't as heavy.

Dummies; It is personal preference if you want to give your baby a dummy or not. New evidence now shows that settling your baby to sleep with a dummy, even for naps, can reduce the risk of cot death. However if you want to breast feed your baby and give your baby a dummy before breast feeding is well established it can make it harder to breast feed because the baby gets used to sucking on a dummy and therefore will try and suck your nipple instead of your breast. However there are some situations in which babies are given dummies by medical professionals when breastfeeding has not been established:

As a general comforter for babies it may be helpful to provide a dummy when they are receiving procedures or when on ventilators.

It can also help to develop oromotor (mouth muscle) skills and bowel mobility in premature babies so they learn to suck

For babies receiving a certain kind of ventilation called CPAP a dummy helps to keep their mouths closed and hence to maintain upper airway pressures.

You may also find when you are breastfeeding that baby may use your breast for comfort, rather than just feeding. In this situation a dummy may also be beneficial.   It can also be argued that babies that don't have a dummy will put their fingers/thumb in mouth which some people believe may misshape their teeth, although babies with a dummy may also suck their thumbs later on and then you also have the added stress of removing the dummy from them. Also baby may cry at night if it falls out so you may have to get up more.

Therefore there is no right or wrong, it depends on you and your baby's circumstances if you want to use a dummy or not.

If you do decide to use a dummy, here are some do's and don'ts;

- Don't use a dummy every time baby cries, to shut baby up.
- Don't give baby an unsterilized dummy
- dummies are good to help babies suck and to calm them before nap times but shouldn't be over used.
- Don't worry if the dummy falls out while your baby is asleep, and don't force your baby to take a dummy if he or she doesn't want it.
- Never coat the dummy in anything sweet.

- Always have spare dummies, sterilise them and keep them in a sterile pot when out and about (or a sandwich bag). Some dummies come with caps.
- It is a good idea to get an orthopaedic approved dummy.
- Some dummies have caps to keep them sterile (if not you need a pot for them, or sandwich bag).
- You may want to buy an additional microwave steriliser if using dummies, this is because if your steriliser is full of bottles you may need to quickly sterilise some dummies.
- You may find it useful to use a dummy that is the same brand as your bottles so the teat matches, or even find one that is your breast shape.
- Avoid using a dummy too much, especially in the day when baby is trying to speak to you, as this may affect their speech development.
- Dummies must be orthapedoc - orthapedic dummies can stop babies teeth being mis shaped which they would be if they sucked their thumb or fingers (although your baby may suck his/her thumb and fingers).
- Dummies - ones with own cap are good because they are more hygenic.

- Don't suck your baby's dummy as this is also unhygienic, instead use steralising wipes.

- Take dummy away if keep waking for it.
- Let cry & will get used to it.
- May get stressed only take 1 thing ie dummy away at a time
- Dummies stop baby being able to self sooth

Even if you haven't decided if you want to use dummies or not it may be worth buying some before the baby comes. That way you can see how it goes, follow your instinct and if you feel that you need it, it will be there.

I found using the tommee tippee closer to nature dummy helped my baby latch on.

Dummies;

It is important to use the right size dummy for the right age.
Bigger dummies - next size up may stay in your baby's mouth but if stay in all night nay give a rash, you can get airflow dummies to reduce this. Different brands are different shapes and you can get glow in the dark or just put glow in the dark stickers on.
Be careful that baby can't take the dummy out and turn it around and put the whole thing in their mouth. My son did this with the mothercare glow in the dark dummy.

Weaning off dummy - If a toddler cut it down gradually then just uses it at sleep time, you can then gradually wean them off it. But in order to keep your baby off the dummy you will have to keep your child preoccupied, distract him/her with toys etc. Then say dummy fariy needs all dummies find them all and get your child to help tie them to a tree. The next morning have a glitter sprinkled on the ground and a present and thank you letter from fairy to your child.

After you have started weaning your baby off the dummy, don't go back and give into your child by giving them a dummy again.

It's ok for baby to have dummy for sleep until first birthday but shouldn't have dummy during active time after 9 months as it may stop speech development. Substitute with a comforter or teddy to help with the transition.

Comforter; It is common for babies and young children to have comforters, that help them sleep etc. When choosing items to give to baby that they may adopt as a comforter. Ensure that you have two identical ones (in case one gets lost), also ensure that it is something that is safe for baby to sleep with, preferably made from breathable material in case they put it over their face. It should also be reasonably small and should be something washable.

Nappies and changing your baby's nappy;

Changing baby's nappy; The first nappy is not nice known as Meconium. It is the earliest stools of an infant. Unlike later faeces, meconium is composed of materials ingested during the time the infant spends in the uterus: intestinal epithelial cells, lanugo, mucus, amniotic fluid, bile, and water and can be particularly unpleasant. Bottle fed and breast fed poo is different, nappies on breast fed babies aren't as smelly.

A newborn will have 6-9 wet nappies in a 24 hour period. It is important to keep a record of the amount of wet nappies, to ensure that your baby is going enough and is not dehydrated (you may want to keep a log of nappy changes, what is in the nappy and the colour). Urine should be a pale yellow to clear colour (if it is dark baby may have a urine infection). It is hard with disposable nappies to see the colour of the urine, therefore put a tissue in the nappy; this will make it easier to tell if the nappy is wet and what colour the urine is.

Nappy rash – change the nappy more often, clean babies skin with lots of water, dry and also leave a nappy off for the air to get to it. Barrier cream can offer some protection.

Change nappies at feed time and also in between if it is dirty, sitting in a dirty nappy will result in a sore bum.

It is recommended that you should change your baby right before or right after every feeding, after every bowel movement, before bedtime, when he wakes up, and before you go out.

Although some mums day don't change the nappy before the feed, only when needed (it is a waste changing the nappy before the feed because the baby will usually dirty the nappy after the feed), although the hospital recommends you change the nappy first so that the baby is more comfortable, baby is also alert for the feed and because baby may fall asleep after feed.

It is really up to you what routines you adopt and when you think it is appropriate to change the nappy, you may decide that you will only change the baby's nappy if it has dirtied it. Although it is important to note that with modern nappies being so advanced you may not notice if baby has wet the nappy and the ammonia in the urine irritates baby's skin, therefore regular nappy changes will help to avoid this.

I used to change my baby after feeds because he would often fall sleep ½ way through feeds (ehn I stoped to wind him), a nappy change would wake him up so sometimes I would hange the nappy ½ way through a feed.

Although if lay flat on change mat after eating it will make baby sick.

Another point to mention is that boys wee as soon as you remove their nappy as air hits their winkle so be prepared for this and on standby with the next nappy. Willy tipi - pee pee tepee

As you remove the dirty nappy, loosely hold it over baby and he should wee straight into this, then you can put the nappy back on. With boys you also need to tuck their willy down, otherwise they will wee up all over themselves.

Get organised, have everything layed out already and don't leave baby on changing table.

Don't forget to give baby some free time without a nappy on; to allow the air to circulate and reduce the chance of nappy rash, it also lets them kick around freely. Lay a towel or some plastic down (or loosely lay a towel over baby), especially boys who are likely to wee everywhere, (you may even be able to time when it is best to have no nappy time i.e. after baby has just weed and isn't due a feed). You may want to do this for up to an hour a day (depending on your schedule etc.).

Have a basket with all nappy equipment in, inc. kitchen roll.

When changing nappy;

Clean as much of the faeces off with the soiled nappy and roll down
Lift legs and put fingers between ankles, so that ankles don't rub together and bruise.

If baby gets stressed i.e. cries when changing just pick baby up, give a little cuddle to soothe and calm then try again and carry on, it usually works, they may be upset or uncomfortable and need comfort.

When bathing and changing nappies on a girl always clean front to back to avoid germs from faeces entering the vagina or uretha. Keep clear of the vagina and never clean inside the lips of the vulva.

With a boy hold his penis up to clean underneath and wipe the testicles, never pull the foreskin back. Rememeber boys wee when you lift the nappy off so hold it over the penis for a few seconds after removing the nappy.

Some babies have an allergic reaction to certain nappies (hence it may be best to buy a trial pack of nappies first). The reaction shouldn't be confused with nappy rash, nappy rash is normally localised where as an allergic reaction will show all over the skin where the nappy touches.

If the ash stays for more than a week and is very bright red with a scaly edge, s/he may have a fungal infection.

Change on knee; If your baby rolls around a lot you may want to change your baby on your lap, it is more hygienic than laying your baby on some change stations when you are out and it stops your baby rolling away. You could also give your baby a toy to stop rolling him/her moving away, or put your hand on their chest. You may still want to use a mat, or blanket, when changing baby on your lap so that you stay clean.

Nappy rash;

Nappy rash is where the skin becomes inflamed after being in contact with urine and stools in a nappy. It can vary from a slight reddening of the skin, a shinny patch or scaly skin, to fiery red spotty skin, which may be infected. It is sore and uncomfortable for your baby.

It is caused by urine, nappies rubbing against the skin and washing detergents not washed out (terry nappies), some babies skin may also be more sensitive than others.

Triggers can be – weaning, change of milk, diarrhoea (this could occur following immunisation), teething, antibiotics.

To avoid nappy rash;

- If using terry or re-usable nappies, wash in mild non-biological detergent.
- Follow a good skin care and hygiene routine for your baby; change nappies regularly, keep baby clean and treat sore skin with an emollient cream (one that has been specially formulated for nappy rash), also prevention is better than cure so put on a cream to also act as a barrier and protect the skin.
- Avoid tight fitting plastic waterproof covers (towelling nappies).
- Lay baby on a towel, remove nappy and allow air to circulate for a while each day.
- Change baby's nappy regularly
- Wash baby's skin with water only
- Dry thoroughly, including in creases
- Let baby have time without nappy on to get air around that area.
- If bottom becomes red and sore, cover with barrier cream, when changing until the rash clears up.

Often babies hate being changed; when changing baby focus on baby, maintain a steady dialogue and change baby as quickly as possible (it is uncomfortable for them being pulled about). You may also want to place your hand, or a small soft toy on babies chest when they are naked, this helps to stop baby feeling too exposed and vulnerable. In the first 3 or 4 weeks have baby grows that snap at the bottom and are easy to change in the night.

Baby's also don't like the cold of the changing mat, so put a muslin cloth on the changing mat first (this stops the baby getting cold and crying).

Nappies come in different sizes, unlike clothes the exact size is crucial, it does matter if the nappy is slightly too big it will leak and if it's too small it will be uncomfortable and restrictive for baby. If you get newborn nappies this maybe no good if you have a big baby, or if you have a little baby you will need smaller nappies. Make sure you have enough of each size. Some brands offer trial packs, which are a great way of checking the size. Supermarket's own branded nappies maybe cheaper than other brands.

Every baby is unique and it is important that you find the system that is right for you. Most nappies can be mixed and matched so it is not essential to stick to the same brand.

There are claims that eco nappies are far less likely to irritate skin, cause nappy rash or an allergic reaction, as there are no unnecessary deodorants, dyes, lotions, antioxidants or nasty chemicals. Changing a nappy as soon as it is soiled also helps to prevent nappy rash, the main cause of which is the mixture of wee & poo.

Types of nappies;

- Reusable
- Disposable
- Disposable – organic/biodegradable

Some parents use reusable nappies and disposable nappies in a mixed system. For instance they may use re-usable nappies at home and disposable ones when out and about. If you plan to use a mixture of disposable nappies and washable nappies you will need about 8-10 washable nappies and 2-3 covers. i.e. when out disposable and re-usable at home.

Check your reusable nappies are pre-washed before first use as this makes them fluffed up and ready for action. Check you have the right size nappy and cover and that the cover is covering all of the nappy and is fitting snuggly around the legs. Add booster liners - some parents add two booster liners or a muslin nappy liner at night times for extra absorbency. Note, leakage will happen from time to time, especially in the newborn phase, even in disposables.

Some biodegradable/organic nappies can be used in a compost pot. As they have fewer chemicals in they are supposed to be better for baby. However they do also work out a lot more expensive. Re-usable nappies are supposed to be cheapest, are better for the environment and kind for baby, however they require a lot of messing about and are time consuming. By the time you have also taken into account washing costs it is not always worth it, which is why most people use normal disposable nappies. Everyone has different ideas and you just need to use the system that works for you.

It is worth bearing in mind that if you are using re-usable nappies there are companies that offer a nappy laundry service. They provide a nappy bin for the soiled nappies and they collect this once a week and deliver clean washed nappies.

Changing babies (disposable) nappy;

1. Undo your baby's clothes and pull them up so they don't get soiled.
   Un-stick the tabs of the nappy and fold them back on themselves (so they don't stick to your baby).
   Keeping the nappy in place, use the front of it to wipe away any poo. If your baby's a boy, cover his penis with a cloth to keep it clean (and avoid getting weed on). Or keep the soiled nappy placed over the willy, and slide the clean nappy underneath so that it can go straight on.
2. You may want to do this whilst laying your baby flat on the change mat.
3. Take your baby's ankles in one hand and lift their bottom off the table, then fold the nappy in half underneath them. It's a good idea to keep it there just in case there is more to come! Clean your baby's bottom and front with a baby wipe or wet cotton wool ball. If your baby's a girl, wipe from front to back - away from her vagina - to avoid infection.
4. Once you have cleaned the baby and removed the soiled nappy apply a barrier cream
5. Take the dirty nappy away and if you haven't already done so, slide a clean one underneath. The back of the nappy goes under your baby's bum, and the front goes between their legs. The nappy goes with the wider part at the back and the picture at the front.
6. Fasten the sticky tabs at the sides, ensure tabs are tucked in so they don't rub and nappy doesn't become loose.
7. The nappy should be tight enough that it doesn't move but not too tight that it is restrictive for baby.
8. Stick the tabs of the old nappy back together again to keep it closed, and put it in a nappy bag and then in the bin.
9. Dress your baby and wash your hands (the baby's vest and sleep suit has longer piece at the back). You may find it easier to put baby's arms and then legs in the baby grow first, and then do all the poppers up.

Put a barrier cream on (such as sudocream) every time you change babies nappy. It doesn't matter if it is not completely rubbed into the skin it is just good to stop urine etc. getting into babies skin and causing nappy rash. You may want to use a fresh spoon or applicator to get cream out of the tub to keep it sterile (rather than keep putting your hands in the cream and getting germs in the pot).

For the first 6 weeks you should use cotton wool and not wipes. This is because baby's skin is sensitive and the wipes have chemicals in, which may sting the skin. However you can get wipes which are just water based. If wipes or water used is too cold it may make baby cry.

As baby gets older and slightly chubbier check that the leg creases are clean. Sometimes they get sweat caught in the creases in their legs, the skin chafe's or the nappys rub where they hang down (especially if your baby is in between sizes), you need to keep this area clean and apply cream where necessary.

- Roll dirty nappy down as you wipe baby
- Hold babies legs up but not too tightly
- Put your fingers between their ankles so that they are not held together and brusing.

When baby older and moving…
- Don't leave on a high surface (even when new born they can still roll)
- Put nappies in bags before putting in the bin, it stops the bin smelling

As your baby gets older and moves around more it will be harder to change him/her with them laying flat. You can instead lay you baby over your knees, put a fresh nappy under their dirty one, take the dirty one off and wipe the bum clean.

Changing your baby on your lap is more hygienic then laying them on a change station when you are out. The change station maybe dirty and they roll of your change mat. Also it saves you bending soen and hurting your back, or getting saggy knees in your trousers etc.

Constipation; how often should poo; It is normal for baby's to cry and grimace when they poo. Exclusively breast fed babies are rarely constipated. Formula fed babies sometimes become constipated. If stools are hard you may need to give baby cooled oiled water. If stools suddenly change colour and smell different from normal and baby seems unwell, consult your doctor or health visitor. Give baby a warm bath and a tummy rub to soothe baby, you can also knead their bum, or give them some water to drink, all of these things help to ease constipation.

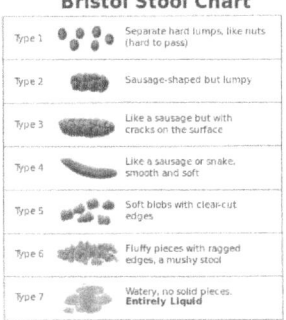

The Bristol stool scale or Bristol stool chart is a medical aid designed to classify the form of human faeces into seven categories. Sometimes referred to in the UK as the "Meyers scale",[1] it was developed by Dr. Ken Heaton at the University of Bristol and was first published in the *Scandinavian Journal of Gastroenterology* in 1997.[2] The authors of that paper concluded that the form of the stool is a useful surrogate measure of colon transit time. That conclusion has since been challenged as having limited validity, and only in types 1 and 2 when the subject is not constipated.[3] However, it remains in use as a research tool to evaluate the effectiveness of treatments for various diseases of the bowel, as well as a clinical communication aid.

The seven types of stool are:

- Type 1: Separate hard lumps, like nuts (hard to pass)
- Type 2: Sausage-shaped, but lumpy
- Type 3: Like a sausage but with cracks on its surface
- Type 4: Like a sausage or snake, smooth and soft
- Type 5: Soft blobs with clear cut edges (passed easily)
- Type 6: Fluffy pieces with ragged edges, a mushy stool
- Type 7: Watery, no solid pieces. Entirely liquid

Types 1–2 indicate constipation, with 3 and 4 being the ideal stools (especially the latter), as they are easy to defecate while not containing any excess liquid, and 5, 6 and 7 tending towards diarrhoea.

Does your baby have wind?

Thanks to an immature digestive system, it's quite normal for babies to have wind and sometimes seem to have trouble passing it. If you're breastfeeding, you may notice a link between what you're eating and how it affects your baby. Some breastfeeding mums find their baby can be unsettled, irritable or even constipated if they drink lots of coffee, strong tea or cola, or when they eat vegetables such as cabbage, sprouts or onions. If your baby has a blocked nose it may cause wind so give nose drops before you give milk to help them breath and stop wind.

Interacting

- Put baby in car and drive around to send baby to sleep.

- Don't put things behind babies head, because baby will try and look behind him/her and it is not good for babies to strain their eyes backwards.

- Always support babies head when holding new born baby (when they are new born their necks are weak and therefore their head needs to be supported at all times).

Tickling;

Although tickling a baby gently is okay, it is not a good idea to tickle a baby too much. Babies have not fully developed their body's nervous system and because of this tickles may feel uncomfortable. Additionally a baby will feel very distressed due to the potential discomfort and they can't tell you they don't like it.

Tummy time

"Tummy time" is important so that babies can learn to push up and eventually crawl. But during waking hours, tummy time is essential from day one. Experts find that babies who don't spend time face-down often have some delays in their development of motor skills.

"The experience of being on their tummy helps babies learn to push up, roll over, sit up, crawl, and pull to a stand," explains Danette Glassy, a pediatrician in Mercer Island, Washington, and chairperson of the American Academy of Pediatrics' committee on early education and childcare.

Most babies spend much time on their back, for instance when sleeping not to mention time spent in car seats, swings, and bouncy seats so it is important to ensure that they also get time on their tummy.

Tummy time is not only an important developmental opportunity for your baby, it's a great time for you two to bond and play together. Make a point to schedule some quality tummy time into every day.

Play with baby, and lay on your tummy too.

Stay with them whilst they are on their tummy.

Some parents find that giving their baby a new perspective — by propping him on a rolled towel or nursing pillow, for example — makes all the difference.

If your child has some neck strength and head control (by age 3 or 4 months) but can't get up on his forearms, simply place the towel or pillow under his chest and armpits, with his arms in front of it. (If he tends to roll forward, keep your hand on his bottom.) When he can get up on his forearms independently, remove the pillow and let him work on his motor skills without it.
Some babies enjoy rolling on a big exercise ball. Hold him on it tummy-down while you gently rock the ball back and forth.

Make sure your baby isn't full, too hungry or tired when you try tummy time. When he gets upset, try to entertain him and see if he'll stay there a bit longer; but if he's really unhappy, pick him up and try again later. Your baby may only tolerate tummy time for a few minutes at a time until he gets used to it.

Give baby tummy time during each awake periods

At first, s/he may not like it because she is so used to her back. Lie down facing her and entertain her with your face and toys as she is getting used to it. Slowly increase the amount of time she spends in this position start with a few minutes and work up to a 10- to 15-minute stretch as she gets older. Infants who get plenty of "tummy time" avoid significant head flattening and often learn to roll, sit up and crawl sooner because of these trunk work-outs. The stronger their head is and the more they can support themselves the more tummy time they can have.

They are more likely to like tummy time once they can lift their heads; however before then they still need some tummy time, even if it's a minute each day and then you can build it up gradually each day.

Trimming nails; New borns nails are soft, especially when wet and peel off. Peel them (or chew them off) rather than cutting when new born. Babies nails maybe long, especially if baby is late. Ensure that you also have scratch mittons so that baby doesn't scratch themselves with their nails.

Nose aspirator; When baby is born it gets covered in lots of mucus that can get in baby's nose, you may need to use a nose aspirator to clean out the nose and also if baby has a cold.

Cradle cap; (infantile or neonatal seborrhoeic dermatitis, also known as *crusta lactea, milk crust, honeycomb disease*) is a yellowish, patchy, greasy, scaly and crusty skin rash that occurs on the scalp of recently born babies. It is usually not itchy, and does not bother the baby. Cradle cap most commonly begins sometime in the first 3 months. Similar symptoms in older children are more likely to be dandruff than cradle cap. The rash is often prominent around the ear, the eyebrows or the eyelids. It may appear in other locations as well, where it is called seborrhoeic dermatitis rather than cradle cap. Some countries use the term *pityriasis capitis* for cradle cap. It is extremely common, with about half of all babies affected. Most of them have a mild version of the disorder.

Cradle cap requires no specific treatment and will clear up on its own with time. However, gently washing your baby's hair and scalp may prevent a build-up of flakes. Massaging a small amount of baby oil, olive oil or petroleum jelly into the scalp at night may help soften the patchy scales. In the morning, using a soft baby brush or cloth, gently remove any loose particles, and then wash the hair with a baby shampoo. Shampoos that contain ground nut oil or peanut oil are best avoided in children under five years old. There are shampoos available over the counter at pharmacies to loosen cradle cap. Check the patient information leaflet before you use these for any ingredients your child is allergic to, and follow the instructions carefully. You should avoid getting any in your baby's eyes as these shampoos are stronger than baby shampoo. Speak to your pharmacist for advice.

If the cradle cap becomes inflamed or infected, a course of antibiotics or an antifungal cream or shampoo, such as ketoconazole, may be prescribed by a doctor. A mild steroid cream such as hydrocortisone may be recommended for an inflamed rash. If the cradle cap does not improve with treatment or your baby has signs of cradle cap on the face or body (seborrhoeic dermatitis), see your health visitor or GP for advice.

Cradle cap; try smothering coconut oil or simple vaseline all over head where cradle cap is and it will all come off quickly and naturally when gently brushed with baby brush about two hours later across a week - it should all go.
Rough towel or hairbrush for cradel cap, should be gone by 6 months, although don't worry if it isn't as some babies continue to have it after this.

Baby swim – Most babies like water, in fact babies gravitate towards water. It is a good idea to get your baby swimming as soon as possible, (once s/he has had his/her vaccines). I preferred to wait for my son to have his first 3 set of vaccines before I took him swimming although they do say that as long as the water is warm and they are only in for a max of 30mins that they don't have to have had their jabs before they can go. The sooner they learn to swim the better, swimming is a valuable life skill, it will allow them to be social and attend swim parties with other children, undertake water activities when they are older such as canoeing. If they ever fall into water and can't swim they could drown so learning to swim is also a skill that may save their lives.

Babies can swim under water because they have a mammailian diving reflex which closes the windpipe to prevent breathing in water, however after 9 months the reflex lessens so unless they know how to hold their breath under water it is not good to make them dive as it can be very dangerous.

It is a nice idea to get a water camera to take pictures of your baby when you go swimming, you can buy disposable waterproof cameras quite cheap but always check with the swimming pool if you can take photos. Some pools will take photos for you, which you can purchase.

It is a good idea to either take someone with you the first time you take your baby swimming or go and carry out a recconicance of the swimming pool first or phone up and ask if you can take your pram, if they have lifts etc. The first time I took my son swimming it was during the school holidays and was very busy (not the best time to go). I didn't think I could take the pram so I carried my son in, the family rooms were full so me and my sister went in the ladies with my nephews. My oldest nephew then decided to go in the mens on his own. We had £1 for the locker to find it took 20p of which we didn't have any. When we finally got change we had to re-open the locker to put my nephews stuff in, and lost our 20p. Then we lost my oldest nephew because he was waiting in a different place to where we said, it was a nightmare. The next time I went with my husband and it was much less stressful. We had lots of 20p for the locker. I also took an extra towel for my son so we could wrap him up and warm him ½ way through and then take him in for a bit longer again and still have a dry warm towel for afterwards. I also brought a microfibre dressing gown that folded small in my bag, I put this on and kept warm whilst I dressed my son then I got dressed. I had decided however that going alone would be very difficult (therefore swimming lessons were less appealing) because who would hold my son whilst I got dressed? I then saw other mums with their purchairs. I also found that there are special cot type things that you can put in the changing room and lay your baby on. It also became apparent that you can take your pushchair, there is then a lift to go down to the family area, you can then wheel your puchair to the side of the baby pool and see it whilst you swim. That way you can lay your stuff out in your pushchair basket as you need it. You can then dress your baby and strap them in the pushchair whilst you get dressed. Once you know what your doing the whole process, like anything else when it comes to your baby, is much simpler.

I woud suggest that before you go swimming with your baby you phone the swimming pool and check if they allow prams and if you can lock them up somewhere or take them pool side. Also check what change the locker takes etc. You may also want to check what the tempreture of the baby pool is.

Swimming check point;
- You may want to ensure your baby has their vaccines first.
- You will need a swim nappy in the correct size (and some spare swim nappies)
- You will also need normal nappies to put baby into after swimming
- Anti-bac wipes to clean the cot table before putting your baby on (you may also want to put your change mat down).
- 2 towels for baby so that you can use one to dry baby and the other to wrap around baby whilst you dress him/her. I would put my baby in for 10-15 mins and then take him out and warm him up/fry him off then we would go in for another 10-15 mins otherwise he would get cold.
- A microfibre towel with a hood to put around you whilst you dress your baby (you will need to dress your baby first and then yourself so that your baby doesn't get too cold).
- You will need warm clothes for once you get outside as you will feel cold after swimming. However it maybe warm in the pool so layers and a blanket are good.
- Snack and drink for afterwards
- An extra set of clothes (just in case)
- A wet suit – to keep baby warm so you can stay in the pool longer
- A baby seat float – that way you can push your baby around and swim in order to get some exercise.
- It is a good idea to only keep your baby in the water for 15mins at a time and a maximum of 30mins in total, when they are young.
- Change for the car park and lockers
- Pack wet wipes and nappies near the top of your bag and take your towels with you to put on the side of the pool. Take as least bags as possible and pack so you know where everything is, put everything in, in the order that you need it when you come out of the water.
- Get swim nappies in advance (stock up as they are sometimes hard to get). Most pools do sell them but you don't want to get there and find they have run out. They are also more expensive if you buy them at the pool.
- Don't put the swim nappy on until you get there and take a few spares, in case your baby messes it.

- Have the exact change to pay, to save time at the till.
- Take change for the hair dryer
- Encourage your baby to move around, splash about etc. to keep warm and try and keep his/her body submerged in the water, otherwise s/he will get cold.
- Once s/he has got used to the water, try and get him/her to mimick swimming moves so that s/he will be able to start learning to swim, but most of all make it fun so that s/he enjoys the water.
- After swimming always ensure that your baby's ears are completely dry and always bring a hat to pull over the ears. Bring a towel to poolside too as temperatures may vary slightly, as you transfer to the changing areas.
- Don't let go of baby on the change station in case s/he rolls off.
- Swimming tires baby/child out so they may want to sleep afterwards.
- Wear a high swimming costume so that your baby cant pull it down.
- Hold baby on your chest and walk into deep water with baby the first time you take him/her. If the baby is held tight against you s/he will feel more secure.
- Wet suit/dry suit – baby can stay in water longer (with a dry suit you could put a normal nappy underneath), with a wet suit you will need a swim nappy.
- Keep your swimming bag packed – Once you come home wash the towels etc. and put them in your swim bag and stock up the nappies etc.
- Keep a plastic bag in your swim bag for the wet costumes and towels etc.
- **keep eye contact with your baby, keep looking at them and smiling to reassure them. Swimming is fun, it also helps them to develop and strengthen their muscles, it stimulates their heart and lungs and helps to improve their co-ordination.**
- Move around when swimming and keep your baby moving, to keep warm.
- Take change for the hair dryer
- They need a snack and drink after swimming (using up the energy swimming in the water will make them hungry and thirsty).
- Wrap them up warmly and let them sleep after swimming (once they have had a snack and drink will probably sleep as swimming makes them tired).
- Take a toy for them to play with whilst you are getting dressed.
- If you are taking your baby swimming before s/he is 12 weeks or 12lb, the water must be at least 30-32 degrees, any cooler will be too cold.
- Take your pram in the pool area with you. When you go to change your baby put a towel in the pram and change your baby in it.
- You can go in the water for 10 minutes, then take your baby out and wrap in a towel and hold next to you to warm with your body heat, then go back in the pool for a while (that way you can go swimming for longer without just staying in the pool and getting cold). You can also get wet suits to keep your baby/toddler warm.
- Foam swim disks are better than traditional arm bands for swimming because they save blowing them up, as your child gets more confident you take disks away (as they get older and their arm get bigger they may become too tight).
- It is a good idea to get a poncho towel, you can then put this on them, pull their wet cozzie off from underneath and give them a snack or toy whilst you get changed and then dress them. You could take a bath toy i.e boat swimming.

Swim safety;

- **Never let go of your baby in the water, even for a second**

- **Never leave them unattended near the pool**

- **Keep their mouth and face above the water as chlorinated water is bad for them if they drink it.**

- **Don't go swimming if your baby has a cold or temperature. If s/he has a tummy bug leave it for 48 hours after last sickness/diarrhoea before going swimming.**

- **10mins in the water is plenty of time for the first few visits, after this a max of 30mins. Newborn babies need heated pools. From 6 months your baby can go in a normal pool (although some babies may get cold quicker – my son did). Wet suits are good and if outdoors a UV suit, sun hat and lots of sunscreen (sun block of at lest factor 50 is necessary).**

To have lessons or not ?

When babies are young they don't need swimming lessons, you can take them yourself to get them used to the water. However it is nice to take them to lessons. Some of the private ones are good as they do nice under water photos etc. however they are expensive and a lot of public swimming pools now offer swimming lessons for babies too at a much cheaper rate. The only thing with swimming lessons is you have to take them every week, and they may get cold etc. making it difficult where as it maybe easier to just go yourself and then give them lessons when they are old enough to take it in and learn how to swim properly.

Always have a spare swim nappy and keep a stock of the next size up in case they have a growth spurt, just when you are planning to take them swimming (they can catch you out and you don't want to be rushing out at the last minute to get swim nappies.

It is a good idea to keep a spare towel and some spare swim nappies in the back of your car. Perhaps even a small microfibre towel and swim nappy in your change bag, then if the mood takes you, you can go swimming in a splash pad when out and about etc.

Items that you need for the summer/if you are taking your baby on holiday;
- Sun hat
- Sun cream
- Pram parasol
- Uv protection swim suit / wet suit (if swimming outdoors or in a cooler pool)

If you are flying with your baby you will need some toys to distract him/her. The cabin pressure may hurt their ears, especially when landing. It maybe a good idea to give your baby some calpol just before landing to keep off any pain.

Going on holiday with your children can bring about tensions. Especially if you are not used to being together all day. If they are used to being at school or nursery they are being kept active, they may get bored they may also get tired with the change in routine and tempreture,food (maybe extra treats and sgar may make them hyper) etc. children like routine and boundries and they may need some time to adjust, you may find as a result they play up. Try no to get too frustrated and try and give them time to adjust.

Days out;

When going out, always have extra clothes (at least one spare set) and nappies, just in case. A snack and drink and toys / book for entertainment in ques.

Theme park;
When visiting a theme park it is advisable to;

- Take a water bottle, most parks have water fountains so you can top your bottle up for free. Food and drinks are expensive, you may also want to take some snacks and a picnic. Some fruit or cereal bars are good to keep your child going if you are stuck in a long que.
- You may want to take some toys, quizzes to keep the kids entertained whilst queuing for the rides.
- Take a water proof jacket / poncho. Save the water rides until last and have some dry clothes to change into. It is a good idea to wear flat shoes, layered clothes and clothes that will dry easily. You may want a light rain coat and separate jumper as the weather may change throughout the day.
- Take some change – a lot of theme parks have dryers that you can dry off in, after going on the water rides.
- If you have a pushchair take a draw string bag to leave on the pram, and a small handbag to wear, with your valuables in, which you keep on you.
- Wear a track suit, or cotton so it will dry when wet, don't wear jeans.
- If your baby is walking, take a small push chair for when they are tired (some park may also have push along cars/carts that you can rent), take baby reins.

Teething; Babies can cut their first tooth at any time, some babies are even born with a tooth but usually teething starts at around 6 months. When babies are teething they swallow more saliva, their bowels are looser and they are more susceptible to tummy upsets and nappy rash.

When your baby begins teething it will be drooling more and will constantly want to chew on things. As teething usually causes them pain they will tend to become very irritable. Tender and swollen gums can also cause their temperature to rise, but if the temperature is very high there maybe another cause so it's best to consult the doctor just to be sure. Other symptoms of teething include red gums and poor appetite.

Signs that your baby is teething, include red cheeks that may become swollen and excess dribble. Teething also causes runny poos (this is ok if the frequency is as per normal, however if they are doing poos more frequently and they are all runny then you child maybe ill so you should get him/her checked out).

As the tooth starts to break through the gum it will usually be the most painful time, they may also get tummy ache and some dihoreah.

Helios combination 21 or asthtons and pastons teething powder is good. Teething gel and calpol.

You will find that before the teeth start to break through the gum and show your baby will feel pain. This is because the pain is created when the tooth pushes through the jaw; the pain is in the jaw and not the tooth (hence why chewing helps and teething rings are effective).

Order in which teeth usually appear;

Age	Teeth	Position
6-8 months	Incisors	Two central top and two central bottom teeth.
9-12 months	More incisors	Two more top and bottom, making four top and four bottom teeth.
12-16 months	First molars	Double teeth for chewing.
16 – 20 months	Canines	The 'fang'
2 – 2 ½ years	Second molars	The second set of double teeth at the back.

Some teeth may come through staright away and others may take their time. My son got his bottom 2 teeth straight away at 3 ½ months. Then the next lot took a while to come through with lots of symptons and no signs of teeth at first. They didn't come through in the prescribed order, he had 2 bottom ones that came through with the normal symptons and then a 3rd bottom one that came through later, when this one came through he wasn't as unsettled and didn't have a rash but dribbled a lot and kept putting his finger there (it seemed to be coming through for about a month by the way he kept pulling there with his finger). When his 3rd tooth did come thorugh I could see a hole in the gum and then gum looked dark, before I could see his tooth (it looked more like an ulcer than a tooth at first), where as his first teeth (which arrived together) apperared like white lines and then the teeth were there staright away).

Teeth don't always come through in the prescribed order and they may all appear differently and cause different symptons and some maybe more painful than others. The gums may look black as the tooth is coming through, this is usually okay; it may just be where the gap is, or if there is blood on the gum, but the actual tooth shouldn't look black so if it does you may need to visit a dentist.

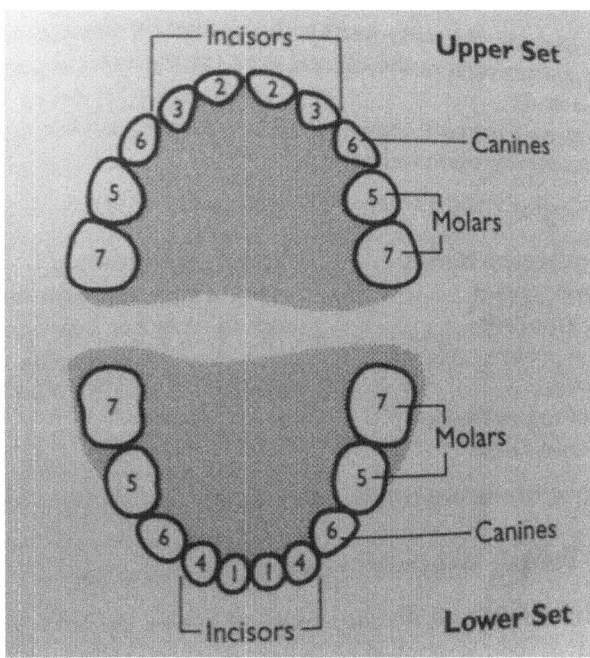

Above is a diagram of the general order that they come through in, although teeth can come through in a different order this is generally how they tend to come through.

Teeth also will come thorugh and then stop and then come through again in phases, rather than it being continuous. Therefore they might be teething and then you may not see the teeth for a while. They will be teething for a long while but will have a brake in between the phases of teething.

Some teeth hurt when they come through and some don't, apparently eye teeth hurt a lot when they come through. This is why your baby may react differently when they are teething will different teeth.

You can get teething rings that have resevoirs for the teething gel, or you can use a clean finger to massage your baby's gums. This is a more accurate way of getting the teething gel where it is needed. You may find that they will calm down and keep the dummy in longer if you put the teething gel on the dummy, although this won't target the teeth so accurately. I found that my son didn't really like his teethers but he liked turning his dummy around and chewing on the back of it instead. He also used to bite my husband when he was teething, but luckily not me. When babies are teething they do try and bite everything in sight (or anyone, so take care they don't bite other children).

You will need to practise good dental hygiene for your baby and your baby should see a dentist from age 1. Also don't let baby fall asleep with bottle in its mouth as the liquid may pool against the teeth and increase plaque. Dilute juice drinks, don't add sugar to your babies food and use a special baby toothbrush and baby toothpaste.

To help soothe babies who are teething;

- Use teething gel

- Chill a teething ring in the fridge and give it to your baby. Or if your baby is old enough give strips of cooled cucumber.

- Give a soothing drink such as cool boiled water

- You can use teething gels, teething powders and herbal remedies, aromatherpahy oils or a mixture i.e. anbesol liquid, Helios combination 21, teethers gel, calgel etc.

- Some people also believe that having amber on the baby helps.

- You can also give pain relief such as paracetmol i.e. calpol or nurefon.

- Lavender oils or tummy oils are good. Cheeky money do a teething oil you rub on babies cheeks (on the outside) and a tummy oil to soothe their tummy. I also burn lavender oil in my babies room to soothe him.

- You can also use a tummy wheat band (for babies) to soothe any tummy pain assoiscated with teething.

By 6 months old, your baby should start to show signs of teething. This is when the first teeth, known as milk teeth, start to break through the gums.

Timing can vary amongst babies with some babies showing their first tooth as early as 4 months old or as late as a year. Some babies suffer from a lot of discomfort and others have no problems. All babies are different but most children have all of their milk teeth by the time they are 2 ½ years old!

Teething Stages:

- **bottom front teeth (incisors)** - 5-7 months old
- **top front teeth (incisors)** - 6-8 months old
- **top lateral incisors** (either side of the top front teeth) - 9-11 months
- **bottom lateral incisors** (either side of the bottom front teeth) - 10-12 months
- **molars** (back teeth) - 12-16 months
- **canines** (towards the back of the mouth) - 16-20 months
- **second molars** - 20-30 months

Symptoms

- Dribbling
- Irritable
- Flushed cheeks
- Chewing on their fingers or objects to ease discomfort can be a sign too!
- Cold like symptons
- There gums may also be itchy so they bite down on everything
- They may cough when teething/sound throaty due to excess saliva/chemical reactions in their mouth. Spitting and blowing raspberries could be a sign of teething (although they often do this when they are playing games, or if they don't want any more of their food).

- They may get an upset tummy and have runnier poos, they may also get a slight rash (although most other common illnesse will also cause a rash and loose stools).

Treatment

- Biting on something hard such as a teething ring can help & it can be even more soothing if kept cool in the fridge;
- Gentle massaging of the gums with a clean finger can also help;
- Teething gel (if more than 4 months old);
- Paracetemol or Ibuprofen can help your little one feel better!
- Keep your little one's skin dry with a soft cloth following her dribbles to prevent her getting sore!

Plenty of grizzling and dribbling are a good indication that teething might be happening

Baby will also try and put things in mouth and put their fingers in their mouth when they are teething, they may even pull on the gum where the tooth is coming through. I have been able to track my son Ritchie's teeth from where he pulled at his gums.

N.B. Teeth sometimes come through in different order to the norm.

As teeth are coming through you may see a white line under the gum and feel a bump. For 2 days as it cuts through the gum it maybe at its worst but will be painful before as growing out of bone. They hurt when first cut through the gum and may bleed. Use ashton and parsosn powder, teething gel and you may need calpol.

Use calpol sparingly for the night dose, if they have a good sleep they won't be so ratty in the day. You can always give them teethers, apply more gel and distract them in the day so best to save the calpol for the night, just give 1 dose before you put them into bed.

Amber is supposed to be good for teething, not eating it but wearing it. Be careful little ones don't try and eat it, also cords and necklaces can cause strangulation.

Some teethers you can steralise. Like bottle teats, don't keep for more than 2-3 months.

Never coat tethers or dummies in anything (especially not anything sweet). Although teething gel is okay. If you put teething gel on the dummy you should swirl it around their mouth to get the gel on their gums.

There are many different types of teethers on the market. From traditional teething rings to water filled ones that can be cooled, ones with pockets for teething gel, ones that are like toys (such as the Sophie Giraffe) and ones that look like dummies. There are many different sizes, ones for different teeth as they come through etc. The key thing is to ensure that they are lightweight enough for your baby to hold themselves and not too big for their mouth. Avoid anything that's too long that they may push too far back in their mouth. You may find that with some newborn babies who may be teething early some teethers maybe too big for their mouths. Most teethers can't be steralised; you can however buy steralising wipes. It is a good idea to check if they can be put in the dishwasher. You can also pour boiling water over them (unless they say otherwise).

When teeth come through first of all the gums look bubbly and then they might look slightly white. Just before the tooth breaks through the gum you can usually see a white line underneath, this means a new tooth is imminent. Teeth come through and flair up at different times, they come through in stages and not all teeth at once. Therefore you may have some teething pain, then it will ease, then it will come back etc. it will come and go for the first few years until all the teeth are though. Then you will start all over again when the milk teeth (baby teeth) go and the adult teeth come through. Although apparently when the adult teeth come through they are not as painful as the baby teeth, cutting the first teeth are always worse.

Instead of using a teether you can also get teething biscuits such as bikki pegs, or even cold raw carrots (although you will have to keep hold of them so that they are not a choking hazard). Ice made with cooled boiled water put in feeding net is also good.

When your baby is teething they will dribble a lot and at night this will cause them to cough. When their back teeth come through they get ear ache and may pull their ear. It is a good idea to keep extra teething gel next to the cot at night.

Teething in summary;

Why teething is uncomfortable?

Teething is uncomfortable because there is a lot of movement and change in the jawbone as the teeth move into the gum. That's why you can often see signs of teething long before the pearly whites break through. This should stop as soon as the tooth appears. The molars (back teeth) can be especially uncomfortable because they are larger teeth.

Signs and symptoms of teething

The common signs and symptoms of teething that you may notice in your baby are:

- · **being bad tempered or irritable**
- · **crying more than usual**
- · **having trouble sleeping**
- · **having problems feeding, changing what they want to eat or not wanting to eat**
- · **wanting to chew on things e.g. toys, fingers, or a GUMIGEM! etc**
- · **drooling or being more dribbly than usual**
- · **having swollen gums**
- · **having red, hot cheeks**
- · **pain**

However there are a whole host of symptoms that many feel are also associated with teething:

- **Runny nose**
- **Nappy rash**
- **Diarrhoea**
- **cough**

Cool to drool! Few babies go through teething without some level of drool! Some however can be like Niagra Falls and a bib an essential to prevent changing tops every five minutes! Try and keep the chin and neck dry by using a soft dry cloth to wipe, but don't rub as their skin can be sore, some develop quite a nasty rash. It may help to use a barrier cream for particularly dribbly babies.

Teething does not make your baby ill

However it has been proven that teething doesn't make a baby unwell. The signs and symptoms that you may notice occur partly because teething begins at the same time that your baby's immune system is changing. At this time many babies will have lost most of their protective antibodies passed from their mothers. This can make them more susceptible to infections and illness until their own antibodies increase.

Health problems not likely to be caused by teething include:

- · **waking a lot at night**
- · **being restless and irritable in the daytime**
- · **infections**
- · **a temperature (fever)**

If your baby seems unwell, seek medical advice.

It's interesting that we refer to teething as 'cutting a tooth', when in fact the emergence of babies' teeth doesn't actually cut through the flesh. Instead, chemical signals between the cells in the gums cause some cells to selectively die and separate, allowing the teeth to push through.

The list of teething remedies is extensive but in my view the most effective is to take your baby's mind off the discomfort. Giving your baby lots of cuddles and playing often works. However that's not a tactic you can or want to employ in the middle of the night! You can also massage your baby's gums, using a wet finger or soothing gels and other products from the chemist: experts caution against the excessive use of teething gels as they contain benzocaine - there is a risk of allergic reaction.

Teething rings are also very effective - especially when first placed in a fridge and cooled. And generally chomping and chewing on things helps too, you'll often see them sticking a whole fist in their mouth or any other object they can find and biting down on it.

You can use natural, old-fashioned solutions, such as bagels, bread or even vegetables. There are many natural and homeopathic teething remedies you could try, but these should only be used in conjunction with expert medical advice. Homeopathic teething remedies include: Apis mellifica (meaning whole bee) - used to ease swollen gums before and after the eruption of teeth; Kreosotum can ease a child's stress when she has irritating saliva and severe discomfort during teething. Kreosotum is very beneficial if a baby's teeth succumb to decay soon after erupting from the gums; Pulsatilla is especially good for teething babies who are nervous, clingy, or tearful. There are more homeopathic teething remedies you can try. What teething remedy is best depends on you and your baby. Some babies can be distracted from the discomfort of teething, whereas some can suffer much discomfort. If one teething remedy doesn't work, then try another. If your child's discomfort is excessive you should talk to your doctor about further information and advice on baby teething.

So what causes all the pain?

It's mainly from all the pressure exerted on the gum tissue in the mouth, otherwise known as the 'Periodontal Membrane'. This membrane contains blood vessels and sensory nerve endings which stimulate pain and touch. Understandably this pressure and pushing can cause swelling of the gums. This is why a baby's first instinct when teething is to chomp and bite down on everything. This helps relieve the pressure and can assist the teeth in breaking through. While this process happens, the gums start to produce excess saliva, this is supposed to help them by lubricating the tender gums. Drooling brings with it another set of issues! Soggy tops and rashes on the chin and the neck. The best thing is to try and keep the skin as dry as possible and tops dry by using a bib!

Caring for teething toys:

- You can chill a teething toy in the fridge – but never freeze as it may damage it.
- Wash them regularly – check whether they can be sterilised or put in the dishwasher, not all can.
- If the teether gets damaged throw it away! Tears and breaks can be a hazard.

Breastfeeding & Teething;

Amazingly, breastfed babies of 6 months or more who have teeth never bite their mums if they are latched on correctly, due to the position of the tongue during feeding, so you can carry on breastfeeding.

Dental care

It's important to get your child into a good dental hygiene routine asap. You can get special baby toothpaste and even a baby toothbrush (this is like a dummy with bristles). You can use a small toothbrush and brush the gums and give the toothbrush to the baby to get babies used to toothbrush, let them chew on it etc. It is also a good idea to get a timer for toddlers when they are cleaning their teeth themselves, to ensure they are cleaning them for long enough. You can get them electric toothbrushes with different characters on, such as winnie the pooh etc. It may also be a good idea to get them a tablet to chew on, that goes pink, if there are areas they have missed. This can help them to see where they need to focus their cleaning.

Don't allow them to take bottles to sleep, apart from the fact that they may choke it is also bad for their teeth as the drink is just sitting on their teeth. Lollipops and fizzy drinks are also bad for their teeth. If their teeth are damaged at the front it is due to drinks and if they are damaged at the back it is due to foods (certain medication can also affect their teeth). Once baby is weaned if you decide to give juice only give this at meal times. This way they are getting sugar at one hit and teeth can recover in between, lots of sugar in one go is better than having sugar little and often on teeth i.e by eating sweets (because your mouth isn't getting time to break down the sugar). Your body can only cope with 3 sugar attacks a day. Juice should be watered down to at least 10 parts water to 1 part juice. Encourage your child to eat savoury foods and not sugar.

As soon as baby has teeth use a toothpaste mint flavour is best. There is no need to rinse the toothpaste away and it doest matter if they swallow some. Use a toothpaste for babies it should have a max of 1,000 ppm.

Brushing new baby teeth

- Brush milk teeth as soon as they start to show;
- Clean your baby's teeth twice daily with a toothpaste containing fluoride. Initially this can be done using a bit of gauze on a clean finger;
- As more teeth appear, a toothbrush specifically for babies should be used;
- The first Dental check-up can start from around six months of age or from when the first milk teeth start to show
- You only need a tiny amount of fluoride toothpaste when your child is a baby & a toothpaste with a fluoride level of at least 1,000 parts per million is suitable for babies and children up to three years old.

- Teething

- Cutting teeth isn't one of those milestones a baby reaches all at once. Transitioning from that gummy grin to a mouthful of gleaming teeth is a rite of passage that can take your little one three years to complete. Whenever the first tooth peeks through, celebrate it by taking pictures and noting its arrival date in your child's baby book.

-

- By the time your little one is 3, he'll have a mouthful of choppers that he can brush himself, a basic step on the road to self care. (Because he won't have the skills to do a good job, though, be sure to lend him a hand until he's at least 6 years old.)

- When it develops

- The journey starts in the womb. While you were pregnant, your baby developed tooth buds, the foundation for baby teeth (also called milk teeth). Rarely, a baby will be born with a tooth or two or grow a tooth in the first few weeks of life. The vast majority of babies sprout their first tooth between 4 and 7 months of age.

  If your baby's an early developer, you may see her first white cap (usually one of the bottom middle teeth) as early as 3 months. If she's a late bloomer you may have to wait until she's a year old or more. The last teeth to appear (the second molars, found in the very back of the mouth on the top and bottom) usually begin coming into place by your baby's second birthday.

- **By age 3, your child should have a full set of 20 baby teeth.**

It is a good idea to visit the dentist from when the first tooth erupts but no later than first birthday (visit dentist at first birthday even if don't have a tooth) use a soft toothbrush and special baby toothpaste (the size of a rice grain), you don't want baby to swallow too much fluoride (and baby toothpaste is specially formulated to be lower fluoride), otherwise they will get fluorosis. *Enamel fluorosis* is systemic fluoride which is where fluoride is taken into the body and laid down in the tooth structure as it forms. This can cause can cause white, yellow, and brown spots of discolouration on the tooth.

It is a good idea to carry some sandwich bags to store spare dummys and teething rings in. You can also use the sandwich bags to put snacks in, or put around beakers if they leak.

If your teether can't go in the steriliser as well as using steralising wipes or boiling water you could also put them in Milton tablets or use a cold water steriliser.

Teeth cleaning;

- Your babies first 'baby teeth' will usually start to appear from 6-8 months (although some babies get their teeth much earlier, my son got his first tooth at 3 months and my friends son was born with a tooth), by 8 months my son had 8 teeth.
- By age 2-3 your baby will usually have all 20 baby teeth.
- Start brushing your baby's teeth as soon as they start coming through, brush them twice a day. You can use a baby finger toothbrush (it goes over your finger) or gauze cloth, once your baby gets to 8 months you can use a 'normal' style child's toothbrush.
- Choose a small headed toothbrush with soft bristles.
- Change the toothbrush every 3 months or sooner of it gets out of shape.
- Choose a toothpaste that is specially formulated for babies (it must contain fluoride).
- Use no more than a smear or pea sized blob (don't use too much because it is bad for children if they swallow it, therefore you also need to keep tubes of toothpaste away from your child).
- Apply toothpaste to the dry toothbrush, after brushing spit but don't rinse (you need the fluoride to carry on working). Fluoride is a mineral that strengthens tooth enamel and helps to protect teeth from decay.
- Brush your teeth in front of your children so that they can learn from watching you. Always supervise teeth brushing until at least the age of 7.
- Take your child to visit the dentist regularly.
- Brush your child's teeth by moving the brush gently backwards and forwards in small circle movements, bristles angled towards the gums. Be gentle but brush around including on the gums. You might find it easier to brush their teeth from behind, rest their head on your chest and cradle their chin in your hand, this way you can see in their mouth and reach the bottom and top teeth well.
- Make teeth cleaning part of the bed time routine and don't let them drink anything sugary after you have cleaned their teeth at night.

Types of toothbrush;
- Baby – finger toothbrush
- Child normal toothbrush (non finger) from 8 months

- Electric from 3 or 4 when can do themselves

Teething:
When babies are teething, they tend to put any new item directly into the mouth. Partly curiosity and partly an attempt at pain management, infants feel the urge to bite and chew. As the teeth are growing, the cells in the gum tissue above the teeth begin to break down, which helps the teeth slide through. The urge to bite or chew is a good thing, because the added pressure helps break down the gum tissue. Give your child something to chew on! You can find homeopathic ice pops, teething cookies, tablets and gels to help relieve your baby's teething pain. Some remedies sound exotic, using strange ingredients like whole honeybees or infinitesimally small doses of belladonna; others include the use of chamomile or pulsatilla (pasqueflower). They are all quite safe.

Other natural remedies include herbs and oils, which can alleviate pain or help your baby calm down and get to sleep. One common remedy for the pain of toothache and teething is clove oil. Cloves contain oils that have warming, numbing properties, so that even holding a whole clove against a sore tooth with your tongue can ease the pain long enough to get to your dentist. Clove oil can be rubbed on sore gums to relieve pain, but only use a tiny amount: too much can upset your baby's stomach. Other homemade remedies include letting your infant chew on a natural licorice stick (the herb, not candy!) You can find natural licorice in health food stores: real licorice feels cool and also numbs the gums when your baby chews on it. Wild fennel, a relative of licorice, grows in disturbed areas in Northern California and other parts of the country: you may be able to harvest it yourself along the bike paths. The feathery, fern-like leaves and hollow stalks can be chewed or sucked for a cooling, licorice-tasting treat.

Some parents find that rubbing a little pure vanilla extract on the baby's gums can soothe the crying child: this home remedy may work in three ways. First, merely rubbing baby's gums can ease the pain by creating opposite pressure; second, the alcohol in vanilla extract will create a warm sensation that is temporarily comforting. The third way this remedy may work is in the calming properties of vanilla itself. Vanilla is known as a soothing yet energizing agent that reduces anxiety and promotes feelings of well-being. Besides that, vanilla has long been used to cure stomach distress: a baby whose stomach is mildly upset from crying or swallowing large amounts of drool may find vanilla soothing to the tummy as well as the nerves.

You should supervise them brushing their teeth, and help them with brushing up until the age of 7. You can let them brush your teeth to encourage them to let you brush their teeth. Let your child choose their own toothbrush, to make it fun for them.

Dental advice for children;
- Children up to three years of age should use toothpaste with a fluoride level of at least 1,000ppm (parts per million).
- After three years of age, children should use toothpaste with a fluoride level of 1,350-1,500ppm. The level of fluoride can be found on the pack.
- Children should be supervised when brushing their teeth until about seven years of age.
- The amount of toothpaste your child uses is important. Up to the age of three, a smear of toothpaste is sufficient, and from age three to six, a pea-sized amount is recommended.

- Encourage your child to spit the toothpaste out after brushing their teeth rather than swallowing it.

- Wash teeth after having milk, milk is bad for teeth if not washed away (although drinking milk helps teeth because of the calcium that is absorbed in the body, the actual milk itself can erode the teeth, the same as any drink if teeth are not cleaned regularly and especially before bed).

TIPS FOR MOVING FROM BOTTLE TO CUP

Here are some practical tips which may help.

- As soon as they can hold things, **give your child a cup to play with.**

- When you start weaning at age four to six months, **introduce a cup** even if very little is taken from it.

- **Sit your child upright** before offering food or drink.

- **Mess is normal** – be prepared. There will be less mess if food and drink are kept in one place.

- **Keep the bottle out of sight,** especially when offering a drink from a cup.

- Remember that **milk** may be given from a cup but **don't give too much.**

- **NEVER leave your child alone with a drink at sleep times.**

- As your baby gets older, if he or she wakes during the night, a drink may not be necessary – **give a cuddle instead.**

- Older children may **give up their bottles for a new toy.**

- **Moving on to a cup** may not be easy, and may take longer than you think, but **it will be worth all your hard work!**

If you want any more information on feeding your child, contact your local health visitor.

HEALTHY SNACKS

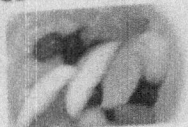

Making available good nutritious snacks is just as important as providing good nutritious main meals

Sugar is harmful to teeth when taken between meals whether in drinks, sweets or snacks

Try some of these healthier snacks

FRESH FRUIT	Apples, Oranges, Pears, Bananas, Peaches, Grapes
RAW VEGETABLES	Carrots, Celery, Tomatoes, Cucumber
BREAD	Sliced, Rolls, Pitta. With savoury spread.
NIBBLES:	Breadsticks, Rice Cakes, Corn Snacks, Cream Crackers or Ryvita
DRINKS:	Water and plain Milk.

INGREDIENTS TO AVOID: Dextrose, Glucose, Syrup, Invert Sugar, Sucrose, Fructose, Maltose, Hydrolysed Starch.

How to Brush Your Teeth

1. Use a pea sized amount of toothpaste for children over the age of 3 and just a smear of toothpaste for children under 3 years old.

2. Ensure the bristles of your brush point towards the edge of your gums and also cover your teeth.

Gently brush the edges that face outwards of 2 or 3 teeth at a time.

3. Move your brush in backwards and forward or circular motion.

4. Gently brush the edges facing inwards. Again brush 2 or 3 teeth at a time touching the gum.

Brush the insides of your bottom and front teeth by tilting the brush upwards or downwards.

5. Gently brush the biting surface of your teeth.

Spit out and remaining toothpaste to finish and do not rinse with water.

Toys and development;

- Playtime develops your child's creativity and encourages hand to eye co-ordination and dexterity. It also promotes a sense of achievement.
- Toys should stimulate their imagination.
- Versatile toys that adapt as they grow are best.
- Interpreting sensory information while playing expands a childs ability to reason and problem solve.

N.B. Don't let them have thin toys, straws or spoons that they may push down their throats

It is a good idea to get your baby used to other babies, noise & boystrous behaviour from other kids. That way you can g out with other kids running around, they will join in and won't be scared of loud noise. Dont fuss them and instead let them get messy. That way they won't grow up fussy and won't be scared to try new things and join in with other kids.

Alternate toys 20 mins in jumperoo and then play on mat with toys out, regularly rotate your toys too. This way they will have wider experiences and won't get bored.

Once they get older and play with toys they are easier to distract and less wingy – 6 or 7 months is usually the golden age. Once they get older and can move around more they aere more of a handful.

Ofen the 2nd child gets passed toys, from their older sibling so it takes longer for them to learn to crawl. However they may develop in other areas quicker because they are watching and copying the older child. Each child develops differently and in their own time, they will do things when they are ready.

They learn from movement, from picking things up and putting them in their mouth. Therefore it is important that they have a safe place where they can crawl, explore, move around and feel different textures and see different things. It is also nice to take them to a sensory room every so often (if you have one near you). A lot of children's centres and soft play areas do have sensory rooms.

Communicating with baby;

- Babies when born appear to have a film over their eyes. They can't see far at first (only approx. 25cm), they can't see much detail so its good to get close to baby so s/he can focus on you. Touch and skin to skin contact is also a good way of communicating. As the weeks go on you will see babies eye become brighter and less 'misty', s/he will focus on more in the distance, will track movement and will start to turn and respond to sounds and will look for where they are coming from. Babies like bright objects and you will see your baby will start to stare at lights or the TV. Give your baby bright coloured or black and white toys to play with, show objects and pictures to your baby. Your baby will love the contrast. Put a mobile over his/her cot, babies love this. It is also good to give your baby a toy with a mirror on or put baby in front of a mirror. Your baby loves to have your near. Hold him/her close and sing to him/her, talk to him/her and stimulate him/her.

- At 2 months s/he may turn his/her head towards you and gurgle and at 3 months baby may reach out and grasp objects. Baby is very sensitive to touch, sound and textures. Give baby different toys to play with and let him/her experience different textures and toys. Surround baby with age appropriate toys to encourage him/her to reach out and develop movement skills. Let baby experience different textures. Let baby play in the bath, have different materials and toys with different texture etc. some children's centres now offer 'messy play' where children can get their hands into various products from sand, water, paint etc. to experience different textures.

Encourage speech;

- Make sounds baby can copy/speak in silly voices etc. (some people don't like the way adults speak to babies in silly voices but it has been proven that a sing-song style of speaking to a baby makes it easier for them to understand).
- Talk to baby from birth
- Get down to your child's level, point at things and say the names of them
- Keep talking whilst making eye contact, repeat sounds and give a running commentary on what is happening.
- Look at books and talk about the pictures
- Avoid background distractions, such as radio and TV, which can be confusing
- Ask lots of questions and start sentences with your child's name
- Take babies dummy out when talking so that s/he can talk back
- They shout and make scream noises when first learning to talk, sometimes its hard to tell if something is wrong, if they are upset, or if they are simply finding their voice.
- Read to your baby.

None verbal communication;

Your baby speaks to you in two ways, through verbal and non-verbal communication. Your baby is born with the capacity to do both, and as he or she grows older, verbal and non-verbal communication skills will advance. You have grown accustomed to your baby's cry and may have learned what different cries indicate in your child, but there is another area where you baby communicates his or her needs, and this is through body language.

Verbal communication skills will continue to advance throughout babies' lives, and while babies may not be able to speak and clearly express their needs, they are still communicating through their body language. Parents and child care givers who learn to read a baby's body language, or non-verbal communication clues, can better address situations and ensure that a baby is comfortable, happy and peaceful.

Understanding your child's non-verbal communication is imperative for understanding how your child is feeling on a deeper level. When reading your child's body language, pay attention to his or her facial expressions, rate of breathing, the way his or her eyes are moving, how he or she is utilizing personal space and distance and how he or she holds his hands and arms. In younger babies, look at whether they are kicking their legs, rubbing their eyes, arching their back or squinting their eyes. Each of those body movements may indicate something that the child is feeling or experiencing on a physical or emotional level.

Talk to your child and express what they want when they can't so that they understand the words. If you understand them too much and just do things when they point they may not bother talking, but others won't understand them so they will have to talk to them. If your child talks to others a lot but is lazy at home this could be why.

Think about how you act and react around your child. They will pick up on and mimic your behaviour. They will also react according to how you treat them.

Arching the Back - Infants that arch their back while keeping their eyes wide open often do so due to physical pain and discomfort. You may notice your baby does this when he or she is experiencing colic or bouts of gas. The fingers and toes may be flexed, and your child may let out a loud cry while arching his or her back.

Rubbing Eyes - When baby rubs his or her eyes, it may be a sign of sleepiness. You'll know if you catch your baby yawning that it's time for a nap. Sometimes older babies will rub their eyes or keep their hands up to their eyes as a way of saying they want to play peek-a-boo.

Kicking - Babies that kick their legs may do so because they are happy or they want to be picked up in order to see you face to face. If your baby is kicking his or her legs, this is a great time to play.

Squinting - Older children may breathe heavily or rapidly when angry, and their eyes may squint.

Wrinkling the Nose - A baby that wrinkles his or her nose is indicating disgust.

Moving Toward You or Away - Older children that move close to someone is stating they would like more affection while a child that moves away may be saying they need some alone time.

Wide Eyes - When a child's eyes are bright and wide, it indicates your child is ready to play.

Babies may also reach out their hand, pull you close, point, nod their head etc.

If a small baby diverts their gaze they maybe saying "im tired and need a break.", where as an older baby or toddler may divert their gaze if they have done something wrong.

If a child covers his/her face when meeting someone new it maybe because s/he is anxious.

You can tell if a child is full of energy and wants to play or is tired and needs a rest from their body language. Babies also mimic other babies behaviour. They don't play together when they are young, instead they play in parallel and may mimic other babies behaviour.

Psychologist and author David Chamberlian observes; "Both premature and full-term babies read faces so well that they can immediately imitate a wide-open mouth, a pretuding tongue, or mimic expressions of happiness, sadness or surprise."

Children are natural communicators and by two to three months can give you a smile.

By learning how your child expresses his or her emotions facially, such as smiling, grimacing, or how he or she holds his or her eyes, you can more readily determine what your child is feeling. Through watching and learning your child's body language, you can ensure that you are in tune with your child's physical and emotional needs.

It is also important that you use body language when you communicate with your baby to help him/her understand your words. For instance smile when you are pleased, shake your head when you say no, hold up a cup when asking if your baby wants more juice.

Encourage yor baby to communicate;
- Talk to your baby and give him/her time to respond
- Repeat your babies sounds
- Encourage your baby to wave 'bye bye' to people
Crawling;

Your baby may start crawling (may go backwards or forwards), may stand and walk and not crawl or may scoot on bottom. To help baby crawl when s/he is on all fours, remove socks and trousers to help him/her grip with knees and fit in order to push off. Also put toys slightly out of reach so that s/he has to move to grab it. Use a ball to roll in front of him/her etc.

It is quite common for babies to learn to crawl backwards before they can learn to crawl forwards. Some babies just roll and bum shuffle and some never learn to crawl and go straight to walking.

When your baby will be walking;

By 18 months your toddler will normally be walking, by the age of 2 s/he will be running, can also walk sideways and backwards but may find it hard to change direction or glance over his/her shoulder when running.

You need to set boundaries for safety and say "you must hold my hand when we are out because the road is dangerous". It is a good idea to have your baby walk on the inside of the path and consider using reins if there is traffic about. It is also important for your toddler to have the freedom to run around on their own in a safe environment, parks and soft play areas are great for this.

N.B. When babies first learning to stand babies often stand on tip toes / may walk on tiptoes but if they continue to walk on tip toes all the time you may want to get this checked out.

Encourage walking;

-   Letting child go barefoot allows them to grip better and allows feet to develop.
-   Arrange stable furniture close together, so that this can be used to balance
-   Use push along toys but not a baby walker
First shoe;

If baby has been walking unaided for 6 weeks then it is probably time to get the first pair of shoes. Get them fitted properly, somewhere that does width fittings too. A shoe that doesn't fit properly can slow down the process of trying to walk.

When buying first shoes check that they;

-   Fit correctly (feet should be measured every time and they should fit the largest foot and still have some growing space at the toe). They should also be correctly fitted on the width too.
-   They should stay on when the child walks or runs.
-   They shouldn't be too heavy
-   They should be flat and comfortable to support the feet
-   Shoes should be flexible and not too stiff so that babies foot can move as near to barefoot as possible. Hard shoes can constrain a toddlers feet and lead to flat foot and other such problems.

- Its best to let your child go barefoot as much as possible so that they can grip the ground, feel different textures, develop balance and strengthen foot muscles. However you need to be careful as they may step on wasps, glass or rusty nails. It may be a good idea to put a blanket down in the garden or park that your child can walk on.

  N.B.

- Over 97% of babies have flat feet due to a thick wad of fat in the soles of their feet. Arches develop as they gradually gain muscle.
- Some toddlers walk on tiptoes, an instinct that helps them develop balance, but a sign of persistent tip toeing maybe a sign of muscle damage.

First shoes;

- Get their first shoes once they have been walking for 4 weeks
- They may find their shoes feel strange at first and may not like them/may find it hard to walk but they do offer them support and keep them steadier.
- Babies feet seem wide because they have flat feet/chubby insteps
- Get shoes fitted somewhere where they also do width fittings and where they keep a record of their shoes, a proper shoe fitters who does it all the time is good – they have different thickness insoles that go in the shoes, you may need thinner ones if their feet are wide, to allow the feet more room in the shoe. You need somewhere that measures their shoes using the WMS system.
- ¼ inch gap is needed in the shoe (push the foot forward and you should be able to put a finger in behind it).
- When children are age 1-3 years old, their feet should be measured every 3-4 months.
- There feet may grow in width as well as/or instead of length, so as well as checking the length, you will need to keep an eye on the width.

Ask nursery not to put shoes on all day, just when going outside when baby is first wearing shoes to give his/her feet chance to develop without being restricted by shoes.

Babies development

Babies /children all develop at different weights and may even miss out on some stages i.e. may not crawl but may just pull themselves up on the furniture and start walking straight away.

Weight;

Within 6 months your baby becomes twice its birth weight, and it triples 6 months after this. After a year its growth settles down.

At one year of age an average child is about 30 inches in length and 20 pounds in weight. At 2 years old it is approx 33 inches in length and 26 pounds in weight.

Development;

Babies grow at different rates so rest assured that his/her rate of development is almost certainly normal and if s/he seems not to have reached the same stage as others her age, s/he very soon will do (although if you are concerned it may be a good idea to speak to your doctor/health visitor). In general girls tend to develop faster than boys. All children are individuals and it isn't a competition. Some children maybe slower in some areas, yet more advanced in others. This is also the case between twins and triplets too.

In some circumstances your child may not reach development in normal milestone range. For instance if baby was born prematurely then s/he should be measured by their due date (not their birthdate), rest assured premature babies soon catch up. If your child has a medical condition or special need then you will need to get advice on his/her development.

Below is an average development guide;

At 3 months your baby will study faces and try and grasp toys and moving objects, and will respond to voices and volumes.

By 6 months most babies will be able to stand and sit with some assistance.

At 9 months of age your baby will be able to sit alone, and will be able to pull himself/herself up on furniture.

By 1 year old your baby may start walking. Will be able to recognise faces, will show a greater preference for using one hand over the other and maybe able to crawl up the stairs and out of the play pen.

Help your baby to explore by singing to them, playing with them, give your baby different shapes, colours and textures.

Your baby doesn't know what's harmful or the difference between right or wrong and you must therefore be firm with and protect baby.

Babies have emotions from one month. Be calm and happy and keep your baby calm and happy. In a calm happy state your baby will develop better.

Soothe your baby by gently rocking, stroking head or pat her/his back gently, swaddle baby (but not too tightly), communicate with your baby and make soothing noises.

Multi-languages do not confuse your baby. It maybe good to teach your baby sign language or another language at the same time as teaching your baby to talk.

Ensure that you get regular breaks so that you do not become over stressed (baby will pick up on your stress and it could lead to a vicious cycle). It is also good to get baby used to other people.

Keep a record of all your babies milestones, first smile, first word, first time he/she sat up etc.

Average baby Milestones

Mastered Skills (most children can do)	Emerging Skills (half of children can do)	Advanced Skills (a few children can do)

Child's Age : <u>One month</u>		
• <u>Lifts head</u> • Responds <u>to sound</u> • <u>Stares at faces</u>	• Follows objects • Ooohs and ahhs • Can <u>see black-and-white patterns</u>	• Smiles • Laughs • Holds head at 45-degree angle
Child's Age : <u>Two months</u>		
• Vocalises sounds - gurgling and cooing • Follows objects • <u>Holds head up</u> for short periods	• <u>Smiles responsively, laughs</u> • Holds head at 45-degree angle • Movements become smoother	• Holds head steady • Bears weight on legs • May <u>lift head and shoulder (mini-pushup)</u>
Child's Age : <u>Three months</u>		
• Laughs • Holds head steady • <u>Recognises your face</u> and scent	• Squeals, <u>gurgles, coos</u> • Recognises your voice • Does mini-pushups	• Turns towards loud sounds • Can bring hands together and may bat at toys • Can <u>roll over</u>
Child's Age : <u>Four months</u>		
• Holds <u>head up steadily</u> • Can bear weight on legs • Coos when you talk to him	• Can <u>grasp a toy</u> • Reaches out for objects • Can roll over	• Imitates speech sounds - baba, dada • May <u>cut first tooth</u>
Child's Age : <u>Five months</u>		
• Can <u>distinguish between bold colours</u> • Can roll over • Amuses himself by playing with hands and feet	• Turns towards <u>new sounds</u> • Recognises own name • May be <u>ready for solids.</u>	• May sit momentarily without support • Mouths objects • <u>Stranger anxiety</u> may begin
Child's Age : <u>Six months</u>		
• Turns towards sounds and voices • <u>Imitates sounds,</u> blows bubbles	• Reaches for objects and mouths them • Sits without support • Is <u>ready for solids</u>	• May lunge forward or <u>start crawling</u> • May jabber or combine syllables • May drag object towards

		himself
• Rolls in both directions		

Mastered Skills (Most children can do)	Emerging Skills (Half of children can do)	Advanced Skills (A few children can do)
Child's Age : seven months		
• Sits without support • Reaches for things with a sweeping motion • Imitates speech sounds (babbles)	• Combines syllables into wordlike sounds • Begins to crawl or lunges forward	• Stands while holding onto something • Waves goodbye • Bangs objects together
Child's Age : eight months		
• Says "dada" and "mama" to both parents (isn't specific) • Begins to crawl • Passes object from hand to hand	• Stands while holding onto something • Crawls well • Points at objects	• Pulls self to standing position, cruises around furniture while holding on • Picks things up with thumb-finger "pincer" grasp • Indicates wants with gestures
Child's Age : nine months		
• Combines syllables into wordlike sounds • Stands while holding onto something	• Uses pincer grasp to pick up objects • Cruises while holding onto furniture • Bangs objects together	• Plays patty cake • Says "dada" and "mama" to the right parent (is specific)
Child's Age : 10 months		
• Waves goodbye • Picks things up with pincer grasp • Crawls well • Cruises	• Says "dada" and "mama" to the right parent (is specific) • Responds to name and understands "no" • Indicates wants with	• Drinks from a cup • Stands alone for a couple of seconds • Puts objects into a container

	gestures	

Child's Age : 11 months

• <u>Says "dada" and "mama"</u> to the right parent (is specific) • Plays patty-cake • <u>Stands alone</u> for a couple of seconds	• Imitates others' activities • Puts objects into a container • <u>Understands</u> simple instructions	• <u>Drinks</u> from a cup • Says one word besides "mama" and "dada" • Stoops from standing position Baby will be ready to play with simple puzzles such as Jigsaws, this helps them to recognise how patterns come together. You can help baby to recognise colours by describing them when playing with baby. Babies are burning off lots of energy as they play so may need to snack in between meals.

Child's Age : 12 months

• <u>Imitates</u> others' activities • Jabbers wordlike sounds • Indicates wants with gestures	• Says one word besides "mama" and "dada" • Takes a few steps • <u>Understands</u> and responds to simple instructions	• <u>Scribbles</u> with crayon • <u>Walks</u> well • Says two words besides "mama" and "dada"

Journey of baby's development & major milestones record		
Baby's achievement	Date	Additional comments

1. In the first 6 months your baby's weight will double and by 12 months it will have triped.

2. At around 6 months a baby will learn to passthings fom hand to hand.

3. A baby's brain can lean in its sleep – it organises what they have learnt in the day to it in with existing memories.

4. Some babies crawl backwards before they learn to crawl forwards.

5. A baby's gurgling is the beginning of a real language – they are trying to work out how sounds are made.

6. At around 7 months your baby will recognise and respond to your voice.

Baby sign language

When we talk, we often use gestures as part of our communication. Babies are very good at picking up on these gestures and, in turn, using them to communicate. Think of a baby pointing or waving "bye bye", or asking to be picked up by raising his arms. So, it's not surprising babies can learn how to sign.

Your baby's understanding of language and gross motor skills develop much faster than his ability to speak. As a result, he will use gestures to let you know what he wants before he can talk.

The idea of taking this one step further, and teaching babies a range of signs, was inspired by child development expert Dr Joseph Garcia. He found that hearing babies of deaf parents easily copied their parents' signs and used them to communicate.

Garcia also noticed that these babies appeared less demanding than non-signing babies because they could express their thoughts and needs more easily.

It is best to start with a few signs at a time and to be repetitive and use the signs a lot.

You can make up your own signs, by using gestures that comes naturally. Or you could go to a proper class so that your baby can learn proper signs. I started off doing simple gestures for my son so I knew when he wanted to b picked up, my friend claps befor playing with her baby, she then knows that when he claps it means he wants to play. When my baby was 5 months I started taking hin to tiny talk and by 6 months he started signing for milk, which he also did when he wanted water, this was useful as I knew when he was thirsty. It is good to know some signs, even if they only use a few it's handy to know if they want milk or food. This is good because otherwise it is hard to know wha your baby wants, this way you cut down on fears or fustration.

If you want to use formal signing systems such as Makaton or Signalong you will need to attend classes or a course. These systems of signing are normally used with children who are struggling to communicate for a variety of reasons although it is good for all children parents of children who have deafness or significant hearing difficulties may need to learn a signing system, such as British Sign Language. It may well be their child's main way of communicating.

If your baby has no hearing difficulties, you can still use signs based on British Sign Language but there's no reason why you can't make up your own signs. Any gesture that obviously mimics the meaning of the word works well, for example:

- **More**. Hold your hands open, palms facing toward body, with one in front of the other. Move the hand in front forward a short distance.
- **Food**. Put your finger tips to your lips.
- **All gone**. Move your hand, palm up, backwards and forwards.
- **Happy**. Draw an exaggerated smile over your mouth with your finger, while smiling.
- **Hot**. Put your hand out and withdraw it quickly.
- **Where?** Shrug your shoulders, with your palms held out.
- **Rabbit**. Wrinkle up your nose or hold up two fingers.
- **Car**. Steer an imaginary wheel.
- **Book**. Hold your hands flat with your palms up.

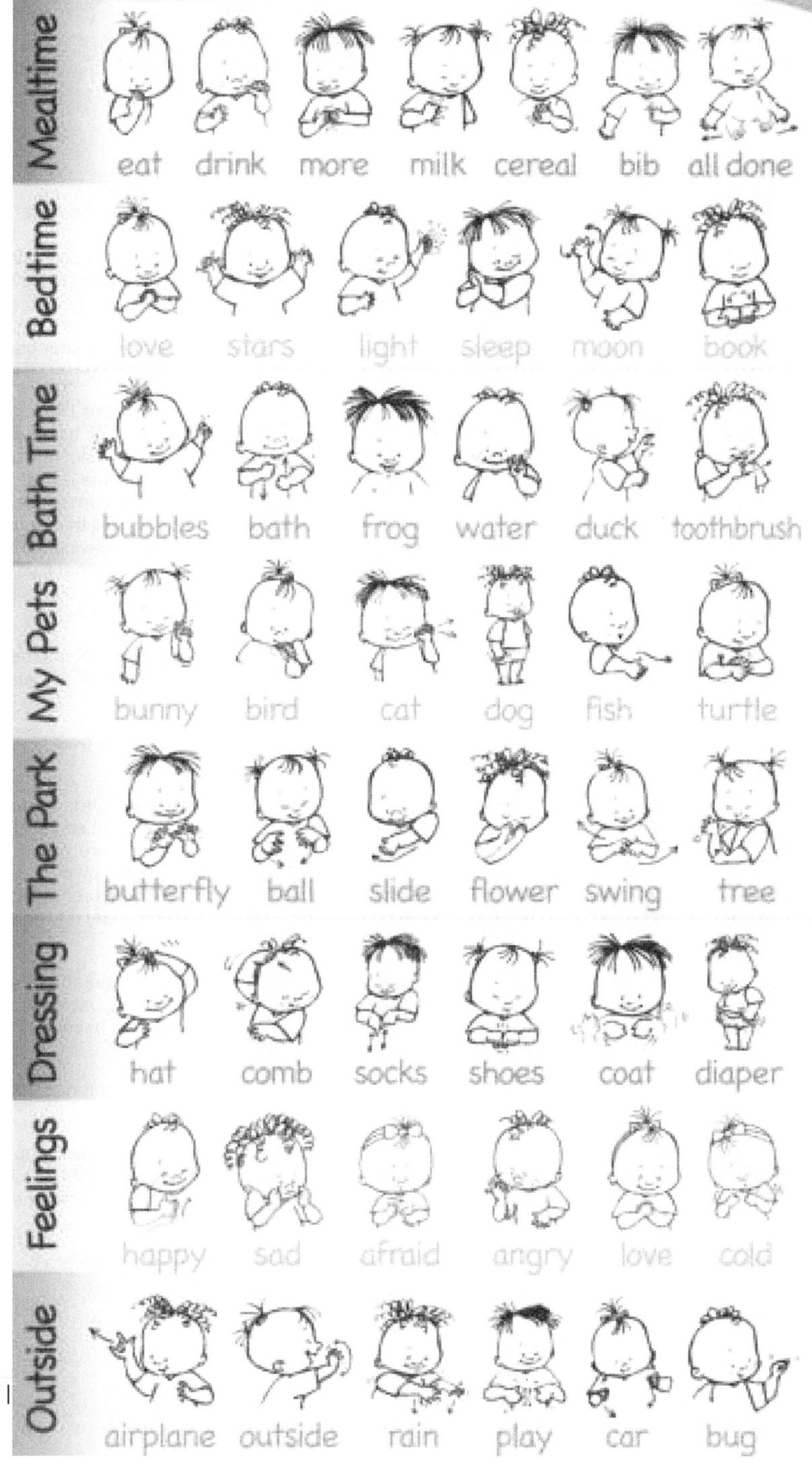

Mealtime	eat	drink	more	milk	cereal	bib	all done
Bedtime	love	stars	light	sleep	moon	book	
Bath Time	bubbles	bath	frog	water	duck	toothbrush	
My Pets	bunny	bird	cat	dog	fish	turtle	
The Park	butterfly	ball	slide	flower	swing	tree	
Dressing	hat	comb	socks	shoes	coat	diaper	
Feelings	happy	sad	afraid	angry	love	cold	
Outside	airplane	outside	rain	play	car	bug	

Weaning babies onto solids

Just when you're beginning to get your head around milk feedings and rotines, the next challenge of getting your baby onto 'solid' food.
Most people refer to weaning your baby onto solids as 'weaning' (which can get confusing because other people think weaning is persuading your child to give up the breast or bottle, which is related but not exactly the same).

At approx 6 months you will wean your baby. Weaning is the process of moving your baby from a milk-only diet to a combination of milk and solid food.

In 2003 the Department of Health issued guidelines (based on recommendations by the World Health Organisation and UNICEF) that weaning should start at 6 months. It is now thought that, in general, babies under 6 months have kidneys and guts that are not mature enough to cope with a more diverse diet and that early weaning can increase the risk of infections and the development of allergies like eczema and asthma. Babies born pre-term (before 37 weeks of gestation) may not quite be ready to wean at 6 months and therefore it may be best to speak with a health visitor before solid foods are introduced. Having said all that, babies do develop at different rates and the Department of Health advises that if your baby is showing signs of being ready to start solid foods before six months then you could try some solids. So keep an eye on your baby at meal times and look out for clues.

All the health visitors I have seen are very insistent not to wean until 6 months. Rememebr this is not 6 calender months it is 24 weeks. / 6 months is 26 week ie;52 weeks of the year halved.

However by 6 months the iron supply is down and so it is not a good idea to go over 6 months.

Dr Rana Conway in her bookweaning made easy says that The World Health Organisation recommend this because in developing countries the hygiene standards are not so good and prior to 6 months a baby's immune system is weak and they are likely to be more vunerable and develop allergies etc. therefore before 6 months they will be more effeced by poor hygiene standards. Therefore to protect all babies around the world exclusive breastfeeding is recommended until 6 months. However in developed countries it maybe okay to wean before 6 months.

Also when the guidleines were to wean between 4-6 months many people misinterpreted this and believed that they had to wean their babies by 4 months, which led to babies being weaned early and subsequently having issues. Therefore the new guidelines became 6 months.

If you do wean before 6 months you need to steralise spoons and bowls. After 6 months you just need to wash them and not necessarly steralise them.

There is a lot of debate whether children in the UK should wait until they are 6 months to be weaned. Many baby's may need more than just milk before 6 months, even the WHO said so in their 2001 report. In fact Sweden has reverted their guidelines back from 6 months to 4 months as the time to start weaning.

In the future it will be interesting to se if guidleines change, to wean your baby before 6 months.

It is debatable that gluten should be avoided until 6 months, there is an argument for giving gluten prior to 6 months avoids intolerance later (as per studies in Sweden according to Dr Rana Conway).

In Sweden, parents used to be advised to introduce gluten, which is found in wheat, at 4 months. Then in 1982, the official advice changed to 6 months. It was then found the rate of coeliac disease (gluten intolerance) increased. They thought that this increase suggested that babies needed to have gluten earlier, in order for the bodies to get used to it. So, in 1996, the Swedish authorities decided to change the advice back to the recommended weaning from 4 months again. They also adviced parents to introduce gluten slowly whilst breastfeeding. This seemed to result in the incidents of coeliac disease, back to previous levels.

I think that teeth could be natures way of saying your baby is ready to be weaned. Therefore if your baby has teeth you may want to consider weaning, but this is just my personal opinion.

Although the official guidelines are ver clear not to wean before 6 months;

The official guidelines are actually pretty clear: you should wait to introduce solid foods until your baby is six months (26 weeks) old – whether he is breastfed or formula-fed (or both). The trouble is, these guidelines are relatively new (2001/2003) and many of the people you may be relying upon for advice – your mum, your sister, your friend, your parenting-book 'expert'.

Why six months?
Until 2003, parents were advised to wean between four and six months. This was changed to six months after worldwide research (endorsed by numerous health bodies, including the World Health Organisation and the Department of Health) showed, if you wean before six months:

- There's a very real chance your baby's digestive system and kidneys won't be developed enough to cope safely with solid food
- Your baby may absorb fewer nutrients from breastmilk (if he's breastfed)
- There is no positive health benefit for your baby
- Your baby's risk of developing infections and allergies – and going on to have digestive problems and obesity in later life – can increase
- Also if you wait untill six months you can do baby led weaning instead of baby led weaning, which is said to be quicker and easier. At this age, your baby is very likely to be able to sit in a highchair, take food easily from a spoon and/or pick up and hold food to feed herself. Because of this – and because you can offer him a wide range of foods straightaway – you can move very quickly onto a good, varied diet. If you start earlier than six months, you will go have to go much more slowly and carefully and the type of foods you can offer your baby will be quite restricted.

Why doesn't everyone wait till six months?
Despite the official advice, nearly half of all babies in the UK are weaned before four months – and one in ten has their first taste of solids at six to eight weeks. There are probably all sorts of reasons for this but some of the most common are:
- Label confusion; Go into any supermarket and you'll see jars of baby food with 'suitable from four months' written on the label. Kind of leads you to conclude that four months is the right time to start, doesn't it? Manufacturers are free to label baby food in this way because the relevant European Union Directive allows them to (although some governments and many agencies are working to change this).

- The it-didnt-do-my-kids-any-harm argument which you'll hear from all and sundry, old and young. And maybe it didn't, but who can tell? The point about the new guidelines is that they're based, in no small part, on research into adult outcomes of early weaning.
- The Department of Health guidelines and weaning booklets do include advice for parents who wean early. It's there because 'mothers who are unable to or choose not to follow recommendations should be supported to optimise their infants' nutrition'. Roughly translated, that means it's there because there are certain foods that babies under six months should not be given and those parents who don't heed the official advice need to know what they are. The guidelines also state (for those parents who might be tempted to wean extremely early) that no baby should be started on solids before the age of four months (17 weeks). This, of course, is not the same as recommending you start your baby on solids at 17 weeks.
- It can be rather weird to be the only one hanging on till 26 weeks when every other mother in the neighbourhood seems to be busy spooning purees into their baby's mouth. Especially if they're suggesting that, by not being on solids, your child is falling behind in some way (which isn't true, of course).
- The 'it's only for babies in the developing world' myth. Actually, of the 20 studies the World Health Organisation reviewed when considering its six-month recommendation, slightly more were conducted in developed countries (11 studies compared to the developing countries' nine). As hunkermunker says: "This is such a red herring: gut maturity isn't geographic."
- The magic sleep 'solution' Perhaps the biggest – and most-trotted-out – weaning myth is that starting solids will help your baby sleep through the night. Or that solids are the magic solution if your previously good sleeper starts waking again in the night. If, through your sleep-deprived haze, you think that sounds too good to be true, you're right: it is. "There is no evidence that the introduction of solids is linked with sleeping through – in fact, the evidence we do have shows it makes no difference. Any apparent coincidence is just that: a coincidence. To use the perfectly developmentally normal behavior of waking in the night as a 'sign' for the need of solids is to mislead people." Tiktok
- The fussy eating mistake. Defenders of early weaning often insist there's research showing that babies weaned at six months turn out to be fussy eaters. In actual fact, the latest research shows no difference in appetite or food acceptance between babies weaned at four months and babies weaned at six months.

The readiness signs that actually matter include being able to sit up unaided, being able to reach and grab (and put things in his mouth) and the loss of the tongue-thrust reflex (small babies instinctively use their tongues to push objects out of their mouth; until this reflex fades, you're not going to have much luck putting a spoonful of food in there).

If your previously settled baby's suddenly become ravenously hungry, it's not a sign he's ready for weaning (though plenty of people will tell you it is). The most likely explanation is that he's having a growth spurt – many babies seem to go through a hugely ravenously patch at about four months – and simply needs more milk for a while (more milk in his bottle if you're formula-feeding; more frequent feeds if you're breastfeeding).

Exceptions to the 6 month rule;
- Premature babies: The Department of Health weaning guidelines are for term babies and do not apply to babies who were born prematurely. Experts at special care baby charity Bliss recommend that babies who were born prematurely should be weaned between the ages of five and seven months (calculating from your baby's birthdate, not his corrected-age date). Very occasionally, a premature baby may benefit from weaning before five months but this should be discussed with your healthcare team first.

- Babies with feeding problems: If your baby has particular feeding problems, such as reflux, or a medical condition that makes feeding difficult, the health professionals you see will sometimes – but not always – advise weaning before six months.

If you think you do need to wean early you need to speak to your health visitor. I started weaning my son at 5 months, under the advice of my health visitor because he was demanding hungry milk every 2 hours (a full 8z) and was a large bvery hungry baby who was showing lots of signs of readiness. He also had some reflux which got better when he was on solids (although I did give him big bottles of milk, which then caused reflux so I was adviced to reduce the milk to little and often too).

However whever you think your baby should be weaned at 4 or 6 months, you should not wean before 4 months (17 weeks).

I think that this makes a lot of sense and I also think that you have to take a common sense approach. Look at your baby, the weight etc. the min you can wean is 17 weeks but the nearer you can get to 24 weeks the better. There needs to be some flexability, trust your instinct.

All babies develop differently so I don't think that you can so rigidly apply guidelines in a general way.

You can switch your baby onto hungry baby milk before weaning to keep your baby going longer. It isn't recommended to put rusks, cerial or baby rice into milk bottles.

If you wean before 6 months you will have to puree food (traditional weaning), where as if you wait until 6 months you can just give mash food and finger foods (known as baby led weaning). You will have to move through the food groups quicker but you can give your baby more variety, you can give lots of foods straight away so its easier for you, baby can join in more at meal times and is likely to be less of a fussy eater.

Or you might want to mix the 2 methods.

Speak to a pedetrition, if your baby has certain medical conditions such as reflux they may let you wean earlier.

Because guidance is always changing it is best to speak to your health visitor before weaning to ensure you are doing it in line with the current guidance. They can also look at your baby and offer persnolised advice.

Before 6 months you might want to give some hungry baby milk and baby rice. However this may cause constipation and some health visitors say baby rice has no nutritional value. Another view point is that it's good because it's bland so it's easy for your baby to digest and gets them used to another texture and something other than milk. They do suggest that you don't put baby rice in their bottle, instead give it to them on a spoon.

I did this for 6 days and found my baby was constipated so I alternated between hungry milk and normal milk, I then gave some water. After this I gave fruit and veg.

Some people say try one food at a time to start, which I agree with. However they say try for 3 days. I believe everything in moderation and if you give something they will usually react the same day, therefore I gave a different fruit and veg each day.

However think about the type of fruit and veg. Is it easy to digest and is it full of fibre? Try to mix types ie don't give citrus all week or it may cause tummy ache. Don't give too much,especially if food is rich.

If you give something rich or want to bulk something out you can mix with bay rice. Baby rice only keeps for a month after opening.

Mix milk in with food i.e. milk in with banana to make it softer and make sure baby gets his/her milk allocation for the day (the milk at first is the main source of vitamins and minerals – if breastfeeding you could express).

Try giving food on a spoon and feeding net. My son took off a spoon but didn't like the feeding net at first.

The feeding net is good to put ice in when baby is teething.

I found it easier to use a flatter spoon at first, that way he could get the food off (and try and find some that aren't too wide).

I cooked fresh food but just use packets when out – you only need small packets to start with otherwise it's a waste.

At first they may pull a face. It might not be that they don't like it. It could just be that they are not used to it and are unsure. Or it could be the texture. Keep trying and keep smiling. If you pull a face it will put them off. If they are unsure they will look to you for reassurance and if you smile they will feel at ease to carry on.

Babies have extra taste buds; it's also all new and exciting to them so something we may find bland is fine for them.

Just give them a little bit on the spoon at a time. Don't worry if they gag this is normal. Instead keep smiling so baby is calm and reassured. You don't want to stress them out.

Strap baby in but also know how to get baby out in a hurry and how to deal with chocking.

Don't waste money – cook food yourself and cut up normal pasta instead of buying baby pasta. Use natural yoghurt instead of other yoghurt which is sweetened and ignore the ones that say calium as all yoghurts have this in.

When you start weaning your baby, if you have been using hungry milk you can can come off hungry milk and go to normal baby milk, especially if you find that your baby is getting constipated.

After 6 months your babies Iron supply (the iron from you / the placenta) would have depleted so they need food to get the iron. You can also go onto the next stage in milk – follow on milk which is said to have more iron etc. however if you give the right foods you may not need this. You can also use stage 1 milk for the whole of the first year. You can have cows milk after 12 months but not before and mix this into foods. Once you come off baby milk you need to ensure baby is getting a balance diet to get all the viatamins. Even before a proper feeding routine is established and baby is relying on milk you should vary the foods to get baby used to liking a variety of different foods. You can have products with cows milk ie yoghurt before your baby is 12 months but not cows milk to drink until your baby is at least 12 months. The health professionals say as long as your baby is having a varied diet cows milk is sufficient but the manufacturers of baby milk do follow on milk which is said to have more vitamins, however this shouldn't be necessary if you are giving your baby a balanced diet. After 12 months using cows milk is cheaper than baby milk and babies should get all their vitamins and minerals via their food but to be doubly sure you can buy special milk for babies 1 year old. Personally I prefer follow on milk to ensure baby is getting enough vitamins.

After 6 months you may want to give your baby vitamin drops. Breastfed babies should have vitamin drops containing vitamin A&D and non breast fed babies who drink less than a pint of formula a day need drops too.

At 1 year your baby can have cows milk but still should have 500ml of milk a day, because s/he needs the calcium content, be it milk or in food (until approx. 5 years old needs calcium but may only have a bottle at night and after 2 may not drink much milk but may have it on cereal etc).

From 12 months they can have tap water (water doesn't need to be boiled). However if you are abroad you may want to boil it. Some people say in the UK that after 6 months you can give tap water.

Your baby is ready to wean onto solid food if they can:

- Stay in a sitting position and are able to hold their head steady.
- Co-ordinate their eyes, hands and mouth, can look at food, grab it, and put it in their mouths all by themselves.
- Swallow their food. Babies who are not ready will often push their food back out, so get more around their faces than they do in their mouths.

Other signs may include;

- Your baby may seem unsatisfied after a full milk feed and cry or demand more
- You may find your baby starts to demand milk feeds more frequently
- Your baby may begin sucking and chewing their hands and toys (although they may also do this when they are teething).
- They may start showing a real interest in food; following what you are eating with their eyes or even reaching out and trying to grab it! Although this is not necessarly a sign that your baby is ready for weaning.

The following are not signs of being ready to wean;
- Baby seems hungry or wakes for feeds at night (this may mean that your baby needs more milk teething or other things can wake your baby at night or they may simply be having a growth spurt, which may unsettle them at night and may mean that they need more milk at night). However if they are getting hungry they may wake at night so although it in itself is not a sign of needing weaning, it may, with other signs be an indication that your baby needs weaning. Daytime sleeping may also become disturbed, with your baby waking earlier or not settling down as easily. Although again this could also be caused by teething, illness or growth spurts.
- Your babies weight gain slows down (this is no reason to take them off milk, because the milk is full of calories). After 3 or 4 months babies weight gain will naturally slow down as their growth steadies out. Once your baby gets to around a year old and starts to move more and burn more calories their weight gain may slow down (they may start to lose their baby fat).

- Baby watches parents eating (this doesn't mean they are ready, nor does because other babies of the same age are weaning as this doesn't necessarily mean your baby is ready. Babies are individuals and will be ready at different stages.

Giving your baby food won't necessarily help them sleep through the night so you shouldn't wean them in order to keep them full at night, if anything it may give them tummy ache and disturb their sleep further. Babies often wake in the night when they are developing because their minds go into overdrive, processing their thought from the day. If baby wakes in the night hungry then give a bottle of milk. They often go through growth spurts and seem extra hungry and may need food at night. This will then normally pass and may then happen again when they have the next growth spurt. They may just take on more milk and be satisfied with this, don't confuse this with needing to wean your baby.

I personally would say if your baby is draining their bottle and wanting more, if they are on the max amount (8 oz) then try hungry milk, if they are still hungry and weight gain has slowed down they need to be weaned.

They say not to wean when teething, however babies are always teething. Once you are ready to wean your baby if they seem particularly bad with their teeth perhaps wait a week for teeth to calm down before starting weaning.

The advice is not to give your baby food before 6 months as before 6 months they are more likely to develop allergies. Therefore if your baby has a milk allergy (it is more that they can't break the milk down rather than being allergic to the milk) they won't usually get allergy tested until they are 6 months, because after 6 months they may not have the same allergies. If your baby has reflux you may be advised to wean your baby earlier, only do this on the advice of a pedetriain.

When you start weaning the amount of milk you give and the milk intervals will change. Your timings will need adjusting and it will be confusing at first.

Too much milk when weaning can cause constipation. 500ml is the min amount of milk a day that your baby should have although they may need more. At the start they will be getting their nutrition from milk and just having food to get used to the taste and textures and to experiment. They maybe having their normal milk intake and then just one small meal or peicie of food a day, this is gradullay inceased and as time goes on they will have less milk and more food and will get their nutrition from food. This is when you are less worried about follow on milk (but until then they need the right milk for nutrition). At this stage you can worry less about milk but baby still needs at least 500ml. Even though your baby may get the nutrition from food they need milk for their calcium. However rather than getting them to drink milk you can get them to eat milk by giving them foods that contain milk such as cheese and yoghurt, a small bowl of cheese may be equivalent to up to 300ml of milk. You want them to end up having enough food to fill them up and give them nutrition so you don't want them filling up on milk and not having enough food. You will need to increase your baby's water intake and substitute the milk for water. The less milk that they have the more water they will need, in order to stay re-hydrated.

Items that you may need for weaning;
- Mini food blender / hand blender
- Masher
- Food storage pots/tray/ice cube trays/freezer bags
- Labels for the storage pots/marker pen

- Beakers x 2
- Trainer cups
- Bowls (bowls with suction pads stop baby throwing bowls across the room).
- Soft spoons
- High chair (its good to get one with an adjustable height, and adjustable tray, you can even get them so the back reclines slightly, or stackable ones if you have twins).
- Splash mat
- Bibs – long sleeved bibs and aprons are great for baby led weaning, which can be messy. They are also good for arts and craft i.e. painting.
- Muslin cloths
- Wet wipes (for when traveling) / Sterilising wipes
- High chair toys
- Booster table seat (for travelling with older babies) / Travel/pocket high chair
- Sandwich bags to sore spoons in to keep them sterile.
- A bumbo seat is great to help babies sit up.
- A suitable bib, a floor covering and hand held hoover are essential.
- Don't give your baby metal spoons as they have sharper edges and can hurt your baby if s/he bites down on it.
- Normal hand held blenders will do you don't need specialist baby food grinders (you can get some that take the skin and seeds off that could be good, however the skin and seeds also hold the goodness and these types of grinders can be fiddly and messy to use, not to mention expensive).

Choosing a highchair;

Highchairs come in all shapes and sizes, but far more important than whether or not it complements your kitchen decor is whether it can fold away (if you need it to), comes with a tray (if you want it to) and is easy to clean.

When looking into getting a highchair think about what features you want i.e. one where the seat goes up and down so you can adjust the height, a shelf that you can put wipes on. It is also a good idea to consider if it can fold up and how much space it takes up.

It is a good idea to get a portable highchair and keep it in the boot. Its great for holiday, for visiting friends and if you go to a restaurant and they have run out of highchairs.

You can get a highchair that goes into a desk and table afterwards. Although it maybe better to get a better highchair and then get a separate desk and table later.

Using a highchair;
It is a good idea when you have your baby in the highchair next to the table not to tuck your baby into the table in case your baby grabs your food & drinks from table.

You can get some without straps that lock the baby in with the tray that, they don't have gaps and are more hygienic.

How much food and milk to give;

From 6 months old you may want to give 2 tea spoons of chosen food in the morning, then babies milk for lunch and then again in the evening 2 tea spoons (once you have established there is no reaction). By giving food at night you are giving extra calories to stop baby getting hungry in the night. By 7 months you can increase it to 4 tea spoons and by 8 months old 8 to 12 tea spoons per meal (depending on your baby and his/her requirements).

Cow and gate recommend from 6 months your baby will need between 600-800 calories a day

When weaning a baby onto solids;

- Never leave baby alone with food as this can cause a choking hazard.
- Make your own fresh food rather than buying it.
- Start by weaning your baby gradually – start with a tea spoon or two once a day.
- Its better if the food is smooth so puree or mash the food and mix with some breast milk. At this stage the baby still needs to get it nutrition from milk (until it starts eating properly).
- Offer the food ½ way through a milk feed so that s/he is not too hungry or full to try it.
- At first offer no more than one or two new tastes every few days. Once your baby is happy with these you can introduce new foods and eventually start mixing the foods together.
- Once you know what baby can eat and s/he is safe with most foods you will need to mix them up to ensure that s/he gets all his/her nutrition.
- If baby obviously doesn't like something, don't force it on him/her. Give it a week or 2 and then try it again.
- The first foods should be bland and smooth. Baby rice or root vegetables such as potatoes and carrots are good, also banana, cooked apples and pears.
- When weaning have ice cube trays stocked up. Fill them with some of each food i.e. one potatoes and one carrot etc, pop it out into a tub when you go out and then it will stay cool and defrost whilst you are out.
- You may also want to collect jam jars to save the baby food in.

When you first start weaning give baby rice at night in order to get your baby to sleep through the night.

They know when their full so don't keep feeding them or force them to eat more if they are not interested in their food.

Once weaning is established give your baby a good mix of foods in order that s/he gets a balanced diet include;

- Startchy foods (i.e. bread, ceral, rice and potatoes)
- Dairy products (i.e. cheese, yoghurt)
- Protein foods; Meat and fish, eggs and lentils etc.
- Vegetables
- Fruit (apples, plums, apricots, pears and bananas are good but citrus and berry fruits such as strawberries should be introduced with caution).

- Probiotics and prebiotics are beneficial to your babies health. Probiotics are great if your baby has constipation, colic, colds or is on antibotics.

Vitamins;
- Make sure the omega 3 are long chained and not short chained
- Only give vitamin supplements that are specifically for babies, and do not give more than one type at a time.

Avoid;

- Salt (don't add this to the food and be wary of food that may include this especially processed foods that aren't specifically for babies).
- Sugar
- Honey (occasionally honey contains a type of bacteria that can cause infant botulism so don't give honey to a baby who is under a year).
- Egg whites (egg whites shouldn't be given before 8 months old, egg yolks can be given if cooked thoroughly to avoid salmonella)
- Tea, coffee and soft drinks (these are not suitable for babies)
- Nuts – until age 5
- Mineral water and other bottled waters may not be suitable for your baby due to the high mineral content. If using bottled water look for one that says suitable for babies or contains less than 200mg of sodium per litre.
- Don't give your baby low fat foods such as skimmed yoghurt. Babies need full fat milk, cheese and yoghurt until they are 2 years old. This is because they need the fats to give them calories, which they convert to energy.
- Foods with added dietary fibre should be avoided i.e. wheat germ, all bran and bran flakes, this is because they may fill the up before they get all the calories and nutrients that they need.
- Saturated fats and trans fats should be avoided.
- Shark, swordfish and marlin should be avoided. Due to their high mercury content they should not be eaten by anyone under the ae of 16 otherwise this could affect their nervous system.
- Try to avoid foods with artificial colourings

  NB. Make sure you cut the skin off of grapes and tomatoes and cut grapes in half (otherwise they can become a choking hazard). Rice maybe too hard to start off with so coo it for slightly longer.

Before 6 months avoid;

- Fish & meat
- Raw seafood/shellfish
- Foods containing gluten e.g wheat bsed breads, some cerials, pasta and rusks *
- Eggs
- Beans and pulses
- Citrus fruits
- Dairy products especially blue and unpasteurised cheeses

Foods to avoid in the first 12 months;
- Honey

- Salt – babies under one year should have no more than 1g of salt and one to three year olds should have no more than 2g of salt a day.
- Sugar
- Whole nuts (until age 5)
- Low-fat foods (until age 2)
- High fibre foods
- Uncooked or partly cooked eggs and therefore ice ceam
- Blue and unpasteurised cheeses
- Raw shellfish (after 6 months cooked shellfish is ok)
- Shark,marlin and swordfish (until age 16)
- Smoked and salted meats and fish
- Fizzy drinks
- Caffeine
- Cows milk (apart from small amounts in food which is okay after 6 months, but cows milk can't be drunk in large quantities until your child is at least a year and then you may want to go onto cows milk or the next stage follow on milk).

The issue of giving cow's milk to babies is one highly debated by inexperienced mothers, however experts do not recommend this type of milk until the baby is 12 months old. After the baby has reached a year old, there are a number of advantages where cow's milk is concerned.

Reasons as to Why Cow's Milk Is Inappropriate in the First Year of Life

There are multiple disadvantages and risks associated with the use of cow's milk for babies who are less than 12 months old, therefore its introduction must be delayed until the baby is above the advised age. The first reason as to why mothers should avoid feeding their babies cow's milk is because a baby's digestive system is not mature enough to digest the proteins contained by this type of milk. In addition to this, cow's milk also comprises large quantities of certain elements that can affect the baby's kidneys such as sodium, potassium and chloride.

Another reason as to why cows' milk does not benefit babies is that it lacks the vitamins and minerals that are essential for a baby's harmonious growth and development during his first twelve months of age. This deficiency is best illustrated by the lack of vitamin E, zinc and iron with cow's milk being a cause of iron deficiency and even internal bleeding for babies under 12 months old.

The importance of iron in a baby's life translates into its role of helping the body make red blood cells, a decreased level of red blood cells being known to cause anemia. It's true that newly born babies have enough iron in their bodies however by 3-4 months of age the iron supply gets depleted, requiring extra iron which needs to be obtained from the baby's diet. If by any reason the mother is unable to breast-feed her baby, iron-fortified formulas are available on the market to ensure infants get the proper amount that their body needs.

Extended studies have proved the often occurrence of iron deficiency anemia in babies less than a year of age which in some cases has related to developmental delays that could not be reversed by a late iron-rich diet.

The Advantages of Feeding One-Year-Olds With Cow's Milk

Once the baby reaches the adequate age for cows' milk consumption, mothers are advised to feed cow's milk as this type of nourishment is great for building and adding strength to the baby's teeth and bone structure, as well as for improving blood coagulation and muscle control. Cow's milk is a good source of vitamin A, calcium and phosphorus, and most milk products contain high amounts of vitamin D which is necessary in aiding the body absorb calcium. The latter decreases the risk of suffering from fractures later in life and also reduces the chances of getting a stroke or suffering from high blood pressure and colon cancer. Another benefit of cow's milk is that it contains protein that contributes to the baby's growth, as well as carbohydrates for giving the infant enough energy to last a whole day.

Making the Switch Towards Feeding Babies Cow's Milk

Babies are not used to the taste of cow's milk, so some infants may take a while before they get used to the new type of milk. In order to facilitate the switch, mothers are advised to mix cows' milk with their usual one, be it breast milk or formula, paying attention to the amounts so their babies will be willing to drink the new milk just as easily as the one they were used to. Hence, the first few mixtures should contain larger amounts of formula, over time the amount decreasing until the baby is fully happy with drinking cows' milk only. Another way of helping babies get used to the dietary change would be to alternate bottles of formula with cows' milk until the transition is finalized.

The Amount of Cows' Milk Recommended for Babies

The American Academy of Pediatrics has stated the importance of avoiding feeding the baby too much milk as such a diet would increase the risk of getting anemia or nutrient deficiencies. This is explained by the fact that too much milk will prevent the baby from eating the whole foods that his body needs, therefore the above mentioned organization has recommended the amount of 16 ounces of milk per day as being the most adequate, larger quantities of 16 to 24 ounces being also accepted in the case of infants of one to two years old.

Milk Allergy

A milk allergy is a rare food allergy that affects only 2 to 3 percent of babies, 95 percent of them outgrowing it by the age of 3. A milk allergy has two common causes, one of which is genetic. The latter is explained by the occurrence of food allergies or allergic diseases in family members, this situation increasing the baby's risk of developing an allergy such as the one related to milk. Another reason that explains a milk allergy is the baby's early contact with cow's milk protein, either before birth through the mother's diet or in the following months.

Children who are used to drinking cow's milk-based formula won't develop a milk allergy, and neither will babies who were exclusively breastfed due to the exposure of cows' milk protein existing in their mother's milk. In order to detect the occurrence of milk allergies in babies, mothers ought to know the main symptoms associated with this kind of allergy. Therefore, parents should contact the doctor if they notice blood in the baby's stools, or if the baby suffers from diarrhea and vomiting. Other irregularities such as eczema, hives, rashes in the mouth and chin area, a runny nose, coughing, wheezing and other breathing difficulties may point to the fact that the baby's respiratory system is disturbed by a milk allergy.

What Kind of Cow's Milk Is Best for Babies?

When the switch towards cow's milk is made, parents should know that skimmed milk must be avoided in the case of babies who are under two years old. Only full fat cow's milk is the proper nourishment for helping infants obtain a healthy growth and development. However there are other beneficial types of milk aside from regular cow's milk that are being sold in babies' stores.

Some mothers purchase organic or hormone-free milk to feed their babies with, this option coming with a significantly higher price tag. Although studies are inconclusive as to whether these types of milk are a lot more beneficial than regular cow's milk, it is advisable to purchase organic milk if possible since the certified organic type of milk is free of hormones, antibiotics and other harmful additions that are given to some dairy cows.

Food allergies;

Keep a food diary of what you give baby and how s/he reacts to the food. That way you can tell what s/he likes, ensure that s/he is getting a balanced diet and if s/he is ill you can trace back what s/he has eaten and identify possibly allergies.

Food allergies are rare however if anyone in your family has eczema, asthma or hayfever you need to be vigilant for allergies. If you or your partner has a food allergy your baby may also have it so discuss this with your health visitor.

An allergy is….

An allergy is when the body's immune system tried to attack something that is normally harmless, such as food or pollen. This can be immediate or take several days for sympton to present themselves depending on the severity, symptoms may include;

- Swelling (possibly of lips and tongue)

- Sneezing and watery eyes

- Rashes, eczema, or itchy skin

- Asthma or wheezing

- Vomiting or diarrhoea

- Anaphylaxis (in rare cases)

Peanuts should be avoided until age 5 but if your child has another allergy or there is a family history of allergy check with the doctor before giving peanuts, even if your child is over 5.

A food intolerance is...

This does not involve the immune system and is the body being unable to digest something properly, such as lactose. Symptons tend to be less immediate and may include;

- Diarrhoea

- Bloating

- Wind

Eating too much of the same food may cause a food intolerance or allergy.

Soluble fibre is better for you as its easier for the body to digest than non-soluble fibre. For instance oats, fruits, seeds, nuts and vegetables.

Choosing a cup;

It is a good idea to get your baby used to drinking from a cup from about 6 months, its best to start with a free flowing cup and ideally one with a lid. When your baby is older and is used to drinking if you want you can get an anti spill cup with a valve.

New research is continually updating and leading to changes in advice. There are currently two schools of thought on weaning there is the traditional method of weaning and now the current advice is suggesting baby led weaning...

Baby-led weaning's for you if... You don't mind mess. Because there will be loads of it.

Getting started;
- When you decide to start weaning, time it right. Choose a quiet time when your baby's probably a bit peckish but not frantically hungry. And you're feeling calm and collected.
- Think small. One or two spoonfuls (or mouthfuls) is all you're aiming for to begin with. If your baby's just not interested, leave it and try again another day.
- Don't be put off by funny faces. Babies can pull the most amazing grimaces at new tastes and flavors – even if they actually really like them.
- Stay with him. Never leave a baby alone when he's eating: you need to be there to make sure he doesn't choke (unlikely but not impossible).
- Milk's still the main thing. Starting solids is not a cue to start dropping feeds. For a considerable time to come (and at least until he's established on three decent meals a day), your baby still needs to get most of his daily nutrients and calories from breast or formula milk
- Have a camera ready. To catch those first gummy, carroty smiles!
- Know when to stop. If your baby turns her head away from your spoon or loses interest in the food on her tray, it's time to call it a day.
- It may take your baby a while to get used to the whole idea of swallowing food. Let him set the pace.
- Have a good supply of bibs, a splash mat and face cloths to clean your baby afterwards.

First tastes;
What to dish up: Whatever your approach of choice, good first foods are gently cooked vegetables (carrot, parsnip, potato, cauliflower) or fruit (melon, banana, avocado, pear).

Spoon-feeders could also try plain natural yoghurt (but not before six months; see A word of warning for anyone starting before six months) or plain baby rice mixed with your baby's usual milk. This last option has the advantage of tasting reassuringly familiar, but the collective Mumsnet opinion about it is rather withering, as summed up by mears: Forget the baby rice: it is like wallpaper paste. Go straight for carrot!

How to dish it up: If you've decide to wield a weaning spoon, you'll need to blend or mash the food first to quite a smooth consistency. Think yoghurt or milkshake.

Pour the extra puree into ice-cube trays, then transfer the cubes to a freezer bags. Now you've lots of 'meals' from not very much effort.

Cut veg into chip-shaped batons or divide into baby-fist-sized florets, and cut firm but ripe fruit into wedges big enough for your baby to grab. Put them on your baby's highchair tray and resist the urge to interfere any more.

"As a first food, most people steam carrots, cut up cucumbers, make toast fingers or crinkle-cut bits of mango but there's no reason whatsoever why your baby can't have a pile of spaghetti bolognese or mashed potato to dig into if that's what the rest of the family are having.

If you're spoon-feeding, Allow a couple of weeks for your baby to get used to the idea of taking a few different-tasting foods from this round plastic thing you keep waving in front of his mouth. Then you can gradually increase the amount you give and the number of times you offer it each day.

Aim for three 'meals' a day by seven months (see Weaning Timetable). You should also start leaving the food a little lumpier now and introducing new tastes, such as fruits and veg you haven't tried yet and (assuming your baby's over six months) well-minced meat or fish, cooked and mashed lentils, (thoroughly cooked) eggs, rice, porridge, cheese and chopped pasta.

And now's also the time to bring on the finger foods, if you haven't already. Offer your baby sticks of food he can hold in his fist and suck/gum down on.

"Finger foods my son loved – and still does – include strips of toast, cheese, avocado, cooked carrot, banana, sweet potato (roasted in oven), rice cakes, and fish/chicken goujons." Sunshineymummy

For baby-led weaners, it's simply a question of keeping on offering the veg and fruit and, as your baby gets the hang of the whole gumming down/swallowing thing, gradually introducing more frequent meals and a wider variety of foods, including meat, fish, bread and dairy products.

Your baby may not eat anything much to begin with. He'll probably just squish it all about. But, once he discovers that his new 'toys' taste nice, things will start to take off.

Even so, it won't be long before you're amazed at what your baby is able to cope with...

"You can just plonk cottage pie or fish pie in front of him. Or a roast – potato, Yorkshire, big strip of thick meat and all – and let him gum at it.

Don't let people get you paranoid about gagging (often used as an argument against baby-led weaning). It's not the same as choking and, in fact, babies are more likely to choke on runny foods than something more solid.

They do gag for the first few days but it stops that after a week or so. Anything they cannot cope with, they spit out.

If you decide to wean before six months (having understood the official guidelines and taken advice), you must:

Avoid all the following until your baby reaches six months: foods containing gluten (wheatflour, bread, breakfast cereals made from wheat, rusks, spaghetti or other pastas); eggs; fish and shellfish; citrus fruits, including citrus fruit juices; anything made with cow's milk (yoghurt, fromage frais, cheese). This is in addition to all the other foods to avoid in the first year. Puree all food very smoothly until your baby's six months old. Sterilise all your feeding spoons and bowls until your baby is six months old.

By seven months, your baby should be eating three meals a day and sampling a wide variety of different foods. If you're still mainly spoon-feeding, you shouldn't need to do much more than roughly mash the food up with a fork first; by nine months, you should really only be chopping or pulsing up the bigger lumps.

Whatever approach you're using, you can also now take advantage of your baby's fast-developing pincer grip (the ability to bring her thumb and first finger together to pick stuff up) to offer her smaller finger foods, such as raisins, berries, peas. At some point between nine months and a year (probably a lot sooner if you're baby-led weaning), you should find that your baby is eating more or less the same food as you – with daily portions of starchy foods, fruit and veg, dairy foods, and meat, fish, egg or pulses (see our sample menu to get an idea of the kind of thing you're aiming for).

What about milk?

Breast or formula milk is still a key part of your baby's diet while he's starting solids. This is not the time to start cutting out milk feeds. Only when your baby's on three good meals a day should you begin to think about reducing the amount of milk he has, And even then, it's wise to try to follow your baby's appetite and go at your baby's pace – let him decide how much milk he wants each day.

Your baby should still be having breastmilk on demand or 500-600ml of infant formula a day until the age of one. After his first birthday, you can replace formula (or breastmilk) with cow's milk but you can (and some would say should) continue to breastfeed for as long as you want.

And other drinks?

Apart from milk, the best choice of drink for your baby is water. Other drinks tend to contain sugar and/or fizz (both of which damage developing teeth). If your baby won't drink water and you want to give her fruit juice, dilute it well with water first and always serve it in a cup, not a bottle.

Introducing a cup

The earlier you get your baby used to drinking from a cup, the easier your life is going to be later on. Remember: at some point, you're going to have to wean your baby off the breast or bottle (for more about that, see our breastfeeding or bottlefeeding feature) and if she's already a dab hand with a cup by then, you've something else to put his milk in and one less thing to worry about.

Weaning timetable

When What How often Texture** Breastmilk/formula?

Weeks one and two Veg/ fruit/ yoghurt* 1/2 a day Puree/ mash well Yes (no change)

Weeks three and four Veg/ fruit/ meat*/ fish*/ cereals*/ cheese* 2/3 a day Lumpy puree/ finger foods Yes (no change)

From seven months Wide variety 3 a day Mashed with fork/finger foods Yes (can reduce amount)

From nine months Family food 3 a day Chopped or pulsed/finger foods Yes (can reduce amount)

* Not before six months **Not applicable for baby-led weaning (obviously)

Most nine-month-olds should be capable of (and excited about) chomping their way through this little lot in a day (milk feeds not included).

The spoon-free crew will do better with 'pick-uppable' cereal shapes soaked in milk and may prefer a few cubes of cheese to the otherwise inevitable fromage frais facepack but, that apart, will manage just fine with their fingers.

Breakfast: Breakfast cereal with formula, breast or cow's milk
Lunch: Mini sandwiches (tuna/chopped chicken/cheese) or pasta shapes with tomato sauce; melon chunks
Supper: Well-minced meat/fish fingers with mash and broccoli or veg risotto; yoghurt or fromage frais

Some cultures have weaning parties and some children's centres have weaning parties. In Asian culture at the weaning party they place objects on a tray and the object that the child picks dictates what they will do when they grow up ie. If they grab a stethoscope they will be a doctor and if they grab a pen they will become a writer.

Traditional weaning;

5 step programme or you may know it as Stage 1 is runnier food, stage 2 is thicker, stage 3 is food that they can bite;

Step 1 (stage 1) – introduce baby rice – food packets maybe labelled stage 1
Step 2 (stage 1) – introduce purees– food packets maybe labelled stage 1
Step 3 - increase the amount and variety of purees
Step 4 (stage 2) – introduce protein rich foods– food packets maybe labelled stage 2
Step 5 – introduce lumps i.e. mash rather than puree / establish 3 meals a day
After this between 9-12 months your baby should be moving onto chopped or minced family meals. (stage 3)

9 or 10 month old babies may refuse to be spoon fed and may decide to feed themselves, where as others may continue to want to be spoon fed after a year.

Baby led weaning (BLW);

Baby led weaning is when you let baby pick food up themselves, rather than spoon feeding them.

If you wean at 4 months you need to spoon feed and do pureers this is slower, between 4-6 months they do lots of development and at 6 months they can eat finger food so if you do baby led weaning you wait until they are 6 months and then go straight into finger food and skip purees and spoon feeding.

There is no need for blenders or storage pots. They need to learn to chew and not suck, if they push food out then they are not ready to swallow food and it's too early for weaning. When you put food in it goes to the back of the mouth where as when they eat finger food themselves they chew propely at the front of their mouth and there is therefore less chance of choking. Therefore the advice says wait until they are older and can swallow and then give them finger food so that they can feed themselves, its also much easier for you.

You can introduce them to a spoon with yoghurt and let them spoon feed themselves (use soft spoons and dippers).

Baby led weaning is good for hand and eye co-ordination.

See Jill Raplin – Baby led weaning (book is on Amazon).

You can mix both methods of feeding although once you start to feed baby they will be lazy and not feed themselves because they will want you to feed them and if you give pureer food they may not learn to chew and may have issues with finger food.

Baby may gag, this is normal, don't make a face in front of baby as this may put baby off, also if they see you frowning at certain foods they may pick up on this and may not want to eat it. They will lead from your example and if you don't eat something, they will be less likely to. Babies have the gag reflex at the front of their mouth, not at the back like adults so they are much better at dealing with unwanted food.

Baby led weaning allows babies to develop their jaw (because the food is not mashed they have to learn to chew) this helps them learn to talk.

BLW involves offering babies a range of foods and allowing them to explore and select their foods and self feed as soon as they are ready. It can be seen as a natural extension from breast feeding, but bottle fed babies can baby led wean too.

Initially your baby might only touch and play with the the food, before moving on to licking, tasting and finally eating some. When offering foods such as rice and cereals you can give your baby a spoon, but they will probably start eating it with their fingers first, before mastering the use of a spoon. Be warned, this can be a messy process, so you might want to invest in a messy mat and some bibs first!

It is good to let your baby play with food be messy and experiment. It stops them from being fussy eaters as they get older. Also when they feed themselves they know when they are full.

There is a time and a place for food – ie. high chair /mat – picnic. But I wouldn't let my son run round playing with food or eat in the car. I thought it dangerous and that it was better mannered and more controlled to have set areas and times for eating.

Once your baby has developed enough to sit up unaided (or with minimal support) - and can grasp and pick things up and guide them accurately to their mouth - they can be encouraged to start handling food. However, they may not be able to chew and swallow it efficiently yet, so don't be surprised if they don't eat much at first. Start with pieces of food that are big enough for your baby to hold their fist with some sticking out (babies can't open their fist to get at something hidden inside it until they are about eight months).

It's important that babies are allowed to learn to move food around their mouth safely in their own time, so don't place pieces of food in your baby's mouth for them. This way your baby will only pick up and attempt to eat foods which they are capable of managing.

Once you have established your baby on foods and ensured there are no food allergies you can then mix foods up, even give them curry and get them used to a range of foods and tastes, this way they won't grow up to be fussy eaters. Give them what you have, this way they will be used to eating different things and you won't have to cook separate meals.

Gradually you will have to make food lumpier to get baby used to solid textures.

If your baby doesn't like vegetables, try sweeter vegetables first. Keep trying other vegetables and baby may take to them later. Babies learn by copying the food that you eat, they learn to like food (the more they are give a food the sooner their taste buds will acquire to it). After 12 months it takes longer to learn to like new tastes. Sometimes you will have to offer a food up to 12 times before your child will try it. It's important not to get into a battle and to offer the foods to your child in a positive way. If your baby doesn't want to eat it maybe that s/he is drinking too much milk or juice. This can lead to iron deficiency, so you may want to moderate what you child is drinking or just give water instead of juice.

Weaning chart - a basic guide

Stage	Can Have	Can't Have
4-6 months	Baby Rice Basic fruit and vegetable purees Lentils **Note:** *babies can digest yellow/orange vegetables more easily than green vegetables initially.*	Gluten (avoid wheat, rye and barley-based foods e.g. bread, flour, pasta, some breakfast cereals, rusks and oats.) Eggs Nuts and sesame foods (like sesame oil) Fish or shellfish Soya-based products Honey Cows, goats and sheep's milk Soft and unpasteurised cheeses Chicken or meat Salt
6 to 9 months	Fruits and vegetables Oats and other gluten foods. Avoid very high fibre foods though Cooked eggs Peanut butter and ground nuts (only if no history of allergies in family and not whole nuts as they're a choking hazard) Chicken Fish Meat (including beef, pork	Honey Salt Shark, swordfish or marlin (due to high mercury levels) Goats and sheep's milk Mould ripened soft cheeses Raw or lightly cooked eggs Sugary foods and drinks (these can encourage a sweet tooth and lead to tooth decay when your baby's teeth start to come through. Only add sugar to

	and lamb) Cheese and cow's milk for cooking **Notes:** *It's best to start giving mild tasting chicken and white fish before introducing the stronger flavours of beef or lamb.* *While cow's milk is suitable for cooking, it shouldn't replace breast or formula milk as a drink until your child is 12 months old as it is too high in salt and protein and too low in iron and other vitamins.*	foods if it's really necessary. Sweet puddings, biscuits, sweets and ice creams are not recommended.)
9 – 12 months	As above Finger foods and bigger lumps	As above

Cooking fruit & vegetable purees; The easiest way to make your own purees is to wash, peel, chop and then steam whichever fruit or vegetable you're using until it's soft. Be careful not to overcook as the food will lose its taste and texture. Then blend it in a liquidiser or mouli. You can control the texture by adding a bit of the reserved cooking water or breastmilk / formula milk.

Always allow the food to cool and then test it yourself to make sure it's the right temperature before giving it to your baby.

Freezing purees; Homemade purees can be made in batches and then frozen. Once you've made the puree allow it to cool before freezing. You can use ice cube trays (just make sure you cover them so they don't get contaminated from other food in the fridge) or individual ice cubes with lids. If using ice cube trays, once frozen you can pop the cubes into labelled freezer bags. This way you have a ready supply of different frozen purees that you can mix and match once your baby is happy with single-ingredient purees.

When re-heating, you must make sure the food is piping hot, and then allow to cool before giving to your baby.

Do not reheat foods more than once and never refreeze uneaten food.

Texture and consistency of food;

Start by whizzing it all in a food processor to a smooth consistency (using the veg juices form the bottom of the steamer) as they progress, you can then use less juice so the consistently was thicker. Then we progress to half in the processor totally smooth and half mashed with a fork so we have a rougher consistency and then gradually whizz up less and less in the food processor. Then mashing it all, and then leaving a bit more lumps in until you eventually progress to all just chopped very small.

Try starting with some basic purees;

- Apple puree
- Pear puree
- Mashed bananas – no need to cook
- Mashed avocados – no need to cook
- Mashed papaya – no need to cook
- Mango puree - no need to cook
- Peach puree - no need to cook
- Butternut squash puree
- Sweet potato puree
- Carrot puree
- Courgette puree
- Swede puree
- Green beans puree
- Parsnip puree

Puree Combinations; Once your baby is used to single flavours, you can start trying out different taste combinations.

These points may help when your baby starts to eat solid foods:

Eat with your baby – eat together as a family

• It needs to be a relaxed time – not when you are in a hurry or the baby is unsettled.

• To eat solid foods your baby has to learn to move food from the front of their tongue to the back so that they can swallow it. Some seem to do this really quickly and others take longer – that is OK, it's more important to go at your baby's pace.

• Your baby should be sitting up straight and facing the food. This will make it easier for them to explore foods and they will be less likely to choke. A high chair may be useful.

• Everything you use for feeding your baby should be really clean (see page 43 for more information about safety and hygiene). It's better to spoon out the amount you think your baby will eat and heat this, rather than heating a large amount that then goes to waste. You can always heat up more if it's needed. Some babies are happy to eat food that has not been heated.

• At first your baby will only need small amounts to try.

• Cover the floor with newspaper or a protective mat and use a bib to catch food spills – introducing solids can be a messy business!

• Feeding your baby is a great opportunity to communicate, so keep talking to them the whole time. This will help them to relax while they are eating. You will usually be sitting facing them, so they can really concentrate on what you are saying.

Initially, your sentences can be very short ('More?'). As your child gets older, you can start offering more choices and using more complex language ('Do you want milk or juice?').

• Babies love to explore and do things for themselves – it is how they learn new skills – so encourage your baby by giving finger foods so that they can do it for themselves.

• **Never** leave your baby alone when eating as they could choke.

How will I know when my baby has had enough? Most babies know when they have had enough to eat, so don't try and persuade your baby to take more food than they want. Babies are telling you they have had enough when they:

• turn their head away

• keep their mouth shut

• push the bowl or plate away or on to the floor

• scream or shout

• keep spitting food out, and /or

• hold food in their mouth and refuse to swallow it.

It doesn't really matter how much they eat; the important thing is to get them trying lots of different things. Give your baby plenty of attention, chat and enjoy meals together, and don't pressure them when they refuse food.

It is nice to eat together, if your baby sees you eating s/he will eat better, because theylearn from copying you. It is therefore important that you have good eating habits too. When you start weaning your baby it is a good time to start having a healthier diet with more fruit and veg yourself.

Fussy eaters; Get going as soon as possible with offering them a variety of foods after weaning is established. Research shows that if your child has been introduced to a wide range of foods straight from weaning, they are more likely to accept them. Only 4% of new foods are accepted after the age of two. A delay in offering textured, 'lumpy' foods or chunks of food can contribute to later faddy eating. Almost all children aged around 2 - 3 have their food favourites and will take against certain other foods that they have previously liked. Many use food refusal as a way to get attention. If they are not underweight and seem healthy, and are eating some foods from each of the groups don't worry too much. If they see you get agitated, or if you try to force feed this will make the situation worse. Children who will only eat a few different foods can be a worry but seem to do better on such limited diets than you might think. Try to build on a favourite food and work others in.

Tips on getting children to eat;
- Show by example. If everyone is eating it and there is no alternative then there is more chance they will eat it.
- If you only have healthy food available and don't have junk food in the house then they are limited to when they can eat junk food.
- It is a good idea to also eat sit round the table and eat together as a family.
- You can also try having tea with another child who is a good eater and don't criticise your child but be amazed and delighted by the other child "Wow X you are such a good eater." This is a form of practising the positive parenting rule about using positive language to praise and encourage a child, rather than criticise.
- Don't be too tense, as children can be put off their food by tension - or learn to like the attention that food refusal brings. Sometimes if you turn things into a big deal it can make them worse.
- Tastes for salty and sweet foods are developed early on - though they can be reversed, it is harder when entrenched. However, there is nothing wrong with many puddings - things like custards and fruit desserts can offer a range of nutrients such

as vitamin C, calcium and protein, and if your child eats a balanced diet, the small amounts of sugar in such desserts are acceptable.

- Get children involved, children enjoy preparing food - washing fruits, mixing, kneading, and then taste testing.
- Reduce their milk intake so that they are not filling up on milk, if they are hungry they will soon eat.
- If your child is becoming increasingly selective with food, it's always worth asking a health professional for advice.

Nb. Always stay with your child whilst they are eating in case they choke.

Hygiene;

Protect your baby by practising good hygiene;
- Wash and dry your hands before preparing baby's food.
- Check that your baby's hands are clean before feeding.
- Keep work surfaces clean and clear of pets
- Keep raw meat at the bottom of fridge
- Cooked food should only be reheated once
- Cook foods thoroughly and cool it as quickly as possible to a lukewarm temperature, before giving it to your baby.
- Wash and peel fruit
- Avoid raw eggs and raw shellfish

NB. Grapes and tomatoes skins can be a choking hazard. Peel grapes and/or cut in ½ or mash up before giving to your child. You may also want to lightly cook hard foods until your baby has enough teeth to cope with them safely. Be careful with foods that have skins, such as chicken and sausages and fish with bones.

Vitamins;

If your baby is 6 months + and has less than 1 pint of infant formula then they may need vitamin drops (of vitamin A, C an D) until they are age 5, check with your doctor/health visitor.

When it comes to vitamins and babies who are on formula, it's a different story. Formula is already fortified with vitamins A, C and D, and many other super nutrients, so as long as your infant is getting 500 ml (18 fl oz) of formula each day, he's getting all the nutrients he needs at this point in his young life. But once he starts solids – especially when he's eating them regularly and drinking less formula – it'll be a whole new nutritional ball game. He'll start to get less of his nutrition from formula and more of his nutrition from foods, so at that point, you'll want to have a conversation with your health visitor about supplementing vitamins A, C and D. The Department of Health recommends that all children between six months and five years take vitamin drops containing these vitamins.

Other vitamin variables to consider: There are a few more caveats to consider when it comes to vitamins and babies. Talk with your health visitor if these conditions apply to you or your baby:

• Your baby was premature or has health problems.

• You're breastfeeding and you're a vegan, which may mean that you're not getting enough

B12, iron, zinc or calcium.

• You're breastfeeding and you think your diet is lacking some important vitamins and minerals.

How much food? To give you an idea of how much food you need to understand that a baby's stomach when you start weaning them onto food is the size of a walnut and by the age of 2 it is roughly the size of a pear (or the size of the baby's fist). Therefore small regular meals are best.

However my baby had more than a fist full....

Your baby is used to milk and unlike food milk is easy to digest because it is liquid, therefore a baby can have more milk than would fill its stomach as it gets absorbed in quickly. As your baby starts crawling and is getting more exercise they will burn off more calories and will want more food (the same as a milk feed a baby that has had a busy day or is having a growth spurt will require more milk).

Milk and food may bloat and cause reflux so give little and often

Further advice when weaning;
- Let children be messy so that they will be less fussy (get a painting apron for baby to wear rather than a bib).
- The more foods you introduce the less fussy your baby will be. If your baby/child doesn't like a food keep trying it on them. It takes 12-15 times of trying a food to like it. Often they may reject food due to texture and not taste. It is good to offer baby everything that you eat, especially between 8-12 months. At one year they may get fussy as they find other things to do such as crawling/walking and may loose interest in food, therefore if they only have a few foods they eat they will then have even less so its best to start off with a good variety of foods. They fussy stage is usually between age 1-5 years old. Let them have some choice (but you can pick what they choose from i.e. pick healthy options), this way they feel involved and interested but don't give too much choice as they may get confused.
- It is also good to have a variety of food so that your child is getting a balanced diet and all the vitamins they need.
- Make your own food, try to avoid jars as they are processed and are bland in one texture, instead make fresh food and freeze (this is cheaper). However when you are out and about it's a good idea to use jars and packet food so that you don't have to worry about keeping it cool and heating it adeqauetly to avoid food poising. You can get organic convience foods that don't have preservatives in. These convienience foods are more expensive but easier when you are out and about.
- The NHS have healthy start vitamins you can buy these at clinics or you may qualify for them for free if you are on benefits and meet the criteria.
- It's good to get baby to sit round the table and join in with family meals (especially easier if you are doing baby led weaning).
- When weaning you can continue with milk to give fluids, breast milk is good to continue with to keep giving your baby antibodies.
- Only give soft foods raw, not hard food i.e. not raw carrot
- When giving finger food give it in large stick shaped portions so that they have plenty to hold onto and can reach mouth easily (i.e. the length of a pen).

- When you start weaning don't worry about the quantity of the food because they can get the calories from the milk, to start off with its more about getting them used to foods, you can then increase the quantity of the food later.
- Introduce foods alongside milk, eventually as the food increases the milk feeds will decrease.
- They don't eat a lot to start but will self-regulate, they will eat what they need. Give milk first so that they are hungry but not too hungry, once they get feeding half their milk. After 8 months they should be on food and have milk reduced, they should however still have 1 pint of milk, this can be from a bottle of milk or can include yoghurts and other milk sources, rather than just milk.
- Get in a routine of breakfast, lunch and dinner, feed separate to milk so they don't fill up on milk i.e. give milk and then some food 2 hours later.
- Eggs – should be cooked so white and yolk is solid
- Nuts and seeds may cause allergies, avoid before 6 months
- Nuts can be a choking hazard until 5, but smooth peanut butter maybe okay from 6 months although some people recommend to avoid nuts.
- Babies need full fat yoghurt to get enough calcium
- High fibre foods fill babies tummy too quickly so stop them having more foods with the nutrients that they need, from other foods and should therefore be avoided
- Your baby needs; Iron, vitamin C, Calcium, Vitamin D.
- Grapes should be skinned and mashed
- When your baby smells food they may get hungry for their milk, this is what my baby used to do.
- Don't just feed your baby when s/he cries, without checking what else is wrong or your baby may use milk for comfort and therefore want to eat every time they are upset.
- Salt is really bad – adults should not have more than 6g of salt in a day, children you should avoid processed foods high in salt and should not add any extra salt into the foods.
- There is no set time table for weaning your baby and you should follow your babies lead, don't rush your baby. The ultimate aim is for your baby to have 3 meals plus 2 snacks a day, most babies will have this established at around 12 months.
- Babies are born with a natural gag reflex and will normally cough or spit out any object that they can't manage. However it is worth knowing how to deal with a chocking baby just in case.
- Your baby picks up on your expressions so kee smiling, this will make your baby feel safer and more enthusiastic about trying the new foods.
- Get a spoon case for your spoons when out and about (if you have one with 2 compartments you can keep the clean and dirty spoons separate, until you can get home and clean the dirty spoons.

- Steam vegetables are heailthy and they can hold them themselves and eat them, if you are doing baby led weaning (and there is no need to puree them).

- Babies prefer sweeter food because breast milk is sweet but don't just give them sweet food because this is not good for them. They need to get used to eating savoury foods.

- Rusks are good because they melt however they are sugary. You can get other foods that are soft and melt down such as carrot sticks, other biscuits that are less sugary rhan rusks, rice cakes. Breadsticks are good but if your baby has teeth they may bite a big chunk off and try and swallow a whole lump rather than guming it until it melts. This is what my son did so I wasn't a big fan of giving him breadsticks.

- Soft bread, such as the inside of a roll is good. You can soak the bread in olive oil or soup. As baby gets older you can give long dtrips of bread with the crusts on and toasted and s/he will hold it and gum it.

- Steamed vegetables and chopped fruit also makes good snacks.

- It is a good idea to make up a snack pot so that when you are out and about your baby can have a snack, it will be something to calm your baby whilst s/he is waiting for his/her food. It is also nice to have your meals togther with your baby . However you will usually find that your baby wants his/her evening meal earlier than you. The best thing to do is feed your baby in his/her highchair at the dinning table. Then leave your baby in the highchair, sat at the table with you and then give him/her some snacks from the snack pot whilst you eat. That way s/he will get used to sitting around the table with you. S/he will also be able to go to a restaurant and should be quite happy with snacks to keep him/her occupied. Some toys that attach to the highchair (and can't be thrown may also be a good idea).

- Check that your baby's hands are clean before feeding, especially if s/he is using his her/hands to eat or puts his/her hands in mouth whilst eating.

- You can also give your baby a spoon to hold whilst s/he is being fed so that s/he gets used to the idea of holding a spoon (just supervise him/her so that they don't ram the spoon down their throat).

- Introduce a new food in the morning, in case baby has a reaction to food (that way you have all day to see it, rather than them being left alone at night in their cot with a reaction). Don't mix foods to begin with either, until you have established that there is no food reaction to each type of food, then you can mix them.

- You should always feed baby in a high chair and not a bouncer as their stomach maybe squashed in a bouncer and as they won't be upright there is more chance of choking.

- Ideally begin to offer solids 30 mins or so before milk so that baby isn't too full, equally you don't want baby to be too hungry or his/her tolerance for trying something new maybe limited.
- Babies will regulate what they eat and will stop when they are full – which is why baby led weaning is good because spoon fed babies maybe over fed. I also found my baby self-regulated well with milk so when he wanted 2 bottles at a time I knew it was time to go onto hungry baby milk.
- When going onto hungry milk still give same quantity and amount of feeds a day as you would have done with normal milk. This should just hold your babyb off from going onto solid food for a few extra weeks. Although this didn't work with my son because he needed solid food earlier than 6 months and hungry milk wasn't enough to satisfy him.
- Start by weaning your baby onto solids when you have time and you are not rushing – meal times will take longer when you first start, it won't be like just giving some milk, so you will need to re-adjust your timings and schedules when you go from milk onto solids.

- It is good to cook in batches and then freeze the food in in ice cube trays. Use frozen foods within 8weeks and only re-heat once. When you freeze food it expands so you should not fill tubs to the brim .
- Don't buy too many small weaning pots because as your baby gets older you will need to increase the size of the pots (although you can keep the small weaning pots and use them for herbs and spices etc afterwards).
- Give a balanced diet - Gradually you are aiming to give your baby a starchy food, a fruit, a vegetable at each meal, with one daily portion of protein rich food such as cooked meat, fish, tofu or pulses.
- Drinks – offer cooled boiled water from a beaker fruit juice must be diluted one part juice for 10 parts water. Offer juice only at meal times and not sips all day, otherwise baby's teeth will get damaged. You don't really need to give them juice milk and water is fine. Even when they get older avoid fizzy drinks and tea and coffee especially with added sugar, they are bad for the teeth and also have caffine in which is bad for their tummies. Between 4-6 months baby can use a free flow beaker. You can give some water to get used to drinking from a cup? Although they probably don't need to until after 6 months, also bottle is sterile and you can measure.

They recommend that you use a beaker from 4 months because it flows faster and there is less contact with the teeth and therefore it is better for the teeth. Use one with handles for 5 mins a few times a day. Breastfed babies can sip water from a beaker. Check baby is producing enough wet nappies to ensure that s/he is getting enough fluids.

- You should be taking vitamin D from birth if you are breast feeding, especially in the UK, (bottle fed babies don't need this because there is minerals and vitamins in the formula / carton milk). All women are recommended to take supplements containing 10 mcg of vitamin D each day during breastfeeding . However if you are breastfeeding and have not taken a supplement containing vitamin D through your pregnancy, your health visitor may advise you to give your baby vitamin drops (containing vitamin D) from the age of one month
- Until your baby is a year old s/he will still need breast or formula milk after which s/he can have normal cows milk, goats milk or sheeps milk. Some milk feeds will be dropped as baby has filled up on solids however, s/he should still have 500-600ml (17-20 oz) of milk a day.
- Allergies are more likely if there is a family history of eczema or asthma. Introduce foods one at a time in the morning, so that you have all day to gauge baby's reaction.
- If you change breast milk to formula milk your baby may find it hard and maybe unsettle because breast and formular milk are very different and this can upset your baby, however changing from one formula to another shouldn't be too different and therefore shouldn't upset your baby.
- If your baby has reflux when you go onto hungry milk and then start weaning it should help to reduce the reflux as it will be heavier and will stay down longer. By 7 months as the muscles etc. have developed the reflux should go. It also helps to build up tummy muscles by giving tummy time to help with this.
- Natural yogurt is a good thing to give your baby, natural full fat yoghurt is healthy and has less sugar than most baby milks.
- If your baby demands more milk and his/her weight gain slows down than s/he may need weaning.

- You can mix any type of baby milk (or normal cows milk) with food to make it less dry and therefore easier for your baby to eat.
- It is great fun weaning your baby, seeing their reactions to different foods. When they are on solids and can sit in highchair etc it makes your life easier, you can take them out to dinner etc. It's a good idea to get your baby used to sitting in a highchair and going out to dinner etc.
- You don't always have to warm food. It is a good idea to sometimes give your baby food cold i.e. you can give food cold when out and warm at home so s/he gets used to different temptetures. Can cook sweet potatoe cool, store in fridge & take out uncooled or unwarmed because no dairy it will keep.
- Give your baby lots of different food to try and get them used to eating lots of different things, to stop them getting fussy.
- When first weaning give food for penultimate meal, and milk for the rest of the meals.
- When giving baby hungry baby milk and also when weaning baby may get constipated so you may need to give some water and also massage tummy.
- When you cook food yourself you have to heat it up when out so pipping hot and then let it cool down so its cool enough for baby to eat. Therefore have things that are fresh and don't need cooking ie bananas are a good idea (make sure it's a soft one so it mashes).

- It is a good idea to put a plastic table cloth or splash mat under the high chair when weaning.
- Boys tend to be more hungry and eat more, they also tend to be bigger than girls.
- When can hold own bottle can hold food net, put iced pineapple chunks in.
- I think that bigger/hungrier babies need weaning earlier than smaller ones, however this is just my opinion, the experts say that it is all age dependant.
- If baby is gaining weight on milk then may not need to wean yet. Don't rush, keep checking weight regularly, increase milk to max ie. If on 240ml 6 times a day, this is the max, most bottles hold and therefore baby maybe ready to be weaned (especially if weight gain has also slowed) as long as they at least 4 months. You can wean at 4 or 6 months, not before 4 months. From 4 months you will need to do traditional weaning i.e. puree from 6 months you could try baby led or a mix of both. You will know if baby spits food out s/he may not be ready yet. Don't confuse teething with needing weaning.
- In developing countries where hygiene is bad its best not to wean before 6 months, in developed countries you can wean from 4 months.
- It is a good idea to have lots of flannels when you are weaning your baby in order to clean hands and face (baby wipes may irritate your baby's face).
- Start off introducing one food at a time, for a few days of each food group and then once you know your baby is okay on the basic food groups you can then start mixing and introducing more food.

- They say a baby's stomach is the size of their fist, however my son always eat large bowls of food that were certainly more than the size of his fist.

- Introduce a sipping cup as you start weaning, as you increase solids and reduce milk you will need to increase water intake to prevent dehydration. You will also want to give your baby vitamin drops. The healthy start vitamin drops are available from the clinic and are cheaper there (they are also free if you are on benefits).
- Don't buy too much of one type / flavour of food in case baby doesn't like. Your baby also needs some variety to get a balanced diet.
- You can get a snack pot and sipping cup in one, which make a handy addition to your change bag when you are out and about.

- After 12 months you don't need to steralise bottles – the official advice is that after 6 months you don't need to cool boiled water, instead you can give your baby tap water. You also don't need to steralise your baby's bottles after 6 months. As long as you wash them well. I however preferred to steralise the bottles and use cooled boiled water until 12 months. I find it's safer to do this, especially if you are going somewhere new where the water is different because the change in water can upset your baby's stomach. However after 6 months I stopped steralsing babies bowls and spoons, I just washed them in hot soapy water.
- When giving lumpy food stand next to the high chair and don't strap in so that you can lift out in a hurry.
- Start with puree then increase the texture, after pureer make mash etc and introduce finger foods such as toast and rice cakes.
- Some probiotics may have sugar and addetives in – don't give for under a year. However you can give natural yoghurts that have probiotics in.
- Bread sticks may stick to the roof of the mouth.
- If your baby has a cold or sore throat they may not want food and may just want milk. Even if you have started weaning them and they have reduced their milk, if they are off their food, you may want to increase their milk. As long as they are having milk they are getting enough fluid and substance from this. Water alone will not be enough if they are not eating. Milk has the vitamins etc that they need. If your baby is not taking food and water and/or milk they may be in danger of dehydrating / mal nutrition so if this goes on for more than a day or 2 you need to seek medical attention. It is better to be safe than sorry and go to the doctor if you are unsure, 100 wasted visits is better thann not going the one time that you need to and having a seriously ill baby as a result.
- Water is okay to give your baby when your baby is on solids but when your baby is on milk only you don't want to give your baby too much water becaue otherwise your baby may fill up on the water and not want the milk, which has the nutrients that your baby needs.
- Once your baby is on solids you can give water with fresh OJ for constipation.
- Vitamin drops are good to give if not on follow up milk or just give an iron enriched balanced diet ie spinish iron needed for brain development. In theory you shouldn't need to give vitamin drops if you give a balanced diet although it maybe best to give vitamin drops to be on the safe side.
- Every child should have their own beaker (its not hygienic to share) and periodically you should throw away ones with spout and replace with new ones, because germs could build up in the spout
- A bumbo chair can be used to feed, and it is portable.
- You can put toys and soft balls on highchair to keep baby entertained whilst being fed/waiting for food.
- Between 6-9 months make sure you give wheat and other food to stop allergy. If you don't give certain food groups your child may develop allergies later on.
- Babies will instinctively stop feeding when their nutritional needs are satisfied. Although this is true with milk my baby did take on a lot of food and was then sick.
- Keep highchair clean – especially when baby adds some food to the tray or is teething and starts to bite the tray.
- Protein keeps baby full and babies sleep at night once they are on proteins so it's a good idea to introduce proteins as soon as you can.
- When deciding when to start weaning your baby onto solids bear in mind that for a week after having their jabs your baby gets grizzly so don't wean then, wait to see if settle first and then start weaning onto solids when they are calm and don't have anything else going on.
- There is an argument that if you start weaning later you have to work through the food groups quicker.

- When weaning keep a food diary

- Baby needs nutrients from milk, as wean they may not want milk.
- When weaning – baby rice/baby powder meals have wheat in, you may want to avoid certain things such as wheat and gluten until baby is 6 months old (before then they are likely to be susceptible to allergies).

- Raw red pepper and veg is cold and is good for them to suck when teething

- Rusks go soggy and have sugar in. biki pegs are good and you can tie string on so you can pull out so they don't choke.

- They say not to wean when they are teething but they teeth for a long time and sucking on the teat may bring blood to the gums and make them sore.

- May make baby happy when wean – maybe grumpy and cry a lot if hungry. My son seemed much happier when he was weaned onto solids (before this he was unsettled because he was hungry).

- If baby doesn't take to milk once weaning – add formula milk in rice instead of water.

- As baby gets older you don't need to steralise everything so much but should still steralise the bottles because they have milk in so need to be totally clean so the bacteria in the milk doesn't develop.

- If still gaining weight on milk don't need to wean yet. – if going on weight make sure that you get your baby weighed at the same place and the scales are calibrated etc. otherwise you might get a false reading.
- Clean out baby food jars and use them to store your baby food in.

- Do mashed sprouts and other healthy food.

- Grind down pumpkin seeds and mix in with greek yoghurt.

- Mozzarella cheese has the least salt in.

- Mix baby rice in with food to bulk it out.

- When weaning if baby has less milk give milk at night only as baby needs milk to sooth and food maybe too heavy to give before going to bed.

- If you want to give some hungry milk but your baby is constipated you can alternate the feeds between hungry formula milk and normal formula. It is a good idea to give hungry milk for first and last feed.

- pears are easy to digest and are good for weaning. Avadcdo is good. Carrot, sweet potatoe and butternut squash are good.

- Get milk and water in by adding to cerials, so if your baby won't drink all his/her bottle give weetabix with milk mixed in or cerial with milk mixed in etc.

Top tips for getting started;

- Eating is a new experience and requires your baby to move their tounge in different directions than when they are drinking milk, therefore they may spit food out to begin with, just be patient and don't rush them.
- Pick a time when they are not too tired.
- Choose a location where they will feel safe and relaxed.
- Let them hold and play with their food and the spoon.
- You may want to give them a drink of cooled boiled water to help them wash the food down.
- Test the temperature of the food on the inside of your wrist to ensure that its not too hot. Your baby's food should be served at body temperature so it shouldn't feel either hot or cold on the inside of your wrist.
- Freeze excess foods so that you can re-use them.
- Keep a record of what foods your baby has when, and what reactions your baby has, do they smile and want more, are they sick afterwards? Etc.
- If certain foods are too sour for your baby try adding baby milk or a sweeter vegetable or fruit such as banana, that way your adding vitamins and calories and not sugar.

When introducing fish and meat;
- Oily fish such as salmon, herring and mackerel, sardines and trout provide special omega 3 fatty acids, which can help your baby's development, especially their brain and nervous system.
- Use the best quality, tender cuts of meat or mice and trim off the excess fat.
- Check fish, meat and chicken before cooking and remove any bones.
- Don't give your baby shellfish before 6 months or raw shellfish before 12 months.
- Don't use processed foods and meats as they contain salt preservatives.
- Don't add stock or gravy as this is high in salts and disguise the flavour of your baby's food.
- Lean meat and fish can be steamed, grilled, roasted or fried. Try not to add too much extra oil or fat.
- Meat should be well cooked with no pink bits.
- Fish should be firm and flaky.
- It is a good idea to get into healthy habits and start cooking healthy foods before weaning your baby, that way you will instinctively cook health meals.
- Try and keep to a routine with meal times and eat with your baby.
- Babies are like us and have likes and dislikes. It is quite normal for them to have a sudden change in taste and suddenly hate something they used to love. It may also take a few attempts to get them to like something. Therefore never rule anything out, instead try re-introducing it at a later date.
- Choose a breakfast cereal that has additional vitamins and minerals.
- Al yoghurt contains milk which contains calcium so don't just go for ones that say contain calcium.
- It's normal for babies to spit food out at first (it doesn't mean that they don't like it), it is also common for babies to gag so try not to panic (never leave a baby eating or drinking alone).
- When out and about alwas have extra food with you because they may want more if they are having a growth spurt.
- Take care when giving your baby chicken or fish because of bones. Don't give them chicken on the bone.
- Take care when your baby gets teeth that s/he doesn't then bite off the finger food that s/he used to suck and instead puts it all in their mouth in one go which maycause choking. My son would bite up strips of food but put it all in his mouth like a hamster so I would have to remove some. I would also have

to check that he didn't store food in his mouth after meal times. Sometime he would keep a small piece of food in his mouth which was then a choking hazad when I layed him down to change his napp.

- Only let children eat when they are sat still at the table or in their highchair, don't let them run around with food in their mouth (it makes a mess and can be a chocking hazard).
- Don't mix food up on the plate lay it out separately. That way your baby can distinguish between the diferent foods. You can then mix some of the food in a corner but at least that way if your baby doesn't like one of the foods they still have something else to eat.
- As you child gets older try and keep to the good food habits that you have developed. Junk food is bad and may raise the risk of asthma, as well as adding on weight and not giving goodness. Make your own lollies with fresh fruit juice, this way you know that there are no sugars or additives.

Feeding babies fish;

You can introduce fish to most babies as early as 6 months, says Frank Greer, a pediatrician and former chairman of the American Academy of Pediatrics' (AAP) Committee on Nutrition. But if your baby shows signs of an allergy of any kind – such as eczema – hold off until you've checked with your baby's doctor.

Fish is one of the top eight allergenic foods, and experts used to advise parents to wait until their baby's first birthday before introducing it. That advice has now changed.

In 2008, the AAP released a report stating that there's probably no reason to wait to introduce allergenic foods until your baby reaches a certain age. "There is no evidence that delaying their introduction prevents food allergies," says Greer.

If your baby has a strong family history of food allergies or asthma, Greer says it's probably safe to introduce fish at 6 months, but advises checking with your doctor first.

As with any new food, watch for signs of a food allergy: swelling of the tongue, lips, and face; skin rash; wheezing; abdominal cramping; vomiting; and diarrhea. Allergy symptoms can be mild or severe. If you notice mild symptoms, call your baby's doctor right away. If your baby seems to be having trouble breathing, has swelling of the face or lips, or develops severe vomiting or diarrhea after eating, call 911 or your local emergency number immediately.

After introducing any new food, wait at least three days before moving on to the next new food. That way you can monitor for any reaction and know what's causing it.

Always make sure the fish is thoroughly cooked, to avoid food-borne bacteria and virusesthat can thrive in raw or undercooked fish, and properly deboned and minced or pureed. Offer a small amount and introduce only one type of fish at a time.

One important caveat: Certain fish contains high levels of methylmercury, a metal believed to be harmful in high doses to a child's developing brain and nervous system. That's why the U.S. Food and Drug Administration (FDA) recommends that you avoid feeding your child shark, swordfish, king mackerel, and tilefish – large predatory fish that contain the highest levels of mercury.

Tuna is okay in moderation but has some mercury so its best to be limited until your baby is a year old.

What to be doing and by when;

0-6 months; It is recommended that you give your baby milk only (although you may want to start weaning from 4 months).

6 months; You need to start weaning your baby onto solid foods and start introducing a sipping cup (you may want to introduce a sipping cup from 4 months especially if you have started weaning).

From 8 months your baby should be moving towards 3 meals a day (a mix of finger foods, mashed and chopped foods). My son was having 3 meals a day from approx. 7 months.

From 12 months; Your baby will be having3 meals a day plus snacks and your baby can now have cows milk (they need to have full fat milk until they are age 2 years old, after that they can have semi skimmed milk and from 5 they can ave skimmed milk). However before age 2 they must have full fat dairy products because they need the extra fat and vitamins in these products.

n.B

When you start weaning baby can get cause nappy rash or constipation. You can give some water to help with the constipation, also changing nappy regularly and using nappy rash creams or barrier creams such as Vaseline, can help reduce the nappy rash.

Feeding toddlers;

For toddlers make your own homous, have with sliced vegetables and pitta bread. Make your own mix with low-salt pretzels, wholegrain cereal, banana chips, shaved coconut etc. (only for toddlers that can chew thoroughly). Dried fruit, vegetable crips, cheese and yoghurt. Smoothies are also fun to make and healthy.

Toddlers food requirements can vary to day to day depending on what activities they are doing.
Toddlers need food little and often (they stomach is the size of their fist and if they say they are full they probably are). Healthy snacks between meals are vital, especially if your toddler is very active.
- Let your toddler feed himself/herself, where possible.
- Try to involve your child in choosing the food (give a limited choice between healthy items). Teach your child where food comes from and take your child food shopping, let them cook with you etc.
- Use your imagination and make the food like varied and delicious because toddlers are very visual.
- Use lots of different colour fruit and veg (each different colour represents different vitamins and minerals), think rainbows.
- Make the dessert delicious but healthy and don't use it as a reward for eating the main meal otherwise the dessert will be viewed as a treat and therefore wanted more often than the main meal.

- For toddlers try and keep meal times short – to 20mins, otherwise your toddler will become restless.
- Try to have meal times together as a family and have picnics in the garden etc.
- Try andbe enthusatic and eat a variety of meals without pulling faces so that your child won't develop food issues.
- Let baby hold spoon, baby can also try and feed him/herself
- If weaning early - start baby rice & then one food at a time only veg, fruit or baby rice. Purée & then try mash as will take it
- Store spoons in a sandwich bag
- When wean on solids you need a bigger bag for bowl etc
- Don't give food last thing at night as may lay heavy, having said that a good meal in the evening followed by milk keeps your baby full until morning.
- When you first start weaning you might want to store the food in small weaning tubs, you can use these instead of bowls but as baby gets older you may want to use plastic bowls. You can use ice cube trays to store and freeze baby food that you have made.
- You may want to hide the bottle first and then give baby some food first otherwise baby may just wan the bottle and no other food.
- Steam vegetables so that they are soft, that way you don't need to mash them up. Instead you can just give them to your baby in long strips to hold and feed themselves.
- As soon as your baby is old enough put them in a highchair. Babies like to join in so they will feel better once they can sit at the table with you, in their highchair, and be the same height and see whats going on/join in and interact with you.
- When weaning dont forget to sterilise the knife and chopping board if you are weaning before 6 months (after 6 months a good wash will do) boiling water is better than chemicals to steralise utensils etc.
- Give water in a doydi cup. It is important when you start weaning baby that s/he won't doesn't get dehydrated, therefore you need to get baby to have small sips of water through a cup. It is good to introduce a cup because later you want to give milk and juice through this as its better for the teeth than a bottle.
- After 1 year they may become more fussy with their food.
- Iron deficiency suppresses hunger, vitamin drops or follow on milk may help.
- You may find that your babies may not want to leave play to eat food, try winding down before meal times or putting toys in their highchair and making meal times more fun by doing aeroplanes etc.
- Keep hungry baby milk for the days when your baby is eating less, on those days give the hungry milk to bulk out, especially at night.
- Don't leave food lids on highchair tray as baby may grab them and try to eat them, some of the pouches have small lids that could be a choking hazard.
- Try and spread feeds out, don't overfeed i.e. feed and then give milk or custard and then milk straight after as this may make baby sick. If you have a sicky baby feed little and often.
- If your baby is having less than 600ml of milk you may need to give vitamin drops, your baby should get all vitamins from food but in reality probably won't so it's a good idea to give vitamin drops as an extra boost, in their food.
- If your baby won't take water – mix with juice or increase the milk that you give.
- Mix savoury foods with sweet foods if your baby is resistant to savoury foods i.e. carrot and sweet potatoe can be added to brocali. However try and give as much savoury food as you can. Don't just give your baby sweet foods because s/he will just get used to these and always want sweet food. It is a good idea to get your baby used to savoury food.

- Increase lumpy textures gradually . Babys's have a good gag reflex and will bring up food they can't break down. They need to gag a bit so stay calm, undo highchair straps for first time lumpier food in case you need to take them out and pat them on the back. If your baby is struggling, fish it out and give them something softer. However take care with finger foods, make them thin in case they eat them all in one and choke. Break rice crakers down and try and give finger foods that are soft and melt down.
- You can change the consistency of food as you need to. Weetabix can be added to purees to bulk them out. Or boiling water or milk can be added to make food softer and easier to digest. A hand blender could also be used to break food down further.
- Talk to your baby and tellthem when the food is all gone, ask them if they want more and say food and milk to them. That way they understand what you mean and will be able to ask for more, for food and milk etc.
- Give your baby a spoon to hold when feeding them. That way they get used to holding a spoon, which makes it easier for when they come to feeding themselves.
- You can grind seeds etc. such as sunflower and pumpkin seeds you can then add these with natural yoghurt.
- It is a good idea to feed your baby at same time as the rest of the family, this helps with the timings and its good for children to see you eating with them, it encourages them to eat.
- Introduce new textures when your baby is alert and happy i.e. for breakfast. Try not to introduce too many new tastes and textures all at the same time – although I did and it worked for me.
- On a hot day, don't worry if your baby is not eating too much, dont count the feeds just give water when you can. Obviously try and still give feeds but don't worry if your baby doesn't want to eat as much as normal when its hot, as long as s/he has fluid.
- When your baby's food is cooling you can give rice cakes or a healthy snack (just a small amount) or you can feed your baby and then keep him/her at the dinner table and give some healthy snacks that they can hold and eat themselves, whilst you eat, so that you are all eating together.
- It is a good idea to give finger food in big chunks. Finger food, at first, is all about giving them something to hold and taste rather than filling them up, instead the sunstance comes from milk.
- Don't let them get too fussy, If they are hungry they will eat.
- Once you start weaning onto solid foods expect changes in bowel movement. Stools maybe more smelly but they will be thicker and this may make nappy changes easier.
- As your baby gets older give them lumpier food, less milk and more water until by 12 months they are eating and drinking as a child would.
- Perhaps make one meal more substantial i.e. at lunch time you could give a bigger portion.
- You can test the tempreture of food on your top lip.
- Only give your baby plastic spoons, at first you may want to give your baby flatter spoons that are not too wide, as your baby grows you can move onto deeper and wider spoons.
- When introducing lumpier food use food that is soft and will melt in he mouth to get baby used to textures.
- BLW – is to get used to feeding self and not to take food in i.e. a chicken drumstick to gum, therefore need to give other food and milk for nutrition. I used to puree food but also give my son strips of steam carrot which he would hold and eat himself; this is because it was soft.

- When feeding your baby try not to mix food up too much. Instead put food in separately sections on the plate, in case your baby doesn't like something, or has a reaction. It also gets them used to eating different flavours.
- Babies often store small amounts of food in their mouth, after feeding check your baby has finished all the food and if necessary remove small particles. It is a good idea to check and remove food from your babies mouth before you tip them back.

Don't give your baby too much water;

- Adding too much water to your baby's formula not only risks water intoxication, it means that your baby is taking in fewer nutrients than he needs. Carefully follow the package directions for mixing powdered or concentrated formula and don't try to stretch formula by using more than the recommended amount of water.

- In some instances – if your baby has gastroenteritis, for example – the doctor might advise you to give him an electrolyte drink like Pedialyte or Infalyte to help prevent dehydration.

- Once your baby is 6 months old, it's okay to give him sips of water when he's thirsty. You still don't want to overdo it, though, or you might give him a tummy ache or make him too full to eat well. After his first birthday, when your baby's eating solids and drinking whole milk, you can let him drink as much water as he likes.

- Give your baby a drink of water when they wake up, after you have been out etc.

The brain may mix hunger with thirst; if your baby/child is crying for food but shouldn't be hungry i.e. they just eat, give them water. Its best to give water after food, rather than before so that they don't fill up before their food. Although they may need some sips first.

Don't force your child to finish all their dinner (they should know when they are full), otherwise you may make them over eat and their may then have weight issues when they get older.

If they don't want their milk, give them cheese or yoghurt for them to get their calcium.

For more information on weaning;

http://www.cornwallhealthyweight.org.uk/
www.eatsomegoodfood.org
The change for life web site also has tips on healthy eating.
www.realbabymilk.org – this is a charity set up to promote breastfeeding. They have lots of resources including a DVD on weaning called ready, steady, eat.

N.B. **The latest guidance out is that you should wean your baby onto solid food from 4 months**

Weight

As an average guide your baby may gain a 1lb a week, once weight gain is established when small (obviously when new born they loose weight at first) then eventually around 4 months weight gain may slow down.

They maybe chubby until they start crawling and loose their baby weight. Often they may start to get fat reserves before they start crawling, that they build up beforehand to keep them going.

You may find that your baby will grow outwards and get a tummy then they will reach a certain stage and will then stop growing outwards and will start growing upwards only. They will also loose baby fat as soon as they start crawling. Thererore you may want to keep clothes that are too tight but the right length for later on when your baby looses his/her baby fat as you may find that they then fit.

Potty training

Each child is different and they are all ready at different ages to start trying. 2 – 2 ½ is a good time to start trying. If your child can pull up his/her own pants and only wets its nappies every 2 hours then it's probably time for potty training. Sometimes potty training takes longer with disposable nappies as child doesn't realise that they are wet.

Children get bladder and bowel control when they are physically ready for it, and when they want to be dry and clean. Every child is different, so it's best not to compare your child with others.

• Most children can control their bowels before their bladders.

• By the age of two, some children will be dry during the day; however, this is still quite early.

• By the age of three, nine out of 10 children are dry most days. Even then, all children have the odd accident, especially when they are excited or upset or absorbed in doing something else.

• By the age of four most children are reliably dry.

It usually takes a little longer to learn to stay dry throughout the night. Although most children learn this between the ages of three and five, it is estimated that a quarter of three-year-olds and one in six five-year-olds wet their bed.

It helps to remember that you really cannot force your child to use a potty. If they are not ready, you will not be able to make them. In time they will want to use it; your child will not want to go to school in nappies any more than you would want them to! In the meantime, the best thing you can do is to encourage the behaviour you want.

Most parents start thinking about potty training when their child is around 18–24 months, but there is no perfect time. It's probably easier to start in the summer, when washing dries better and there are fewer clothes to take off, and at a time when you can have a clear run at it, without any great disruptions or changes to your child's or your family's routine.

You can also try to work out when your child is ready. There are a number of signs that your child is starting to develop bladder control:

• They know when they have a wet or dirty nappy.

• They get to know when they are passing urine, and may tell you they are doing it.

• The gap between wetting is at least an hour (if it's less, potty training may fail and at the very least will be extremely hard work for you).

• They know when they need to wee, and may say so in advance.

You will probably find that potty training is fastest if your child has started to show any of the above signs before you start. If you start earlier, be prepared for a lot of accidents as your child learns.

How to start potty training;

• **Try leaving a potty around where your child can see it and get to know what it's for.** If you have an older child, your younger child may see them using it, which will be a great help. It helps to let your child see you using the toilet and explain what you are doing.

• **If your child regularly opens their bowels at the same time each day, try leaving their nappy off and suggesting that they go in the potty.** If your child is even the slightest bit upset by the idea, just put the nappy back on and leave it a few more weeks before trying again.

• **As soon as you see that your child knows when they are going to wee, encourage them to use their potty.** If your child slips up, just mop it up and wait for next time. It usually takes a while to get the hang of it. If you don't make a fuss when they have an accident then they will not feel anxious and worried and are more likely to be successful the next time.

Your child will be delighted when they succeed, and a little praise from you will go a long way. It can be quite tricky to get the balance right between giving praise and making a big deal out of it, which you don't want to do. It's best not to give sweets as a reward, as this can end up causing more problems. When the time is right, your child will want to use the potty, and they will just be happy to get it right.

Some common problems with potty training, and how to deal with them

My child is not interested in using the potty at all

Try not to worry. Remind yourself that, in the end, your child will want to be dry for their own sake. If they start to see the whole business as a battle of wills with you, it will be much harder.

My child just keeps wetting themselves

You have two options. You could go back to nappies for a while and try again in a few weeks, or you could keep going but be prepared to do a lot of changing and washing of clothes. Whatever you decide, try not to let it get you or your child down and don't put pressure on them. Try talking to other parents about how they coped. You also don't want to confuse your child by stopping and starting too often, so if you do stop, leave it for a little while before you start again.

Just when I think things are going well, there is an accident

Accidents will happen for a while, so it's always good to make sure your child knows how pleased you are when they use the potty or manage to stay dry, even if it's just for a short time. Even though accidents can be

very frustrating, you should try not to show this to your child. Explain that you want them to try to use the potty or toilet next time. If your child starts to worry, the problem could get worse.

My child was dry for a while, but now they have started wetting again

If your child has been dry for a while either at night or during the day, or both, and then starts wetting again, there may be an emotional reason. Disruption – like moving house, or a new baby arriving – or a change of routine can often have such an effect. The best thing you can do is be understanding and sympathetic. Your child will almost certainly be upset about the lapse and will not be doing it 'on purpose'.

My child's about to start school, and they are still not dry

By this age, your child is likely to be just as upset by wetting as you are. They need to know that you are on their side and that you are going to help them solve the problem. Talk to your GP or health visitor to get some guidance. They may refer you to a clinic for expert help.

Further tips on potty training;

- At first you may want to use pull up pants (similar to nappies) rather than regular pants and you may want to keep a nappy on your child at night, until they progress enough to not need nappies and be able to use normal pants instead.
- You may want to purchase disposable potties
- Always keep a potty in the car
- Always carry spare pants and a change of bottoms, you can buy lots of cheap pants and track suit bottoms (keep some in school bag and also at grandparents house etc.)
- Also note with boys, boys may sleep walk and wee in strange places (like in their wardrobe).
- Your child may say poo and wee and pull their nappy, this is a good start but they are not ready for potty training until they can tell you every time they wee or poo (it is bad to start too early but equally you don't want to miss it, apparently there is a time that is just right, and this time is different for each child).
- Buying several potties means you can have one in each room, so they're close to hand when your toddler needs to go. Getting them used to sitting on their potty is a good idea too. You can make this more fun by telling stories or singing songs while they sit. A routine can also help, so try using the potty first thing in the morning when they're bound to need a wee!
- Start by encouraging your baby to tell you when s/he has done a poo. Praise them when they do a poo and avoid saying ugh. Once they start squatting to do a poo and if they are regular you can get them a potty. Start getting them used to doing a poo on the potty first, and try wee later. It helps if they can talk enough to tell you they have done something/need the toilet before you start potty training. First just get them used to what the potty is and sitting on the potty etc.
- When you first start potty training take a week off of work if you can, if you can and stay home for a whole week you maybe able to get your little one trained in a week.
- You can usually only begin once baby is advanced enough to talk and can tell you they need the toilet etc. its not usually until they are at least 18 months. They also have to know when they have done a wee or poo and need a nappy change, so usually when they start crying when they have soiled their nappy and want you to change it, you know its time.
- Its best to use pants only and not pull ups in the day. You might want to start with pull ups at night and then use pants and plastic sheets, under the normal sheet and have extra sheets on standby. When you first start potty training you may want to put a nappy on when you go out, this may get confusing but may be the only practicable thing to do.

- Potty training; Don't use pull up in nappy training just pants, lots of spare clothes & spare cheap trainers that can go in the wash. If children are in nappies i.e. pull ups when potty training they may not bother because they may get confused and think they can just wee in the nappy.
- Before you are potty training you may want to use pull ups instead of normal nappies if you have a wiggly baby, you can put them on with one hand. Although normal nappies can be put on without taking trousers off (which is obviously quicker if your going out and they have shoes on etc). Most nurserys insist on normal nappies and won't let you have pull ups. You can always order both and alternate between the 2.
- You can get a car seat/ pram seat liner for when you potty train so that you can take it off and clean it easier if baby has an accident. It is also handy if your baby has food in the pram etc.
- You will need a big change bag again for spare clothes when they are potty training.
- There will be a window when your baby is ready for potty training, if you miss the window of opportunity it is not the end of the world but may take longer. It can be from 18 months to 3 years to get your baby potty trained. When they are ready to start they may show signs by pulling at their nappy etc.
- 18 months is generally the earliest to start potty training – use plastic matress protector for the bed at night and put normal sheets on top.

You shouldn't push children to do things too early. You need to wait until they seem ready, or at least show an interest. Some children start later tha others, as they all develop at different rates in different areas. Some children maybe quicker at some things and slower at others. My son was slower than other babies at sitting up, but could crawl quicker. They need to develop at their own pace. You als need to think about what is going on in their life at the time, it is no point toilet training your child if you have just had a new baby and your child is feeling insecure/regressing etc.

The usual signs that your baby is ready are;
- Increased interest when passing urine or a motion; s/he may pretend play on the potty with her toys;
- S/he may tell the carer when s/he has filled a nappy, or may look embarrassed.
- S/he may start to be more regular with bowel motions or wet nappies may become rarer.

- Toilet training should be carried out in a relaxed, unhurried manner. You shouldn't force your child to sit on the potty too long otherwise s/he may rebel. It can take a few days or months, dry nights take longer but most children should be potty trained by the age of 5.
- Have the potty at home so the child can become familiar with it and include it in play to make it more fun, so your child is more relaxed about potty training.
- Some children feel insecure when sitting on a potty with no nappy on. Try it at first with a nappy on, if you need to.
- It is easier to start potty training when the weather is good and your baby can run around without a nappy on.
- It helps if your child sees other children using toilets or pottys.
- Don't make faces or show any disgust, instead be encouraging when your child succeeds and don't show anger if your child doesn't.
- Encourage good hygiene, with hand washing from the start.
- A child may prefer a seat fixed onto a normal toilet rather than a potty, although you may need a potty for car journeys etc.
- don't rush, do it in their own time. Give treats when they use the potty. Mix using the potty and the toilet, to get them used to using the toilet. You can get a special seat that goes over the toilet, so that they can sit on the toilet properly.
- When potty training – start with just getting dry in the day and then use the nappy at night until the nappies are dry, meaning they can hold it until the morning. Praise them when they do a wee in the potty or toilet. Take potty when you go out and about. When you first start potty training, stay at home for at least 2 days to get the hang of it. Its good to do it in the summer. At first your child may wee every 15 to 20 min. They might not understand the wee, where it's from and that its them doing it and they can control it, once they understand this you can move forward, you may need to show them in the potty once they have done a wee/poo and praise them at the same time.
- When they are potty training; don't shout at them if they have an accident as this may put them off.
- Ritchie used to tell me when he had done something in his nappy and so I thought he was ready for potty training, then he stopped telling me and would want to keep a dirty nappy on and not change it (especially if he was having fun playing and didn't want the distraction).
- When potty training you will need extra clothes (for your toddler and possibly for you and floor wipes/mop on standby).
- If you can keep their trousers or pants off so they get used to the sensation and understand they are weeing. Then take them to nursery in pants or no pants with

extra trousers. Line your car and pushchair with towels or seat protectors and / or put your toddler in training pants for a long car journey.

If out or on a long car journey you may need to put a nappy on, when you first start potty training.

- Some say that they don't know when they need to toilet/have done a nappy. Once they start potty training and have their nappy removed they soon get to realise when they wee/poo and what it is and therefore they get used to the sensation and recognising what it is, which helps them to quickly potty train.
- When potty training, get lots of track suit bottoms because they will have accidents and you will be getting through lots of clothes.
- To encourage your child to use the potty you could put ducks/toys on the toilet and get them to pretend to use the toilet, you could use maltesers chocolate and drop it in the toilet and pretend they have pooed.

- If you potty train too early it takes 10 times as long to get potty trained.
- Potty training – encourage them to tell you when they need to go, praise when they go and get them used to sitting on the toilet / potty first. You can even get signing potties, let them watch you and their friends go.
- When potty training pants are better than boxes because they help your child feel more supported/holds in.
- When potty training you will need a potty, potty training pants, a potty training story book, potty liners, toilet seat and disposable/travel potty, underwear and lots of tracksuits/trousers.
- When potty training are you going to start by using pull ups at night? Do you have a plastic sheet to go over the mattress?

Bedwetting;

This affects 1 in 10 children up to the age of 9.
- Reassure the child that it is not their fault
- Makesure your child drinks plenty of fluids in the day, teach them to recognise the signs of needing the toilet
- Encourage them to use the toilet regularly
- Use reward systems such as star charts for dry nights
- You can get alarm systems that wake the child when they come into contact with moisture.

General tips thoughts, observations and comments for life with a baby;

- As your baby gets older s/he can sleep on his/her tummy, and s/he may prefer to be put on his/her tummy or may just roll over, to sleep.

- Babies need naps, they are happier in the day and sleep better at night if they have had naps and aren't over tired.

- If you are doing something ie cleaning your babies nose and your baby crys & chokes. Stop, give your baby a cuddle, distract them with a toy and then try again after a while when calmer.

- You could light your baby's Christening candle at their 1st birthday

- You should tumble dry baby's clothes otherwise you will have a house full of washing; however you may need to buy the next size up clothes if they shrink.

- Don't buy baby's toys from abroad as they may not have the same safety standards.

- Your baby's soft spot may pulsate but after 18 months it should have healed/stop pulsating.

- Try selling your old toys at NCT sales, selling them to a nursery or do a toy swap.

- Get your child play dates with other kids and don't be too overprotective. They need to play slightly rough because the other children maybe rough with them at nursery. However try to teach them to play nicely and share etc.

- Its good to pick a nursery where they don't wear shoes in the baby area, one that has a baby monitor in the sleeping area as well as well as doing 10 minute checks. Some nurseries also have computers for the babies. Check what the age range is in the baby area, smaller age ranges are better.

- When you get baby's hand prints you may also want to get all different generations, done in the same go i.e. great gran-parents, granparents, parents and baby.

- You could give calpol before your baby's jabs to stop your baby getting distressed. However it might be best to give the jabs first and only give calpol if they get a tempreture as you may find that your baby maybe okay.

- If your baby is ill put calpol in abottle and warm slightly, only put a small amount of milk in, so that you know it all gets drunk and warm it before you put the calpol in.

- Tell your child to speak out what is wrong, if they are having a tantrum tell them to say what they want (speak it out).

- Having a baby puts strain on your relationship. You often argue over who is doing the most because you are so tired and need a break. It is important to support each other – you both have different stresses you need to recognise you are both stressed and help each other where you can.

- Babies like to be naked so try and give them time to crawl around on a towel naked to give them a break. They may start to cry when you get them dressed, especially when you put their arms in clothes. They hate having their arms in clothes so you may need the next size up clothes so that they are not tight on their arms.

- They sense when something is going on & don't want to miss out so won't sleep.

- It is a good idea to get a heavy cot in case a light cot may tip/move. Check your travel cot because it might have a weight limit and you may not be able to use it for as long as you can use your regular cot

- Dummy wipes can be used to clean the highchair.

- Hold your baby on chest, to calm him/her as s/he finds your heart beat soothing.

- Dontpour all jar in bowl in case baby doesn't finish and you want to keep it.

- When you change something to do with your babies routine i.e. put your baby in their own room. Do it on a weekemd, or other time when you are both off, in case your baby is unsettled. That way no one is being kept up on a work night and you can support each other, if you need to.

- Your baby may go through a phase of being silly with food. If so say no and stop feeding, then hold the spoon of food and pause just by babies mouth. That way your baby will need to open their mouth and lean forward to take it better.

- You will have less time for your partner; you will also have less patience and will get annoyed with dithering. You will find because you have a lot to do and less time that you will use short orders and may forget to have conversation. Try and communicate to each other and understand why you are being like this, be tolerant of each other and make time for each other when you can. If you get the chance, have a night out or a family holiday together. Even just one night out alone will make a big difference. You will both have different stresses and find different things hard. Don't get caught up into a competition of who works the hardest or who is most tired. Try and put yourselves in each others shoes and be tolerant of each other. I used to get annoyed that I would do things on auto pilot and much quicker where as my husband wouldn't always know what needed doing, he would have to ask. Then I realised that because I was at home all day with our baby I had more practise so found things easier. Where as he was less experienced, perhaps how I was a few months prior. The first time he had our son alone he was stressed and I thought well I do this everyday. Then I remembered how stressed I was when he went back to work and I was first on my own, then in time I found things easier. I then realised how he felt, and that he just needed some time and patience so that he could find his feet, just like I had to.

- It is a good idea to get a pram that folds down easily but also has a stroller section that folds down. I found my pram really sturdy and I could hang my bag on it but it wouldn't fold as flat as my stroller. You use your pram everyday and it will cause you so much greif if you don't get one that's right for you. Therefore it is important to spend time on choosing one that works for you (not the most expensive or the most fashionable). Think about where you live and where you will use it. If you live down a lane and have to travel over gravel paths etc get a pram with large wheels. Large wheels are better for when you are not on tarmac, so going on grass, cobles etc.

- Parenthood is like everything in life, at first until you get used to it, its hard. When you have a new born baby they scream with colic, they wake every 2 hours for feeds and its all new to you. As baby gets older s/he becomes more settled, is less deamding and you get into a routine yourself. Even breastfeeding gets easier with time, after a while they get quicker at breast feeding as they learn to get better at it and they need it less regularly. Patterns change just as you get used to them and as your baby gets older s/he will sleep less. However even though s/he sleeps less the times s/he does sleep its for longer and it's at more reglauted times and it becomes easier to change as baby's patterns change. Therefore even though you still have worries as your baby gets older and its hard when you go back to work etc. nothing is as difficult as the first couple of months. They seem so long and you think you won't get through them. However they soon pass and things do get easier. If you can try and savour the first few months (this is hard because you will feel ill from the birth and it is stressful), however your baby grows up so quick and you will soon look back on the newborn stage in fondness (you will usually forget how hard it was).
- After you have given birth it maybe painful to wee, you may find it easier to wee in the bath, and then shower afterwards.
- Grapefruit is lovely and fresh to get in a hand clenser.
- It is a good idea to get a steady, heavy cot, especially if your baby grows big and fidgets. It's a good idea to try and leave your baby in their cot as long as you can. Once they are in a bed they can get out and wonder around the house and get in your bed etc.
- If you are breast feeding, once the feeding has been established you may want to express and use a bottle. It is easier for a baby to take from a bottle and so because they don't have to work as hard, if your baby is tired and needs milk but doesn't want to take it, in order to keep baby full so s/he sleeps try giving a bottle. It is also handy so that your partner can share night feeds because you need a break in order to get all important rest.
- It is a good idea to get a stair gate once your baby is crawling, in case s/he trys to crawl up the stairs.

- Get a lightweight hoover/carpet sweeper so you can quickly go over the floor after meal times (babies make a mess when they are on solids), it is also good to keep the floor clean when s/he is crawling
- Stock up on vanish and also colour catcher. That way you can throw all the baby clothes into one wash. But always wash bright colours separately for the first time (after a few washes they should be okay). Stain removers work well on cotton baby clothes but becareful if you have got clothes such as wool, test the underside first and don't leave them to soak in stain remover too long, I damaged a couple of cardigans that way.
- If you have lots of hair loss you can get clip in hair extensions, pony tails and other peicies, they save time and make your hair look thicker.
- It is a good idea to put sunscreen on you and baby, especially the face, on a daily basis, mineral podwers maybe better than cream when its not too hot. When its sunny you will need factor 50 kids waterproof suncream. However you may need some time to get the sun on your arms so that you can get vitamin D (or take vitamin D drops).
- If your baby is very dribbly or you are in and out a lot (going from hot to cold) you may need to put cream on your baby's face to stop it drying out or getting a rash.
- At 4 or 5 months they may start going through a pinching stage and pinching your arm. Just say no and gently pull their hand off. You may find as they get older and start jumping they may jump on your legs and bruise them. As baby starts crawling and has falls and you try and hold them and dodge out of the way of things you will both end up covered in bruises.
- Keep an eye on the weight for swing chairs, car seats and jumperoo as they have weight limits.
- Makesure jumeroo is on a flat surface and make sure baby is on tip toes and not flat footed when using it.
- Give your baby floor time - put toys out & let him choose ones to go for. I usually give my son 20 mins in the jumperoo (I don't like him to be in it for too long in case it pulls on his hips), then we have 30mins floor time, crawling practise and playing with toys. The he has a nap, then more floor time and then some story time etc.
- It is quite normal (although very annoying) if your baby puts the dummy in their mouth ½ way through feeding, it doesn't necessarily mean that they have had enough. Often they may spit during meal times, this could mean they don't like it or have had enough or in the case of my son he just thought it was a fun game to play.
- Try and keep your baby shaded as much as possible in the summer, but try and get outside with baby for the fresh air. You could get a mini gazebo, pop up tent or just get a pram parasol, you could also use the pram parasol on the back of the highchair, if feeding your baby in the garden.
- If your baby keeps headbutting the side of the cot and is too young for a proper cot bumper you could use a travel cot that has mesh sides (although this isn't a good idea for a long term soloution because the travel cots don't have proper mattresses).
- You can hang a music machine or toy on the pram to soothe your baby to sleep when you are out.
- If you use accessories on your pram, such as cup holders, take them off before collapsing the pram. If you use weights on the front of the pram, it may still tip with the weight of your bags if your baby fidgest so don't hang bags on the pram.

- You will need a foot muff on your pram, you can also get a knitted one or use a blanket but a proper one that comes with the pram will be water resistant.
- Plastic bibs are great for when you are weaning, or are out and about as they just wipe clean. Disposable bibs are a waste.
- If not using milk as food source but for fluid do 1/2 milk & 1/2 water.
- Be there for your children and spend as much time with them as you can. You don't need to spend a lot of money, do simple things hire DVD from library etc. it is all about quality time, not the amount you spend. Its nice for them to have a break from technology and go for walks, visit a farm etc.
- A handy item to have is a bath thermometer that is a room thermometer too. Although I had a bath thermometer duck I used to test the temp with my elbow (I found the themostats were cautious and my son liked his bath slightly warmer as he got older). I also had a room thermostat on my baby monitor.
- Put your baby outside to get fresh air to help him/her sleep when you can.
- Every day is different some days things that worked another day may not.
- Time goes too quickly so try not to feel that you have to do too many activites, intead spend time enjoying your child. The interaction that they have with close family members is the most important thing.
- When they start standing they may seem ok then after a while legs may go.
- They seem to take a while to learn something ie crawl or speaking but as soon as they have got it they then seem really quick. One minute they can just crawl and then next thing they are speeding off.
- Have familiar items with you when you go away ie don't wash cot sheet before you go so that the baby has baby's smell, take familiar toys etc
- Babies work on associations so they may associate a certain toy with bed time or they may associate that their parents are always at home so if they aren't there they may get unsettled or they may find they can't sleep in another cot etc.
- They learn groups of sounds first i.e. dada, baba, muma, then they learn words, and eventually sentences. It helps if they have good Jaw and mouth muscles; they get these from chewing their food so it is important that they develop onto lumpy food.
- Get a bath mat when your baby can sit up in bath, that way they can sit in the bath without sliding. You still need to keep an arm around them in case they slide backwards, or lunge themselves forward.
- Babies get frustrated when want to move and they can't. I found my son was much happier in himself when he was able to crawl & explore. Before this he got fed up and upset. Think he also had colic when he was new born so once he got bigger and could get his own wind up he was much more settled.
- Before 6 months everything needs to be steralised. After this and when baby is crawling s/he will pick up some germs. Try and remember to clean babys hands when s/he has been crawling before giving food, and at regular intervals. Before 6 months you need to steralise the dummy after this it isn't so bad if you suck it, although this won't clean it and will give the baby some of your germs it is better than nothing.
- Check the bottles and make sure that the valves in the bottle don't get damp and mouldy, you may need to change the teets regularly.

- Your baby will try and fight against sleep. They will cry a lot when they are tired and fidget in your arms, hold them firmly but not too tightly and rock. Eventually they should then fall asleep.
- It is nice when they get older and can interact with you, they learn how to smile etc. When they are old enough to sit in highchair you can then enjoy your dinner etc and even though they are hard work they are not as demanding as new borns so you can feel like your life back.
- When they sleep their body temp goes down so carry a blanket to put over them when they have an afternoon nap.
- When you go on holiday don't forget to pack your baby sling (if you use one).
- Kids have to behave at school so when they get home they need to let off steam. Need to run.
- Don't worry if your baby is slightly chubby. Babies start to build up fat before they start crawling so that they have reserves. They should then start loosing some once they get crawling (if they don't then check with the doctor). Milk makes them put on more weight than food but babies need a balanced diet so don't put them on a diet just makesure they only eat healthy things and no salt or sugar.
- Relax - don't get too hung up on getting things right. Babies survived lots of things in the past. Use love and common sense. If you worry about everything you will drive yourself mad and the things that will go wrong are probably the things that you hadn't even thought of.
- Get a paddeling pool and put balls in it. Your baby can play with this as soon as s/he can sit up.
- Get a fold up stool for your toddler to be able to reach the sink etc.
- If you are really busy get some hired help, or take it in turns with swapping favours for friends. If you can afford it get a cleaner, that way its one less thing to worry about – even if you only get them to clean once a month it just helps you to stay on top of it.
- Get a stair gate that you can open one handed so you can open it when carrying your baby.
- On the stairs you may want one that screws to the wall or you could try and lay it out so that it isn't over the wall, like in the picture below; this will be sturdier than placing it directly on the stairs.

- When you have finishedusing food pots use them for herbs and spices (when your baby gets too big for the smaller size)
- When you wash dummies, squeeze the excess water out.
- You think that you can't cope with things, but you do, you find a way, take each day as it comes.
- I found by about 9 months things were much easier. My son was eating what we were eating and didn't need food blended, he could play by himself so didn't need me to pick him up all the time (although he was a little explorer and was into everything so I had to keep grabing him –but he would go in his play pen for a while), he slept through the night and I only had 2 bottles to make up in the day and I knew the exact times he would want them (I also stopped steralising th bottles at 8 months). His

health was better and because he was bigger and more robust I didn't worry about him so much. His nappy chages were also more predicatable (30 mins afer food). So it was much easier to get into a routine and get organised. That said if we went out he wouldn't get naps but he would then go to bed ealier and he coped quite wll with this. We would often go out all day so he would miss naps. Things always seemed to change because then I had to go back to work by 12 months, so that was another re-adjustent for both of us.

- People may treat children differently from their age depending on their size. A bigger child may get treated as if they are older, and will have more expectations placed upon them and may get into my trouble if fighting with another child where as a smaller child may get treated more like a baby and so may do less for themselves. Try to be aware of these sterotypes and dispel them where you can.
- Everything can be a hazard for babies so use some common sense to avoid accidents.
- Things need to be steralie but as they get older they need some germs, gradually steralise less.
- You only need to sterilise bottles and boil water until your baby is 6 months old – although some people say 12 months. It depends on where you live; water can sometimes become contaminated so it may be best to do this until 12 months (especially if travelling to a different region).

- Baby has mums immunity until 6-9 months old, it wears off then and then they start to develop their own, during this time they may become unwell.
- Don't wash your child too much – let them make some mess or they may get a cleaning ocd.
- Patterned clothes hide the marks babies make on clothes, which is useful if your baby is always dribbling on you.
- Don't put blanket over the pram for your baby to sleep in case your baby can't breathe
- In your labour bag have the baby grow and vest and nappy near the top so you can easily get it out when your baby is born.
- When you hold your baby becareful in case they put their arms up and slide through your arms.
- They go through a phase of spitting and spitting their food out, they think that it is fun. It could also be that when they are teething the extra saliva etc in their mouth irritates them.
- Make the most of cuddling your new born baby, once s/he crawls they won't want to just lay there and have cuddles all the time.
- If your baby won't drink water, try giving it on a spoon, or syringing it into his/her mouth.
- Don't rest a bag over the back of your stroller, even if you get the weights for your stroller if your baby is laid back and your bag is heavy it may still tip.
- If you need to make up a bottle and you don't have any hot water in the flask, use some cooled boiled water from the kettle (approx ½ of the amount required), then boil the kettle and add the boiling water straight in. This should give you the same tempreture water as if you had boiled the kettle 30 mins before. It is therefore a good idea to keep your kettle full and leave excess water in there to cool down, or put some cooled boiled water in a jug and keep a flask of boiled water. You may find that your kettle is more prone to limescale and may wear out more, the more you use it. It maybe a good idea to have a spare cheap kettle (in case yours breaks), or you can just boil a pan. If you also keep a stock of carton milk / pre-mixed formula you can use this in an emergency. I used to use the ready mixed cartons when I was out and about, at night and if baby was screaming for a bottle and I hadn't made one (rather than making him wait for it to cool down). The ready mixed milk is much

easier but it is more expensive. Its hard to use formula because they recommend that you don't pre make it and keep it in the fridge so you have to predict when your baby wants it, make it and then cool it, which takes a while. In the old days where you would make feeds and store them in the fridge it was easier because it's quicker to heat a bottle rather than cool it. Once my baby got past 6 months I used to make feeds up, cool them in cold water and put in the fridge. As your baby gets older it gets easier because the feeds are less frequent and the times they will be needed are more predicatable.

- Have somewhere to store babies toys so that you can get them out easily in the day you're your baby can get them out when s/he gets older), yet you can throw them into tidy your lounge to make it an adult place again in the evening. A large ottorman to match your other furniture is a good idea. You can also have a playpen in the corner and throw some toys in there.
- Steam your floor to clean hygienically without chemicals.
- Don't be too hard on yourself or stress about things too much, most things aren't as important as you think and most problems can be resolved. Things are never as bad as they seem once you have had some rest. Eat well, drink fluids and rest and keep things in proportion. Just spend time with your baby and give your baby lots of love.
- When you read to your baby at night. If you have a good imagination you can make up stories rather than having to read, that way you can have the lights down low and lay in bed and snuggle your baby, without having to try and read from and see your book (if your stroty is good remember it and you can even self-publish it into a book).
- If your baby is having a growth spurt or coming down with a cold s/he may be unsettled at night and may be a bit restless and not him/herself during the day, then you know they are going through changes or sickening.

Practise good time manangement;
It will take approx an extra 20 mins to leave the house. From getting up it takes me 2 hours to get myself and baby washed, dressed, breakfast and ready to leave.

To save time;
- Keep a change mat and basket with creams and nappies upstairs and downstairs so you have everything to hand and don't have to keep running up and down the stairs everytime your baby needs changng.
- when you go upstairs think of something that you can take up or one thing that you can do
- keep a note book to hand so you can write things down as you rememer them
- Have an app for your food shopping and scan things in when they run out/ have a manetic list on the fridge
- cook meals in a batch and freeze or have a monthly meal plan
- Have a box or bucket that you can just throw toys in at the end of the day
- Do chores the night before - get your and baby clothes out, fill up the nappy bag and baskt etc.

Other general tips;
- Keep extra dummies near the cot, have a position in the cot where you put the dummy so you can find it when it falls out in the night.
- Keep stocked up on formula, always have some extra in case you can't get out and get some when you need it or the shops sell out etc.
- Alternate toys with ones in the loft so that you have less items out at one time and have more space in your living areas.
- Once your baby is crawling and moving around more you may need to change the nappies to active fit ones.

- As your child gets older and goes in and out of the door you may need a door bell for backdoor.
- Never swear – even in front of a baby as they take in more than you think.
- If your baby has their arms up, they are waving their hands and reaching out they normally want something, or want picking up.
- Get a handbag/purse alarm and be careful as you maybe targeted whilst you are struggling with baby, never leave your handbag on the back of the pram or your purse near the top in case it gets snatched.
- Show your baby photos of friends and family and watch their reaction, they also love seeing pictures of themselves and other babies.
- Only change 1 thing at a time, nappies or wipes etc. in case they react, so that you know what is causing the reaction.
- Jam jars are good to keep, wash out and use them to store home made food in.
- When you are organising a holiday check the times that you can check in/check out and check that there is somewhere for baby to sleep etc. you don't want to have a long delay from leaving the room to catching your flight with no where for your baby to sleep and be changed etc.
- When you are going on holiday think about the flight arrival times and check the check in/check out of room times so there are not long gaps where you don't have a room and have nowhere to wait / sleep / change etc. check if they have courtesy rooms.
- Have fun with your baby make an obstacle course for crawling with cushions, blankets, towels, tunnels and dot toys along the way to make it more fun.Toys that you think are fun maybe not be toys that they think are   fun.
- When purchasing a haighchair get one that can fold up, for better storage. You can then keep it in the loft for the next baby. It is handy if it is lightweight enough to move, if it has a storage tray and if it has varable heights. You can get ones without straps that are very easy to clean (instead of straps the tray moves to lock your baby in).
- Throw away pouch food and jar lids so they can't be eaten. Don't undo the food and leave the lid in arms reach.
- Even in a small house a baby monitor is good, so that you can use it in the garden etc.
- Don't get hung up on what you should do, just do what you can. Coulds are better than shoulds.
- Fill a flask of hot water before you go to bed, so that you have hot water to make a bottle in the morning.. You may also want to boil a kettle before you go to bed so that in the morning you have cooled boiled water to put in your babies water botlle for your baby to drink throughout the day.
- Use the resources that you have, if people offer to help let them. There is no point struggling to do everything yourself.
- Don't let your baby chew your beaded necklace the beads may have toxic paint on them, they may also break off the beads, swallow them and choke. Seed beads are poisonous.   This also applies to beads on clothes etc.
- It is a good idea to keep a spare dummy next to the cot.
- If you have a drinks holder on the pram be careful that it doesn't tip and spill on your baby (as your baby gets older s/he may kick it.
- Don't let your baby stand on his/her legs before s/he is ready as this may cause him/her to get bow legs.
- Watch your baby doesn't pull your earings, necklaces or glasses.
- Take care with pets, especially dogss, around your baby as they may get aggressive.
- Perhaps get a routine going before signing up to classes and activities. Get to know your baby first, take time out for yourself and each other and then start going out etc.

- Don't let yourself get hungry because you need to be able to function, keep fed and re-hydrated and so you keep your energy up, don't leave things like eating until the last minute, otherwise you might not get chance.
- Let the kettle boil, leave it to cool and fill up your babies beaker the night before and then pack it in your baby bag so that you don't go out without the water bottle.
- The best feeling in the world is cuddling your sleeping baby (and not just because s/he is quite); they look so peaceful when they sleep. Make the most of your cuddles and spend time cuddling them as they grow up fast and cuddling them doesn't spoil them, it makes them feel loved and secure.
- Keep a stick in the soak bucket for your baby's solied clothes so you don't have to keep putting your hand in.
- Each baby/child will have different problems at different stages i.e. one child may not sleep well, one may take a longer time to feed etc.
- Keep spare baby and adult clothes in the boot of your car.
- If you are holding a bigger baby with one hand put hand under bum so doesn't slide down.
- When your baby is ill put in organic cotton, your baby will sweat less and the temperature will be easier to control.

Download such as the following, on your phone/ipod;
- Mumderground
- Wowmum
- Baby sign etc
- The essential parenting company

- You can now get special ipad cases so your baby can play games on your ipad and you can get special apps for babies and children.

- When travelling instead of taking a steriliser it is a good idea to use milton sterilising tablets. When using water abroad boil it in a kettle and boil the water twice so that it is boiling long enough to kill all of the germs.

- When you go on holiday your childs routine gets thrown out, this can make kids play up when you are on holiday and also when you get back, until they get back into their routine.

- If you get an isofix base for your rear facing car seat, you can tip it back slightly as the baby gets older and therefore get more use out of it, (just check wirh manufacturer for that particular one).

- To stop your baby being sick leave a slight gap between liquid and food, that way your baby will not get too full too quickly.

- You may want to give your baby a spoon to hold when you are feeding him/her this will stop him/her from grabbing the spoon that you are feeding him/her with.

- Keep a 24 hour grab bag by door in case you need to go out in an emergency.

- When you first have your baby it gets stressful because at first you only get sleep in 30 min bursts as your baby wakes for food and it takes you a while to get back to sleep etc. as baby gets older and sleeps longer and you get used to things it gets easier.

- The first few months at nursery your baby picks up all thhe germs and may get a lot of illness but this helps them to build up their immunity (just make sure that they have all of their vaccines before they start going to nursery).

- It is a good idea to take your child to a crèche so they get used to being left before they go to nursery / day care full time.

- Babies under 2 months - don't give insect repellent with deet in. You may want to try natural insect repellent. Lemon is supposed to keep insects away so you could put some of this on the edge of the cot sheets.

- Once your baby starts crawling, s/he will get germs. Try and keep the floor etc as clean as you can but they need some germs to build up their immune system. Don't wear outside shoes in the house but equally you can't have your house too clean as your baby needs to get some germs to build up their immunity.

- Wear practicable clothes, don't wear strapless tops etc. as they may get pulled down whilst you are lifting your baby etc.

- From 10 months you need to talk normally to your baby talk as they copy what you say now so talk and listen carefully.

- Juggling the demands of life with a baby can be tricky - it's all too easy to let your relationship take a back seat. If you haven't had much time for your partner lately, you could ask a friend to babysit so you can go out together.

- You will find as your baby gets older and more independent, they want to do things themselves and they get frustrated when they can't. They also get frustrated when they can't express themselves - it helps if you learn to pick up on their ques, sign language may help too so that you can understand them before they learn to speak. My baby got fustrated from 9 months because he wanted to give himself a drink, he couldn't hold the cup properly so I got him a sippy cup with handles and helped him to drink it himself. Before this he would try and grab the cup but push it away when I tried to give it to him.

- It is a good idea to purchase a microfibre towel for the splash pads. This way it folds up small and goes into the change bag without taking up as much room as a normal towel.

- Every day your baby will do something new -it's very exciting watching them grow up.

- As baby gets older you may want to bath everyday especially in the summer.

- It's a good idea for the summer months to get an air con unit for room. You can get portable units or hire a unit.

- Can go to the children's centres for a break - they will hold child & give you a break if your struggling.

- They do say that you should wean your baby off of the dummy by 12 months. However I think its fine for them to stay on the dummy until they are walking or at nursery or whenever you think they no longer need it (its an individual decision) its is best to wean your baby off of the dummy in day first, and eventually wean it off at night.

- They pick up germs from nursery and will tend to get more illness in the first few years, but certainly the first few months. However this is not a bad thing because it builds up their immune system. Just be careful to save some annual leave when you go back to work in case you need to take sick days.

- When you are referring to your parents call them granparents names i.e. nanny or granma so that your children don't get confused.Call parents by their grandparents names so kids don't get confused.

Mummy Cards;

Mummy Cards are the newest and trendiest way to share important contact, allergy or emergency info and keep in touch. They're perfect for busy mums and dads.

Top 5 Uses for Your Mummy Cards;

- Hand out when setting up play dates
- Leave one with the babysitter
- Put one in your kids' backpack
- Use them for changing bag tags
- Tuck into Christmas cards and invitations

- Re-stock the nappy/change back as soon as you get in after an outing, then put the bag by the front door, in the pram shopping basket or the boot of the car (but always keep it in the same place so you know where it is) and then you are ready to go, especially important if you need to rush out unexpectedly. However don't leave things in the car if you car share otherwise one of you may take the car and the other one will be left holding the baby without a change bag, and always check the car before going out to ensure that they are in there.
- Have a small bag and a larger change bag so you can interchange in accordance with the daily activities and don't have to carry a big bag for a short journey (have a neutral colour to match all your outfits).
- Get a fold up play mat that you can take when you go out and about.
- Get a steam mop for the floor, its quicker and easier than moping and keeps your floor more sterile for when baby is crawling. It is also a good idea when baby is crawling to get people to take their shoes off and leave them at the door. It is also a god idea to get play mats and blankets and cot duvets to make the floor soft, for when baby starts to roll and crawl, especially if you have a hard floor.
- Get a baby memory book whilst you are pregnant so you can start to fill in, with your pregnancy information and put scan pictures in it etc.

- Write a storybook for your baby about the different activities you do and include picture.

- Wear nice socks because when you go to baby groups and people's houses you will have to take your shoes off a lot. It is also a good idea to keep a spare pair of baby socks in your change bag as they often fall off (the sock-on products are okay but I found that they were tight on my baby's feet and it says not to wear them when they are asleep and new borns sleep nearly all the time and you can't take them off every time they doze).

- Allow extra time when planning to go out, actually allow extra time in everything you do. You will find that just as you are about to go out your baby will need a nappy change and then may wee on their clothes and then you have to change their clothes etc. and this can add 20mins delay into your schedule and if s/he also needs a feed this could add a further hour, and this doesn't include the time putting them in their car seat and packing the items you need to take (this is another reason why its good to keep the change bag stocked up). Then there is the time it takes loading the pram, change bag, toys and travel mat etc into the car. If you are out all day you may also want an extra bag with extra bottles , formula and a flask in. Depending on the size of your boot it could take a further 10mins to load everything in.

- It is a good idea to have an organiser that you keep a full flask in along with formula and clean bottles, spare dummies, infacol and teething rings. You can keep this in the kitchen so you know where everything is and if it has handles you can take it with you when you go out visiting family for a long day.

- Always keep a camera handy and take lots of photos and video clips. Always remember to download pictures from your phone and camera and back up regularly.

- It is normal for a baby to have an unsettled time each day and an unsettled day a week. Often it's tiredness. You will get through and the next day they will be OK again! Babies are like adults and have different moods and maybe hungrier at some time than others or if they have been out and looking at different things one day they may get extra tired and be grumpier that evening. It may be a good idea to note down sleep times, activities, feeds, nappy changes etc. and babies moods then you may notice that your baby has a natural routine and you can identify things that make baby happy or unhappy. For instance you may decide that you will only do one activity a day otherwise baby may get too tired or baby maybe grumpy if s/he doesn't have a morning nap etc. But remember you may have to compromise what suits baby with what suits you and vice versa, there is no point going out shopping all day everyday if baby gets grumpy afterwards, perhaps just do it one day a week instead. Equally you don't want to stay in all day just because baby likes to nap. You also need to prepare for the long term if you are going back to work etc and try and get a routine that suits you both.

- Do what you feel is right/what works for you and the baby.

- It's not easy traveling on a plane with a baby, so perhaps go on a cruise.

- Enjoy your baby! Cuddle your baby (s/he won't get spoilt or manipulative). Don't stress the little things, housework can be done tomorrow.

- Let your baby led you and let you know when their hungry, tired etc.

- Do what YOU feel is right and never be afraid to ask for help., it is true mums do know best.

- Be there for, talk too and reassure your baby. When baby wakes up talk to him/her in a reassuring voice and smile at him/her.

- It is a good idea (especially in the early days) to have your phone on silent.

- Wash babies bibs separately as the Velcro on them may catch on your clothes.

- Also be wary of change mats etc. that may have Velcro which may catch on your clothes and silk scarfs etc.

- Listen to all the advice given to you, be polite and respect each word of wisdom but only take on board what you think will work for you and your baby/ies.
- Sleep is more important than housework, if you are tired and stressed baby will pick up on this. Look after yourself as well. If you are not well you won't have the energy to look after your baby.
- It may take longer than you expect to recover after birth and you may find it hard adjusting. With a baby you get less done so you may feel like you haven't achieved things with your day but you have probably achieved more than you think. Don't set your goals too high. After a few months and gradually as things settle down you will get more and more done, you will also find as time goes on you will get quicker at things and will get in a routine without thinking. At first its tiring because you have to concentrate and little things take a long time and its easy to forget things, after a while it comes automatically and you find things take less time and baby is more settled so you have more time to yourself and can get more things done, pick up on projects etc. so in the beginning just be patient with yourself, take your time, and drop other things off your list to give yourself time to adjust, to learn about your baby and give your baby time to get to know you. Have time together and put everything else on hold. Sleep when they sleep and when they get older and sleep through the night, you won't need to nap in the day and this is when you can then get things done when they nap. Your lucky if you get one thing a day done with a newborn.
- Respect to mums - you will get through anything, be confident you have strength to do anything in life. Believe in yourself.

- Having 2 babies is harder – with the second child you may no more but have less time with your newborn, need to rush the feeding to pick up next baby etc. try and get people to help out so that you can give your new born the time they need to get to know you. Also have a break to spend quality time with your older child/other babies/children so they don't feel left out.
- All you can do is try your best and show love and affection. Love is the most important thing.
- Having a baby puts a real strain on your relationship and you will find that you snap at each other / argue when tired and over who will do what. You need to stay strong and you need to work together as a team. Talk to each other, good communication will help you to get through it togther, empathy of each others position is important. It's good if you have been together a long time because you know each other, but things change so you will need to re-adjust.
- When you have finished with your nipple cream , don't throw it out because it is expensive, instead use it as lip balm

- It is useful to have travel wash to hand wash clothes and keep a bucket in kitchen for soaking clothes (don't put your own delicate and wool clothes soaking too long in stain remover as it may take the colour out).

- You may want to use essential oils - Lavender helps your baby sleep – put this by the cot, wash blankets and put a drop in the machine or mix the lavender oil with some with olive oil and use it to massage your babies feet.

- Wash your baby's bottles separately.

- Your baby may go through a stage when they start grabbing they may pinch you, you need to gently pull their hands away, or tickle their palms of their hands to get them to open them.

- When you use an alarm clock to wake you up, put it onto start on a low beep and get louder, so that it wakes you without waking your baby.

- Try not to worry about things, you will manage better than you had thought and financially it won't be as tough as you would expect because you will go out less and therefore save money.

- Have lots of clothes for you and your baby, with vomit and other spilages you may find that you both get through various sets of clothes (maybe 3 changes a day).

- Once you have made your babies bottle, hide the milk until you hve changed your baby's nappy etc and are ready to give the milk, otherwise if your baby sees it s/he will cry and not co-operate with anything else, s/he will just want the milk.

- You can't have gripe water until s/he is a month old.

- Watch that your baby doesn't throw his/her head back /fall backwards and hit his/her head. They have a tendancy to start thowing themselves backwards off of your knee, once they start to move. When they first start sitting up they may also fall back or throw themselves backwards so they need cushions behind them etc. When they first start standing and walking they may fall too and have lots of bangs to the head. My son used to head butt the cot bars and then pull himself up on the cot bars and then let go and fall backwards. When they first learn to stand it also takes them a while to learn to sit down so they hold on for dear life whilst their legs get weak, or they fall backwards, until they learn to lower themselves down onto their bum. At this stage you need to let them explore (and accept their will be some bumps), however you will need to keep a close eye on them and follow them around (and get ready to catch them). You will find that you will never always catch your baby, not matter how close you are s/he will forwards if you are behind him/her and backwards if you are in front (they always seem to be just out of your reach).

- It is a good idea to in the morning as well as filling up the flask for bottles fill up a bowl of boiled water to cool for washing, and once you start weaning put some boiled water in a beaker or jug to cool so that you can give your baby some water with their meals throughout the day.

  - Your know when you don't need to support baby's head. It wil be obvious as they will be able to hold it up themselves without it wobbling. Before this you will need to support their head otherwise they may strain their neck and damage blood vessels in the neck and brain (like shaken baby syndrome).
  - If you use a 'jumperoo' make sure that you move it so that it is on the right setting/height for your child' height so that they don't get any damage to their feet and legs (they should be jumping in it on the balls of their feet, not the flat of their feet).
  - Everyone should do a parenting course / lots of local authorites offer these free of charge. There is triple p which is quite prescriptive but is the most indepth course and then there is the family trust and caring course. Ask your

health vistor to see if there is one in your area. There are many private companies offering courses too but they may charge.

- Chalk board paint is good for your child's play room, they can then draw all over the walls and you can wipe it off (be sure to tell them though that they can't draw over other walls).
- The sound of a ticking clocks is soothing to a new born baby as it is similar to the heart beat sound that they hear in the womb.
- Hoover up at least once every day, if you can, once your baby is crawling in case there are tiny stones or debris on the floor that your babymay pick up and eat.
- It is nice to have a play room with sliding doors off of your lounge so that you can open it up to still interact with your baby whilst you are doing stuff in your room, but then close the playroom off at night when your baby has gone to bed and you want your own space. Or you could just take your lap top into the play room and supervise your baby whilst checking your emails, although its nice f you can leave that until nap time so that you can focus on your baby.
- Even though its scary when your baby is learning to eat and they start gagging but they have to gag to learn to swallow.
- Its best to just give your baby water but if they won't take it you can give baby juice, avoid normal squash as this has too much sugar.
- Make the most of new born cuddles once they start crawling they won't want to stay still for long enough for cuddles. When they are new born forget everything else and just sit and cuddle them all day.
- Rather than buying the pocket size sun cream buy the large size for the same price and pour it into.
- Everytime I eat something I gave my son something to eat. Even if he had just had lunch I gave him a snack when I had my lunch. This then meant that he wanted to eat everytime he saw someone else eating and he used to beg for food and shout if you didn't give it to him like a little puppy. Babies in some ways are like puppies.
- If found it useful to keep flannels in my babies highchair and I would also keep a pack of wet wipes nearby. I also kept baby wash by the kitchen sink so that after my baby had eaten (and got very messy), I could quickly clean him up.
- To get baby to drop the night feed you can give them water instead of milk at night.
- Keep wiping your babies hands because they put their hands in their mouth after crawling on the floor etc. although you want them to have some germs to build up immunity you don't want them to have too many. At the very least you should clean their hands before and after meals.
- As they get older and crawl around and get messy it is a good idea to give them a bath once a day, especially in the summer. I found my son would get food everywhere and milk under his neck, his hands and nails would get grubby etc.
- It is a good idea to get your baby used to drinking from a sippy cup (one without lids), it is handy for them to have a beaker too as they may find it easier. I tried lots of beakers but my son struggled so I gave him water in his bottle and then a sippy cup with handles. However it is easier to use a beaker when you are out and about because you need to store the cooled boiled water. I carried a water bottle and a sippy cup. I found that the water bottle with a spout was easier for him than a beaker. Some babies I know managed with straws and had a cup with a straw attached.
- With a baby time goes fast, you don't realise because you are focusing ahead for the next thing i.e. when they will be walking or doing x,y,z.

- Baby sick is just milky and doesn't normally smell. If it is thick and lumpy and smelly this indicates it maybe a bug. This is how you tell if they have a bug or just reflux (however once they are on solids their vomit will usually be thick and smelly dependant on what they have eaten so look for other symptons such as a rash or tempreture).
- Babies needs sleep to build up their immune system so try and give them a nap in the day and put them to bed at a regular time (not too late in the evening). My son at 9 months would have a short morning nap after his bottle and then sometimes a mid morning and afternoon nap, although as he got nearer 10 months he would nap less in the day, I would then put him down at 19:30 and he would sleep until approx. 6:30am through the night.
- If you don't have a bib you can use a muslin cloth.
- Let then get messy, a bit of mess is good for them otherwise they will be too fussy about keeping clean.
- If your baby has a dummy they may find it hard to breathe with this in, so they may spit it out a lot at night and keep waking up, never attach it to them as this is really dangerous, they need to let it fall out when they need to breathe
- It is important to set a good example because your baby will learn from you and will copy your behaviours. Share jobs with your partner so that your child will learn that it's important to all do the jobs, don't smoke in front of kids etc.
- Don't overgive calpol or other pain relief, it only brings down a tempreture or gets rid of pain, it won't cure illness. Therefore if your baby is in a lot of pain or has a high tempreture give it to them but if they are just a bit wingy try not to as the less often they have it the more effective that it will be when they really need it. If you do just give it once in the day give it at night so that they can sleep better. Sleep will help the body to heal.
- If you don't fuss your child and make it a big issue when they have a little bump they will be less fusyy. 'just say your okay' and pick them up because they look to you for reassurance and if they see you are upset they will get upset. Often the 2nd child is tougher and less fussy because they get less fussed over. Although they should still have cuddles for each bump.
- They may react differently to things on different days, one day they may like something, the next day they may not. It all depends on their mood, noise and tempteture of the environment that they are iin and who they are with etc.
- Don't make work for yourself, use the dishwasher for the babies bottles (pu them on the top shelf because this is cooler). I washed all the bottles by hand and then found I saved loads of time putting them in the dishwaher (although it did discoulour them, it was a small price to pay in order to have save time).
- Don't nag only shout about the big things in order to be listened too / make an impact
- It is important to have a break, absence makes heart grow founder and a short break, even if just for an hour will make you appreciate your baby more.
- Having children helps you make friends – its nice to make new friends with children the same age.
- Change you baby into their night clothes before the bed time routine i.e. before their bottle but after their bath and dinner, in case fall asleep i.e. if you are out change them and then give them their bottle, they may then fall asleep in the car on the way home and can be lifted into bed. You can always make a small extra bit of milk to have on standby so that if they wake up when you get them out the car you can top them up with some milk to get them back to sleep.
- Portable DVD etc are great to entertain kids on long car journeys
- It is good for them to play with other kids the same age in order for them to develop their social skills.

- It is a good idea to put their clothes in layers for inside and outside, different environments, especially in the Uk as the weather is always changing, that way you can easily add or take away a layer to keep them at the right tempreture.
- Get as much sleep as you can before the baby comes, although having said this you can't store sleep so it is just as well to get used to having little sleep, because you won't be getting much sleep once the baby arrives.
- Respect the rules of whoevers house you are in i.e. grandparents their house their rules, even if they are different to yours.
- Over the summer holidays give your children some work to do, make it fun such as writing their name in the sand pit or writing a diary of what they have been doing each day and get them to ready books to you. Otherwise if they do no reading or writing for 6 weeks they may slip back in their skill level.
- Try to take your shoes off before bending down to change your baby, keep bending over may ruin the toes of your shoes.
- Plan ahead to avoid traffic & delays (things take longer with a baby and you want to avoid traffic as much as possible, there is nothing worse than being stuck in a car with a screaming baby). Pull over where it's safe and soothe baby. Plan feeds and try to feed before a journey or avoid travelling around feed time (where possible).
- Pack your baby bag the night before, that way you are ready to leave the house the next day, and its one less thing to do if you are running behin. It also means that if there is an emergency in the night you have a grab bag ready to go. It also helps if you decide what your wearing the night before whilst your baby is sleeping to make your hectic mornings easier.
- Always have a spare set of clothes and have lots of extra blankets and muslin, especially if you have a sicky baby. You can always keep a bag of extra things in the boot of your car.
- Before your period comes back it is a good idea to carry sanitary towels in your bag as your period may come anytime & wear panty liners.
- Babies smile more for dads because they don't seem them as often but they tend to be more reliant on their mums because of the bond from being in the womb and so it easier to feel disheartened for either partner whe the baby wants the other one, but remember they still love you both.

- When baby gets older s/he will grab your hair and jewellery etc. so you may want to tie hair back/wear less jewellery etc.
- Encourage team sports - discipline & exercise, start them early on activites that they show an interest in so that they have the opportunity to be the best that they can, encourage them to try their best and do well but don't push them into doing something if they are not enjoying it.
- Get comfy/stretchy clothes that are easy to put on baby and allow baby to move
- Its exciting for parents because they give you something to look forward to every day. Everday they do something new, they develop and learn something new as they grow and learn to smile and interact its great fun.
- Demonstrate things to your baby in order to get them to eat or take medicine etc. as your baby gets older you could demonstrate on a teddy and say 'teddy is having his medicine'.
- Growth spurt may make them wake up in night, also if teething wake up in night.
- Baby's don't like lying flat because they can't see whats going on but its good for them to move about on floor, you could alternate between lying on floor, holding them and putting them in the chair.
- Baby brain - scientific fact your body slows down to cope with lack of sleep

- Your own baby's cry you are tuned into and it startles you. Crying is meant to be annoying, in order to get your attention/make you do something.
- Babies will only drink the amount of milk that they need in most cases so if they are demanding more milk, give them more milk. If they persistently drink most the bottle then you need to make an extra ounce in each feed. They will usually drink what they need however they don't always drink enough so you will need to keep an eye on the amount they drink and if they are ill give them little and often. They can never drink too much so keep feeding as much milk as you can, until you start weaning them onto solids and then you will reduce the milk to give solid food instead.
- When you have a baby its important to be near your family and friends so that you have a support network.
- It is often a good idea to do baby sitting circles so you take it in turns in looking after each others children, but make sure you only do this with people you trust. The down side is that it is hard to look after 2 babies as they want to sleep and eat at different times so you will be extra busy none stop. Having twins must be a nightmare.
- Take it in turns going to friends houses and hosting a dinner party. Get each person to bring a dish so that there is one less thing to cook.
- Babys sleep in your arms because of the body heat – pre-heat their matress with a hot water bottle before putting them in to keep them asleep, but makesure their room is not too hot and don't leave the hot water bottle in as this is dangerous (babies musn't over heat). With older children if you want to give them something give them a wheat bag not a hot water bottle, because if the hot waterbottle splits the boiling water could scald them.
- Have a safe place to leave your baby in case you need to leave the room to go to the toilet or take a moment to calm down etc. This could be their cot or a play pen. If you are struggling to cope go to your local children's centre and they will offer you advice or can take your baby for a moment to give you a break, they often run classes where your child can go in a crèche, that way you get a break and get to interact with other parents.
- Smell food at dinner time makes babies hungry – they are like us sometimes they may be hungrier than they are at other times.
- Be persistent, keep trying different things to see what works although you need to give each thing time to work. If you don't stick with one method and keep changing the way that you do things you may not know what works.
- Sometimes hearing you talking when baby is sleeping is soothing for baby.
- When looking for a car you may want a large boot to fit your pushchair in but you may want to also fit your friend's puchair and other items in so it's best to get the biggest car that you can.
- Close eyes & pretend to be asleep to get baby to sleep (if you look at baby s/he may want to get up & play).
- Perfume disguises natural smell so try and avoid wearing perfumes also when massaging baby use olive oil because baby's are less likely to have a reaction and again it isn't perfumed. It is good for baby to have your smell to bond with you.
- Wash your hands before holding baby
- Don't hold baby in standing position before they can stand, if you let baby stand when they are too, before their legs have developed it can be harmful for them (it can make them bo-legged). However once they start standing themselves, its fine to let them stand as much as they want. Although at first they learn how to stand they may find it hard to sit back down from a standing position.
- All babies go through a clingy stage, don't worry it will pass. Let baby interact with other people so they get used to other people too.
- Wanting a regular nappy change is a sign of good clean baby.

- Get your baby sitter to wear your jumper or have a muslin or something with your smell on.
- Balance food and sleep. If your baby is ill and not eating enough you may want to set an alarm in order to wake them so that you can feed them.
- Don't wrap your babies hands in their blanket because it inhibits movement - cold hands okay as long as your babies core temperature is warm, you can use scratch mittons if your baby's hands get too cold.
- New borns will be snuffly in the winter, because of going from the cold outside and having central heating inside. New borns can't cough and clear themselves so instead they may get sick.
- If you have been breastfeeding you may leak milk for upto 6 months.
- From around 4 weeks your baby may start recognising people
- If one baby starts crying often it may set other babies off and start them crying too.
- It is a good idea to have your baby's room as near to your room as possible.
- Babies learn by using their hands and mouth: putting things in their mouth.
- They say that you should sleep when your baby sleeps but this is not always possible because you need time to yourself/time to get things done too.
- If your baby is finding it hard going from a small moses basket to a large cot you may want to roll up a blanket around the sides to make them feel cosier in the cot, however this could cause a hazard so you need to use a cellular blanket only. Fresh air & outside play is good - tv like everything in moderation.
- If your new born is ill or dehydrated the soft spot on his/her head may look sunken in.
- You can get headphones for baby for fireworks night.
- Don't leave keys in car / turn elect windows off if you have an older child so that they can't do any damage in the car, it is also important to have and use child locks.
- Babys develop their personality early, its lovely to watch their individual personalities grow.
- keep your spare dummy in a sandwich bag, in your babies change bag.
- If your baby has a bloked nose it can cause wind. So if your baby sounds snuffly use saline drops.
- If your baby is sick one hour or later after food and the sick is thick and curdled rather than just looking like normal milk then it is an indication that your baby may have reflux.
- If you have stitches or piles you may want to sit sideways in order to ease the pressure.
- Try and give your baby slightly more in their night time feed to get them to sleep through the night.
- Babies dont like being changed because they don't like being cold, put a warm cloth on the mat, you can also get wet wipe warmers.
- Babies like bouncing
- Prepare to be out of action for a while after had baby; don't make any immediate plans just in case.
- You may want to put vaseline on your babies neck to stop dribble, milk and sweat irritating the skin. Its also a good idea to use a dribble bib too.
- You maybe able to disability allowance if your baby has an illness i.e. bad asthma.
- Steralise dummy – 10 mins in boiling water and then leave to cool.

- Listen to what people say, say thanks & only take in what you want, don't get too hung up on other peoples advice.

- Mood swings are normal after baby, especially when you feel fed up being at home - Speak to your partner you may feel that they take you for granted. Find ways of sharing the jobs and giving yourself time for a break.

- They rub their head/eyes when they ar tired but will try and fight it and stay awake (except when they are new born when they will fall asleep when they are tired). Driving them around in the car or pushing them in the pushchair will normally send them to sleep.
- Get food in that is quick and you can eat with one hand and keep in freezer i.e. pita bread, pancakes, sausage rolls so that you can eat when feeding baby. This will be really useful when you first have your new born.
- It is normal for a new born to sneeze a lot, it doesn't mean baby has a cold (it is often their body clearing out and also the changes in environment, for instance new borns are sensitive to central heating etc.
- Boys more likely to get asthma
- It is good for babies to cry sometime in order to exercise their lungs Sometimes new borns cry and they are okay they are just finding their voice.
- Watch your hair doesn't fall into your babies eyes.
- Sometimes they may confuse wind & hunger
- Nurse on side, rock, swaddle & rub head & top of eyes for comfort
- Sometimes you have to let them cry for a minute & then they settle themselves. When you are letting your baby cry you will know the difference between attention and pain cry and how long they can cry for. Sometimes it good for them to cry it out. Especially if they are tired they may need to cry then they will sleep.
- When they first learn to move they start moving around more in the cot and may bash into the sides and wake themselves up. My son still moves around a lot in his cot and hits the side and has a cry, he also head butts the bars and sometimes when he pulls himself up and jumps on the materress he slips back and hurt himself.
- A quality of good parent is patience but the most important thing to have is love.
- Empty and dry the sterliser after each use in order to stop the limescale build up.
- If you put your formular into pots, use the pots in order so that you don't have formula in pots that is old and out of date. The same when you steralise bottles, roatate the bottles in your change bag (don't steralise them and then leave them in your bag for 2 weeks otherwise they won't stay sterile), use them in the order you steralised them.
- You need to clean your baby's eyes everyday, if your baby has a sticky eye - wipe with water Dry
- Tidy as go and have a place for everything. Show your baby how you tidy and encourage your baby to tidy.
- Don't give your children grapes or cherry tomatoes with the skin on.
- Your senses are heightened when your pregnant and after having a baby.
- Most hospitals provide milk but you can get some ready made to take with or in case you need rather than buying bottles.
- You may find that your appetite is less before giving birth.
- Before and after having a baby record your menstral cycle so that you know your pattern, can check that everything is regular and okay etc.
- When you change a boos nappy they wee as soon as you remove it so carefully take it off and hold the nappy over the boy for a moment to catch any wee.
- Having a baby is a balancing act, dealing with competing demands and the are all indviduals and will react differently so take their lead and follow their cues, a lot of it is tria and error.
- White noise calms new born babies.
- Most babies start to cry less when they're about eight weeks old.
- Have a spare pair of glasses in case your baby breaks yours, they have a tendancy to pull them off of your face.
- Their routine changes as get older, at each new stage of their life (say every fews months at first, then every 6 months, then every year etc. the routine and their needs and demands adapt).

- Sometimes you won't be able to comfort or calm your baby and other people will be able to hold and calm your baby down. This is because sometimes the baby picks up on your stress or just likes a change of scenery.
- Work out how long the bottle warmer takes and put the milk in for that time so it doesn't get too hot. I would always struggle to get my babies milk to the optimim tempreture, it would either be too hot or too cold. You can also use the bottle warmer to warm jars and packets of food (obviously this may take a different amount of time to what the milk did).
- It is easy to get distracted when you are out and about with your baby and become a victim of crime. Think about what your doing and you and you babies safety. Never leave your baby, don't put your bag down on the floor and if you have your change bag over your pram don't have your purse, phone, keys or other valuables near the top and never rest your purse on the top of the pram or in holders or pockets on the pram.
- It is good to try your baby at modelling but be aware of fake model agenies and don't pay anything up front.
- Secure items in the car so there are no loose items to fall & strap baby into car securely, double check fitting.
- Dont arrange anything hectic for the first month ie don't move house etc (or even the first few months as it may take you a while to get used to things, especially if it is your first baby.
- Just because you have just changed your babies nappy doesn't mean that your baby is clean, it may soil a nappy just after you have changed it and you may need to change it again. When my son was newborn as soon as I changed his nappy he would wee in it and he wanted his nappy changed everytime he had a wee. Which was sometimes every 30 mins and sometimes every hour.
- To get your baby into a proper routine of having a decent nap in the day you will need to start putting them in their cot to sleep (although when they are new born they will sleep anywhere, in the bouncer chair, in the moses basket and in the pram etc)
- Don't put the baby to sleep in bed with you, although you can lay baby on bed with you to get baby to sleep and then lift baby into the cot.
- Makesure you wash your hands every time after changing your baby. It is also a good idea to learn to change your baby on your lap. When my son started crawling he wouldn't stay still and would run off so I would have to change him on my lap. However if you are going to do this it is a good idea to put a muslin over your lap first (I also keep a spare outfit in the car).
- It is a good idea to get a pram where the stroller can face both ways. You will want to have your baby facing you, especially when s/he is younger. As s/he gets older they will want to face out to see whats going on (and facing the direction of travel is more comfortable) and as they get older they will start kicking too. When they are facing out the strollers with the windows in the hood are better so that you can see your baby. I had a pram that went into a stroller. I preferred this to the stroller because it was sturdier and I could put my bag on it and it was easier to lay it flat etc. however the stroller was lighter and took up less room in the boot. The stroller also had a window to see my son when he was facing outwards and it had a UV cover to protect my son from the sun (it was a Maclaren XT) so I would take the pram and my husband had the stroller (he had a smaller car). I used the pram as long as I could and then later went onto the stroller. I also took the stroller with me when on holiday.
- Babies form habits so be sure that you do bad practises that form bad habits.
- Don't lift Moses basket by handle with baby in, instead support it from underneath too, in case the handles don't take the weight.
- Take care what you store in your pram basket and makesure that it is stored securely so that it doesn't fall out.

- Don't forget your pram attachments when you go out so that you can put your car seat on the wheels. I went out without the pram section and forgot the attachement for the car seat and had to carry the baby around the shop in his/her car seat.
- Practise with your pram before going out so that you know how it works and can easily put it up or down.
- Think about what you wear for bending to pick up baby etc.
- When your first start giving your baby tummy time for support you can use a pillow or roll up a towel.
- It is important to put your baby in a clean vest at night time to go to bed, this is because changing the clothes for bed is all part of the routine to let them know it is night time and to get them into good night time sleeping habits.
- It is importnant to have set amounts of play time and quite time so that your baby gets some stimulation but is not over stimulated.
- It is important to talk and sing to your baby a lot.
- Some teething powder (i.e. Nelsons) has lactose in and if you are using gel too that can all affect your baby. If your baby is lactose intolerant you need to check everything you give them as things that you wouldn't vene expect may have lactose in, if you are unsure speak to your doctor.
- One technique to calm your baby is to hold him/her like a plane and swish them around, face down.
- When using nasal saline drops the ones with a pippet such as the calpol ones are good and when using the paracetmol the calpol one with a syringe also makes it easier to administer.
- If you wear your normal clothes when pregnant they may stretch, you may not want to wear them again.
- Don't drive too near your due date in case of contractions.
- Try and put your new born in different positions in the chair to avoid flat patches. If your new born has a very flat head your doctor may give your baby a special helmet to wear.
- In the first week or 2 when you are very tired keep guests to a minimum and only have those who you don't need to tidy up for, and those that will help you tidy up and will make their own cups of tea etc.
- Use a damp cloth to around the babies ear, never clean inside them, wax in the ear is natural protection, so leave it there.
- Wash your babys face, hands and neck and their eyes at least once everyday. As they get older, like my 10 month old son you will be cleaning every hour.
- From around 3 months baby can sleep through the night. Give a good feed at 11pm and have a good night time routine.
- Don't rush to pick baby up if they cry in the night, give them time to settle, that way they learn to soothe themselves. But always check why they are crying. The first time I tried controlled crying I was told to leave my son to cry, which I did for a while. I then couldn't leave him any longer and went into find he had put his arm through the cot bar and got stck (this is when a video monitor or hiding outside the door and peeking through whilst they cry is a good idea).
- Milk spots are caused by babies oil production glands, wipe skin with warm water and cotton wool, don't apply products or squeeze the spots. My son had a blocked gland which caused a spot on his nipple, these are usually fine as long as they don't get any bigger in size (if so you need to get your doctor to check it out).
- New born babies eyes can look a bit strange because they are born with a covering like a thin film on their eyes, which gradually dissolves but their eyes look gooyey at first, don't panic this is normal. However if it doesn't go and they continue to have misty eyes check with your doctor or health visitor. They may also have some red in their eyes as they may burst some blood vessels when they are born, again this should clear up after afew weeks.

- Its important to have lots of skin to skin with your baby and make time for your baby.
- After 6 weeks baby should feed every 4 hours and you will have a routine, you may be lucky and baby may sleep through the night.
- Keep your nappy/change bag stocked up - as soon as use something, replace it.
- Babies areok on their back as they will turn their heads to vomit.
- Snoring/snuffling is normal but not grunting for breath isn't.
- Some babies may sleep with their eyes open, or they make peak at you to make sure that you are still their and then go back to sleep. My son used to do this a lot, he would stir and peek at me through ½ open eyes an when you looked at him he would close his eyes and go back to sleep. My youngest nephew thought that this was hilarious and would shout 'he's peeking', 'he is pretending to be asleep'.
- If using cotton wool to apply cream it might be too fluffy, you can always use lint free facial cotton pads which are less fluffy (these are better for babies eyes than the loose fluffy cotton wool, I also found the cheaper the cotton wool the more loose fibres it had, so its better to pay more and get better quality). I also found the really cheap nappies gave my son nappy rash, I would have to change them more and use more cream so they were a false econmy.
- You need your baby's birth certificate to register at the doctors etc. so make sure you get the birth certificate asap.
- When you are pregnant, even if you are not near labout keep a small hospital bag packed in case you are taken ill, I had a few hospital visits in early pregnancy.
- Don't bath your baby alone if you feel faint in case you pass out and drop your baby in the water.
- Before baby is born prepare draft announcement email so you can just add photo & details ie weight etc. and send out. You can also add the receipents in, in advance and save the email in drafts. Facebook is also a good place to do the announcement, but remember not everyone is on facebook so keep a list of who you need to call, that way you won't forget anyone.
- Pack in your hospital bag a blanket (it was 10 hours before I got a room and a bed so the blanket was good to put on the floor when I was kneeling over my birthing ball), a relaxing lavender eye mask is also a good addition to your labour bag and so is a bendy straw.
- Don't be afraid of pain relief when you are in labour, its better to have some pain relif than get stressed and stress the baby out, take 1 contraction at a time.
- Some babygrows have scratch mittons attached, these are a good idea because my son just threw his scratch mittons off and I was worried about them being on his face.
- Have diff size baby grows or bigger than new born for your hospital bag because you might have a big baby or a small baby (it is better to have the baby grow slightly too big rather than too small).
- Drink lots of fluids after birth to make up for fluids and blood loss in labour and fluid loss from breast feeding.
- Steralise bottles ready for coming out of hospital (if you know when you are goingin, are in labour and can manage to do this). You can also use the already sterlaised starter bottled for the first few days (these are bottles with milk already in steralie disposable bottles).
- After 24 hrs your baby shouldn't go longer than 4 hrs without a feed. At this stage a breast feed will last approx 40 mins. You should then feed every 2 hours to get milk in - for 10, 20 or 30 mins.

- For the first 12 hours you baby will be full of mucus and will feed less and will cough up a lot.
- If your baby keeps throwing the scratch mittons off try putting socks on their hands instead of scratch mittens.
- Be prepared for your body swelling after giving birth, it will look awful and shock you but it will then settle down and you will be back to normal before you know it.
- If you smoke, wear a smoking jacket or T-shirt so that you can then take it off, rather than holding your baby against smoking clothes and always wash your hands after having a cigarette.
- Big babies may need a diabetic test, if they are born very large there is a risk that they maybe diabetic.
- Put your babies car seat in the passenger side so that its safer getting your baby in and out.
- After you have had a baby you can get a premium cool pad & cushion to help ease discomfort.
- Put your hand on your babies chest so that they feel secure without their clothes on i.e. when you wash/change them.
- Use baby oil to remove the sticky stuff on your skin from plasters.
- Keep places of interest and postcode in the notes section of your phone so that you have ideas of places that you can go on a day out with your children.
- Use a bendy straw so that you can put a drink on the table and still drink whilst breast feeding.
- Before your baby's 5 day heel prick test, that day, put 2 pairs of socks on your baby in order to keep your baby's feet warm. Warmer feet make it easier for them to do the test.
- Rub your baby's toys and blanket on your chest to make it get 'mummy's' smell, they will then find them soothing.
- If you don't bath your baby ever day at least give a top to toe wash every day to make sure sweat and dirt does not build up in the skin creases, otherwise the skin may get irritated.
- Pack spare pads for your ten machine in your hospital bag because they may come off if you are sweating or moving around a lot.
- After you have given birth soak your stitches in bath with milk and tea tree oil. Use 1/2 cup of milk and 3-4 drops of tea tree oil in bath twice a day, don't use the tea tree oil neat as it will sting (the milk helps the tea tree oil dissolve into the water).
- Keep a jug of cooled boiled water in your bathroom with tea tree oil or salt for your stictched and use it to wash yourself after every time that you go to the toilet so that your stitches don't become infected.
- If you have stitched use cotton only maternity/sanitary pads because the standard ones will irritate you.
- Jaundice starts at head and works down.
- Drink lots of fluid and milk when you are breastfeeding, don't eat anything too spicy such as curry because the curry may come out in milk. I had a strong chilli and it really affected my son the next day.
- Cut name tags off as soon as you get home so that they don't irritate your baby, they are nice to keep in a memory box.

- Have a thermometer in each room so that you can check and regulate the tempreture.
- Don't use ear thermometer on new born - use under arm
- Heels have no nerves:feeling but baby doesn't like the pressure
- Clean around neck and under arms regularly
- Yoga is good; they say 4 mins of complete relaxation is akin to hours of sleep. Mum and baby yoga is a great thing to do togther.
- Gripe water is good for hiccups
- Don't leave your baby on surfaces as they can move when you are not expecting it.
- make sure the back up batteries in your monitor are fully charged in case there is a power cut.
- When your baby doesn't drop off in the day because s/he is looking at things and then gets overtired you know that this is the time that you will need to start putting your baby down for a set nap each day and you will the need to plan your day accordingly.
- Your baby may need extra sleep when ill but make sure that s/he is still being woken for feeds. You may not ordinarily need to wake for feeds as this may interfere with sleep patterns.
- The temperature drops in the night and when your baby is asleep his/her tempreture may drop so it is a good idea to go in and check on your baby. Even if it is really hot and you just put your baby to sleep in a nappy (I would recommend that if its 27 degrees or over that you just put your baby to sleep in a nappy), you then need to go in a few hours later when the tempreture has dropped and cover your baby with a light blanket.
- Avoid spreading infections, don't cough on your hand and touch things. Cough and sneeze into a tissue and wash your hands frequently. Otherwise you will just keep passing germs throughout the family.
- Over the body handbags are good so that you have got your hands free. I used to have a change bag and then a small handbag. Then I had a change bag with 2 compartments one for me and one for baby's stuff. Now I have a Miche bag because it has interchangeable handles and covers. I have the extra long shoulder strap with it and can easily change the outer shell to match my outfit for the day. I have some for sale on my web site http://soinspire.weebly.com/
- In the winter leave the heating on constant but low so house stays warm when you get up in the night.
- It's okay to have cold hands and feet as well as core temperature is warm (feel chest and back to check that baby is warm enough).
- It's a good idea to have cartons of ready made baby formula in case there is an electrical fault/power cut and you can't heat the kettle etc. otherwise you will have to boil water on the stove and put it in a flask.
- In winter cartons maybe too cold to serve at room tempreture and you may want to warm them slightly.
- Give a fresh dummy in the morning & clean night one.
- Steam gets on the formula spoon and some powder may get stuck, tap it out fully & regularly clean & sterilise the formula scoop soon.
- When baby sleeps through the night, in the morning s/he may need more frequent foods to make up for less feeds in the night.
- Try powders & medicine yourself first to make sure that they are okay before giving them to your baby.
- Growth spurts and development may make your baby sleep more.
- If you are using a sensor pad and metal travel cot makesure that it is compatible.
- New borns legs stay curled up until at least 8-9 months when they start standing and straightening them.

- A rash that comes and goes if it feels dry and prickly could be sensitivity (try changing washing powder), if its flat and smooth it could be a heat rash but always check it, especially if there are other symptoms. If the rash doesn't disappear with pressure i.e. by rolling a glass over it, then it could be meningitis.
- A new borns gums /roof of mouth will appear white, this is okay.
- At night oxygen levels in your babis blood may be lower when ill so may be worst at night. If it drops below a certain level hospital will admit the baby.
- Themometer – don't use in ear at first until older. Tempreture not true indicator because they can be ill and don't always get a tempreture.
- Its good to have friends with kids, then you can take baby to their house for dinner etc.
- Be organised with bottle timings, predict time next bottle is due and make in advance.
- Heat is lost through head so keep it covered and put muslin over change mat to stop the head getting cold.
- The soft spot on your baby's head will pulsate, if they chew, suck or drink etc. this looks alarming but is quite normal.
- If you get a rocking mosses basket stand, they are quite nice to rock a new born to sleep but after a few weeks (especially if you have a bigger baby they may tip to the side, if your baby lays to one side of the moses basket), a flat one that can fold up for the car is best.
- If you have a dummy you may find that when your baby is sleeping s/he keeps wanting the dummy and will wake when it falls out.
- It's a gamble if you feed your baby early if you then put him/her down early for a nap if s/he will then wake early for another feed but if you wake your baby to do a dream feed s/he may not settle afterwards for a while. Its best not wake your baby at night for feeds, once you have got your baby into a routine of sleeping through the night as will disrupte your routine and your baby may get used to waking. However if it is still quite early another feed at 11pm may ensure your baby sleeps through the night. Most people do recommend dream feeds, sometimes hungry baby milk will also keep them fuller for longer and keep them sleeping through the night.
- Rotate your babys clothes so that you are not just washing and putting at the top of the draw the same things and then wearing the same clothes.
- Don't forget to use spare nappies in car etc before running out.
- If your baby appears to be sick a lot, keep a diary of this to show the doctor.
- When you go out if you know your babt will be due a feed soon, make a fresh bottle with warm water as soon as you are leaving, that way it will have cooled by the time you get to your destination.
- It is a good idea to keep an inventory of what you have (and where it is stored) and what you need to buy fresh for your next baby. That way you can keep track of things and won't waste money buying things that you already have. If you lend things out also keep a list of who you lent them too.
- Plan your journey or your day around sleep and feeds – you can tailor babys feeds and sleep around what you are doing with some clever workings out. When you know what you regualry do and what works best for you, you can tailor routine but will need to change when your life changes ie going back to work etc.
- When you take your baby to get their vaccines make sure that you put loose clothes on them so that the clothes don't pres on the jab site.
- Cots with sides that fold down are easier when baby gets bigger so is better – but ones with a higher base are better for new born.
- Even when baby is older, when you go out walking you may need a stroller if going out for a long time because your toddler may get tired.
- Put ribbon on their toys & tie to harness on pram or reins so they don't fall on floor & kids can pull them back up.

- If you can't afford private school send to state school but supplement with a few private lessons.
- Most nurserys won't mix powder & formula so you have to pre- make bottles or use cartons. Not such as issue as your baby gets older (by 12 months your baby will be on formula milk).
- Watch your baby closely when they first learn to roll over in case your baby rolls over and can't roll back again. My son used to want to sleep on his side, as soon as he could roll he would roll over in his cot onto one side, the trouble was he would always roll into an akward position and trap his arm, he would then get stuck and cry until I went in and rolled him back. We had a period of a couple of weeks where this would happen several times a night and I got no sleep at all. In the early stages there is always something to keep you awake. If its not waking for feeds or nappy changes its teething or moving in the night and bumping themselves or getting suck in akward positions, or colds and other viruses keeping them awake. For my son this went on until he was about 9 months. Sometime he would start sleeping through the night and then this would last a few weeks but stop due to something else. You soon forget how tiring it is and the affect the lack of sleep has on you and other people who have had babies forget. Sometimes people really don't realise how hard it is. Stay strong and it will all pass and before you know it you will be getting full nights sleep again and you will have forgotten what all the fuss was about.
- A larger cot (and heavier one) maybe better if you have a baby that is large or moves around a lot, but you won't realise this until you have already brought your cot and you also need to think about what works in the space that you have and what is within your budget.
- You dont need to know all the words to nursery rhymes you can make up your own words/rhymes, you will also learn them as you go along or you can buy CDs with them on. I got really worried before my baby that I didn't know anything about children and couldn't even remember any nursery rhymes. You soon pick things up as you go along and after a year of having your baby you will be a wealth of knowledge, you will be giving other parents advice and won't even remember when you didn't know what you know now.
- You may be worrying about the time of your labour but you will loose all concept of time and a long labour won't seem as long as it actually was.
- Get as much sleep as you can whilst in hospital so u have your energy when home looking after baby
- Imagination is good for babies and children, play games, tell them stories and feed their imagination.
- If there is a lot of sound and lots of things for your new born to look at, s/he will get tired much more quickly from taking all of it in. You may find at first they can only go in a sensory room for a while, after a while they will become over tired, as they got older they can manage longer.
- They move their arms and legs around and kick their legs when they are excited, as they get older they may add to this with a squeal or laugh too.
- Constant crying could be a sign of illness. Usually the doctors say your baby hasn't got an infection/isnt'till if they have no tempreture but this isn't always the case, your baby could get ill without a tempreture so always get baby checked if in doubt. Usually if they hold the side of their face and pull their ear it could be ear ach either caused by an infection or by teething. If it carrys on it is worth getting them checked again, or getting a second opinion.
- Get the balance right, have fun activites for your child to keep them stimulated and help them develop but let let your child rest too and don't be too pushy for them to join in with things.
- Babies continuous whinning can be annoying and distracting when you are trying to do your monthly paperwork etc. so store up your jobs and send to the granparents for

a few hours so you can have some space to concentrate on your admin without getting stressed.

- Dont be near anyone in labour when pregnant as hormones released & stress may bring on your labour early.
- Keep the out of hours doctors numbers near the phone
- It's prudent to phone ahead to the hospital when you are in labour to check that they have beds.
- In the car park if you can't get in a parent and baby space park at higher level or in an end space, where you have space around you.
- Work out the best way to put your pram in the boot so that it will fit and you can pull it out easily (I used to pu my handle and back wheels to the right so that the pram clip was at the front, so I could unclip it and open it as I was pulling it out of the car).
- If your baby goes rigid/straightening and tensing or curls his/her legs up it could be wind
- Crying in sleep - could be bad dream, cold, hungry or wet nappy. Shh back to sleep but don't wake & get up unless really crys, if settles leave to go back to sleep.
- Rattling in chest = asthma, in the back = a blocked nose.
- Doctors don't always write to you re; vaccines so you have to remember to book appointments yourself
- Pass toy to both sides/give both hands a chance so child can use either or both don't be bias & stifle a child to have a certain preference of what hand they use.
- Keep a spare dummy near the cot
- Cross the road with the pushchair further up, not on a main junction.
- Leave a bucket & brush outside the front of your house in order to wash your pushchair wheels.
- When baby has vaccines (first lot), baby gets a fever (doesn't from others as they are not live), therefore baby needs calpol as you need to get the temp/fever down.
  Every few months go through clothes, check size & get next ones out.
- Try Medicine & powders before giving to baby - if you are allergic they maybe too. Before a year they are sensative to allergies but you don't know what allergies they may have so be cautious & assume they maybe allergic to what you are allergic to.
- It's good to have 2 baby chairs so you can leave baby in 1 whilst you move other chair around & then put baby in it, for instance rather than moving baby up & down the stairs in the chair which is dangerous.
- Keep a stock of generic children's toys for birthday parties.
- Check weight/size for car seats & pram etc new born car seat - up to 13 kg/29 lbs usually upto 12-15 months. Some bouncers only go up to 9 kilos (when you are looking to buy them you may want to purchase some that go up to a higher weight).
- At Christmas (once your children are old enough to understand) make reindeer footprints in the garden and scatter reindeer dust (glitter). Get kids to write to santa and write a letter back yourself on the computer (there are companies that also do this for you).
- Even with a stair gate don't let them play near the top of the stairs in case they push the stairgate out or manage to jump over it.
- Take a picture of your babies first bath & the first time they have food. They can't have messy cake pictures until they are a year old due to the sugar in the food.
- When you go into labour it is a good idea to eat when you have your first contrations because you need your energy & won't want to eat once full contractions come on, so it maybe a while before your next meal (but only eat something light otherwise you will throw it up, you will also have lots of bowel movements as your body tries to empty your stomach – if you can eat early enough you can get the energy and nutrients before your body flushes the food out).

- Don't let children play unattended in the garden because of foxes and cover your cat flapin case they come in at night
- Stroke and cuddle your baby to calm baby him/her.
- Put bibs and socks in a washing bag to keep separate from the rest of the wash so that the socks don't get mixed up and the velcro on the bibs doesn't damage the other clothes.
- Get toys that make them develop in ability (something that stretches them slightly is good but nothing too advanced because it can also be bad too make them advance too much too early. It is also a good idea to put their toys just slightly out of their reach so that they have to move to get them; this encourages them to start crawling.
- Every baby does things at different paces and your child may seem to be lagging behind at developing some skills and then all of a sudden may pick things up, at nearly 8 months my son could not sit up unaided but he could crawl backwards, then in the space of a few weeks he started crawling forwards really fast, hhe could not only sit up but he could stand up and could walk around furniture.
- Try to alternate what they do so they get to develop lots of different skills. They may want some time in the jumperoo (but no more than 40 mins), they may then need some floor time so that they learn to crawl etc.
- If you shop around you can often get deals such as 3 for 2 on dummies etc. but check the till receipt if you get lots of 3 for 2s to make sure you get the full value off (when I was shopping in mothercare because they didn't put through each type of item together I got 2 expensive things put through and then a cheap dummy through twice rather than 3 of the expensive items going through together and 1 dummy free and then the rest of the dummies going through together and another dummy free), so always check your recipt. Furthermore if you are on a price plan where they price match with any further discounts the offer, check on the web before you pay. I had a mothercare baby plan with 10% off, then I saw that they had 20% off on the web site so I printed it out when I went instore to pay and they gave me a further 10% off to bring it upto 20% off.
- Babies loose their dummies in the cot at night and might not get back to sleep without it. It's a good idea to put extra dummies in the cot, you can also get glow in the dark dummies.
- It's a good idea to exercise when you are pregnant to increase stamina and build muscles will help with labour. You should do gentle exercise only don't overdo it otherwise baby can over heat and it can be dangerous.
- You will want to get a nice coat with a hood to wear when its raining so that you have your hands free. You can't really hold a pushchair and push a pram, you can get umbrellas for the parents that clip onto the pushchair but they often fall off or get blown off by the wind. You may also want to keep gloves nearby in the winter as your hands get cold when pushing the pram.
- Teethers – use spray or wipes to clean them, then put them in the fridge in a sandwich bag (most can't be electrically sterilised or be put in the freezer or microwave).
- Don't forget to clean babies neck (and in between wrinkles when new born).
- Keep a spare change of clothes for you.
- Some people wind their baby ½ way through a feed to stop them getting too much wind, however if you do this and your baby gets too distressed with their feed being interrupted you might as well carry on feeding them and then wind them when you have fisnished feeding them, because if they are excessively crying they will be taking in more wind and there is no point stressing them out.
- It can take upto 12 months for your babies soft spot to fully heal.
- Children are little people with less experience of the world trying to find their way and are easily influenced by their peers.

- Clothes size may come up small / shrink so try them early, don't wait until your child is 12 months to put them in their 12 month clothes, try them at 6 or 9 months. My baby was in 12 month clothes when he was 7 or 8 months.
- Babies hate getting dressed and will cry when you dress them or try to change their nappy. It was a shock to me when I tried to dress my very placid 1 day old baby and he screamed so much, I soon learnt this was normal. At 10 months he still screams and fusses when I try to dress him.
- Children don't understand things so you need more understanding for them.
- If your baby drinks his/her bottle too quickly and gets tummy ache, to low down the drinkin process, take the bottle out and wind your baby at regular intervals. You may also find that when you move to next stage teat they may seems too fast until baby gets used to them. If your baby is still drinkin too fast then just use a slower flow teet. If this still doesn't work your baby may be hungry and need hungry milk, more milk or may need weaning onto solids.
- Your baby may dribble and find it hard when going from breast to bottle. My son used to drible ½ thw bottle out whilst he was drinking. This was okay because it was from the change of going from breast to bottle but sometimes this could be a sign of muscle weakness so its something that you need to keep an eye on and may need to get checked out.
- Outings with toddlers; before going on a day out, look up on the web site for special offers and deals to the attraction that you want to go to. Check the opening times and if any parts of the attractions are closed. It is also good to check where to park and how much parking costs etc. Put a label on your child with your phone number – perhaps a sticker or arm band, in case they get separated from you.
- Keep a muslin and wipes handy on the pram, if you have a tray or you can get a holder for wipes that clips to the side of your pram.
- Keep bottles of water and snacks in the car so that you can keep yourself and your toddle re-hydrated.
- Some babies like to be tight/swaddled where as others like room to move around in the cot. If you have a small cot and your baby doesn't like it, you could put your baby in a travel cot that maybe wider and then get a better mattress to put in it.
- When you are going on holiday check what type of travel cot will be where you are going and if in doubt take your own. If using a borrowed travel cot you may want to take your own mattress. When your baby gets older you could use a bath seat. Also put some toys in the bath and fill it so that s/he is submerged enough to stay warm.
- You baby may not like being held on their back in the bath. If you get in the bath and then put your baby in the bath with you s/he may prefer it as s/he can sit up.
- Take a blanket /coat when you go out, even if it's hot and your baby doesn't need it. Just in case it suddenly turns colder (especially in the UK as the weather is so unpredictable). In the winter if you put your baby in a snow suit, take a thinner coat in case it gets warmer and your baby gets too hot in the snow suit.
- When you and baby are in the car, if you stop the engine and it's a hot day, open the windows as the car will heat up without the air con on. On a cold day don't stay in the car without the heating running either. Remember even in the winter your baby may get too hot in the car, with the heating etc. so you may want to remove a blanket whilst in the car.
- It a good idea to get your baby used to other babies, noise and boisterousness. Try not to fuss them too much either, that way they will play with other babies, won't mind noise and won't be too fusy.
- Anything new/new place etc is a nightmare until you get used to it. Try to be organised and plan ahead as much as possible in order to take the stress out of any new places/situations.

- If you don't have a bath you could try putting your baby in the shower with you, some babies like showers (if you are planning to have a baby and are re-designing your bathroom try to keep a bath in your bathroom).
- When your baby starts moving and gets too wiggly to change on a change mat you may want to change him/her across your knee. This may be easier too if you are out and the change station doesn't have a seatbelt. It is also more hygienic than laying your baby on a change table that s/he may touch, or roll off of your mat onto. Changing your baby on your knee also saves your knees and stops your trousers from getting knee marks in them.
- Your baby has to know that you are there. If baby knows you are there for him/her and that when you go away/are apart you will come back then s/he will sleep better and also be less clingy and settle for other people etc.
- If your baby seems unsettled in the pram try turning the pram around to face the other way. Sometimes baby's like facing outwards, also with car seat may prefer facing outwards towards the direction of travel, motion feels more natural and then they can see what is going on.
- It is a good idea if you are going out to baby group/to meet friend that you tidy your house before you go, in case you want to have your friends back.
- When babies play together they have to be watched as they may bite if teething and they often pinch/scratch each others faces – they don't mean any harm by it but like to grab soft skin and it can be harmful if they scratch each other's eyes.
- If you have a messy baby it may be good to put on an apron when feeding your bay so that s/he doesn't sneeze and/or flick food all over you.
- You c buy mini bottles of sunscreen – these are great to keep in your handbag in the summer.
- It is a good idea when you are going on holiday to pack a travel kettle, (you can pack other things inside it to save room in your case), to boil drinking and formula water
- Permanent marker – write instructions on things and/or your baby's name. It is great to write instructions for use on your travel steriliser (if it's not used very often you might not remember the amount of water/time it takes etc).
- Wear cheap scarfs to catch sick and dribble from your baby, rather than having to keep changing tops.

- If your blender breaks you can always mash the food through a sieve.

- You can always give your baby a small amount of milk for comfort maybe a few ounces but don't make a habit out of it, otherwise your baby will need milk to settle.

- Lthough you need a big naapy changing bag to have your nappies, nappy mat, milk, change of clothes for your baby in you don't necessarily have to carry a big bag. You will always have a pram or the car with you so you can keep an overflow bag with spare bibs, muslin, outfits and extra nappies in. You can then just keep the scaled down bearessentials in a handbag/smaller nappy bag. As your baby gets older and gets heavier you will want to carry less weight in your bag. You may also need room for your own essentials such as makeup, purse, phone, notebook etc.

- Having kids gives you an Excuse to do stuff – play in the park etc. with them, go on rides and act like a child yourself, you can have loads of fun.
- Take them to waky warehouse or the park its good for them to run around.
- Steam clean the floor, its hygienic and saves cleaning chemicals.
- Keep the clothes that they are growing out of as when they get moving and loose the baby fat they may fit into them again.

- It is normal for young babies to breathe slightly erattically, which can seem concerning but I am told is normal. They also hold their breathe sometimes, if they do this you should blow in their face.
- Gently hold and rub the back of their hand if they pinch you. For them its like a comfort thing, if you gently remove their hand and stroke it instead they will soon stop doing this. My son went through a stage of pinching.
- When you pack your travel cot don't forget to pack the sheets and blankets for your travel cot
- Every day you will learn something new, even if it isn't your first child.
- Sometimes, especially at first it feels like one thing after another. I felt like this with my son, he had colic, was then teething, then had RSV, then started loosing his dummy in the night and waking up and then started waking into the sides of the cot and hurting himself, things eventually got a lot easier. Remember everyday is a new day and you will feel better, take each day as it comes and let others help you.
- You may find that your new born does wet farts, these are okay, they are not the same thing as having diahrea and a small amount of dioreah is okay, especially if you are breast feeding and have eated something spicy. Your newborns poo will be runny and different colour because they are just drinking milk. When you go onto solids they will smell more but will be a normal consistency so it will be easier to clean their bum.
- If you want to wean your baby onto solids before 6 months it is up to you. Babies are now much bigger than they used to be and they are similar to adults, it is just the hormones and protiens that are different and the way they break down enzymes, therefore baby rice as it has been developed for babies should be okay. Therefore if you are unsure just give your baby some baby rice. If something doesn't agree with them you will see this in their poo or they will be sick.
- Keep a bottle of baby wash by your kitchen sink to wash your baby after s/he has eaten and keep a bucket of water by the sink to soak any soiled clothes in.
- When you go back to work and your baby starts nursery you will need to chage you routine, it maybe worth changing it a month before you need to so that you are settled in the routine for when you need to be.
- You will find that you will get 'mummy rage' as I call it over things that you didn't notice or wouldn't bother you before, i.e. you will get annoyed over mother & baby parking spaces. You will find that you need a large space so that you can lift your baby in and out (you will need to open your door right out to life the car seat out/lean into strap bay up) and have space to safetly put them in their pram. You will find that there aren't many parent and baby spaces so you may wait a while for one, or risk parking in a normal space and someone park so close that you can't get your baby back into the car, or have to risk putting the pram in the path of oncoming traffic. You will see people park there that don't have babies and you will get very angry (mummy rage). Another thing that annoys me is when you go swimming and go in the family room and can't get your pram in, yet the change table doesn't have a seat belt (I found another pool that had a larger family room). When you go shopping you can always use the disabled changing room to take the pram in with you except when the shops use the disabled changing room to store their stock & boxes in (this happens quite frequently). On one recent shopping trip when I couldn't get in the chaging room I said I will just keep the curtain to the cubical open to take my baby in (thinking

its inside a changing area only for women, the sales assistant confirmed that was okay and the turned around to welcolme in the male shop assistant to sort the rail, what was she thinking!).

- If you have a cot toy, that attaches to the side of the cot. When your baby wakes s/he can play with it and will stay in the cot longer in morning, before screaming to get out.

- Rechargable batteries are cheaper than keep buying normal batteries.

- It's a good idea to have your phone on silent but keep it close by so that it doesn't distrurb your baby.

- Why not put a poem in your photo book that you get for your baby.

- In the summer give your baby a coolish (but not too cold) bath before bed to make him/her feel nicer.

- If your baby does a regular poo at the same time every morning why not put him/her on the potty for this. I know a friend who would put her baby on the potty in the morning from 1 month and by 8 months she was potty trained.

- Babies and puppies are alike

- Bannana stains clothes, so soak anything with bannan on straight away.

- Cats may get in through the window so don't leave your baby's window open at night.

- Cruising is where they walking holding onto furniture, once they start doing this it is not usually long until they are walking.

- If your baby is not drinking you could give him/her some water in a syringe and squeeze it into the mouth.

- Sometimes they fight sleep & won't settle so have to be left to cry it out- sometimes they need to cry to tire themselves out & cry to sleep.

- They don't like being restrained and having their arms held, they often won't sit and cuddle you and instead want to run off.

- Don't let them chew your phone, apart from the fact that it may break, it will be full of germs.

- Jogging bottoms are good for babies when they are potty training.

- Thin hair out in summer with thinning sissors so that it isn't too thick and warm for them.

- Do a photobook of your baby's first year and if you have 2 children or more do a picture of each child next to each other at same age.

- Wean off dummy at 12 months

- Nct sales are a great place to sell your old toys and buy new ones or why not organise a toy swap.

- Don't leave batteries in toys in loft as they may corrode.

- Don't get 2nd hand soft toys - only plastic that can be sterilised

- You need a break, you are always thinking of the kids and timings and don't get chance to switch off. The husband always has the wife there to help and prompt him what needs doing. Its good for you to go away so that he has to think for himself, sees what its like and learns what to do so can cope if something takes you away.

- Do a folder and daily schedule of what needs doing to prompt him.

- Keep a list of daily schedule in bag / for emergency carer so they know what needs doing.

- Keep babies toothbrush by the highchair.

- Carry a spare food pouch in your car/change bag.

- It's a rollercoaster ride having a baby some of your best and worse moments, your life will be full of highs of the joy of your little one and lows when your heart is in your mouth when they are ill or have accidents you never stop worrying but equally you laugh and love a lot too. They also make you have fun, stay young and live life to the full. My best and worst day was when Ritchie was born (bad labour, I thought he was going to die then I thought that I might die but I was so pleased that we both pulled through and I had my wonderful baby), then I was too tired to feel. Then there was some scary moments when he was taken ill, some near misses etc. but loads of laughs and cuddles. The best feeling in the world is when your baby crawls over to you and cuddles up to you.

- When you are travelling if your children are too old to be in your room get adjoining rooms for child.
- When you go away, take your red book and do a route card for each place that you are staying at to the nearest hospital.
- Get your child registered for the European Health Insurance Card (EHIC), if you are going outside the UK. This can be used to cover any necessary medical treatment due to either an accident or illness within the European Economic Area (EEA). The EHIC entitles the holder to state-provided medical treatment within the country they are visiting and the service provided will be the same as received by a person covered by the country's 'insured' medical scheme. The EHIC is the replacement for

the E111. As of 1 January 2006, E111's are not valid. Also ensure that you have the correct medical insurance. It is also a good idea to research where you are going – check it is safe and the vaccines that are needed etc.

- Take all opinions into account but be cautious about whom and what you consult, get a balanced view and trust your instincts about what is right for you and your family. What may have worked for someone else, may not work for you.
- Have lots of spare white vests and baby grows and a couple of spare sleeping bags and sheets, that way you won't have to do some much washing if you have a sickly baby (although you may not want to get too many new born clothes as they will grow out of them quickly). You could have a bucket outside with water and bleach in and throw really mucky baby grows in, then rinse them out and put them in the wash.
- Blood in baby sick could be from your breasts bleeding so don't panic but get it checked out, bright colour is superficial blood but if it is dark in colour this could be an issue.
- Just because you have a baby/child it doesn't mean you can't have a tidy stylish house. Get storage to put things in, an ottoman to put toys in, leather sofa wipes clean and you can have a new car and put car seat protectors in. Have things organised in cupboards etc.
- You don't have to have all the toys out at one time, you can rotate the toys (keep them in baskets/boxes and swap them around), just ensure that baby is getting a good mix of toys/good mix of development opportunity.
- When you go out take baby's pushchair so that baby can sleep if s/he feels tired and grumpy.
- If you have a boy when you take its nappy off the release of pressure may make it wee so hold the nappy over it, until you put the next one on (or be ready to jump out the way). Some people say that you may also need to pull its foreskin back to clean its winkle to stop it getting an infection. However pulling it back too far can cause damage so its best not to and instead just ensure that you clean the area well. Be sure to lift up the willy and clean underneath it and the testicles, otherwise baby may get sore. Sometimes they may get sore so use water to clean and a good cream with antiseptic properties such as sudocream. Apparently bepathan is good and is stronger so its great for sores but sudocream is best for more frequent use as its not too strong.
- It is good to take babies nappy off and lay baby on a waterproof sheet (in case they pee), this gets air to baby and reduces nappy rash and lets them move more freely. You could always cover him/her in a towel if necessary. Perhaps do this for an hour, just after a nappy change (its then less likely that s/he will need to toilet again straight away). Therefore you may want to buy some PVC sheets and small towels.
- When going out, take a change of tops with you or a spare dress in case you leak milk.
- When baby starts to crawl s/he will be into everything, therefore it is a good idea to keep important documents and tickets etc. in a box or organised folder outside of babies reach. You may also want to get a letter box guard that collects all the post, that way baby won't pick up and hide important letters.

- Don't leave muslin cloth in reach of baby because baby may grab it and put it in their mouth and choke / over their mouth and may struggle to breathe.
- Blacked out windows on car means you don't need a sunshade,
- Flat head/rash on back of head is common from where baby has been lying on head
- Have extra vests
- Have a break between kids for your body to recover
- Keep labels on clothes until baby needs to wear them in case you need to change them. You get through new born clothes so quickly, if baby doesn't get chance to

wear them you can then sell them, change them or give them as gifts if they still have the labels on.

- Check sale and second hand price of items, sometimes it is better to buy things new if you can get them in the sale.
  - Make noise and hoover around your baby so they get used to it.
  - Put different toys out every day so that they get used to playing with a variety of toys and have some toys in a basket that they can reach so that they get to choose what toys they want to play with.
  - Change mat on front of bag may get lost easily.
  - Babies cinema; some cinemas have special sessions that you can take babies, get front seats and then you can put out the play mats.
  - Buttons – make sure that buttons are swen on securely so they don't fall off/become a choke hazard
  - Bottle water - keep small bottles that you can fill with cooled boiled water and take out with you.
  - Keep a bottle of water for cleaning baby's face
  - U- tube is good for looking up nursery rhymes
    When are they out of first car seat - different ages for different seats. It goes on weight for first baby seat and then weight and height – first ones are usually up to 20kilos.
    It's hard when you go back to work & put baby in nursery - after 2 weeks it gets easier & nursery is good for baby because it teaches them how to interact with other children.
  - Don't tie ribbon/string onto toys etc where baby can strangle themselves.
  - Sensory rooms are great places to take babies.
  - Babies need their sleep to develop so sometimes let them sleep, don't do too many activities.
  - After vaccines they maybe tired and grumpy etc.
  - Don't keep baby held or in chair too long, put baby on mat so s/he can move around unrestricted and give 'tummy time'. Even time laying on their back allows them to move around, kick their legs and develop muscles, move to side etc. have things that they can reach for too (a play gym mat is good).
  - The more informed you are the more confident you are - although you can get info overload / confused with conflicting advice
  - Record activites and log any ilness/reactions to see if there is a pattern/cause ie if unsettled, sleep less, eat or wee less, sick, cranky etc
  - Babies nails grow long quickly - soften in bath before cutting
  - Financially it maybe better to have kids close in age so you pay for chilcare for less time.
  - Its hard work looking after baby and is all rush but at least you get to sit down and slow down when you feed them, they force you to slow down and appreciate what's important in life.
  - Get dressed first, as soon as you can, then put bottle on and whilst waiting for kettle sterlaise next lot of bottles, then feed and then take up ready milk and bottles for next night.
  - We don't know what they take in, it could be more than you think, therefore think about what you say. Speak to them and teach them as they they absorb the information.
  - some teething medication is suitable from birth, some isn't so check it. Check what is in each item, especially if giving 2 medications i.e. calpol contains paracetmol so don't give with anything else containing paracetmol.
  - Wash hands when picking baby up, wash hands after nappy change before touching baby face or feeding etc.

- It takes time to bond with baby – not always instant – but over time love will grow each day.
- Try different genres of music to see what soothes baby
- Keep a snack and drink for you, you are always on the go and need to keep your energy levels up
- Have stock of childrens presents and birthday cards, for birthday parties
- 2nd child harder because you have 2 to look after, but you will be more confident and know what you are doing so in that respect things will be easier.
- Take care with bright lights and camera flash around your babies eyes and avoid strobe lights
- Happy parents means happy baby
- Put your address in when searching eBay for baby stuff and look for local items, because people don't always post baby stuff that maybe bulky so you may get some good deals locally if you collect them.
- Don't wipe you baby's mouth with wet wipe as it may effect the skin on the face instead use a water wipe or a flannel, if you can.
- Aquious cream is good for cradle cap, olive oil is also good.
- Use the toy libraries at children's centres.
- Have a file for all your babies important documents and keep red book in there, that way you know where everything is when you need it.
- Swap mix and match stuff around so it looks like you have more outfits
- Diff types of toys & balls: foil blanket, peecaboo material - chiffon, massage ball, light up ball, o ball
- Weaning bowls / will help you measure amount of food
- If you have wipes in a box its hard to see how many are left – although it is cheaper to buy a big pack and put in a travel case then to buy travel packs of wipes.
- Most children's centres you will have to leave your pram outside, therefore you need a lock. And a light car seat if just carrying baby in, in car seat (which is what most people do).
- You will find that you get an inner strength, now your a mum, so that you can look after your baby.
- Set up an ipod play list for your baby. That way if you are in the car or out and about and your baby needs soothing you can play some lullaby songs. You can also have some fun songs for your childs party etc.
- Let baby get used to putting himself to bed – he may wake when dummy falls out. Don't get into bad habits of rubbing when put dummy in. Just put dummy back in and let him get used to self soothing, don't rush in and get into bad habits etc. when s/he can put dumy back in by himself/herself put extra dummies in the cot so that they can find them.
- Learn cues of when they want what i.e. when my son is sleepy he puts his hands by his face, rubs his face and eyes and looks at his hands and rubs them together, like he is counting his finger. I have taught him sign language for milk so I know when he wants a bottle, he sometimes uses this sign when he is thirsty and wants water too. I don't need to predict when he wants food, he has his regular meal times but loves his food and is always hungry, so if he is wingy I feed him, he never turns food down.
- Write notes / keep logs of your own observations – what you may want to remember in case you have another baby (otherwise you might forget things). It is also nice to record when your baby does things and record any major milestones or any cute things that you want to remember (they do lots of cute things). My granny wrote a book about her life before she passed away, I

then added to this to develop it into a book about the family with a family tree etc. for a wedding present to my husband I wrote one about him and his family and when my son was born I wrote a book for him and recorded everything from his birth to major milestones and added pictures of where he was born etc. I am hoping he will then carry on writing it to record his life store, and will then pass this down to the next generation and so on. I also got him a 100 year diary for his first Christmas present and will fill it in until he is old enough to take it over and start filling it in himself.

- When your baby is new born try and put him/her down for a sleep for 2 hours between feeds.
- You loose all concept of time when you have a baby – especially at first with a new born.
- Things change, one minute you know what you are doing, you find things okay and are getting some sleep through night and then it changes, they need more milk or weaning onto solids and you start the learning process again. Everything is new, it's a constant learning curve. All children are different, all individuals and develop differently and different things work. There are so many stages, just as you get your head around one stage you enter a new phase and so on. At all stages of their life they will cause diff problems/issues but the hard work will be worth it.
- With your baby something that works one day might not another, depending on their mood, the environment etc.
- You may want to limit the time they play with certain toys i.e. I used to limit my son to 40 mins in the jumperoo so that he didn't damage his legs by too much bouncing. As they get older you may also want to limit the time in front of the TV and playing computer games etc.
- Put a smile on when your baby wakes up. You need to be reassuring and smile for your baby so that s/he has a happy environment. This is not always possible but no matter how tired and bad I feel when I go to get my son out of his cot in the morning I go in with a big smile and make a big fuss of his, so that we are starting off the day in a happy way and he feels happy and secure, (not that I managed to do that for night time feeds but for those you don't want to be making eye contact, and certainly not smiling otherwise your baby will think that its playtime).
- Make friends with other people with baby's so that your baby has friends the same age. It will also give you people to talk to who are facing the same issues; it's a nice support network to have.
- Don't clean bath just before putting baby in because of chemicals. Instead try and clean your bath as regularly as you can so that it stays hygienic for your baby.
- Kids tv – a limited amount of children's TV is good for them. It will usually keep your baby calm, and they might learn something from it. However don't put your child in front of the TV all the time, instead spend time playing and interacting. Also think about what programmes you watch in front of them and try to avoid anything inappropriate.
- Don't give your baby a toy that is too heavy in case they hit themselves on the head.
- Get name labels and sew onto babies toys, mats, cots and snow suits etc. if you are going out to baby groups/other parents houses so that the don't get muddled up. However when they start school if they are being passed down a siblings items don't forget to update the name labels. My newphew created all sort of confusion at school when he lost his coat and it was found with his brothers name on it.

- Don't worry too much about the development stages and comparing babies, some babies may skip crawling ad go straight onto walking. Some will be slower at some things and faster at others.
- Don't compare yourself with other parents – some may seem to cope but you don't know how they are under the surface. Also one stage maybe easier for them but then other things maybe harder i.e. they maybe able to breastfeed but then may struggle with giving a bottle when they want to express or bottle feed or weaning may be harder etc. their baby may sleep now but then they may struggle at the teething stage. Other parents may like to show off so take what they say with a pinch of salt and don't ever feel like you are not good enough / don't let what they say worry you. They may not admit that its hard and you may feel like you are the only one finding it hard, this is not the case.
- A new lifestyle with less freedom can be hard to adjust to but as one door closes another one opens, focus on all the joy you will have with your new baby and all the things you can do with a child, all those precious moments to look forward to and its lovely to have a family, especially when you are old and grey and have your children around to look after you.
- Baby's are perceptive; they will pick up on your moods etc. children know whats going on around them too and take in more than you think. Don't swear etc. or be angry in front of them.
- The room tempreture may get colder in winter in night so bear this in mind when deciding on how many blankets, perhaps keep the heating on constant and turn down low (the thermostat should regulate it). But make sure your baby doesn't overheat; overheating is more dangerous than being cold.
- Rub over your babies head and down the top of their nose to make them close their eyes and soothe them off to sleep at night.
- When you have a new born get dressed first thing, as soon as you are able. Otherwise you may find that a whole day goes by and you haven't even got dressed, this will get you down. Just having a shower and get dressed, this will make you feel better. Try not to aim to do too much because you won't get it all done and will get upset but equally you need something to aim to achieve so aim to do 1 thing per day. Even if it is just something simple as first such as get dressed or put your makeup on.
- When you need to get petrol go to a garage where you can pay at the pump, that way you don't have to get out of the car and leave baby alone while you go into pay, or have to drag the baby in with you.
- When choosing a baby sitter, ask them, what activities will they do, will they take baby to groups etc.
- Get a note book and get people to write messages, tips advice etc for baby to read when older.
- With a baby there is always something to look forward to, their smiles and reactions to things, the cuddles etc It's amazing the older they get how much more alert they become. Its important to make the most of your time with your baby, you don't get it back and they grow up so quick, so spend time nurturing them, everything else can wait
- Do photo books and scan in important things such as child's first drawing etc. On line photobooks can always be re-ordered if the company is still in business, that way you have a lovely record of your memories. You can also make your own scrap books and add poems in etc.
- Encourage your children to mix with other children their own age on a regular basis to learn sharing (sharing is caring) and get them to sit with adults too and take them out to dinner so they know how to behave when out, can interact and have good social skills.

- Steralised bottles don't stay sterile for long so you must use them that day, otherwise they need to be re-steralised.
- Don't pull faces or make a fuss over things i.e. if you eat something that you don't like, otherwise they will be put. Babies/toddles will fall and get bumps etc. 'say your ok and don't fuss' otherwise they may cry. If you are calm they will get up and get on with it and be braver (unless of course they are hurt).
- You don't know what/how much they take in so its good to read to them, play music etc.
- Reins are important to keep toddler safe
- Normal household items - sponges etc can be used for baby play and learning. You don't have to spend a lot on expensive toys you can use your imagination and what you already have (children love playing with cardboard boxes), your love and time and interacting with them is what is important.
- Separate pram blanket
- Don't give your baby something to eat or medicine etc. for first time at night in case react badly, give it in the day, when you can monitor them.
- Regular weighing helps you keep an eye on your babies health, it also gives you the chance to meet the health visitor and ask questions it also helps you know when they will be in the next size nappy and when they will be too heavy for their car seat, their swing chair etc.
- Don't stock up on nappies too much because they grow quicker than you think. I used to put my baby in the larger size than the pack recommended i.e. once he was crawling he was in 4+ (he was 10kg and the nappy pack said that it went up to 14kg but the size 4 seemed tight and were rubbing him so I would have one size bigger and I never did it up too tightly).
- It is a good idea to get a spoon case or use a sandwich bag to keep the spoons in.
- When your baby is new born they will feel exposed when they have no clothes on because they are used to being swaddled in the womb so a flannel over their front in bath to help keep them warm and soothe them. A hand on their chest when you change their nappy will also do the same thing. You can buy a fancy cover for your baby in the bath but a flannel does the same thing and is less than a tenth of the price.
- A women life changes more with a baby because she is the one that is pregnant and usually spends more time nurturing the baby when it is born so she takes leave from work etc. where as the man still goes out and has less of a lifestyle change, but equally they miss out more on stuff so each role brings its challenges.
- Wipe mouth with gauze to get used to it before teeth come through, then use a baby toothbrush once your baby gets a tooth.
- You can go to any clinic to get your baby weighed as long as you have your red book, even if you forgot your red book they can give you a form with all the details on so that it can be recorded in the red book later on.
- Children are more tactile and are in large social groups, mix with toys, put things in their mouths etc. so spread infections.
- Your hair doesn't fall out when pregnant so after you have your baby it falls out, and your baby will do a good job of trying to pull it out too.
- Some nappy rash cream is too thick and then the skin can't breathe, Vaseline is good because acts as a barrier without being too thick, some people also find bepathan better than sudacream, although I like sudacream.
- As you get older your skin is less elastic and therefore harder for your tummy to spring back after a baby.

- Take plain change bag to crèche as you will have to leave it, with baby so don't leave valuables. Keep your nice change bag for when you have your baby with you.
- Dentinox cradle cap shampoo is good if your baby has cradle cap.
- Hot air rises so where baby is low down s/he may feel cold and may therefore need a blanket when playing on the ground on the play mat etc. also when your baby is sleeping and is still his/her temperature drops.
- PND will pass in time so try to focus on the positive and don't let it get you down.
- Babies love mirrors, play with baby in mirror.
- Clothes – after you have had a baby, even if you loose all the weight, you will change shape so you may want to buy new clothes (if you can put away a fund for this, it will cheer you up). But don't buy too many new clothes within the first year, because after a year (especially when your baby is crawling and you are chasing him/her) you may loose more weight.
- Have a system – in the morning get up and fill the flask ready for the bottles for the day. Fill up your organiser of what baby needs. When baby has morning nap it's a great time to get organised, get fresh clothes out for baby etc. My routine is that we get up (if im organised I can get up shower and dress before baby wakes, at the very least if I can get a shower then I can get dressed and do my makeup whilst he sits up on my bed after his bottle, without leaving him), if not get baby up, change nappy, give a bottle (carton), then I get dressed and do my makeup while baby lays on my bed (sits up in V cushion for his milk to settle). My baby then has a nap I come downstairs, have breakfast, empty the dishwasher from the night before, fill up steriliser and wash night bottle, lay out clothes and a bowl of water for washing, pack bag for the day (if not already done the night before – I try and keep bag stocked at all times but sometimes have to add in last minute stuff) etc.

- We have kept a weekly routine – like being at work mon-fri we have our routine activites, catch up with other mums and friends, go out every day to courses and baby groups, dentist appointments, doctors appointments and other meetings, then at the weekends we chill at home, do the housework, see the parents and have family time etc. having weekly activites and a routine helps, we aren't just stuck at home with all the days the same.
- When going out in the cold wrap baby up well with snow suit, hat and blanket etc. if in and out shops use a blanket and remove it when inside so that bay doesn't get too hot.
- A month is classed as 4 weeks i.e. 2 month calpol is 8 weeks.
- If you just have a job its easier to leave, if it's a career its harder to get back into after a break.
- Just because you have complications with bone child/baby labour or pregnancy it doesn't necessarily mean that the next one will be like that. Usually the subsequent pregnancys and labour get easier.
- Always carry more then you need, have a spare outfit yourself in case baby pukes or urinates on you. Equally you don't want to be carrying a heavy bag so if you can have a secondary bag in the boot of the car that is better.
- Feed with one hand (so that you can eat at the same time);

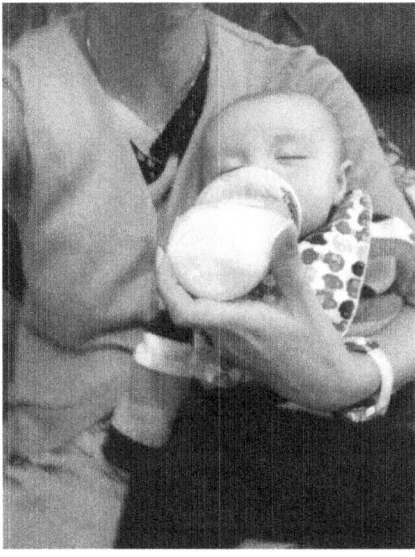

- Get a passport for baby in case you want to go away

- New born should sleep before feeds, feed, wind, change nappy and put down for a nap (after 20mins of letting milk settle).

- Spend as much time as possible with your baby but also give your baby some time on their own so they get used to their own company.

- The first few months are so hard its difficult to enjoy but try not to be anxious and try and enjoy the time because it goes quickly and you can't get it back.

- Keep muslin by cot so that you can wipe up babies dribble etc.

- You will find that babies kick their blankets off so grow bags are good. However if your baby falls asleep before you can put him/her into the grow bag you will need to use a blanket. When it got really hot in the summer I used a thin blanket because I would put my son to sleep in just a vest or a nappy and then when the tempreture dropped in the middle of the night I would cover him with a blanket (I couldn't manouver him to put him in a grow bag without wakin him.

- Only get baby grows that are easy to get on & off, not funny shape ones. I had some given to me for my son where the fastenings were at the back, this made it hard to change him and was uncomfy for him to lay on. My husband didn't like the ones that went over my son's head because he cried; it was eaier to use the ones that buttoned all the way down at the front. Although I found the ones that went over the head and just had the poppers at the bottom were easier once you had the over the head and getting the arms in battle.

- At night if baby is ill, turn light on and check baby properly for rash, colour of skin and check breathing etc.

- After birth have dental check up – prescritotion and dentist is free for a year after the birth. Make the most of it and get all your dental work done before this benefit expires.

- After birth it's a good time to get a dishwasher if you haven't got one. It saves washing all the bottles by hand, you need to save as much time as possible so just buy extra bottles and put them in the dishwasher.

- New borns clench a fist and don't open their hands much and they get sweaty and dirt, saliva and milk trapped so you need to try and oopen their hands and clean them properly.

- Often babies can learn to say words that are similar to their name because they hear their name so much. Its great when they finally recognise their name and when they respond and come over to you and bring you toys when you ask them to. It is suh fun when your baby can interact with you and you can see the bond that they shar with you.

- Health visitor are good source of information and can refer you on, sometimes youn may rather see health visitor rather than a GP. Because it maybe quicker, especially if you need a referral for something specific. They may even give you a referral over the phone i.e. with my sons ingoing big toe nails the health visitor refered us to a specialist clinic.

- Don't allow your baby to play in the cot otherwise may feel cot is time to play and not time to sleep. Having said that once my baby was sleeping well in his cot in the morning, after his bottle I would put his soft toys in his cot so that he could play and then eventually have a short nap whilst I got showered and dressed. When I went back to work I had to get up early to shower etc before he woke up because we didn't have time for anything else. Because he was older and had a routine and set wake up time, otherwise it would be more difficult (another reason why you should take as long as you can for maternity leave).

- Babies need to lay down, kick about and not be just held and in their bouncer chair all day.

- Don't make eye contact when you put to bed/at night, otherwise they will want to wake up and play.

- If you spread feeds out/do longer between feeds ie every 4 hours baby may not sleep through night as may have had less millk & maybe hungry at night because they have had less food in the day.

- If you have a choice put baby in a bigger room and get a spare bed in there so you can sleep in with baby if baby is ill.

- Don't drink alcohol if looking after baby (or just have a small amount so that you are still in control and can drive, you can get low alcohol wine and beer).

- It is a good idea to carry a snack for you in your change bag ie a ceriel bar (and if you have not long given birth carry a spare pair of pants).

- Dont always pick your baby up as soon as s/he cries (except when new born), otherwise they will not learn to self soothe themselves back to sleep.
  You know your baby better than anyone else - by about 6 to 7 weeks you will understand/know your baby.
  Some germs are needed, gradually as get older to build up tolerance.

Have a small kit of items to keep in car - torch, tissues, water, nappies, food, jump leads etc.

- Eat, sleep & shower when you can. Because you don't know when you will get the chance again.

- Babies get hot when they cry, are held to feed etc.

- Seahen changing clothes

- Avoid bright lights & camera flash as it's bad for eyes, also avoid strobe light and certain flashing films on the TV etc (especially if there is a risk of epilepsy in your family).

- Don't get them too many toys because they need some different toys to play when they go to their friends or nursery if they have too many they won't appreciate them and won't play with them all.

- **Whilst playing with his ball boo did a forward roll. Then when going to bed he wouldn't stop screaming when I went in he pulled the blanket over his head really forcefully like he was mega angry for ages I thought on my goodness he is so upset he is hiding from me, then he popped his head out & started laughing, then did it again kept doing it and laughing I then realised he wanted to play peek a bo it was so funny.**

- **This goes to show controlled crying can't upset them long term.**

- **He was just screaming for attention and then playing when I went in. It just goes to show how they try it on.**

- Stock up on gifts for their friends for when they get invited to birthday parties etc.
- Use summer dresses in winter by adding tights/leggings and chunky cardigans.
- Deal with bad behaviour there and then (children have a short memory) and if you try and punish them later and refer back to their bad behaviour they won't understand. Never get physical with a child, instead explain what they have done wrong and give them time out, be firm but fair. When child is having a tantrum try distraction techniques.
- Stand by what you say – if you make a promise uphold it.
- Teach child concentration by making them concentrate for short periods of time and then gradually increasing this.
- Put coconut oil in hair, leave overnight and wash off in the morning.
- Don't let your child see you in pain. Disguise a scream by pretending it's a dinasour roar.

Tips to help develop your baby's brain

Children's needs;

- Children need security; they need a familiar place and routine.
- Some children develop a need for a favourite toy or comforter that helps to soothe them. They often need this at bedtime or in stressful situations.
- You children don't like change they like their world to be predictable and ordered. This is why nurseries need to follow your child's own routine.
- Babies need new experiences to learn and develop.
- Children need to develop language skills for emotional and social development as well as to communicate and participate in society.
- Children need praise and recognition; children need encouragement and a reasonable level of expectations to act as an incentive for perseverance. Children who are set too higher level of goals and made to feel like a failure when they don't achieve will adopt a low level of effort and achievement.
- Children even babies need a level of responsibility, even as babies they can hold their spoon and learn to feed each other etc.
- We are role models for our children and they are influenced by us far more than we think.

Babies brains;

A new borns brain is only a ¼ the size of an adults, but will have grown to 80% of an adults by the age of 3. The newborn brain is only 25% developed. As most growth happens within the first few years experiences during this time have a profound and lasting effect on the brain's structure, function and performance.

Science suggest that toddlers brains act in a similar way to adults watching a movie. It is as if children view the world as a movie. They struggle to concentrate and can't focus on one single thing. Which adults often find frustrating. However this is so that they can absorb as many stimuli as possible from an environment. It is amazing, they view everything with excitement and enthusiasm. They have a heightened ability to adapt to new events.

The first few years of heightened brain activity are the best time to learn an additional language. If teaching 2 languages you need to be consistent and try to compartmentalise speaking each language. At age 2-3 the child should be able to differentiate between the languages and use them in the correct context. Language development can be slower in bilingual babies because they are trying to learn 2 different languages and it can be confusing. However being bilingual is highly beneficial for brain function, it gives the brain a workout, especially as the brain is often trying to decide what language to use (bilingual has been known to reduce dementia).

As the child becomes a teenager the brain functions not used will shrivel away.

To help your babys brain develop in the right way give your baby love, attention, a good balanced diet and offer plenty of positive stimulation, such as conversation and play. You can play at home and you don't need to have lots of toys instead you can use every day items, such as a muslin cloth to play peek-a-boo etc. Children learn through experience so reading to them is good, as is performing routines, exploring and playing.

What you can do to encourage them to develop;

- Lots of love and a good diet is key.

- Let children learn at their own rate and don't force development.

- Don't be too pushy

- Encourage them to do things that they like.

- Love them.

- Talk to them and listen to them and show them attention.

- Make sure baby gets enough sleep.

Maslow developed a hierarchy of needs;

A Theory of Human Motivation, A. H. Maslow (1943)
Originally Published in Psychological Review, 50, 370-396.

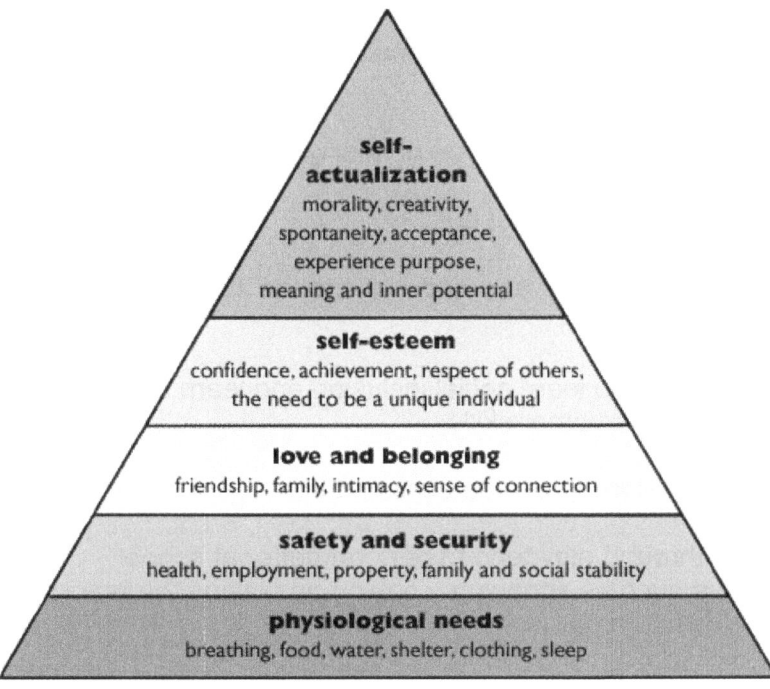

Maslows theory is that human needs arrange themselves in hierarchies of pre-potency. That is to say, the appearance of one need usually rests on the prior satisfaction of another, more pre-potent need. Man is a perpetually wanting animal. Also no need or drive can be treated as if it were isolated or discrete; every drive is related to the state of satisfaction or dissatisfaction of other drives. Therefore babies needs to feel safe, fed, happy and warm before they can develop learning, gain self confidence etc. it is therefore important for your to be involed and develop a good relationship with your child, let them be able to trust you. Keep a healthy lifestyle and do things together. With young children set rules and with older children don't give up on talking to them, with them and reason with them so thnat they are empowered to make the right decisions themselves.

All children need to feel secure, loved and valued – this is the basis of self esteem and confidence.

Notcice good behaviour and praise good behaviour in order to have a positive impact on your child.
Be realistic about what you expect from your child
Do fun things together with your child, hve fun with them, spend quality time, talk and listen but also be theor parent not just a friend and have disapline and routine.

Bring out the best in your child by listening, understanding, prasing ad encourage their efforts. Praise effort rather than achievement alone.
Give positive feedback that is constructive when you did x it was good because of Y it would be even better if you could add z.

Use praise in the right direction – try not to give attention to bad behaviour.

Children have to learn how to make their own decisions and gain independence from their parents. There decisions may not always fit what you want them to do. Choose your battles and let some go. Try and be supportive, listen to their rasons and explain yours.

Ensure that your child recievd enough stimulation (but not too much that they become warn out).
Make time to have fun and play with your child, introduce as many new experiences as possible.

Try and dicover what sort of play interests your child as you go along.

Find things to do all year round – even in the winter get out.

Play with them but also let them get to play on their own and with friends their own age, encourage them to mix with other children.

Play is very important to help them develop –to learn social inclusion and learn and develop creativity, and motor skills, communication and other skills.

Keep children healthy and active, active children become active adults.

Children who can express themselves through play tend to perform better at school.
Involve children in normal daily activites such as shopping, cooking and laying the table so that they can learn real life. Turn things into a game.

From birth your child learns how to use their senses, mobility, language and social interation through play.

As your child becomes older you need to set ground rules about playng outside, teach stranger danger etc.

Teach your child about safety and the bassics – what their address is, what to do in a fire etc.

The importance of love;
Loving smiles, kind words and cuddles help your baby to develop. According to Sue Gerhardt author of why love matters "being lovingly held is the greates spur to development".
Physically holding your baby helps your baby to know s/he is supported and will feel safe.
As babies the part of the brain that understands and expresses emotions still needs to be developed. Dr Allan Schore, leading American neuropsychology reasercher believes that in infancy loving smiles and looks, actually help your baby's brain grow and that positive looks are the most vital stimulus to the social, emotionally intelligent brain. Furthermore positive

experiences early on help with growth and genetic development. Therefore it is important to making learning new skills, meeting new people and going to new places as fun and positive as possible also try and be as encouraging as possible.

Other things that you can do in order to help your baby develop include;
- Talk, laugh and sing along with your baby. It will help them to recognise words and encourage speech.
- Read to them, they are never too young to hear stories and they will ind the sound of your voice soothing.
- Use your hands, babies find hands fascinating; clap, wave, tickle and use finger puppets.

Diet;
A good vitamin rich diet is essential to help the brain develop. Iron rich foods are key.

Brain Rules for baby; How to raise a smart child by John Medina is a great book to advice you on ways to help develop your babies brain.

John Medina suggests a number of things he says that the fist five years of life are the most influncal

www.brainrules.netpractical

His practical tips are as follows (in his words, as adapted from his aboe web site);

"In pregnancy;

- *Leave the baby alone at first. The best advice neuroscience can give a mother-to be about how to optimize her baby's brain development in the first half of pregnancy can be summarized by a single sentence: Do nothing. You don't need to speak French to your embryo at this stage, or play Mozart. Your baby's brain is not yet hooked up to her ears anyway. Neurogenesis, the major preoccupation of a baby's brain at these early stages, proceeds in a mostly automatic fashion. Just find a calm place where you can throw up on a regular basis, and take your doctor's recommended amount of folic acid, which prevents neural tube defects. Later on in pregnanc you can then talk to the baby and play music etc. They think babies can feel in the womb so gently touch and bond with your baby bu don't poke your tummy too hard too often (they might be able to feel pain).*

- *Take in an extra 300 calories a day*

- *Eat fruits and veggies*

- *Do 30 minutes of aerobic exercise each day*

- *Reduce the stress in your life; Pregnancy is stressful, and the body is equipped to handle that. But excess stress can do damage to you and the baby. An overabundance of cortisol targets a baby's developing neurons, interfering with proper brain development. Remove as much toxic stress as possible—for you and for baby.*

- *You can 'flavour programm' your baby yto like certain foods by eating them when you are pregnant, this is a good reason to have a healthy and varied diet in pregnancy.*

- *Take in lots of Omega 3 when you are pregnant.*

- *Physical fitness will help you when in labour so gentle exercise in pregnancy is good (exercise also helps you to reduce stress) but don't do too much exercise otherwise your baby may overheat.*

Once the baby is here;

- *Babies can smell in the womb, your perfume, garlic on the pizza you eat etc. Your baby will then develop a preference to the smells s/he experienced in thewomb. Immediately after your baby is born rub her down with her own amniotic fluid, it will calm her down by providing a familiar smell.*

- *Develop a good relationship with your partner and friends so that you have a good support network.*

- *Breast feed for a year if you can.*

- *Describe everything you see*

- *Talk to your baby a lot. This is as simple as saying, "It's a beautiful day" when you look outside and see the sun.*

- *Have a nice play room/play environment where your baby can develop; A place for drawing. A place for painting. Musical instruments. A wardrobe hanging with costumes. Blocks. Picture books. Tubes and gears. Anything where a child can be safely let loose, joyously free to explore whatever catches her fancy.*

- *Play 'opposite day'; After my children turned 3, I employed some fun activities to improve executive function, roughly based on the canonical work of Adele Diamond. I would tell them that today was "opposite day." When I held up a drawn picture of the night, an inky black background sprinkled with stars, they were supposed to say "day." When I held up a picture with a big blue sky inhabited by a big yellow sun, they were supposed to say "night." I would alternate the pictures with increasing rapidity and check for their responses. They had a blast with this; for some reason we always ended up rolling on the floor laughing. I did a kinetic form of this exercise with my elder son, who was a natural drummer, when he was 4. We each had a spoon and a pan. The rule was that when I struck a pan with a spoon once, he had to do it twice. When I hit a pan twice, he had to strike it three times. Or once. (I changed it up quite a bit.) The idea for both exercises was to a) give the boys a rule and b) help them inhibit what they would do automatically in the face of this rule—a hallmark of executive function. We had a certain place in our Chocolate Factory for these types of play. There are a ton of exercises like these you can do with your kids. For a list of nearly 20 great ones, check out Ellen Galinsky's Mind in the Making.*

- *Make play plans; See if elements of the Tools of the Mind program will fit in with your lifestyle. Here's one way this worked at my house: Our boys might decide that they wanted to make a construction site. (They had a favorite video that featured various construction machines, which*

  we watched ad nauseam. We still take it out for birthdays, as a funny nostalgia piece.) We would sit down together and plan the elements of what would go into the construction site, what might occur there once it was built, and how cleanup should best be handled once finished. Our imaginations ran wild, but a linear list of goals would be created from the exercise. Then the boys would play. A full description of the Tools program is available here: __http://www.mscd.edu/extendedcampus/toolsofthemind__

  - *Do not hyper-parent; Give children the choice and freedom in play, don't stifle them too much.*

  - *Take a critical look at (gulp) your behaviour Children will imitate your behaviour so lead by example.*

  - *Say, 'Wow, you really worked hard'; Praise effort rather than achievement.*

  - *Trade for digital time; Knowing full well the need for our kids to be digitally conversant, yet fully aware of the dangers, we came up with a few rules as our boys became preschoolers. First, my wife and I divided digital experiences into categories. Two of the categories involved things necessary for school work or for learning about computers: word processing and graphics programs, web-based research projects, programming, and so on. The boys were allowed to do these as homework required. Recreational experiences—digital games, certain types of web surfing, and our Wii gaming system—we called Category I. They were off limits except under one condition. Our sons could "buy" a certain amount of Category I time. The currency? The time spent reading an actual book. Every hour spent reading could purchase a certain amount of Category I time. This was added up and could be "spent" on weekends after homework was done. This worked for us. The kids picked up a reading habit, could do the digital work necessary for their futures, and were not completely locked out of the fun stuff.*

  - *Chart your child's emotional landscape; Most infants have a limit to how much stimulation they can take at any one time. Make a list of your baby's "can we stop now?" cues, which can be as subtle as head-turning or as obvious as bawling. Then get into a rhythm based on that, interacting in response to your baby's cues, withdrawing when she's had enough. Continue to monitor your child's emotions as he or she gets older. Jot down a few sentences describing your child's likes and dislikes. Update it continuously as various emotional responses develop. Making a list gets you in the habit of paying attention, and it provides a baseline, allowing you to notice any changes in behavior.*

  - *Help your child make friends of the same age but social experiences must be tailored to individual temperaments.*

  - *Speculate on another's point of view; In front of your children, verbally speculate about other people's perspectives in everyday situations. You can wonder why* the person behind you in line at a grocery is so impatient or what the joke is when a stranger talking on a cell phone laughs. It's a natural way to practice seeing other people's points of view—the basis of empathy.

- Read together

- Develop an empathy reflex with your children; When faced with a strong emotion, turn to empathy first: 1. Describe the emotion you think you see. 2. Make a guess as to where it came from. Remember, understanding someone's behavior is not the same thing as agreeing with it. It is just your opening response to any situation, especially when intense emotions are involved. If you want to have empathic children, they will need to see it modeled on a regular basis. Empathy comes from being empathized with.

- Determine your meta-emotion style; What are your emotions about emotions?

- Practice verbalizing your feelings; If your children are surrounded by people who can talk about feelings, they will be able to verbalize their feelings, too— invaluable to you when they reach puberty.

- Get your child involved in music; Instruments, singing, whatever—make music a consistent part of your child's experience. Long-term musical exposure has been shown to greatly aid a child's perception of others' emotions. This in turn predicts your child's ability to establish and maintain friendships.

- CAP your rules;Rules delivered with certain characteristics have the best shot at instilling moral awareness in children. You can remember them with "CAP."

  "C" stands for Clarity. The rules are clear, reasonable and unambiguous. It often helps to write them down. Chore charts are good examples. Many families simply shout out a rule as a reaction to a frustrating experience: "From now on, you are going to bed by 8!" But what happens to the rule when the emotions die out? Write down important rules, and post them in a public place for the whole family to see. They can serve as a point of negotiation and a source of humor—as anyone who has read the Harry Potter series and the edicts of Dolores Umbridge can attest.

  "A" stands for Accepting. The rules are delivered in a consistently warm and accepting environment.

  "P" stands for Praise. Every time a child follows a rule, reinforce the behavior. This includes praising the absence of a behavior, such as when a child learns not to yell in a restaurant.

- Eplain the rationale behind the rule; Explain verbally to your children the reasons for your rules. This allows kids to generalize the lessons learned to other situations, which leads to moral internalization. If all they have is "Because I said so," only a primitive form of behavior modification takes place.

- Effective punishment FIRST

- *"F" stands for firm. The punishment must mean something. It has to be firm and aversive to be effective.*

  "I" stands for immediate. The closer the punishment is delivered at the point of infraction, the more effective it is.

  "R" stands for reliable. The punishment must be consistently applied whenever the noxious behavior is displayed. Inconsistently applied rules are confusing and lead to uneven moral development.

  "S" stands for safe. The rules must be supplied in an atmosphere of emotional safety. Children have a hard time internalizing moral behavior under conditions of constant threat.

  "T" stands for tolerant. Actually, it is a call for patience, something we addressed only obliquely. Children rarely internalize rules on the first try and sometimes not on the 10th.

- *If you argue it is important to reconcile in front of your kids. Children need to feel safe in order to be able to develop and they need emotionally stable homes (hostility in the home is very bad for them).*

- *Babies, children and even teenagers need lots of sleep.*

- *The ability to question things and think creatively and see if there is a better way to do things is important. You need a willingness to explore. Its important to develop your childs creativity.*

- *If the childs brain detects social interaction i.e. with language, it will take it in. Children learn better from people than DVDs etc*

- *Your baby needs relationships and social interation in order to develop, warmth and love will make your child emotionally stable and more intellectual than anything else.*

- *Learning sign language may boost cognition by 50%. Non verbal and verbal skills are closely linked.*

- *Babies need facial expressions, its important for them to be able to read faces. Therefore babies need human time and not computer time in order to develop important socialskills and be able to read people and situations in later life. Communication skills are vital for your child to succeed in adult life. Its important to talk to your child a lot.*

- *Your child needs a healthy diet for his/her brain to grow.*

- *Kids learn through play and need to be encouraged to explore and play.*

- *Too much pressure on children can stop them being curious, creative and may even stop them trying.*

- *Good friends and loving relationships are what make people happy soteaching your kids social skills so that they can make friends is one of the most important things that you can do for them. Helping them to develop emotional regulation and empathy will go a long way to helping them succeed in life. Teach them how to be thoughtful, kind, sensitive, outward focusing, accomadating and forgiving (remember lead by example).*

- *Its important to teach your child self control in order for them to become successful in life.*

- *Young children are not always aware of the emotions that they are experiencing and find it hard to 'label an emotion', his may leave them confused, frustrated and even scared so it is important to help them to learn to label their emotions and instead of getting cross, try to understand them and help them deal with their emotions. They may act out anger if they are sad, because kids often express their emotions indirectly, it is useful to consider the environemental context and try and de-code their feelings so that you can help them deal with them, and resolve whatever issue is making them sad.*

- *Teach them optimism, positive thinking is a powerful tool*

- *You yourself as a parent will need to be flexible and adapt to your childs ever changing behaviour.*

- *Your main focus of your parenting should be your childs emotional wellbeing (read your child's cues and help them verbalize and label how they are feeling, give them some freedom to develop by giving them limited choices and teach them empathy, let them see you makeup after an argument etc). Watch, listen and respond to you child.*

- *As parent you should teach your child rules and boundaries. Give clear and consistent rules and rewards, swift punishment, rules that are reasonable and explained and offer praise eveytime your child follows the rules. "*

John Medina

Activities to do with children

Games and activities to encourage your baby to learn and develop;

Time spent with your baby is precious, but often parents worry that they spend so much time caring for their little one they are too exhausted to actually play and have fun with them. And sometimes they're not even sure how to.

Parents are natural teachers, but it can help to have some inspiration to direct your baby's energies as well as guidance on what games to play and how to play them.

We've picked some of our favourite baby play games, from birth up to 12 months old, and ranging from quiet observational activities to more lively games.

All these activities are first and foremost meant to be fun. Development and learning will naturally follow as a stimulated baby can't help but absorb skills and knowledge, improving their memory through repetition and observational skills through a desire to take part and not miss any of the action!

Through active, hands-on play your baby will learn language, develop problem-solving skills and master social relationships. And you will benefit from it too. It's thrilling when your baby reaches out for you, giggles and claps her hands together for the first time!

Have fun with your baby while getting her off to a great start in life...

The Bright Sight Game

To engage your baby's attention and stimulate her senses, lie baby on a rug and hold a small brightly coloured ball or toy about 15 inches above her face until it gets her attention. Then slowly move the toy from side to side matching her pace to focus and follow the object. Move the object nearer and further away so she sees it getting bigger and smaller. Let the object stroke her arms (but don't go too close to her face). You can also play this game with a cloth handkerchief, a piece of cloth or a balloon blowing on it to create movement.

Dancing with baby
This helps calm her and make her feel loved, hold your baby against your chest and dance slowly and smoothly around the room to any kind of rhythmical music (not too loud). The movement replicates what she felt in the womb and also stimulates her sense of balance. It's good exercise for you too!

Change of face
Intimacy with your baby depends as much on touch and eye contact as it does on giggles and toys. Time spent gazing into your baby's face is actually time well spent.

Cradle your baby in your arms or lie her down on a mat or rug and gaze into her eyes speaking or singing her name softly. Introduce some facial expressions (open mouth, raised eyebrows, stuck out tongue) then return to your normal face. You may find your baby attempts to imitate you. If she starts to turn away, stop the game and give her some quiet time to process what she has just seen.

Who's that?
Babies are fascinated by seeing their own faces in a mirror, even though they have no idea who or what they are looking at (and won't recognise themselves until they are about 15 months old). Hold a hand mirror where baby can see her reflection and say her name. As she gets older she will start to smile at her reflection.

Texture treats
You can turn nappy changing time into fun time by introducing your baby to different textures. Gather swatches of different materials and objects (like velvet, feathers, sponge, corduroy or silk) and gently rub the different textures across her arms, legs and tummy. You may be able to tell from her expression which textures she likes best.

Swing time
Lie your baby on her back in a blanket and with you and your partner holding opposite ends of the blanket, gently swing her from side to side. This replicates that wonderful feeling of weightlessness she experienced in the womb and teaches her about balance and trust.

Ball balancing
Many babies don't like lying on their tummies for very long. Try placing her face down on a slightly deflated beach ball then, while holding her securely, rock her slowly forwards and backwards and from side to side (always supporting a newborn's head). When she is older and sitting up by herself you can hold her sitting on the ball and gently bounce her up and down.

What's that sound?
You can make a fun sound game by stringing together a number of noise-making objects (jar lids, rattles, plastic spoons) on a rope or ribbon. Dangle this about 15 inches in front of your baby and jiggle the objects for her (never leave her alone with this kind of toy).

Other ideas…hold your baby as near as possible to a bird table in the garden and let her watch the activity; lie baby on her back and pedal her legs in a bicycle movement (it feels good to stretch and kick); sing lullabies and fun songs to baby and vary it sometimes by singing close then further away so she gets used to the variation in loudness; hold baby on your arm face down and swing or sway her in a rhythmical movement (supporting a newborn's head). This will help strengthen her neck and give her a whole new view of the world!

Other things that you can do include;
-Stack cups up in a tower
- prop baby up with cushions for sitting practise
- hold a toy about babies head whilst s/he lays on his/her tummy, that way they will learn to lift their head
- puppet shows
- finger games such as round and round the garden
- put dried rice in plastic bottles
- use a torch to make shadows and shapeson the ceiling
- make an indoor pool filled with balls and toys, use cardboard boxes to make tunnels
- different toys (colours/shapes/sizes/noise) - motor skills - hand and eye co-ordination and learn shapes and colours. Pans and wooden spoons and homemade shakers are better than expensive toys.

Give your baby plenty of opportunity to exercise and develop whilst awake. Put out a large mat that baby can roll around and play on safely. Place different textured toys and baby safe mirrors to make it more fun.

Roll it; Roll a ball to each other, use different size and shaped balls. This helps your baby to develop hand and eye co-ordination and develop muscle tone in arms.

Build it; Using plastic building blocks is great for developing problem solving skills. Practise building towers and try putting 4 bricks in a simple pattern and see if your baby can copy the pattern, or try sorting blocks into groups of shapes and colours.

Tidy it; At the end of play get your child to help tidy the toys away, this is good to teach them about tidying up.

Play groups are also good so that your child gets to play with different toys and meet other children, it is also a god way for you to get out and meet other people, a change of scenery does you both good. Some children's centres also operate a toy library which is useful for you to try before you buy or just have a good mix of different toys.

12- 24 months;
- Play with water;
> Assemble a variety of toys and containers for bath time.
> Get your child to help you water the garden.
> Fill up the paddling pool in the garden in summer.
> Have a tea party with water.
> Let them wash up.
- Walking;
> Practise walking by setting up an area with supports to hold onto or set up a simple obstacle course with things to crawl on, under, or over.
- Hand games;
> Hand puppets and games like pat-a-cake and songs with actions. Sit opposite baby so s/he can see you and sometimes sit him/her on your lap so that they can watch your hands.
- Bring a toy to life;
> Use a teddy or favourite toy to imitate things. Walk teddy around the room, give teddy medicine, put teddy to bed etc. This will stretch his/her imagination and allow them to express emotions. Also if teddy has his medicine your child will be more inclined to take theirs too.
- Get physical;
> Go for walks and take a ball to play with in the park or a bucket to pick things up.
> Go swimming, to soft play or mummy and me yoga in order to get him/her exercising.
> Play hide and seek, chasing games and dance around the house together.
- Independence;
> Although it is important to play with your child it is also good for them to learn to play on their own and be independent, put him/her in a play pen or other safe area with toys (not for too long), and watch your child play.

From 18 months; Children from 18 months old love games that involve dressing up and using their imagination.

Fun activities to do with kids;

- At Christmas make Christmas cards and crakers with the kids
- Bake cakes
- Keep a list of good places to take the kids (go on net mums and look places up).
- Cook with your child
- Go for bike rides and picnics

Get them involved

When you're washing up, let your child join in, for example by washing the saucepan lids. When you cook, show them what you're doing and talk to them as you're working.

Getting them involved in the things you do will teach them about taking turns to help and being independent. They'll also learn by copying what you do.

Sometimes, things have to happen at certain times and it's important that your child learns this. But when you're together, try not to have a strict timetable. Your child is unlikely to fit in with it and you'll both get frustrated. There's no rule that says the washing-up has to be done before you go to the playground, especially if the sun's shining and your child's bursting with energy.

As far as you can, move things around to suit your own and your child's mood.

Tips for playing

- Get together lots of different things for your child to look at, think about and do.
- By making what you're doing fun and interesting for your child, you can get your household jobs done while they're learning.
- Have times when you focus completely on your child. Talk about anything and everything, even the washing-up or what to put on the shopping list. By sharing as much as possible your child will pick up lots of new words.
- Give your child plenty of opportunities to use their body by running, jumping and climbing, especially if you don't have much room at home.
- Find other people who can spend time with your child when you really do need to focus on something else.

10 baby games for baby's first year

Baby games that are fun and can boost your child's skills and development don't need to be complicated. In fact, they shouldn't be. You may even find that many of the best games you can play with your child to help him or her learn about the world are what you already do naturally.

To help you and baby get the most out of playtime, make sure that you recognise signs your little one is sending that indicate when it's time to play. These signals might include:

- Watching you or other people with interest
- Reaching out for you
- Smiling

It's also important to recognise when your infant has had enough of baby games and needs a break. These signs might include:

- Crying
- Regurgitating
- Looking away

To help your baby have fun, bond with you and learn about the world, try playing the following 10 development games. You may also want to make up your own variations or combine games when you sense baby is ready for an additional challenge.

Baby game 1: Peek-a-boo

One of the best baby games to play with infants is also one of the easiest. Simply hide your face behind your hands and then move your hands away while you say, "Peek-A-Boo"!

Until babies are about nine months old, they don't realise that you're still there when your face is covered. So your child will be fascinated by your disappearing and reappearing act. This baby game may even help your child become more comfortable in the world when he or she realises that you'll come back even when you "go away".

After your child begins to understand the game more, they may try to "find" you by reaching for your hands when you hide. Try playing this development boosting game to make tasks like changing nappies and getting dressed more fun for you and baby.

Baby game 2: Mummy see, mummy do

Just as you can read baby's signals to know when to play baby games, you can take your lead on how to play from your little bundle of joy.

For example, if your baby is vocalising with "coos" and "ga-gas", try imitating your baby's sounds. That will help your baby develop a foundation for conversation skills. Similarly, when baby smiles, smile back. This will help your baby develop self-confidence as he or she realises that you're having fun and enjoying their company.

Baby game 3: Dance around

All babies need plenty of cuddling time to help them feel secure and build emotional attachments to the important people in their lives.

Try dancing around with baby to foster bonding and respond to your baby's needs. If he or she's in a playful mood, do a gentle, silly jig together to get them laughing. If your baby is tired or upset, they might prefer a slow dance around the room to help to soothe them.

Baby game 4: Pat-a-cake

"Pat-a-cake, pat-a-cake, baker's man, bake me a cake as fast as you can. Pat it and roll it and mark it with 'B'. And put it in the oven for baby and me". This clapping game may seem silly, but it's a great way to help your baby develop a number of important skills.

First, the rhythm and repetitiveness of the tune will help your baby develop language skills. Additionally, the feel of your touch as you gently clap your hands against his or hers in time to the rhyme will help stimulate sense of touch. As baby gets older, they'll probably try to imitate the movements you're making with your hands, which will help develop their gross motor skills and hand- eye co-ordination.

Baby game 5: Where's your nose?

Want to work on developing language skills and make baby giggle at the same time? Then this silly, simple baby game is perfect for you.

To help boost your baby's development, ask, "Where's your nose"? in a singsong voice. Then gently touch your baby's nose as you say "There's your nose"! with great delight. Repeating this game and playing it with different parts of baby's body or nearby objects will help your baby start to learn the meaning of different words.

Baby game 6: Fabric fun

Provide ways for your infant to explore their environment safely.

Watch how your baby plays when you give him or her pieces of fabric with different textures -- such as burlap, corduroy, satin, and velvet -- to handle. The variety of textures will intrigue and interest your baby. At the same time, holding pieces of fabric and waving them around will help build muscle strength and coordination.

Baby game 7: Shake, rattle and roll

There's a reason why baby rattles are so popular. Not only do they help baby develop, but they're great fun to play with too.

When baby is little, try shaking a rattle as he or she watches you. You can then move it out of sight and continue to rattle it after you're sure you have their attention. Very soon, they'll turn their head in an attempt to find the source of the rattling.

Baby game 8: Rhyme time

Babies love to listen to the voices of people they know, and they're also intrigued by repetitive sounds. Give your baby the opportunity to hear both by regularly reciting nursery rhymes or other child-friendly rhyming poems.

You can have rhyme time anytime -- in the bath, during cuddles, or when you're out in the car. These are all perfect opportunities to entertain baby and boost language skills.

Baby game 9: Have a ball

You can play ball with baby long before your little one is able to catch and throw.

To keep things interesting, find a ball designed for infants that has different textures and colours. First, try giving the ball to your baby and see what he or she tries to do. You can show your baby different ways to play by gently rolling the ball or putting it in a container. As babies develop muscle tone and learn more about how the world works, they'll start to imitate you and make up their own games.

Baby game 10: Sing a song

Babies love music, from soothing lullabies to rhythmic drums and silly tunes. Even if you don't think you are musical, baby will love you to sing and it will help you deepen the mother-child bond.

Give your baby the opportunity to listen to a variety of different types of music. Based on how he or she responds, you'll probably be able to determine their favourite kind of music.

Songs don't even need to be "real" songs to create a development boosting game. Make up a tune about what you're doing while you bathe baby or go for a walk in the park. The exposure to language will help your child build their vocabulary.

Early play

As your child grows older, the kind of games you play together may develop. Nevertheless, Sue advises not to be too prescriptive about early years play.

During the early years, children's play often comes from themselves and parents just need to provide the environment where that can happen in a natural way.

One and two year olds

Children can make a game out of anything. That sort of play is vital. Many parents may feel they have to supervise and organise everything, but that kind of play often comes from the child.

Simple, low-cost games are the best way to encourage creativity.

Baby games: Top 10 baby games for one and two year olds

Here are top 10 games suggestions for one and two year olds:

Fill a bucket: If you're going to the park of the seaside, take a bucket and fill it up with the things you collect: shells, leaves. Bring it home and make a collage.

Tidy-up time: Got chores to do? Try making them into a game. Your house won't get as clean but part of playing is you get to know your child and trust each other. Give your child a little cloth and let them help with 'polishing' or 'cleaning'.

Play on the pans: Turn an empty pan upside-down, give your little one a wooden spoon and - bingo - they've got their very own drum kit. Teach them how to tap out a rhythm and get them to copy you. Warning: you may need ear-plugs by the end of the day.

"Do" the dishes: All you need is a bowl of lukewarm water, with washing up liquid in it, and some plastic cups. Then your little one can enjoy filling and emptying out the cups to their heart's content. Make sure you supervise them while they're playing with water.

Shaker makers: Half-fill some plastic bottles with dried pasta, rice or beans, then do some serious shaking with your little one.

Don't let rain stop play: Puddle jumping is great fun. Make sure your child is wearing wellies and there's a nice, big towel to hand when they've finished.

What's in the box? If you're wrapping up birthday or Christmas presents, don't forget that children love boxes. Put together a little collection of shiny paper, tinsel, baubles and toilet rolls in a box and allow your child to pick them out and discover all the different textures.

Get the paints out.

Read teddy a book: Get your little one to draw their very own story book, with lots of pieces of paper folded together, then they can "read" the story to teddy.

Skittle alley: Make your own skittles out of small, plastic water bottles and line them up, a few feet away from your child. Give them a plastic ball and watch them roll the ball to knock over the skittles. You can make it slightly harder by filling some of the bottles with a bit of sand, to make them trickier to knock down.

Fun games for three year olds

For three year olds, getting active is definitely the name of the game as your busy toddler tests their ability to dash about - often picking up a few bumps and bruises along the way. When parents sigh about how their little one runs rings around them, often they mean literally!

Fun and active: Games for three year olds

Turn a family walk into a game of tag.

Fun, free games for three year olds

As well as helping your family have fun - and get active - running-around games can also help with child development.

"Children at this age love running around, so active games such as hide and seek and simple treasure hunts are very popular ways of promoting social development," says psychologist Dr Amanda Gummer, who has developed an online guide to children's play named the Good Toy Guide.

Games for three year olds: Child development

At three years old, children are starting to make friends and play with - rather than just alongside - other children. Promoting interaction with other children will help develop a range of social skills that will stand them in good stead for starting school or nursery.

So what kind of games can you play with your three year old? Look for inventive games that capture your child's imagination.

"Play is messing about and having a good time and the games you make up together are often the best ones," says Sue Palmer, a child development expert. "The tried-and-tested games are usually pretty cheap or free. The point of playing games is to help you connect more and more with your child and to give your child a chance to play."

And, if you feel exhausted at the prospect of more high-energy play, don't worry - it is possible to keep your toddler entertained without embarking on an Olympics-style athletics programme for them!

Games for three year olds

Chasing shadows: Warm, sunny days are perfect for this one. Show your child the different shadow shapes you can both make. Try chasing each other round the garden or pretending to be different "shadow animals - birds, elephants, or join together to make a pony. "We play a game where we have to try to jump on each other's shadow..

Summertime snowballs: Scrunch pieces of old newspaper or magazines into balls, then have a "snowball fight". Try ducking and diving as your toddler tries to pelt you with paper - and then they have to run and hide while you try to get them back.

Build a cam inside.

Go disco dancing:

Get cooking:

Treasure hunt: Hide a few little treats around the house and ask your child to go and find them. Give them little clues like "Go and ask Teddy - he might know" - and hide one of the treats near Teddy. They'll love telling you all about how they found everything you hid.

Water the plants: Use squirter bath toys to water all the plants in the house.

Have a picnic: Put a picnic rug down - either outside or, if the weather isn't conducive to eating outdoors - the living room floor. Then do your baking - get your little one to stir up some biscuit mix, put chopped fruit into a salad and use star-shaped cutters to make sandwiches. Then pack it all into a basket and head to the living room for your big day out!

Easy-peasy kites: A great one for those windy walks in the park. Get your toddler to design their very own kite on a small piece of paper - about the size of a Post-it note. Then simply tape it to a long piece of ribbon and wait for the wind to blow.

Sock it to them: Spend a morning making some new sock friends out of some old (preferably washed) socks. Use a bit of glue to stick on eyes, a mouth and maybe a bit of glitter and wait for it to dry. Then crouch behind the sofa and put on your very own sock puppet show.

Starting nursery: Games for preschool children

"As children start nursery, they may well be a little anxious - especially if parents are worried about it," adds Dr Amanda Gummer.

Dr Gummer says simple games can help children acclimatise to the experience of going to nursery.

"Role play games and small world play (puppets, little figures etc) can help children understand what is likely to happen in nursery and identify any areas that they are particularly worried about," she says.

"Try letting the child take the role of the teacher in these sorts of games, as this will make the real nursery adults more approachable and increase a child's confidence as they enter a new phase of their lives."

Nursery and preschool games

As you're taking your little one to nursery for the first time, Sue suggests playing games along the way can help remove some of those first-day nerves.

"Try spotting things or playing alphabet games, such as 'Mrs Brown went to town and she bought...'" she says.

And, of course, once you arrive at nursery, suggesting games for your little one to play with their soon-to-be friends can help them settle in early on. If there's a sandpit in the vicinity or a favourite book on the shelf, encourage your child to explore this new environment.

Games for preschool and nursery children

Here are our top 10 suggestions for games nursery and preschool children can play with their friends:

Pat-a-cake: Clapping games are a great way to get your little one interacting with others and pat-a-cake is an old classic. In case you don't know the words, they're: "Pat-a-cake, pat-a-cake, baker's man. Bake me a cake as fast as you can. Roll it and pat it and mark it with 'B'. And put it in the oven for baby and me." Two children playing together can pat each other's hands and make a B shape in the air.

Let's put on a show: Act out Britians got talent, or make up other shows etc.

Hide and seek: "Coming to find you... ready or not!" This classic game is lots of fun - and the more who play it, the merrier the game.

Kids' games: Top 10 preschool games
Dropping your child off at nursery for the very first time can be tough – particularly if you're used to spending lots of time together.

Hand painting: Most nurseries have paints and paper available, so get your child to practise making hand-butterfly or foot-print pictures. All you need is a little tray filled with different-coloured, non-toxic paint, a few large sheets of paper, lots of newspaper (to protect your home) and old clothes for you and your little one. It might be good to run a big bucket of soapy water as well, so you don't get painty footprints trailing through the house to the bath when you've finished!

Have a sing-song: Sing-songs are a great way to help children get to know each other - particularly songs that include other children's names. Try "Five current buns" or "Good morning (insert child's name). How are you? How are you this special day? We're so glad you came to play. Good morning (insert child's name again). How are you?" (sung to the tune of "If you're happy and you know it").

A day at the zoo: A great way to teach your children about animals. Each child has to decide which animal they are (e.g. a monkey, an elephant, a mouse, a giraffe, a fish), then locate themselves around the room imagining themselves in the place where that animal lives (a tree, a lake, a burrow), and make appropriate animal sounds. You can walk around the "zoo" with some snacks at "feeding time" or switch all the lights off and walk round with a torch, trying to "discover" the animals.

That's not my name: All the children sit in a circle, apart from one. The person who is "it" walks around the circle, placing a hand on each child's head and saying their name. Then, when they decide the time is right, they pat one child on the head and shout: "Scooby Doo!" The chosen child has to scramble to their feet and race the other one round the circle. Whoever is first back gets to sit down - the other one is then "it" and the game starts over again.

Ice breakers: This is, essentially, an old-fashioned game of "tag" but with added spice. When somebody gets tagged, they have to stand still with their legs open. The other children can "unfreeze" them by crawling beneath their legs. The game finishes when everybody is "frozen".

Be in a band: Get your tots performing with air guitars and drums (upturned biscuit tins and plastic storage containers always make good ones). Put CDs on and get your children to rock along.

Superheroes: Give each child a superpower - maybe they're invisible, or they can fly or see through walls. Whisper their superpower so that only they can hear it. The game is that the group has to guess the other's superpower - and each child can only answer "yes" or "no".

Fun games for four year olds

By the age of four, children will also be able to play some games without adult input. You'll also see them starting to interact with other children.

"Allowing children to play with minimal supervision gives them the opportunity to practice skills such as negotiation, compromise, persuasion and empathy," says psychologist Dr Amanda Gummer, who has developed an online guide to children's play named the Good Toy Guide.

"Young children find these skills difficult and will defer to an adult to sort out disagreements if there's one readily available."

Games for four year olds

Dr Gummer recommends giving children space to develop these key skills. This may prove difficult for some parents, if you're used to getting stuck into your children's play.

"By giving children space to play parents are not being neglectful," reassures Dr Gummer. "They're helping children develop important skills in preparation for independence."

Games for four-year-olds

Here are our top 10 games suggestions for four year olds:

The hair salon: There's a lot of fun that can be had with some towels, some water, a comb and a small mirror. Wet your little one's hair and then watch them twist it up into all sorts of styles. Try a punk look, spikes or pin-up curls if she's a little princess. Bring them some magazines to browse so they can select their favourite looks.

Raid the dressing up box: Put old clothes, feather bowers and items from charity shops in a dressing up box, its much more fun for children than having expensive ready made dress up outfits.

Have a jigsaw competition: Set each member of the family up with a puzzle to suit their skill level, all helping each other finish, or create teams to work on puzzles together.

Get baking: Get them involved with mixing up pre-weighed ingredients and using plastic cutters to cut out cookies or scones. You can take over at the oven part while they go and set the table for afternoon tea!

Junior disco: Put on a favourite CD and get the children to rock around the clock. Different coloured lightbulbs will help create that party-night atmosphere. Teach your children different dance moves (e.g. the congo, the moonwalk or the Saturday night fever strut) to get them in the groove. If you've got a camera to hand, get some pictures or video to play back to them later.

Water world: There's so much fun to be had with a big bucket of water. Give your little ones watering cans, funnels, small buckets or bottles punched with holes and watch them get splash-happy. They can use empty margarine tubs as little boats and fill them with pebbles to see how many it takes to sink their ship. Outside space and old clothes are a good idea for this one!

Finger counting: A great way to introduce your child to numbers. You and your child put your hands behind your back. On the count of three you both shout out a number between one and ten and bring out your hands with some fingers raised. The person who guessed correctly (or closest) to how many fingers would be raised gets the point. Keep playing until you have an outright winner.

What do you like? A great way for you and your child - or you and a sibling - to share your interests. You start with "My name's Mummy and I like dancing." Your child takes up the story: "My name's (insert name) and I like chocolate. My mummy likes dancing." Then it's your turn again: "My name's Mummy. I like dancing and yoga and (insert name) likes chocolate." You go on, trying to remember each other's hobbies. If anyone forgets, you can always mime to help each other out. This game also works well with multiple players.

What's in the sock? Fill several large socks with small household objects (e.g. a coin, a toothbrush, a spoon). Your child has to stick their hand inside the socks and guess what object is hidden in there.

Make home-made play dough: "My son and I spend our time modelling anything from aeroplanes to rabbits," says Fay Wheeler from Norwich. This is the recipe Fay uses:

- 250g plain flour
- 50g salt
- 140ml water
- 1 or 2 tablespoons of cooking oil
- Few drops of food colouring

Mix together the flour and salt in a large mixing bowl. Add the water and oil. Knead well until mixture is smooth about 10 mins. You might need to add a bit more flour or water until the consistency is smooth but not sticky. Add food colouring and knead until the colour is fully blended. Store in a plastic bag in the refrigerator until chilled enough to use.

ACTIVITY	HOW IT WORKS
1. HAVING FUN AND GAMES TOGETHER	Both Dads and Mums create happy memories and security for their children when they make time for fun, sometimes as a family and sometimes on a one-to-one basis – even twenty minutes a week for each child. For this 'special time,' it may be best not to tickle, to take the emphasis off winning or losing, and to let the *child* take the lead in deciding what to play – for babies, watch and you'll see.
2. STORIES, SONGS AND RHYMES	When a child sits cuddled into a parent, listening to or making stories, followed by a chat together, she is not just being 'stretched,' having her imagination, intelligence and language development fed – her sense of security and values are also being formed, and her emotional development is thriving. (Television is good, but can never replace all this for a child.)
3. 'NOTICING' CHILD AT PLAY – WITH WATER, SAND, TOYS...	Children develop through play – even with a simple basin of water and empty yoghurt containers on the kitchen floor. Wait for interest so that you avoid 'pushing' with unsuitable toys, but, above all 'notice' the play. 'Noticing' includes listening, looking, showing an interest, and generally giving good attention when it is *not* being demanded. You might join a child at play, forget about 'helping,' supervising, or even suggesting, and just enjoy watching quietly – with an occasional comment that *reflects* what you see.
4. 'NOTICING' CHILD WITH SMILES, HUGS, KISSES, TOUCHING.	Show affection regularly. It is said that all children need at least four hugs a day to *survive*, and sixteen a day to *thrive*! Cuddling, smiling, touching say, *You are good; you are loveable; you are beautiful.* You might cuddle in closely for reading a story, or get down on the ground and let your baby crawl over you.
5. LOOKING AFTER YOURSELF	Plan 'quality time' for yourself too. You have more to give your child when you've taken exercise and fresh air, and when you have relaxed, done something you enjoy, laughed, and had some fun. Planning for yourself includes planning time with a partner and/ or adult friends (even joining a parent and toddler group). Remember that children learn a great deal about love and life from watching adult relationships.

Throw your chiffon scarf up into the air and over yourself and your baby, they will find it fun.

-
-
-
-

Through the eyes of a child

Being born must feel like being abducted by aliens and taken to another planet.

Adults want to be children and have less reposibility but children want to be able to do things and be grown up.

Between 12 – 18 months your babies' sense of identity strengthens and they recognise themselves in the mirror, rather than thinking it's another baby and they respond to their own names and may become more curious about other people. From 18 months your baby will learn to interact more but will probably play alongside, rather than with other children and will still not undertans the concept of sharing.

Your child views the world from their own viewpoint and will not be able to understand others viewpoints until they are much older.

Between the ages of 18 months and 2 years your child becomes very curious and continually wants to explore.

Have empathy with your baby, they are small people and have their own moods and may want their space or time to explore, having someone bigger than them keep grabbing them and getting in their face maybe annoying. How would you like it?

As they start to get aware of their surrounding they may push you away because they want to be off and explore, it doesn't mean they don't love you. Just be there for them i.e. lay on the play mat next to the toys, don't interfere and let your baby play. You baby will approach you when s/he wants to, or will give you ques to join in with the play. Your baby even when grown up will always need you, even when they are an adult, but they sometimes need space too.

Babies get bored easily. They need to learn how to do independent play but will need you to play with them at first. Do things in blocks of 20 mins i.e. jumperoo for 20 mins then play on the mats on the floor and do crawling, then read a story etc. in between have meals, milk, naps, nappy changes etc.

When they get to 2 and start to develop they start to experience more and more emotions. They don't know how to express themselves and get upset and have tantrums. It is hard enough for us when we are tired and we get irritable, imagine how they must feel.

Terrific toddlers and beyond

Terrible toddlers;

As your child goes from a toddler to a baby s/he will become very curious and will therefore try and push the boundaries. S/he is still learning and developing. Toddlers have raw emotions that they will display and a quest for independence. S/he will try and exert his/her will and as his/her brain is working twice as fast as that of an adults s/he may get tired quickly. Because s/he is still learning and can't express himself/herself s/he will have tantrums. Try not to intervene at the peak of the tantrum, instead let them get it out of their system. Try using word so that they can express themselves next time and if all else fails distract them.

Reaserchers at the univeristty of Minnesota discovered a vocal rhythm tom tantrums, with certain emotions having their own vocal features. Peaks of yelling and screaming signify anger, while fussing and whinning indicates growing sadness.

It is important not to give into tantrums as this will encourage further attention seeking tantrums. Give your child a limited reasonable choice i.e. a choice between red or blue socks.

If you want your child to sit still for an appointment let them go for a run first in order to get rid of their energy.

Children have an unquestioning confidence in their own abilities, this is why they get frustrated when they can't do something that they want to do. They are very determined to learn new skills, be independent and copy others.

Be age 3 they are aware of their gender.

Toddler sleep time;
- Your toddler should sleep for 11 hours at night, if your toddler wakes early try shorter naps in the day or a slightly later bed time. Also get blackout curtains so that the light doesn't wake your child early in the morning.
- If your child wanders into your room keep putting them back in their bed until they break the habit.
- When they can climb out of the cot its time for their own bed.

Other tips;

- Keep a box of craft items for playing with your child, in case they have to make things for school such as glue, felt material, colouring pens etc. Fabric pens and washable paints.

- Get a batch of name labels for your child printed up that can be swen into their clothes when they start school or use fabric pens.

- When you have a child you have more opportunity to try new things and join in with things that you wouldn't normally get to do, you can volunteer at school, join their theatre group doing costume design etc.

- Keep children busy and entertained to stop them getting into mischief

- Joint birthday parties are a good way to save on costs

Pregnant with your second child and toddler in tow

When to plan your next child – when is the best time? Some people like a bigger gap so you don't have 2 young ones to deal with, others like to have them close in age so they will be at school together etc. You may want them close together to get it out the way and the you can focus on your career or you may find it hard paying 2 nursery fees so may want to wait until one is old enough to go to state nursery. When they are younger it is easier with a bigger gap because the older sibling can help (although if you have a big gap you may find it hard getting back into the baby phase again), as they get older they may bond together and play better if they are closer in age. Two young ones maybe a handful but as they get older they may go to classes and football together if there is a smaller gap so it maybe easier then. You need to also work out when you can financially afford to have a second baby. You may need to go back full time for a year if having another baby so get full maternity pay and can save up to take time off again. However there is never going to be a great time financially to have another baby and you don't want to leave it too long in case you get too old. Your children may get on if they are close in age but it is nice to have a big age gap ie. At least 3 years so that you can enjoy your baby and don't get too stressed with 2 young ones, it also gives you time to save up enough money to take further time off work for the second one. However sometimes if they are close in age they go to school together etc and you can have a career break in one go and then go back to work. It depends on your situation, different age gaps suit different families. You may find that your body needs a long break after your first baby, or if you are older you may not want to leave it too long before your next baby.

How long should you leave it before having the next baby?

This depends on your circumstances. There are reasons for and against small gaps and large gaps, similar to the debate on having children when you are younger or older. This is subjective because different age gaps will work for different families. Also you can't always plan when you will have another baby, sometimes nature decides this for you.

Some people like "back-to-back babies". The idea being that you can have your children in a single batch lasting just a few years and then move on. Women starting a family in their 30s might not have the luxury of spacing their children out. For the mother's health, two to three years is "probably perfect" says Sarah Jarvis, a GP who regularly appears on the BBC's Jeremy Vine Show.

However it can be stressful having a baby and a toddler. As long as you have enough of a gap, to allow your body to recover and you are happy with the age gap, that is all that matters.

A woman goes through a lot giving birth, especially if they breastfeed afterwards. In nutrition terms, it takes a year to recover, says Jarvis. They will need to have time to rebuild their pelvic floor, she continues. Two years is good because it gives a bit of leeway. And anything over three years may be too long as it can cause sibling rivalry, Jarvis suggests.

Some parents talk of two years as being ideal. If you plan ahead, it means siblings will be approaching A-levels and GCSEs at the same time - allowing the family to have an intensive "exam" year, followed by a year off.

There are pros and cons with any gap, says Justine Roberts, who co-founded Mumsnet. She once read of research suggesting that the ideal age gap for developing a child's intelligence is 11 years as the older child becomes like a third parent. But that's not practical or desirable for many.

At the other extreme, having children one year or less apart is likely to be a huge strain. The advantage of having babies close together is that your children will play together and become close, developing shared interests, Roberts suggests. But having a new baby while you have a toddler is hard work. "It depends how your set up is, how drained you'll be."

Some tips to help you survive pregnancy with a toddler;
- Nap when your toddler naps
- Give your toddler lots of opportunities to burn his/her energy
- Make rainy days fun, visit the library, go to a museum etc.
- Batch cook healthy meals in advance
- Help your toddler to be independent, potty train etc. so that you have less to worry about when your new born comes along.
- Save time by ordering things on line
- Take your toddler to your hospital appointments and explain this is where you will have the baby, this will de-mystify the situation for your toddler.
- Prepare your toddle by reading books on babies together, give him/her a doll and get your toddler to help with preparations for baby. It is also important to manage expectations as a baby maybe boring for a toddler.
- Set rules ie. Hold baby gently etc.
- Have time alone with your toddler before and after the baby arrives.
- When you go on maternity leave it you are getting statuatory maternity leave and already have child care vouchers your employer must continue to provide these and can't take the money out of you statuatroy materity pay. If you ge paid over and above your statuarory maternity pay they can however take the money for the child care vouchers out of that.
- With the 2nd child it is a good idea to still go to bay groups, put your first child with minder so that you can have some time with your new baby and also go to NCT classes to meet new people etc.
- When you have another baby your older child may get jealous and start acting like a baby for attention. Try and set some time aside for your oldest child.

It is harder at first having another baby, there will be sibling jelousy, twice as much work with 2 to look after and you will have ebven less time with your partner. However as they get older it will be worth it because they will have a friend. The other child will help to occupy their attention and may help you out and when you are older and need lookin after they will be able to share the load, hopefully your child will not be alone, because they have their sibling. Only children get more attention but brothers and sisters learn to share. If you only can have one child, don't worry your child will make friends at playgroup and will still be a happy child, they will get more attention and maybe brighter, just take them to play groups so they get to meet with other children and that way they will learn to mix in and will learn to share too.

Parental Guidance

- Enjoy your time with one baby before you have the next, do it when it's right for you. Don't be pressurised. I think a 3 year gap is nice so that one is walking, talking and is potty trained etc. If you have your current baby in nursery you may want to keep that arrangement even when you are off with your second child. That way you can spend time with the 2nd baby, you don't loose your nursery place if you are returning to work and your oldest keeps the same routine. However when you are on maternity leave with the second child it maybe financially hard to keep paying for nursery/day care, but when they are 3 you get 15 hours paid by the government.

- You are not supposed to smack children but there is a difference between smacking and hitting children. If you do have to smack/tap your child only do it in a controlled manner, be in control, don't do too often, give a warning. ie on 3rd give a tap ie on hand if child touching plug socket.
- Baby/children are distracting and it's easy to forget things such as getting a parking ticket, locking your door etc. so you need to be as organised and focused as possible so that you don't forget things. You may want to be extra organised and get a year planner and put re-newal dates on, that way you won't forget anything.
- Encourage your children to be what they want to be/do what they want to do. You might think something else is better for them but they need to be happy and this will occur by being who they want. Things may have worked out, better than you could have expected.
- Still do all the things that you did before, with your children.
- Take lots of photos of your pregnancy and baby and then as your child grows up etc.
- If you make a rule, such as holding your hand near a road, stick to it. By giving into tears and tantrums you will teach him/her that s/he can his/her own way by pushing you.
- Praise your child for saying please and thank you.
- Explain your reasons so that they can understand the rules.

10 golden rules;

1. Remember you are dealing with a child not an adult. It is easy to have high expectations and forget that children have immature emotions and their cognitive skills which help them think things through are still developing. Toddlers are naturally egocentric.
2. Praise your child for his/her efforts, to boost his/her self esteem.
3. Try to ignore less appealing behaviour, tantrums are inevitable and you don't want to feed them by giving attention to their tantrums.
4. Be consistent to show you mean what you say. Think 3 Cs – Calm, consistent and clear.
5. Be a good role model. Be patience, take a deep breath and keep calm, speak gently and firmly.
6. Make your child feel important. This will help to encourage positive patterns of behaviour. If you listen to your child so that s/he feels heard will make him/her less likely to throw a tantrum.
7. Choose your battles – let him/her win on trivial things but ensure s/he knows that safety matters are non-negotiable.
8. Distract to diffuse – Look for signs that your child is getting fed up and then use a toy to distract him/her, or use humour as a distraction.

9. Don't just say no – try not to be positive. Show what s/he should be doing in order to nurture positive behaviour.
10. Be realistic – manage your expectations about your child's behaviour. Children are often not being naughty but trying to be independent.

Turn choares into fun games. Set a challenge i.e. the first one to tidy their toys away is a winner, inject some make believe and feed their imagination. Ask him/her to pick out adifferent colour socks each day or count how many strokes when they brush their hair etc. From 2 or 3 set mini routines for your child to do, get them involved in housework. Get him/her into habit of makin bed, putting toys away or tucking pygamers under pillow etc. Put music on to distract child whilst getting dressed etc. to make them more co-operative. Resist doing everything for your child, they need to learn, try and be patient and let them have a go at doing things.

Here are some tips on parenting;

Talk to your child directly; Use your child's name to get his/her attention before asking him/her to do something. Use eye contact and bend down so that you are at the same level as your child (especially important if they are under 3).

Use positive language; The human brain even as adults can't process negatives. If we are told not to think of an elephant we will then think of an elephant. Therefore don't say don't drop that plate instead say please pass that plate to me.

Praise rather than critise; to help self esteem but still be fair and say no when you need to so that they understand no. This is especially importrant so that s/he will listen to you when it counts. Therefore rather than nag and saying no all the time use it when it counts. Also if you continuously give orders like come here, go there your child won't understand why and may not listen to you. Instead ask I would like you to come here please.

Give notice; You may also need to give your child some notice because children find it difficult to switch their attention, especially when they are absorbed in play. For instance say we will be doing x,y,z in 5 mins so start putting the toys away, its nearly time to say goodbye.

Toddlers can't always understand what 'if' means so try using 'when' instead i.e. when you have cleaned your teeth you can play with teddy rather than if you clean your teeth you can then play with teddy.

Think about how you behave and what you say; Toddlers are born mimics so bear in mind your own phrases and actions, be a good role model and mind your ps and qs.

Give limited choices; Asking your child open ended questions will make it hard for them to answer you as this will be overwhelming for them. Instead give them simplified choices i.e. would you like yoghurt or toast for breakfast. This way you are still giving them some choice and independence without over complicating things, this will help them to gain confidence.

Remember it's natural to worry about being a good parent and its natural to worry about your child and his/her safety, happiness, future etc. You usually worry about your baby from the moment you find out that you are pregnant and this continues over their life, even when they are adults and you are old and grey you will still worry (and they may worry about you too, its love).

You have to teach them good values / diff between right & wrong & then trust them to make the right decisions. Don't let them play parents off against each other, stand firm together, both parents need to agree 'be singing from the same hymn sheet'. Never contradict each other or argue in front of the children. But most of all follow your instincts and do what you believe in your heart to be right!

The age old question is it nature or nurture that predicts how our children turnout? *'The human brain and heart that are met primarily with empathy in the critical early years cannot and will not grow to choose a violent or selfish life.' – Robin Grille (Parenting for a Peaceful World).* The way we bring up our children influences the people that they come as adults; and how they subsequently care for their children. As humans we display a great range of emotions and the maternal instinct does not always come to everyone. If we have good role models and are nurtured by our families and communities we are more likely to love and care for our own children. Our life experiences influence how we are as parents. Therefore how we bring up our children is an important job and can have an impact on future generations for years to come. Although some people are naturally more maternal than others we all have the ability for parental instinct, it just comes easier to some than others. *'Tomorrows' world is already taking shape in the bodies and minds of our children'* - Kofi Annan

'Most human 'instinctual 'behaviours have to be learnt in a social context… The experiences that we have in infancy have been shown to have permanent affects on brain development. Some of our deepest, pattern likes aspects of our personality, and our fundamental dispositions regarding relationships, are shaped in childhood, babyhood and possibly even in the womb.' - *Robin Grille (Parenting for a Peaceful World).* Therefore children are heavily influenced by the way they are brought up the environment, their communities and their surroundings. Although there are expectations to the rule, against the odds people who have had a bad upbringing can prosper.

Our children are individuals and as such want to do with their lives what they want and not what we want them to do. *'If there is anything that we wish to change in the child. We should first examine it and see whether it is not something that could be better changed in ourselves' – Carl Jung*

Anything that's worth doing is hard work, kids are hard work but worth it, they are fun and your hard work will be rewarded.

Your life will change but it can't stay the same. Things always have to change, your life will be different but more enriched. Have a family is just a new chapter in your life, that will be different to before.

Teach your children kindness and compassion, love courage and the difference between right and wrong. Teach them love and responsibility and keep them close but also let them find their own way and also have your own life. Be there for your children and do as much as possible for them but also teach them how to do things for themselves, make the responsible and don't let them act in a spoilt manner. Also have your own life, hobbies and interests don't just base your life around your children and give them something to be proud of you and inspire them, so that they will want to achieve things for themselves. Be honest and open with them, tell them how you feel and that you love them, cuddle them and show them affection, don't push them away. Let them love you and take time to love them. Teach them the importance of integrity. It is also very important to teach your child empathy (a very important skill).

Develop your childs skills by reading to your child and talking to your child. Just because they are a child doesn't mean that they don't have opinions. Discuss matters with your child and get them to put a reasoned argument together, get them to think logically but also be imaginative and think outside the box. Give your child puzzles and get them to come up with solutions. Encourage play that develops creativity. Get your child to mix with other children in order to develop social skills and learn to share.

Give the child discipline, but if you tell them off in the day later on talk to them about it, explain that you love them and why you had to discipline them and get them to understand why their behaviour was wrong and alternative courses of action.

People without kids often don't understand which is why it's good to have friends with children too.

Grandparents are often softer with grandchildren and sometimes have different ideas, which can be confusing for the kid. They often want to help and may feel left out at times, try and include them and talk to them.

Take care of yourself – If you are not fit, healthy and happy how can you take care of your child? If you are stressed and upset your child will feel it too.

Be a good role model – Children will watch you, they will imitate how you behave and if you do something they will think that it is the right way and that it is acceptable for them to behave like that.

Never ask them to do something that you wouldn't do yourself. Get kids to obey you but empower them to eventually make their own good decisions. Reason with them & explain why so that they have a good understanding of situations and circumstances and develop good reasoning power and decision making skills.

Give children the space to learn to do things for themselves.

Don't give in, follow threats through and don't back down on promises.

- Give children limited choices i.e. choose between 2 items to buy
- Give instruction (Clear), no swearing/yelling, no tv in room, take something away, replace it with something.
- Spend time bonding with your child; especially when they are young they just need you. Your time is more precious then anything money can buy. But as they get older don't forget that how ever old they are (even adults) still need you.
- Kids will attention seek/misbehave if they are bored so keep them entertained and teach them how to make their own fun and find positive things to do.

Dealing with children's bad behaviour;
- look them in the eye, to say, "Look at me: I'm very pleased when you do that," to get these children to understand the emotional components of interaction,
- 'Give children clear consequences. you have to be strict about following through with threats such as: "If you do that, you're being sent to your room." And it all needs to be said very calmly.
- lots of positive talk, such as: "Well done for not losing your temper," and quick rewards like: "Because of that you can choose pudding tonight." Fast responses and calm, consistent parenting.
- 'It's also important for parents to gain their children's respect and have lots of positive interaction together. Ten minutes of special time a day makes a huge difference.
- 'The other thing is when they're being naughty, don't get into lengthy discussions. Just say: "You've done this, there's the consequence," and turn away. As soon as they stop showing any anger, turn back, and talk normally again.
- Give them attention for normal behaviour.
- As children get older you still have to be strict with their sleep - don't leave computers etc in room to distract them and stop them from sleeping.

Positive parenting and positive discipline;

Do not lose control, if you feel your child is not conforming and needs discipline. Instead encourage better behaviour through positive parenting and positive discipline;

Not all parents can get it right all of the time so if you do something wrong say that you are sorry, this teaches children a valuable lesson, make up and try again.

Avoid smacking as this may lead children to hit or smack others, to become resentful and it gives a bad example of how to handle strong emotions.

Give warmth and love as much as possible.

Have clear simple rules and limits (once the child can read these can be written out and stuck up). Get the child to negotiate and help to set the rules and write up a pledge that they agree to stick to (especially if there is a certain way that they are behaving and they know that they shouldn't behave in that manner).

Be a good role model and set a good example.

Discipline children but don't be harsh or judgemental.

Keep your promises.

Spend more focused 'quality time' with your children.

Don't bring work stresses home

Listen and talk to your children (listen and observe more) and find out what's going on in their lives.

Even if children act like they don't want to talk to you often they want and need you to talk to them but maybe struggling to express their emotions and may therefore push you away.

Teach your children how to work and do something that they enjoy (often children learn more about work from their mothers more so than there fathers).

Children worry about their parents too when they are away, just like adults worry about their children.

You children need to be able to trust that they can talk to you about issue and you will listen to them.

Praise good behaviour

Criticise bad behaviours, not your child.

Distract younger children to avoid a certain behaviour.

Don't give them attention when they are being naughty (as they often do it to attention seek), however don't ignore bad behaviour, they do need some discipline otherwise they will think that they can get away with bad behaviour.

Use 'time out' or 'removal of privileges to' discipline.

Explain why at the time what they are doing is wrong, if the child is very young use simple and concise repetitive language and say no. When they are old enough to reason, ask them why what they did is wrong, that way you are getting them to recognise their actions and take responsibility.

Often children 'act up' for attention. Therefore you need to teach them that they can't have attention all the time and don't let them interrupt adults, equally they need enough love and attention at the right time which will make them feel secure, this should reduce their need to 'act up.' Ensure that your child does get some quality time with you, especially if there are other siblings. Children tent to 'act up more' when they are jealous and feel they need to fight for your attention, for instance if you have another child, or start a new relationship. It is important to explain to them the situation and that you don't love them any less, get them involved, make time for them and try to avoid rewarding bad behaviour by giving into the tantrums.

If child tries to interrupt stop and say firmly, "mummy is talking now, wait until I have finished", then remember to turn to your child and ask them what they wanted as soon as you have finished talking. This way they are clear that they can't talk when you talk and they get their turn too. If you don't give them chance to speak they will feel neglected/rejected and then will develop behavioural issues.

Discipline is important; Change your tone according to when you are talking to child nicely and disciplining (but always be polite and don't swear), just be firm when you say no so that it is clear you mean no. This way they will be clear and know the difference between right and wrong.

The younger the child the less reasoning power they have, therefore the more concise and assertive you need to be i.e. short sharp commands like no, put down etc. as child gets longer you can start to explain why, then reason and bargain with them and eventually include them in the decision making process, or get them to think for themselves, answer the questions and tell you why (use a coaching technique such as "what do you think would happen if you did x, y, z?"

Behaviourism is a concept of psychology that children's (and adult's) behaviour can be changed through learning and association. If they associate certain behaviours with bad outcomes they will avoid it, and if they associate certain behaviours with good outcomes they will repeat it. This is also true when training animals and they are given rewards for certain behaviour. This is why we mustn't give in when a child has a tantrum for something as they will see this as a reward and will continue to have a tantrum every time they want something. We can use this concept with our children, in the form of star charts. Star charts are rewarding behaviour over a certain time. This way you are not just saying you do this once and you get a reward instead you are encouraging a pattern of behaviour, for instance if you eat your dinner every day at the end of the week you get a reward, therefore encouraging good patterns of behaviour. To re-enforce this further get the child involved with discussions about the behaviour and why certain behaviour is good and why certain behaviour is bad.

Key life changes can cause uncertainty and upset for children, which may lead to behavioural issues. Star charts and other such reward systems can be short lived, especially when there is an underlining issue or reason for the child's behaviour. Often the child may not understand themselves what this is and they often find their feelings hard to express too, especially if it something new to them and they have no experience of how to deal with it. In this case it is important to be gentle with the child and explore the issues together. The root cause of behaviours can be complex and multifaceted. Listen to your child and help him/her understand and talk through the issues that s/he is facing.

Young children cannot always identify and verbalise their motives. When a child cannot be forthcoming, parents and teachers have to become detectives, looking for clues as to possible causes and trying to hypotheses tentatively in the process of working out a solution.

Help children to recognise and name feelings. Use simple diagrams of happy and sad faces (you can buy cards with these on or make your own), use toys, pictures and the arts (visual and performing). Play is a more familiar way of communicating, for children, and then talking is.

Use a 'child centred 'approach for interaction;

When trying to get a dialogue with children, set up a child friendly context, which is good for listening to children.

Help children feel comfortable; think of the 'place' and 'pace' of interaction. Sit at the child's level (always try to come down to their level when interacting with them), make sure that you are both comfortable.

It is important to have lots of patience. Patience and empathy is important. Everyone has different skills in different areas and some people may not be as good at understanding certain things as other. Don't get frustrated; just recognise their lack of understanding and show patience and empathy, not irritation.

Give them extra time and support and don't expect too much from them.

Children are little and are still growing and developing and therefore things are harder for them and take longer, so be aware of this and offer support and patience. For instance simple things that need to be recognised are that there legs are shorter so when walking their little legs have to work 3 or 4 times harder than yours and therefore they will feel tired much sooner, the level of tiredness you may feel after a long walk, they will feel 4 times as much.

Furthermore things that seem insignificant to you will have a huge impact on children and may also affect them later on in life. Little trials of childhood – can have a huge impact.

Recognise this, be sympathetic towards this and talk things through with children to reassure them that this is normal, that its okay embarrassing things happen to everyone and they will get over it.

Try and see things from child's point of view.

Although adults need to take the lead, get children involved in a small part of the decision making, even if it is to do with a star charts, or asking them what story they want to be read etc.

Alfie Kohn provides a step model for solving problems between parents and children (known as the 3 c's);

Content – First look at the content of your request to the child and your child's expectations – is it reasonable? Or are you asking your child to do something that s/he can't. Does the child have a just cause for objection? Look at this from the child's viewpoint.

Collaboration – Involve your child in the process of deciding whether a request or expectation is reasonable. Involve the child in the process of problem solving (this involvement should increase as the child's age increases).

Choice – Problems need solutions which involve the child, for instance offer 2 alternative choices. For instance ask the child - would you like to go to bed now and read for 10 minutes or would you like to play a game now for 10 minutes and then go straight to bed without reading?

Negotiation – negotiate with your child and even ask them "what is your desired outcome?", then discuss this with them and explain why or why not this is reasonable and where you can compromise, then together come up with a suggested course of action/outcome and discuss the consequences of not carrying out the agreed actions.

When should children make decisions – An outcome in the case of Gillick v West Norfolk and Wisbech Area Health Authority (1985), referred to as 'Gillick competence' states that;

As a matter of Law the parental right to determine whether or not their minor child below the age of sixteen will have medical treatment terminates if and when the child achieves sufficient understanding and intelligence to understand fully what is proposed." Lord Scarman

The ruling holds particularly significant implications for the legal rights of minor children in England in that it is broader in scope than merely medical consent. It lays down that the authority of parents to make decisions for their minor children is not absolute, but diminishes with the child's evolving maturity; except in situations that are regulated otherwise by statute, the right to make a decision on any particular matter concerning the child shifts from the parent to the child when the child reaches sufficient maturity to be capable of making up his or her own mind on the matter requiring decision.

You can consult children without them having the responsibility for the whole decision.

Often children want to be listened to and consulted but equally understand that they need guidance from parents.

Parenting is about negotiation and recognizing the power adults have and children do not have. Children's views should be sought as much as possible but their more limited life experience has to be taken into account too. It should also be explained to children why they cannot have the final say in decisions, so that they understand the reasons.

Studies have found that children understand the complexities of family life and expect to have to negotiate their position in decisions. Often children have strong and clear feelings about what they want and it is important that their feelings are considered in decision making.

Families; most children are not worried about family structures and who looks after them, as long as they are loved.

Independence; Children need to learn how to do things in order to develop and be prepared for adulthood, get children involved in chores around the house, teach them about responsibility and get them involved. Teach children to be helpful and the value of contributing.

Development – Even though all children are individuals develop differently there is an 'average' often shown in development charts. This helps to evaluate a child's development. Although there other factors that come into play such as social and economical factors it is good to have an indication of a child's progress and a way on monitoring it. This is why they have tests and assessments at school, it also helps to determine what they already know, areas to develop and where they need support and therefore what groups they need to be placed into.

As the current school system groups children by ability. Although this can be beneficial it is also important to note that if they get out in bottom groups, although they get support, if they are borderline it is hard for them to progress. Therefore its natural to want them to do well in exams but you have to balance this against the pressure they may be under and how much stress they can handle.

Nowadays society places more pressure on children than ever and this can lead to all sorts of difficulties and school life may have conflicting aspects to home life, such as expecting children to be more independent, perhaps rushing their lunch etc. this can be confusing and unsettling for children. There is a lot of pressure on children to do well at school and to grow up quickly, when sometimes they need time to relax and play. It is important for children to learn to relax as this is something that is important for them to be able to do when they are adults too. Try not to impose your will on them too much.

Friendships;

As humans we are naturally social and most children will have a strong desire to fit in.

From the age of 4 or 5 they will start to form friendships - Before the age of 4 children usually play alone or with adults or 'alongside' rather than 'with' other children (solitary and parallel play), once they start to develop social skills they start to select who they want to play with and develop friendships with this becomes 'co-operative' play.

Children, like adults select friends that they have things in common with, therefore children who are different from their peers find it harder to make friends (and can often find themselves subject to teasing, hostility or exclusion). Negative attitudes that children develop towards other children often stem from what they learn at home and in the world around them, such as stereotypes they see on the tv etc. Although children do also have patterns of friendship that do not conform to what is expected and they often challenge our assumptions, they may be more accepting because they don't have pre-conceived ideas. It is important that children learn to keep that 'open mind' rather than taking on stereotype views from the outside world. We should encourage them to be accepting of others and to continue to use their imagination and think outside the box.

The quality of friendship is more important than the number of friends.

It is important for children to have some independence and to have quality time with friends away from the home.

Further tips on brining up your child;

- Think about road safety, don't let your child play in the road and teach them the green cross code (stop, look and listen). The Royal Holloway University of London, research scientist vision reaserch shows that primary school children (up to age of 11). Can't Tell accurately speed of cars above 20mph and can't tell the distance of how far away they are.

- They have to do things for themselves so that they will learn, but they also need guidance and protection, as well as rules, boundaries and lots of love.
- Monitor them to make sure that they are safe using the internet and social networking sites.
- Always have a backup plan for child care in an emergency (such as another parents number) in case something happens and you can't pick them up from school or you need someone to look after them, in an emergency.
- Don't have favourites out of your children.
- Don't let them see you lose your temper and get angry, instead talk things through with your children.
- Take time out to spend with your children, if they want to talk to you and you have no time then schedule some in and agree with them a time that you will sit down with them, and stick to the agreed time. Children need reliability and consistency and they need to be able to trust you.
- Ensure they get a good mix of love, fun and discipline. If they are naughty punish them by taking away privileges such as tv, ipod etc. if you threaten something then follow it through otherwise they will never take you seriously. If they are very young give them a minute on the naughty step for every year of their age, so if they are 5 they get 5 minutes. Children need to know boundaries. Often children will play up for attention so it is best not to give in. It is important to spend time with your children. If you are at a restaurant sit adults with the children to supervise them and ensure that the learn to sit at the table sensibly. Remember to teach children that it is rude to stare.
- Children need discipline (it doesn't damage them it teaches them right from wrong and stops them being spoilt. When the parent takes them to other people's houses, they should also discipline them so that they learn to respect others and behave. Don't let them run riot at other people's houses. As well as parents backing each other up and not arguing in front of the children, this is also true with friends and family who look after them. Teach your children to respect them, discipline them and back up the person in question if your children don't do what 'the adult' says and if you disagree to them discreetly but not in front of the child. The child should respect all adults especially grandparents and aunts and uncles and shouldn't get away with being rude to them.
- It is important that parents work together and put up a united front; children will try and play them off against each other to get their own way, if they think that they can get away with it.
- Teach them to take responsibility for their actions, also teach them manners. Sit around the table together as a family and make the children stay there until they have eaten all of their dinner, make them ask permission before leaving the table. It is also important to teach them good moral values. Teach them to be truthful and honest. Also teach them not to have pre-conceived ideas about things and to judge everything and everyone by their own merits.
- Ensure that they eat properly.
- It is also important to teach children about their roots, show them photos of the family and do a family tree with them.

- Teach children compassion and show them people who are less fortunate. Show them poor countries abroad and get them to volunteer with you at homeless shelters and other places where there are less fortunate people that need your help.
- Don't let them swear or use slang, create a good example and don't use slang or swear in front of them.
- Don't shield children too much from reality, let them see the bad things that go on as well as the bad things, in a gentle way, perhaps in a school play and then you can discuss them with them. (i.e. death). Otherwise they will get confused and when they get older will find it hard to cope as they won't have the coping skills, won't understand what's going on etc.. Explain the bad things and the difference between right and wrong.
- Kids - all need to be treated differently according to the individual and their individual personality. However it is important to have a good bedtime routine with all children. Spend some play time with the children bonding with them, then read them a story, to put them to bed.
- Give children new experiences and activities to try. Spend time with them to teach them well and make them feel loved, this way they are more likely to come to you with their problems and less likely to go off of the rails.
- There is a need for discipline & parental control, children need structure and discipline, but also always tell kids why so that they understand and also show them kindness, compassion and fun. Remember what it was like to be their age, we all made mistakes, its all part of growing up. We always think the next generation are worse that we were but that isn't necessarily true, it's just our perception because we have forgotten the things that we got up too when we were that age. Kids should be given limits, kids that are spoilt and not given limits don't know how to react when they finally get limits. They need to know difference between right and wrong, as a child their brains aren't fully developed so its important to teach them properly otherwise it can have serious consequences that can impact on their adult life.
- Children need a routine – they need to get into a pattern, this will also help with their behaviour, if they stay up to late or doesn't have a pattern they will get stressed and act up.
- Give kids a carrot, an incentive to do well, teach them to respect – do this by setting an example and showing respect to them and to other people around you, as well as respecting yourself. Also teach them about reasoning and the consequences of actions and why things should be done in a certain way.
- Children need lots of cuddles and affection. They need sympathy at times and they need to be shown things but they will get lazy if too much is done for them and they need to be taught how to think for themselves and to be given some responsibility too.
- Don't expect children to come to you with their problems unless you encourage them, make time for them, are there for them and remind them that they can talk to you. Make it easy for them to turn to you and let them know that they can so that in times of hardship they will.
- Hug them and show them love and ensure that they feel loved and that all of your children feel equal. Especially if you are pregnant with another child they will get jealous so you need to include them so that they feel part of it, let them help out and bond with the other child and reassure them that you will always love them.
- Young children find any change hard. Moving house or gaining a sibling can be very traumatic to them and cause problems sleeping etc. because they feel the safe world that they knew has been changed and they are unsettled. It is important to be aware of this and do all you can to reassure them.
- A simple way to encourage a young child is to do a star chart, every time the child does something good they get a star in the box and when the chart if full they get a treat. This can be done for general behaviour or to encourage a particular activity for

instance they could get a star every time they eat their dinner and at the end of the fortnight they could get to choose their own special plate if they have eaten their dinner all week. They should be encouraged to eat healthily and be made to eat what everyone else is eating and should try new food. Take them out to dinner from a young age and at home all sit around the table and eat together making them eat what is on the menu rather than them choosing the usual chips and chicken nuggets, and they should be taught table manners and not be allowed to leave the table until everyone has eaten and if they don't eat their dinner they shouldn't get pudding.

- Teach them the value of money, don't always buy them things, make them earn what you give them (although it is also important to make it clear that they should automatically help out in the family, do things around the house etc. without expecting to be paid or given gifts). Explain to them that you have to work hard for things and that money doesn't grow on trees, and that these are nice things and not everyone has such things, teach them about other children who are in poverty and do things together, as a family, such as fundraising for people in poverty. Get them to do odd jobs around the house, give them a money box and put money in this each time they do a job, then make them save this up so that they can buy something that they really want.

- As a parent you will also have to accept that you may make mistakes and what works for one child may not work for another because everyone is different and therefore responds to things differently too.

- It is also important to recognize that all children are different and will respond differently to different treatment, you will need to vary your approach according to the child and the specific situation, all you can do is follow your gut instinct and do what you feel is appropriate at the time.

- Children need discipline and do need to be shouted at on certain occasions, however don't shout at them all of the time, or nag them, instead reason with them and ask them what they did wrong and why it was wrong so that they get to understand the difference between right and wrong. They need to be aware of the consequences of their actions and take responsibility for their own actions, without excuses.

- Don't argue with anyone in front of kids, set a good example for them to follow. Parents should show a united front, both agree on the same thing, once a decision has been made you need to support each other and don't undermine each other.

- Kids need to know the difference between right and wrong, they will get their values from their parents and that will set the tone of how they will act in later life. Its not fair on them if they are not brought up properly and don't know how to behave because later on in life they will then have difficulties, sometimes you have to be cruel to be kind and discipline them, its for their own good and they will thank you when they get older.

- Protect them and try and keep them safe but don't wrap them up in cotton wool and do too much for them as they will be too dependant and not independent or confident enough, and they may worry and be fearful a lot, they may then be afraid to do things instead get a balance, and teach them ways of keeping them selves safe, find practical things so they can still go out but be safe i.e. a mobile and ask them to call home, a personal alarm, teach them the green cross code and tell them not to speak to strangers etc.

- Supervise them using the internet, it can be very educational and useful for them to use but it is important to ensure that they use it safely. Discourage them from meeting people on the internet; if they do you should go with them too. Encourage your child not to give out any personal information that could allow someone to find them, only use moderate chat rooms and don't add people they don't know to their buddy list. Use safety filters on the computer and keep computers in family areas and not bedrooms so that you can see what is going on.

- Discuss drinking, drugs and sex with your children and talk through the associated dangers. Explain to children the facts of life as soon as they get to an appropriate age prior to puberty, in case they go through puberty early or hear the wrong information from their peers, it is important for them to have all the correct information in relation to puberty and sex education.

Bullying; Talk to children about bullying. Your child may not tell you if they are being bullied but may not want to go to school and may seem anxious. Signs of bullying can include running away, not attending school, other learning and behavioural difficulties and/or marks on them with no plausible explanation. Bullying can be physical and verbal. Talk to your child calmly and make a note of what they say; who was involved, where, when and how often? Reassure your child that they have done the right thing by telling you, tell your child to report any further incidents to the teacher straight away, talk to the teacher yourself about what can be done. Advise your child to walk away and to try and avoid getting in a fight.

It needs to be reported because the bullies may be experincing problems that are making them behave in such a way and as a result they will need help.

Teach your child respect from a young age, tell them not to discriminate against others and if they know someone is being bullied to report it, because the person whom is being bullied may not be able to report it themselves.

If you are told that your child is being disruptive at school or is involved with bullying, take it seriously. They maybe are being led astray by the wrong crowd or they maybe unhappy about something. The sooner you talk to them and deal with it the better, otherwise the problem may esculate. Work with the school in putting an action plan together and seek independent help where appropriate, get as much support as you can.

Stranger safety; Also tell your children that they shouldn't always do what adults say, that they should talk to you if they are unsure about something that someone has asked them to do and that they must never keep secrets. Tell your child not to speak to strangers and if they get lost to ask a police officer or someone behind the till in a shop for help. It is important for children to learn things from a young age so that they can deal with any situation that they may face. Also if you learn things from a young age you are likely to retain it. Repetition and visual aids increase learning and retention of information.
- Encourage them to be able to talk to you, this way if they are unsure about doing something they can discuss it with you, rather than sneaking off behind you back and doing things, which of course will be more dangerous for them.
- If you have children, ensure that your house is child friendly, don't leave medication or chemicals such as bleach in reach of the children.
- Children need something to do to keep them active and focused, they will play up and cause mischief when they are bored. Sometimes all they need is a bit of encouragement and support and they will excel. They need to feel loved and supported and need affection as well as discipline, there needs to be a balance. They need to know the adults are in charge and know their boundaries – it is natural for children to try and push them, they are just being children but you need to set the limit otherwise they will be naughty all the time if they think that they can get away with it. Sometimes children play up because they have a lot of energy that is not being channelled in the right direction for instance if they are not being stimulated and they find school too easy they will be naughty, the same goes if they find it too hard as they will switch off, you should always asses what the child is doing and why they are behaving that way, you need to steer and encourage them to channel that

negative energy into something useful, perhaps get them to take up sports, join a club or team to burn off some energy etc.

- They need to exercise and play outside to get fresh air but you need to take they somewhere safe so they are not in danger playing in the road, they shouldn't be sat inside playing computer games all day either.
- They need to be taught how to sit still, concentrate and listen and they shouldn't be allowed to run wild. If they are not used to sitting still they won't. Don't let them have too much sugar and encourage them to sit and listen, keep engaging them, be imaginative and capture their minds and slowly build up the amount of time so that they can gradually concentrate for longer. But remember each child is different and they all have different personalities and learn and develop at different rates, don't compare one child against the other and expect them to behave the same or discipline them for not being as well behaved as other children.
- They need routine and security and they need a pattern of when they eat and go to bed, children do need their sleep (research has shown they do need more sleep than adults as their brains are developing). When they get older they shouldn't automatically be allowed out, they should earn nights out and have strict curfews.
- It is important to spend time with your kids and do things as a family, to bond with them.
- Learn what the child's abilities are from a young age and encourage them to develop these skills and abilities. Encourage them to do well but don't push kids into doing things that they don't want to do. They have got to have fun and be happy, their childhood should be enjoyable not stressful.
- Many skills have to be developed from a young age, for instance many famous ballet dancers have been dancing since they could walk. Therefore if your child develops an interest in something it is important to encourage them from a young age, however you also need to recognise that they are a child and it needs to be fun so you shouldn't push them too much and as children often do they will probably change their mind and want to move onto something different, you must also let them do this.
- Encourage them to have their own personalities and think for themselves and to become confident. Get them to stop and think about things and make them use their imitative, be independent and do things for themselves.

- Get them to mix with people from all ages and teach them to respect their elders. Get them to develop communication and social skills by encouraging them to play with other children and share toys and not be selfish.
- Encourage them to do some charity work, perhaps help out during the school holidays in a homeless shelter and at Christmas send gift boxes abroad, this will teach them about what others don't have so that they will value what they do have.
- Ensure that they get a good education and set a good example and give them something to aspire to. They also need to learn how to concentrate, children do find it hard but start them off with giving them breaks and getting them to do something physical such as moving around, this will wake them up and help them concentrate, start with short concentration periods and lots of breaks and then gradually increase the time that they can concentrate.
- School is important but it is not everything, some children don't do well in school academically or may have issues at school if they have trouble mixing with the other children, always try and find out what the root cause of the problems are and see if they can be resolved, if your child is unhappy at school there must be a reason and this should be capable of being worked through.
- If they are really behind on their work you may want to get help from outside of the school such as private tuition, children usually switch off only when they are de-motivated which is usually because they find something hard because its not taught

in a way that they understand it, one to one tuition to bring them up to speed may be enough.

- It is important that if they are struggling it is recognized early on and they get help straight away as the longer they feel they don't understand something the harder it will be for them to pick it up as they may start developing a mental block for the subject. Core subjects like English and Maths are important and will affect the whole of the rest of their lives, however at school they will fail to see the importance and may become bored. Try and make the subjects relevant to them by showing how they work outside the class room and are linked into everyday life and how they will affect them.

- It's important to get them to become rounded individuals and to teach them social skills and morals and compassion as well as the academic knowledge. Encourage them to join clubs and to try lots of different things to find what they like. Allow them to try something without pushing them and expecting them to stick at it so that they are not scared to try something just to see if they like it, although they will need to eventually stick at something and they also need to learn the value of committing to something.

- When deciding what to teach them/when to tell them something bear in mind that if they are old enough to understand something they are old enough to be told and learn. There are certain things they have to learn at some point so its often better to teach them properly, the right way, rather than leaving them to find out for themselves even though some things they will have to discover for themselves.

- Encourage them to work hard but also have fun; do fun activities together as a family. Quality family time is very important.

- Encourage them to take all opportunities and send them to groups and clubs where they can develop and make friends outside of school, drama groups are good to give confidence or if they don't like dram they could join a theatre group doing lighting or stage work. Get them to join in with community projects and do something productive for their local community. Scouts or cadet groups are good, if they join a cadet group they can do Duke of Edinburgh courses and also BTEC in public services (equivalent to 4 GCSEs), these are valuable qualifications which they can do whilst they are having fun and meeting people. If you are religious or got to church try sending your children to Sunday school.

- It is important for kids to join a group and learn how to do things and learn values and also feel valued and make new friends, especially if they are not getting that from school. There are lots of opportunities out there for children and young people, it is important to take all the opportunities that you can in order to develop and grow, so don't waste valuable opportunities for your children.

- Teach them to respect everyone and teach them about other cultures.

- They also need regular testing to see what they don't know, so that you can teach it to them in order that they don't get behind as if they do they may lose confidence.

- The same techniques that psychologists apply to advertising should be applied to education to get children to learn, such as aromas in the room, creative colours in class rooms etc.

- They say children develop a personality from age 7, but you can still teach them and develop that personality at any age i.e. if they have an aggressive personality you can challenge the negative energy into something good and they will be very focused and become successful, if you don't they may end up using that aggression later on in life for negative purposes.

- Try and understand your children and why they behave the way that they do. Listen to them and believe them and believe in them too. Be honest with them and teach them the importance of honesty, encourage them to always tell the truth.

- It is also vital to teach them important life skills from a very young age, they should learn how to swim, if you can't teach them then get them to have swimming lessons.

This is very important because without being able to swim they may get excluded from many groups and activates and as there is so much water they need to swim as one day it may save their life. You should also teach them the dangers of water and not to go off swimming in deep water or diving in shallow water etc. They should also know basic first aid and should know what to do in an emergency, even as a small child they need to know how to evacuate the house, their name and address and what to do if they get separated from their parents etc.

- Teach children about finance from a young age, how to earn pocket money and budget, priorities etc. Also teach them about sex, drugs and alcohol so they know the truth before they may get to the age where they may be given the wrong information and influenced into taking drugs and alcohol etc.
- It's okay to teach children to fight back in self defence but you must also teach them that sometimes you must walk away and violence isn't the answer and that they shouldn't hit out especially at those younger than them no matter what they do to them, getting the balance is a fine line but you don't want to create a child who is a bully and thinks its okay to fight.

" Don't worry that children never listen to you; worry that they are

always watching you."

Robert Fulghum, American essayist (born 1937)

" The trouble with parents is that by the time they are experienced, they are unemployed."

Anon

"The truth is that parents are not really interested in justice. They just want quiet."

Bill Cosby (born 1937)

What do children need?

While no one has ever maintained that positive parenting is easy, there is a strong case for suggesting that the basic principles are surprisingly simple. The pioneering British psychiatrist, John Bowlby, described the ideal state for children as one of "secure attachment". The securely attached child, he said, experiences his or her relationship with their parent as solid and reliable. This means that the child does not feel overwhelming distress if temporarily separated from the parent and can react positively when they return. So what is required to achieve this state? Interestingly, Bowlby and his colleagues discovered that while a warm and loving atmosphere was certainly necessary, it was far more important that parenting be responsive and consistent. In practice, that means that children will gain much more from a parent who can understand and acknowledge different moods and feelings than from one who just tries to keep smiling, whatever the situation. By the same token, a parent who ignores a child one moment, then showers them with presents the next, will be perceived unconsciously as unpredictable and neglecting. Consistent loving attention, which is both kind and firm is far more important. Securely attached children will be more likely to form trusting, lasting relationships in adulthood, they will also seek out social support and will tend to have good self esteem.

One critically important factor that all parents need to understand is that attachment styles are often passed from one generation to the next. That means that people will often act towards their own children in very similar patterns to the ways their parents treated them. Paradoxically, this can include what appears to be completely different behaviour. Someone who felt very neglected by her mother, for instance, might vow not to do the same with her own children, but ends up smothering them with attention, leaving them equally unable to establish a coherent and stable sense of self.

Self-knowledge is by far and away the most powerful weapon against unproductive patterns. Talking through the issues with a friend or a counsellor can make all the difference.

What do parents need?

Many parents might quite justifiably feel that these kinds of theories are all very well, but ask where they fit into the often chaotic reality of modern family life. Every parent may want to be perfect for their offspring, but life is of course much more complicated. We're all familiar with the proverb, "It takes a village to raise a child", but that can seem like a distant fantasy for many busy working mothers and fathers these days. So if parents are to stand any chance at all of being able to provide a secure and consistent environment, what is going to help them do it? Put simply, they need a combination of reliable information and solid support, but that can be a hard combination to access. Surveys of parents have shown that isolation is a common problem for a variety of reasons. In an increasingly mobile society, grandparents are often not close by to lend extra support and advice. There are also increasing numbers of single parents, who can quickly feel alienated and overwhelmed. Childcare can also often be prohibitively expensive, even when both parents are working.

Perhaps a more serious block to accessing information and support, however, is stigma. A recent inquiry into the needs of parents and children in Wales, for instance, uncovered what it described as a "cultural perception" that parenting support was something that only "failed parents" looked for. Many parents who spoke to the inquiry said they felt embarrassed or afraid when asking for parenting support, because of how that might reflect on them. Childcare experts believe, of course, that it takes wisdom and foresight for parents to look for the best possible help available, and there are in fact many charities, voluntary agencies and governmental organisations dedicated to offering just that. Research shows that the key antidote to parental stresses is contact with other parents and there are numerous groups offering this kind of interaction.

Pretty much every culture in history has acknowledged the need for community support in raising children. So don't try and go it alone. Between friends, family, support groups and paid help, there is always a way forward.

Parents often may not be completely clear about what their needs are, and a conversation with a trained impartial observer can help clarify exactly what's required.

Why are children so difficult?

From the moment we are born, we are trying to accomplish one central task; to figure out who we are. In our earliest years, this means establishing first that we are actually separate, individual people and second that our needs will not always be met instantly. The task of the parents is, of course, to make sure that the most important needs are met, but it is also up to them to cope with the child's anger and confusion when it does not get what it wants. Children get upset and misbehave for all sorts of reasons, rarely just to annoy their parents. More often than not, they are trying to communicate in some way. As well as wanting to receive attention, they are also trying to work out what is permissible and what those around them can tolerate. When children become delinquent, it is often because even negative attention is better than being ignored. In order to develop healthily, children need to know that they have a certain freedom to express themselves and that these feelings will be accepted, but they also want to know that they are safe, supported and contained. It's a delicate task for parents. They need to allow children enough room for manoeuvre without making them feel that they've been completely left to their own devices. But they also need to

Provide discipline and structure without making them feel completely controlled and manipulated. Both extremes will leave children feeling neglected and insecure. But establishing a stable environment that gives children both room for exploration and a sense of safety will set them up for life with a strong sense of self-esteem and the ability to form close reliable relationships in adulthood. All of that is, of course, easier said than done, so here a few tips based on the latest advice from government family policy units and children's charities.

Talk and Listen; Communicating with your child is the single most important thing you can ever do for them. Long before children learn to speak, they start communicating. In the earliest years, this involves the baby looking at the face of its mother, seeking recognition and reciprocal attention. A mother who is watching television or talking on a mobile phone might as well not be there. It is also incredibly important that parents learn to tune into the moods of their children. If a child is upset, it wants to know that its parents can recognise this. Help them find the words to describe their emotional states. Tell them you love them all the time, but also tell them when you are cross with their behaviour. If you say no to a request, explain why.

Play; It can be very tempting for exhausted parents to leave their kids in front of a DVD. But making time to play with children can be refreshing and rejuvenating for Mums and Dads as well. All the research shows that play is absolutely essential if children are to develop their own sense of creativity and self esteem. The key is to keep it simple. For busy parents, play can also be incorporated into daily routines. Messing around with a cup and a sponge at bath time is huge fun for little ones, or give your toddler a bowl and a spoon to play with while you are cooking. A child wants to know that you are interested and involved in their world, and play is one of the most effective ways of doing this.

Make time; Increasing numbers of households contain either only one parent or two parents who are both working, so making time for the kids can be a real challenge. Again, it pays to keep it simple. Get up ten minutes earlier so you can sit and play or talk with your child before the day gets busy. Have one night a week when you make sure you all do something together. Even just eating dinner together regularly can make a huge difference to a child's sense of support and belonging.

Set clear boundaries; There are few things more unhelpful to a child's development than inconsistency. Parents need to agree on rules and stick to them. When you say no, mean no. Mixed messages are incredibly confusing to children. Never threaten what you can't deliver and if you are going to punish a child, do so straight after the behaviour so they can understand cause and effect. Help children to take responsibility in constructive ways. If they break something, for instance, find a job for them to do to make up for it. If they hurt another child, help them make amends with a kind gesture and an apology.

Notice and reward good behaviour; All too often, children are only noticed when they are behaving badly. Try giving them praise for doing something right. Real encouragement like this can provide a huge boost to kids' self-esteem and confidence. It also shows them that rewards can be emotional as well as material, which can make a huge difference in their capacity to build caring and giving relationships with others.

Time-outs; One of the most useful ways of dealing with tantrums or difficult behaviour is the time-out. This involves putting your child in a dull but safe place for a period of time (like the corner of a room), giving everybody the chance to cool off and regain their composure. The time limit should be one minute for every year of the child's life. Once the timeout
is finished, so is the punishment.

Allow consequences. Parents quite naturally want to protect their children from the dangers of life. But they will always be doing them a disservice if they try and shield them from the consequences of their own actions. For instance, if they haven't done their homework, there's no use in doing it for them and depriving them of an important life lesson.

Be a role model. Young children learn far more from what they see their parents do than from what they say. Be aware that you are being constantly observed by your children, and they will absorb the way you respond to the world. Model the traits that you wish to cultivate in your kids.

Look after yourself. Self-care may seem like an unattainable luxury to many parents, but you will pay a high price in the long run if you do not look after yourself as best you can. No one is pretending it's easy, but it's crucial to take periods of time for yourself, even if they're short. Find the help you need to make that possible. Maintaining interests outside the home can also be difficult, but it is vital that your children do not completely swamp your life. Sleep may be hard to come by, but you can certainly take responsibility for eating properly and getting plenty of gentle exercise.

Love and nurture your children but don't over spoil them. As a family eat dinner together every night, this will help you to bond, to understand each other and to spot if anything is wrong.

- If your child has a favourite toy – buy a spare one in case they lose it.
- Influence your children to achieve more than you.
- Children like discipline; they need to know the boundaries. Children also respond well if you give them responsibility, if you give them opportunities they will perform.
- Children like most adults if you treat them with respect, they will treat you with respect.
- Do a photo book of your children growing up and then present this to them on a significant birthday i.e. 21st or 30th or 40th. When your child is born start a baby book, also get a 100 year diary for them to fill in.
- All children are different and some need extra attention – don't get angry with them, instead sit down and talk to them and reason with them.
- Childcare – if you work for a local authority look into having child care paid straight out of your wages – that way you pay less tax.
- If you can't get out because you have children and can't get a baby sitter, or you haven't got much money. Don't sit at home by yourself, get friends to come over and each bring a dish of food or a bottle. It's good to have a family life and do things with your kids but you need your friends and your own social life too.
- Teach children values from young age
- Teach children to respect people and property. Don't let your children climb all over your furniture, even when it is old because then when you get new furniture they will think they can do the same. It's like the broken window theory, if a place is run down and has a broken window, people will respect it less and soon that broken window will turn into more than one, graffiti will appear, people will be less likely or willing to care and it will become a downward spiral. Respect yourself, those around you and

the area that you live in. It is also important for you to lead by example and for you to protect the area where you live, do your bit to keep it nice and don't drop litter.

- Children needs discipline that is consistent. If you are not consistent they will be confused and not know the boundaries. Really in all aspects of life this is true, when managing others etc.
- Activities to do with kids – make cup cakes etc.
- Check out your local adult education college, they may run free family learning sessions.
- Build up a network with other mums, go on net mums, go to mother and toddler groups etc.
- Select some recopies and get the kids to go through them and choose what they want to eat for the week ahead. Buy the ingredients at the start of the week. This way you can budget, you know what you are eating is healthy and because you are more organised and you know what you are doing you have more time. You can then cook together with your children in the evening, or even have baking day where you all cook together, then freeze the food for the week. That way you have more time of an evening to help them with their homework etc.
- Children need a balance, they need to be given some chores and need to learn about hard work but it's not good for them to have too much work as they need time to be kids, to play, learn and explore. They need to do some activities and sports but also they need time to relax. Children and teenagers need more sleep than adults. They need to be protected but also need to be allowed to make mistakes so that they can learn.
- When your children leave school if you have no one to sell or give the old uniform to, give it to the school so they can give it a child who may need it.
- If you are disciplining children for fighting, tell them both off (they are usually both to blame, sometimes one may be secretly winding the other one up so that they will hit out and get told off), you don't want the children to feel that you have a favourite.
- Don't feed on demand – instead have a routine (distract them so that they get in the habit of going for 4 hours without food, that way they will be more likely to sleep through the night).
- When correcting your children's homework don't rub out what they have written, instead cross it out in a different colour pen (so that their teacher can see where they are going wrong and give them extra support. Also have a look back through their work yourself to see if there is a pattern of mistakes emerging and if there is discuss the extra support they need with their teacher). Also explain to the child what they did wrong and why, but be constructive with your criticism and praise them for their efforts, so that you don't de motivate them.
- If your child has problems sleeping, discuss with them what is worrying, also get them dream catchers and worry people. This will help them to feel more positive about going to sleep and may break the cycle.
- Encourage your child to do things, use star charts or give them coloured stones when they do something well. When they have received a set amount they get a treat, equally if they do something wrong they lose a star or stone, which means they then have to work harder to get their treat.
- If you have kids young and missed out on going travelling, go with them when they are old enough, you could even take a gap year with them.
- Parents should work together to display a united front and not let children play the parents off against each other.
- Take away their privileges as a punishment i.e. mobiles, play stations. The more they break the rules, complain about the punishment or are none compliant, the longer you should take the stuff away for.
- Look out for offers of free concerts and TV recordings that you can go to. Most TV stations allow you to apply to go to studio audiences for free.

- The first year at school/nursery they will get sick a lot because there will be lots of other children and germs flying around, they will not be used to all the new germs because it is a new place and they have not been with so many other children before. After the first year their immunity will then build up. It is a good idea to gradually introduce children to some germs (in a controlled environment), but only gradually when they are ready i.e. as they get older and their immune system develops (not when they are babies), this will help them to develop a strong immune system.
- Parents need to realise that children especially as they grow up may need their space, Children also need to realise that parents are people to and not just parents, they also need space to be themselves. Grandparents need to play a supportive role but remember that they are not the parents, and they need to let the parents make the decisions (with their support and guidance). Even families need some space and privacy.
- Teach your children curiosity, ethics, and self-belief. *'We make a living by what we get, but we make a life by what we give'* **Winston Churchill.** We do make lives for ourselves by giving our love, devotion, time, attention and treasure to others, especially our spouses and our children.
- Gradual independence, supervised as they get older is a good thing.

- Ask the child what they want to do, then negotiate a plan so they feel included and listened too, it will also help them to develop their negotiating/compromise and decision making skills. For instance; child wants to play game, say well lets play game for 10 mins and then its bed time (don't then give them longer as they will then keep trying to push the boundaries).
- As they get older, get them involved. They like responsibility and to think for themselves but they still need to be shown and have supervision. They need boundaries and like to know where they stand but don't be too authoritative, its about getting the balance. For instance you could put a selection of healthy snacks in a low cupboard and if they ask they can go and select their own, that way they feel like they are getting a choice but it is only from healthy things that you have picked for them
- Take charge, you still need to be in control. As parents you need confidence and self belief and need to give a confident aura. Don't let others criticize you, you are the parents and should therefore do things how you want (as long as you work together and have a joined up approach). However you should admit when you are wrong, and that no one gets everything right. Talk to them and explain why i.e. sorry if I've been moody today I've had a really bad day at work etc. Listen to them, share and talk with them and they will listen to you. Apologies when necessary, be honest and teach them integrity and empathy.
- Try and understand them, listen to them and find out the 'why' behind their behavior and reasoning. They are like normal people (expect their brains are growing more and trying to learn more), therefore they may have bad days and mood swings etc. some days they may react differently to others so some days things may work and other days they may not.
- Watch them and get clues of how they are feeling and predict what's going on, be perceptive to them and their needs as they may not always talk to you. As much as possible encourage them and make it easier for them to talk to you.
- Listen to your child and don't force them to do things (unless necessary), often they have their own ideas and ways of doing things, which are not wrong they are just different to your ways. Sometimes you have to let them learn and do things their own way in order to develop their independence. Its important that children grow up learning how to think for themselves and being able to use their own initiative.

- Focus on the positive things and what the child like and can do, not what they can't (although you also need to develop areas they are weak in you also need to nurture and develop areas that they are strong in). It is also good to focus on their strengths in order to give them confidence. However although it is good to reward your child, don't reward them too much as then they will feel that they have to do things to get your approval and will do what they think you want and not what is necessary best for them. You don't want them to be constantly seeking approval. Furthermore when they are not rewarded they may get upset and if you give out too much praise you are de-valuing it. However a certain amount of praise is important but they also need to be able to deal with failure. When giving praise or constructive criticism instead of being general be specific and give specific feedback. Like anything you need to get the balance right and all feedback should be balanced, constructive and specific. Notice the detail and avoid generalizations, this will also show that you are paying attention.
- Star charts can be useful but if used too much they may lower self esteem.
- Look at what's important for them and not you (don't get caught in your own agenda and be over controlling, let them think for themselves and do things their way).

- Gather as much info from as many different sources as possible but there is no right and wrong way so don't follow it to the letter, instead be well informed but also follow your heart and your own instincts and do what you think is right for you and your family.
- Kids have a lot of energy so let them have physical activity, run around the park etc. Boys often find it hard to concentrate so you need to give them eye contact and get their attention first before giving them an instruction. Most boys can't multi task so you need to give them one instruction at a time.
- Children are perceptive and pick up on parents emotions, negative vibes may make children want to avoid parents, they may even feel it is their fault. In order to have happy children you need happy parents, that way you can create a calm harmonious atmosphere for your children, which will make them feel secure, well balanced and happy.

Childs behaviours

A lot of children's behaviour is to do with the environment that they have been brought up in.

If child has an issue with food lay out lots of different foods on the table , walk away and let child pick the food themselves.

Do a star chart – be realistic i.e. don't make it too easy for them or the reward too expensive and always deliver on promises otherwise you will lose the child's trust.

If your child is having difficulty behaving;

Identifying the reasons for difficult behaviour

There are a number of possible reasons for difficult behaviour. Here are a few suggestions:

• Any change in a child's life, like the birth of a new baby, moving house, a change of childminder, starting playgroup, or even something much smaller, can be a big deal. Sometimes children show how they are feeling in the only ways they know how.

• Children are quick to pick up on it if you are feeling upset or there are problems in the family. Their behaviour may be difficult to manage just at the time when you feel least able to cope. If you are having problems, don't blame yourself – but don't blame your child either if they react in a difficult way.

• Sometimes your child may react in a particular way because of the way you have handled a problem in the past. For example, if you have given your child sweets to keep them quiet at the shops, they may well scream for sweets every time you go there.

• Could you accidentally be encouraging difficult behaviour? Your child might see a tantrum as a way of getting attention (even if it's angry attention!) or waking up at night as a way of getting a cuddle and a bit of company. Try giving them more attention when they are behaving well and less when they are being difficult.

• Think about the times when your child's behaviour is most difficult to manage. Could it be because they are tired, hungry, over-excited, frustrated or bored?

Changing your child's behaviour;

- **Do what feels right** - It's got be right for your child, for you and for the family. If you do something you don't believe in or that you don't feel is right, the chances are it will not work. Children are quick to pick up when you don't really mean what you are saying!
- **Stick at it** - Once you have decided to do something, give it a fair trial. Very few solutions work overnight. It's easier to stick at something if you have someone to support you. Get help from your partner, a friend, another parent, your health visitor or your GP. At the very least, it's good to have someone to talk to about what you are doing.
- **Try to be consistent** - Children need to know where they stand. If you react to your child's behaviour in one way one day and a different way the next, it's confusing. It's also important that everyone close to your child deals with the problem in the same way.
- **Try not to over-react** - This can be very hard! When your child does something annoying, not just once but time after time, your own feelings of anger and frustration are bound to build up. It's easy to get wound up and end up taking your feelings out on your child. If this happens, the whole situation can start to get out of control. Of course, you would have to be superhuman not to show your irritation and anger sometimes, but try to keep a sense of proportion. Once you have said what needs to be said and let your feelings out, try to leave it at that. Move on to other things that you can both enjoy or feel good about. And look for other ways of coping with your feelings.
- **Talk to your child** - Children don't have to be able to talk back to understand. And understanding why you want them to do something can help. Explain why, for example, you want your child to hold your hand while crossing the road, or get into the buggy when it's time to go home.
- **Encourage your child to talk** - Giving your child the opportunity to explain why they are angry or upset will help reduce their frustration.
- **Be positive about the good things** - When a child's behaviour is really difficult, it can come to dominate everything. What can help is to say (or show) when you feel good about something they have done. You can let your child know when they make you happy by just giving them some attention, a hug or even a smile. There doesn't have to be a reason. Let your child know that you love them just for being themselves.
- **Rewards** - You can help your child by rewarding them for behaving well, for example by praising them or giving them their favourite food for tea. If your child behaves well, tell them how pleased you are. Be specific. Say something like, 'I loved the way you

put your toys back in the box when I asked you! Well done!' Don't give your child a reward before they have done what they were asked to do. That is a bribe, not a reward, and bribes don't work!

- **Use positive language** and encourage child to use positive language and be optimistic about life and situations as a positive outlook on life is an important virtue.

Assist baby's/child's development

Play with them, talk to them. Get pre-school syllabus and teach them etc.

IDEAS FOR PLAY

You can support your child's development by:

- teaching them songs and nursery rhymes. You may want to invest in a nursery rhyme book yourself so that you can sing them to them (or download them free from the internet).
- playing with letters and numbers (for example with building blocks)
- painting and drawing
- reading storybooks and
- talking about the pictures
- taking them to a toy library
- going to your local library and children's centre – they have lots of activities.

Read; Spending time reading to or with your baby or child will help them develop good language skills, support their emotional well-being and help you bond. Bookstart is a national programme that offers free books to children, along with guidance materials for parents and carers, at around:

• eight months

• 18 months, and

• three to four years.

Ask your health visitor, Sure Start Children's Centre or library for more information. Books are carefully selected to give young children an introduction to the world of stories, rhymes and pictures. Books are also available for children who have problems with hearing or vision. For more information, including about activities in your local area, go to www.bookstart.org.uk

- Interact with your baby/child as much as possible, sing and talk to them. This will help them to learn their communication skills. Also spend lots of time reading to them and helping them to read and write.

- **Toys;** Use a variety of toys that educate and stimulate them i.e. bright colours and sounds etc.

  - Wrap toys in cling film if they have loose parts when you store them
  - Have a toy box that you can throw toys in or plastic storage boxes and cover with material (it is better to have a toy box without a lid for younger children, to avoid any accidents with the lid).

- **Teach life skills;** As well as teaching a child the basics; reading and writing, and teaching them to be creative and explore with paints and colours (which is also very important). It is a good idea to teach life skills such as how to swim and as child gets older teach them basic first aid.

- **Teach your child sign language or another language;** If your child is doing well with his/her current language skills you can teach them another language or even sign language as this is a very useful life skill.

- **Teach your child to be able to use both hands;** If your child can manage it, it is good to be able to use both hands, that way if a child gets an injury in one hand s/he can use the other without having to learn all over again.

Baby development;

90% of your child's brain is developed by age 3, therefore what you teach them and how you develop them from a baby is very important;

- It is therefore a good idea to participate in lots of activities which will stimulate and develop the baby's brain. Be creative and play with paint and colour, let your baby explore different textures too.
- Music and sound is also good to develop baby. You can play music and sing to baby, or you can use everyday house hold items as instruments (such as pans and wooden spoons to make drums).
- Join mother and baby groups and attend local children's centres so that your baby/child gets exposed to a wide range of activities and also gets to mix with other children. Ask your health visitor about local children's centres. They are looking to put midwifery into children's centres instead of doctors. If you have a query go to the children's centre and if they can't help you, they will sign post you elsewhere. Children's centres also have drop in centres and you can have child's development (speech and language checked).
- It is important that your child gets to mix with other children to develop his/her social skills and give him/her confidence.
- As your child gets older, speak to your child like you would an adult and have discussions on various topics, that way your child will be able to hold conversations with adults and will be able to have well structured conversations.
- Keep talking to your child and encourage your child to talk back, in order to develop good communication skills.
- Encourage baby to move to develop co-ordination skills, lay toys around baby so baby has to reach for them.
- Don't keep your baby lying down, get your baby moving and sitting up asap in order to develop motor skills. The head will need supporting at first (it varies from child to child when they will be strong enough to hold their head but it will need supporting for at least the first 6 weeks).
- Sing and chat to your baby and encourage him/her to raise his/her head.
- In the night you have to put baby to sleep on his/her back but in the day you should put baby to sleep on his/her side and give baby tummy time.
- **You can do courses such as caring and trust or triple P.**
- The youngest in year may find work at school harder than the other children because s/he will be younger, sometimes the teachers may forget the age gap and think that the child is not developing as much as the others in the class. You need to rember the age gap and bear this in mind. On the plus side s/he will be with older children and may therefore be pushed more and so may develop quicker for his/her age.

Returning to work and Childcare

Maternity leave

- Whilst on leave you may want to suspend any trade union subs, check pension implications of not earning wages etc..
- Prepare for going back (as well as making the most of KIT days), get a next years diary and write in a to-do list of this to do when you come back, you may want to include things such as;
    - Think about going back to work and child care, you may want to have child care vouchers come out of your wages (you and your partner may want to do this, out of both your wages in order to get the maximum benefit).
    - Check any policy/structural changes
    - Don't assume knowledge – get refresher training and updates.
    - Get set up on new systems / new software updated on your pc
    - Get re-issued with PPE & lap top etc
    - Take out of office/filters off of your email
    - Perhaps set up a new folder for any old emails and file them in here, then check the old ones some at a time when you have free time, so you can therefore concentrate on new emails only.
    - Do forward/development plan for projects and training etc.

- 3-4 months before arrange when you are coming back to work and speak to your line manager/HR and do your return to work form;

Options can include taking off a full year as maternity pay and then either saving the leave you accrued whilst you were off to take later, or taking this at the end to give you longer off, or using this leave to go part time. Alternatively you may want to take less maternity leave i.e. 11 months and the rest as annual leave. Before going on maternity leave you may also want to see how much leave you can carry over, as you may want to take the maximum annual leave at the end of you maternity leave. Check with HR that your manager submitted forms/get confirmation from HR of everything in writing.

Before starting back you may want to go in for a refresher/update. You will need to;

- Know your passwords and door codes
- Ensure your password works and you have access to car park (know where to park and are aware of changes etc).

When start getting your full pay again;

- check tax code is correct, re-instate trade subs (if appropriate) and check pension comes out correctly.
- Re-do direct debits and accounts to make necessary adjustments for new income, i.e. re-instate mortgage payments to full amount (if you had reduced them whilst you were off).

N.B. It takes 2-3 months to get back into it after being off for a year

Before going back to work check out different scenarios of how many hours working, what you will earn, what benefits you will be entitled to and what child care costs (that way you can decide when its best to go back to work and how long for etc). Bear in mind that you may need to register with a nursery up to a year in advance.

WOMEN IN BUSINESS; MAKE MATERNITY LEAVE WORK FOR YOU SAYS
WHILE YOU'RE ON MATERNITY LEAVE, BE SNEAKY ABOUT WHO REPLACES YOU
"Tempted to choose a replacement who doesn't do as good a job? That's a mistake says
Suzanne Doyle-Morris, author of Beyond the Boys Club: Strategies for Achieving Career
Success As a Woman Working in a Male-dominated Field. "If something goes wrong, it's the
person on maternity leave who get the blame, so you want someone competent." Avoid an
ambitious competitor by finding a recommended replacement with a history of doing
maternity cover. "Overlap with her for a few weeks" says Doyle-Morris, "Build up a rapport
and make her a gatekeeper who will keep you informed." and when RETURNING FROM
MATERNITY LEAVE "KEEP BABY TALK TO A MINIMUM "Talk to your boss about how
keen you are to get back to work, not about how you're missing your baby" advises Doyle-
Morris. "Flagging up your problems can make you look less committed. Keep everything
work focused. Say 'The baby's great – what's going on in the office?"

TAKE CONTROL OF YOUR FIRST DAY BACK

Only 10% of women surveyed by the NCT had a re-introduction on their return to work. Ask
your boss or office ally you provide you with door codes and computer passwords so you
can enter seamlessly on your first day and avoid the feeling that you no longer belong."

I packed all my work stuff in 1 box and put it in the shed. I put on the top a to do list of all the
things I wanted to do when I got back, admin that had to be sorted out, projects to start,
courses to sign up to & catch up refresher training to organise (you can do some of this on
your KIT days too).

Career/work life balance;

- Once you have had the baby your priorities change, you can have a career but it may
  take longer, don't let your family suffer. You can't do everything as you need time to
  rest and relax and don't want to be ratty and not be there for your kids either. You
  can do everything but something will suffer, you can't do everything well and be
  happy without stressing yourself out.
- Think of the bigger picture and what you want out of life, then decided what to do and
  plan how you are going to do it, what hours to work etc. Do a high level plan first by
  looking at the bigger picture and what the goals are, think about the main aim that
  you want to achieve and why you are doing something, looks at the Ws and H
  (what?, where?, why?, who? and how?), rather than getting bogged down with the
  detail.

- It is hard trying to achieve everything and thinking you can do it all when you have a child, learning how to manage a child is a learning curve in itself and sleep and rest are so important and time for you to just 'be'. Life is not always about 'doing' but you need to make time for just 'being' as well. I've realised you can get balance in life, priorities do change but you make it work.
- Your life changes but this is not necessarily a bad thing, instead enrich your life. Take on other activities with your baby, meet new friends etc. - the more you put in the more you will get out.
- Many parents worry that going back to work will have a detrimental effect on their child's well being. This is not true, sometimes it is better because you may be happier and have more security for your family by working, as long as you ensure that when you are at home that you spend quality time with your child/children; A study conducted by Ellen Galinsky of the Families and Work Institute in 1999 found that the greatest wish for children was not to spend more time with their parents but to spend more 'quality time with them' 34% of those surved said that their biggest wish was for parents to be less stressed when they are with them. Children accept working parents as a normal part of life, but want their needs recognised by busy and stressed adults. Ensure that if you go to work, when you come home you have time with the baby, perhaps put baby to bed etc.
- When you get in from work change out of your work clothes as these have smells of the outside on them, which the baby can pick up on and maybe upset by.
- Working from home can be lonely and hard to concentrate with baby, you will be isolated as to what is going on and might get passed over for promotion.

- Even if you earn a small out by going back to work you will keep your skills current, may get more opportunites and will be out meeting people but equally you will see your child less so part time for a small wage maybe a compromise.

- Also when you go to get a mortgage you may do better if earning a wage. You may also get the proposed child care allowance.

- Make sure you get the bank holidays back from your maternity leave.

Whist on maternity leave, stay skilled up to keep it easier to return to work;

- Undertake Continued Professional development (CPD) and update your CV, and keep a CPD log, even if the CPD is only reading articles, it still counts towards your CPD and should be recorded.
- Do online courses and conferences.
- Evolve in your job, when you get the opportunity, work on extra projects that give you extra skills, especially in the areas where other jobs are requiring it.
- Even when not at work you should meet people, keep up with current affairs, keep your confidence up and thus your employability.

RETURNING TO WORK;

- Be organised when you go back to work - go to loo before leaving work and have a cup of tea and a snack in afternoon so that you are not too hungry and rushing to get baby sorted with hunger pains etc. because once you rush to the nursery to pick your baby up, then travel home your baby maybe demanding after not seeing you, will need dinner and attending too and you won't have chance to eat, drink, or go to the toilet for a while.

- After a couple of weeks you will feel more used to having your baby in the nursery etc. but the first 2 weeks are hard with rushing about and getting used to a new routine and also missing your baby.

- Phased return to work; you could use some of your leave to go back a few days at a time.

- Check if you extend your maternity leave by taking paternity leave that it doesn't count as a break in service and therefore affect your maternity rights.

- Get as much help, at home, as you can when you go back to work; get hired help to do the cleaning etc and batch cook and freeze meals so that you have less to do and you have more quality time on your days off to spend with your baby. It will also be more important than ever now that your partner does jobs around the home too.

- Be consistent - get baby sitter to be consistent with your methods (also both you and your partner need to be consistent with your methods and routine).
- If you are thinking about home working – can you work with the distractions and will you feel isolated? You may also find that the time you spend on your work creeps up and eats into your home life and time with your baby.
- Keep calm, especially when you first take your to nursery as your baby will pick up on it if you feel sad/stressed and will feel unsettled and won't want to stay.

Giving notice about returning to work

Your employer should assume that you will be taking your full entitlement of 52 weeks unless you tell them otherwise. You will be due back to work on the day after the 52-week period of maternity leave.

If you want to take all of your leave, you simply go back to work on that day.

If you decide not to take some or all of your maternity leave, whether Ordinary Maternity Leave (OML) or Additional Maternity Leave (AML), you should give eight weeks' notice to return to work early. Even if you only wish to take OML, or you just want to be off work while you still

get maternity pay, you must give eight weeks' notice of your return as you will in fact be returning early.

If you don't give this notice and just turn up at work before the end of your maternity leave, your employer can refuse to allow you to work for up to eight weeks or until the end of your leave, whichever is earlier. If you change your mind and wish to continue taking your maternity leave, you must give your employer eight weeks' notice before the earlier date of return.

The law does not allow you to work for two weeks (four weeks if you work in a factory) after childbirth. This period is known as **Compulsory Maternity Leave**. You will not be allowed to return to work during this time.

Your job when you go back

When you go back to work after AML, you have the right to return to the same job. But if your employer can show that this is not reasonably practicable, you have the right to be offered a suitable alternative job on at least the same terms and conditions. If the job no longer exists, this could be a redundancy situation and you should get advice. You should also be offered any suitable alternative vacancies if your post is made redundant while you are on maternity leave.

If you need more time off work

If you stay off work after your maternity leave has ended, you will lose your right to return to the same job. If you need more time off you could do one of the following:

• Ask your employer if you can take annual leave immediately after your maternity leave. Your paid holiday continues to accrue during maternity leave so you may have some holiday owing to you.

• Take some parental leave at the end of your maternity leave (see page 172). You must give 21 days' notice to take parental leave, and it is usually unpaid, unless your employer offers paid parental leave.

• If you cannot return because you are ill, you can take sick leave as long as you follow your employer's sickness procedures.

If you are not able to take annual leave and don't have enough notice to ask for parental leave, you can still ask your employer if they will agree to a further period off work (this will usually be unpaid). You should ask your employer to confirm this agreement in writing and to confirm that you will have the right to return to the same job. You should also check whether your employer is counting this as part of your parental leave entitlement.

Other entitlements

Most employers offer 3 days dependency leave for emergencies such as nursery etc. Most nursery's adopt a policy where if the child is sick the nursery may not let child go in but may still charge you.

NB. Check if your employer offers child care vouchers/contributions if you work during school holidays as some employers offer this.

Separating from baby to go to work

Separation anxiety – being upset when you leave is very common because they don't understand when you are returning as they have no concept of time. Make good byes short and reassuring with a kiss.
Separation anxiety can start from around 8 months and last for up to 2 years. It can be triggered by new unfamiliar environments for instance your child may be happy to be left with granny but not happy to be left at the nursery. Thankfully it doesn't affect all children. Don't sneak out instead go with a jolly goodbye and then come back when you say you will. Your child may not feel safe and so needs you, as your child's memory develops they will realise that you go and then return when you say, each time will get a little easier and the independence is good for them too.

Why sudden clinginess happens; You have become the most important person in your baby's life, and he feels safe and happy when he is with you. When he was younger, you could leave the room and he wouldn't notice; out of sight, out of mind. But now that he's a bit older, he realises when you're not there and becomes upset. If he sees you leave, he can't be sure when you'll come back again. For all he knows, you have vanished into thin air and may never return. You know where you are going, what you are going to do and how long you will be, but he doesn't. When your baby becomes a little older, he will learn that you will always return when you leave the room or drop him off with the childminder, but right now he will cry for you every time you go. Psychologists and child experts call this 'separation anxiety'.

How to cope; The best way to cope with a clingy baby is to accept that for this period of your baby's life he will be happiest if he can be with you while you go about your daily routines. This can be easy if you are mostly at home. However, if you have returned to work, or have to leave your baby with someone else while you attend to other things, then you will have some difficult goodbyes.

If you ignore your baby's need to have you nearby, he may keep an even closer eye on you, and be less able to play on his own while you get on with things.

Working at home; If you are at home, you may find it easy to fit in your baby's need to be with you as you get on with what you need to do. Position your baby so that he can see you getting on with your things, while he plays with his. If you have to go into another room, take him with you or give him time to follow you if he's crawling. You may have a small area in each room where he can play happily: the high chair in the kitchen; a play mat or playpen in the living room; a selection of toys in the bedroom; and bath toys and sponges that he can play with in the bathroom.

Leaving your baby to go to work. The frantic rush to get everything ready for work, to get your baby's things ready for nursery, crèche or the childminder, and to get there on time, can be hard work. It's even more difficult if your baby becomes very upset when you leave. You may be torn between comforting him and knowing that you should be on your way. It will help if you know you are leaving him with another 'special' person who your baby likes, knows and trusts. Perhaps he has a key worker or designated carer, or maybe there is one friend or relative who you know your baby enjoys being with. He may still be upset when you leave but if he is usually happy with that person he will soon settle down once you have gone. Many parents who leave a screaming baby feel anxious and guilty… only to find out that their baby was playing happily within five minutes of being left. Arrange to call the nursery or childminder when you get to work so that you can be reassured. If your baby doesn't settle, then it is always worth reconsidering your childcare arrangements for peace of mind.

Hello and goodbye; If you mark the end of each separation with a 'Mummy's back again now' or similar greeting, this will help your baby to learn that you always do and always will return.

Losing your patience

There may be times your baby's constant need to be with you becomes too much; you can't even go to the loo in peace! If you start to get impatient or irritated, it may help to think about the situation from your baby's point of view: he loves you and it really matters to him that you are nearby. Remember, he won't be like this forever; this phase will pass.

It may also be hard for you leaving your baby, sometimes it maybe harder for you leaving your baby than it is for your baby.

Other tips;

When you go to nursery/crèche they stick a sticky label over your bag with your childs name on it. If you have a nice change bag that you don't want to get ruined either take a cheaper change bag for those days or get a luggage label and put your childs name on it, or you could even go one step further and get a personalised luggage label with your child's name and photo on.

If you have a day off on Wednesday you only work for 2 days at a time before having a break. They say that your child should do 2 days at nursery at least in order to settle and get a routine, apparently one day isn't enough, but 2 times ½ days is okay.

It is a good idea to get a nursery get one near your home not your work in case you have a day off and are sick, move jobs etc. when looking at nurserys think about the next stage up – do they take older children, its nice if the can stay at the same one for consistency.

Going back to work/regular activities gives you structure and focus and something else to think about which is good. As babies can be distracting and it is easy to get consumed into baby world so you need a break and change of scenery.

Here are some tips to help you and baby with the transition;

- Before you go back to work and leave baby gradually get baby to spend time with other people, perhaps leave them longer with grandparents, so that get used to being left.
- Visit the nursery/childminder with your child and stay there with your child, a few weeks before child is starting to get him/her used to the surroundings. Then leave him/her there for a ½ day and then increase this to a day (when you are not at work and can pop in to settle him/her).
- When you do eventually go out to work don't sneak out, wave and tell your baby that you will be back, otherwise your baby won't understand. S/he will feel abandoned and will feel insecure and may think that s/he may be left again, s/he won't trust that you will be back and as such will become insecure and cry when you are not there. Whereas secure confident children who recognise a pattern that parent says bye, then leaves, and then comes back will know that you will come back and will be more likely to play and not worry. Having said this all babies will cry at first but once a pattern is developed your baby will become more settled. You could try at first leaving baby for short burst, say I am going now and kiss baby goodbye, go out for 15mins and then come back and say hello I am home. Baby will soon learn that you came back and that goodbye is followed by you leaving but s/he will be okay and you will be back.

Consider and plan carefully any separations from your baby. *'Hellos and goodbyes are important and should be lovely moments of connection, rather than hurried non-events'* – M Sunderland, The Science of Parenting.

- When you are returning from long term leave to catch up on your work - Start from what you need to achieve today and this week (which is your everyday job and not reading old emails) and then work backwards if you have time, then you won't have a feeling of always playing catch up. The classic and very good response to someone challenging you about work not completed from 2 months or so ago is that you've been out of the office for x months, what did they do when they realised you were not available to respond or sort out their query? If they answer 'nothing' just reply 'that's a shame' and ask what they still need and when by.
- Before you are due to go back to work arrange to go in to have a catch up, then schedule in some refresher time, refresher training and ask for a smaller workload for the first few weeks whilst you catch up (don't arrange to start any new large projects in the first few weeks, whilst you settle in).
- It may be a good idea to use some of the holiday that you have accrued to go back into work part time for a few weeks whilst you ease into it.
- Check with your work if they offer child care vouchers and check what benefits you may be entitled too. Some companies operate a scheme where you pay your child care directly out of your wages, this is pre-tax, so you will only get taxed on what is left on your wages and therefore are getting a small amount of tax relief.
- If you are breastfeeding you will need to get into a routine of expressing at least 1-2 months before. You will need time to work out how much you'll need to express, and

to let your body adjust. If you are switching to a bottle your baby may need time to get used to it.

- Ease yourself in gently and meet friends for lunch before you go back.
- Let your baby settle in at a relaxed pace.
- Your baby will pick up on how you feel so try and be positive.
- Don't rush them in the moning. Get up early before your baby and get their breakfast and yourself ready first. Spend quality time with them over breakfast.
- Create a special goodbye routine so that your baby knows when it is time to go.
- Make sure that your baby has familiar toys and food etc. to help them settle.
- Babies like routine so try and find a nursery where they will implement your own routine so that your baby isn't disprupted too much.

Tips when looking for a childcare provider

Inevitably, there will be times when you need to arrange for your child to be looked after by someone else, perhaps because you have decided it's time to go back to work. Ideally, whatever arrangements you make should give your child plenty of opportunities to spend time with other children. So, for example, you could think about using playgroups and nursery classes as well as a childminder or nanny.

Note that all childminders and daycare providers (except nannies who work in your home) should be registered with Ofsted. Your local FIS will be able to give you information about the care options available in your area. Your local information service can provide additional help to parents of disabled children in finding suitable childcare. You can also get information at www.childcarelink.gov.uk or at www.familyinformationservices.org.uk

N.B. You may need to register with a nursery to go on the waiting list at least a year before, you may have to pay a holding fee. You may want to register for 5 days and you can reduce it later, it may not be possible to increase the day's later if you only choose to pick a few days (check what the holding deposit will be if you book extra days).

Types of childcare;

- Child minder
- Nursery (private, state and independent school nursery's)
- Play groups
- Pre-school groups
- Nannies
- Before and after school clubs
- Mobile child care (mobile child care are mobile nursery, this is very good for childcare at large events such as weddings, where there will be lots of children).
- Agencies that match you with childcare (you have to pay a fee but it can help to eliminate some of the stress, however they will only search with nursery on their books and there may be a good local nursery that is not on their books).

High quality childcare enables children to fulfil their potential by learning about the world around them through play in a safe and supportive environment. A childcare setting providing high quality care will ensure children are safe and well cared for at all times, whilst also encouraging children to be conscious of their surroundings and develop more awareness of their own safety. They should also actively encourage children to make healthy choices. In a high quality childcare setting, children will be given a variety of learning experiences, both through activities that they initiate as well as ones given to them by staff.

Choosing a childminder;

Do you pay someone to look after your child or children in their own home? If you do and your child is under five years old, they must be registered on the Early Years Register with Ofsted before they do this. If they wish to look after children between the ages of five and seven, they must join the Childcare Register. Failure to register is a criminal offence and illegal childminders can be fined.

If they only look after children who are aged eight and over, joining the Childcare Register is voluntary.

There are around 500 registered childminders in Hillingdon. If you use one of these you may be eligible for tax credits to help pay for your childcare.

There are risks around using someone who isn't registered. These include them not having had a CRB check or any first aid training; their house may not be safe for children. They will not be insured, so if, for example, they have an accident while driving your child or something happens to their house while they are caring for your child, their car or home insurance will be invalid.

All registered childminders and everyone over-16 who lives with them will have been CRB checked, and their house will be safety checked by Ofsted. They will also have had first aid training and hold a certificate, and many of them will have official childcare qualifications. They are also required to follow the Early Years Foundation Stage, meaning they will provide activities that are appropriate for your child's age and promote their development.

Anyone registered to child mind will have a certificate provided by Ofsted that you can ask to see.

Childminder pros and cons	
Pros	Cons
Your child will be in a home environment	Your child may not be mixing with other children the same as at a nursery.
Childminders can support families for years as children grow up	There is no one to supervise what the child minder is doing so you have to trust them totally.
Can be flexible hours	If the child minder is off sick there is no one to cover, where as a nursery will have other staff.
Childminders can make the most of local parks, playgrounds, toy libraries, drop-in groups and community centres. Often children have the chance to make good friends with the other children who go to their childminder. Every childminder is different so look for someone who will suit	It may be harder to change the contract if you want to increase/decrease hours.

your family and your child's needs.	
Childminders can often be flexible about the hours that they work and they should provide your child with lots of care, fun and learning.	There is no one to complain to if things go wrong (although you can complain to Ofsted there is no manager as such, as there would be with a nursery).
	If the child minder decides to have a baby or move away etc. you are stuck looking for another childminder.

Because its one on one care your child will develop strong emotional bonds with the child minder. This can be a good thing and you may stay in contact with the childminder for many years, as a family friend. However if it doesn't work out with that child minder it can be very hard emotionally for your child.

Questions to ask

How many children will there be with a childminder?

Childminders can care for up to six children under the age of eight at any one time. Most childminders are registered for three children under five and three children under eight. They are normally limited to caring for one child under twelve months at any one time. However childminders who work with an assistant may be able look after larger groups of children.

The childminder's own children are taken into account and counted in these numbers.

What age range are the children with a childminder?

Children can go to a childminder from a few months old right through until they reach secondary school. Check with the childminder what ages they are registered to care for.

When are childminders open?

Childminders are self employed and so they decide on their working hours. Most childminders will provide you with childcare between the hours of 8am and 6pm. Some childminders will work early mornings, evenings and weekends as well. You will need to negotiate hours, terms and conditions with the childminder.

What about part-time childcare?

Many childminders are happy to provide families with part-time places for children. They often drop children off at school and pick them up. Childminders can also take your child to a playgroup or school nursery as part of the routine.

How much does a childminder cost?

Childminders set their charges themselves. Charges vary in different areas.

Nurseries;

Most nurseries are registered with Ofsted and inspected at least once within three to four years of the implementation of the Early Years Foundation Stage (September 2008). They are usually open all day for most weeks in the year. Part-time places are often available.

Nurseries are run by a team of staff and activities should be planned to help children enjoy learning. At nursery children can enjoy making friends, playing outside, sharing meals and trying out new skills.

There are different types of nursery with different ways of operating so look around for one that suits your child and you.

Nurseries must be registered with Ofsted. This means checks are carried out to make sure the staff are suitable to look after children. At least half of the staff in a nursery must be trained.

A check on the nursery premises is carried out to make sure the building is safe and suitable for children. The nursery is inspected at least once every three or four years to make sure the nursery is continuing to provide a safe and suitable service.

There should be a set number of staff at each nursery to work with the children.

You should find one member of staff for every eight children aged three to five, one member of staff for every four children aged two to three and one member of staff for every three children aged under two.

You can ask to see the nursery's registration certificate and latest inspection report.

Pros	Cons
Opportunities for children to learn and play with friends around the same age	It is less personable, there are lots of different staff who may come and go making it harder for your child to form relationships with them.
Usually geared to the needs of children with working parents	They will have strict rules about when you can and can't bring your child and won't be as flexible as a childminder.
Some nurseries offer free, part-time early education or pre-school places for children aged three and four	There are lots of other children so your child will get less attention, it is also more like a school setting than a family one. This can be good if it's just for a few days as the child will then be used to mixing with other children ready for school, however if it is everyday your child may miss out of forming close bonds that s/he would have formed in

	a family setting.
The nursery will be regularly inspected	

There are different types of nursery:

Private nursery - This is designed to cater for the children of working parents and the type you are most likely to find in your area. They are independently run and fees do apply, even though your child may be entitled to a free part-time place.

Local authority nursery - Run by the local authority for children in the local community who need support.

Workplace nursery - Some employers run childcare schemes for children of their employees

How many children will there be in a nursery?

Most nurseries provide places for between 26 and 40 children although some are smaller and others larger. Children are usually divided into much smaller groups based on their age.

What age range are the children in a nursery?

Nurseries are for children aged up to five. Some nurseries have places for babies and toddlers as well as for children aged three to five. Some nurseries are part of childcare schemes which also provide childcare for older children.

When are nurseries open?

Most nurseries open at about 8.00am and close at around 6.00pm. Some offer different hours for the children of people working shifts. Most nurseries are open all year round except for public holidays.

What about part-time childcare?

Many nurseries are happy to offer you part-time places. Often they organise these into morning and afternoon sessions.

How much does a nursery cost?

Nursery charges vary in different areas. If your childcare provider is part of the Nursery Education Funding scheme, you may be eligible to receive either a free part-time place or, if your child is attending for longer than the free entitlement, you may receive money off the cost of the place at the nursery.

Visiting the childcare setting

It is important to visit the setting more than once, preferably at different times of the day, prior to your child starting. Trust your instincts and your first impressions. You will get a sense of what the setting is like from seeing it for yourself and meeting the staff.

These are some of the areas you may wish to reassure yourself about:

- Will my child have one key person responsible for their care?

- Do my child and I feel welcome?

- Do they value my child as an individual?

- Will I be kept up to date about their learning and progress?

- What are the 'settling-in' arrangements?

- How many staff are first aid trained?

- What are the staff ratios?

- What meals are provided? (you may want to check the cooks qualifications and look at the cleanliness of the kitchen area).

- If my child doesn't eat will an alternative be offered?

- Is food re-heated and if so how?

- What are the times/routines for food, sleep, activites etc?

- Do they have a weekly plan of activites? What activites do they do? Do they take your child on trips? What are the policies for taking children out – do you need to giver permission for each trip?

- Do they have free flow in the garden area?

- How secure is the garden area?

- Is there a separate quiet area for your child to sleep if they want to sleep at a different time to the other children?

- What is the age range of the children?

- Can your child take his/her own beaker?

- Do they have a daily diary?

- What things are recorded and how often? i.e. do they do a log each day of when your child has a nappy change, what they eat, when they slept, how they played and felt etc.

- Is the changing area open/do they have 2 staff that change them?

- What toys are put out?

- How often are the toys cleaned?

- How often is the area cleaned?

- What cleaning chemicals are used?

- Do they have their own separate matresses and blanket?

- How often and where are the matress and bankets cleaned?

- What is the security for collection like?

- Is the manager always there? Is the manager there to speak to at the beginning/end of the day?

- Is the nursery easy to get to? Is there parking nearby for drop off & collection?

- Do they have long/ appropriate hours and do they have flexible drop in sessions if you need extra days/hours?

- Do they do sleep checks? How often? (it should be every 10 mins). Where is this recorded? Do they have a visable sleep chart? / Whos job is it to do the checks – is their a rota.

- Is the manager always on site? If not is the manager there at the beginning/end of each day?

- Do they use trainees or bank and agency staff and if so are they used as additional staff or are they used to make up the ratios?

- What do they do on snow days, do they close?

- Do they have a highchair to feed your baby? How is food given, is it at the table, do they all sit together etc.

- Is there a separate area for babies and how do they ensure that they toys are age appropiate (i.e. babies don't pick up toys for older children and choke).

- Does someone keep an eye on the babies in particular i.e. when they are learning to walk?

- Do they also have a monitor in the sleep room?

- What is the age range of the babies?

- What activities - day trips do they offer?
- Do they have free flow where the children can go outside (Ofsted says that all nurseries should have this).
- What facilities - toys do they have?
- It is good if the nursery writes everything down, however it maybe better that less time is spent making notes and more time on children.

N.B.

- When your baby gets older its easier to leave them.

- The difference between a state nursery and day care is the hours. If you work full time you will have your baby in day care, then when your baby gets to 3 years old they will still need to be in day care if you are working full time, but if not they can get into a state nursery. So you also need to think about where you are putting them and where they can go until they are ready for full time school. The nursery where my son is going provides day care until they are old enough to go to school (once my son turns 3 he will get 15 hours paid for). So you need to think based on your circumstances you may want a private day care, or you may want a state nursery that offers nursery or day care. You may want a state nursery attached to that school to get him/her used to it. That way s/he will go to school with the same friends tha s/he met at nursery.

- You may want to change your routine to fit in with the nursery. Although most nurserys will fit in around your babies schedule it is best if they are in the same routine as everyone else at nursery, so find out what the routine is before you take them in. That way they can join in with the activities and won't miss out. Otherwise they may be sleeping when activites are going on an when the other babies are playing they will want to sleep.

- Check that they have a no mobile phone policy for the staff on duty.

- It maybe a good idea for you to write down/tell the nursery if your baby had a change of routine the night before i.e. if your baby was up late the night before you need to tell them because they need to know in case your baby is tired and needs an extra sleep that day.

- Larger nursery purpose built nurserys are better in some ways because they have more staff going through and more resources etc. It is better if they have more staff than the ratio although they may not.
- **Nursery rules are changing there will be less workers per child but greater govt tax relief for childcare regardless of earnings.**
- Nursery is good for a child but not at a year, they are better with parents for the first few years. However they do need interaction with other children, especially if they don't have any siblings. Most people have to put their children in nursery at a year, or younger so that they can go back to work.
- When looking for a school look at social side of it as well as just the educational side because social skills are important too.
- Boy/girl learn differently so educationally single sex schools are good however mixed schools are good to develop social skills for boys to be able to deal with girls etc.
- Check the amount of food that the nursery gives them is enough. A lot of nurserys won't give them an evening meal so you may want to work your timmings out so that you can leave work, get your baby home and all have dinner at home together.

Things to consider

• Do the premises look safe? For example, is the front door secure?

Look for covers on plug sockets. Are children able to access the

kitchen area?

• Was I asked to sign in and out when I visited?

• What are the arrangements in the event of an emergency, such

as the building needing to be evacuated?

• Are the children told and explained any rules and expectations,

which are in place to keep them safe?

• How do staff raise any concerns about safety? Are there any

examples of what has happened as a result of concerns raised?

• Are the activities challenging but safe?

• What are the arrangements for child protection? Who is the member of staff with responsibility for this?

• How do they make sure people working with children have a Criminal Records Bureau check (police check)?

• Do the meals, snacks and drinks look healthy? (A menu should be displayed.)

• If my child wants a drink of water, can they get one when they want it?

• Have they asked me if my child has any dietary/medical/cultural needs and likes/dislikes? How do they take account of these?

• How many members of staff are qualified first aiders?

• Do the children look happy and secure; are they having fun?

• How are they helped to feel confident, secure and encouraged to enjoy themselves?

• Do the staff look interested, relaxed and as if they are enjoying being with the children?

• How are children's feelings acknowledged and are they encouraged and given the opportunity and time to talk about them?

• How will I be involved in my child's learning and development? Are there opportunities for me to talk to my child's key person? (They may have workshops for parents or open days, for example.)

• What will be the routine be for my child's day? Can this be flexible to suit my child's needs?

• Is there a variety of things for them to do that are appropriate for their age?

• Do staff and children play together? Are they taken outdoors daily for as long as possible? Do they have activities such as sand play/water?

• Are children encouraged to be independent in all aspects of their everyday activities and learning?

Pros & cons with nursery & family:

- easier to say what you want to nursery
- nursery know all new research & can give development advice
- they mix with other children
- it's not 1-2-1 attention although that can be good to stop your child getting spoilt
But nothing beats time bonding with family & the rate you learn with 1-2-1 they also learn morals & values from family members .

Check if the nursery has training days it closes and when it closes after Christmas. You shouldn't have to pay when they are closed but if your child doesn't go due to sickness or holiday you will usually still have to pay.

Check your nursery's sick policy to ensure that they are not sending your child home all the time when they should be keeping him/her at nursery. For instance some may send home with conjunctivitis where as some may say if your child has had it for over 24 hours and has got medication they can stay, ensure you have a copy of the policy and they are not fobbing you off, sending your child home too often.

There's no single type of childcare that best suits every family. Many young children have a mix of early learning and childcare from nurseries, childminders, playgroups and friends and relatives. Grandparents often play an important role in helping different elements of childcare fit together, for example by looking after children after nursery until their parents come home from work.

It is good for your child to have a mix of childcare. They need close bonds with carers and family members but also need time mixing with other children. Even if you are looking after your own child full time it is a good idea to take your child to a children's centre to play with other children or attend play groups. However if you can don't leave your child in a nursery all day every day, perhaps get a friend or relative to care for the child for one day a week. Furthermore if you are away from your child all week ensure you set aside quality time for your child at evening and weekends.

It is great to have family members or friends look after your children, however bear in mind that it is harder for you to tell them how you want your child brought up (they maybe soft on them and sneak sweets) and if you do pay them unless they register as childminders you can't claim any money back for what you give them, you can't use childcare vouchers either. Also they will not mix with as many children and they will not be aware of the early years curriculum and won't have as many toys or offer as many development activities as a nursery. They will however love and care for your child and you can trust them.

You may find that having a nanny is the best form of childcare, if you have two kids. A nanny or childminder will be cheaper than a nurdery if you have 2 children. It means that your children are in their own home and you don't have to take time off if they are sick, like u would if they were at nursery and were sick and therefore not allowed to go. However if your nanny is sick there will be no one to cover and you will need to take time off.

Some nurseries do a discount if you have a sibling at the same nursery. Bear in mind that at the moment (feb 2014) the 15 hours the government offer for day care (when your child is 3 instead of going to a state nursery, or 2 if you are on benefits) is term time only and doesn't include food. Also state nurseries close in the school holidays so you will need childcare.

- When you have kids rather than just considering working full or part time look at other options such as portfolio career - Get a well paid contracting job and work for 6 months then have 3 months off etc. Or do freelance teaching and freelance beauty work etc.

Extra things to know as a mother;

Norland College teach their nanny's driving skills and self defence, among other things. These are all good skills to have. It is good to do a driving course, especially a session on a skid pad, before the icy weather in the winter.

You may want to do a skid pad driving course. It is a good idea to have good driving skills, possibly and advanced driving licence, personal safety skills and first aid skills. Most children's centres provide first aid courses free. Also if the grandparents look after a child who is under 3 they can attend first aid courses.

GETTING IT IN WRITING

If you're signing a written agreement, check all the details. Examples of contracts for childminders are available from the National Childminding Association (NCMA).

Help with costs;

Every three- and four-year-old is entitled to 12.5 hours of free early learning per week, for at least 38 weeks of the year. (From September 2010 this will go up to 15 hours per week.) These sessions are available in Ofsted-registered Sure Start Children's Centres, nurseries, preschools and with some registered childminders as well as at some private nursery schools. You can use these places to take a break, even if you are not working or training.

From September 2009, there will also be some free targeted early education places for two-year-olds in all parts of the country.

Tax credits

Families who are in work and who pay for Ofsted-registered childcare can get financial help with those costs through tax credits. Depending on your household income, tax credits can give you back up to 80 percent of your childcare costs, up to a maximum cost of £175 a week for one child and £300 a week for two or more children. It's worth checking out with HM Revenue & Customs (HMRC) or with your local Families Information Service.

Childcare vouchers

Some employers offer childcare vouchers or 'salary sacrifice', where you offer up part of your salary in return for help with the cost of childcare. These schemes give you the first £55 a week of vouchers free from tax and National Insurance. Some families will be able to get tax credits as well as vouchers. Check it out with HMRC and see how much you could get.

Flexible working

As well as all the high-quality childcare arrangements that are on offer, if your child is 16 or under (17 or under if disabled) and you've worked for your employer for at least 26 weeks, then you're entitled to ask for flexible working. Flexible working is designed to help you cope with your family responsibilities. It can include options such as flexi-time, homeworking, job-sharing and compressed hours, and is built around your own needs. If you're entitled to make the request then your boss will have to consider it, and can only say no if there's a clear business reason, which must be given in writing. These days most employers recognise that flexible working for staff makes good business sense.

At Work;

• Talk to your boss about your work and your family needs

• Think flexible working – why not see if you qualify?

• Don't be embarrassed about saying: "I've got to go home now to collect the kids"–everyone has commitments outside work.

EMERGENCY! It happens sometimes: your childcare provider falls ill, or there's a problem at the nursery, so you've got no childcare. All employees have the right to take unpaid emergency leave (sometimes called compassionate leave) at very short notice when there's a crisis.

Hiring a baby sitter;
- If you haven't got friends and family you could ask you may want to ask staff at the nursery, that way you know that they are qualified.
- Leave checklists on the fridge with important numbers, medical information and what to do if you can't be contacted on your usual numbers, who to contact next etc.
- For a nursery you will need to provide your routine too, you may also want a log book for the nursery to record things such as nappy changes, what food, drink and naps your baby has. You could make up your own book with a photo of your child on etc.
- If you are having a nanny come to your house show her where everything is or lay all the items out. You could also include a list of fun places to take your child.
- You could spend time with your child and nanny so they can see how you do things and can follow your lead.
- As well as providing a folder with your child's routine, fun places to visit, contact details etc. you may want to include some basic first aid instructions. It is best to get a nanny who is first aid trained but it is good to keep some instructions to hand, as people often panic and forget things in that sort of situation.

- Have a book with routines/schedules where your children need to be when, with maps etc. what they need to take (where their bags are), passes etc. can be in plastic wallets with this. Have medical information and important contact information in with this.

It is a good idea to…

• Give clear instructions to the nursery
• Do a dummy run drive to the nursery to see how long it takes to get there with traffic in the morning
• Drop your child off just before the other parents, avoid dropping off and picking up at the nurserys busy times

Being a working mum

It's hard working full time and being a mum. You think you won't be able to cope. It gets easier as you get used to it. Once you get in a routine and do things on auto pilot its easier, it also gets easier as your baby starts sleeping through the night.

You can do things to help yourself i.e. cook meals in batches at the weekend and freeze them into little tubs. That way when you get home late after work and picking your child up you can zap the meals in the microwave. I put my son in his highchair, put Cbeebies on, give him a drink and a snack and then cook my pre-prepared meal. You can also prepare a meal the night before i.e. prep the raw ingredients, when your baby is in bed, leave it in the fridge and then put it in the slow cooker in the morning, then when you get home from work dinner is done (spag bol is great for this).

As soon as you get in the door, re-stock your babies nursery bag/change bag, get the clothes out for the next day for you and baby especially for baby because if his/her clothes are in their room you don't want to go in when they are in bed. I also have a nappy box downstairs I stock up, I also bring down my babys PJs and check he has spare dummies and a milk carton and bottle upstairs (in case he wakes in the night). I do this first, whilst he plays. I then put him in his highchair with a snack and prepare dinner. I usually find it easier to eat with him, that way he eats better and I know I get to eat. Although sometimes if my husband is home late I wait until he is in bed to eat, although this means I eat very late if he hasn't settled (I tend to only do this on Friday nights).

Once your baby is in bed you can get your clothes and other items ready for work the next day, make some sandwiches, paint your nails and do any other jobs etc. but get an early night if you can, especially if you have important meetings the next day. That way if your baby wakes in the night you have had some sleep and if your baby doesn't wake you can get up early and get sorted before your baby wakes up.

Do your food shopping on line, carry a computer tablet in your handbag and do your online shop between meetings at work etc keep adding to it when you remember things (you can also do the same with on line apps). Then you can order it to come Saturday morning. You can steal time i.e. do your online food shop when you are walking from one meeting room to another. Take advantage of your lunch break to go clothes shopping without your child, to the gym or the bank. If you eat a sandwich whilst at your desk you can then pop out for 30mins to an hour and have eaten in works time whilst working so you don't waste time for food but be sure to still go out so you get a break from your desk, even if its for a walk to clear your mind – it will make you more productive in the long run, also keep your desk clean if you are eating at it, clean the crumbs off your desk daily etc. (I keep tissues, baby wipes, and anti-bacterial desk wipes, and hand sanitizer in my desk along with bottles and cartons of drinks and snacks and cereal bars as I often miss breakfast, nuts are a nutritious snack, also graze boxes also keep bottles of water so if you are rushing around you can take them to meetings and stay hydrated).

Have your emails and a list of quick 5 min tasks, emails to send on your phone. Always arrive at meetings early so you feel prepared and look professional. Whilst you are waiting for late comers to your meetings you can discreetly do your 5 min tasks/send emails, catch up with face book or text your friends.

Have a blue tooth function on your car, you can then make calls on your way to/from work, use time sat in traffic to your advantage and don't waste a single second of time. The more you multi task the more you get done and the more spare time you have with your baby at the evenings and weekends.

No matter how bad your morning is before work have a good morning routine at work to get your sorted.

Arrive at work and turn your computer on. Whilst it is loading up get a cup of tea and snack. Whilst the kettle is boiling you can also check yourself over use your baby wipes to remove smudged make up or milk or baby dribble from your clothes (you could always keep a spare outfit at work or in your car boot). Then have your tea and snack whilst you read your emails and double check your calendar. Fill up a jug of water (so that you can monitor you are drinking enough and don't forget to get up from your desk, walk around and exercise and don't stare at your screen for too long, swap between computer and written work). Write a list of things to do that day/week, highlight the most important and try and do these first. Also write in any jobs you need to do at lunch time i.e. phone through the meter readings etc.

Things to keep in your desk draw;

-mirror, makeup, bodyspray, hairbrush, toothbrush, hair tie, mints.

- hand sanitiser, tissues, cutlery, tea, coffee and cup

- snacks and water, seasoning for food, emergency torch

-baby wipes, anti bacteria wipes (to clean your desk), female products (don't get caught out without them) and headache and intergestion tablets.

- Water jug, cartons of drink

-pens, spare notebooks, celloptape, sissors, stapler and other stationary

- Have scrap paper to write things on whilst you remember

Start winding down for the day and finishing tasks, getting ready for the next day and get ready to leave about 30 mins before you need to leave. That way you won't suddenly remember you had to make a phone call or finish something, which then takes longer making you late. Wash up your cup, empty your bin and leave your desk tidy, that way a. you will feel better when you come into a tidy desk the next day and b. if your child is ill and you are not in the next day you won't have a smelly bin or mouldy cup to come back to. During this time you can also plan out what meetings you have the next day, what you need for them (get this out ready) think about what outfit you need to wear the next day and write a to do list to keep on your desk/or to take home with reminders as appropriate.

Make the weekends full of fun activities so you are spending quality time with your child. That way you will have fun and feel relaxed and you will get to enjoy your child and won't feel like you are missing out and will feel less guilt from being at work. You can do things that involve exercise i.e. swimming, that way you can double up fun time and exercise and save time on having to go to the gym.

Be organised at home – file post as soon as you can. Have plastic draws so toys can be organised in an orderly fashion.

Cut out wasted time, in order to maximise time and keep your home tidy so that you can feel calm. Get flowers to brighten up your time.

Have a place for everything and everything in its home, so that you know where things go and don't waste time looking for things.

Maximise your money, save as much as you can so if you need to take unpaid days off work or later decide you want to go part time you have some money set aside. With kids you always need money for things that you forget i.e. nursery photos (that they forgot to tell you about) etc. save money on other things so you can spend money on important things that you won't be able to get later i.e. nursery photos.

Spend as much time as you can with your child, they grow up too quickly and time with them is precious.

Use your phone note pad to record notes on things they have done/said, you can then copy and paste them onto a word doc and have a book of memories etc to keep as your child grows up.

Try to compartmentalise things i.e. when you are at home don't think about work and when you are at work try and focus on what you are doing, that way you can get everything done and get out of work as quickly as possible, without having to take work home.

You might find even though it is tempting to put your baby to bed earlier so that you can have some time to yourself, if you don't put your baby to bed too early s/he will sleep in, in the morning for longer, giving you longer to get yourself ready before having to attend to your baby.

From bounty; Mums at work - a juggling act

Do you feel that you're treated differently at work these days, or that no-one takes any interest in your precious baby?
While working mums shouldn't expect special treatment, your new status as a mum as well as an employee shouldn't mean you are treated badly.
Luckily, the majority of employers embrace the skills that working mums can and do bring to the workforce, but there will always be a few who ignore it. Legally, like any other employee you shouldn't be bullied or discriminated against as a result of being a mother, or sidestepped for promotion.

Work and families

Although attitudes to working mums have changed dramatically over the past few years, mums still report feeling excluded or resented by colleagues who are not parents. Problems might crop up because you have flexible hours, have to leave on time to pick your baby up from childcare, or are off when your child - or the childminder - is ill.
If you work part time you may miss out on meetings, and you may also miss out on the 'social glue' that helps to make us feel part of a team - impromptu drinks after work, and gossip over lunch or a coffee break. You might feel concerned that you'll miss out on promotion if you work part-time or flexible hours, or don't do the networking outside of work. Your experiences will also depend on your colleagues' situations: if you work with lots of other mums - and dads - they may be more understanding than an office full of young men, for example. Mum of two Melanie says she has a good relationship with all her colleagues 'although I don't join them for drinks after work sadly anymore! There are quite a few part time mums here so they do understand and are very supportive if I am having a wobbly day because I am either missing them or feeling guilty.'
So what can you do when you return to your old job or start a new one to ensure a good relationship with people at work?
Know your legal rights around flexible hours and discrimination.
Try and give your confidence a boost before you step into the workplace so any negative comments or treatment are less damaging to your self-esteem.
Ensure you communicate extremely clearly. If anything, over-communicate. Make sure everyone knows exactly where you are, when, and where you are with your projects. Follow-

up verbal agreements with an email. If you work part-time, make sure everyone knows where to find information on the days when you're not in, and get an update of what's been going on while you were away.

Do some of the social stuff - you might not be able to - or want to - be out for drinks after work every night, but joining in from time to time will keep you in the loop.

The expert view

Gillian Nissim, who founded workingmums.co.uk to connect employers with women returning to work, says it's crucial to develop good communication with your manager and build a network of support from other colleagues and friends in similar positions. 'You may go through bad patches, for instance, when your child is ill or you have been up for several nights with a teething baby, but remember you are not alone, that all things with children go in stages and things will get better.'

And mums' coach Amanda Alexander adds: 'As a working parent, there's always going to be someone somewhere judging you. Get used to it and build your own self-confidence so that you build your immunity to other's opinions. Treat being a working mother as a choice rather than as an impediment and it will help you to deal with the inevitable obstacles positively.'

Education and School

Early education for free

All three and four-year-olds are entitled to a free part-time early education place for two years before they must start school. These free sessions are available in a variety of settings in the public and private sectors, including nursery schools and classes, day nurseries, childminder networks and playgroups. From September 2009, the children from the most economically disadvantaged families in every local authority will also be entitled to up to 15 hours each week of free childcare and early learning. You will also be able to access it more easily at a time that suits your family's needs.

Early years structured learning

Schools and early years providers have to follow a structure of learning, development and care for children from birth to five years old. This is called the Early Years Foundation Stage (EYFS) and it enables your child to learn through a range of activities.

All maintained/independent schools or registered early years providers in the private, voluntary and independent sectors caring for children from birth to five must use the EYFS. This includes:

- reception and nursery classes in maintained and independent schools
- day nurseries
- childminders
- playgroups
- after school and breakfast clubs
- holiday playschemes
- Sure Start Children's Centres
- The following groups are not covered:
- mother and toddler groups
- nannies
- short-term, occasional care (eg crèches)

The EYFS ensures:

- children learn through play
- providers work closely with parents
- you are kept up to date on your child's progress
- the welfare, learning and all-round development of children with different backgrounds and levels of ability, including those with special educational needs and disabilities

After the first day

- If your child has been to a nursery or reception class, they may have had some preparation for primary school and so their transition may be smooth. However, they might still find their initial weeks a period of change and stress.
- Your child may be more tired than usual and need time to relax. You may find that rather than becoming more 'grown up', they may regress or become more difficult or defiant, in response to the stress of a new routine.
- Your child may also have concerns about making friends or be more withdrawn than usual.

What you can do

- In order to provide support or help your child through what can sometimes be a difficult first phase, it may help to:

- set aside time with your child to talk about school and take an interest in what they have been doing
- listen carefully to any worries your child might have
- find out as much as possible about your child's school and what happens there during the day
- try to keep a regular routine at home to keep stress to a minimum
- make sure your child knows what is happening on a day-to-day basis and is informed in advance about any changes to their routine
- encourage your child to build friendships with children in their class
- keep positive as some problems may be resolved as your child adapts to a new way of life
- If you cannot sort out problems your child has by talking to them, you may find it useful to talk to your child's teacher about your concerns.

Starting school;

Legally, children must start formal education no later than the beginning of the school term following their fifth birthday. Many infant and primary schools admit children to their reception classes at four. The reception class will also be following the Early Years Foundation Stage.

If you are offered a school place for your child when they are four, but you would rather they started school later in the school year, you can ask the school to defer entry. But you must take the place during that school year. You cannot hold it over to the next year.

Ofsted reports; All preschools in England are now required to be registered with Ofsted which means they must be inspected every year and at least 50% of the staff are required to be formally trained. Ofsted reports are a great way to find out more about what the playgroup offers and will equip you with detailed info on everything from the quality of care and education to the cleanliness of the building and opportunities for play.

Types of schools;

There are many different types of state school as well as independent schools. To help you make a choice for your child, this page provides some information on each type of school and their admission procedures.

- **Mainstream state schools;** All children in England between the ages of five and 16 are entitled to a free place at a state school. Most go to state schools. Children normally start primary school at the age of four or five, but many schools now have a reception year for four year olds. Children normally leave at the age of 11, moving on to secondary school. Most state schools admit both boys and girls, though some are single-sex. The four main types of state school all receive funding from local authorities. They all follow the National Curriculum and are regularly inspected by Ofsted.
- **Community schools;** A community school is run by the local authority, which: employs the staff, owns the land and buildings, decides which 'admissions criteria' to use (these are used to allocate places if the school has more applicants than places). Community schools look to develop strong links with the local community. They can do this in a number of ways, including providing use of their facilities, or providing services like childcare and adult learning classes.
- **Foundation and Trust schools;** Foundation schools are run by their own governing body, which employs the staff and sets the admissions criteria. Land and buildings are usually owned by the governing body or a charitable foundation. A Trust school is a type of foundation school which forms a charitable trust with an outside partner. For example, a business or educational charity aiming to raise standards and explore

new ways of working. The decision to become a Trust school is taken by the governing body, with parents having a say.

- **Voluntary-aided schools;** Voluntary-aided schools are mainly religious or 'faith' schools, although anyone can apply for a place. As with foundation schools, the governing body: employs the staff, sets the admissions criteria. School buildings and land are normally owned by a charitable foundation, often a religious organisation. The governing body contributes to building and maintenance costs.
- **Voluntary-controlled schools;** Voluntary-controlled schools are similar to voluntary aided schools, but are run by the local authority. As with community schools, the local authority: employs the school's staff, sets the admissions criteria. School land and buildings are normally owned by a charity, often a religious organisation, which also appoints some of the members of the governing body.
- **State schools with particular characteristics;** Within the state schools system described above, there are a number of schools with particular characteristics. As with other state schools, admissions are coordinated by the local authority. However, some may have different admission criteria or funding arrangements.
- **Academies;** Academies are independently managed, all-ability schools. They are set up by sponsors from business, faith or voluntary groups in partnership with the Department for Education (DfE) and the local authority. Together they fund the land and buildings, with the government covering the running costs.
- **City Technology Colleges;** These are independently managed, non-fee-paying schools in urban areas for pupils of all abilities aged 11 to 18. They are geared towards science, technology and the world of work, offering a range of vocational qualifications as well as GCSEs and A levels.
- **Community and foundation special schools;** Special schools cater for children with specific special educational needs. These may include physical disabilities or learning difficulties.
- **Faith schools;** Faith schools are mostly run in the same way as other state schools. However, their faith status may be reflected in their religious education curriculum, admissions criteria and staffing policies.
- **Grammar schools;** Grammar schools select all or most of their pupils based on academic ability.
- **Maintained boarding schools;** Maintained boarding schools offer free tuition, but charge fees for board and lodging.
- **Independent schools;** There are around 2,300 independent schools in England. These schools set their own curriculum and admissions policies. They are funded by fees paid by parents and income from investments. Just over half have charitable status. Every independent school must be registered with the Department for Education (DfE). To ensure the school maintains the standards set out in its registration document, standards are regularly monitored by either Ofsted, or another inspectorate.
- **Home schooling;** You can also register to home school your child, you will need to seek permission to do this and will need to follow strict guidelines. Most parents send their child to school, but you do have the right to educate your child at home. As a parent, you must ensure your child receives a full-time education from the age of five. You do not need to be a qualified teacher to educate your child at home. Your child is not obliged to follow the National Curriculum or take national tests, but as a parent you are required by law to ensure your child receives full-time education suitable to their age, ability and aptitude, any special educational needs your child may have must be recognised. You do not need special permission from a school or local authority to educate your child at home, but you do need to notify the school in writing if you're taking your child out of school. You will need to notify the local authority if you are removing your child from a special school, you do not need to observe school hours, days or terms, you do not need to have a fixed timetable, nor give formal lessons. There are no funds directly available from central government

for parents who decide to educate their children at home but some local authorities provide guidance for parents, including free National Curriculum materials.

To chose a school;

1. Think about what type of school you would like your child to go to
2. Search the schools in your area
3. visit the schools
4. read the schools' most recent Ofsted reports
5. read the local authority's and schools' prospectuses
6. School performance: test results and Ofsted reports
7. Check the admission criteria, how and when to apply etc.

You may want to apply for a state school in your borough and also a public school (if you can't afford public school some do offer scholarships, grants and funds so it is always worth checking these out).

Think about if they go to primary school what secondary school their friends will go to and what secondary school you want them to go to. It's best if they go to a primary school that progresses to the secondary school that you want. Think about moving house in terms of schools.

<u>Tips for older school children</u>

Football boots – Studs are good for real grass hard or soft and studs can be replaced. Moulds can be worn on all surfaces and worn out. Flater ones are for astro turn and indoor surfaces.

Don't let them take expensive gadgets to school

Label all their school kit with their name (in one more than place and use a hidden mark, so that if someone does try and remove the name tag and take the item you can still see it is yours).

Kids school bag;

- Lunch box & drink

- Jumper

- Hat

- Homework

- School diary (you could get kids to carry their own diary as well as writing their appointments in your own PDA).

- Any notices/letters to be handed in

- Tissues

- Sports uniform

- Library books to be returned

Other

Pregnancy advice;

- Be prepared that your plans may go out the window, as your baby may come early or late so be prepared and things that need doing get them done in advance. You also don't know what baby will be like or how you will feel after you have had the baby. You might think you will go out but you may not feel like it and may not want to leave the baby.
- It's a good idea to do something on your due date, to distract you; otherwise you will be wondering if baby is coming (that is if baby hasn't come already!). Only 5 percent of people give birth on their actual due date.
- You may find it comfortable to get a bean bag to sit on when you are pregnant; it is also good to lean on because you can't bend down.
- If you go into hospital before you have the baby you can request sleeping tablets (as ward maybe noisy and it may be hard to sleep).
- It is a good idea to pass the baby around so s/he gets used to different people holding him/her, cuddle him/her a lot but also get him/her used to be put down for naps to sleep on his/her own.
- If you are short of space in your car get a roof box or trailer.
- Take rings off & put in safe before you go to the hospital or when you are near your due date. You may be asked to remove your jewellery in hospital and don't want it lost or stolen.

Create memories;

- Take a photo in your bikini month by month of your bump and then put all the pictures side by side to show how you grew, you can then show this to your baby when s/he grows up.
- Take lots of photos and get them made up into photo books, you can scan in any other relevant information such as birth certificates.
- It is also nice to make a scrap book of when the baby is born, and include things like his/her first lock of hair, a newspaper from the day s/he was born, the baby's hospital band etc. you may want to order an additional birth certificate to put in here, you could also include a photo of the hospital where s/he was born, a family tree, christening certificate and photos etc.
- As your child grows older keep a scrap book of baby's achievements and explanation of what's what.
- Look at getting professional maternity and parent and baby photos done. If you can't afford them, then look for offers such as one free photo, many studios offer a free photo shoot and a free photo in the hope that you will buy more photos, check that there is no obligation to buy more photos and go to various photo shoots and get your one free photo, scan it in and get them made into a digital photo book. Or there are photographers who will take the photos at varies stages of baby's development and keep them for you, you can then wait until you have enough photos (or enough money and order a book), you could go once a year and then go back in 3 years and have the book made (not many offer this service and you would have to check what would happen to your photos and what you have paid if they close down), or you can pay in instalments.
- A memory box with babies baby grow, first passport cover etc.
- It is also nice to get a photo of the mother and father as babies and put it next to the babies photo as a comparison to see who s/he looks like most.
- Buy and keep a copy of the newspaper for the day your baby was born.
- Put an announcement in your local newspaper of your baby's birth (and keep a copy of it).
- Keep a record/photo album for your baby, memory box, family try and do an autobiography of both parents for baby. Do a short video clip of your baby each

week that you can later put onto a DVD for your child. Children love watching videos of themselves, it will keep your baby fascinated for a while.
- 'Smash the cake' photo shoots are lovely, this is where they get baby to get stuck into a pretty cake and it is photographed.
- You can do photo books and photo calendar for gifts for friends and family, for instance at Christmas.

Financial / security;

- Make a will now you have a child so that there are provisions, life insurance, who will get custody of your child if both parents die etc.
- Set up a savings account/isa for baby
- Add your baby onto the critical life aspect of your life insurance that way if baby becomes ill and needs and operation you will get some money to cover this.

Tidy old stuff away/Plan for the next baby;

Put baby stuff in loft labelled by age for next baby. It is a good idea to put it in clear re-cycle bags that are double bagged. Put it in your loft with the oldest age stuff at the back and the youngest at the front, that way you can get it out in the order that you need it for the next baby. It is also a good idea to have a full written inventory of exactly what you have kept, each item, age it's for and quantity (and even a photo), that way when you have your next baby you will know what to buy and what you already have (you won't either run out of items or waste money on duplicate items that way). Ensure all the items are cleaned when they go in the loft, you will still have to clean them when they come back down but if you leave them up dirty the stains will set in and will be harder to get out. You may also want to buy a vacuum seal bag so that you can safely store all of your maternity clothes in the loft too, once you have had the baby. Although immediately after having the baby you may find it comfortable to wear your maternity clothes.

If you are planning to have more than one child, think of the age gap between them and plan when the best time will be for you to have your next child.

Baby show and exhibitions;

Look up when baby shows and exhibitions are. There are national shows and local ones, they are a good source of information and you get many giveaways and goodies too.

Important dates you need to be aware of other than your baby's birthday of course, are mothers and fathers day as you will need to buy presents for each other, and prompt your child when s/he gets older. Mothers day (mothering Sunday) in the UK, is always on the fourth Sunday of Lent. Mothering Sunday is a time when children pay respect to their Mothers. Children often give their Mothers a gift and a card.

Mothering Sunday church service;

Many churches give the children in the congregation a little bunch of spring flowers to give to their Mothers as a thank you for all their care and love throughout the year.

Mothering Sunday is not a fixed day because it is always the middle Sunday in <u>Lent</u> (which lasts from Ash Wednesday to the day before Easter Sunday). This means that Mother's Day in the UK will fall on different dates each year and sometimes even fall in different months.

Mothering Sunday has been celebrated in the UK on the fourth Sunday in <u>Lent</u> since at least the 16th century.

Father's Day is held on the third Sunday of June in the United Kingdom. There are some suggestions that the idea of Father's Day may originate in pagan sun worship. Some branches of paganism see the sun as the father of the universe. Since the summer solstice occurs around the same time of year as Father's Day, some people see a link between the two.

The idea of a special day to honour fathers and celebrate fatherhood was introduced from the United States. There, a woman called Sonora Smart Dodd was inspired by the American Mother's Day celebrations to plan a day to honour fathers. Father's Day has been celebrated in June since 1910 in the USA. The celebrations in the United Kingdom are thought to have been inspired by the American custom of Father's Day. This is in contrast to Mother's Day, which has a very different history in the United States and the United Kingdom.

Other children and pets;

If you have pets or other children it is natural for them to feel jealous. Older siblings, especially if they are still toddlers, react to the arrival of a new baby sibling in different ways ranging from jealousy, through complete indifference, to a sudden transformation into mum's grown-up helper. Getting off to a good start with their new sibling is crucial to developing a good relationship later. There are a number of things you can do to foster close sibling bonds and prepare your child for his new brother or sister. Read our article Sibling relations: Coping with sibling rivalry and Helping your toddler adjust to a new sibling for handy hints to foster sibling harmony.

Getting your old child used to baby -

Your older child, no matter what their age, has to adjust too, and some children find this difficult. The following suggestions may help:

• **Try to keep up old routines and activities.** Going to playgroup, visiting friends and telling a bedtime story might be difficult in the first few weeks, but sticking to established routines will help reassure your older child.

• **Your first child might not love the baby at first.** They may not feel the way you do. It's lovely if they share your pleasure, but it's best not to expect it.

• **Be prepared to cope with extra demands.** Your older child may want and need more attention. Maybe a grandparent can help out. But they will still need one-to-one time with you so that they don't feel as if they have been 'pushed out'.

• **Encourage your older child to take an interest.** Children don't always love babies, but they do find them interesting. You can encourage this, by talking to them about what they were like as a baby and the things they did. Get out their old toys, and show them photos.

• **Provide distractions during feeds.** An older child may well feel left out and jealous when you are feeding the baby. You could find something for them to do, or use the feed as an opportunity to tell them a story or just have a chat.

• **Be patient with 'baby behaviour'.** Your older child might ask for a bottle, start wetting their pants or want to be carried. This is completely normal behaviour so try not to let it bother you and try not to say 'no' every time.

• **Expect some jealousy and resentment.** It's almost certain to happen, sooner or later. You can only do so much. If you and your partner, or you and a grandparent or friend, can sometimes give each other time alone with each child, you will not feel so constantly pulled in different directions.

- **Encourage your child to engage with the baby.** Try to turn looking after the baby into a fun game and encourage your child to talk to the baby.

- Get prepared and before the baby comes along show your child book with babies in, show your child pictures of the babies development, discuss each stage and practice looking after your child's doll.
- When baby is born give them gifts (from the baby).
- Niece and nephews may also get jealous (not just siblings), try and involve them as much as possible, buy them gifts when baby arrives etc.

If your pregnant and have pets;

Before baby is born;

- Don't forget about them and have someone on standby to care for your pet when you go into have your baby.
- Wash your hands after stroking your pet (wear gloves and take care when emptying the litter tray).

According to the Centers for Disease Control and Prevention (CDC), toxoplasmosis is the main concern when it comes to pregnancy and cats. The infection can lead to birth defects and miscarriage in pregnant women. Cats can get the infection by eating contaminated raw meat, birds, soil, or mice. Cats then pass the contagious stage of the infection through their feces. The CDC recommends pregnant women take the following precautions:

- Avoid having the pregnant woman change, clean, or come in contact with the litter box. If there is nobody else to do the job then she should be sure to wear gloves and a mask, and wash hands thoroughly when finished.
- Keep cats indoors to avoid them possibly eating contaminates.
- Avoid handling or adopting stray cats.
- Feed cats only canned or dried commercial cat food. Never give them undercooked or raw meat.
- Do not bring a new cat into your house that might have been an outdoor cat or might have eaten raw meat.

After baby is born;
- Introduce them to your baby slowly and keep them out of the room where your baby sleeps.
- They may become jealous so don't leave them out and never leave them unsupervised around the baby, especially at first while they get used to each other.
- Naturally, in a small percentage of cases, the baby will in fact be allergic to pet dander. Official statistics differ, but the total population of allergy sufferers is about 10%, only a small portion of which is allergic to dander. Also, of that 10%, only a very small portion is an infant. So, the overall chances are very low. In such cases, just as with adults, steering clear of contact is best. A lot of parents won't want to get rid of a loved pet from the household completely. The state of affairs is not an irresolvable dilemma, though. Very little pet dander remains airborne for long. Repeated washing of bedding and a once-per-month wash of the pet can assist a lot.
- Generally speaking, it's all right to allow your pet near your new baby, as long as the pet is well behaved and you are there to supervise.

It's common for a pet, who has until recently been the focus of the family's attention, to become jealous of a new baby. You should allow your pet to become accustomed to this new member of your household while in your presence. Continue to give your pet plenty of attention, both when your baby is present and when you have time alone with your pet. This will keep the jealous behaviour to a minimum.

If your pet shows any aggressive or hostile behaviour toward your infant, you should quickly reprimand him. He'll learn fast what behaviour is allowed near the baby. If your pet doesn't respond well to your reprimands, though, get help from a professional trainer.

When your baby is very young, I'd recommend not allowing the family dog or cat to lick your baby's face. This could transmit infectious material (such as feces) into the baby's mouth or eyes. As your baby grows older, her immune system will get much stronger and she can play with and even be licked by your pet without any consequences.

Family life;

Buying a new car;

- You may need more space so look for a car with a big boot to fit the pushchair etc. in. (you may want to have 1 car seat for each car to leave in).
- You don't necessarily have to buy a bigger car; you can just organise a smaller one better.
- If you only need the extra space in your car occasionally, for instance when going on holiday, you can hire a larger car for that short period instead of buying a larger one, which will cost more to run.

Buying household items

- Now is a good time to invest in a dishwasher
- If you are buying a new washing machine buy one with a large capacity (especially as you will be doing more washing now).

Moving house with a child;

1. Pack in boxes where everything goes i.e. each kitchen draw goes in a box so it is in the right place ready to unpack.
2. Clearly label the boxes.
3. Keep toys out handy – boxes with baby stuff near top
4. If possible stay with a relative or friend & pack a case with everything you need then you can go to house at your leisure to unpack and decorate.

Family holidays;

If there is a lot of you going you may want to hire a villa or apartment and then family members can chip in and come and go as they wish.

Some holidays young children are free. Cruises are good with young babies because you don't have to fly, they may be free and many large cruise companies offer a crèche facility.

Caravan holidays are cheap and often have discounted deals in the paper (or last minute on line); If going on a caravan holiday take in a plug in heater (some caravans get cold and even though they have heating it may not be sufficient). You may also want a clothes airer to put swimming coz on and take a carbon monoxide / gas detector with you if you have one. For the first night you could cook a meal in advance and freeze it, then when you go put it in a cool bag in the car with no ice so that it can defrost whilst you get up there, you can then heat it that night or if it needs longer to defrost, put it in the fridge and heat it the next night. It is easier to cook meals to take in advance although the freezer in the caravan will probably be small so you will also have to take some fresh food and cook, if you are not eating out (it may be cheaper and easier to self cater if you have fussy kids – check with the caravan company what facilities and equipment are provided and what you need to bring with you). It may be worth getting a programme of activities in advance so that you can plan out what you are doing and how much it costs. Otherwise you may arrive to realise that the activity that you want to do is only on once a week and you have missed it but if you knew in advance you would have left an hour earlier to get there in time. It is also worth checking height restriction before you get there. If you have 2 children with an age gap bear in mind that they might have to different activities at different times. Always look at what is going on in the surrounding area and what attractions there are and when they are open, before you get there.

If travelling with a baby/young child by car plan lots of stops, take CDs and toys to distract them. Have snacks and water in the car and if possible an adult in the back to supervise them. Be prepared for travel sickness and have sick bags in the car. Try and set off just before they are due a nap, that way they are likely to sleep in the car. If they have a dummy have lots of spares and clip them onto them. Take extra food and milk in case you hit traffic. Check where the services are along each route of your journey so that you know you can stop when you are approaching meal times. You can roughly work out how long it will take to get to each services. It is best to stop sooner rather than later, to stop your baby getting too irritable. I found that playing Brahms lullaby (my son's favourite song) helped to soothe him. I also had spare dummies in the front of the car, that I could lean over and give to him. If I had packed better when we went on our first holiday to Scotland I would have left space on the back seat so that I could jump in the back with him, rather than only being able to use the front passenger seat. Its also useful to pack your stroller/pram and change bag last so that they are easily accesable for when you stop at the service station. I found that when you arrive at your destination the best thing to do is unpack your travel cot first. I put his travel mattress, sheet, sleeping bag, musical toy and his favourite sleep toy all togther in a bag so that I could make his bed up quickly. I tried to organise my bags so that I knew where all my baby's essentials were. I recommend that you take 2 sheets and 2 sleeping bags or a sleeping bag and spare blanket in case your baby soils one in the night. It is also a good idea to take some travel wash so that you can wash some muslins or bibs in the sink, should you need to. Most places have laundry facilites but it is good to take some extra clothes just in case they don't, also you may not want to spend your holiday to do washing. It is also a good idea to try and be organised and have a large cloth bag for dirty clothes, at least if you can keep your items sorted its easier when you come to unpack at home.

If travelling by plane try and book an aisle seat near the loo. Babies suffer with their ears when they fly, giving some food or drink on the way up and the way down helps with their ears, you can also give calpol just before landing and take off (just ensure there is a 4 hour gap between doses). The heated hand pads you get may also offer some reflief from the warmth held to baby's ear (ensure the pad is warm only and not hot), you could also try massaging behind the ear. Your baby will need a passport if going overseas.

Think sun safety. Keep heads covered and babies out of the sun and keep applying plenty of sun block (even in the shade).

A play shade and swim nappies are good items to have. If you are going near water you will also need a swim vest. A UV suit is also good to keep the sun off and stop your child burning, you will however need to still use sunblock on the exposed areas.

A cruise is good with a baby because you haven't got the worry of flying and you can take what you want, you also know the standard of the ships etc.

When going on holiday with a young child/baby;
1. Make a list of what you need to pack and then tick each item off as you pack it, this way you won't forget anything.
2. Pack just in case essentials such as teething gel and calpol
3. You can rent car seats but its better to take your own
4. Take some toys to distract baby

5. Pack ready made formula and pre-steralised bottle liners
6. Car sun shades
7. Use sun block
8. Slings for all terrain travel
9. Make regular stops and walk around with baby (change of scenery should calm baby).
10. practise with travel cot putting it up and down before you go on holiday.

Don't forget to add cot sheets to your travel cot.

N.B. When going away you may need to hire a car seat – even if not going in a car you may want to catch a taxi, or you may want to do a coach trip. You may find it useful to get a protective bag for your car seat and a protective bag for your stroller.

Holiday pack list;

- Cot sheet and spare cot sheet (mattress protector if applicable)

- Travel wash

- Sleeping bag and spare sleeping bag

- Blanket

- Coat/snow suit

- Stroller/pram

- Travel cot

- Steriliser

- Bottles

- Formula and cartons of milk

- Red book

- Medicine; Gripe water, calpol, nose saline drops, teething gel and powder

- Flask

- Food / baby rice / hand blender

- Bottle brush

- Feeding diary

- Bibs and muslin

- Intercom monitor

- Spoons / weaning pots and labels

- Vests/baby grows/outfits

- Nappies / wipes / change mat

- Spare dummies & dummy sterilising wipes

- Toys & teethers

- Comforter

- Toothbrush and paste

- Hair brush, olive oil, cotton wool, nail clippers, thermometer and other grooming items

- Baby shampoo, body wash, bath bubble

- Play mat (travel)

- Chair

- Music device

- Travel high chair

- Drinks clip and accessories for pram

- Potty if potty training

- Reading books and games

- Towels

- Swim nappy and swim stuff

Have a pack list for your holiday that you can follow when packing, that way you won't forget anything; Pack a UV swim suit to protect your baby from the sun when swimming and a wet suite for when it is a bit cooler. Babies get cold quickly when they are swimming or if there is a breeze in the air when they get out. Take spare batteries for toys and monitor and extra wipes and nappies, you don't want to run out. Sun screen is needed at 50+ You may want to pack washing up liquid so that you can wash out the water bottle and bibs etc. in the sink. Towel with a hood/poncho towel for around the pool. Don't forget nappy rash cream, baby spoons, bibs and a spare sun hat. Nappy sacks can be used for dirty bibs and spoons when out and about. Take a reading book and some crayons and colouring pens for when at dinner or in queues to keep baby entertained.

A rubber ring is good for swimming because they can use their arms and legs freely, however they can tip upside down and get trapped so they must be used with supervision.

Always carry snacks and toys and a book so that your baby is less likely to stress out when you are out and about. Take a spare water bottle on holiday, or carry straws.

You can still burn through glass so you need to wear sunscreen. You also need to wear sunscreen in the shade. Your baby's skin is very sensitive so try and keep out of the sun and ensure s/he has lots of water. You may want to carry a muslin to cover your babies legs. A pram with a UV sun screen hood is good to have. Keep a sun hat on your baby/child in the pool. Be wary of hot and cold temperature changes i.e on a hot day jumping in a cold pool may cause a big shock to the system and be harmful.   Pack dummy wipes to clean spoons etc.

Even dark/tanned skin needs sunscreen.

Under 5 or 8 year olds shouldn't go in Jauzzi's because they may cause too much pressure on their body.

Check if your holiday resort has somewhere you can loan toys, this means less to pack. It maybe a good idea to take balloons, these will keep your child occupied without taking up room in your case.

PRE-HOLIDAY CHECKLIST

- ☐ Sort the travel insurance
- ☐ Check passports are valid
- ☐ Make phone number list for hotel/villa/campsite/car hire company
- ☐ Pay bills
- ☐ Car (oil, tyres, water, screenwash etc)
- ☐ Check if/how you can use your phone abroad
- ☐ Sort out jabs/malaria prevention, if needed
- ☐ Sort out who's looking after the hamster, rabbit, goldfish, cat, dog, chickens etc
- ☐ If you're going abroad, tell your bank and credit card company
- ☐ If you're getting a taxi to the station/airport, pre-book your journey there (and back at the end of the holiday)

Before you leave

- ☐ Water the plants
- ☐ Check/re-check flight/crossing times
- ☐ Cancel papers/milk, if delivered
- ☐ Empty the bins
- ☐ Lock doors and windows
- ☐ Set timers for lights (burglar-prevention etc)
- ☐ Draw curtains upstairs
- ☐ Switch on voicemail/answering machine
- ☐ Switch off alarm clock
- ☐ Switch off/turn down heating
- ☐ Turn on burglar alarm
- ☐ Leave key and contact details with friendly neighbour

And then just as you're about to set off...

- ☐ Re-check if your passports are valid
- ☐ If you're driving, check you've got your driving licence and documents
- ☐ Check flight details
- ☐ Rush back in to check you haven't left oven on/taps running/forgotten a child/dog/cat etc

<u>Holiday pack list;</u>

For the pool;

- Swimming UV suit
- Arm bands/rubber ring/life jacket
- Sun hat
- Pool shoes / sandals / crocks
- Sun hat & spare sun hat
- Sun glasses
- Poncho towel
- Swim nappies
- Suncream and after sun
- Beach bag

Medicine;

- Calpol sachet
- Paracetmol, Imodium, gaviscon
- Savlon
- Plasters
- Nurofen
- Dylorite
- Thermometer

Feeding;

- Bib
- Spoons and spoon pot or sandwich bags
- Dummie wipes
- Straws
- Water bottle
- Spare dummies

- Washing up liquid
- Lunch box
- snacks

Clothing

- Tooth brush and paste
- Toys, books, coloring pens and travel games.

Sleeping;

- Pjs
- Travel cot matress and sleeping bag?
- Night light
- Night music
- Mosquito net for pram and cot?

Other;

- Photocopy of everyone's passports
- Milk cartons
- Bottles/sippy cups
- Change bag/mat
- Nappies & wipes
- Sudocream
- Water steraliser
- Towels and flannels?
- Baby wash
- Cotton wool
- Thin rain mac
- Tissues
- Muslin (for shade)
- Pushchair

- Blanket

- Snacks

- Baby monitor

- E11 card / Insurance documents/red book or medical details copied out.

- Plug adapter

- Car seat?

- Snacks

- Sponge

- Lunch box (foldable)

- Dummies

- Room thermostat

- Baby UV sun tent?

- Neck pillow / eye mask

- Trainers/flat shoes

- Travel cot? / bed guard

- Calculator

- Fleece

- Hand bag / evening bag

Camera

Batteries

Adult;

Gym clothes/trainers

Notebook and pen

Camera

Plug adapter

Swimming coz

Microfibre towel and dressing gown and head turban

Sunglasses

Hat

Wrap/cardi for the plane

Light waterproof jacket

Beach bag

Suncream

Insect repellent & bite cream

Driving licence

Credit card (plus cash card/spare credit card).

Spare glasses?

Phone & charger

Money – both currency & snacks (baby food and snacks)

- **bath non slip mat**
- Car seat for coach and taxis? /Booster seat
- Portable high chair
- Microfibre beach towels, swim stuff, wet suit, UV suit etc.
- Cot sheet and spare cot sheet (mattress protector if applicable) (x2)
- Sleeping bag and spare sleeping bag (x2)
- Blanket
- Coat/snow suit
- Stroller/pram
- Travel cot
- Steriliser
- Bottles
- Formula and cartons of milk

- Red book

- Medicine; Gripe water, calpol, nose saline drops, teething gel and powder

- Olive oil and nail clippers

- Flask

- Food / baby rice / hand blender

- Bottle brush

- Travel wash

- Feeding diary

- Bibs and muslin

- Intercom monitor

- Spoons / weaning pots and labels

- Vests/baby grows/outfits

- Nappies / wipes / change mat

- Spare dummies & dummy sterilising wipes

- Toys & teethers

- Comforter

- Toothbrush and paste

- Hair brush, olive oil, cotton wool, nail clippers, thermometer and other grooming items

- Toothbrush

- Teething gel

- Nappies, wipes and nappy sacks

- Baby shampoo, body wash, bath bubble

- Play mat (travel)

- Chair

- Music device

- Travel high chair

- Drinks clip and accessories for pram

- Potty if potty training

- Reading books and games

- Reading books and games

- Towels

- Swim nappy and swim stuff

- Jar baby food

- Large play mat & blue chair

- Portable high chair

- Cot and cot mattress

- kilt

Highchair
Play mats & toys
Kindle
Update iPod with play lists inc ritchie's
Swim nappies & swim stuff
Nappies
Spare dummies
Nail polish

Medicines – paracetmol and gaviscon and plasters / St's

Dressing gown - microfibre

Underwear

Make up / makeup remover and ponds cream washkit –toothpaste and toothbrush, shower gel, shampoo and conditioner and razor, deodorant and perfume.

Hair straightener and hair dryer, hair bands and pins and hair brush

Phone charger

Net book and note book

Camera

Kindle and charger & torch

Coats & flat boots, trainers, walking boots

Blk heels

Blk boots – high and flat

Summer wedge shoes

Silk neck scarfs

Handbag – clutch and shoulder bag

Umbrella and pram umbrella

Swimming stuff?

slippers

towels

hat/scarf/gloves and sunglasses

jewellery & hair extensions

Further notes;

- When they are tired they try to fight it and push you away, they then cry worse and you may wonder if you are hurting them, if laying back puts them in pain, usually its just them fighting the sleep, keep rocking them and they will fall asleep.
- Some TV is good if it is educational, it may also help them develop language skills.
- There are music festivals and events for kids such as lollibop, a festival for kids (its been dubbed as the children's version of Glastonbury).
- As your baby gets older and can put the dummy back in themselves put loads of extra dummies in the cot so that they are easy to find.
- Boys tend to weigh more than girls
- You may find that nappies change and your nappy preference may change as they change size (natural nappies with less chemicals may cause less skin irritation, although they maybe less absorbent and may need changing more).
- With car seats an iso fix base fits into the cars anchor points so is the best, but the most expensive. Other base uses the seatbelt to fix them in, but are just as good.
- Spending quality time with your child is important, don't worry if have less time just make time you gave special. Quality time is better than lots of less quality time.
- Yoga or pilates exercise to stretch and be flexible is important as lifting your baby plays haveck on your body
- Blanket instead of coat in car means you can throw it off if your baby falls asleep in the car, which it makes it easier to lift your baby straight into the cot without waking him/her.
- Approach things calmly, confidently and consistently to succeed.

- If you are doing an activity, give them something to do at the same time so that they feel that they are joining in.

- Toddlers go through stages and go back to their baby toys (especially with a new arrival in the family) so it's a good idea to keep some of their favourite baby toys.

- Its good for a baby to have weight reserves so don't worry if they are slightly large.

- Take own food/drink and toys when go out visiting people, so that you have everything tha you need for your baby.

- Have lots of hand cream because you will get dry hands from washing so much
- Keep boxes of some items, in order to put stuff back in when storing in loft
- Check baby grow still fits when legs are stretched out. The baby grow may look like it fits but their legs need to be able to stretch out and they need some room to grow too.
- Wear glasses on & off to get baby used to you with/without
- Before getting pregnant have a nice photo of yourself taken, because after having a baby your body will change.
- Keep a record of when you take medication (especially after giving birth you may become forgetful).
- Stock up with lots of tea, coffee, and milk for you visitors.

- Have a nice outfit ready in case you want to go somewhere nice, because time it limited, to get ready, with baby.
- Don't make baby look backwards/up over the head when they are newborn as it may cause them to strain.
- Have comfortable clothes to wear after the birth
- Baby milk stains clothes so wash off immediately, clean clothes with stain remover (especially before putting clothes in the loft for the next baby).
- Get special outfits for baby for special occasions i.e. Halloween or Christmas outfits.

- You can crystalise your babies first booties or get a deep memory box frame and put your babies booties and other precious items in there.

- Open packets, set up equipment such as monitor and steriliser bottles before your baby comes so that you get used to it. You can also get baby starter kit with bottles that are disposable and contain pre-mixed formula, they are great for when your baby first comes home (they are also great to keep in the car for emergencies), (these are the same things that they give out at the hosipital).

- Take lots of photos and videos and do a photo book of babies first year, name and date photos in folders/file name when saving them.

- It's easy to loose confidence after having a baby and being stuck in. Therefore you need to get out more, meet new people, do new courses etc. and get out and be confident. Make an effort to get out. Don't get stuck in a rut.

- Rub forehead and down babies nose to soothe them and close their eyes for sleep.

- Get a roll of blue roll and put it over the babies changing mat

- Don't let your child see you put your bank pin number in as they may shout it out.
- Have throws on your sofa or get a leather sofa tha you can just wipe clean (and purchase lots of leather wipes).
- You can spend all day just looking at your baby and waching him/her so that you don't miss something – take lots of photos /video clips. First moments, such as first smile are special and should be recorded.

- Christening – If having a reception afterwards in a hall without much facilities, set up a kids corner with toys and play mats, you may also want to use screens or put up a large tent and make a quiet area and/or a baby change area/place where mums can have some privacy to feed etc.
- Children's Parties – party bags with books instead of sweet
- You may find that when your baby starts talking s/he may say a word/name and then may not say again.
- If have c section have to wait before having natural birth for a while to makesure that your scar heals properly inside.
- Even up to a year you may still feel emotional and weepy, while your hormones are still settling.
- You would never employ someone to look after your child who wasn't first aid trained and child care qualified, or at least knew about children. Therefore if you have no previous experience with children you should do a paediatric first aid course and a parenting course. I did because I hadn't had much experience of children and I wanted to do everything that I could to be the best mum and give my child the best possible start in life.
- When new born need more nappies and a bigger nappy bag. Can down size as gets older although may want to pack jars of food and toys. Put snacks in a snack pot rather than carrying the whole packet, in order to save space in your bag.

- Babies hate being dressed and also having their noses wiped. Turn wiping their nose into a game to make them more acceptable to it.

- Organic cotton is best and to have blankets from breathable material, with holes in. Also think about moses basket lining etc and other things that they might press their face up against the side of or try to eat etc.

- Babies feet sweat more than adults so you need breathable material for their socks.

- Socks, sleepsuits, tights etc. that are too tight can stop your babies feet developing properly.

- Veri-flow teets are good because your baby decides how fast the milk comes out, depending on how fast they suck.

- When getting your baby dressed roll the sleeves down to put arms in - roll sleeves up like tights to put arms in or gentle guide hand ' push elbow through.

- Exaggerate expressions for your baby, and watch them copy your expressions.

- Use cushions to support your baby when s/he is learning to sit up.

- Your child may learn to talk quicker if you have older children, they will learn from them. The children may also develop a special language together.

- Be wary of small items, especially other children's toys that they don't swallow them don't leaving pens lying around and bewary of caps /lids from pens and teething gel etc.

- If baby wigles when you are changing give a toy to hold or book to read

- Discipline – you can start saying no i.e. from 6 months, they understand the tone.

- Toddlers – set an an alarm clock/get a night and day alarm clock – to stop them getting up early i.e. in the summer when its light. Teach them that they can't get out of bed and wake you up until a set time.

There are many different activities to do with a baby including;
- Buggy fit
- Theatre tots
- Water babies
- Monkey music
- Gymboree
- Bollykids – Bollywood dance class
- Art classes

For back pain (in pregnancy and after labour);
- Keep active to stop fatiguing muscles in the lower back
- Get up every 40 mins and stretch
- Sit on a gym ball, its also fun for your baby to play and roll on the gym ball and it can be used as a birthing ball.
- Yoga, pilates and swimming also helps your back

Getting help / creating a support network

- Invest in a doula or other paid help if you can afford it.
- Be sociable - Meet other mums on line / Set up a mummy group
- Ask at clinic for groups - nct, sure start etc. It's important to socialise and meet other mums to be/other mums. Hospital classes/NCT & other private classes or groups. Net mums & net mums forums (meet other mums on line). Go to coffee mornings and mother and toddler groups when baby is born. Read books, go on line and social networking is important.
- You could even take it in turns with other mums to baby sit.
-

It can be hard getting them to sleep in their bed after being in a cot, especially when they discover they can get out and move around. My son, with his first night in his bed decided he wanted to sleep under the cot. Then he decided to sleep in the bed, then got up and slept under the bed and then woke up and hit his head etc. My nursery manager told me she put a sleeping bag in her daughters room she slept there and then eventually after a while slept in the bed. Its best to try and settle them in their bed over a weekend, so you haven't got to be up in the morning. Explain how fun a big bed is. Have a bed guard (and I kept the cot up for a while so if things got too much I could put him into the cot, at least that way I knew where he was).

It may take 3-5 days to get them to settle. You may have to sit outside their room and keep putting them back to bed when they get up.

A memory foam mattress for the first mattress is better than springs. Springs may dig into a small child and a sprung mattress is bouncier so there is more temptation to jump on it, where as a child is less likely to jump on a memory foam mattress.

If you are keeping the cot up for a while, whilst they adjust to their bed (or have a cot in the room for another child), don't put them next to each other as your child may jump in and out of the cot from the bed.

When your child first goes into a bed put a mattress on floor, or spare duvet and padding next to the bed, in case they fall out. This is also a good thing to do if your baby tries to jump out of the cot, you may also want to put a stair gate on their bedroom door, lock their door or use stair gates at the top and bottom of the stairs.

If they are coming down with a cold or other illness or having growing pains or growth spurts, this will alos affect their sleep.

- **If your child starts bed wetting when s/he was prevuisly dry, it could be that s/he is upset about something or it could be that s/he has a urine infection, especially if it is smelly.**

- **If your child is sleep walking or waking at night s/he may be cold, it maybe worth getting a bigger duvet, or slightly heavier one.**

Dealing with bad behaviour;

Dealing with bad behaviour;

The first tantrum or few that your child has are shocking. When Ritchie had his first tantrum I didn't know what to do I thought there was something wrong with him or he was in pain, he just screamed for over ½ hour, it turned out he was tired. In the end I put him to bed and he fell asleep.

It's not easy being two. You want to be independent, but you can't quite manage that zip; you want juice but mum says it's teatime; you want to explain something but just don't have the words yet. The result? A tantrum: screaming, crying, shouting, kicking, throwing things – and a very embarrassed mum if you're out in public.

Dealing with tantrums is part and parcel of being the parent of a two-year-old. Or a three-year-old, as tantrums often continue until a child is nearer four.

Dealing with a tantrum

The best way to deal with a tantrum is to stay calm and ignore it, which is obviously a lot easier to say than do, especially if you're in a public place!

Your toddler's meltdown is a cry for attention, so if you can absolutely refuse to give any attention – including shouting or negotiating – then it will die down more quickly. Stay calm and carry on with what you were doing – chatting to a friend, shopping or whatever – and check to make sure your little one is safe every couple of minutes.

Ignoring your child is very hard, but if you answer back or smack them, you are giving them the attention they are demanding, advises the Royal College of Psychiatrists.

Early stage tantrum

In the early stages of a tantrum, you can often divert their attention ('oh look, there's a ladybird!') which can take their mind off the impending explosion. And because a toddler's attention span is so short, they may well have forgotten that tantrum trigger within a few seconds.

Full flow tantrum

But when they're in full flow, distraction is unlikely to work. Stay outwardly calm, ignore them and wait for it to pass.

Never give in

It's really important never to give in to the demand that caused the tantrum as it will teach them that having a meltdown gets you what you want. That's a recipe for more tantrums.

It's tempting in the supermarket to say 'ok, ok, I'll buy those sweets if you'll just stop crying and screaming' just to stop the embarrassment, but stand firm. You may think others are judging you for having a screaming toddler, but they are probably just relieved they've passed that stage or have left their kids at home. Most likely they'll admire your refusal to give in.

Once the tantrum is over

When your child begins to calm down, talk to them in a low voice, advises family psychologist Linda Blair. Don't try to pick them up (unless they are in danger) and reassure your child that they will be fine. She says: "Naming the emotion can also help here. Say, 'I know you're angry/upset because X happened, but you're okay, we'll sort it out. Mummy is here'."

Don't try negotiating or reasoning – there's no point. And don't punish them after a tantrum, either: move swiftly on and give them lots of positive attention as soon as it's over, without referring to the tantrum. Give your toddler your full attention and talk to them warmly as if nothing has happened. If you can find ways to notice and reward good behaviour, your little one is more likely to stay calm for longer.

How to avoid a tantrum

The best way to deal with a tantrum is to avoid it in the first place – sometimes easier said than done.

- Are they hungry or tired? This can tip some toddlers into a meltdown, especially if they can't tell you what they feel.
- Try not to rush them all the time, especially when trying to leave the house in the morning. This can stress them out and start a tantrum. Start preparations 10 minutes earlier if you find you're always running late.
- Are you saying 'no' a lot? Sometimes we have to say no ('no TV now, it's bedtime') but check if you're saying it as an automatic response to their requests because it makes your life easier. If there isn't a good reason for saying no ('can I do finger painting?'), find ways to say yes sometimes.
- Your toddler is desperate for some control over their life, so give them a choice within a choice. So, rather than saying 'hold my hand when we're crossing the road please', say 'would you like to hold my hand or the buggy?'
- Learn to spot your child's triggers. Some children have tantrums when they feel anxious, if they're worried you're leaving without them, or if their coat zip isn'tquite pulled up to the right level. Deal with the underlying problem to avoid the tantrum.

- Have a time out areas, (I used the porch), you can also get a roll up matt and egg timer (1 minute per age), you can then creat a 'time out space' wherever you are.
- Record things so you can see behaviour changing/triggers
- New methods take a long time - if you have done something over 20 times a habit forms so takes longer to change.
- Give your child gentle messages at night, as you are settling them down to sleep, what you say will sink in. Give them nice gentle positive messages such as; tomorrow be kind to your friends.
- Deprive of toy / say to go away - when bad and ignore the bad behaviour. But be careful don't push your child away and say they are horrible, just show them you don't except bad behaviour.
- Have less toys out and rotate the toys. This way they will get to play with things, rather than just the toys on top. It will also be easier to take toys away as punishment if you don't have too many.
- Give praise for good behaviour and over exaggerate the praise for good behaviour. If your child hurts you, over exaggerate the hurt too so that they understand.
- Wait out temper – If they are getting frustrated and having a big temper it is a good idea to leave them be, then disucss it with them and deal with it once they have calmed down, otherwise (especially if they have anger management issues) they may lash out. As they get older give them strategies to help them control their anger i.e. walk away, count to 10, take a deep breath and smile etc. think about strategies that are realistic and age appropriate.
- Toddlers from the age of 2, test the boundaries, they are so used to being served and having everything brought to them, that they think the worls revolves around them and they think people are there to serve them, they are king. They are also finding themselves / learning independence and get frustrated if they ca't say what they want to, do what they want to etc.
- You need to be tough and in control, be firm but kind, show strength when they are sad, praise good behaviour etc.
- Over exaggerate praise & hurt etc If they hurt you over exaggerate this, get their hand and stroke yourself with it and say 'gentle' and then stroke them gently to get them to learn to stop hitting and to do gentle touching.
- Don't confuse actions that they need to do with play ie they run away when you are dressing them because they think it's a game.
- Reward and give prizes for good behaviour, i.e. if they are good all week they get a prize at the end of the week.
- Explain/talk and reason to them – even if they don't understand , it will help as it will eventually sink in.

- I found smacking Ritchie made him hit me, so we stopped using this as a form of discipline.
- Use toys and say their behaviour is naughty i.e "the dinasour is bitting the other diansour, that is naughty behaviour, we don't bite do we..", this is taking them away from labelling them and is making them focus on and understand the issue.
- Gentle restraining – If your baby is having a tantrum or is just jumping all over the bed and refusing to sleep gently restraining and rocking may help to calm and soothe.
- Ignore tantrum and cuddle then, when it is appropriate try reasoning with them.
- If your toddler is throwing - give soft toys only to play with so it does less damage when they hit things, this phase will pass. It is important to give other toys so they get a balance of learning and play. They can play with hard toys under supervision at set times, until they stop throwing.
- They want to be independent so let them think they are in control doing x,yz i.e. say you do x and mummy will help you i.e. you dress yourself like a big boy and mummy will help you.
- Give them limited choices i.e. milk or water to drink. This T shirt to wear or that t-shirt.
- Appropriate boundaries, don't useboundries that are not appropriate for their age ie don't stop messy play, this is good for them.
- Use firm voice / face – they will see it if you don't mean it or are unsure.
- Let them dress themselves in their room, have a room for dressing such as their bedroom, don't let them get dressed in the kitchen etc.
- They need control - restrain & rock through tantrums
- They copy you and the behaviour they see, so create a good example for them to follow.
- All children are diff erent and react differently to different things so there is no set answer, they may act differently depending on their mood. What works on one day may not work on another so you need to be flexible, also what works for one child may not work for another. Therefore you have to try different tactics and see what works for you and your child. You may find one style works for you but not for your partner or a style/approach they have may not be one you are comfortable with. Do what works for you, as long as both parents / carers are being consistent in what you are saying/doing, you can find your own style of delivery.
- Phases happen - they may become more irritable before learning to walk or before more words come etc most issues are a phase and will pass. There are always phases, one phase leads into another i.e. bitting, not sleeping, not getting dressed etc.

- No one wants their kid to be one not invited to party because they hit other kids so its important to nip it in the bud.
- Teach children to stand up for themselves and don't hit first
- Children want to be independent before they can crawl they get frustrated because they want to move around but can't.
- Watch them carefully – recognise the signs of mischief in their face (register the signs that they are about to do something) and distract the before they can.
- You will have bad mornings with kids, be organised helps, try to let go. Don't hold onto the frustration, move on and focus on your next task. Do something to help you focus at work and get from the stressed mummy zone to the work zone. Try lunch time yoga as this helps for inner peace and relaxation and is good for your body. It is good to do exercise and stretch out your joints and muscles, especially after carrying babies and bags etc.
- Everyone has opinions on everyone else's kids, don't take them to heart.
- Children grow out of stages and you forget these differecult stages as time passes.
- Give your child lots of praise for good behaviour be specific with your praise
- Give child love & they will trust you, be more open with you
- Have a small low table in kitchen for drink so your child can help themselves and put the drink back in a tidy place and know where it is.
- Teach them to sit down to eat a biscuit/snack; don't wonder around with food in their mouth.
- Talk to with respect like an adult
- Both siblings are different, try not to compare them and expect them to act the same way, react to the same things.
- Age appropriate rules & boundaries are necessary – don't set rules that aren't age appropriate i.e. a too early bed time, too restrictive, or too difficult to understand.
- Don't spoil a friend/family member, the more you do the less they do, sometimes you have to stop doing too much and pushing and step back to make them do it for themselves, to give them some confidence and independence.
- You child m**ay hit you after you have been away to express anger at being left**
- **Don't have naughty space as bed room, the bedroom should be a nice relaxing place they enjoy, not somewhere they associate with bad things, otherwise they will not want to relax/sleep there.**

To get to sleep at night – have a good bedtime routine, gradually cut their day nap and think of inventive stories to tell them to help them want to sleep (I made up a story for Ritchie that his bed was a magic cloud and if he closed his eyes and thought about and imagined what he wanted to see the cloud would take him there).

Try different things but give them time to work, use your imagination.

When I had trouble dressing Ritchie – he would run away. I found the following helped;

- Got him to pick his outfit / chose fun things i.e. a dinosaur cardigan and said do you want to dress as a dinosaur today, that will be fun. I then went onto distract him whilst I dressed him by saying all the fun things he was going to do, what friends he would see and how they would be so impressed with his dinosaur outfit.
- I dressed him as a soon as he woke up (so he was a bit dozy).
- I dressed him on the bed so it was easier for me to lean over him and hold him. I laid him down and held his legs up/put a hand on his chest to keep him in place. I got him to join in and hold his baby/change his baby, think he was dressing himself and mummy was helping and I got him to hold his legs up whilst I changed his nappy.
- Stopped chasing him when he ran away
- Gave him a prize for getting dressed
- Some days some things worked and some days they didn't, you have to keep calm and keep trying and be imaginative, patient and fair.
- I reasoned with him and showed him its quicker and easier when he co-operates.
- Once his trousers are on, I sit him on my knee and cuddle him to change his top (although sometimes he throws his head back and head-butts me).
- Sometimes I say **"if u get dressed quickly we will go downstairs and get x toy" this encourages him if he wants to play with the said toy.**
- **Another tip is to over exaggerate the fun of getting dressed. Wow you can wear your dinosaur cardigan.**
- **Instead of a change station, put a change mat on a chest of draws. To make him stay on the change mat say if you lay still I will play x,y,z and play his favourite song on the iphone and if he moves, take the iphone of of him so that he learns he must stay still to have his nappy changed.**
- **If you take something away because he is naughty, don't give it back. You must stick by your punishment and follow threats through otherwise he will think he can get away with it and won't take you seriously/show him you mean what you say. Even if he is good don't give his toy back/let him go to the park until the next day, say now you are being good you can have x toy back tomorrow or we can go to the park tomorrow, follow through with promises too. Make it clear why you are cross, be specific and use a sad face, don't say naughty because then they will see this as a label and act up to it. Don't keep going on i.e. lecturing or nagging your child, sternly say what they have done and then move on. After the issue has been dealt with move the focus to**

something else, focus on something fun to divert their attention away from the negative, always focus on the positive i.e. say lets go and do x, y, z now.

- **If he throws food take the food away (he will soon learn not to do it again, no child intentionally goes hungry).**
- If he gets angry give him a way to vent his anger i.e. a specific cushion to punch or put a timer up and say at the end of this timer you will be calm.
- Give praise when he is good but ensure the praise is specific so that he knows why he is being good and is encouraged to repeat the good behaviour.
- Try a sticker chart – use a chart to focus on one thing at a time i.e. getting dressed, start with a target of 5 stickers (this can later be gradually increased). This also helps with counting. Make a laminated sheet with days of the week and then get his favourite stickers. His prize doesn't have to be something expensive – it can be some bubbles or crayons etc.
- A time out area is an area where he gets no attention and there are no toys / stimulation i.e. a quiet area.
- Never call him naughty
- Give a 5 minute warning before stopping him playing and moving onto another activity i.e. dinner. He likes to do things his way and doesn't like to be interrupted so warnings are important to him.
- Encourage him to tidy up and make tidying up a game.
- You want him to be compliant, if he doesn't' do something after 5 minutes of trying , go away and then distract him and steer him towards something else. Don't focus on the bad, just focus on the good. Distract from bad behaviour and focus on what you want him to do. Its less about discipline for a toddler and more about distracting away from bad behaviour and focusing their attention to something good. i.e. taking toy off them and getting them to read a book if they are throwing.
- They easily form habits both good and bad, the more good things you can encourage them to do the more good habits are formed and less bad habits.
- Use a timer / time out for 1 minute per year of their age.

- If your child doesn't take your instructions, then make him sit down somewhere. If he refuses to sit to ignore him (ignore bad behaviour until he complies), when he then does something good to give him over exaggerated praise.
- Another tip is to pretend to be an aeroplane and give your child a cuddle.
- Encourage your child to have 'kind hands' and if s/he he his say no have kind hands and demonstrate a gentle touch.
- Everyone needs to be consistent, work with the nursery and draw up a behaviour plan. Use their knowledge and guidance.
- Ritchie easily copies what he sees (copies scar from the lion king, even though it is a U rating). Some children are more subseptible to certain things and some children copy more – always watch a film through furst before showing them. Although they

will pick up on the smallest thing you wouldn't even notice so you can't account for everything, they will also see things and copy other children at nursery etc.

Most toddlers go through a stage of hurting mummy out of frustration/temper, for attention or because they are cross ie if mum has been away when mum comes back they realise how much they missed her and get cross.
Usually they grow out of it but you must ensure they don't do it again.
Over exaggerate you hurt mummy and act out being sore. If they laugh say you don't like it if you are hurt, you wouldn't like it if mummy hurt you.

When they say sorry get them to also explain why they are sorry. This way they will understand what they are sorry for, and will associate it rather than seeing sorry as a magic word.

Child behaviour – tantrums

- If giving them time out, have an area that is just for time out i.e. a special rug that you get out for them to sit on, or a special different colour chair. If you use a high chair or cot they will associate this with being naughty and won't want to eat/go to sleep in it.

- You could use an egg timer for time out

- If they are too young for time out – distract them with a toy when you see them about to go into a tantrum/the tantrum coming on. If they are having a tantrum, ignore them. Hold them if you need to pick them up so that they are facing away from you and can't pull your hair etc. If you can move to a different room, area of the room or place them on a bea bag etc, until they stop.

- Be consistent with discipline - if your child goes to different carers you all need to have same plan for discipline, what treats your child can eat etc so there is consistency and your child know what the boundaries are. This will stop confusion and stop them getting upset at one place because they can't do something that they can do at another place.

- Kids might show off / play up in front of friends.

- Each day they react diff / diff triggers. Go with the flow, be flexible. Don't try too hard or expect to get anything done, just focus on looking after your child and having time to follow their ques - then anything you do manage to get done is a bonus. If you have a list of things to do, it may not be possible, especially if your baby has a bad day and then you will feel stressed that you didn't get those things done. Having said that sometimes you have to have a plan and you have things you have to do, otherwise the days would just go and you wouldn't get anything done.

- If you have issues with your child's behaviour, write down when they have tantrums and what trigges them etc.

- Food colouring and e-number may send your kids hyper (not just sugar).

- They go through different stages of tantrums etc at terrible 2s but usually grow out of it. Although you do need to manage their behaviour try not to over analyse, or over worry.

- Don't smack your child; it makes them confused and violent towards you. Be consistent with discipline.

- Be assertive when telling your child. They will look for signs of weakness/will detect if you are unsure and they will try and push the boundaries.

- If your child is very intelligent you have to appeal to their imagination and keep them stimulated otherwise they will get bored and this is when they will be naughty.

- Other children will influence them, even as toddlers they copy, don't worry just keep teaching them good behaviour. At school they will come across bad influences and have to learn how to ignore bad influences and practise bad behaviour. From approx. age 2 they copy each other, if not before but from age 2 they copy and play together, rather than just around each other.

- Tell off firm - they will then cry/ have tantrum. Don't comfort them at this tantrum stare or they will continue to have tantrums when they don't get their own way. Stage will pass. Be persistent and consistent.

- When they get over tired they get hyper and can't calm themselves. Sometimes you have to hold them and they fight. It seems cruel holding them tight whilst they fight but sometimes it's the only way and then they will sleep. Ritchie did this, even as a baby. He hated being held when he wanted to move. At first I thought he didn't want to be cradled because he had acid reflux and needed to sit up/was in pain. Then I realised it was because he didn't want to sleep, and even as a baby new how to fight the sleep. He is quite hyper and can't settle. He says no mummy hold he doesn't like it, but it's worst letting him not sleep and getting over tired.

- Hold arms down if hitting and naughty & have area to go / naughty step.

- When naughty – short sharp and firm commands to say stop or no put down and don't cuddle, distract with a toy if the tantrum lasts too long.

- Baby biting - He will be doing it out of frustration and it's quite a normal stage for them to go through. The best thing to do is when he bites firmly say 'no', put him down if you are holding him and move away from him for a moment. It could take a while but he will grow out of it eventually. If he is in any kind of childcare let them know and find out if they have the same problem and find out how they handle it. You could if your child continues to bite, warn them that if they continue to bite they will have to bite soap, then get your child to bite on soap if s/he bites again, this will soon prevent them doing it again in the future (you could also use a similar technique to stop swearing).

Tips & tools

EVERY YEAR, MY WIFE AND I DEVOTE THE MONTH OF NOVEMBER TO CONVINCING OUR CHILDREN THAT, WHILE THEY SLEEP, THEIR PLASTIC DINOSAUR FIGURES COME TO LIFE.

It began modestly enough. The kids woke up to discover that the dinosaurs had gotten into a box of cereal and made a mess on the kitchen table.

The next morning, the dinos had climbed onto the kitchen counter to raid the fruit bowl.

The morning after that, they had managed to breach the refrigerator and help themselves to a carton of eggs. "Uh-oh," we heard our girls whisper. "Mom and Dad are not going to like this."

Things quickly escalated from there. More often than not, the dinos' antics were less than tidy. They are dinosaurs, after all.

To be fair, they did clean up after themselves from time to time.

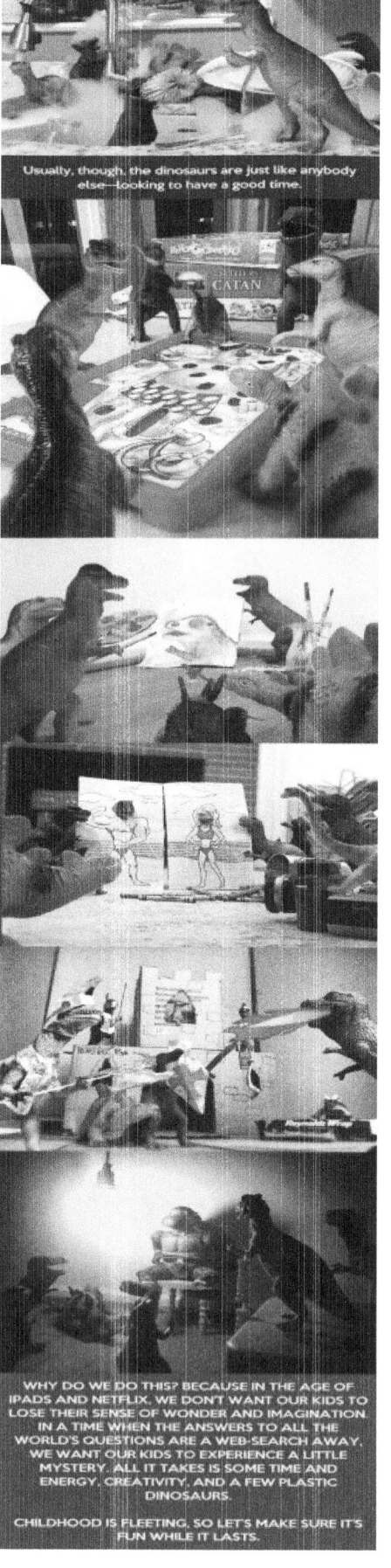

Usually, though, the dinosaurs are just like anybody else—looking to have a good time.

WHY DO WE DO THIS? BECAUSE IN THE AGE OF IPADS AND NETFLIX, WE DON'T WANT OUR KIDS TO LOSE THEIR SENSE OF WONDER AND IMAGINATION. IN A TIME WHEN THE ANSWERS TO ALL THE WORLD'S QUESTIONS ARE A WEB-SEARCH AWAY, WE WANT OUR KIDS TO EXPERIENCE A LITTLE MYSTERY. ALL IT TAKES IS SOME TIME AND ENERGY, CREATIVITY, AND A FEW PLASTIC DINOSAURS.

CHILDHOOD IS FLEETING, SO LET'S MAKE SURE IT'S FUN WHILE IT LASTS.

Stereotyping

But snap judgments can often be very unfair or misleading because they are over-simplified and based on such small amounts of evidence. Another word for over-simplifying in this way is **stereotyping**.

Gahagan defines a stereotype as a belief about the characteristics possessed by some group and possessed, therefore, by any member of that group (e.g. "all politicians are crooked, therefore Tony Blair must be crooked").

Our very names can also provide stereotypes. If we know that someone is called Wayne or Sharon, we may well expect less of them than if they were called Charles or Eleanor. **Harari and McDavid** (1973) showed that teachers marking essays by unknown students are influenced by the name on the bottom. If an attractive or intelligent-sounding name was found on the bottom of the essay, marks tended to be a full grade higher.

Physical attraction is a key aspect of the process of stereotyping. If we find someone attractive, we are likely to attribute a large number of other positive qualities to that person.

Our stereotypes tend to be entirely positive or entirely negative. Once we have attributed one positive quality to a person, the rest of the stereotype may well also be positive (remember the halo effect!) or negative. But that is not true of all stereotypes. Our stereotypical picture of a Frenchman, for instance, may be a mixture of good and bad qualities.

Here are a few ideas that may be adopted by the working teacher:

1. **education** — explain the lifestyles and differences of the different groups in a non-judgmental way. Prejudice thrives on ignorance and a sense of 'otherness' so anything which draws on the common humanity and interests of 'different' individuals should help.

2. **co-operation rather than competition** — as we saw in the last unit, competition for scarce resources can be a cause of prejudice. Instead of pitting the children against each other, devise activities where they can be split into multi-racial groups so that they have to employ teamwork in order to achieve common goals.

3. **equalisation** — make sure that you are seen to treat all individuals equally, whatever their group. Encourage them to see each other as equals. The very theory of 'comprehensive' schooling is linked to the idea that equalisation has positive social benefits.

But are all these techniques likely to have the same positive effect? Or are you doing more harm than good? Psychologists disagree on the best approach for tackling prejudice and we will look in more detail at the pros and cons of different strategies.

Positive and Negative Expectations

Labels may not refer to a specific job-title or set of tasks. A label may simply be an adjective that someone else has applied to us, e.g. "John is a lazy so-and-so" or "Mary is good enough to make it as a concert pianist". But such labels have great power to affect our decisions and our level of performance. You have already come across the idea of the **self-fulfilling prophecy**. If John is conscious that he has been labelled "lazy", he is more likely to conform to it than to fight against it. Mary, meanwhile, may become one of life's over-achievers.

Hence the importance of encouragement and approval in all learning situations. Success breeds success, they say, and there is no doubt that the expectation of success is a key component in performing at one's best. Athletes are encouraged to visualise the moment of their own victory and to believe that nothing can stand in their way.

There are limits however. There is a thin line between super-confidence and complacency, the feeling that you are so good that you don't really have to try. But this is only a problem in a small minority of cases. In the real world, the problem most of the time is to create positive rather than negative expectations.

expected to be incompetent and unmotivated at needlework, domestic science, and perhaps even mainstream subjects like English.

Later in life, we still face the stereotype that the man is the hunter and the woman looks after the home, bringing up the children. Men often expect themselves, even today, to be the breadwinner for the family, and if they are thwarted by unemployment or some other problem, they expect themselves to be bad at child-rearing. So the wife ends up doing two jobs at once while the man does neither.

Strategies for Modifying Negative Expectations

Such problems are difficult to tackle because they are a combination of society's expectations of the individual and the individual's expectations of themselves, each leading to reinforce the other. The circle needs to be broken at some point and one decisive event may be enough to break it. Perhaps the child gets surprisingly good marks in one test and, from then on, the teacher expects them to do much better.

Good teachers with a new class will often start the year by giving no more than moderate marks even for good pieces of work (e.g. 10/20, 11/20) and then gradually shift the marks upwards as the year goes by. With luck, nearly all the pupils in the class will get the feeling that they are making concrete improvement, especially if they are unaware of everyone else's marks. This is one of many ways of boosting self-confidence. If it is apparent that the teacher has genuinely high expectations for all the pupils, they will do their best to prove them right.

When psychotherapists are called in to tackle the problem of low achievement and low self-expectation, they will probably try to tackle the patient's poor self-image directly. It is usually a good idea to negotiate realistic short-term and medium-goals that the person can work towards, making it clear that the therapist fully expects them to succeed. Success is duly rewarded and the targets are set a little further away. But a psychotherapist has no particular advantages over a good teacher or even a sympathetic friend. The key points are that someone should expect you to do well and cares that you do well.

Sex-Rôle and Racial Stereotyping

Sex-rôle stereotyping refers to the way we have expectations of people simply on the basis that they are men or women (or boys/girls). Girls might be brought up to do the washing up after meals while their brothers are never asked to do the same job. Men are often assumed to know more about computers or electrical wiring or football. So if someone has an electrical wiring problem, they may contact a male relative first — this kind of stereotyping may save time in the long run, and time-saving is the principal value of all forms of stereotyping.

Stereotypes like this can become **self-fulfilling prophecies**. Because a girl or woman is expected to be better at sewing buttons, for example, it is more likely that she will have been asked to do a job of this kind and so it is more likely that she will have developed the skills necessary to do the job successfully, and so on. In this way, the stereotype proves itself to be a useful working theory and so it is reinforced. If on

- Sleepwalking can affect anybody, but it is more common in children. Children may just sit up in bed and go back to sleep again or they may actually get out of bed and walk around. If your child sleepwalks, make sure they'll be safe by using stair gates, locking windows and doors and removing any obstacles they could fall over. If you find your child sleepwalking, lead them back to bed but avoid waking them up.
- **Cut grapes in ½ for your baby/child, otherwise they are a chocking hazard.**
- **They may put raisins up their nose, so it is a good idea to watch them when they have small peicies of food. Ritchie always put raisins up his nose. If they do get them lodged in their nose, don't poke up there it will make it worse, calm your child and take them to the hospital.**
- **Get a larger size Halloween costume, when you go trick or treating to go over coat. Otherwise you will find your child is all dressed up nut cold and when you put their coat on you can't see their outfit. Skeleton dresses are good to go over coats and jeans, or you could put a black fleece under it.**
- **Spend as much time as you can with your kids whilst they are young, you might regret having only a little time with them later on when if you work full time. There first few years are important and when they get older if you still work part time it's nice to have time to yourself too.**
- **Don't let your child sit in the W position (on their knees with their legs out to the side), because this puts pressure on their hips and knees and can cause them problems when they get older.**
- **Try giving your toddler fruit tea / green tea / jasmine tea, make it up like tea with boiling water and then mix in cold water. As long as it is naturally caffeine and sugar free it maybe a healthy alternative t juice and squash.**
- **Your child may stop drinking water if they want juice - they are clever. Don't give in and give them juice, keep them on the water, its healthier. Keep them entertained sit and play educational games, teach them the alphabet, colours etc spend time sitting and playing one to one, this will reduce their urge to run about and throw things.**
- **Play gentle music / pregnancy hypnotherapy music to calm baby.**
- **Put a blanket over 2 chairs to make a tent/camp, put toys underneath, to keep your little one entertained.**
- **Massage to keep calm / bath & low lights etc**
- **May sleep better/longer in bed**
- **Theme park - avoid busy times**
- **Units to go under bed to stop them crawling under**
- **Check when go in room, check not behind the door**
- **As a mum you feel guilty about everything ie leaving your baby to go to work, the advice you give etc**
- **Get a canopy/cover over your patio so you child can play out in the rain & hot sun and will be protected.**
- **Stair gate across door - then can't open the door, perhaps a lock.**
- **If your child spits out their medicine/won't take their medicine – pinch their nose, or blow on their face.**
- **If your child has too many toys keep presents for gifts for other children and give your child the money you would have spent. Or ask for money instead of gifts.**

- **Get your child used to tidying toys. Tidy in front of them / get them to tidy toys away.**

- Broccoli makes kids behave. If they eat lots of broccoli it is supposed to help to keep them calm. If you also keep your child entertained, they are less likely to misbehave. If they are very active they may need lots of fresh air and exercise to burn off excess energy. Lots of exercise, lots of activities (a good mix of activities – active and calming things like reading) , and a good diet all helps to keep your child's behaviour in check. Set a good example and practise good behaviour yourself. Also speak to your child and if they seem upset find out what is wrong. If they are upset and unsettled this will affect their behaviour.

- It's a good idea to put a bed in your baby's room. That way if they are ill in the night you can go into them and sleep in their room. Or lay down and read a book and rock them in their bed, before putting them in their cot.
- Don't give pillow - pillow age
- Though they're often sold with crib bedding sets, pillows are not recommended for children under 2. Kids that small can easily suffocate while using one.

- Actually, older kids don't need pillows either. Parents often think a pillow will provide their child with extra comfort, not realizing that their child was doing fine without it.

- If you want to introduce a pillow, it's best to wait until your toddler moves from a crib to a bed. But if you want to give him one while he's still sleeping in a crib, go with one that's small (the size of an airline pillow) and firm. Stay away from feather pillows, which are too soft, can set off allergies, and can smother a child if his head sinks into it while he's sleeping.

- When you buy curtains for the babies room, get a cot duvet, sleeping bag (X2) and sile duvet covers and pillow cases all to match. That way as you baby progresses from cot to bed you don't have to change the room décor and curtain (or hunt for a similar set, if that design is no longer in the shops). If you buy it all together it will be matching.

- When you have a baby, treat yourself to some jewellery with the birthstone of that month in.
- Do fun things with other mums / children, arranged and spur of the moment i.e. a MacDonald's dinner after nursery etc.
- Make education fun - turn learning into games.
- The best feeling in the world (and the best tonic for depression and illness etc) is snuggles with your baby/child.
- Get feet measured regularly because they grow quickly.
- They go through phases ie when acting like a baby.
- When Ritchie was 2 he became unsettled at nursery when the older children went up and he was left with the babies. In September when the older children go up to the next group and new children arrive they may find it hard. If they go to a nursery only 1 or 2 days a week, they may find it hard to remember the routine, they maybe used to one to one attention the rest of the week and they may have more discipline or different rules so try using the same approach to avoid confusion, they may find that they have less attention because it is not one to one. Or they may have separation anxiety or get into a routine of being upset. Try and be positive when you take them to nursery, explain how fun it will be and don't let them see you feeling sad. Don't fuss the and make a big deal about asking why they don't want to go, giving attention to it will make it worst (although at first it may be important to talk to your child to establish any

possible issues), after this distract from the negative and make it positive. When they arrive find toys that they like and give them the toys that they enjoy, this will distract them when you go. Say bye but remind them they will have fun.

- Be careful with chicken bones as they splinter / have gristle on etc.
- Back to back labours are more painful.
- Now that you have to stay in in evenings can do online evening courses, not at first but perhaps after a year or 2 when baby starts sleeping through the night.
- When they are really little babies they put everything in their mouth, then they stop and start again as they are teething. Then just as you think they are safe at approx. 2 years when they know what food is and what they shouldn't eat. They then start again putting things in their mouth and trying to swallow them because they think that they are sweets.
- If your child is naughty use short firm commands. You could use symbol/sign cards.
- They start having tantrums from a year. They may have a tantrum if they are frustrated or tired or hungry thus the way to deal with it is take them away from whatever is frustrating them/move area, cuddle and distract with a toy and use reassuring but assertive words, feed/give water, or out in bed for a sleep.
- Don't be quiet when they sleep – that way they get used to noise. Otherwise they will become light sleepers.
- Its important to have other mums to talk to, who know what you are going through. Friends without kids don't understand.
- If you are going to a museum / day out you will end up in a toy shop, the are usually over priced so it is a good idea to take a toy with you (buy something in advance), take your child out of the shop and give them that.
- Dried fruit sticks to their teeth and fruit has sugar, so be wary. Don't brush their teeth for 30 mins after eating fruit, because of the citric acid.
- If your child won't eat their food you can give them food off of your plate as they may eat this, or make plane noises to make their food entertaining. This can lead to bad food habits but maybe okay for a short while just to get food down. Or you can add sweet foods like carrot to make the food more appealing, although again you don't want to get them too used to just eating sweet food.
- If you think that your baby/child has hurt their arm but you are not sure if they are attention seeking, to test their arm give them something and see if they take it with that hand.
- Put in baby swing / high chair in front of TV so they are strapped in whilst you get dressed.
- Keep banners, balloons, party bags etc & table cloths for the next party. Keep a party box ready for all occasions.
- Have a cake carrier and a cake tin full of goodies to decorate your cake.
- It's good to keep the baby in your bed room for the first year.
- Green snot - infection. Clear - no infection.
- Feed on demand for first few weeks then establish a pattern of feeding.
- If they are hungry they will wake up for feeds so try giving more milk or if they are on solids cut the milk down and give more solid food (give cheese and yoghurt to add calcium and make up for the reduction in milk).
- If they are tired they will become hyper and naughtier and whingey, if they behave like that try and put them to sleep. Even when they are tired they may fight their sleep.
- Stairs – teach them to go down the stairs backwards or on their bum. If you are on your own with the pushchair, go backwards and pull them u the stairs,

bumping the wheels up. Going down, go forward and bump down one step at a time by tipping the chai back and just using the back wheels.

- Start weaning / feed b4 6 months i.e. advice is at @ 4 months now. Could start with baby rice b4 then.
- Feed liquid don't do baby led weaning, can try some baby led weaning but they won't get nutrition straight away, until get used to eating. Once they have finished eating, don't try and give them more food. They know what they need and when they are full.
- You sometimes need to be firm, don't shout/raise voice, just say 'no' and distract them. They will try and push your limits, they know what they can get away with.
- When you put your baby/child in the car seat, make sure they are sat back, not leaning forward when you put seat belt on, otherwise it is loose and they get their arms out.
- Don't tell your child off too much, so that when you do tell them off it has more impact. Over exaggerate and praise them when they are good, but ignore them when they are bad.
- If your child doesn't hold your hand - keep putting them back in car, until when they get out they hold your hand.
- If they refuse to get into the car seat, in a safe place, pretend to get in the car and go without them, you can do the same thing with tantrums at the shops (but keep them in sight and near by).
- If s/he refuses to lay down for nappy changes, change him/her in the same place so that its not seen as a game and keep in the bathroom until s/he lays still. Or use a book, or toy etc. to distract your baby whilst you change their napy.
- Asparatame sweetener is artificial so it is hard for your body to process. It stays around longer and after 30 min your body craves sugar again. You are better with full fat. Sucralose is better than Asparatame. This is why full fat is better for children. Plus they need the fat/sugar/energy and calcium from milk and they burn the energy off.
- Expose your child to as many things and experiences as possible so that they have more options of what they may be interested in and want to do later in life i.e. play lots of different music, take them to the ballet and theatre, let them try ice skating and lots of varied sports, let them play in a gymnasium (some run soft play and toddler sessions), if they show interest in a particular area, then encourage this.
- If your child looks older, carry a photocopy of their passport, so that you pay for tickets based on their age, and aren't charged for an older child/charged more.
- Say to your child good girl/boy, rather than clever girl/boy.
- Watch your child with your handbag to make sure that they don't put your handbag straps around their neck.
- Before your baby is walking use thick socks or slippers in the pram. You can get pram shoes, but there are harder to get for boys.
- Bribe with food to get in car seat, or if your baby tenses up and won't go in it, tickle him/her gentle to get baby to move enough to put the straps around. Also loosen off the straps first and have them out the way of the seat so that it makes it easier to put your baby in.
- Do voice record of your baby
- If you keep tablets in your handbag get a purse with a double headed zip that you can put a combination lock on.
- Have a high bolt on your garden gate, my son from the age of of 2 could open the gate latch.

- From the age of 2 they say more and more every day.
- Huggies (pure) the green ones are the best.
- Babies sleep patterns keep changing. They change a lot in the first year and then even at 2 they may start waking in the night, maybe due to teething and they may then get into bad habits and keep waking. From 4-6 they get night terrors.
- It is lovely when they get to the age that they interact with you and as you start understanding what they are saying/what they want, it makes life easier.
- When you are out and about watch your baby doesn't pull off and throw his/her shoes/hat etc.
- Paracetmol i.e. calpol can be very dangerous if you take too much within 24 hours, it can also mask the symptons of meningitis, which start off as flu like symptons and don't always have a rash. Most child care providers now have a policy where they will not give such medication to a child. Ritchie's childcare provider won't even let me pop into give him such medication, they say if he is ill and needs it, he is too ill to be at nursery.
- Remember to save some of your annual leave for nursery closure, such as training days and for sickness days. If you child has vomiting and diohrea they will have to stay off of nursery for a while (usually 48 hours).
- get first one potty trained & get terrible 2 out of way before you have another.
- a routine is good so your baby sleeps, you can then have time to yourself while they nap. If you do things routinely it gets easier & quicker ie re-stocking the baby bag as soon as you get in.
- top bottle up with extra milk for last feed.
- As your baby becomes a toddler and you start packing up the baby toys, keep some of the teethers back as you may need them until your baby is 2 ½ , as s/he sporadically continues to get more teeth.
- If your baby runs away and doesn't let you change him/her and runs away, change in the cot, so that s/he can't run away.
- Use duct tape to cover sharp edges, fix toys etc.
- Make things easy for yourself, don't do things the hard way. Except help when it is offered. If you can afford a cleaner, get one. Make bottles in advance, just cool them off and store them at the back of the fridge. Or if you can afford it buy ready made cartons. Use disposable nappies and have spare sheets and lots of vest and clothes so you don't run low. Tumble dry clothes rather than hang around the house. Clean bottles in the dishwasher (and then steralise them) if they are stored outside the sterliser/after 24 hours they are no longer sterile. Your time and sanity is more important than saving money or electric.
- Children start kicking off at nursery - clingy in the morning. At approx age 2 when they are aware their parents are leaving them.
- They will cry but are usually fine 10 mins after you have gone.
- They go through a stage where they do their own thing and tend not to need their mum, yet when they are ill/need something they always need their mums to be there for them.

- Nightmare/dream to brain growing/developing & processing so much info

- Grandparents get to enjoy kids more because they can devote their attention, have less to do, can give them back & have experience.

- Set time aside to devote to them. Make the most / enjoy them.

- **Get a play pen / gate to stop toddler getting to your baby**

- **Only do something if it feels instinctively right.**

- **Try your own way of doing things- learn for yourself - do what is right for you.**

- Face painting is good to get children talking and out of their shell. Its great to take face paints to a party. Bowls of water and paint brushes also keep them entertained. Snazaroo face paint is good.

- At a certain time your baby / child may develop a fear of the dark. My son Ritchie had a subtle night light but at age 2 wouldn't sleep, we put his side lamp on and then he slept in his cot. Things in their room that cause shadows and coats and dressing gowns on he back of their door can also scare them. A warm red/orange light is better than a white colour night, because this is better for the body to sleep. Human beings have evolved alongside these daily light patterns, developing biological mechanisms to trigger sleep and wakefulness. When the light starts to fade at night, our bodies start producing melatonin, aka the 'sleepy hormone'.
- As morning approaches, the daylight becomes a signal to stop producing melatonin, which makes us feel alert and awake. It's a beautifully balanced symbiotic relationship with nature.

- Your baby's sight; Up to a quarter of children have problems with their eyesight, so if you've noticed any tell-tale signs, for instance if they hold objects up very close to their face or one of their eyes moves inwards (called a squint), or if you have a strong family history of poor eyesight, it's a good idea to tell your GP and ask for an eye check. It is a good idea to take them to the optician from the age of 2.
- Activities for all ages – swimming, ice skating, theme park, aquarium zool. These sorts of things all children can do.
- Painting and face painting are goo to do
- You can make your own play dough
- Mustard seed oil and camphor oil mixed with eucalyptus make a great rub for coughs and colds, you can also burn it in an aroma stone, glycerine can also be given for coughs.
- Prune juice, fresh fruit and tummy massages are great for constipation.
- If you go on a day trip don't buy the toys at the museum, try and get at a local shop, otherwise they will cost more, the same goes for the theatre (i.e. buy a peppa pig toy at a shop or online before going to the show).
- Get a catch on your DVD box, children love posting things in the DVD / CD player.
- You used to be able to get a fold up pram which became a ruck sack/child carrier, which was great for the beach.
- If you are flying you will need to book your pram in, it is a good idea to label it and also make it stand out so that no one else takes it. Especially if you have a maclaren, which most parents have.
- Create a nice space at home so that your child/teenager will want to hang out at home and you know where they are and what they are doing i.e. get a log cabin in the garden, with a TV and bar in.
- **You need to get as much rest as you can, when you can so you are on peak performance to look after your child. If you are tired you may miss things/ accidents occur or you get run down & ill. You owe it to your child to be the best that you can as often as you can.**

- Babies can choke on liquid i.e. milk or mucus, not just food, be ready to tip them up and pat them on the back (see first aid notes).

- Give your children love but teach them to be independent and think for themselves too. You don't want them to be clingy & needy they need to be loving & open but confident in the themselves in order to form good relationships in the future & become successful.

- Sensory party – you can have someone come to your home to arrange a sensory party for your childs first birthday

- Ask the nursery who your childs friends are and who close in age & give invites to the nursery. Set up a nursery mums face book group to stay in contact with other mums.

- They stop having milk when they are ready they will just not drink it/push it away. Ritchie stopped his night feed but likes his morning one as he is thirsty after night.

- The height that they are at, at 2 doubled will be their height when grown up?

- Be careful of your children having named items such as bags and pendants with their name on, because strangers may call their name and they may think that they know them and may then go with the stranger.
- Think carefully about what you name your child and what you dress them in etc. other children are cruel and you want to make sure you don't give them any reason to get bullied.
- Have a small bin outside the back door to keep nappies in.
- As your baby gets older s/he will pay and entertain themselves, they will be easier to look after in some ways and more fun. This is a good time to go part time at work so that you can take them out on fun days out (although if they are hyper they will be harder to look after because they can run away when you are trying to dress them).
- If your under 3 is naughty and is too young to understand the naughty step, instead of smacking put him/her in a corner / ignore so that s/he knows that the behaviour is not acceptable. It is especially important to discipline if they are violent.
- As your child gets older you can give them a technology ban i.e. no computer, no tv, no phone for a week. Give 3 warnings and on the 3rd warning and they get a ban (like 3 strikes and you are out).
- Between 2 – 2 ½ years your child has a review.
- Your child may get cradle cap upto 4 years (don't pick cradle cap), if it gets really bad then get medicated cream from the doctor.
- If there is someone your child likes/looks up to say they do x, y, z in order to get your chid to do x, y, z i.e. so and so eats their dinner, are you going to eat your dinner?
- Items with re-chargeable batteries such as baby monitors and phones will eventually fail and after a year or 2 the re-chargeable batteries will need to be replaced.
- Nurofen can be given with calpol to help bring the temperature down.
- You have a bad heachache caused by a sinuse infection but don't want to take pain killers – rub vicks on your head.
- If your baby doesn't eat at night, take some milk up with you, in a carton, to give him/her should s/he wake in the night.
- Get medicine in pesserie form, it works faster and if they vomit it stays in.
- Give a bottle of milk on the aeroplane when landing, to help ease their ears.

- Get them reading books from a young age, take them to the library. Make props to make stories come to life i.e. the bear hunt story, use brown paper on cardboard to walk over it as if walking through mud etc.
- Have an alarm on your door so they can't just go out, without you knowing.
- Keep the water tray/sand pit in the garden upside down, so that it doesn't fill with rain water and become a hazard.
- Make sure they don't dribble on library books, wipe them clean so that the pages don't stick.
- Keep low windows closed, so that your baby doesn't climb out.

- If your child / baby goes through a stage of throwing things, or hitting toys against items, say no and a short clear command i.e. no don't throw or no don't hit then take the item off them/get it from where they threw it and say now you can't play with it, take it off them for the rest of the day but leave it somewhere prominent where they can see it but can't get to it, so that they can see they can't have it because they threw it.

- Buy clothes a size bigger, so that they last longer (they grow so quickly and you want them to get the maximum wear out of them). When they are younger they don't wear the clothes out so much because they grow out of them quicker (and maybe less active) so you can buy good condition early years 2nd hand clothes / keep the clothes for the 2nd child. As they get older this is less of the case.
- ……………………………
- ………………
- Monitor cord; If you use a baby listening monitor/video/sensor pad ensure that the cord is not somewhere where the baby can pull it into the cot etc, as this may present a strangulation risk, tommee tippi now do a cord cover for their monitors.

- Mattress - zip off; Get a mattress that has a zip off cover that can be washed, you may also want to use a separate mattress protector. You can get duvet & pillow protectors, which are useful. Soak blood soiled sheets in salt and cold water to get rid of the blood.

- Give advice to your children but teach them independence, be there for them but you both need to have time apart on occasion.

- Follow your instinct and your own parents advice

- Some germs are good, an over sterile environment may stop them from developing their own immunity.

- In the bathrooms have door locks that can be opened from the outside so that your child can't lock themselves in whilst locking you out.

- You can buy things later but can't buy back time with your baby & you don't know what will happen/be around the corner so spend as much time with your children as you can (you still need a break to yourself every now and again).

- Be there & give them security, security and love is the best thing you can give your child, without this they cannot grow and develop.

- 10 second rule. Don't go to them straight away when they fall. Give it 10 seconds, talk to them and reassure them, if they are still crying they may be hurt and need a cuddle. If they see you panic and go to them straight away when they fall, this will make them feel frightened and cry every time they fall.

- They need a secure home to develop & be independent

- Sibling jealousy – this is normal, try and give equal attention, buy a new toy for your child when there is a new baby (this includes cousins too), encourage them to play nicely with each other and be kind to each other.

- Don't try & be a hero, accept all the help you can

- Don't let go of pram without break on, wind / incline may blow it away

- Sun cream – ensure to use water proof for dribble face, otherwise it will wear off when your baby dribbles and they will burn.

- Babies are nocturnal, don't panic they will grow out of it in their own time.

- Make a lava lamp with water then mix food colouring and oil, add salt to make it bubble and add glitter too, mix it in a plastic bottle (seal the lid tight with cello tape and supervise your child with it).

- You can get colour free calpol (as well as sugar free), this may stop your child from being hyper.

- If your child is hyper encourage him/her to read books and have quite time, ensure your child doesn't get over tired (this makes them hyper) watch what they eat and when and give him/her plenty of exercise and fresh air, to run off the excess energy.

- If s/he won't take milk in a bottle put it in a beaker, straw or sippy cup. Warm it in a microwave dish, stir it & pour into the desired cup.

- Change the nappy in bathroom, otherwise it may make the whole house smell. Use essential oils and natural air fresheners so that they don't irritate the baby.

Isn't the above just common sense? I always ask my son what he wants to do, what he likes etc. even at a year, before he can speak properly he can tell me what he likes and wants to do by nodding. Although sometimes he has to do things he may not like, like eat healthier food, put his toys down to go out etc because I have to be practicable and although a little of what they like is good for them you also have to balance this with being healthy, it's not always too good to let them have their own way all the time otherwise they will grow up to be egocentrically maniacs unable to handle stress and deal with rejection. We all have to do things we don't want to do at times and we need balance. My son doesn't like having his nappy changed but it wouldn't be good to leave him in a dirty nappy. I try and distract him with toys to make the process more fun for him, but it still has to be done. It's good to try and make things as fun as possible for them, children need to play and have fun but also to have love and feel loved, I think that's more important than anything. I try and cuddle Ritchie lots, although he trys to run away and play. He likes cuddles on his terms and will play and then just come over for a quick head on my knee and then he is off again, he is very active and that is how it should be. Cuddles when your child wants them, not when you need them (although I do often feel better after cuddles with my baby, it's the best therapy ever, it makes you realise what is important i.e. them and everything else is insignificant).

Don't try too hard to be supermum, this isn't possible. Don't beat yourself up about things. Do what you can but don't over do it, otherwise you will get stressed. Just be yourself and you have to be practicable and do what you need to, it's okay to let your child watch TV so that you can have some time to prepare the dinner etc.

If your baby is having a bad tummy or is unsettled keep a note of what your baby / child eats and when and his/her toilet habits and any other symptoms.

Sometimes it is good to write things down. If something occurs every day you may get so used to it you think its normail i.e. my son had loose stools all the time and I thought that this was normal, because they had always been like it and I had got so used to it, until someone else pointed out that this maybe an issue. I then started keeping a food and stool diary, just to see if there was a pattern that may indicate a dairy issue etc or if certain foods set it off.

Collapsible water bottles are great to keep in your handbag or in the car

If you want your child to let go/give something up you may have to swap it i.e. give a biscuit to get them to spit something out, swap an item for a toy etc.

Every child is unique. Don't compare them to other children or wish they were different, accept and love your child for who s/he is i.e. if you have an energetic child, just accept that, don't wish you had a quite child that likes to sit still, later on that quite child may come with other issues, no child is easy all the time, just be grateful for what you have and love who your child is.

Before the start of term school shirts go up in price, half way through the term buy the next size school clothes, in advance, to save money (as long as they don't grow too much and skip a size this is good, perhaps buy them slightly bigger).

....

- Be careful that natural sponges might be broken apart and can then become a choke hazard if your toddler breaks them up and then eats them.
- If nappy keeps leaking, it could be too small.
- When using a thermometer – head strip thermometers are less effective, it is best to use a digital thermometer. When using a digital ear thermometer use it in both ears, if baby has been leaning on one ear it maybe warmer.
- Get a water bottle clip so you can attach it to your change bag or pram;

- Be cautious of metal park slides in the summer, the sun ay really heat them up, which may burn your child.
- With children its better to have a nigh flight, so that they sleep on the plane.
- Its better for your baby to have bare feet as much as possible
- Always run a bath with cold water first, don't leave your baby/toddler near the bath un-attended as they may jump/fall in, don't let them near the taps and have a lock on your bathroom that you can open from the outside, in case they lock you out and run the taps etc.
- Ensure that there are no hard toys in the soft play area.
- If they are using their dummy it stops them putting things in their mouth and eating them.
- Calpol can make them hyper (it did with my Nephew and son).
- Put toys they kneel down to play on, on a rug if your have wooden floor so it is softer for them.
- Get large chalk to play outside.
- Think ahead of them, before you know it they will suddenly be able to do something new that you hadn't expected or safeguarded against i.e. climb up the kitchen units, on the dining table, take things out of the bin etc. therefore get locks for cupboards, take vases off even high tables, don't say words they may repeat etc. it is a good idea to keep your front door locked, otherwise your child may open it and run out. Use a stair gate upstairs as well as downstairs, in case your baby climbs out of his/her cot. You may also want to lock windows, and don't have windows open near a sofa etc. where your toddler may climb up and jump out.
- With my son I used to always keep reins on him, especially if we were near a road or water because he would often wriggle out of my grasp and was a fast runner.
- Kids do thing in their own time, don't worry if they appear to be slow in their development. Often ones that take their time learning to talk end up talking more and being better at talking later on.
- After holiday get your baby back into a routine as soon as you can.
- At your home you can't baby proof it so your baby needs one to one attention, where as at nursery although it is only one member of staff to every 4 it is a safer environment.

- Fill your baby up with milk in the day and then s/he will need less at night and will sleep better/will wake less often for night feeds. They say not to give a big bottle as the last bottle at night because it swells and expands their tummy. I think they only drink what they want and sometimes a big night bottle or dream feed is a good idea to help them sleep through the night.

- Double bag extra smelly nappies so that they don't stink your bin out.
- For constipation; fruit or a fresh fruit drink and a warm bath.
- All babies go through a stage of standing or crouching in the bath, and not wanting to sit in it.
- Kids except and believe what adults say, so avoid telling them negative things as these may stay with them. Try and void identity and labels and instead talk about behaviour and how it can be changed. Instead of saying you are naughty say your behaviour is naughty. Otherwise they will believe it and it will become a self-fulfilling prophecy. It also helps to be specific so that the child can be more effective, this also means that there is no danger of misinterpretation.
- Touching cup – germs – If your baby has a cup they have to lift the top and their hands are dirty they may get germs.
- Snoring - adoniods - may grow out as they get to 7 plus.
- Asthma - hard to diagnose before 5.

- The less time you leave it before having your next baby, the higher the risk of having your next baby pre-term, this is higher for some ethnic groups too i.e. afro Caribbean have a higher risk of pre-term pregnancy, when having shorter gaps between babies.
- Take your car seat on holiday or hire one?
- Take it in turns getting up with the baby and having lay ins.
- When your baby goes into a bed if s/he keeps getting up, put a lock on the outside of the door to keep them in.
- Be careful when you are in the shops as most doors are automatic and your child may run out whilst you are going in your bag for your purse.
- A dummy helps when they are teething, my son chewed his and used it as a teether, more than his teether.
- Its good to have 2 kids close together as similar ages will have similar interests and you can do stuff together.
- A quick healthy meal – tuna or tinned salmon with sweetcorn, scrambled egg and covered in grated cheese.
- Be careful what toys your baby has in the car in case s/he throws them at you whilst you are driving.
- When you first have a baby everything is new. Your mind can't switch off, relax or focus properly because you are looking after the baby. This makes you feel stressed and tense but eventually you get used to it, and all the little things that you have to worry about you tend to do on auto pilot and it becomes normal and gets easier. You then find it weird when you have a break. You do however need a break, some time alone or time out as a couple. Its amazing how relaxed you feel when you have a break, you then realise how hard its been with having a baby, but also how over time you come far and achieve a lot. It takes a while to get used to it, like any new role. Its like having a new job, you have new things to learn and it's a shock at first. However unlike a new job every day everything is changing, every day is different, there is always more to learn and you will never be able to become an expert and you will never get it all right, as there is no right or wrong way. What works one day may not another and what works with one baby, may not with another.
- If your baby seems to be sleeping for longer / having longer naps it maybe that they are going through a growth spurt/about to go through a growth spurt or they are about to come down with something or start teething.
- I've heard it said that if your pour water on your bump when you are pregnant and in the bath, when your baby is born and you go to bath it, if s/he gets upset if you pour water on his/her tummy they will then settle.
- Take lots of photos and videos.
- Get a height chart to plot your child's height. Take photos with objects in the background for perspective, so that you can visually watch your child grow.
- The first year you will need more photos as your baby changes a lot in the first year. Its nice to get a newborn photo shoot and then one at a few months or 6 months and then at a year. After that the nursery and school do a photo every year. If you can get an electronic copy that is best, or scan a copy and then you can do a photo book of every school photo in chronological order, showing how they have grown.
- 18 months to 3 years of age they might get night terrors, this is normal.
- If you forget your childs sun hat, get a large hankie and knot the corners.
- You can get doors with blinds inside the glass, this way the blind and the cord is contained in the glass and is not a hazard for your baby.
- Calpol has lots of sugar in and might make your baby hyper. It also isint always the sugar sometimes the E numbers from the colouring are worse. You can now get calpol without colouring.
- Cut nails short in case they scratch you
- Pram that can face both ways are great, you can turn it around and use it as a high chair

Extra water bottle on hot day – carry 2 water bottles so that you don't run out, if you are going somewhere without a water source.

For a boys christening why not have a white tux;

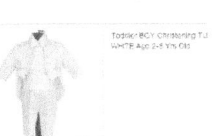

- Aqua mats are great/safe toys

From the age of 2 they are more aware of things around them, they start saying more words and trying new things and being more interactive. From 23 months Ritchie started holding my hand and taking me to where we wanted to go and saying play with me and mummy hold Ritchie etc. He also started playing with his friends in a much more interactive way, rather than playing around them.

- Glycerine is great for coughs

- You can make glow in the dark bubbles by mixing liquid from a glow stick into the bubble mixture (blow it away from your child and in the garden as it maybe toxic).

- Make sure your child has another MMR vaccine when they are 15 years old (apparently the MMR that they have as a baby only lasts 15 years.

- The NHS doesn't provide children with the chicken pox vaccine (except in special circumstances i.e. if they or family members have a weak immune system). If children catch chicken pox it is safer than getting it when they are older (so in a way its best to get it, although it's uncomfortable for them and in rare cases it can have complications). However if you have chicken pox the virus stays in your system and every time you come into contact with someone with it your natural defence gets a booster yet the same virus can present its self as shingles later in life (you can't catch shingles). You can pay privately and get a chicken pox vaccine but it only lasts 15 years so you have to ensure that you get it again when 15, and its not as good as having a natural defense to it. However in some cases its better to have the vaccine and not get the disease, however because it is mild, in most cases, for children it is not routinely given on the NHS.

- Your toddler will go through a stage of refusing to get in the car seat and will go stiff. You need to persuade them to get in car i.e. do you want to play with your toys, if you seat nicely you can go home and play with your toys etc.

- It is good to have a separate cheap bag i.e toddler rucksack rather than your designer baby bag or handbag when you go out. That way you can put a nappy, wipes and water bottle of water and snacks in their bag, rather than a large bag (you can leave the large bag out in the car boot) and put your purse, phone and keys in an over body bag that stays on you. Their bag can go on the side (its not as valuable if stolen) when you are at soft play etc.

- Give water at set times to ensure toddler has enough because s/he won't ask for it.

One of the first ways in which infants initiate **social interaction** is by **smiling**. From about the second to the seventh month of life the infant will smile at whoever approaches and interacts with it. It will even smile at a very crude, oval-shaped piece of cardboard with two black dots painted as eyes (**Ahrens, 1954**).

In the second part of the first year of the infant's life a dramatic change takes place in how readily they smile at a stranger's face. Spitz clearly demonstrated this change.

Age of children	Number of children	% smiling at strange face
0 — 20 days	54	0
21 days — 2 months	144	2
2 months — 6 months	145	98
6 months — 12 months	147	3

This change in the infants' social behaviour is clearly related to their development of specific **attachments** as we'll see in the next unit.

It's important to note that **cross-cultural studies** have noted similar types of behaviour in children throughout the world.

-

- Macfarlane, a psychologist, found that from 10 days a baby recognises and shows preference for its mother.

A plate with a lip/flat bowl are great for toddlers, they can scoop the food off without pushing it off the end of the plate and because they are flat, unlike a bowl, the food can cool quicker.

Try to keep garden items on the grass so its softer if they fall, move them around regularly so that the grass underneath doesn't die.

Even babies and small children succumb to peer pressure. They will be influenced/change according to the children around them, they maybe hyper and copy them etc.

If you get a mini trampoline, cover the bar with the foam that you insulate pipes with, that way your toddler won't hit their chin or head on the metal bar.

Babies all go through phases. Ritchie (my son) went through a phase of screaming (this is normal whilst they are finding their voice) and then spitting food (for them this is a game, although it also normally indicates they don't like something or have had enough food), they tend to know when their full and they tend to prefer sweet food so may spit their main meal but then go onto eat a putting – when they spit don't react, just take their food bowl away for a minute. They will then usually after the spitting phase, stat throwing food, do the same as spitting, tell them no but try not to react (they are looking for attention, in fact most of these things are attention seeking, take their food away for a minute or turn the highchair away to a corner (you may also have to clean their bib and highchair so that they don't grab stray food to throw). It is hard to then put them to bed without any food if they are very young (especially as they may wake in the night) so it maybe best just to take the food away momentarily, although you may find taking it away all together works for you. Try not to worry, the stages although distressing do normally pass, just try whatever works best for you and don't get stressed if people pull faces when you are out, keep calm, all children do this and we were all children once (although some people forget this and stare and make you feel bad – just smile back and carry on as normal. As the posters say 'keep calm and carry on' – a mantra you need with children!).

A sponge football is good because they can hold it and pick it up.

Quillow – quilt that folds into a pillow

Don't stand too close to the end of the road, especially when waiting to cross it. On cross on the green, don't run across, stop, look and listen etc. walk acoss in a straight line, don't J walk.

Kids always play up more for their mums because it is someone familiar.

For a happy baby fit around their routine not yours. Don't drag them to too many groups. Let them sleep and feed when they want. Be aware that each day maybe different and the day that you want to get things done/go out may be the day when they are unsettled.

Most babies have a witching hour when they are tired, it maybe at 4pm for instance. If they are over tired and won't settle, don't get stressed instead take them out of the situation, change their environment i.e. give them a bath, bottle, play soothing music and try putting to bed.

When your baby is older it is ok to put your baby in bed with you if s/he is sick or clingy but if you do it all the time it will become habit and they will only want to sleep with you. Give it a few nights with them back in their own cot/bed and they will soon get used to sleeping in their own room.

If baby spits food – take it away and turn the highchair away for a minute (they do it because they are attention seeking).

Check before changing your babies milk – comfort milk may have less key ingredients.

When the clocks change your baby/child may take a while to adjust to the new routine.

Be more authorities, in control with your tone ie deeper when saying no to baby. Don't show any sign of weakness. Babies are testing the world around them, how it reacts to them, how they should behave etc. so they will try and push the boundaries. If you show signs of weakness they will learn that you will give in if they push hard enough, it is then hard to undo this behaviour.

Make sure your baby/child has a drink after running around/sleeping etc

Rotary washing line – keep a cover over it, otherwise it can be dangerous if your child gets wrapped up in it whilst playing in the garden. Also be careful that they don't have long scarfs when riding their bike that might get caught in the wheels.

Pj better than sleep suit as they don't restrict babys feet, as they get slightly tight.

Don't let them play with your car keys, they may loose them, or they may even unlock your car, even if they press them from inside your house.

Sometimes babies get sleep apnia / hold their breath but also they may snore loudly and be in a light sleep and then suddenly they go into a very deep sleep and when they are in a deep sleep their breathing is very shallow so it may seem as if they are not breathing when they are (if in doubt use a mirror, it's better than poking them and waking them up, having said that if in any doubt it is better to rouse them and be safe than sorry).
If going on a long journey, take snacks and drinks, especially if going on the motorway where the service station is often over priced and has long ques.
Will need stair gate at top of stairs once they can get out of bed by themselves.
You may find that if you don't drill the stair gate into the wall it may push the banisters, putting too much pressure on them and make them loose.

You children need discipline, a lack of discipline can lead to asb
Maternity pillows can be kept and used when your toddler is in a bed, between the wall and the mattress.
Don't use own words others won't understand i.e. call a dummy a dummy. My husband called my sons dummy a 'tus', none of the nursery staff understood this or knew what he was asking for.

They may go through a stage of not wanting to wear their bibs, you could try softer cloth bibs, painting aprons or muslin.
Door finger guards are important
If you are going to give them milkshake – make it yourself with fresh fruit liquidised with milk.
If your baby keeps pulling his/her sun hat off, get one that ties up at the bottom and is more fitted and less flappy.
My son went through a stage of head-butting everything when he was younger i.e. the floor and furniture, he then grew out of this stage but has now started backward head butting so that he hits the back of his head against my chin when I am trying to get him change him, if he doesn't want me to change him.
If you put your tv on the wall get a cable clip that goes flush to the wall, not a hanging one, otherwise your baby may swing on the wires.
They get to a stage where they don't want you to feed them, this isn't necessarily because they aren't hungry, sometimes it's because they just want to be independent and feed themselves, you may have to have 2 spoons and do a spoonful each to ensure that they get some in their mouth, sometimes you just have to let them get messy and accept it.
Always have an emergency bag packed with enough items for your baby in case you have to rush out. It is worth leaving spare essential items with your baby's care givers too. It is a good idea to have a network (emergency contact list) of people that can pick your child up from the nursery if they are sick and you can't leave work to pick them up. It is also a good idea to make sure that if someone else it picking your child up that they have supplys. One day my mum had to pick my son up. I keep a grab bag in my house (by the front door) so as she has a key she could pick this up. I also have spare nappies in my car and a baby grow (but I had my car with me), the nursery have a bag with spare clothes etc. that stays there (to save me taking a bag backward and forward), I forgot to ask them to give this to my mum (and nappies that they keep separately in the change room). Luckily my mum has a cup, and has a few nappies and wipes, this turned out to be enough to pick him up, The car seat wasn't an issue because she has her

own one in the car (all the grandparents do), but it is worth checking who will pick your child up in an emergency and where they will get the car seat and anything else you baby might need from. It may take some co-ordination if someone else if picking your child up, especially if you need the car seat to drop them off. It is often worth having a spare car seat that you can leave somewhere.

Children often catch things off each other including nits (all the family have to be de-liced) and they may get conjunctivitis. If they get conjunctivitis you need to clean their eyes regularly, use cooled boiled water and cotton wool (separate cotton wool for each eye and wipe inside to outside so the germs are being pushed out and not back into the eye). It is good practise to wash their eyes day and night anyway. Dab the eye don't drag it as the skin under their eye may be sore. Conjunctivitis normally clears in a few days but if it doesn't then they may need antibiotic drops. If it is really severe the whites of their eyes will be red too. It is a virus so they may feel unwell with it too. Some people say wash with salt water, although this may sting.

Cut their toe nails straight across and not into the corner, to avoid getting in growing toe nails (this is hard if they get flaky fan nails), which my son does.

Sometimes you have to be strict, they may get into habits of wanting to sleep with you, especially when they are in a bed and can get themselves out. Its ok to let them in with you if they are poorly but if a habit forms you have to be strict for a few nights and eventually they will get used to their own bed again.

You may find their sleeping habits change. If they were sleeping through the night they may suddenly stop for no apparent reason, there are always all different phases that do pass.

May recognise places /get to know routine of where going. Tell him/her where you are going and you may find that when you pull up outside your parents, s/he knows where they are and smiles.

Bad crowd/drugs/owe money – It is easy for teenagers to get in with a bad crowd, try drugs and end up owing money/getting into gangs, try to warn them about the dangers and steer them away from this. Be mindful that it can happen to anyone and look out for the warning signs.

Reins – If your baby runs away you will need reins.

Crawl down stairs on tummy – teach your baby to crawl backwards down the stairs, otherwise if they go down forwards and lean to far forward they may topple over and fall down them, backwards is the safest way.

Out of house - steps / door step – watch when they walk in or out the house that they don't topple up or down the door step.

It's a good idea to have a light weight pushchair for when walking, just in case gets tired if you have far to walk (their legs have to work twice as hard).

Think about your safety and belonging when you are out and about, pick pockets may target you because you have a baby and are distracted. Don't leave your bag in the pushchair and don't leave it on your car seat whilst you strap your baby in the other side, they may snatch it whilst you are distracted strapping your baby in. Put your bag in the boot and lock it first, or put your bag in the footwell by the baby seat so that it is next to you whilst you strap your baby in.

If you put your bag in a bag i.e. put your handbag inside a bigger bag, be careful that it doesn't slip out, particularly when you are moving luggage out of cars, where it may tip out, especially if it is dark.

I won't always cry, Mummy
When you leave the room
And my supermarket tantrums
Will end too soon.

I won't always wake, Daddy
For cuddles through the night
And one day you will miss
Having a chocolate face to wipe.

You won't always wake to find my foot
Is kicking you out of bed
Or find me sideways on your pillow
Where you want to lay your head.

You won't always have to carry me
In asleep from the car
Or piggy back me down the road
When my little legs can't walk that far.

So cherish every cuddle
Remember them all
One day, Mummy
I won't be this small.

Discipline;
- **Take treats away - let them earn them back.**
- **Reverse psychology - I bet you can't do x,y,z**
- **Positive discipline if you are good all week you will get a treat at the weekend.**

When they are hungry, bored or over tired they may get hyper and play up. Avoid sugary food and cheese before dinner.

Babies start off pulling hair and pinching for comfort and as affection. They will soon stop this with some gentle reminders i.e. moving their hand away when they pinch etc. However as they go through the tantrum stage they my start again, out of frustration. Try to distract them to something positive, a toy or point something out to them if you see them getting bored or about to go into a tantrum. Always try and tell them what is happening next and give them a warning i.e. a 5 min warning before leaving the park, this helps to avoid the sudden disappointment. Don't just grab them, when lifting, especially not from behind it will scare them and they will fight out. Instead be gentle, bend down to their level, put your arms out and communicate to them that you are going to lift them.

Its nice to spend time with your baby/child but if you have a break then the time when you are with them is more special i.e. you have more quality time.

You can get a back pack so they can carry their water etc. or a nappy. Back packs with reins built in are useful.

It is so exciting having a toddler, as they explore new things and interact with you, everything is exciting and fun.

If we have a positive self image and are confident we are likely to be happier. People that have been bullied or had negative parents question everything or put them down, may be less confident and may go onto have destructive relationships and end of in a downward spiral of lack of confidence and unhappiness and may therefore think negative thoughts that turn into self-fulfilling prophecies. It is therefore important to be a positive role model, always try and be upbeat and look on the bright side of life. Praise your child but be realistic and don't over praise them, otherwise you are setting them up for a fall later on. Help them to do things but let them be independent so that they learn to do things for themselves and can grow and develop and become confident individuals and therefore happy and positive individuals.

Terrible 2s - Tantrums - usually when they are tired. Last a year usually. Try & ignore them after 5 mins try cuddling them to sleep.

- Instead of buying a cot sheet, fold a normal sheet and use that.
- Regularly check straps on car seat and pram for when they need adjusting. As your baby grows they will need moving upto the next loop point.
- You can buy tops with an anti dribble patch in.
- If using a tie get a baby tie with Velcro at the back so that it is not a strangulation hazard
- You can put baby rice in bottle of milk to fill baby up in the night, use this for the dream feed (although health visitors don't recommend this).
- It is hard when you have a baby when you are older because you are set in ways when older/not in control with a child around, when you are used to having control/need something for yourself so you feel part of the world. Talk about depression, lots of people get postnatal depression, get help and don't see it as being a failure. I felt a failure because my sister had a baby and coped without getting depressed so I was hard on myself and questioned what was wrong with me and why was I struggling to cope. Lots of people don't cope but can't admit it.
- Don't try & do too much no one is perfect and you have a baby to cope with so that on its own is enough.
- As your baby get older s/he will run away during nappy changes, my son is a real wriggler and has a tantrum if you restrain him so I find myself running after him with the nappy. I let him play with his toys and change him whilst he is standing up playing (I use pull ups).
- Babies know when they want food and when they don't, don't force them to eat.
- Pack travel wash, washing up liquid, clean bottles & carton milk & fold up bucket. When you go away. That way you can soak clothes in the fold up bucket and then throw soiled water down the toilet.

There are people that make teddies out of your babies first baby grow, to their exact birth weight, this is a nice keep sake.

Wash your babies hands and roll their sleeves up before you let them eat

24 hours = roughly 10 nappy changes – make sure you have a grab bag of 24 hours worth of stuff for emergencies.

Avoid socks on wooden floor – as this is a slip hazard.

Take old muslin to the park, in case the slide is wet, so that you can wipe it.

Keep tinned fruit so you always have pudding – tinned pineapple is good because pineapple can be used in sweet and sour and in chicken wraps.

Once your baby has finished his/her milk, rinse the bottle. Don't leave the bottle of milk on the side. If you do your baby may get hold of it and try and drink the milk that will be spoilt with bacteria.

If your baby sits food, or throws it – say 'no' and tell them it's 'dirty' take the food away/take them out of the high chair or turn the chair away to face the wall and then tell them they can have the food back when they stop. If they spit their water out, take their cup off them etc.

When using a bottle warmer – put the bottle in first, and then the water (or measure out the amount so you know how much to use), otherwise once you place the bottle in the water may overflow and spill out.

Kids, as with adults (but maybe more so) need to feel like they belong/fit in. They may have something missing 'a hole in their soul' and will need to find something to fill it. This makes them more vulnerable to peer pressure. After the age of 12 they are less influenced by their parents and more so by their friends. It is therefore important to be a good role model and give them a good base and boundaries before 12. After this you still need boundaries but they will need to explore things for themselves and be capable of making their own decisions, they need to be able to talk to you and come to you with issues.

- Talk through things with them and in front of them / don't try to shelter them from things.
- Don't have taboo subjects / be open about everything
- Be curious as to what your child is doing – if something seems wrong and they seem distracted try to find out why.
- Be casual in your enquiries when dealing with teenagers, don't bombard questions at them.
- B honest and tell them the pros and cons of drugs, to re-enforce in them, why not to take them.
- Ensure that they have balance in their life so there is no 'holes in their souls'.
- Raise your child's awareness as to the dangers around them.
- Be knowledgeable yourself / keep up to date with the latest info and what is going on in the world around you.
- You could use reality programs to bring subjects up, 'oh look at what they are doing, what do you think of drinking too much etc.'

Kids know the boundaries with their parents so thy know how far to push them. They therefore play them up more than other people.

young children are better off playing with old fashioned lego rather than computers so that they can develop their imagination and fine motor skills. They need to learn how to use computers, but not too early. 2nd hand toys are ok, if they have lasted all those years, chances are they will last longer (some new toys break easily). You don't have to spend a lot of money. Kids like playing with boxes etc. its about the time and attention you give your child, not how much you spend.

Demonstrate to your child how to brush their teeth by brushing your teeth together.

It always best to go to a reputable shop and get your child's shoes, where they are fitted properly. Even if you get them fitted and then try to buy them cheaper elsewhere it is not as good. For instance hush puppy baby shoes have different insoles for different width fittings. To make sure the hoe fits, push your childs foot to the front of the shoe and you should be able to fit a whole finger between the back of their foot at the back of the shoe.

Cardigans are better than jumpers because you can regulate the temperature by unzipping them. You can see if they have a nice top underneath and baby can pull them off themselves (once they are a toddler).

Check there are no loose threads in socks to get wrapped around babies toes.

When you register the birth – get extra birth certificates they are cheaper to buy at the time, rather than later on.

Special baby snacks/crisps are more expensive and are not always healthier i.e. Organics carrot sticks have the same amount of salt as wotsits. Wotsist are quite low salt/fat so are not too bad. You may find normal biscuits and wotsits the same as the so called healthy snacks, which are more expensive.

Don't eat food that is too spicy when breastfeeding. As baby gets older s/he can tolerate spicier food.

If they pull your hair/bite tell them off to stop it straight away/do it back.

You can get books and DVDs to deal with topics such as berivmenet or having another baby etc.

We get more UV exposure/damage through our eyes when we are kids so it is important that they have good sunglasses.

Take a small suitcase to hospital instead of a labour bag.

Don't be too proud to except help. Even if it's for ½ a day a week get someone to watch your baby so that you can have a break and catch up with washing, housework, sleep or take time to yourself to have a hobby etc.

Having a baby is physically exhausting for your body it takes a year to get over the birth (it felt longer for me, I had a bad labour and then had adenmyosis) and then physically running about after them and lack of sleep and this takes its toll mentally too.

By 2 years old they should be able to say 30-35 words and should start being able to put words together.

By 1 year you should start weaning them off the dummy in the day time and then eventually wean them off the dummy at night.

If they start spitting their food, take it off them.

If they throw their toys, leave them where they throw them (if you are in doors), that way they won't keep throwing them because they will learn that if they throw them they will loose them.

Don't carry a big bag everywhere. Instead keep some stuff in the boot and carry one nappy and some wipes etc. Have a smaller bag that you can take out that can fit into the bigger bag.

As long as you have one spare set of clothes if your baby is at grandparents they can then wash the original clothes that the baby was wearing, after you have put the spare set on (as long as they have a tumble dryer to dry them). Otherwise if you leave lots of spare clothes at their house your baby will quickly out grow them without wearing them and the gransparents house may become over run with baby stuff.

Get your baby/child a library card. If you take them to library its cheaper than buying books and they can have a change of books. Sometimes they get book start packs and other free books and perks if they visit regularly. The libraries often run sessions such as story time etc.

If your babys food is too hot but they want to it eat, get another bowl and put a small amount that has cooled in there, whilst you wait for the rest to cool down.

Laminate rhymn sheets and pictures so that they can play with them without tearing them and getting them messy etc.

Young babies who are sick are at more risk of choking because they can't always bring up their vomit.

When their molers come through they hurt the most. Some babies get very ill and get colds and chest infections etc. and don't sleep when they are teething where as other babies it doesn't bother them too much.

A change to their routine can cause upset and sleep problems. They can get into bad habits and expect things i.e. If they wake once and you let them in your bed they may then keep waking as they get into a habit and expect it. Although a bit of indulgence isn't bad every now and again, if they are poorly you have to do what you have to do to deal with any upset and get by (sometimes that includes bad habits).

You can get baby nests to hold babies up to 4 months in you can use this instead of a travel cot when baby is new born (although a moses basket is practicable and cheaper);

You can purchase sleep positioners/cushions to stop flat head.

Ready beds great for sleep overs and holidays.
Shaped baby spoons are good

- Syringe for medicine maybe easier than a spoon. Calpol comes with a syringe or spoon.
- If you have a baby go to bed as early as you can, ideally when you put our baby down, that way if your baby wakes in the night you might have managed to get a few hours sleep.
- Babies don't understand reasoning so short repetitive commands are great for babies and toddlers. You can then elaborate more as they get older.
- Babies vision is not great at long distance i.e. why they sit close to the TV etc
- Babies/young children have a short concentration span, boys often tend to have a shorter one than girls.
- If you are going out for the day tidy the toys away so that when you come home you are not walking into a mess/there is less to do. Also if its late your baby may want to go to bed, without getting distracted and wanting to play with the toys along the way.
- Get a city grip pram holder protector
- You can now get new baby sensors, which work off of movement without the need for a pad.
- As a parent sometimes you need to relax & go with the flow
- Be assertive, it ia battle of will - they will try & push your limits.
- When changing their nappy if you lift their legs higher they find it harder to wiggle and will be more likely to stay still. Although I never got to master my sons nappy changes, he always ran away so I had to chase him and put him in pull ups, he was like this the whole time he was in nappies, so I never did get fully to grips with this situation.
- Mothercare do part exchange on car seats
- Babies/young children may put food up their nose and in their ears so if they seems to be in pain or pulling at their nose etc. check for food or other obstructions.

- Get a bath tidy for your bath stuff that you can lift off the bath when you put your baby in, so that s/he doesn't touch your razor, shampoo etc.
- When babies spit their food it could be that they are playing or it could mean that they are full and don't want any more food.
- Make pizza with kids, it's fun and you can put healthy toppings on and it encourages them to eat healthily.
- If booking a holiday to centre parks - Book activities before you go because they get booked up and take food for sandwiches and evening meals as the shop and restaurant on site is expensive.
- If you have 2 young babies get 2 moses basket downstairs so you can watch both, crib upstairs?
- Put thick table cloth on when they are old enough to sit at the table & bang cutlery. Or put with tray high hair.
- They like to poo in a clean nappy so always carry extra nappies, one spare nappy is never enough because as you change a wet one, they may do a wee.

Mother's Heart

Author Unknown

(This would be nice to be read by the mother).

I loved you from the very start,
You stole my breath, embraced my heart.
Our life together has just begun
You're part of me my little one.
As mother with child, each day I grew,
My mind was filled with thoughts of you.
I'd daydream of the things we'd share,
Like late-night bottles and Teddy bears.
Like first steps and skinned knees,
Like bedtime stories and ABC's.
I thought of things you'd want to know,
Like how birds fly and flowers grow.
I thought of lessons I'd need to share,
Like standing tall and playing fair.
When I first saw your precious face,
I prayed your life be touched with grace.
I thanked the angels from above,
And promised you unending love.
Each night I lay you down to sleep,
I gently kiss your head and cheek.
I count your little fingers and toes;
I memorize your eyes and nose.
I linger at your nursery door,
Awed each day I love you more.
Through misty eyes, I dim the light,
I whisper, "I love you" every night.
I loved you from the very start,
You stole my breath, embraced my heart.
As mother and child our journeys begin,
My heart's yours forever little one.

The Greatest Gift Of All

Author Unknown

We give you the greatest gift of all,
a headstart that will last throughout your life

We shall do our best to teach you,
but it will be up to you to learn.

We shall try to guide you in the right directions,
but it will be up to you to make the right decisions.

We shall also encourage you to seek your own independence,
but it will be up to you to be responsible.

We shall tell you about 'drink and drugs',
but it will be up to you to say 'no'

We shall teach you about respect,
but you will choose whether to appreciate it's value.

We shall encourage you to try,
but you should want to succeed for yourself.

We shall teach you kindness,
but it will be up to you to be good-natured.

We shall teach you to share,
but it will be up to you to be unselfish.

We shall model values for you.
but you have to develop your own morals.

We give you this knowledge as a gift with all our love.

http://www.babyblessingnewjersey.com/poems-for-baby-blessings.html

Make sure your child can't reach the door handle and get out the front or back door. If you can lock the door but keep the key where you can reach it, in a fire.

Baby will watch you and after a while may work out how to open the stair gate. It is therefore a good idea to get one with an additional catch at the bottom for added security.

If you are going on holiday in the UK it might be a good idea to take a collapsible bucket so you can soak soiled clothes in it.

If you have a bean bag, if it starts to split sew it up straight away. The small polystyrene balls can be dangerous if baby puts them in his/her ear.

In the morning, if baby gets up before you have chance to shower etc. put stair gate on upstairs and open bathroom door, if everything is baby proofed baby can then roam in and out whilst you take your shower. Or you could put the toys in the cot and let baby play, but then s/he may associate the cot with play and not sleep.

When you go playing with your child in a ball pit and other play area, you need to supervise them but don't want to leave your bag – take a money belt or an over body bag to keep your valuables i.e. purse, key and phone in. You can use a carry-a-bag or cloth bag for nappies, drinks and snacks etc that you can leave on the side. My Sarah Jane bag has a large bag you can leave in the car and an over the body bag that is detachable from the main bag.

http://soinspire.weebly.com/

I have also seen wide elastic belts with hidden pockets in (that way you can keep your phone on you and take pic of your child too). You can even sew your own pocket in.

I also found this on the internet that I thought was a good idea;

There are many change bags, or you can just use a large handbag. I found it useful to have a 'grab bag' with nappies in so that I could either put them in my normal handbag if just popping out for an hour, or have them in my change bag and just grab them when I needed to do a nappy change rather than drag a big bag into the changing room. I found that a normal handbag will do but a bag with lots of compartments is useful. I used cartons of milk when I was out so just needed a bag with a separate pocket for the milk and a water bottle for me, so that if it leaked it didn't leak over everything. I also found it useful to have my personal items such as phone, keys and purse in a clutch bag inside my bag, that way I could grab and go if someone else had the baby. It is good to have outside pockets for your phone and keys so you can grab them easily, however you need to also ensure that you protect them from pick pockets. My favourite bags are;

- Miche (they have changeable covers and the big Prima bag with the shoulder strap makes a good change bag, I like the fact most the covers have pockets on the side for bottles and you can change the cover, to match your outfit, without emptying your bag).
- Mia Tui do a nice changing bag with bright pink lining so its easy to see things. There is a clip for the keys and a separate clutch bag inside for your own items. Its also smart enough to use as a work bag.
- The Pacca pod is nice and practicable although slightly on the expensive side and it does look like a baby bag, unless you buy the leather ones, which are even more money.

I designed my own baby bag with a separate smaller bag on the front so that you can have your own stuff in it and clip it off the baby bag. I decided to design this because when I was out with my husband if I wanted to pop in a shop and he was taking the baby with him I needed to empty the bag out to get my phone and purse etc. and then I had no bag for them. I thought having a smaller breakaway bag would be useful. When my son became older I used to leave the big section in the car in case we needed a change of clothes, but kept the smaller bag with just a couple of nappies on me.

I also found it useful to have a coat with a hood and big secure pockets for keys and phone. You can't hold a baby and hold an umbrella and then rummage through your bag when you need your purse and keys. I also found it useful to have a retractable key hook attached on the inside of my bag so I could grab my keys and open the door with one hand, and have child in the other.

You can buy a pram liner/ an insert to go in a pram to keep the baby warm and cosy, great if you have a 2nd hand pram, it also means you can take it out and wash it, so its more hygienic. You can also use this in a pushchair to keep baby's feet warm.

- **If babies vest are tight they are hard to squeeze on over the nappy, especially when you have an older baby who is wriggling. Therefore if you buy the vests a size bigger it makes it easier and quicker to change your baby.**
- **If you have a portable highchair not only is it great for when you go out and about but it is also good if you have other children over to eat and need a spare high chair.**
- **Teach them how to go down stairs backwards, so that they can get back down stairs without falling.**
- **Low vitamin d can damage bones - of fracture get a vitamin d / calcium tes**
- Take a photo of your baby so you can see their hair and then print this out, stick a lock of their hair next to it, write the date and laminate it.
- It is a nice idea to keep a family book with the family tree, copies of birth certificates, death certificates, baptism certificates, marriage certificates and wills, along with photos of where they were born etc
- Get your childs school photos for every year and put them in an album/folder in age order so you can see how they grow. Write the date/ year and name underneath each one.
- Always keep snacks/water or carton of juice in your baby bag and a toy.
- You can have toys that you keep in the car that you can bring out to restaurants etc For instance you can use a Sarah-Jane shoe strap and attach the toys, hook it over the front seat in the car and then your child can play with the toys in the car without throwing them around. You can then just unhook it when you go into a restaurant and can attach it to the highchair without toys getting lost, or being thrown around etc. Therefore it makes your life easier and safer. To get a strap see - http://soinspire.weebly.com/
- It takes a year to recover from a general anaesthetic.

- When writing you will, think about the future if one of your children dies will all the money go to your remaining child or will their 50% go to their children (your grandchildren).
- Retractable key ring clip for keys so you can keep them in your bag & pull your keys out to open the door without taking them out of your bag (this way you won't loose them or leave them in the door and can open the door with one hand).
- **Keep off dummy for speech, try and take dummy away in the day and distract baby so that s/he doesn't need it and can work on speech.**

- Get cheap Tshirt for nursery from primark
- Turn back speakers off when in car so you can listen to music without it being too loud for baby.
- Chunky crayons, colouring pencils are good from 10 months.
- Babies / children's body clocks don't behave like adults until they are at least 5, even then teenagers need more sleep, at least 9 hours, and then as you get older you need less and the elderly sleep fewer hours at night.
- Before a year your baby is growing all the time and will eat a lot, as your baby gets to a year or older the growth stables out and so does their appetite, although it may increase when they are having a growth spurt. Some days they may eat more or less depending on what they are doing, how they are feeling etc.
- Strap your baby into the highchair and then put the long sleeved bib on, this way it goes over the straps and keeps them clean too. However if you put the straps on over the bib you can clearly see that baby is strapped in. Use a plastic sleeved bib or a wipe clean bib over a cloth full sleeved bib for less mess.
- Your baby, when they learn to say a word, may repeat that word because they have limited vocabulary. That's why you mustn't make a big deal if they say a rude word, otherwise they may think it's funny or it brings attention and may keep repeating it.
- Don't give your child time out until they are at least 4 years old, before this they are too young to understand and it isn't good for them.

- If your baby keeps throwing food, say no and hold a plate out for your baby to put the unwanted food on (they maybe bored and attention seeking, they may have not like that food or may not be hungry).
- Be careful with bumbo chairs, don't put your baby in them on high surfaces, don't leave your baby in them for a long time before they can sit up unaided and once they can arch their back and lean backwards stop using them otherwise your baby may tip them back and hit their head, perhaps keep a cushion behind them etc.
- Don't let your child eat an ice lolly straight out the freezer, give it a few minutes to thaw otherwise their lips could stick to it and they could get ice burn. If their lips stick to it, don't pull them off just apply warm water, the ice lolly will melt off.
- Don't put your baby to sleep in a onesiee because the zip is not flexible and it may push into their neck and choke them.
- If your baby is draining a bottle of milk it means that you are not giving them enough milk, they should never drain the bottle dry, if they do start giving them more milk in their bottle, there should always be a small amount of milk left.
- Take all the advice you can, but don't necessarily follow it, just be aware but do what works for you. What works for one person may not work for someone else. You can get to hung up on the information, however it is important to be well informed, take the information in and then make informed decisions based on what works for you. It is good to have all the latest information, especially when it comes to safety information.
- 3rd baby syndrome – they say the labour with the 3rd baby is worse than the 2nd, this is called 3rd baby syndrome. The 2nd is easier than the first and all subsequent births, other than the 3rd are supposed to be easier. The 1st is always the worst.
- Check that your baby hasn't put any toys in the washing machine before you turn it on, also check the bins before you take them out. My boy Ritchie was always putting toys in the bins and washing machine.
- Check that your baby can't open the front door, you may want to put a chime or additional lock on it.
- You can now get dribble bibs with teethers on the end
- Teach humbleness ie via having to apologise, join in with chores, volunteer to help others who are less fortunate etc. Engage your child in discussions about fairness, how to treat others and what's right and wrong.
- Mums be careful that your baby/toddler doesn't get hold of your silk scarf as this maybe a strangulation hazard.
- Boys need more exercise, they have higher levels of testosterone and can be boisterous so need more support to control this. Boys tend to have growing spurts which affect their ear canal as it stretches, which can lead to periods of temporary hearing loss.
- All creatures start life being female the 'Y' chromosome that makes the baby a boy is an 'add on' at around 8 weeks the y chromosome stirs and starts make testosterone. At birth a baby boy will develop as much testosterone as a 12 year old boy and after birth this testosterone stays around for a while, therefore newborn baby boys are prone to have occasional errections, this reduces once they become toddlers. As your boy goes through puberty and also stages of brain growth the hormones can make your boy dozy and forgetful, this is natural and will pass. Boys more than girls need structure, they need rules and consistency.
- Be social and teach your kids how to make friends and be social so that they gradually develop social skills and don't suddenly have to make friends without social skills, this is when you may find they get into a bad crowd.
- When you go to choose a pram, if you normally wear heel, make sure you wear your heels. If you try the pram in flats then it may not be the right height when you put the heels on (so pram handles don't adjust to a very high height so it's worth making sure it's not too high for your partner either).
- Elizabeth Arden 8 hour cream is good for bruises
- Set boundaries and don't change them, don't give in otherwise they won't know where they stand.

- A cot duvet when they are old enough is often easier than a sleeping bag. However if they wriggle a sleeping bag maybe better although you may find that they wriggle less under a duvet.
- Your baby may start talking and then suddenly appear to go backwards and talk less, try not to worry this maybe because s/he is focusing more on what is going on and starting to process what the words mean, rather than just copying them.
- You will find that your baby will go through a phase of rolling over and getting stuck because they can't roll back and may lean on their arm etc. don't worry this will pass, don't use pillows etc. as this will become a suffocation hazard.
- Play dough – make your own, that way it doesn't matter if baby eats it.
- At Christmas make decorations from felt and salt dough, that way they are not breakable and hazardous to small children (the breakable ones can always go near the top of the tree). You can also get biscuits with holes in that you can decorate and hang from the tree.
- To keep your baby content - See 'The Baby Whisperer' have a set routine. Let your baby have lots of sleeps and feed or put to sleep before they cry. Don't go out too much and have a routine so that your baby doesn't get over tired, predict when your baby will be hungry and keep your baby topped up with milk before you put him/her down to sleep so that s/he isn't hungry. Try reflux milk if your baby has reflux. Make up bottles put cooled boiled water in and put in fridge, add formula and rest of water as boiling water (1/2 and ½ 7 mins before a feed is due). Wean your baby when they are hungry ie 4 months not 6 months. Don't let your baby get over tired or over hungry.
- When toddlers are tired they get unsteady on their feet
- Best way to change baby – lay on floor and lean over in front of them, with one hand hold their ankles together and lift the legs, the other hand wipe their bum, if they wriggle just lift their legs higher and push the legs in towards their body.
- The best way to discipline a baby/child is to threaten to take a toy away, as they get older this could become a computer or phone ban etc.
- If you have a young baby its often easier with an older sibling because they can watch the baby whilst you cook dinner and help out with certain tasks etc.
- Keep saying no, even if your baby doesn't understand
- Sometimes they can undo the cot with the sides to let themselves out so be careful with this type of cot.
- Muslin - can be used to wash face/dry if you don't have a flannel.
- Book - keep some mini books in your bag, they don't take up much room and keep your child entertained if you go out impromptu without toys.
- Milk - if your baby doesn't drink all of his/her morning milk put it in their weetabix.
- Radiator - they may burn their hands on radiators.
- Straighteners - when in use keep baby/child away. When not in use unplug and put in a draw, in case they turn them on.
- Hair dryer - careful because the end can get hold and if child touches it, even after it is off, until it cools down, they might get burns.
- Virus - can't have antibiotics
- Don't put your baby to sleep with the dummy clip on, as it may be hazardous, or at the vary least uncomfortable.
- If using a pull up, in order to avoid getting bum cream all over you too; put your baby's legs ½ way in and pull them ½ way up, then put cream on and then pull them up fully.
- Be wary if you hold your baby under their arms to lift them, if they suddenly raise their arms and tip themselves backwards, (something they learn to do when they don't want to be held), whilst you are holding them you may drop them. It may be a good idea to try and place a hand under their bum too.
- Babies will try and pull off their shoes and gloves etc. It is a good idea to have mittens on a cord inside their coat (or on buttons that way if they pull their mittens off they are still attached to their coat. Ensure that they don't pull the cord out, otherwise it can be hazardous.

- If you store your pram in the porch, or behind the front door be careful that it can't fall down across the door and block it, thus locking you out if your door opens inwards and you have left the pram at home.
- At approx. 14-16 months your toddler sees that s/he is an individual (before this s/he didn't realise that they were a separate person to their parents) and they start to develop their self image. S/he will have emotions to cope with. Sometimes s/he will need reassurance and praise, other times they will want to do their thing and do things their own way, when they can't they may get frustrated and this may lead to tantrums etc.
- Toddlers will want to explore the world and may therefore get messy, let the get messy, mess is not a bad thing.
- They go through different phases and these pass i.e. throwing their food. They also go through different phases of who they want to go to ie. Being a mummys boy or wanting their dad etc. one day mum will be favourite, next time dad will be favourite.
- Get a bowl with suckers so it sticks to the highchair and just give your baby a bit of food at a time (not too much as they may throw it all out), have a separate plate with the rest of the food on. That way they can try feeding themselves.
- If they throw things, leave them where they are and don't pass them back to them, they will soon learn not to throw things.
- It's a good idea to have more play together and less tv.
- Don't shout at babies, just say no. They don't understand no until much later on but if you keep saying it, when its time they understand they will be familiar with no.
- Take hard items out of baby's hands when picking baby up, otherwise you may get hit on the head or face with them.
- If using a laundry pen to mark clothes it may eventually fade in the wash, if you use sewn labels you can then take them off and re-sew on another name if you keep the clothes for the next child. Having said that as the child gets older you don't want other children taking their jackets and unpicking the labels.
- Don't let your baby play with hard toys in the car, in case the throw them at you.
- The more baby proofed your house is, the more that you can relax
- Every day your baby/child will grow and without you realising may be able to reach things that they couldn't before.
- It is important to spend quality time with each child. If you have a 2nd child keep them to their child care routine so that their pattern doesn't get disrupted, also that way you can spend time with the new baby. Then get someone to watch your baby so that you can spend time with your other child/children without them feeling left out.
- You might find it easier to fit your pram in your boot if you take your parcel shelf out.
- Have a password if you arrange for someone to collect your child, tell your child the password in advance, that way they know if the person collecting them has genuinely been asked to.
- Tell children to get away from incidents as quickly as they can but also tell them if they can to get a descriptions and vehicle reg etc.
- Tell them not to walk near the back of vans, in case they are grabbed in and get them to walk on the inside side of the pavement.
- Your child could grow up to do something amazing, if you mould them the right way and help them to develop in order to reach their full potential and be the best that they can be.
- Too many of some viatmins can be harmful, so be careful what vitamins your child has. Keep vitamins and other medication out of their reach.
- Put nappy rash cream even if your baby hasn't got nappy rash, in order to maintain a barrier and stop getting nappy rash in the first place, prevention is better than cure.
- Once they can climb out of a cot it is safer to put them in a bed, with bed guards.
- For major life events it is a good idea to get books out of the library that help explain them and help you to discuss things with your child. Most libraries have a family learning section where they have books explaining in a childrens story events such as death, starting a new school, general worries, another baby coming into the family etc. You can also ge DVDs etc.

- Post vaccine fever usually lasts for 24 hours and goes with calpol, if it doesn't go with calpol or lasts longer than 24 hours you need to call the doctor.
- Getting your child used to a cup – as soon as they hold things, give them a cup to play with. When you start weaning, introduce a cup, only if little is taken from it. Always sit your child upright before offering food and drink and make them sit still, don't let them run around with food, drink or a toothbrush (this will reduce the chance of choking and also will keep the food mess to one area). Keep the bottle out of sight, especially when offering drink from a cup. Don't leave your child alone with a drink at sleep times. If your child wakes when older a drink may not be necessary, give a cuddle instead. Older children may give up their cup for a new toy.
- Put socks and colour catcher in a laundry bag so that they don't get caught in the washing machine filter and block the machine, it also keeps socks together and stops them going stray.
- Children often try and push the limits with their parents, with other people they maybe unsure of the boundaries and may be more likely to do as they are told. I heard about a dad who when his baby wouldn't go to bed put his baby in the cot and then put on a wig, changed his voice and told his baby to go to sleep and the baby did.
- Try not to pick your baby up every time s/he cries or every time they fall otherwise they will cry and expect to be picked up all the time. Its ok to cuddle them a lot when they are very young (and when they are older they still need cuddles) but after 6 months they also need to be able to self sooth.
- Loosen the car seat straps when you get your baby out, this will make it easier to put your baby back in later (you can also get clips to clip the seat belt back when you put your baby in, if your car seat doesn't have this already, because some do). But don't forget to tighten the straps, they should be tight enough that you can only get 2 fingers between your baby and the straps (they will need adjusting for with and without coat etc).
- You may find that after a while you will get to understand your baby very well, don't do everything for your baby when s/he points instead say what you are doing i.e. getting milk and eventually get your child to ask for things rather than pointing, otherwise you will get a lazy baby/child that won't bother developing his/her speech etc.
- Put nature programmes on the TV babies love watching the animals.
- Get special tape to tape rugs down to the floor so that they are not a slip hazard.
- Store books within reach of baby/child so that s/he can grab them and bring them to you when they want to read.
- Sweet wrappers can cause a choking hazard so dispose of them and don't leave them lying around on the coffee table.

Safety glass has a kite marks so if it doesn't have this it isn't safety glass, often glass in doors is not safety glass, anything low or in doors or by stairs you should make safety glass. DIY – practise in a hidden/less obvious area first. i.e. putting safety glass film on glass start with the door that isn't in the main area, so by the time you do the door you see the most you will be better at it.

- It is a good idea to teach your child to feed themselves as soon as you think they are able to. Weetabix is good to start with as it stays on the spoon. Stand to the side of your child in their chair so that you are facing the same way as them and imitate what to do, once they have watched you, put your hand over their hand and show them what to do, at first do it together. Then let them have a go, this technique also works when you are teaching them to write their name etc.
  You can also give them a spoon of food and then let them feed themselves a spoonful. At least that way you know they are getting some food in their mouth and they are still having a go at eating themselves.

Childcare: setting the boundaries

Some mums say grandparents are the only people they would trust with their child, while others struggle to accept methods that are vastly different from their own. So to avoid any misunderstandings it's best to set a few boundaries at the outset.

- Be clear about what your children are allowed to eat or how they are expected to behave with their grandparents. It's your right to establish your own rules about how your child is brought up.

- However, do expect to make some compromises and allow for a little natural over-indulgence every now and then. A little spoiling goes with the territory, but if you think it's too much, say so.

- Remember that grandparents have lives too! While they love spending time with your little ones, they are likely to be busy with work and other obligations, so don't expect them to be at your beck and call.

- Many new mums find themselves isolated from their families with grandparents living hours away – make the most of them when you see them, and if they're just around the corner, remember how lucky you are that they will get to see your little ones grow up.

Top Ten Tips if you want your parents to look after your child when you go back to work:

1. Talk through everything as a family. The more planning you can do together the better. Good communication is key!

2. Don't just presume your mum or dad can take on full-time childcare – they may want to keep on working, or feel they haven't got the energy to take on a demanding schedule. You could consider a mix of childcare if you are both working full-time.

3. If you decide that the best way is for both sets of grandparents to share the childcare, make sure you all agree the ground rules that you (as the parents) should set about such essentials as sleep, play, food, discipline and boundaries, and so on. Get all the grandparents together for a special family occasion and chat things through.

4. Grandparents usually prefer to look after their grandchildren in their own home. This might seem to make things more complicated than they could be, but it's good for your child to experience different places, and your parents will really appreciate it. BUT make sure to remind them, and help them, to make their home baby or toddler proof!

5. Most grandparents wouldn't dream of asking for payment but costs can mount up and they could get out of pocket. Why not set a kitty to cover such essentials as snacks, meals, days out, nappies and new toys?

6. Sorting out the necessary equipment needed – from car seats to high chairs – right from the beginning will save a lot of headaches. If you need to double up on equipment, you could offer help in buying this.

7. Work out your holiday dates. Grandparents often want to take advantage of off-peak (and therefore cheaper) breaks, but these are usually during school term. It's a matter of give and take, and planning the year can really help.

8. Discipline and boundaries across generations are all about give and take because different views on discipline can cause friction in a family. Your parents need to understand that you are the ones to set boundaries for your children, but do acknowledge their point of view. Once again it's all about communication.

9. Remember the rest of the family. If you have brothers and sisters who have children, it is important that they get to see their grandparents too, and benefit from their love. Sometimes siblings can resent the situation and once again, an honest discussion is a good way forward. Grandparent childcarers like to try to see their other grandchildren during the weekends and on holidays and it's important to encourage this.

10. Sometimes being a grandparent childcarer looking after a small child can be a lonely time. Grandparents feel they shouldn't impose a baby on their friends or may be ill at ease at 'mum and baby' sessions. There are an increasing number of grandparent and toddler groups being opened around the country. To find out more go to the Help and Support section on**www.grandparents-association.org.uk** or phone 01279 428040 for further details.

Bridging the generation gap

Differences of opinion on how you bring up your children are sometimes inevitable, given the rapid pace of information since grandparents had kids of their own.

What was unfashionable in their day could be all the rage now, with different approaches to weaning, feeding and discipline all likely to cause raised eyebrows or lively debate. But when it comes down to it, you all have your child's best interests at heart, so:

- Try explaining why you do things in a certain way, rather than just expecting them to understand that things are different now.
- Show them articles or web sites you've read so they can see where your ideas are coming from. **www.proudgrandparents.co.uk** has lots of useful tips for grandparents, including updates on child healthcare, age-appropriate toys and which foods to avoid.
- Hear them out – there might be a good reason behind some of their own ideas, but you'll never know if you don't listen.
- Choose your battles. Set boundaries about the important stuff, but use your judgement and let small niggles go.

A battle for control

From visiting just a bit too often, or offering one too many suggestions about how you should do things – it might sometimes feel like grandparents are trying to take over. Here's how to keep cool and help you stay on good terms...

- Grandparents are bound to be excited about your children, and will want to see them often. But sometimes you need time alone with your own family. Agree a schedule for them to see the kids that suits everyone – they won't feel like they don't get a look-in, and you'll be safe from unwanted 'surprise' visits.
- Bringing up children can be hard work, and it's natural that grandparents want to help. But sometimes what's meant as 'useful' advice can feel more like interference. Gently make it clear that you value their opinion, but that you have your own way of doing things.
- Try not to reject advice out of hand. Grandparents have a wealth of parenting experience, and whatever you're going through, the chances are they'll have been there at some point themselves.
- Remember grannies are mothers too. Your mum (or mother-in-law) could be so used to mothering you that she finds it hard to down-tools now you have a child of your own. Show her you're all grown up and can make your own decisions when it comes to caring for your child – when your mum sees you are a confident and capable mother yourself, things will change.

Keeping the peace

All too often, what starts as a minor niggle can get out of hand and cause a rift which takes years to heal - more than one million grandchildren in the UK are denied contact with their grandparents. Sometimes a clash is unavoidable, but take a deep breath and help keep your family a happy one:

- Don't let things build up. A lot of resentment comes from wishing we had said something but didn't, allowing certain situations to crop up again.
- It might sound easier said than done, but try to avoid confrontation or lengthy arguments – the last thing your baby needs is a shouting match.
- It is possible to say no without causing a row. Stand firm on the issues that are important to you, but be prepared to compromise at times and try not to blow things out of proportion.
- Don't let any friction cause a rift between you and your partner. Make sure your own family unit is a strong and happy one, and you will be better equipped to deal with your problems together.

A family that eats together stays together. If you all eat round the table together children will eat more and get better nutrition, it also aids communication and togetherness;

food guru Annabel Karmel suggests:

- Eating at the table, not in front of the TV or anywhere else they fancy!
- Making meals a family event, with conversational fun, so your kids aren't eager to rush off back to the TV or computer.
- Shopping and cooking with your kids so they understand what they're eating at family meal times.
- Having a night a week where the kids decide what everyone is going to eat and - if possible - go with it!
- Remembering that eating together as a family is about communication so talking to your children about their day, and not just to your partner is vital.
- Bearing in mind that meal times are not an excuse to tell your kids off about all the things they have done to annoy you. This is a guaranteed way to put them off family meals.
- If your family has a very hectic schedule (and your kids are a bit older) implement a fun meal time at least once a week, where everyone has to attend i.e. Sunday lunch, or Friday evening.
- Banning tablets, mobiles, computers, magzines and TV. Make the rule for adults too.
- Persevering even if it's tough at first because practice makes perfect!.

…………..

If you have a baby girl, be careful when changing the nappy & wiping. Be gentle so you don't tear & don't pull legs apart too much.

You can put 2 rails to double up the space in the wardrobe: Make space in your wardrobe for your little ones by adding a rail at their height. That way you can turn getting ready in the morning into together-time.

Get a toy with links on (make a long loop of links) so that you can link it together and hook it to a high chair or pushchair without risk of strangulation.

Babies glands are up when they are teething so they may run their eyes etc
In is normal for them to play peek-a-bo and also put things such as socks, etc on their head. They love carrying things on their head.
Velcro dribble bibs are better than tie up or popper ones, because they may get caught on them or try and pull them off and you don't want them tightening around their neck and doing damage.
They lose balance when they are tired so if your baby, who is normally good on his/her feet starts to wobble it may be time for bed.
Glass doors may not have safety glass – you can buy a film that you can put over the glass to make it safe.
Raisins - keep them in your bag as a healthy snack, they are a good distraction when baby gets grizzly.
Use a laundry pen to mark clothes its quicker tha sewing labels on (although you can use sew on ones for the next child).
Furniture touch up pens are also useful for wooden furniture because your baby will chip your furniture with their toys.
Leave water bottle out on a table/side so that baby can help him/herself.
When you have a new born do yourself food that you can eat with spoon without cutting i.e. chilli and rice so that you can eat with one hand and hold baby with the other.
In play pen for discipline i.e. 5 mins in the play pen (this only works if you are not using for play etc otherwise baby may get confused and think s/he is being told off when they haven't done anything wrong and will not want to go in it – for this reason don't use going in the cot as punishment.
The 2nd child will have more tantrums because due to the nature of not being the only child they will have less attention and will be frustrated as they want to do the things the older one does but can't.

Once your baby can have tap water carry a sealed straw, such as the ones you get in Mcdonalds in case you forget to pack your water bottle. You can also get collapsible bottles that you can keep at the bottom of your bag.

Rather than buy everything new when your baby is new born you could hire the items that you need for 6 months - some stuff you don't need after that so it works out cheaper than buying it. However it isn't all new so it may be just as cheap to get 2nd hand items and you could even sell them on later, once you have finished with them (although you may want a new car seat and travel system (pram).

If you breastfeed for 30 mins and your baby then takes a full bottle s/he is not getting enough milk.

Try latching on for 10 mins only, after that if baby isn't drinking then give up.

Once your baby is on 3 meals a day you may want to add an afternoon snack so they have 3 meals a day and make the dinner time slightly later so you can all eat together. Also once they start walking and burning off more energy you may find that they are hungry and need an extra snack to keep them going until dinner time.

......

Baby powder feed is not sterile because once the carton is open the powder is open to air and this is why you need to use hot water when making the feeds.

Different ethnicities break down enzymes differently due to their DNA and have different diets so advice on weaning can vary from person to person and depend on where you live. If your baby is not ready to be weaned s/he will soon reject the food.

You can get warmers that you click them and they heat up, you can use this to warm the moses basket as soon as baby falls asleep so you can warm instantly before putting baby in (take warmer out before baby goes in).

Bottles are only sterile in steriliser for 24 hrs – once you remove them they are not sterile so don't store bottles. Sometimes it is just as good to make feeds and cool and put in the fridge (as long as you put it in the back of the fridge and let it cool properly).

If you are having trouble changing baby's nappy change standing up – you can try putting pull ups on.

On demand feeding is good for new born but you may find that your baby wants to snack i.e. eat little and often so you may need to get a routine and feed every 3-4 hours for your own sanity. Do what works for you.

Baby proof your house – move chemicals away so they can't be reached, the outside of the cooker may get hot and need a cover, get rid of loose cords due to risk of strangulation, put glass safety film over glass i.e. coffee tables and glass doors. **Anything taller than it is wide or with draws needs to be secured to the wall i.e. book cases.**

Elastic bands around door handles to stop child opening

Socket box for extension leads;

Plastic clip that goes over the doors for bio folding doors (also works for Ikea Billy Bookcase doors);

The Kidco Bi-Fold Door Lock is a fast easy solution for preventing finger injury for your curious little ones. To install simply slip it on top of the door and slide over the joint. To open the door slide away from the jointed area. A handy wand attachment makes it easy to reach and operate.The Kidco Bi-Fold Door Lock is designed to fit standard bi-fold doors and comes with an insert to adapt for thinner doors. It's available in clear to allow your door finish to show through for a flawless match to any decor.

I found that these stopped my son from opening the billy bookcase cupboards and tipping everything out.

It is a good idea to leave it 2 years before you start trying for the next baby to give you and your body some recovery (but if not at least a year is good because it takes a year for your body to recover and then another year to build up even stronger). But you will know when is right for you and when you feel ready.

Exercise your tummy muscles and pelvic floor between babies – when you have a baby your muscles are weak and you need to build them up before you have the next baby and they weaken again, that way they will go back, otherwise it will be so hard to get them back and you will have a pot belly for longer after your baby. Always seek advice as you may not be able to exercise for a year after a C-section you may only be able to do gentle exercise only.

- Only ½ fill water bottle so that baby can hold it themselves and it's also not as heavy when they throw it. However when you go out make sure you fill it and if you do only ½ fill it, remember how much water baby has had (i.e. when it's gone remember they didn't drink a full bottle as it wasn't full to start with).
- They say kids get tantrums at 2 years old hence the terrible 2s, however my son Ritchie (and most his friends) started having tantrums at a year, this is because they are aware of their surroundings and are starting to explore but they can't communicate and may not be able to understand why they can't have certain things.
- When you have the down syndrome test it may come back with high results, this maybe because if you are having lots of sickness the same hormone that causes this can also cause a false high results on the down syndrome test.
- Sometimes you think you won't be able to cope with something because you are thinking of how you do things now but you will be more adaptable than you think and find alternate ways of doing things so that you can cope. For instance I had surgery when my son was 1 and couldn't lift him for 4 weeks, my husband was also off with a slipped disk. Luckily my son had started walking a few days before so I just held his hand and walked with him. As he didn't sit still when I changed him I used to change his nappy on my lap, I therefore had to change this and instead I would put his toys on the sofa, distract him and then change his nappy whilst he was stood up against the sofa. Sometimes you just have to do whatever works for you, whether it is ideal or not you just have to do what you can to get through the day.
- Babies often like other babies and children and will like seeing them on TV and looking at pictures of them too.
- Often they behave differently around different people i.e. at nursery they may eat all their food where as at home they may not, because the other children are there eating theirs. Ritchie would lay still on the change mat at nursery but not at home, I think they know the limits and he couldn't get away with things at nursery that he got away with at home (the nursery staff were stronger and pinned him down and he soon learn not to wriggle). They may be better behaved at their grandparents then they would at home, they often tend to play up more in their own home, because its their house they are more comfortable and know what they can get away with etc.
- Wash baby socks in laundry bag otherwise they may go down the washer drain.
- Eating dirt is common in young children, usually from 1 to 6 years of age. It's called "pica," and children may eat many non-food substances including dirt, mud, clay, sand, bricks, paint chips, plaster, chalk, cornstarch, baking soda, coffee grounds, cigarette butts, ashes, match heads, rust, glue, toothpaste and animal droppings. Why does this happen? Infants and toddlers are curious and explore their environment by putting their hands, objects and other materials in their mouths. Most infants and toddlers try eating dirt, and only some persist with the behavior. Sometimes pica is a result of nutritional deficiency (e.g., not enough food, or low iron or zinc in their diet), emotional stress or a developmental problem. But in many cases, a cause is not identified.
- If you can purchase a large drum washing machine i.e.9k and a dishwasher, this will make your life easier as it will save on the amount of washing loads and washing up you have to do.
- If you have a break from your baby, send them to nursery or can't pick baby up, it will make baby less clingy.
- There is always a flip side to everything, there are alternate view points, every cloud has a silver lining and every action has a consequence. I couldn't lift my son for 4 weeks so I couldn't carry him but this encouraged his walking. When I was small and my mum took me to hospital my sister didn't speak to her for a few days after, but she soon got over it and made up with my mum. Sometimes things will happen and you will get emotional and upset, don't worry too much it will work out in the end. If you

have a baby in special care unit it may take longer to bond but you will bond eventually and things will improve so don't worry. Try not to over analyse things and don't let them get you down. Our children make us emotional and if you over analyse things it will cause you to worry, try to relax and have faith that bad times will pass and things will correct themselves.

- Nursery is good because they get to meet other kids, develop social skills, they do activities and don't get bored so you don't have to worry so much about giving them development activities at home.
- Once baby can walk you won't have to carry him/her as much which will be easier for you. They will also want to explore which means you will have to baby proof the house but at this stage they will also become more independent and want to play so they will be less demanding in that way but will want to run around when you go out, which you will find tiring running round after them. More active is harder for you but its good because it means your baby is developing well.
- Even if its cold, as long as they are wrapped up warm its good for them to play outside (if they move around a lot they will keep warm too), they need exercise and fresh air, just because you may find it cold you shouldn't stop them going out.
- Measure children's feet every 3 months
- A healthy appetite is good at least when they eat less you know when they are ill.
- Healthy snacks - pretend peas are sweets
- Especially with boys they may let you do things for them & pretend they can't do things that they can & may do for others so try not to do everything for them (because they will let you) and make them do things for themselves to help them develop and become independent but also don't push them too hard otherwise they may stop trying.
- You can get twin bags with double the amount of space in case you have twins, or in case you just want a bigger bag.
- If you have had a C section you shouldn't exercise for 1 year
- It is a good idea to give your child/baby vitamin D in the winter
- If you buy a spare of their favourite to i.e. something they use as a comforter rotate the toys to get the babies smell on them, otherwise if they loose one they won't like the spare one because it will not feel/smell the same.
- Boys are harder work when their younger but easier when they are older.
- Before baby is in shoes buy some cheap wellies to keep at nursery for when they play outside or some soft cruising shoes so that they can walk outside, play outside and keep dry and warm (or get some pram shoes or wear their slippers in the pram).
- Xmas jumper – get an xmas jumper outfit that they can wear for the rest of the winter too ie. a Rudolph jumper.
- Don't put hot water in bath first or leave baby in bathroom in case baby launches into the bath.
- Feel ill first thing in morning and at night, therefore take temperature first thing in morning.
- Party - Cake pops
- Child proof house before your baby needs it childproofed so that its done (it may take a while to do and you don't want to have to do it in a worry because your baby has caught you out and is into everything all of a sudden).
- Children, including teenagers need more sleep than adults to develop otherwise they may become obese and have other issues.
- Safety gadgets – TV stand with brackets so that you don't have to wall mount it.
- From 9 months socks & baby grows need grips on the feet.
- Baby's naturally put plastic bags over their head and risk suffocation so don't leave bags around.
- They like to try & be independent and do things and they like to feed themselves.
  Forks maybe easier than a spoon for baby to feed himself/herself because it falls off the spoon.
- Babies throw food on the floor when they have had enough. If they see something else they may want that too.
- Have extra spoons because they throw them/loose them.
- Also have spare drinking bottles.

- You have to watch for things you wouldn't expect ie my son Ritchie picks off the plastic screw covers from furniture and tires to eat them.
- Halloween protocol - only go trick or treating at houses you know/where they are decorated with pumpkins.
- Teach to say ta (before thank you because this is easier to say)
- Lining paper (that you use for linning walls) can be ued to roll and draw on
- Give your baby cows milk – full fat – until they are at least 2 years old.
- There are essential / high frequency words, these are different words for different ages that kids need to be able to read and write. It is good to familarise yourself with what your kids should be learning so that you can help to teach them/support their learning.
- **At the moment schools are following the early years foundation framework – it is a good idea to have an understanding of this and speak to your nursery/school about what your should be teaching your child and how i.e. the alphabet should be taught phonetically.**
- Toys should be be appropriate toys - drum stick balls may come off etc.
- Grow bag – restricts their movement if they roll round too much they may get caught up in it and this may wake them up.
- Cling film over plants base to stop baby taking mud out and eating it.
- One day can take a few steps like that for a week then can suddenly completely walk.
- When walking can reach door handle - put a movement alarm or bell on doors so you know when they go through them.
- Make sure trousers aren't too long (roll the bottom up), and have socks with anti slip pads on - when learning to walk.
- 0-5 if children get burnt it increases risk of sun cream
- Don't swadle baby on lower part of body if its too tight it is bad for hips.
- Check all of your appliances before you use them, in case your baby has fiddled with them and changed the settings.
- Get a little car that your baby can sit on, find one that has long handles and can be used as a walker too. Even better if it has wheels that can be moved in all directions and it can be steered wherever. I got a walk and ride by diddicar for my son when he was learning to walk and we found it very useful.
- Delivering a breech baby – don't touch the baby until the head is out. This is because once the baby is touched it will startle the baby into taking a breath. If the baby takes a breath before the head is out it won't be able to breath so if you don't touch the baby it won't need to breathe until its head is out. Just offer support so that the baby doesn't fall when the head is out.
- When they start walking they start walking on tip toes.
- Get plastic draws and storage boxes so that toys with loose parts like shape sorters can be organised together.
- If you are going to give your baby gravy on their food make sure that it is low salt.
- Table protector cloth – this is a good idea for your table as baby will bang things on it.
- Leather chairs that can be wiped clean are better, make sure you treat the leather to keep it clean for longer.
- Wooden floors are good for kids because they can be steamed & wiped clean
- Put child locks on and keep your windows on lock once your baby turns 12 months as from then on they may grab things
- Good for them to mix with all ages & be with grandparents so that they get used to older people & learn patience
- First breath baby breathes is painful so this is why they cry.
- Your body doesn't know it's limits with your first pregnancy so try not to overdo it.
- New food - takes 6 times to like it
- Kids need quite space alone to reflect on bad behaviour
- Don't feed babies when they have had enough, they know when their full

- Baby probiotics are good, you can get ones that you put in their milk or food as a powder (they say for breast fed babies although formula fed babies can have them. There is an argument that this may not be necessary as the formula has vitamins in, however if they have been ill or are on cows milk they may want it as a boost.
- Banana potassium - stops cramps – this is good for you when you are pregnant.
- Once they start trying to walk they may get restless as they want to explore and may not sleep so well. After a while they will soon start settling & sleeping again.
- Get a large washing machine of 8kg drum or more. You will need a large washing machine and tumble dryer with a baby as you need to wash a lot of clothes.
- Red & orange peppers are healthier than green.
- When designing your house think open plan so you can see your baby at all times.
- Compartmentalise things, look at then individually don't stack your problems on top of each other - this is when you loose perspective & things seem worse than they are.
- Learning to walk can affect your child's emotional behaviour:
- They want to be independent and explore but still need their loved ones nearby.
- Eating patterns may also be disrupted, with your baby eating next to nothing at one meal and more than you at the next. Trust him - he'll balance it out provided you don't make a big issue of it. Offer high-energy snacks such as a bread roll or toast with cream cheese or bananas.
- When you have a baby you give up your basic human right to use the toilet, eat, drink, wash and wear clean clothes.
- Ensure that you have a Smear - after having baby, after your first period.
- Cold veg - put veg under water to cool quickly
- Car seat straps- loosen & clip back before putting your child in, then tighten them once they are in
- As babies/toddlers they understanding more than they can say & they get frustrated because they can't communicate. Be careful what you say around them because they take in more than you think.
- Won't sleep/tantrums/fussy eating – all starts happening when they get to a year. They get frustrated they want independence but want to know you are there and may start doing things for attention
- Say no to them when necessary and keep saying it but then reward when s/he is good / show positive attention
- Music channel & music video for baby

- **Be careful because babys arch back/throw self back when you are not expecting it**

- Distract - play with toys to feed
- Check inside of booties for loose threads that may wrap around foot.

- Trousers - adjustable waste – get toddlers for your child with an adjustable waist (you can get nice one with elastic and hidden buttons on the inside).
- Intelligent kids need stimulation otherwise they play up
- Battery – be careful of small lithium batteries if your baby /toddler gets hold of this they may swallow it and it will burn their insides and will probably be fatal.
- Have high up locks on your doors and a bell, in case your child opens the door and goes out. If you have a house alarm set it so that you can zone your doors and have the doors alarmed whilst you are in the house, so that if your child opens the door it will set off the alarm.
- As soon as you have changed the nappy spray air freshener straight away, otherwise the smell will linger.

- **Don't panic if baby is born early - you only need a car seat & moses basket, milk, nappies, wipes, a blanket and some vests a hat and baby grows to start with. The cots and pram etc can be got later.**
- New guidelines babies can eat anything after a year, although still keep salt and sugar down, some babies may not like strong flavours either.
- Cheese – too much may cause nightmares. They may remember the birth?
- Ice cream – avoid dispenser machines ie soft whippy ice cream as this may have germs in.
- Give babies what they like first then try something new otherwise if you give them something they don't like first it may put them off the rest of their food.
- Progress from plastic spoons to plastic spoon and fork, curved cutlery;

If they don't eat their meal don't give them an option of different food otherwise they will become spoilt and fussy, if they go hungry they will soon eat their food next time.
If they don't like it dry then they may like some watered down gravy.

Crying could still be hungry even if not long had a bottle ie growth spurt so check bottle, take temp, top to toe check for rash.
When cry might get too hot
When too worked up wont stop - blow on face

Always worst at night because laying flat / no distractions etc. if coming down with a cold etc maybe cranky at night but fine in the day. Colic & trapped wind also cause these symptoms.

Stern voice/ignore/use mirror

Socks with grips for when crawling

If baby wriggles when changing, rather than put on the change station when you are out, put a muslin underneath and change them in the pram (you may also want to do this when you go swimming and strap them in so that you can get changed etc).

Whilst on maternity leave let relatives look after your child. That way you get a break and they get used to them and being left, this will make it easier when you go back to work.

Don't give them something new i.e. put them on cows milk etc. as the same day as they have something special i.e 1st birthday party in case it makes them ill, you don't want to spoil their special day.

Cardigans may be better than jumpers to wear to nursery. If you put your child in a cardigan and t-shirt they are more likely to take the cardi off when its hot, than a jumper. It is a good idea to label cardigans and coats etc.

What bedtime?
You could put baby to bed later so that s/he gets up later. That way you have some time in the morning and can get dressed etc. before baby gets up. Before I went back to work I wanted time in the evening so I put my son to bed earlier. Would pack his bag for the day the night before etc. and would get dressed when he had his morning nap but when I went back to work I found it easier to get up before him and get myself ready for work then I just had to get him up and ready and go. It depends on what your lifestyle is, how much sleep your baby needs and when you need the most time. Although that said they don't always follow routines and may want to go to bed earlier or get up earlier one day depending on how they feel. You may want a routine even whilst you are off so you can go out and do things, or you may just want to chill. Try different options and do what works best for you.
Give your baby/child time to unwind before bedtime, this will help him/her to settle better.

………

- Both of you may get frustrated when you find it hard to communicate, try and be patient and understanding.
- Try to negotiate, try offering alternatives rather than saying no.
- If your baby gets whinny try distracting him/her with toys or try using music to change the mood.
- Teach them to be independent and sociable
- Reins are useful to take out and attach to the highchair if the highchair just has lap straps, my son managed to get out of those straps and climb out the highchair from 12 months so even if they are strapped into the highchair it is best not to leave them unattended.
- Don't fuss them too much – if you make a fuss every time they fall they will become whimpy. If another child hits them try to just get on with it, otherwise they may become very fussy.
- Young children can only concentrate for a max of an hour at a time, this is why the walt Disney films were no longer than an hour.
- Label everything that you take to nursery, even baby wipes because they may get confused who they belong too.
  …………

First birthday party;

- Take matches for the candles but keep them out of reach of the children.
- If you get a piñata remember to fill it – I brought one and thought it would be filled already and it wasn't, luckily I had some spare prizes for the games so I put those in it.
- Do some extra party bags for younger siblings who may come if appropriate.
- Take a CD player/ipod docker with music on.
- Get a battery operated bubble machine & take spare batteries.
- Have other games and toys as well as a bouncy castle i.e. garden slide, see-saw and bikes/cars, ball pit and balloons, hoops etc. Not all children like bouncy castles but have a crash mat with soft play or toys on for the younger kids, a castle for the older and some extra toys for all ages.

………

If they have medicine they need to take, decant some of the medicine bottle and leave some at home and take the rest to school, that way you will have some at home in case they forget to bring it home from school.

…………

From a year my Ritchie started head butting, which apparently is quite common. He also started getting annoyed with his toys when they didn't do what he wanted i.e. he had a toy that lit up played music, he threw it out the toy box and it broke, so he got frustrated and kept hammering it into the floor because he couldn't understand why it didn't work. They say they get temper tantrums from a year but my Ritchie started early, from 12 months he started throwing himself backwards, nearly resulting in my dropping him. He would suddenly do it when I was not expecting it. He would do the same thing if he didn't want to do something. He would wriggle and jump and not let me change his nappy. He would do the same thing when I put him in his car seat, he would arch his back so that I couldn't strap him in and at 22lb at 12 months he was very heavy and very strong.

It is common for them to headbutt and slap themselves etc.

………………

Once you have packed your baby stuff away, keep some baby toys out in case your friends come round with younger children.

 If your baby goes to childcare you will find that they settle better because they are younger and then find it easier to settle in nursery and school when they are older.

C section risks;
Although it is a common procedure, a caesarean section is still major abdominal surgery. Like any operation, it carries a certain amount of risk.
Risks to you

The main risks to you when having a caesarean section include:
infection of the wound
infection of the womb lining, known as endometritis, which can cause fever, womb pain and abnormal vaginal discharge
blood clot (thrombosis) in your legs, which can be dangerous if part of the clot breaks off and lodges in the lungs
excess bleeding
damage to your bladder or ureter (the tube that connects the kidney and bladder), which may require further surgery
However, a recent change in practice means that infections should become a lot less common. Doctors now give women antibiotics before operating, which reduces the risk of developing an infection more than if antibiotics are given after the operation.
Aspiration
If you have an emergency caesarean section, there is a risk that you will vomit during your operation. If this happens, food and fluid particles can pass from your stomach into your lungs. This is known as aspiration.
This can cause potentially serious inflammation (swelling) of the lungs, known as aspiration pneumonitis.
Eating during labour may increase the amount of food and fluid in your stomach and increase your risk of aspiration if you need to have an emergency caesarean.
If there is a chance that you may need to have a caesarean section, drinking isotonic drinks (that have the same concentrations of salt and sugar as human body fluid) can give you energy during labour without giving you a full stomach.
Risks to your baby

Having a caesarean section has not been shown to increase or decrease the risk of your baby having the most serious complications, such as an injury to the nerves in the neck and arms, bleeding inside the skull, cerebral palsy or death. These complications are very rare and affect fewer than 20 in 10,000 babies.

The most common problem affecting babies born by caesarean section is breathing difficulties, although this is mainly an issue for babies born prematurely. For babies born at or after 39 weeks by caesarean section, this breathing risk is reduced significantly to a level similar to that associated with vaginal delivery.

Straight after the birth and in the first few days of your baby's life, they may breathe abnormally fast. This is called transient tachypnea. Most newborns with transient tachypnea recover completely within two or three days.

Some materials carry less germs than others i.e. germs don't live as long on copper as they do on stainless steel so copper sinks are more hygienic. When you are designing your house bear this in mind. You can make your surfaces in the kitchen and children's rooms from more hygienic materials.

Have plastic jugs with water in at birthday party and squash next to it and then people can mix the cordial in as they desire (don't have glass in case it drops and breaks).

The advantage with having children close together is that they are in similar school years. Also if your first child is younger when you have the 2nd child s/he is less likely to be jealous of the new baby.

It is a good idea not to leave your toddler alone with your baby, until your baby is big enough to crawl away from them etc. because older babies bite and if under 3 they may not realise and may bite your baby or squeeze to hard etc.

Play with feathers.

Before baby is old enough to wear shoes have pram shoes or slippers so their feet don't get cold in the pushchair if they don't want a blanket/kick the blanket off etc.

Some baby food doesn't have much nutritional value, there is not much food in baby food it is filled with water and bulking agents such as wheat etc. it may also have hidden sugars (formula milk has sugars in but breast milk is naturally sweet too). It is best to make your own fresh food.

Soup - add milk to cool it before giving it to a child.
Colic - emopreziol & ratedibe
Get unsettled & don't want to go to school & miss out when next baby comes. Give them a boring day at home.
If you leave your child they may sulk and not come to you for a while.
As they suddenly get taller they can reach things all of a sudden.
They may go through your bag so keep it out of reach.
Rotate toys
Buy toys at a car boot it's much cheaper.
Put down for a nap when grizzly.
Empty water out of toys & bubble solution out of bubble machine so it doesn't go funny.
When can pull their bib off use Velcro only otherwise they may strangle themselves ie don't use popper fastening bibs.
Pens for writing on clothes to label clothes.
Don't leave cleaning chemicals in reach ie in bathroom
Get bathroom locks that can be opened from the outside in emergencies.
Don't understand no until age 3 but still say no firmly.
Different places - act differently / diff routine for diff career
Wean from 4 months now

Give cake and everything except salt straight away - although I didn't give cake & sugar until 12 months.
They need their own European health card – now

Babies will pull your hair

Check with nursery what they do if they don't eat their dinner. Check with the nursery if they have a sensory room.

Sterilise bottles for upto a year
Tap water from 6 months
Sippy cup so swallow not such ASAP. Start to put milk in there from 9 months - mills drunk may decrease because they like the bottle.
They need a pint a day of milk but is ok if in food, they don't need to physically drink a pint of milk they could have some cheese, a yoghurt etc.
If having enough milk & balanced diet they don't need vitamin drops but you can give them drops if they are having less than a pint of milk, low food intake or yo think their diet may not be balanced enough.
From 12 months weight gain decreases/steadys out. If they did carry on putting weight like they do when they are under a year they would be really large by age 2.
go to weighing clinic every 2 months from 8 months and then every 4 months from a year.
Get sippy cup with handles & put them on bottles so baby can feed self.
After a year still give formula when they are not eating a lot of food to give them their vitamins. It is also handy to keep some in case you run out of cows milk (because powedered formaula keeps for longer).

Even if you think your baby's weight is ok still pop into the clinic to get your baby weighed regularly because then you might find out about things that are going on, you might get invited to weaning workshops, get dental packs and advice etc.

Birthday cards packet - keep them for party bags.

First birthday party bags;

- Finger puppets
- Mini books
- Bendy straws
- Bubbles
- Hand clappers
- Wands
- Bath ducks
- Balloons
- Bouncy balls
  (make sure that they are large enough not to be swallowed).

If you are giving your baby packet food you need to give twice as much as you would with freshly cooked food.

When eating out with your baby sit them so that they can see everything that's going on, they will like this and usually therefore behave better as watching everything will keep them entertained and stop them trying to turn around etc.

A lot of processed baby food is high in sugar.

Don't throw baby bottles out. They can be kept for the next baby and sterilised etc. You may also want to go back to the smaller bottles as your baby gets older and has solids and less milk, they may also be easier for your baby to feed themselves from. You may also want to use the smaller bottles for water. Don't put juice in the bottles, it makes them smell and discolours them, also drinking juice through a teet is bad for their teeth as they are sucking on the sugary juice.

Party games – pinata

At age 2 start using sippy cups for milk at night and stop using bottles.

Boys are usually slower at learning to walk and sometimes if they are heavier it may take longer as they have more weight to knock them off of balance.

Don't chase them and get them too over excited.

Once your baby goes onto cows milk you can still give formula for extra vitamins or keep some formula in case you run out of cows milk.

Keep chicken nuggets and some cooked meals in the freezer.

Babies usually start walking between 12 months and 2 years. Ritchie started walking at 13 months, although one of his friends Isla was walking at 9 months, so they all vary.

Encourage your baby / child to be active and move around to avoid constipation.

Push cutlery in, away from the edge of the table once your baby can pull themselves up.
Lock the car windows so that your child doesn't play with them and get limbs stuck. Don't let them hang out of the window of the car and use child locks on the door.
Keep a picnic blanket in the car in the summer.
Get a litter pick, that way you can grab dummies and toys when they are thrown behind furniture.

After a year their growth will usually slow down a bit.
Caesarian has complications including adenomyosois.

Straws to drink with – get your baby from 12 months to drink through straws, you can get a cup with a straw spout. This way if you go out and have a glass you can give them a straw so that they don't bite the glass.

Rubber ducks without holes underneath go mouldy after a while because the water gets trapped inside so go for ones with sealed bottoms and no holes to store the water as they will last longer.

After having baby use the contraceptive pill to balance your hormones so you can get back to normal ASAP

Keep a bowl with lid with breakfast cereal or weetabix so if you need to out in a rush before breakfast you can just grab it and go.

Squeeze your babies cheeks together to make them expel any food they are storing in their mouths so that you can tip them back to change their nappy without chocking etc.

Use a none slip mat in the bath to bath your baby.

Add to pack list – bath non slip mat

You always sleep lightly once you are a mum – natures way of making sure you listen out to your baby.

Gadgets – mini training sink and travel table that goes over a car seat (www.verbaudet.co.uk)

You now need to get a separate European health card for your children

eventually give breakfast early. Give a bit of milk and then mix milk in weetabix etc.
Don't let child play with car keys in case they unlock the car.
Kids born later in the year ie sept onwards are higher achivers at school this maybe because they are older in their year.

Try and put your child in nursery/reception year at the same school as they will be going to –rather than keeping them in day care and then putting them straight into school because otherwise some of the children may have bonded already and they may get left out.
Real breaded fish fingers
You will soon find that your reactions get faster as you learn to run after your little one.

- Move any razors off of the side of the bath before bathing your baby.
- Don't let baby touch taps in the bath
- You can accumulate child care vouchers as soon as your child is born.
- You can get seat belt buckle guards to stop your child taking their seat belt off
- Check with your HR dept how you can apply for internal jobs – that way if you want to you can still apply for internal jobs/have a new job to return to.

A collapsible baby bath is better for storage;

Most babies/young children don't like tomatoes until they get older

They like sweet fruit i.e. Sharon fruit and its good for them (although the natural sugar and citrus acid is bad for their teeth the fruit has vitamins in, get the balance everything in moderation – too much may give them tummy ache).

Toes fan out in babies - cut them straight or file only (don't cut into the corners otherwise they maybe ingrowing).

Babies also have flat feet, no arches, fat toes that point up and don't flatten out until resting and, legs bandy until age 3.

Take them out to be social - get used to mixing with other people (they will usually be better behaved when they go out because there are things to focus on and they won't be bored and the more they eat out the more they will be used to behaving).

Make snack pots of fresh fruit to give them throughout the day/when out & about. Its healthier than other snacks, although the baby organic maize carrot sticks and sweetcorn rings are quite good too and so are the rice cakes.

Twins need to have 2 toys the same so that they can have the same toy each because they will like what each other has and want that and argue.

Their eyes can lighten, even though in most case babies eyes only tend to get darker.

Babies love being thrown in air by don't shake them around too much

It is a good idea to have a christening and first birthday party on the same day, that way you just need to organise one big party and its easy to remember the date.

First birthday Party:
Bubble machine
Ball pool - fill paddling pool with balls
Bouncy castle

- Once you have a baby everyone has an opinion and will judge and have something to say to you. They will be ruddier than they used to, like they can say what they now. As a parent you need to suddenly develop thicker skin.

- Use face book to send generic messages to all your friends after the birth if you are too tired to reply to each person individually.

- Create a family profile on facebook so that you can invitie other mums to be you friend without them being on your main/personal facebook. You can then use facebook to set up play dates for the kids etc. you can also use it to send out birthday party invites etc.

- Get the email address of all class mates mums so that if you don't do school run you still get to speak to the other mums and can send out birthday party invites without missing class mates out etc.

- They sleep better once they start crawling because they use up more energy in the day and tire themselves out.

- When doing activities with your baby/child think about their age and the activity that you are doing and then be aware of the time that they can concentrate for. You may not want to do too many activities in case they become over stimulated, but equally you need to do enough to help them develop and so that they don't become bored.

- When your hair falls out after having a baby your eyelashes may thin out too – put Vaseline on them.

- When your baby starts crawling around outside on the grass, put some white wine vinegar down daily to stop cats urinating in your garden and be careful what you put on the grass i.e. don't let baby crawl on the grass if you have put seeds or pesticide on it.

- A wireless hoover to hoover up the crumbs is a must with a baby/child.

- When baby learns to walk up the stairs teach him/her how to safely go back down backwards.
- Don't say that you need to go for a wee in front of children, i.e. when in a que, otherwise they will want to go too, even though they probably won't need to.
- When you are booking activities for your baby, such as swimming lesons, think about the time and if it clashes with meal times, then bed time etc.
- When booking a nursery think of the area and the types of people etc.
- You can give your baby tuna and liver to eat in moderation.
- At around 11 months your baby may get jealous if you cuddle another baby.

- Put your baby to bed when s/he is tired and not before otherwise s/he will get distressed, won't sleep and will cry.
- If your baby is having a nightmare - sh & rock / teething gel. If s/he wake up after been asleep s/he will have some energy (like power nap) and won't want to sleep again.
- In an emergency instead of using a change mat use a muslin.
- When taking children out on trips during school holidays try and do a trip one day and then have a more relaxed day and so on, that way the children won't get so worn out.
- You give your child one to one attention where as the nursery can't.
- Asian genes weak?
- From cruising to walking is usually approx. 2-3 weeks. They start off walking on tip toes.

Car seat toys that hang over the chair in front make your baby sit forwards in the car and not back in their seat so they are not great.

Don't let them walk with things in their mouth - drum stick toys etc in case they slip and it chokes them.

Musical toys are good

Tap protector

Pack night light & cardboard thermometer, Pack plug for shower so you can bath baby in the shower. Don't forget Bottle brush to brush bottles.

If staying in a caravan door keep the door shut so that baby doesn't crawl out.

Pushchair - drag backwards in sand, its easy to move than pushing forwards

If younger you maybe sad when they go to school earlier / they maybe pushed more

Keep travel cot away from walls & hard surfaces because of bendy sides baby may push them & hit head on wall .

Teenagers need 12 hours sleep

Stop breast feed gradually otherwise you may get pain, maybe better to let your milk dry up gradulally.

Push baby into breast to get baby to come off naturally without biting you

Bright things ie toys on pram may attract wasps

Bump the pushchair down the stairs

If there is noise let the baby see what it is so that s/he doesn't get frightened, usually if they can see what is making the noise its less likely to startle them.

Demand - do everything on demand, feed & sleep etc & get a loose routine

Bottles washed in the dishwasher still need sterilising

Play building blocks - develop spacial awareness & social skills. Needs physical play not computer.

Bendy spoons to feed themselves

Point pushchair away from sun to keep sun out of eyes

Your eyes get bad when pregnant due to water

Teenagers need 12 hours sleep

Tins of mackerel for easy healthy snack

When reading run your finger under the words so that they learn to speak

Have portable high chair at home to save space (if you have a suitable chair for it)

Cyber bullying / complex issues social networking & age. What is written on social network can't be taken back - has more impact

Try & keep up with technology

Make sandwiches & pack healthy snacks for the kids. Pot porridge is good for camping etc.

Lid on can of drink - wasps

Baby in front of car with air bag off If your on your own.

You see yourself each day so don't notice it drop.

Double travel time for stopping & changing nappy.

Feet/socks off to cool down (if your feet are cool you will cool down).

Don't have loose things in the back of the car in case you are in an accident .

A roof rack is great to get extra space if you are going on holiday

Become a nursery or school governor

At children's birthday parties; Canvas finger print pic for names - birthday i.e. get a giant canvas and write your babies name and the date, then get all the children to dip their finger in the paint and make a caterpillar and then write the child's name next to it, it is something fun for them to do and makes a nice keepsake. Also do Games for adults ie making paper aeroplanes etc.

Put your child in bright clothes when they go out and about/to holiday club etc. so that you can easily spot them.

Leave some a/l for nursery training days & winter when have colds.

Bright clothes for kids club - easy to spot.

- keep small change in car for emergencies ie hospital car park
- Leave it as long as possible before putting your baby in shoes. If your baby is just coasting you don't need them. Once your baby is walking unaided (after a few weeks of walking unaided) you can get the shoes but not too long after, otherwise if you leave it too long they will start spreading their toes.
- Your baby's seat belt should be tight enough that you can only put 2 fingers under it.
- Wash your hands & face after eating so that you don't get wasps coming over to your baby
- Don't force your child to do something that they don't want to do i.e. don't force them in the water if they are scared – take it slowly and let them ease themselves in, when they are ready.
- Don't put hot water in the bath first/don't leave baby when filling bath in case s/he jumps/falls in.
- Line pushchair with a muslin if you are feeding your child in the pushchair so that the push chair doesn't get dirty from the food.

- Babies sensitive stomachs may not be able to cope with chilli and certain strong spices.
- Include all the children so that in children's games all the children are winners and all get a prize. During pass the parcel put a sweet on every layer. Have a prize for every child during music statutes and just have a larger prize for the overall winner so that there is still a purpose to winning /competitive element but because everyone gets a prize they will all feel included and will understand the importance and fun of taking part, even if you don't win.
- After 14 months Ritchie didn't want milk, I just gave him a small amount in a sippy cup and made sure he had yoghurt and cheese to get his calcium. I also gave him plenty of water.
- Put stair gates around the Christmas tree – to stop children pulling it over; you can then have story time around the tree etc. this is good if you have older children who want a tree to go up. Or you can have a life size mager with a toy baby/doll in.

- Time baby crying, it won't be for as long as you think. When you are doing controlled crying 5mins seems like ½ an hour.
- Consistency and limits are important
- Give kids jobs to do, to give them responsibility this will help them with the transition into adulthood, it also gives them a sense of pride. Supervise and help them to do the jobs. Gradually increase jobs.

Self Esteem: A Family Affair, by Jean Illsley-Clarke;

Stages of child development

Age	The situation
0-6 months	Can I trust these people?
6-18 months	Explore
18 moths – 3 years	Learning to think
3-6 years	Other people
6-12 years	I did it my way
12-18 years	Getting ready to leave

Think about not just how much tv they watch but what they watch on tv. Watch tv with your children and join in with educational programmes, answer questions for them etc.

....

Chemical dangers and e-cigarettes

Parents need to keep electronic cigarette refills away from young children because of the risk of poisoning; parents should treat nicotine refills like white spirit, medicines and bleach. The nicotine found in e-cigarette refills, can be lethal in high doses. You should also take care when holding a baby is you wear a nicotine patch. You don't want it touching the baby, or falling off onto the baby, or into the babies' cot.

....

 You don't need to know all the homework answers to support your child's schooling... But these tips will help...

To make the most of your child's schooling, it's worth having short and long term aims. Even if your child decides later to take different subjects or courses, being prepared makes changing stream easier.

Help with the homework

Kids get distracted from work just as easily as us adults do. Think about how you knuckle down when you need to do something. Creating the right setting for study and helping your child organise their school work is key.

Get to know the teachers

Talking to teachers regularly is the best way to find out where your child might need help. Don't just save it for school parents' evenings.

Lead by example

If your child can see that you take learning seriously, it will be easier for him or her to do the same. Make time to read a book or acquire a new skill, such as learning another language.

Read with your kids

From first words and learning to count to exploring teenage emotions and new experiences, books are so important for learning and relaxing. Just 10 minutes a day reading with your child can make a huge difference.

Talk to your child about school

Even with teenagers you can crack open a packet of biscuits and unwind just for a few minutes over a coffee or a juice when they get home. The school run can also be a brilliant time to find out what's going on, so chat as you walk or leave the radio off in the car and start a conversation.

Stop the mid-term slump

Kids can start off the school term feeling inspired and full of energy but as the weeks go on their enthusiasm can start to slide. If they've had a tough day, give homework a rest and snuggle together in front of a DVD, or take them on a midweek trip after school. Refuel them with the best-odds snacks, too.

Get a teacher's expert advice

Are you and the kids cramped up over long spells on the computer or tablet? Here's how to get relief

---

1. Take screen breaks

Have a few short breaks every hour and get up from the desk and walk away. Open post, catch up on calls while you're standing up, or make a coffee. At home, unload the dishwasher or do a bit of dusting. With young children, set a timer to go off every 15 minutes. Tell them that when they hear it they should jump up and do something fun, such as run on the spot for 30 seconds.

2. Vary your posture

Sit forward and back on a regular basis. Even at home you should use an office-style chair when you sit at a computer desk – one with a tilt function. Stretch your feet forward or lift them up on the chair's leg supports at regular intervals. Ideally, pick a desk with adjustable height, too, so you can alternate between sitting and standing while you work.

3. Stretch regularly

Sitting still makes your muscles stiff and shortened so it's good to stretch out. Kristian Berg, chiropractor, personal trainer, and author of 'The Big Stretching Book' suggests these stretching exercises:
•**For the neck** – sit on a chair with your feet wide apart. Grab the underside of the seat with your right hand. Rotate your head 45 degrees to the left, and place your left hand on the back of your head. Bend

your head diagonally forward. Then do the same thing on the other side.
•**For the shoulders** – sit on a chair with your feet wide apart. Grab the underside of the seat with your right hand. Lean your upper body and head to the left side, turn your head to the right, and place your left hand against your head. Change sides.
•**For the hips** – sit on the edge of a table, and lie back down. Pull up both legs against your chest. Grab the left knee with both hands around it, and lower your right leg and let it hang freely. Change sides.

4. Use laptops and tablets with care

It's easy to spend hours hunched over portable screens. Try to vary how you use them and sit at a table as often as you can, to reduce the tension in your shoulders. It's also worth thinking about bringing in some **computer time rules**, for more valuable insights.

5. Stay strong

A stronger body helps relieve stress on the joints. Bone strength increases bone density, too, which helps to reduce the risk of osteoporosis later in life. No time to get to the gym?

....

Gina ford although she makes some valid points has no kids of her own some of her techniques are good / some aren't, take from it what you want but don't take it all as gospel.

I think you should have a flexible routine, pick your child up for cuddles as much as you can etc.

May things easier on yourself; put bottles in the dishwasher, make up feeds in advance, use cartons of ready made milk if you can, have extra bottles, clothes and muslins so its less washing and tumble dry the clothes. New borns are in and out of clothes too quickly to be effected by a bit of shrinking from the tumble dryer. As the get in their age 2-3 clothes and have them for longer, you will find that the colours fade and they shrink due to excess washing so you won't be able to save them for the next child. You will have lots of new born clothes, some brand new for the next child, but less of the bigger sizes and basically no clothes will be able to be kept after age 3, as by then they will wear most of their clothes out (they will get holes in them from playing outside etc).

....

Stereotyping; We are judged by our name - **Harari and Mc David (1973)** showed that teachers marking essays by unknown students are influenced by the name at the bottom. This is something worth bearing in mind, when you are choosing your childs name. Think of a name that sounds intelligent, that would work well in a work place. Some names sound sweet on a baby/child but not so great when they are an adult and want to sound professional. Also think about if the name can be shortened, what the initials spell, does a celebrity have a similar name? It is all very well that the celebrity may be 'en vougue' now but in 10 years' time when they are out of fashion. You want to eliminate the possibility for bulling as much as possible, and choosing a name carefully can be one consideration for this.

Think of the Johhny Cash song, a boy named Sue;

'Well, he must o' thought that is quite a joke
And it got a lot of laughs from a' lots of folk,
It seems I had to fight my whole life through.
Some gal would giggle and I'd get red
And some guy'd laugh and I'd bust his head,
I tell ya, life ain't easy for a boy named "Sue." '

When playing your child will:

- Develop imagination
- Extend their language and understanding
- Increase their self-awareness, self-esteem, and self-respect
- Improve and maintain their physical and mental health
- Give them the opportunity to mix with other children
- Allow them to increase their confidence through developing new skills
- Promote their imagination, independence and creativity
- Offer opportunities for children of all abilities and backgrounds to play together
- Provide opportunities for developing social skills and learning
- Build resilience through risk taking and challenge, problem solving, and dealing with new and novel situations
- Provide opportunities to learn about their environment and the wider community

....

Its good to teach your child and play educational games but under 3 should be about learn through play, if its not play/fun don't teach it. i.e. under 3 don't teach the alphabet.

Its good if at 2, or certainly by 3 they know positioning language i.e. under, on can count to 5 etc.

- I was worried about changing nappies because I'm not good with the smell of poo, but when it's your own, after a while you become immune and it doesn't bother you.

- Be informed/make your own decisions, know the school syllabus and curriculum so you can help your child.

- If your informed you can make your own decisions i.e. reading reports, when to feed. You can be informed and make your own decision about what is best for your child.

- Sometimes advisors are not right so do more research yourself. Use common sense and instinct.

Early years outcomes

https://www.gov.uk/government/uploads/system/uploads/attachment_data/file/237249/Early_Years_Outcomes.pdf

Each kid at school / nursery should have an EYFS profile and early learning goals are the areas for different milestones.

Their are 17 early learning goals. With a toddler concentrate on social skills, colours, shape and sharing and fine motor skills which is things with fingers, play dough . Main thing is making sure s/he understands language. Give him/her instructions to follow and work on his/her speech. Get him/her to build towers and fix train tracks and puzzles so s/he has to think. Encourage him/her to be a bit independent. So get him/her to help with dressing and understanding self care, like when to clean hands, tidy up, put things in bin etc. Also introduce emotions. Get him/her to express feelings in words, understand emotions and show empathy to others i.e. hug another child when crying, or give a toy to another child who is sad etc.

For a 2 year old; Get him/her to count objects to 3 to begin with and when s/he can do it to 5. Counting objects to 5 is 30-60 months. Main thing at this age is speech and understanding, social skills and forming friendships and starting to be independent in self care. Don't bombard them though, let them play and be a child – don't focus too much or get too obsessed with learning and development.

Lots of exploring, especially in the outside like bug hunts, how toys work , what telephone and technology does etc. help with washing, put things in machine etc.

Have a good mix of toys, some tv but not too much etc. boy and girl toys, dolls and cars etc. pens, physical toys, books etc.

Learning through play is a great way to encourage independence and exploration as part of early years learning. Discover our 3 favourite activities.

Though sometimes parents may not see the method to the madness, play is a vital part of early years development. Children are fully involved in play and use their bodies, minds and emotions; they learn to be in control and confident about themselves while interacting with others. Here are a few ideas for stimulating activities which get children exploring and encourage independence.

1. Dressing up

Children love to dress up and to pretend to be other people, animals and superheroes in different settings.

Tip: Section off a role play area with curtains to make it more theatrical, and provide for all the senses with special lighting and sound effects.

2. Building a den

Outdoor environments allow for plenty of different types of play with wide spaces for movement, den building, climbing, running, and messy play.

Tip: Provide a box of den building materials such as old sheets and blankets, bamboo canes and ropes, bendy sticks and pipes.

3. Building blocks

Blocks are an open-ended resource and can take many different forms from empty food packets and boxes, to big wooden crates, and traditional wooden building blocks.

Tip: Add small world, people, animals and vehicles to a collection of different types of blocks to help children create situations and stories.

Discover why learning through play is such an important part of EYFS. Get your free eGuide now: Little explorers: How to promote learning through play - A guide for Schools and Nurseries
- See more at: http://www.learningbook.co.uk/blog/learning-through-play-our-top-3-activities-early-years#sthash.dqb5K7zm.dpuf

Skills to develop	Toys/games
Fine motor skills	Play dough, drawing and colouring
Emotion	Baby dolls

More than just play;
At this age, children play all sorts of games. From imaginary worlds and fantasies to rough-and-tumble, games are essential to healthy mental and physical development. As an adult, you may marvel at your child's amazing ability to see the fun and creative potential in almost any object or situation. So take advantage of this to teach your toddler useful skills - such as how to count!

The power of toddler play;

Development
Play comes in many different forms, from building towers out of blocks or feeding a favourite stuffed animal to simply racing around the garden for hours. Trying out different ways to play can help your toddler develop new skills - while having fun.

Why play is vital for healthy development

Development
Your toddler learns a lot about the world through play. Every event, object and action, seen through your child's eyes, is an opportunity for fun. It's through engaging with their environment while playing that children find out more about the world.

Fun with matching

Games & activities

It's important to learn your letters and numbers, but it can also be fun! Matching games are a fun and effective way to introduce letters and numbers to your child. Our game makes learning fun for your little one!

Children take things literally so think about what you say
If giving time out, start with just 1 minute, use a sand egg timer so they can see it.
Take dribble off at soft play, so they don't slip and catch it and pull on their neck.

Baby massage - Don't massage after a meal. Stop once baby gets restless ie wriggles

When changing put a towel down on top of change mat so baby doesn't feel cold on his/her back (or a muslin does the same thing).

Ensure that you have house insurance that covers accidental cove on your content, and replaces new for old, you will need it with a child around. Ritchie threw a toy and broke my dads HD LED flat screen TV when he was 2.

Web cam – ensure people can't hack into your web cam and spy on you / hack into your baby monitor and talk to or harass your child.

At Christmas get a Christmas jumper and matching xmas outfit for your baby

As well as the urine and the rubbing of the nappy being an irritant, chemicals inside the nappy may irritate the baby. In this case get natural nappies like nappy or traditional towelling, non disposable nappies, maybe best.

Discipline – don't shout, talk calmly, and don't smack. Sit your child down, if they are too young for time out just sit them in a set place when they are naughty and leave for a minute or 2. If they get down put them back. If they cry ignore them for a minute or 2 , then calmly explain. If you shout his will upset them and make them worse.

Toddlers want to be independent, teach them to wash their hands, help you by putting their nappies in the bin, passing you the wipes, putting washing in the machine, pulling their socks and trousers off to help you change them (this one works well if they don't like letting you change them).

People independent from the child, unattached i.e. a care worker and not a mother will look at things with fresh eye and may have a more reasoned perspective. Although the mother will understand the child more.

Take control and empower yourself by reading, learning and spending time with your child. If you understand them you will feel less powerless as a parent.

If child is naughty – they may need more stimulation to stop them being bored and playing up, do something to divert and focus their attention. If they are very intelligent they may get bored more easily and need more stimulation. If they are fussy eaters you may need to put a DVD on and then eat them whilst they are not paying attention.

Night terror – could be if sad before bed or something happened in day that upset them, that they are playing in their head. These are very common.

Don't throw things in front of toddler i.e. toys into toy box as they copy

They copy what they see i.e. Ritchie saw a reindeer jumping through a window on a film so tried to put his toy dinosaur through the dolls house window.

Once they are out of their cot into a bed, move the stair gate from the top of the stairs, to over their door and put toys in their room so they can stay and play in their too.

When you go on holiday with baby pack a flannel, as otherwise you will use too many wipes.
Pack extra wipes (especially if you are going to a resort where they will be expensive to buy).
Vacuum pack nappies in your suitcase so that they take up less room
Mix essentials in different cases ie some nappies in each case and some stuff in hand luggage in case a bag goes missing.
When hot your baby will sweat more so you may need more nappies.
If you baby throws toys, take them away, leave them where they throw them or have a special toy bin where they go in and stay confiscated for a while. At age 2 – 4 most toddlers throw toys.

Teach them to play catch for good hand eye co-ordination. Start with a large ball and as they get older and get better at it progress to smaller balls.

Teach skipping, its good exercise.

Baby reins with anchor straps for highchairs are good
Baby play pen that doubles as gate

Take your baby/child's coat off in car, otherwise they overheat and won't feel the benefit of their coat when they get out, also it's not good with car seat straps because they don't sit so well on the coat.

Dealing with a baby/child with a temperature;
- It's not just the temperature but how quickly they get it that causes the issues.
- Distress raises their temperature.
- Cool them down slowly with tepid water, removing clothes. Do not place near an open window or in a cold bath as cooling them too quickly will send the body into shock.

If your toddler is not sleeping much at night you may find that you need to start cutting out their day time nap.

Get a boot liner for your car with a lip so that it covers your bumper, this will avoid scratching your car with your pushchair when you lift it out your boot.

Behaviour issues? – does your toddler obsess over toys i.e. sit there with a car and focus on it, turning the wheel over and over and line his/her toys up and get upset if they get out of line, if so it may be a sign of a condition, such as autism.

If your baby's nappies are dry it is an indication that s/he is not urinating enough. If they are dark or smelly, it maybe an indication of a urine infection.

Watch how they sit, to ensure they don't sit on the floor with their legs out at both sides, because this is bad for their hips.

Put your baby in their room early, in the moses basket in the day – so that they get used to their room/cot.

When Ritchie was new born **all I wanted to do was snuggle with my baby & sleep. You need to snuggle to bond and rest. Cuddle your baby, in a bed and comfy chair and sleep together. There is a risk of suffocation so get someone to keep check on mother & baby, if you are going to do this. But as long as you haven't been drinking/aren't on medication then you should be fine.**

....

Keep spare nappy bags in your bag for dirty tissues, babies spoons, dirty bibs etc. Keep a small pack of baby wipes in your handbag, in case you leave the wipes in the pram.

....

They go through stages as a toddler where they want to be independent and do things themselves, they may not want to get dressed. Give them a choice and let them feel independent. Do you want mummy to dress you or do you want to dress yourself with mummies help? Either way you are dressing them but it makes them feel like they are doing it. This will help them to be more co-operative. You can also say if you don't come here mummy will pick you up, do you want to come here or have mummy pick you up. Then count to 3 and if they haven't done it on the count of 3 there will be consequences.

,,,,,,,,,,,,,,,,,,,,,,,

At xmas out candy canes n the tree, lower down and nicer decorations at the top that way it doesn't matter if your baby/toddler gabs them and throws them.

- **When you have a toddler / small child it is a good idea to get a hand held hoover, dyson is good. That way you can follow them around and quickly zap up the mess without having to drag a big hoover out.**
- **It is a good idea to get waterproof over trousers, that you can put over the trousers so they can run in the park and go on the slide when its damp, without getting them wet.**
- **It is a good to change them into pj before you take them home, that way if they fall asleep in the car, they are ready for bed and you can just lift them in.**
- **Children are always changing, just as you think you have the routine sorted something changes.**
- **Tomato ketchup & most sauces have a lot of sugar & salt & should be avoided.**
- **If they are too warm or too many people may upset them or if over tired.**

- Take them out & get them used to people. Its good for them to be around children their own age to, to develop good social skills as good social skills are the most important life skills, to bring friends and happiness.
- Children like routine, although some flexibility is also necessary.
- Stay calm when pregnant to have a calm baby
- Children always play up more for their children/where they are familiar because they feel comfortable pushing the boundaries

Even if you have a boy, still tell them about lady things / periods etc because when they have a girlfriend they will need to know this. If they don't know and a girl in their class at school bleeds through it may upset them.

Feeding – when I first had Ritchie they told me not to wean until 6 months, despite my instinct telling me otherwise, they then later retracted this advice and changed it back to 4 months. This shows that the experts aren't always right, trust your instinct. He couldn't sit up at this stage, but was ready for food.

They know when they want to eat or not, yet when they are tired they may fight it and pretend they are not, therefore you can't leave them to decide and have to be firm and make decisions for them.

Boys like pink because it is bright and is often the colour that their mums wear, this is okay.

cseeman/Flickr

Make reindeer food with porridge oats, glitter and sequines, put it on the lawn on Christmas eve for Santa and his reindeers.

When trying a new food for the first time, to test if you/your child are not allergic – first touch the product on to the skin i.e. the face, if there is no react test it on the lips, then the inside of the lips and then finally eat it, if no reaction shows at each stage.

Keep a spare dummy in the car & also spare baby reins.

Carry spare clothes and also PJs and a toothbrush so that you can change baby before brining him/her home, in case they fall asleep in the car.

Spoil your baby with cuddles the first year. Give your baby cuddles and don't worry about picking him/her up too much. Don't feel the need to make your baby self soothe. Through sleep training you can condition a baby not to cry out for attention and go to sleep without parental input fairly easily, however this behaviour is not indicative of a baby who is calm, soothed or settled. Self soothing is actually a myth for babies and is dangerous. Self soothing is a developmental stage, a skill that infants gain as they grow older. Just as they become more physically mobile, develop the ability to eat solids and develop the ability to talk. In essence you can't teach something that their brains are not yet equipped for (no matter what the sleep expert promises!).

'Self soothing' is such a misleading term. Whoever invented it has cleverly made it sound like something positive and gentle, similar to the new wave of controlled crying names such as "controlled comforting", "spaced soothing" and "controlled soothing". Clever marketing, same technique. In reality however you are categorically not leaving your baby to 'soothe', you are leaving them to cry, even if it is only for periods of two minutes at a time.

What Happens When you Sleep Train Then?

I know that many who read this will think "but it works, you're wrong!". The real issue here however is our misinterpretation of what is working and what is actually happening.

If you practice sleep training (that could be controlled comforting, spaced comforting, controlled soothing, controlled crying, cry it out, rapid return, spaced soothing, gradual withdrawal or pick up put down – call it what you will, really they're all the same in their intent and actions) are you teaching your baby to self soothe? No. You absolutely are not, unless you have a wonder kid about five years advanced in their brain development!

What is really happening? In most cases something is happening on a very basic primal level. Let's go back to the hindbrain and the fight or flight response. What happens when those stress hormones reach such a level that they are toxic yet you can't take flight........or fight.....another 'F' comes in, this time it's F for 'Freeze'. You freeze all activity in order to try to conserve homeostasis, or more simply put – conserve life. Dr Sears calls this 'Shutdown Syndrome'.

Do you remember that NSPCC advert with Baby Miles?

"Baby Miles doesn't cry anymore because nobody comes".

Or footage of Romanian orphanages with rows upon rows of cots with eerily quiet babies? They don't cry, not because they don't have needs, or feelings, but because there are too many of them for the staff to respond to unless it is for a basic physical need.

They're in Shutdown Syndrome, they have 'frozen' in order to conserve life. They know nobody comes, why cry?

They are obviously extreme examples (and I am not saying that a baby left in an orphanage is in the same position as a baby undergoing sleep training), but to a lesser extent trying to teach a baby to self soothe relies on the same principles. It 'works' for the same reason.

Check out this research which shows what happens during 'self soothing' teaching, highlighting how stressed the baby still is, despite their quietness and apparent 'sleeping'. Chemically we can now prove that the baby is neither soothed or settled.

The Worrying Side Effects of The Self Soothing Myth

If parents believe their babies are 'soothed' and calmed, they naturally relax and think all is OK. But what if it's not OK? What if a 'frozen' baby is in distress yet doesn't call out for their parents?

What if they have vomitted, or slipped down under their blankets? What if they don't cry because nobody comes, what if they become a SIDS statistic as a result?

This is the 'self soothing' myth at it's most damaging and most alarming. Sadly nobody will ever research this, it would just be too unethical, but it's not a wild theory to present despite how uncomfortable it is to think about.

If a baby has been trained to be quiet and to not call for their parents to meet their emotional needs it isn't too far-fetched to be worried that at some point something might happen and the baby may not call out when they have an urgent need.. A baby's brain is not sophisticated enough to know that sometimes the parents come and sometimes they don't – depending on what's wrong.

Nobody knows what causes SIDs, in fact SIDs, is a label given to unexplained infant death and obviously there is no one cause, but likely hundreds if not thousands. I honestly believe however that there is a potential correlation with sleep training though. Don't parents have the right to know of the potential risks when they are advised to teach their baby to self soothe by a baby sleep expert or health professional?

What if the babies are physically OK though? Are there any psychological risks?

What happens in the first few years of life is vital for the development of a baby's brain. As a parent you are effectively an architect building and sculpting the person they will be in years to come.

Remember the limbic system that develops over the first three years? The bit that contains the Amygdala and Hippocampus?

Well there is research that shows that the more nurturing you are towards your child in their early years the greater their hippocampal volume…..and that's important because the hippocampus is related to behavioural regulation. Many argue that science only proves a link with severely neglected or abused children, but that's not true, there is research that looks at children in perfectly normal family situations.

The same is true of the amygdala which plays a key role in the processing of emotions. The chart on the left is from the research I've linked to above- it's pretty shocking isn't it?

The Real Path to Self Soothing

Parental nurturing increases hippocampal volume (and also that of the amygdala). The hippocampus and amygdala are parts of the brain responsible for behavioural regulation and emotional processing. It is obvious to theorise therefore that the best way to ensure a child grows to have good emotional self regulation (or self soothing/self settling skills) is by responding to them as much as they need when they are young.

A close, nurturing relationship with a child when they are young doesn't just predict their ability to self soothe in later life, it also predicts their ability to form empathy with others and pro-social behaviour, which really is just another facet of emotional self regulation. Just as this research indicates, as does this and this and this and this which has just been published.

Is it possible to teach a baby or a toddler to 'self soothe' or 'self settle' themselves to sleep?

No, it is not.

Is it possible to train a baby or a toddler to not call out for their parents when they are in need? Yes, it is, but this is categorically not indicative of an infant who is happy, calm and soothed.

Is it possible to alter the architecture of your child's brain so that they grow to have good emotional self regulation skills (or the real ability to self soothe) when they are older? Absolutely!

What's the best way to do that? Pick them up, cuddle them, respond to them – and your nurturing parenting will pay dividends in the future – that is how you REALLY help a child to develop the ability to self soothe and doesn't every parent want the best for their child? Yes it is exhausting parenting a baby or toddler, I've been there – I know the depths of sleep deprivation, but as parents we have such an amazing ability to shape the next generation! We owe it to our children to seek alternative ways to cope with our own issues (search this blog for many articles of how to cope with non sleeping children!).

Self soothing is not a skill that can be taught, it is a behaviour that develops once the child's brain is sufficiently developed, it can't be hurried – but you can give your child the best chance of it happening by being as nurturing as possible now. The techniques commonly used for teaching self soothing and self settling ironically make the child less likely to develop these skills in later life, now that's food for thought!

Get a realistic baby doll for your child to look after – one that makes noises and has accessories, to make it fun - teach them to be kind to it, to prepare them for a sibling. Also if you want them to lay down to change a nappy lay the baby dill down, give the baby doll medicine etc

For party snacks avoid peanuts, if people drop them on the floor a baby may pick them up and choke.

When getting crayons get none toxic chunky ones for under 3s.

Keep toys in the car so you can entertain your baby when you are out and about. You can even get portable DVD player that can go in the car too.

If you cut your hours at work you might not lose much money after you pay less tax.

- Keep dummy wipes in the car
- Keep extra nappies & wipes - don't run low, you can always use wipes. Keep some in the car, have a basket upstairs & downstairs.
- Swivel car seat
- Avoid choke hazards in the back of car.
- Having 2 babies is hard work because one is sick and awake, then the other one is awake and you get less sleep.
- Plan children around starting school & maternity leave & child care etc you could plan it so you go on maternity leave 6 moths before your oldest starts school, then when you go back to school work you only have to pay child care for your 2nd child and not both, you also get to spend time with your oldest before s/he starts school.

- Use moisturiser on baby face in winter dribble & dummy with cold & wind will cause a rash, face cream will help to protect & repair.
- Keep small pack of wipes/straw or empty water bottle for baby in car.
- Do food shop on line
- What size does stroller go up to, if you have a tall baby you may need a bigger stroller.
- Fingerless gloves are good if your baby doesn't like mittens and normal gloves are hard to put on.
- Watch how you ask children to do things, say put instead of throw, otherwise your child will literally throw.
- Present for baby - 100 year diary, burts bee toiletries & creams.
- Do online courses when baby is in bed.
- The baby will get lots of soft toys so you don't need to buy too many.
- Make things yourself to save money
- Let child choose their own baby doll, plate, bed etc

When you have a child you will soon be overrun with toys and run out of storage space so you need to find clever storage solutions and be as inventive as possible.

Radiator cover with storage;

Use plaques with pegs to display your child's picture, to hang invites, tickets or vouchers etc.

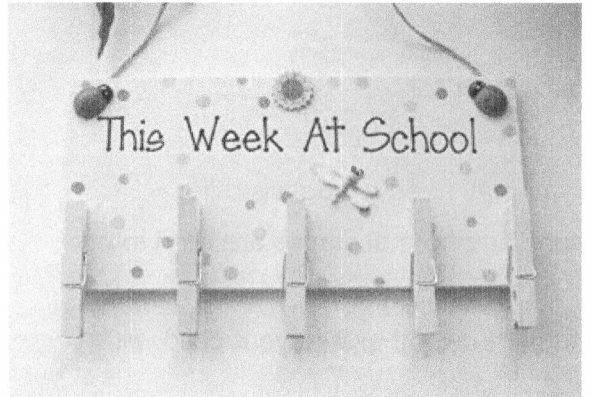

- Have a savings account for your children and put an allowance/ pocket money in, as soon as they are born and ask for money for Christmas and birthdays, it will soon add up to a tidy sum by the time they are 18.
- Be wary of water in vases and fish bowls on tables with cloths & children, in case children pull the table cloth & knock it over.
- Have a tin / box full of cake ingredients & decorations so you can make a last minute cake if you need to, also have a craft box for kids. Keep a cupboard with cards and gifts too, for last minute parties.
- Have a tin / box full of cake ingredients & decorations so you can make a last minute cake if you need to, also have a craft box for kids. Keep a cupboard with cards and gifts too, for last minute parties. Also keep a kit of birthday banners, paper plates, balloons, candles and napkins so that you can organise parties.
- Keep small pack of wipes/straw or empty water bottle for baby in car, for when you are out and about.
- Children copy your mistakes, don't bring them up to follow your patterns of mistakes. At work I see many families where the father beats the mother and then the daughter marries a wife beater. Children will follow your example and choices, they see them as normal and acceptable behaviours. Therefore watch your behaviour and set a good example. Watch what you say as well as how you act, to ensure resentment doesn't get passed on.
- Check if your nursery has a shelter outside so that your child can still play out in extreme weather.

- Keep yourself fuelled - eat protein nuts etc because you can't deal with toddler tantrum if you have low blood sugar and feel stressed. Have a cuppa tea and use the loo before leaving work.
- Keep spare clothes in car and a bag for dirty clothes, you never know when you may need clean clothes if your baby vomits on you or you spill tea on you etc.
- Holding food – some babies hold food in their mouth for ages after eating, make sure that they haven't done this, especially before changing nappies and tipping them back etc otherwise they make choke.
- Super absorbent powder is good for cleaning up vomit and other spills.
- Cool food such as rice by running it under the cold tap before feeding it to baby.
- Biological wash powder is good for cleaning high chair straps.
- Fold highchair away to give you more space in your home
- Top up your pension after maternity leave, to pay back the amount that you have missed paying, so that you don't lose that pension time.
- Work together with your partner as a team. Communicate what needs to be done and assign roles.
- Put dates in your diary to remind you to get your kids feet measures for shoes, in case you forget to check/get re-measured. Also a reminder a month before dentist and optician check up are due.
- At diff stages there is always something to look forward too, when your child is growing up.
- A booster seat high chair is good to have for when you go out, but also to have at home when baby gets older, rather than a large high chair. Although I had tall stools in the kitchen so liked having my tall highchair in the kitchen.
- Name book & lost my name story are great to help children spell their names etc.
- Tell nursery special names for things ie jus, tinkle so that they understand what your child is saying.
- Send to play in room, make room child friendly i.e. no glass doors.

Get a strong phone protector and child proof ipad protector. You can get cases for your children/babies to use the ipad too, which also protects it.

Get a washing machine with a large drum and a separate tumble dryer if you can (if you use a washer dyer you can only dry 1/2 the load that you wash.

Babies/children love looking at photos of themselves and their friends and family.

To do – when have next baby;

Book ante natal classes at children's centre.

Join net mums group

Promote my baby book to fellow mums to be / set up a mums to be group?

Get a maternity and birth scrap book.

Get pregnancy books out of loft.

After birth:

1. Register birth
2. Apply child benefit
3. Register doctors
4. Get passport
5. Do scrap book / 100 year diary / life book & update my auto / make a photo frame /memory box, get a newspaper for the day baby born / print a frame with meaning of name.
6. Vaccines
7. Organise christening
8. European health card
9. Apply child tax & working tax credit
10. Register children's centre / enrolled on baby yoga & baby massage & take red book & get baby weighed.

Plan first birthday party

When go back to work top up pension to cover time pension not paid whilst on maternity leave. Before going to work put name down for nursery.

....

- Just give a small amount of chocolate. Rather than a whole packet of buttons give 1/2 as children are small, otherwise it's a lot for them.
- Don't loose your identity when you become a mum, find things that you can do for yourself so that you keep your identity.
- Once they are toddling don't have a bin in their room with carry a bags in.
- Practise hair on dolls head
- take it in turns doing night feed, stagging on so u both get some rest, don't get up together.
- get rest after giving birth, your body needs time and rest to heal
- Talk to your baby loads to encourage them to talk more.
- Imaginary friend – when humouring them about their imaginary friend, don't promise that they will be somewhere i.e. when you get to nursery kangaroo will be there, in case they are not.

Toddler top tip;

- Work request to change hours - put in formally, this way they have to give reasons to reject your application and you can appeal this, where as if you ask informally they can more easily be dismissive towards your request.
- Train them like a puppy - short commands and repetition.

- If child hits/punches - get their hand and make them stroke with it and say gentle and teach them to be gentle, or push them away and ignore them.
- Do activities to stimulate the brain and stop them from getting bored. If they get bored they will play up more.
- Distract them before they throw a tantrum - prevention is better than cure.
- Give fun things to do and threaten not to do them or to take a toy away if they are naughty i.e. you can play on your own in your room or we won't be able to go and feed the ducks today if you don't behave. When they are older you can use reward charts, to encourage good behaviour but this won't work when they are really small.
- Be confident when you give instructions. Give clear and simple instructions. Use a stern voice and short commands, say please and thank you. If you are unsure in yourself they will pick up on that.
- Come down to their level - get down and talk to them at their eye level.
- If you put them on the naughty step, walk away and leave them on their own.
- Give them discipline at the time they do something naughty, they will not remember or understand later on.
- You can't reason with them until they are age 7.
- They may not understand what they are doing is wrong, may be whinny because they are ill or tired and are therefore not being naughty.
- They will play up if they are over tired
- Have a room them can go I and have down time /quiet time and watch TV, play alone etc calm down if they are stressed etc.
- Have quiet time before bed
- Get someone to video discipline scenarios so that you can watch it back and see how you handled it and decide a better strategy for next time. Have a discipline plan and ensure all care givers have the same routine, methods - consistency is key.
- If you do smack, only do this occasionally.
- Tell them off for important things, don't nag
- Follow threats through, so that they take you seriously.
- Write down tantrum and triggers and so you can analyse what starts them and work out how to avoid them.
- Distract from bad behaviour and praise good behaviour.
- They need routine and boundaries and quite time before bed
- Spend time doing research into different ideologies - what works what doesn't, what your child needs are. Invest time in them. Do yourself a life plan and avoid big career moves / time consuming degrees until they are older.
- Things change - phases pass soon enough, what seems a big problem at one stage will soon pass and be something that you laugh about later on.
- You may have to leave them to have their tantrum and get it out of their system, ignore their bad behaviour and perhaps deal with them once they have got their temper out (some people smack them to shock them out of it).
- Ignore bad behaviour, praise good behaviour.
- Whilst dressing them/changing them - give praise but talk to and distract them at the same time so that you can dress them without them running away etc.
- Let them be independent and involved i.e. choose their clothes from a selection. They want to be independent, because they are finding their independence so will fight you for control and push the boundaries, let them know you are in charge but give them some control and choice.

- Once you have told them off, then go onto do something else (ideally something fun and distracting) and don't mention their bad behaviour again.
- If they don't get in the car - hold them at the side of the car and threaten to go without them.
- Have biscuits and water in the car in case you get stuck in traffic / long journey.
- Use counting - If you don't do X by the time I have counted to 3 you will go to your room
- Give a 5 minute warning, say before going to the park you need to leave nicely, or else you will not be able to go again, then say we will be leaving in 5 mins.
- Attitudes and methods to discipline will need to change as they change / get older etc.
- Take time to keep going through things with your child and deal with issues as they happen. When you are trying to get ready for work and they have a tantrum it feels like it is lasting forever a few minutes seem like a lifetime, allow those few minutes extra, walk away, let them get it out
- Give freedom to play but boundaries i.e. tidy up etc.
- They behave worse for their parents - take nursery with a pinch of salt, they will be better at nursery and school because they have space to play and more toys and there is less boundaries / less scope to be naughty, it's not like at home when they have to fit into chaos and have dinner and get ready for bed etc.
- Children play up for attention. Each child is different so different things work for each child and for different situations so you will need to tailor your approach accordingly.
- If your toddler hits you, firmly say no and put him/her down and turn your back on them, then once they have calmed down move onto another activity, be positive and cheerful so that the tantrum is forgotten and their mood and attention is uplifted and is on something positive.
- Be calm, focused and steer and focus their attention on positive things.
- Make getting dressed fun i.e. put your nappy on so that you look like mogley out of the jungle book.
- Even if its cold wrap up warm and go out – as long as you wrap up and have lots of warm layers, hat coat and scarf.
- They say hurtful things and don't mean them its just a phase, try not to let it upset you.
- Its easy to loose your identity once you have a baby, find a hobby & routine for identity.
- Allow extra time to get ready with baby to allow for tantrums. Get organised the night before etc
- Take them to the door and show them that they will get cold without their clothes on. If they refuse to get dressed / put coat on.
- When they wake up & move around and you are in the shower. Make sure things aren't in their reach that they shouldn't be. Have toys / tv to entertain them so you can get yourself ready in the morning.
- Have somewhere you can send them if they are naughty ie a room with out toys.
- Make sure their room is safe for them to be left in, if they are really naughty take them to their room to calm down / have time out so you can calm down. Ie not glass / mirrored wardrobe doors.
- Have time when they can sit down and watch a DVD, have quiet time.
- If they bite put your hand on their forehead and push their head away.
- Give them incentives, say if you are good we can make a cake together etc
- Consider a stair gate over their room so they can't wonder out.
- Toys / colouring book to distract when your out so they are less likely to be naughty.
- Just focus on getting ready and out the door, leave other jobs until after work/babies nap time etc

- If toddler / baby is restless take for walks in the fresh air, the summer is easier because you can get out more you may need to wrap up warm and still go out, or go to play centres in the winter as they will get restless and play up if they are couped up inside all day with no exercise. They need to physically run off excess energy.
- Put clothes etc away, if you don't leave things lying around its less for them to throw.
- Allow extra time for nursery in case unforeseen traffic.
- Ask them if you miss breakfast if they can give them toast/breakfast at snack time, to ensure they get to eat something on days you are late.
- Nursery - can you see / watch children when you pick up. Stay with when you drop off etc
- Hide remote control / give old remote control
- Threaten to take dummies/favourite toy away when naughty and give back when good.
- Get doll to lay down and get dressed then its toddlers turn or give toddler something to play with or do, including dressing dolly whilst you dress the toddler.
- Try getting their clothes ready the night before and dressing as soon as they wake up, whilst they are still sleeping or you may prefer to get them dressed after breakfast so that they don't make their clothes messy.
- Don't discuss things about them/their behaviour in front of them
- Naughty - for attention or maybe ill, tired, hungry, bored. Deal with the root cause.
- Different things at different times ie don't chase when getting dressed, keep fun times separate otherwise they will start running away when you are trying to dress them and will think its a game.
- Give a warning - 3 strikes policy ie do x, do x or you will get a smack, mummy is going to smack you if you don't, then do smack or time out etc
- Height chart with photos for key development stages & master piece pegs.
- If they refuse to get dressed, take them out in cold without clothes for a few minutes, they will soon change their minds.
- Find ways to how to hold so they can't hit you i.e. pick your toddler up facing out and wrap his legs around you, hold with one arm, and put the other hand around his arms.
- Keep your maternity pillow, use it as a baby nest or breast feeding pillow and later as toddler goes into a bed, put it the side of the bed, against the wall to stop your child falling down the side of the mattress and the wall (if you have the bed against the wall).
- Don't stock up too much on nappies when your baby is getting near the next size or getting ready for potty training etc.
- Don't be condescending towards your children / change with them as they grow.
- Always know where you children are and who they are with at all times. Have emergency plans i.e. if you are out and we get split up meet at this point etc.
- Let your baby / toddler feed themselves, they know what you want and will eat the right amount, where as if you feed them more they may over eat. Don't worry if some days they eat less, some days they will eat less than others.
- Cool food such as rice by running it under the cold tap before feeding it to baby.
- Biological wash powder is good for cleaning high chair straps.
- Throw dummies away after a while and buy fresh ones as they will break down.
- If you take water up to bed with you, take it in a water bottle, to avoid spills, especially if you have a toddler who is likely to knock it over, or tip your makeup or mobile into your glass of water.
- Try giving pineapple juice for a cough
- **If you think you are having problems breast feeding/not producing enough, then express and feed your baby that way. Work out what they need and what you are producing and**

top up if necessary (otherwise they may not get enough). I was expressing for 23 hours a day and wasn't getting any rest, I was so exhausted and couldn't produce enough milk, this made me miserable. There is no point in being stressed and tired, you need energy for your baby and they will pick up on your stress. As long as they have had the colostrum which they get in the first few days, it maybe worth going onto the bottle after this, don't let anyone make you feel guilty about this decision.

- When getting a mattress for your toddlers bed, get a decent one, so that you can sleep in their bed too if you need too.

- If you decide to undertake something like signing up to an evening course, on line course, don't try and take on too much for long because once you think you have got them in a routine and things are under control something will happen and it all changes. For instance with Ritchie we got him settled in his bed and at age 2 he started sleeping through the night, then he hit a rebellious stage and wouldn't go to bed, kept staying up and getting out of bed, wouldn't let me dress him/change his nappy. It was a nightmare getting ready in the morning so I had to get up extra early to allow for the longer time getting ready etc and I had no time for myself in the evenings so where as I could snatch an hour here or there for a window of a few months, this soon went out the window. I had also just applied to do a masters degree at work, in the end I was actually glad that this request had been rejected. Its good to expand your mind and do courses etc but don't put added pressure in yourself. Just sign up to do low pressure / hobby type things that you can pick up at any time.

- Stop and think about things rationally – preferable when you have had something to eat and drink and haven't got low blood sugar. I tend to over worry and think the worse (a nervous disposition). Although it is good to hope for the best and plan for the worse you also need to not over analyse things with kids and you need to rationalise and not make mountains out of molehills or you will be a bag of nerves (which I usually am).

- Keep young kids within an arms reach at all times – so that you can grab them before they fall/run into the road or are snatched. Tell them about stranger danger because there are lots of snatches going on. Tell them not to approach cars or walk near the back of vans.

- If your child won't let you dress them/change their nappy and a toy doesn't work put a cartoon clip on you tube and give them your phone to hold, whilst you dress them. You may find tracksuit trousers (or trousers without lining) are quick and easy for nursery mornings when you are rushing as they are easier to get on, they are also good for late afternoon/early evening so if they do fall asleep, they can go to bed in them, without you having to wake them to change them (this is why soft baby grows and tracksuits rather than jeans are great for babies / young toddlers whilst they sleep a lot in the day – you want clothes that are comfy, stretchy and breathable for little ones).

- If you get your child dressed before breakfast, and for other meal times, muslin over their lap is great for catching food that the bib misses. So don't chuck all your muslins when you pass the baby stage, they are great for the cleaning their face, using as a sun shield, protecting their clothes from food, making a bib out of, using instead of a changing mat (they take up less room, although they will need washing after each use).
- Do a skid pad course to teach you how to dive in the ice, this is particularly important if you have kids you drive around a lot.
- Children like being at home and may protest about going to nursery, not because they may not want to go to nursery but because they may want to stay with their mum.
- You may want to get extra internet allowance on your phone as you will find you use it more with your baby to download music and video clips to entertain them, you also do more emails on your phone as you don't get time to put the computer on to do them.
- They are usually worse behaved for their mums because they see them more so know how to push the boundries, they often miss their dads more as they may see less of them. They tend to be crueller to their car giver and show affection for others.
- If there are older children at their nursery they may copy them and develop faster, as they older kids move up they may become less settled.
- They may sleep better when you cut your toddlers day nap or s/he may get over tired and not sleep so well, its all trial and error.
- Some nursery's give a book of when your child eats / has a nappy etc. however some say its better they spend more time with the children rather than writing and they have the information on clipboards, as long as they can give you the information when you ask, that is what is important and as long as your baby is happy.

The unwritten rules of children's parties?
- Birthday boy/girl must be given preference for starting activity. Small guests pushing past should be restrained by attending adults
- Party bags or gifts for each attending child - the children will always remember "that party" when they didn't get one
- If you don't RSVP don't think you can just turn up. And if you do, don't expect a party bag (see above)
- Avoid party talk around the parents of the uninvited
- Host child MUST win at least one round of pass the parcel. Sweets within each layer for everyone else
- Children must be given 15 minutes at the buffet before adults are allowed to hoover up the cocktail sausages

- from the BBC Magazine on the politics of parties 19/0/2015

Myth: Infants need to be bathed every day.

The truth Babies don't get stinky from sweat the way adults do, so they only need a bath every two or three days (except following a major diaper explosion!). If it's part of your wind-down routine, a daily bath is perfectly okay too--just moisturize afterwards.

Myth: Babies sleep best in a room that's silent and dark.

The truth While some children really are light sleepers, most do fine with background noise and a little light. Plus, if your little one gets used to some activity around him when he's sleeping, he'll be more willing to snooze in a variety of situations.

BananaStock/ Jupiter

Myth: When infants are running a high temperature, rub them down with alcohol to lower their fever.

The truth Rubbing your baby with alcohol won't actually bring down her fever--plus it's unsafe, since alcohol can be absorbed through her skin.

Myth: Letting your little one stand or bounce in your lap can cause bowlegs later on.

The truth He won't become bowlegged; that's just an old wives' tale. Moreover, young babies are learning how to bear weight on their legs and find their center of gravity, so letting your child stand or bounce is both fun and developmentally stimulating for him.

Myth: Listening to classical music will raise your baby's IQ.

The truth Music can enrich a little one's life, but no conclusive research has found that having a baby listen to classical music in particular can result in significant brain-boosting benefits.

Myth: Let your baby cry it out; if you pick her up whenever she's wailing, you'll spoil her.

The truth Babies under 4 months of age have few self-soothing strategies; they know how to suck to soothe and like being swaddled, but that's about it. Picking infants up when they cry helps them learn that parents will always be there to take care of them.

Myth: Babies should be woken up in the night to have a wet diaper changed.

The truth Urine is sterile, and today's diapers are highly absorbent, so it's fine to leave a baby in a wet diaper overnight. However, staying in poopy diaper for too long can cause a UTI or a bladder infection, especially for baby girls--so if you smell one, change it out.

Myth: It's dangerous to immunize your infant if he has a cold or a low-grade fever.

The truth A minor illness won't lower your baby's immune-system response to a vaccination--or increase his risk of any nasty reactions from a shot.

Myth: Never apply sunscreen to an infant under 6 months of age.

The truth The risk of skin cancer down the road from sun exposure is greater than the risk of your baby having a reaction to sunscreen. It's best to keep her away from dangerous UV rays as much as possible from 10 A.M. to 4 P.M., but put on sunscreen with at least 15 SPF if she'll be in the sun. The AAP says that it's fine to apply a minimal amount of sunscreen to small areas, such as a baby's face and the back of the hands.

Myth: During the first month of a baby's life, it's critical that all baby bottles and nipples be sterilized.

The truth Sterilize bottles and nipples when you first take them out of the package--but after that, washing with soap and water is fine. Babies are exposed to many more germs than those that remain on a well-scrubbed bottle or nipple.

Myth: The safest way to put an infant to sleep is on her stomach.

The truth The safest sleep position for a baby is on its back. In the past, doctors worried that babies might choke on any spit-up if they weren't lying on their tummy or side, but studies ultimately linked these positions to higher rates of SIDS.

Myth: Putting rice cereal in your infant's bottle will help him sleep.

The truth Hold off on introducing solids until 4 to 6 months. Research suggests that babies who are given solids before 4 months are actually worse sleepers than their formula-fed counterparts--an studies have revealed a link between the early introduction of solids

Myth: It's critical to keep your baby on a strict feeding schedule.

The truth It's better to feed on demand, as infants' internal hunger cues will tell them when they're hungry and when they're full. By putting your child on a feeding schedule, you may negatively affect your little one's inborn healthy-eating habits.

Myth: Infants need hard-soled shoes to protect their delicate toes and keep their feet properly aligned.

The truth Babies use their toes to grip the surfaces that they're walking on, so they should actually go shoeless indoors. To keep tiny tootsies safe outside, get a shoe with a good grip on the sole--hard-soled shoes can be too slippery.

Must-Read Tips for Your First Week with Baby

- If baby is outside put a sheet over the play pen to keep the flies out
- Put a clip on the back of the highchair to hang bibs on(if your highchair hasn't got a tray/basket) and if your highchair has a basket/ledge etc. clean it out regularly because stray bits of food may drop into it. I had a basket on my highchair and I found t handy to keep bibs, muslin and flannels in, I also kept baby wash next to the sink.
- I kept baby wipes and nappies in a basket upstairs and downstairs and I kept baby wipes next to the highchair to wipe up spills from the floor that the floor mat missed i.e. when my son was throwing food around, I also kept my hand held dyson nearby at meal times.

Give them temporary tattoos in case they get lost during an outing.

Old lotion bottles can be used as faucet extenders until the little tykes aren't so little anymore.

Never worry about losing them in public with these forget-met-not mittens

Source: boredpanda.com

Cut a hole in a pacifier and stick a dropper in it to make taking medicine slightly less traumatizing.

- Put a dummy in milk and freeze it to help with teething.

- A cut pool noodle will prevent little fingers from getting slammed in doors.

-

- Create a kid-sized hammock with some fabric and a table.

-

-

-

-

- Use a woven babywearing wrap (not a blanket) for this one. Find the instructions for how to make one in the link above!

- **If you're super careful, a big cardboard box can be re-purposed into a stair slide.**

-

- **A box fan can help a blanket fort stay up, while also making sure the adventurer inside is getting enough air.**

-

- A baby shower cap will make bath time tear-free.

- Keep their tummies full with this simple cheese rearrangement.

Good Sandwich Guide

Overlap

Nothing in corners

1.

2.

- Better yet, keep two tummies full at the same time by heating multiple bowls at once in your microwave.

-

- Teach them a simple way to make strawberries more enjoyable.

-

- **A cupcake holder around a popsicle stick will keep little hands from getting sticky on hot days.**

- **A spray bottle and cute decorations are all you need to create "Monster Spray" that stops kids from worrying at night.**

- To get them to put their shoes on the correct feet, cut a sticker in half and place it on the insides of their shoes.

- - Share

- - twitter

- I get so worried when the baby coughs all night. Here's how to alleviate that:

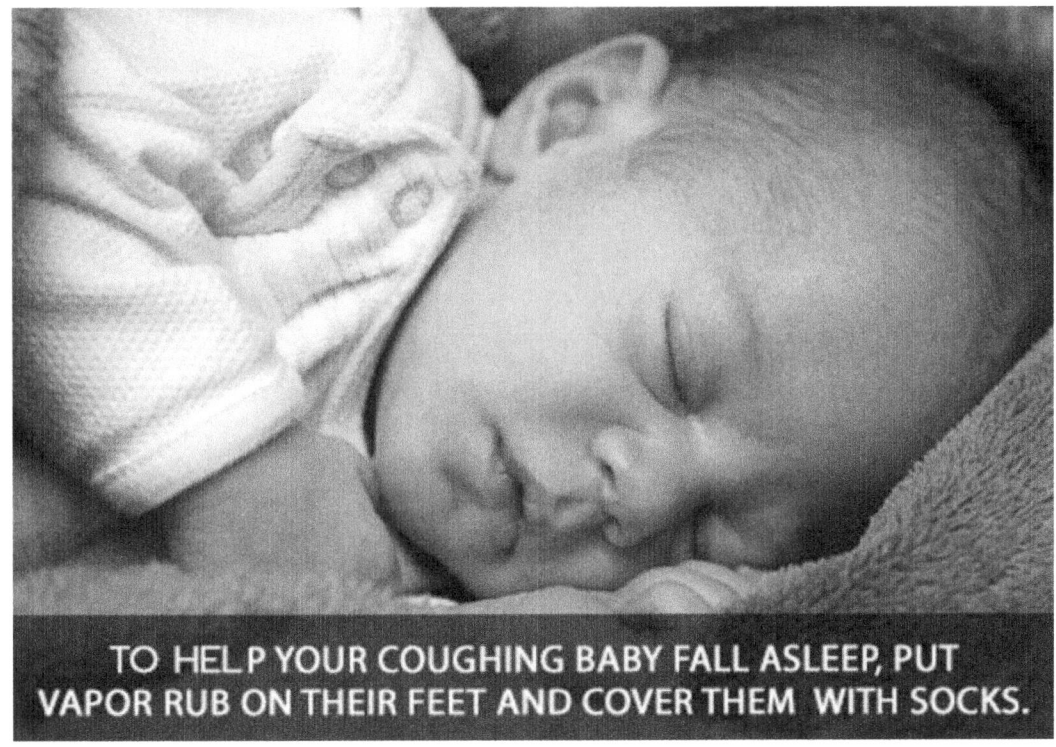

TO HELP YOUR COUGHING BABY FALL ASLEEP, PUT VAPOR RUB ON THEIR FEET AND COVER THEM WITH SOCKS.

- **Prevent spills by inserting a crazy straw upside-down to keep kids from yanking it right out of the cup.**

- **To keep apple slices from getting brown in a lunch bag, put them back together and secure them with a couple of rubber bands.**

-

- **Use an old DVD case to store paper and colored pencils for an on-the-road easel.**

-

- If you're afraid of them falling out at night, create a barrier by putting a pool noodle under a fitted sheet.

Share

- Use a laundry basket to keep bath toys from floating away.

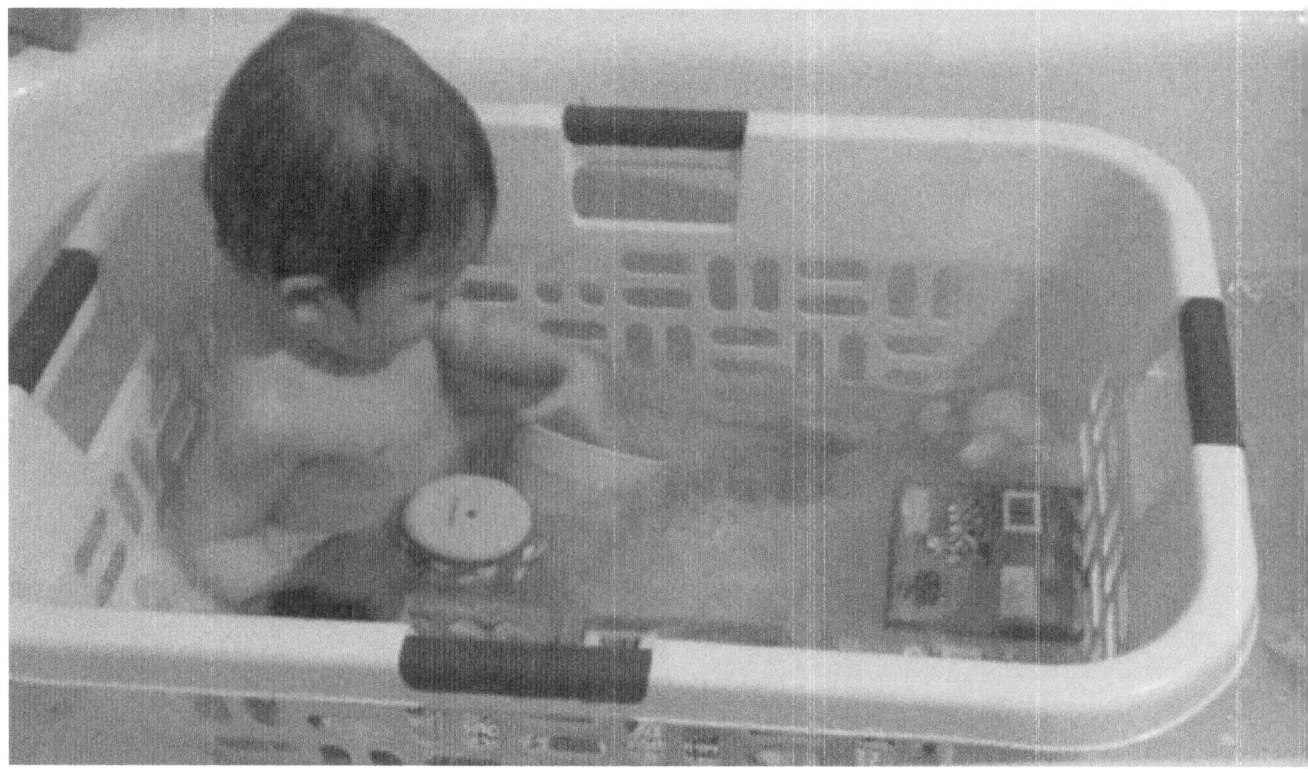

- Instead of damaging your home with nails, use a ziptie to secure baby gates to the banister.

- Some glue and glitter can turn any money into "tooth fairy money."

- **Prevent them from over-squeezing juice boxes by teaching them to hold the drink by the side flaps.**

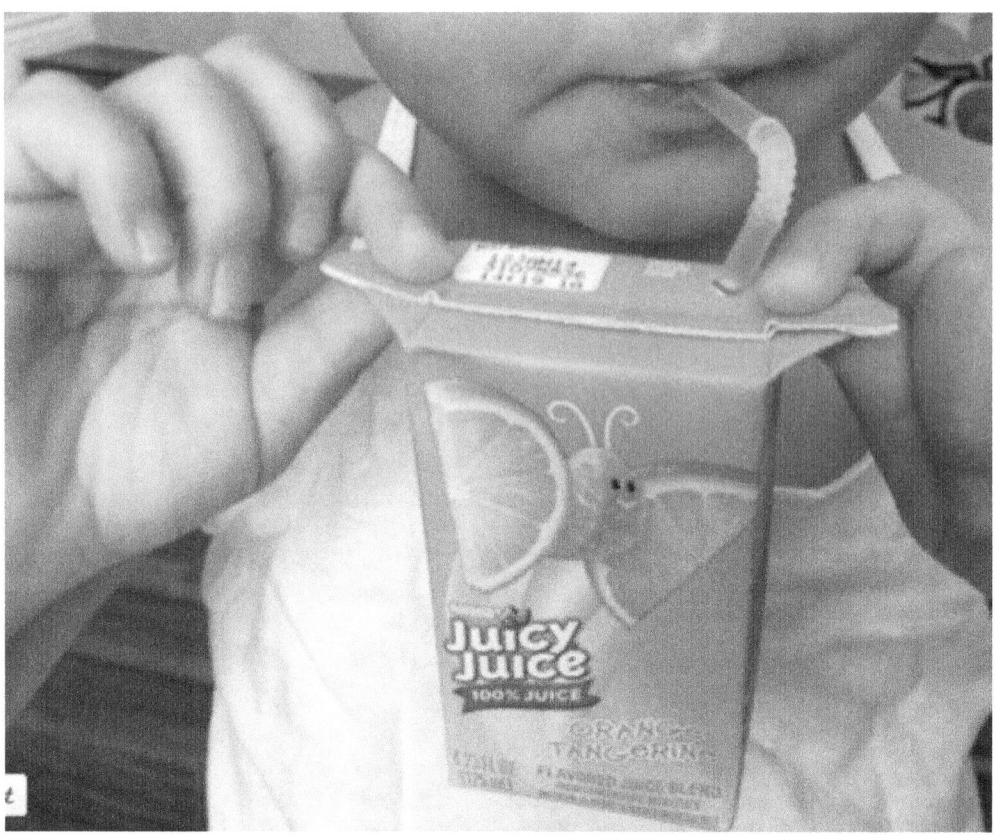

- **To give a more effective time-out, fill a bottle up 3/4 with water, then add a bottle of glitter glue and some ultra-fine glitter. Flip the bottle, and when the glitter settles, their time-out is over.**

- An added bonus to this is that watching the glitter settle can help calm a wound-up kiddo... but if they mess with the bottle and disturb the glitter, their time-out ends up being longer.

- **To clean up pesky vomit stains, wipe up the excess and then spread a paste of baking soda and water over the remaining ick. Let it dry until it takes on a powdery consistency and then vacuum it right up.**

- **Convince them to do chores by offering things they need rather than bonus rewards.**

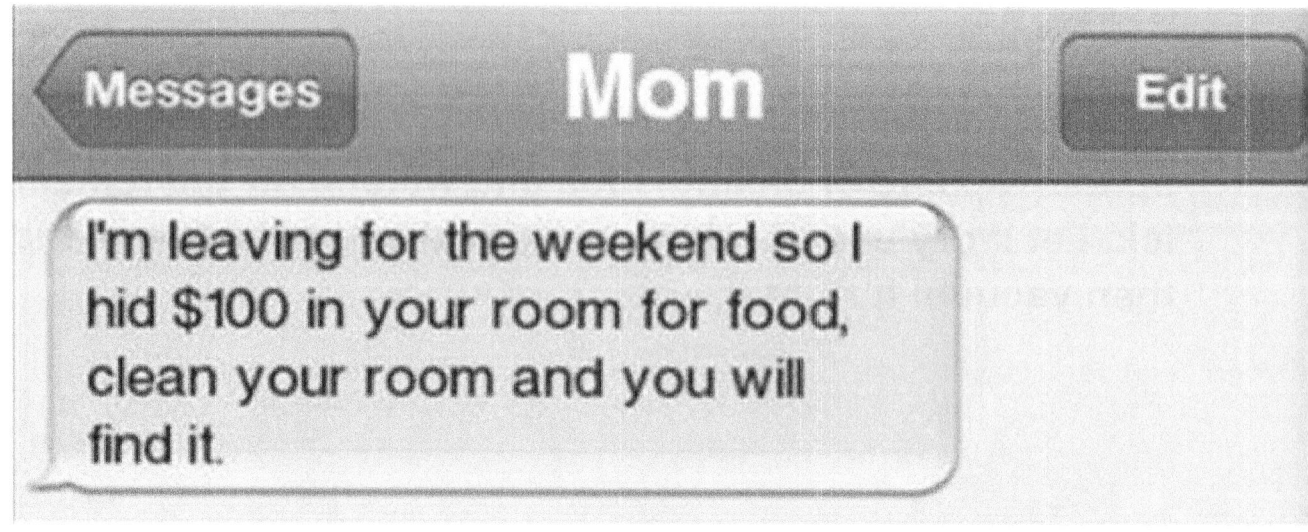

- Share

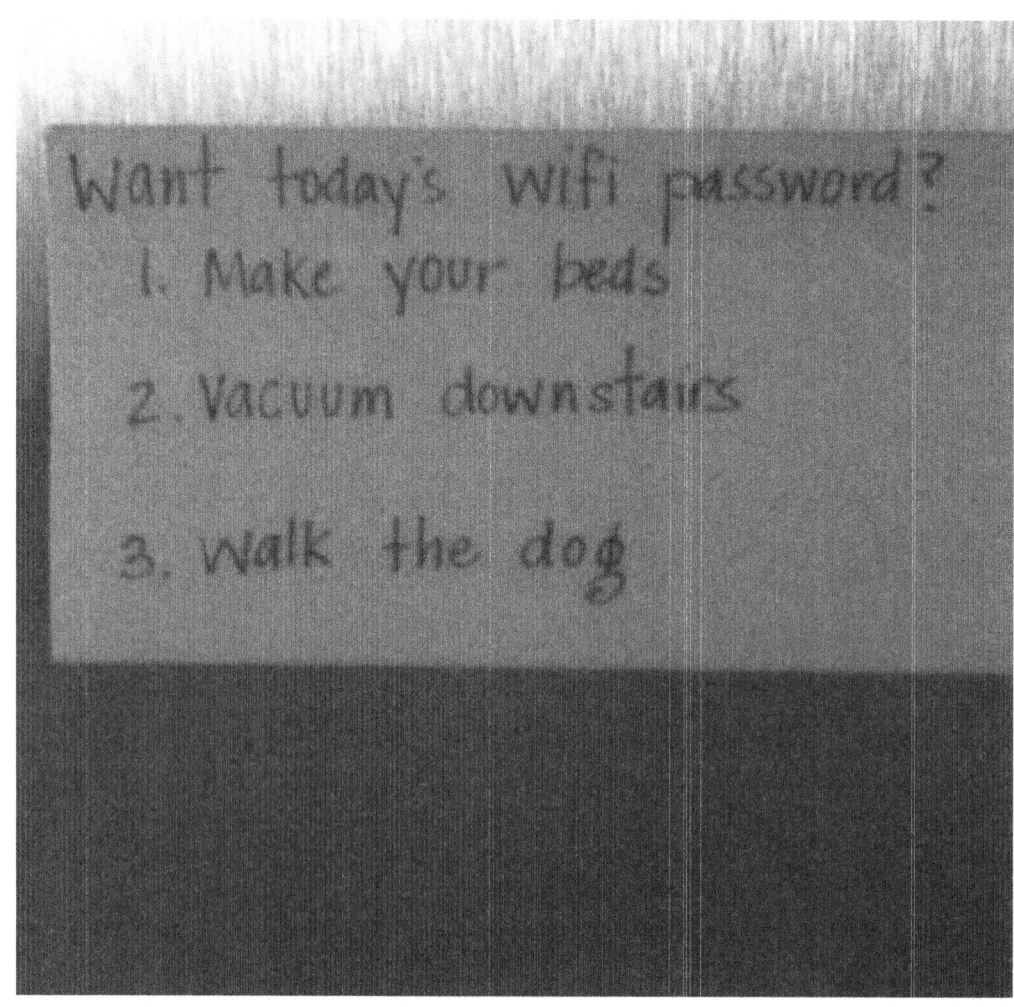

- **If you're flying with infants, there's a simple way to make sure the other passengers are more understanding to your plight.**

- **A lint roller picks up glitter (and just about anything else) like a charm!**

- And when they grow up, teach them how to be resourceful:

Clever trick for the crib when they grow out of it

\- **Thanks for reading! I hope you learned a few things. Here's a bonus baby picture :)**

- Share these helpful tips with loving parents by clicking below.

2. With a little nip, tuck and stitch, his oversized tee becomes your chic and comfy maternity top.

3. Mosquitos have a thing for cute, squishy baby fat. The little buggers don't stand a chance with this hack: A crib sheet placed on top of your outdoor playpen.

4. Until all highchairs come with a hook on the back for bib storage, stick a self-adhesive hook on it and call it a day.

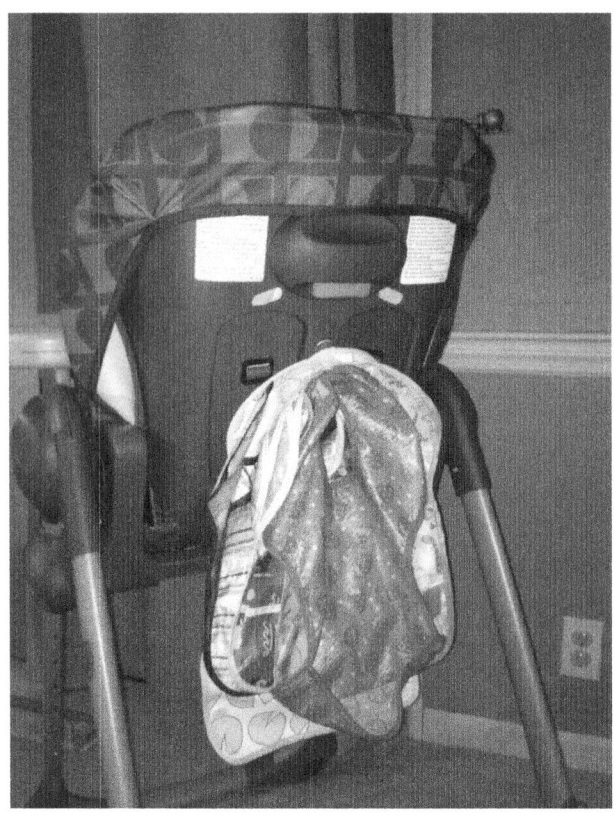

5. Tired of baby snot-covered tissues strewn around the house or stuffed into your pockets? Rubberband a tissue box to an empty tissue box for a convenient mini-waste basket.

6. Baby leg warmers are so cute, practical and easy to hack! Cut the feet off of a pair of grownup knee-high socks, fold the raw edge over and stitch it closed. Voila!

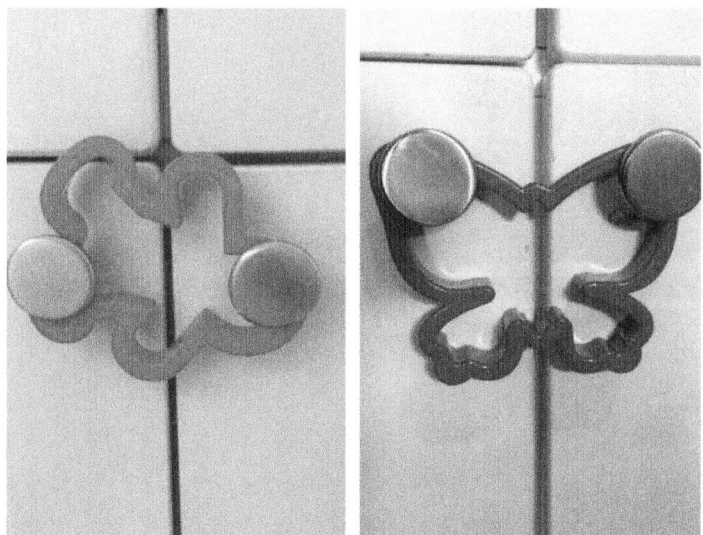

7. When your bambino starts opening cabinets before you've invested in locks, bide your time by slipping cookie cutters over them.

8. Running out of closet space with all of those new baby clothes? Loop a soda can tab on one hanger and then hook another hanger through it to double your space instantly.

9. Part scooter. Part stroller. What's not to love about this Austria-designed <u>Roller Buggy</u>?

10. This snap-on hoodie (that is for <u>sale</u>!) makes wearing a baby on chilly days cozier — especially for you! The front cuddle pocket keeps hands toasty when your coat pockets are covered.

11. Soothe a teething baby's gums by letting them gnaw on a pacifier pop. Pour milk or water into an ice tray, dunk pacifiers in and let them freeze.

12. Some babies require as many creams, ointments and potions as their beauty product-obsessed moms. Keep it all organized by stashing it in the pockets of an over-the-door shoe organizer.

Did we miss a cool parenting hack? Tell us about it in the Comments section below.

— Ayren Jackson-Cannady

add to my play list

Here is my list of must have's for your 0-12 month tackle box...

Pain/Fever

- Infant acetaminophen/Tylenol
- Infant ibuprofen/Advil (for 6 months and up)
- Rectal thermometer and probe covers
- Gentle Naturals Teething Drops

Once your little one hits 6 months, its very handy to have acetaminophen and ibuprofen in your arsenal as they can be given on a rotating basis to keep high fevers at bay. **Always check with your doctor for dosing instructions!**

As for the thermometer, there are lots and lots of fancy no touch thermometers out there, but we rely on a good ol' fashioned rectal therm for the most accurate reading. Especially with tiny ones, a few tenths of a degree can be the difference between Tylenol and the ER, so why not use the most accurate way you can? Scared of hurting baby? There are lots of safety rectal therms on the market that prevent inserting too far.

Cold/Snot

- Snot sucker
- Saline spray/drops
- Little Remedies Baby Rub
- Boogie Wipes

It may be gross, but we LOVE the Nosefrida snot sucker. Look it up, but don't judge us until you try it. Boogie Wipes are also one of our favorite products. These super soft, saline infused wipes clean up the crustiest, sore noses in one quick swipe with far fewer tears.

Tummy/Tushy Troubles

- Gas drops
- Gripe water
- Pedialyte
- Triple Paste

Gas drops and gripe water come in various brands and they all work equally well. Some babies do better with them than others, but C responded relatively well to them. Pedialyte is always handy to have in the case of vomiting or diarrhea that won't let up. Dehydration comes on quickly with little ones and is easy to avoid if cared for quickly.

Now, bear with me - Triple Paste is crazy expensive for something that goes on your butt, but it is literally magic. The absolute worst diaper rash can be cleared up over night with a quick slathering. Just buy yourself a tub when your kid is born and it'll last until potty training.

Skin

- Babyganics Healin Groovy skin protectant
- Sunblock

With all the rest of the chemicals out there, I try to be very careful what I put on my kid's skin. These two products are some of my favorites. Healin' Groovy is basically Aquaphor without the petrolatum, BPA, and other not so great stuff. As for sunblock, read the labels! Sun*screen* is different than sun*block* and not all sunblock is created equal. Each year, theEnvironmental Working Group puts out a report called "Skin Deep" that ranks that year's sun products for hazardous chemicals. You will be shocked at how hazardous some "baby" sun products are. Shocked.

Much of what is in the 0-12 months tackle box is also in our toddler tackle box with a few additions...

- Floristor Probiotics (to avoid antibiotic induced diarrhea)
- Children's ibuprophen/Advil
- Children's acetaminophen/Tylenol
- Droppers and spoons (who knows what he'll accept that day)
- Little Remedies Honey Elixir cough syrup
- Sore throat pops
- Neosporin and character band-aids
- Tweezers (for splinters and what not)
- Red wash cloths

Why red wash clothes, you ask? Because my Mom was a certified genius. What freaks someone out more than anything? Seeing their own blood when they get hurt. Red wash cloth = can't see the blood. Invest in a few, you'll thank my Mom.

Some general tips...

- There is NO cough/cold medication out there safe for infants and young children. Basically, all you can do is suck the snot, turn up the humidifier, and keep them comfortable.

- Honey is a great cough soother, but only for kids over 12 months of age.

- The concentration of medication can be different depending on the brand (i.e. Triaminic vs. Tylenol vs. store brand). Each comes with its own dropper; use it.

- Baby Vicks/chest rub is very different than regular Vicks and yes it does matter.

- Put one parent in charge of medicating and write down dosing times to avoid over dosing and confusion.

Finally, the most important thing about medication and kids (of any age) is to be sure of the dosage and ask your doctor if you have ANY doubts or questions. I'm not a huge fan of giving meds, but having a kid who likes to spike 105 fevers at 3am has taught me to be prepared for the worst.

Here are my favorite tips I've found around the internet about packing for Disney.

- For kids who will have lots of extra clothes, pack outfits together in quart size zip top bags. Socks, hair accessories, etc. included. I was able to fit 14 outfits and 2 costumes in one side of this carry on size suitcase for Ginny!

- Bring your own souvenirs. I actually got this idea from my sister - whenever they bring my nephew somewhere that she knows will sell those carts full of light up toys for $20 a piece, she makes sure to bring some fun light up toy, even just glow sticks, in her purse. It has saved her a small fortune, I'm sure.

- Make spreadsheets. No one needed to tell me this one - I make spreadsheets for everything. It is a good tip, none the less. I have an excel spread sheet with our travel information, packing lists, and to do lists.

- Pack your tickets, Magic Bands, medication, travel documents, and other important items in your carry on. Your bags may take a little bit to arrive at the resort and you don't want to be stuck waiting around!

- Download your apps. There are several apps worth looking into before you head to Disney. The My Disney Experience app links with your reservations and FastPass+ meaning you can make changes on the go in addition to checking wait times, keeping tabs on character meet and greets, and looking at maps. Another handy app is the GPS Transportation Wizardby Our Laughing Place. Just plug in where you are and where you want to go and it will tell you the most efficient combination of transportation (boat, bus, monorail, walking, etc.) across the vast Disney property. And let's be honest - its Florida. Having the Weather.com app is probably a smart idea too. ;-)

• Speaking of rain, being prepared is important. We got caught in many quick down pours last time we went. An umbrella, ponchos, and a clear shower curtain to cover the stroller (from the dollar store) will keep you dry!

• Our party consists of two kids and three adults. Correction, one teething infant, one stubborn toddler, and three adults.We're bringing ear plugs and taking turns wearing them so at least most of us are guaranteed uninterrupted sleep.

• It sounds like overkill, but we're bringing a small pop up hamper. With all of the anticipated clothing changes, if anything it'll keep things organized.

• We plan on gate checking our double stroller and while we can hope and pray, there is always a chance it could be damaged in flight. To minimize the chance of damage, we are removing every part that we possibly can (kid tray, canopies, seat padding, and parent tray) and safely packing them in luggage. It makes the stroller much smaller and less likely to catch on something.

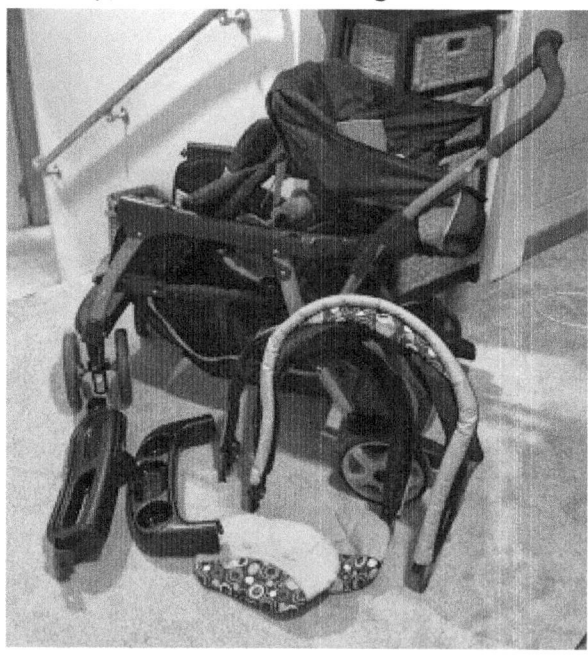

Here is a Google doc of our entire packing list for 8 days in Disney. It looks like a lot, but everything is either a sample size or brought in a much smaller container (i.e. dish soap, laundry detergent) and really, I'd rather bring more things to make the week easier than have to find something last minute!

Another packing tip is to choose your airline carefully. Southwest happened to have the cheapest fairs, but as a bonus, bags (two per ticket) fly free! This was a HUGE cost savings to us with all of the stuff we're needing to bring. We'll be checking four pieces of luggage, which would have cost us $200 on another airline. Ouch!

....

Make your own stickers for scrap books and also make your own cute stickers that you can put on onesies for month to month baby pictures i.e. welcolme home, baby a month, 2 months old etc. Make a cute sticker, put it on their baby grow and take a photo, his looks cute in albums and shows a time line without having to label the photo, which is great for digital photos. Another tip for digital photos is to save the file name as the date / description you want, this makes viewing and sorting photos easier too i.e. Ritchie at 1 month old October 2012.

life
hacks   #684

New parent? Sleep with their
blanket for one night. Result
will be your smell on it, which
will comfort them.

@1000LifeHacks
1000LifeHacks.com

layer his bedding. By that I mean a mattress pad, sheet, mattress pad, sheet. So if he happens to have an accident in the middle of the night, I can just strip a sheet and mattress pad layer off and there's another sheet and mattress pad underneath.

2. Use burp cloths. Everywhere.

This kind of goes along with the above. Whenever I lay Owen down anywhere I throw a burp cloth underneath his head. We always have a burp cloth in his Rock 'n Play, where he currently sleeps. (Did you know they now make a Rock 'n Play that rocks on its own? Amazing.) So if he spits up, I swap out the burp cloth instead of having to wash the Rock 'n Play cover.

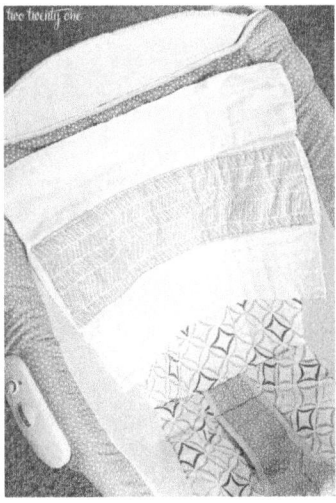

Oh, and while we're on the topic of the Rock 'n Play, remember to air yours out periodically. Moisture can get trapped between the cover and plastic piece, resulting in mold. And don't forget to wash the cover often, too.

As you can see, I also do the burp cloth trick with Owen's activity mat.

In case you're wondering, that's a Boppy Noggin Nest under the burp

cloth.

3. Keep a stocked baby basket in your common area.

To make our lives a little easier, we keep a basket filled with random baby stuff on our coffee table. It's stocked with hand sanitizer (first time parents– wee!), baby wipes, pacifier wipes (first time parents– wee again!), lotion, pacifiers, baby nail clippers, bibs, and burp cloths. I was going to invest in a fancier basket but I decided to go with one of my trusty Skubb organizers.

I found that the basket also helps when family members babysit Owen. That way they don't have to go searching for things in his nursery.

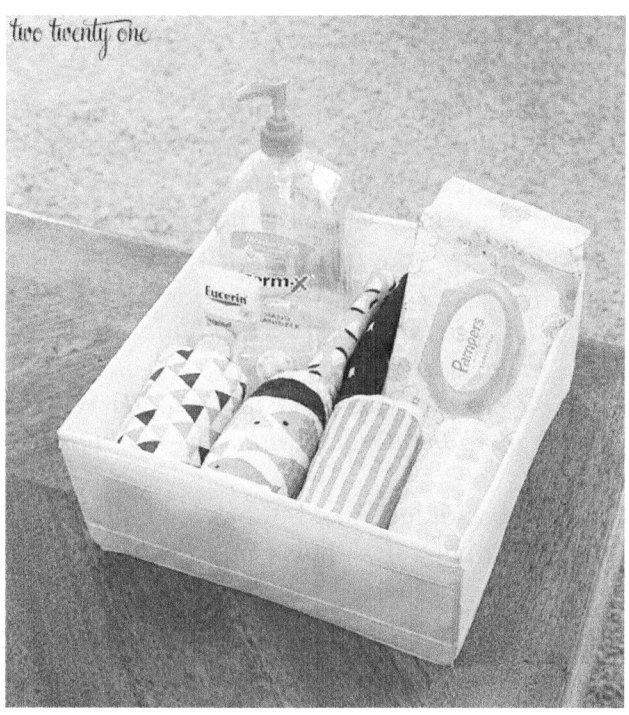

4. Keep a basket of baby toys in your common area.

Like with the baby basket above, we keep a basket of baby toys on the sofa table behind our couch. When we're hanging out on the couch with Owen we can easily grab a toy or book.

5. Prepare for blow outs.

Once upon a time, Owen had a ridiculous blow out in his car seat. Needless to say, it wasn't fun. We had to take the car seat apart, wash the cover, and wait a day for it to air dry. In an effort to avoid this, my friend, Jacque, told me about this awesome tip. I took a changing pad liner, cut it in half, cut a slit in it for the car seat buckle, and put it in the car seat. Now if Owen has a blow out, the changing pad liner will protect the car seat, making clean up so much easier.

Note: I checked with a CPS technician before using the pad liner in the car seat. He said the pad isn't impeding with the function of the straps and it's very thin, so it won't affect the efficiency of the carseat, assuming I have Owen properly buckled in. This is basically a DIY version of a manufacturer car seat protector. He said ultimately it's up to the parent, and using my 'mom gut', I feel okay with using it.

Oh, and in case you're wondering, those orange hand things are called Lulaclips. They hold the buckles open while you place your baby into their car seat. Also a tip/gift from Jacque.

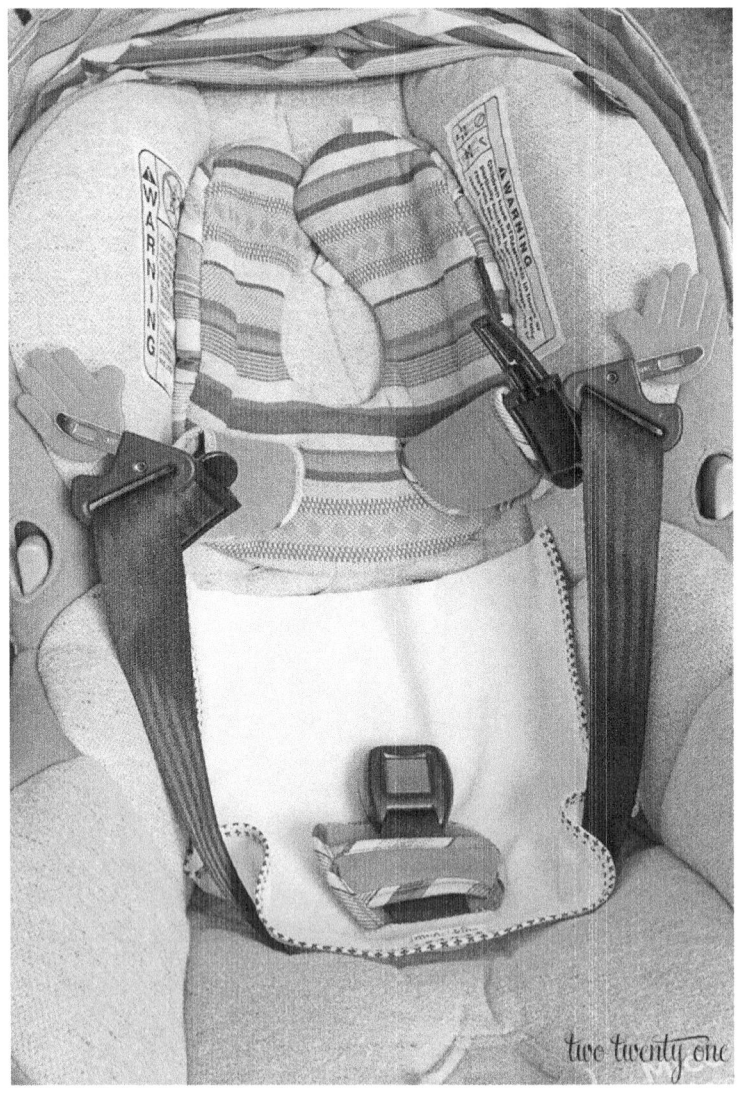

I put the other half of the changing pad liner in his mamaroo.

I must add that when Owen did have a blow out (or three) in his mamaroo before I used the changing pad cover, the material didn't stain at all. Good work, 4moms.

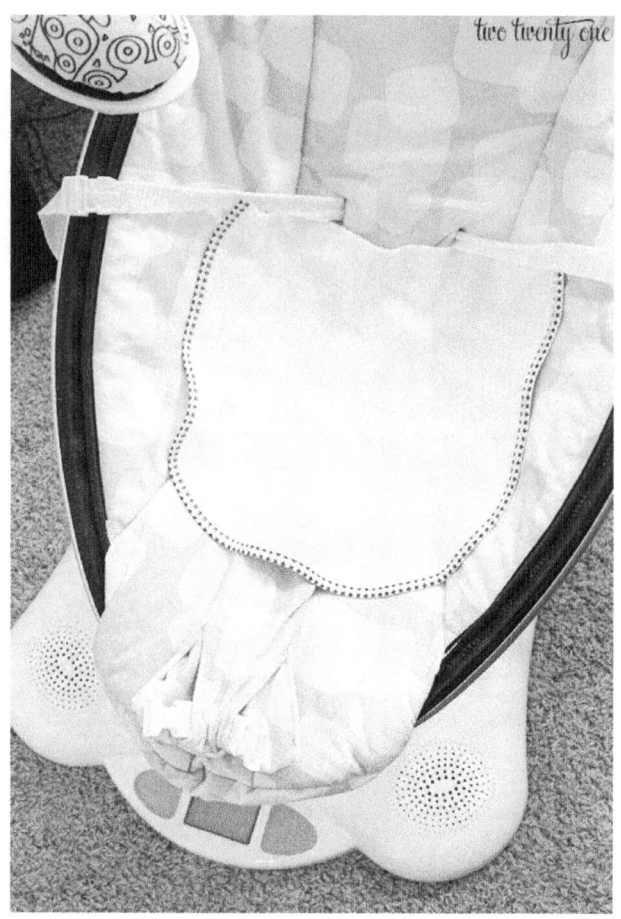

6. Invest in mesh laundry bags.

Ah, the elusive missing baby socks. Corral those socks by using mesh laundry bags. I always keep 2-3 bags in Owen's hamper. One bag is for socks. The other bags are for bibs and his swaddles. The bibs and swaddles have velcro so to keep them from sticking to other items, resulting in thread pulls, while being washed and dried, I put them in the mesh bags.

7. The diaper trick.

When I know Owen has a #1 diaper, I slide a fresh diaper underneath before opening the dirty diaper. This makes changing the diaper faster, and it also helps if he starts 'free peeing', as we call it. If he starts spraying, I can flip the diaper up and block him from peeing all over the wall. I'm sure this can also be helpful when changing girls.

You can also see the washcloth under his booty. This is helpful for when he has a #2. I really don't care if some poo gets on the washcloth (I bought a ton of cheapo washcloths from Ikea). It's so much easier to wash the washcloth than the changing pad. Plus, I don't care if the washcloth gets stained.

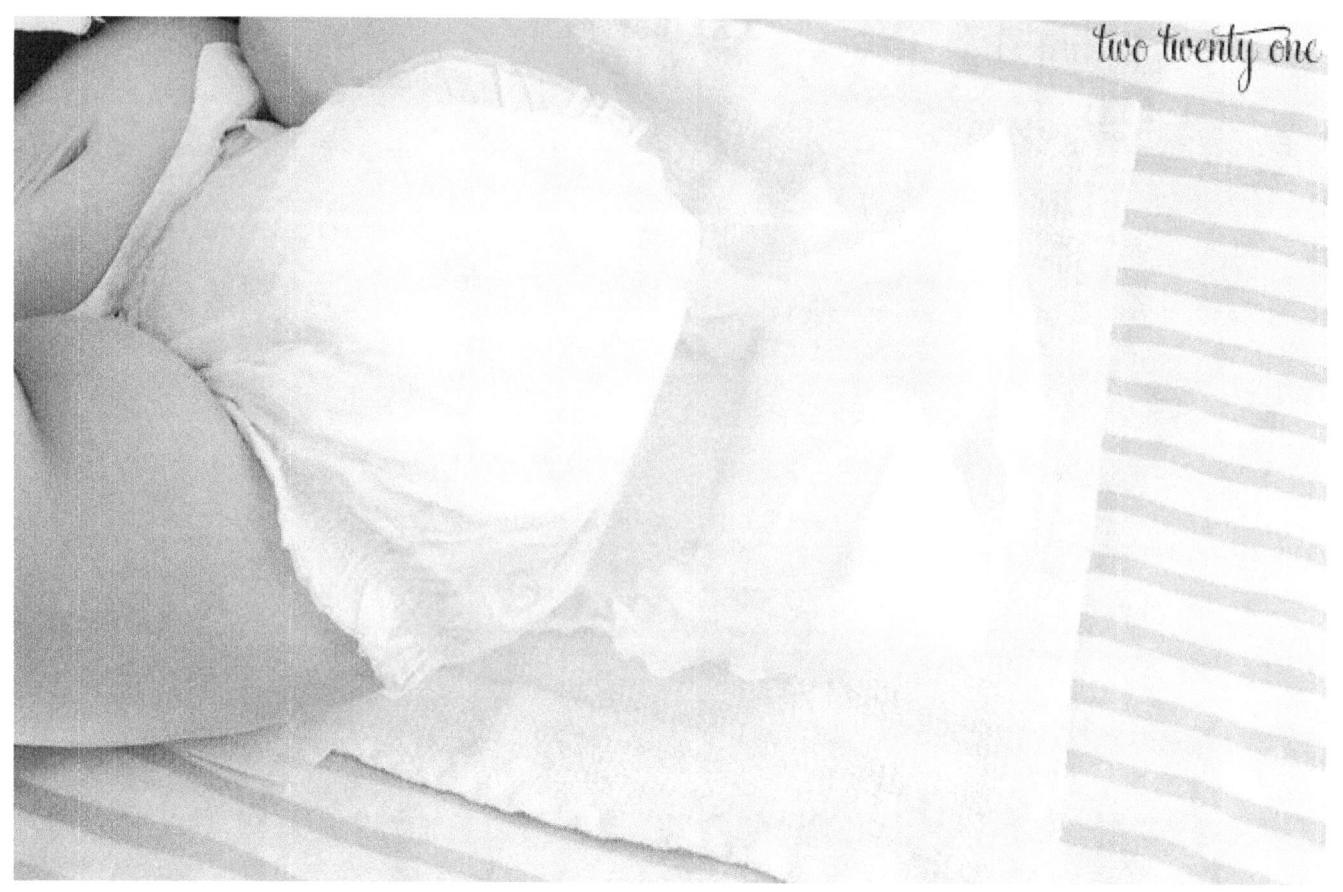

8. Use clothespins to hang baby pants.

More about that tip here!

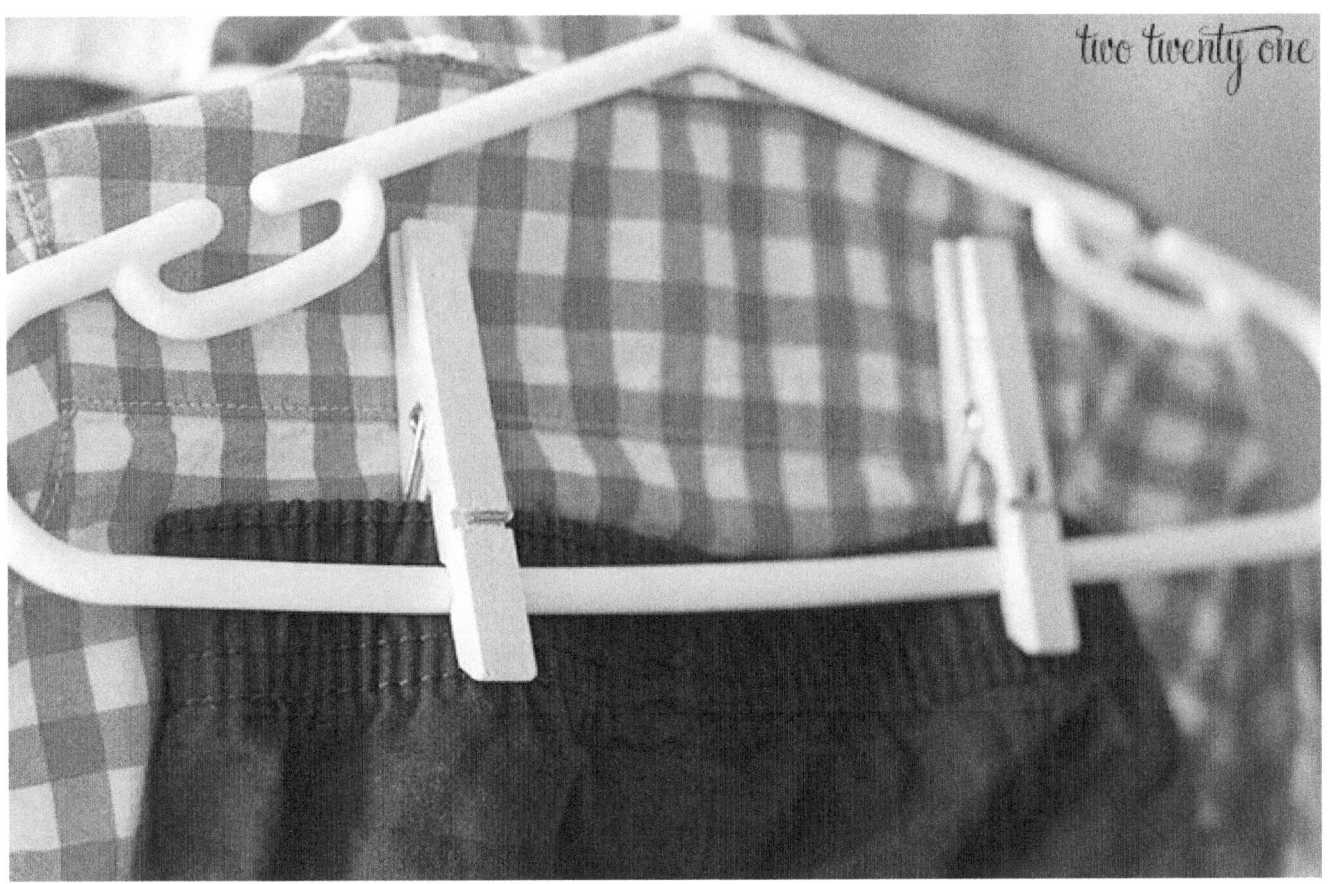

9. Baby car kit.

We have emergency baby car kits in both of our cars. To read more about the car kits and what's in them, click here.

I hope you found some of these hacks to be helpful!

BABY HACKS

make life with an infant a little easier

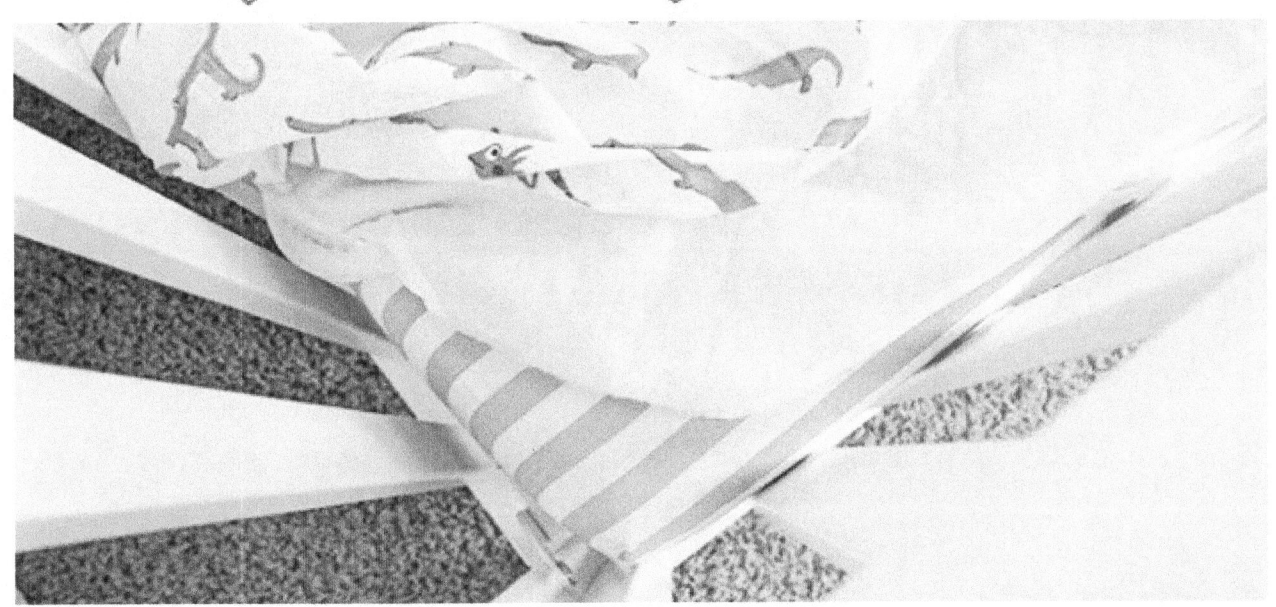

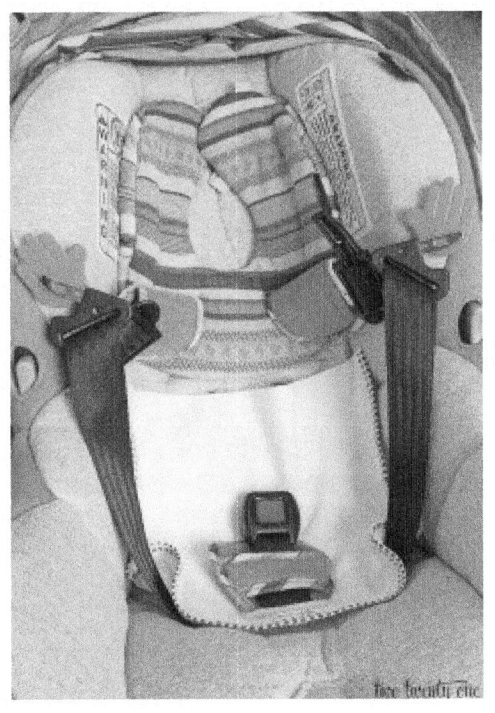

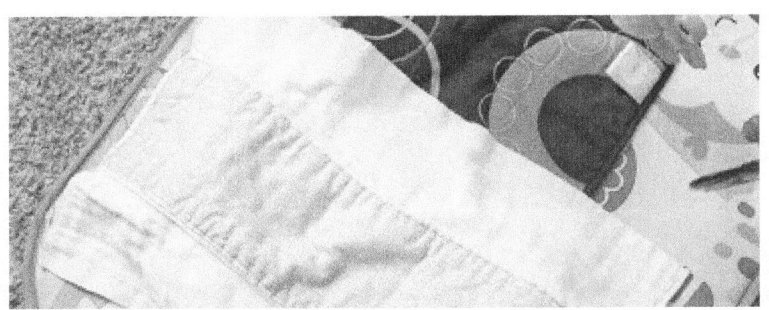

Try vinegar for minor burns.

Just soak a small face cloth or paper towel and apply vinegar to the burn till the skin feels cool. Apply it immediately after the burn and it will ease the pain and prevent a blister.

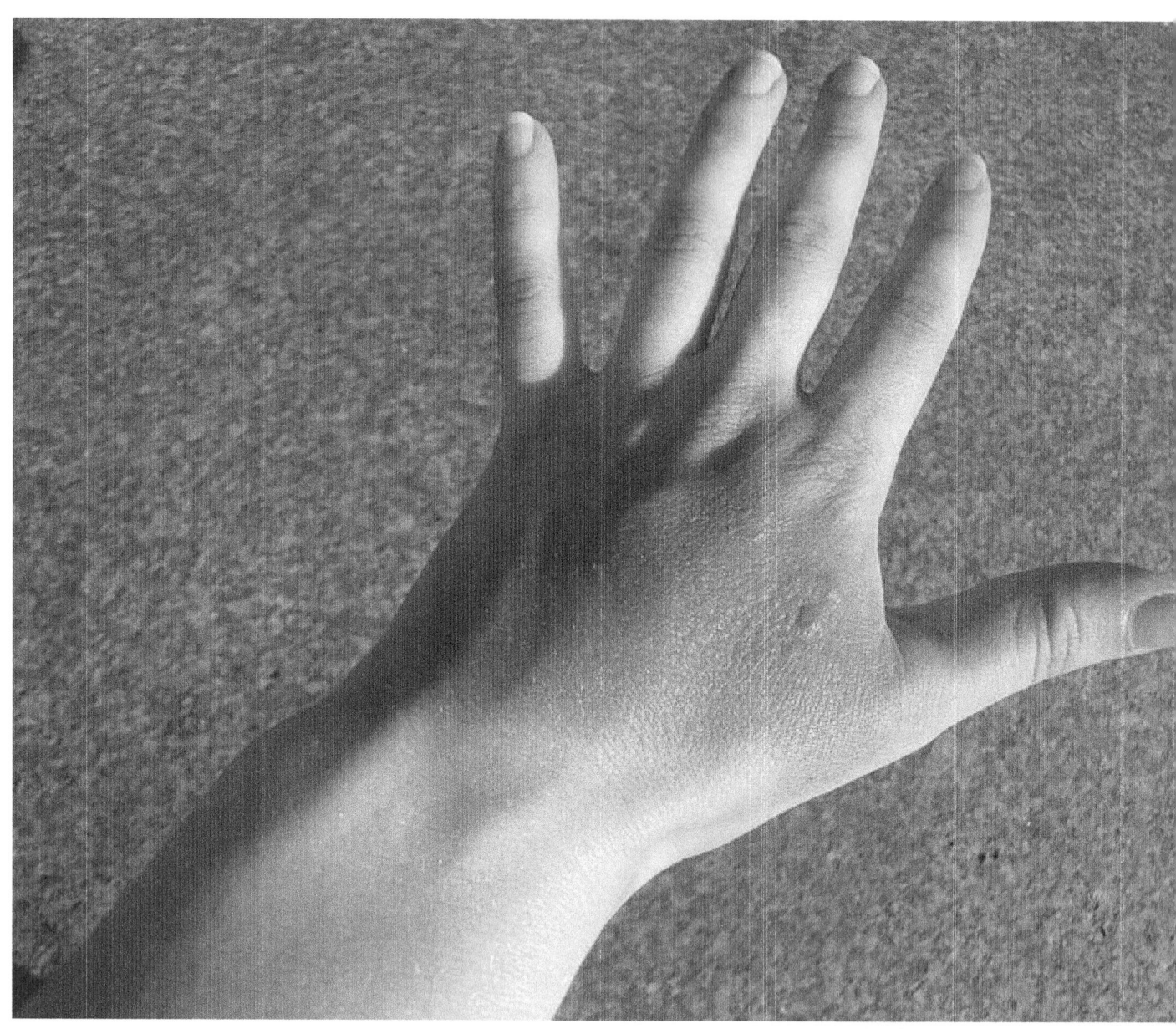

.Keep the kids from locking themselves in the bathroom.

Keep a door unlocked by using a rubber band. You can find more information on this trick here.

http://kidsactivitiesblog.com/54143/2

o-hacks-house

Keep a spray bottle in the car for hot days to avoid scorching seat belts buckles.

Use a fine mist spray bottle to cool buckles. The water doesn't have to be cool. Evaporation will cool the hot plastic and metal quickly.

5. Use pool noodles to improve safety.

Pool noodles offer protection for little hands and feet on the trampoline.

6. A little tape will catch toenail clippings before they make a mess for you.

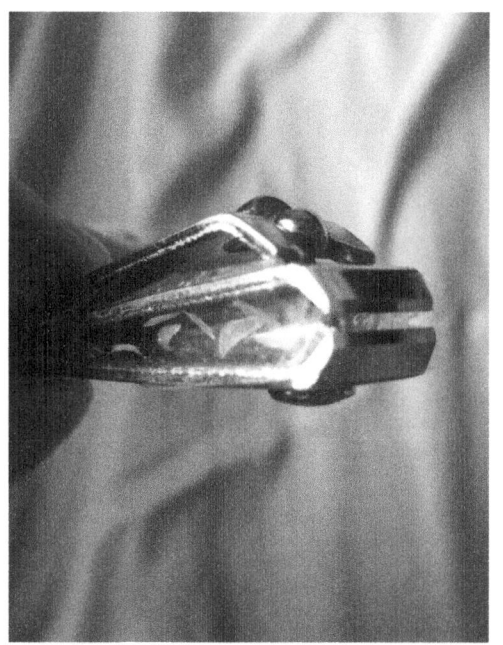

7. Get your teenager to clean their room.

You can get your son or daughter to clean their room by using your cleverness and humor like the mother below.

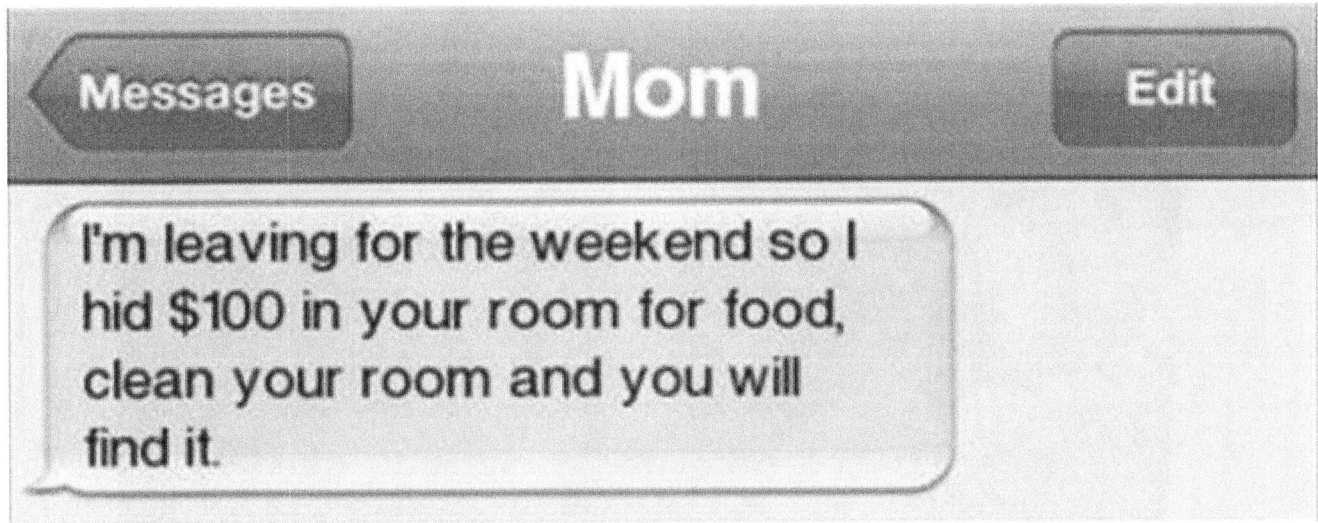

8. Prevent your kids from always using new cups and leaving the old ones lying around the house.

Just give them their own cups with magnets and pin them to your fridge. Your kids will love it.

9. Use this no-mess painting parenting tricks.

Add three dollops of different coloured paint into a ziplock bag and voila! Your baby can create all kinds of designs without any mess.

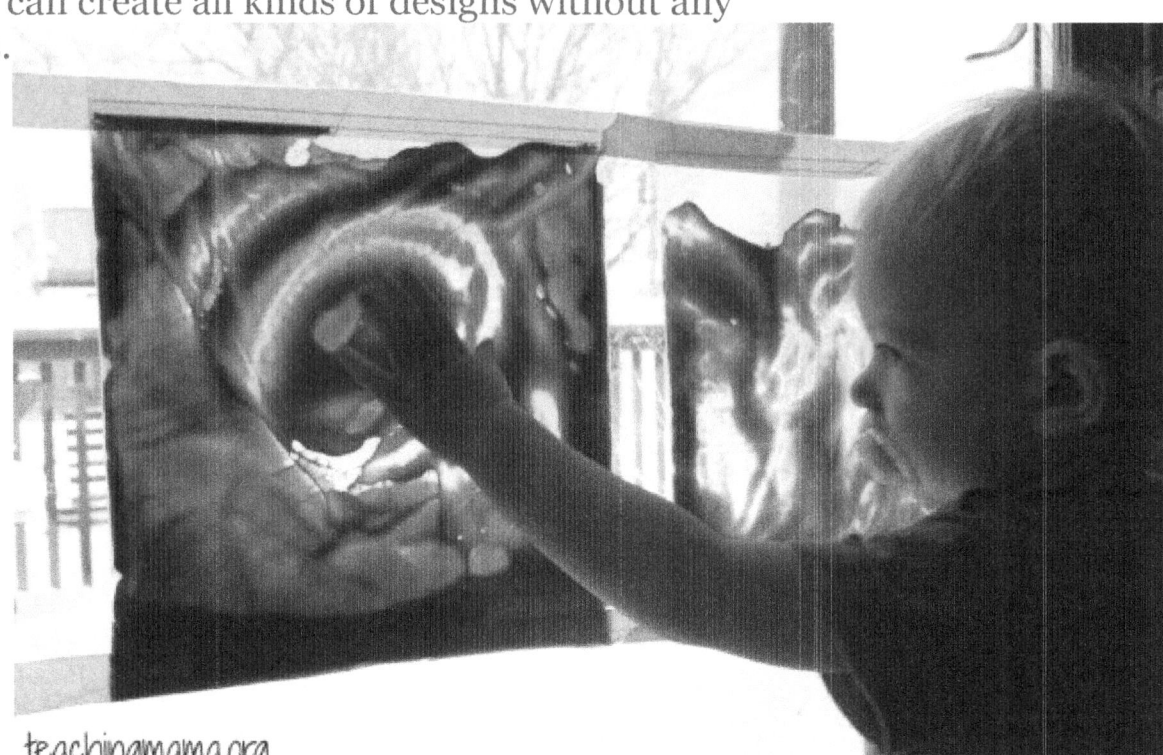

10. Buy a Keep-It-Kleen Pacifier.

This product automatically closes when dropped, eliminating the need to constantly wash it off.

11. Limit Soap by twisting rubber bands around the pump nozzle.

12. Invest in a Baby In-Sight Auto Mirror.

This car mirror both lets you see your baby on long drives and entertains him or her.

13. Use a baby monitor app while on vacation.

Use this app to take care of your kid with your Apple or Android product. No extra equipment needed.

14. To get your kids to put their shoes on the correct feet, cut a sticker in half and place it on the insides of their shoes.

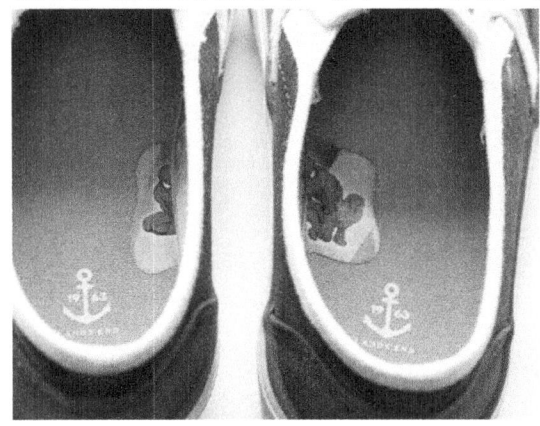

15. Keep apple slices from getting brown.

Put the apple slices in a lunch bag, sprinkle salt over the pieces and give them a quick slosh with water. The salty taste is washed away but the brief exposure to salt keeps them looking fresh all day!

16. Make splinter removals less painful.

Put a paste of baking soda and water on a splinter and leave for a few minutes, the baking soda will push the splinter out saving your child an unnecessarily painful splinter removal.

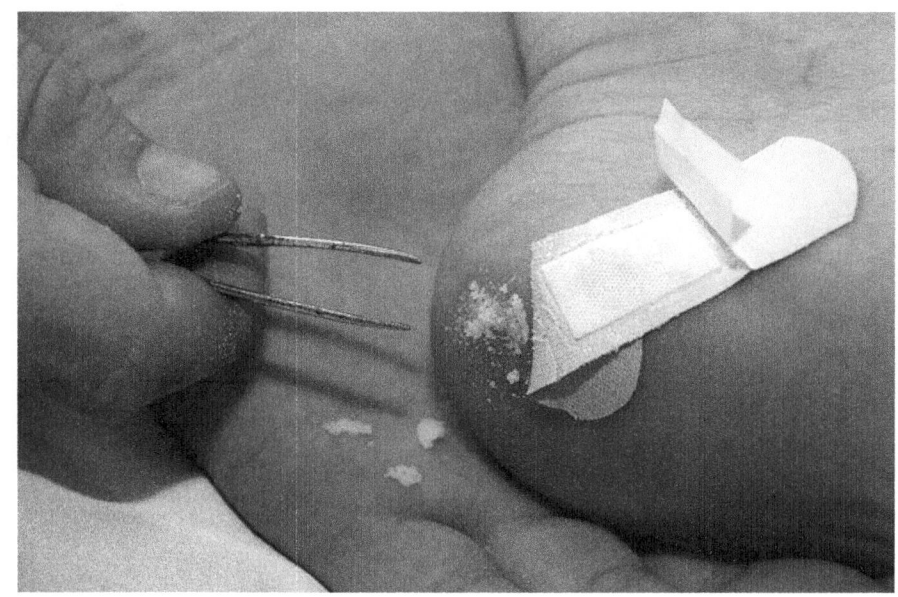

17. Molar Muncher Teethers are perfect for soothing babys' whole gum line.

18. Use a pizza box as a giant sized canvas.

19. WD-40 is the perfect crayon remover.

20. Keep your child's clothes clean.

Tide To Go Instant Stain Remover saves your kid's clothes from stains, even while on the go.

21. Teach your child to hold a pencil the right way with this trick.

With a wad of Kleenex behind their last two fingers this trick will help them keep the right form while writing.

22. Try the Kikko'pilo travel mat.

This mat is perfect when your child needs a clean place to nap on long trips.

23. Use puffy fabric paint to paint a grip on your toddlers socks.

24. Use crayons to cover up scratches on shoes.

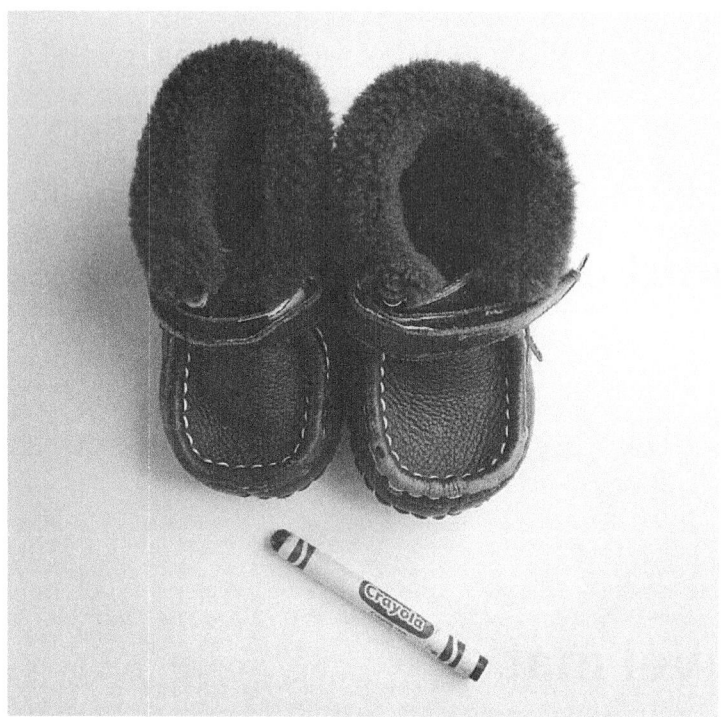

25. Use toothpaste to clean permanent marker off wooden furniture.

26. Try cartoon underwear when potty training your child.

The sight of their favourite character will help them think twice! Also try this link for more toilet training tricks.

27. Use these T-shirts so you don't loose your kids.

Not only do these shirts make your children stand out but also they will lighten up the mood.

28. Make bedtime out of this world!

Make your child love bedtime by using funny and speacial bedding.

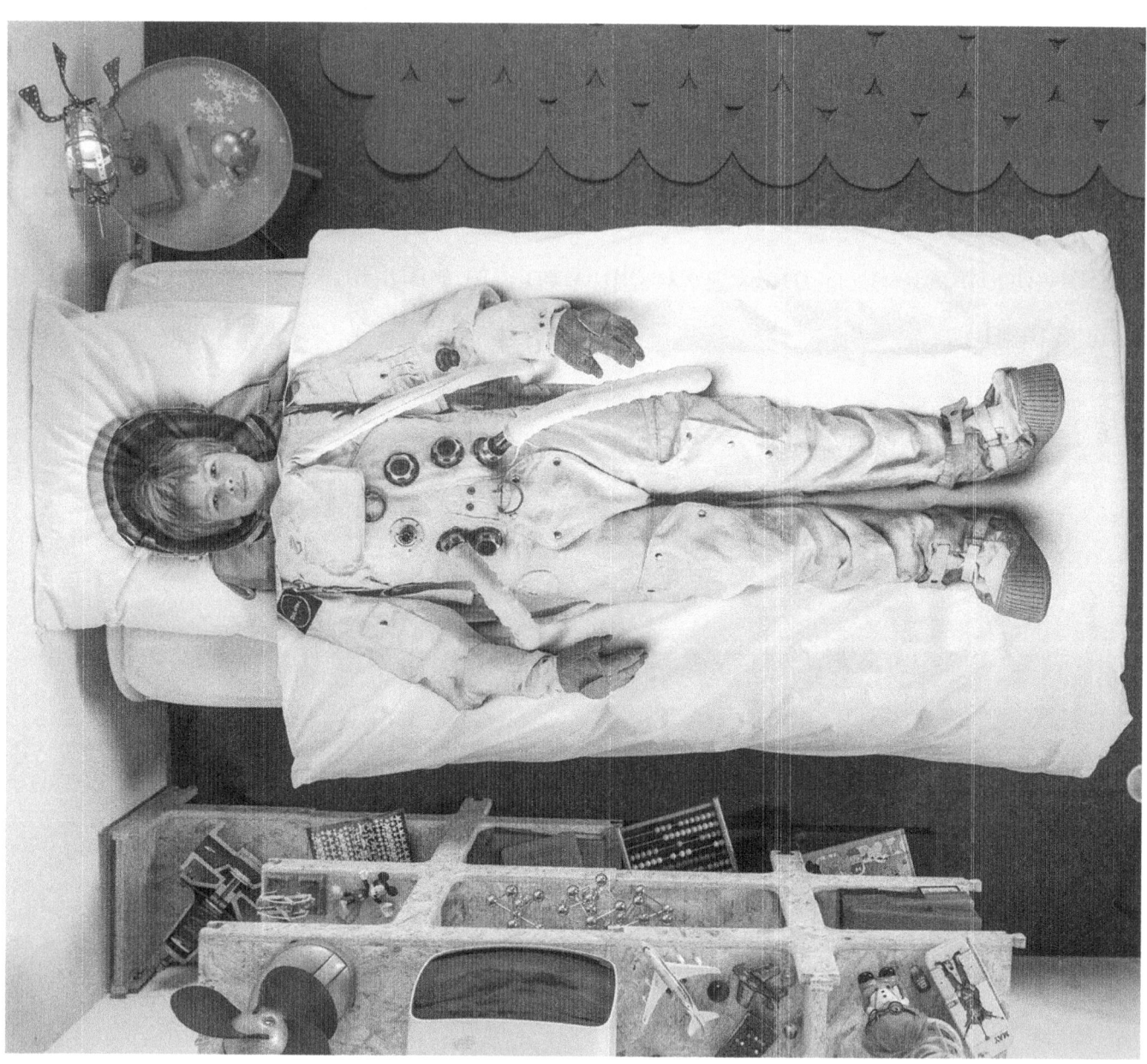

29. The Nursery Spa will warm towels, blankets, and clothing for your baby.

We know that you'll also be using it for yourself but we won't tell!

30. Time to tidy up toys? Play race the clock with an egg timer.

31. Use the toy links from your baby's gym to clip toys to your baby's highchair or stroller.

Save yourself the bending to pick up the toys which the baby throws every five seconds.

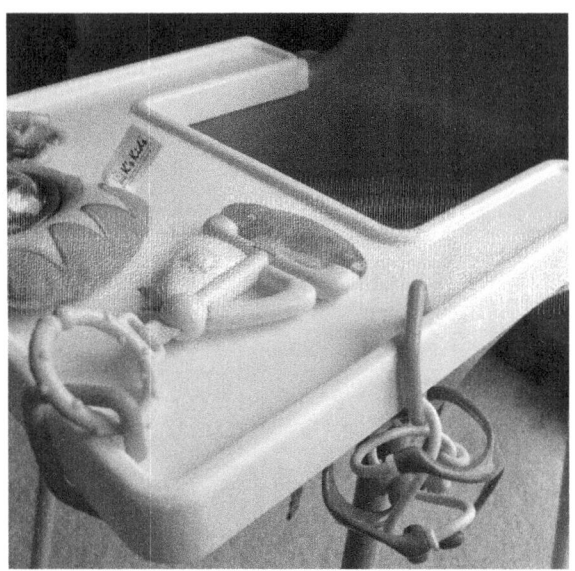

32. Dress your kids in matching outfits so when you go shopping others will identify which kids are "yours". Or bright T-shirts so they are easy to see.

33. Write your phone number on your child's arm when you go on an all day trip.

If he gets lost he can always borrow a phone to call you up.

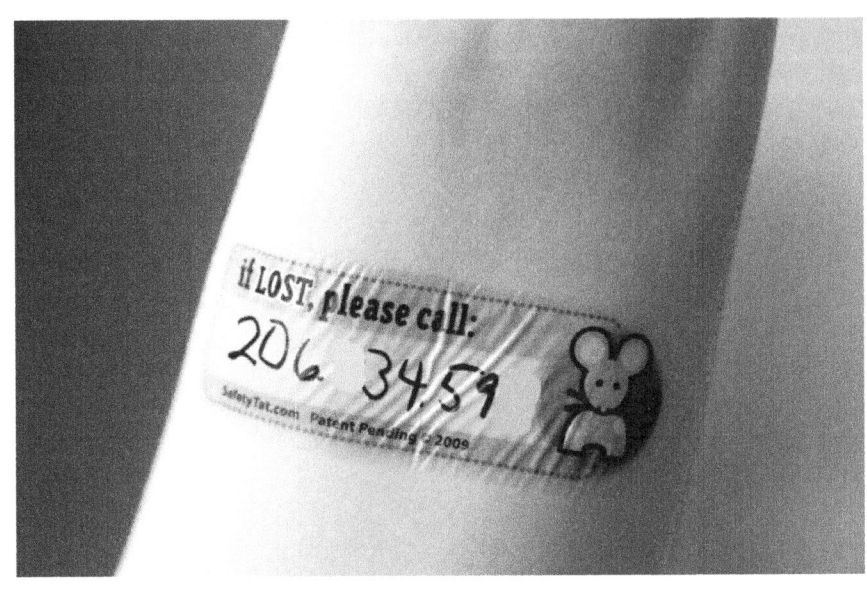

34. Take your baby's temperature while soothing her with this adorable pacifier.

35. Need to wean your baby off a pacifier? Cut away a small piece of the nipple each time your child uses it.

Eventually the baby won't like the feeling and soon there won't be anything left to suck and she'll throw it away herself. (Be sure to keep it extra clean during the process.)

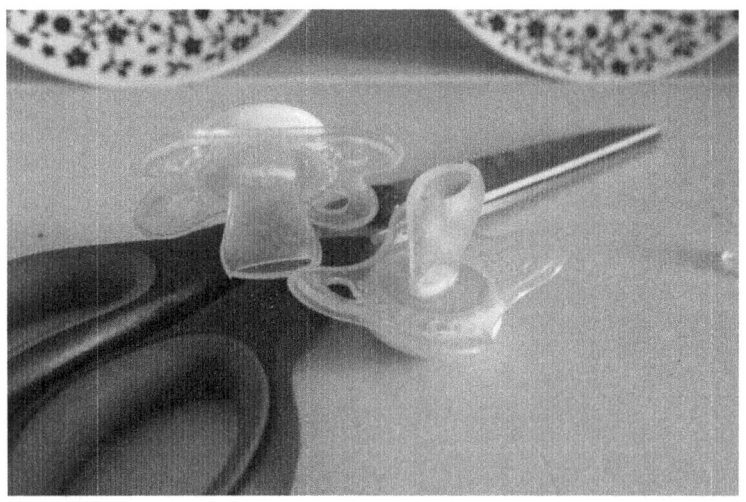

36. This infant diner placemat has a built-in catch compartment for messy eaters.

37. Cover a play table in oilcloth to create a water-resistant outdoor picnic table.

38. Keep pacifiers clean in your bag with sauce-to-go containers.

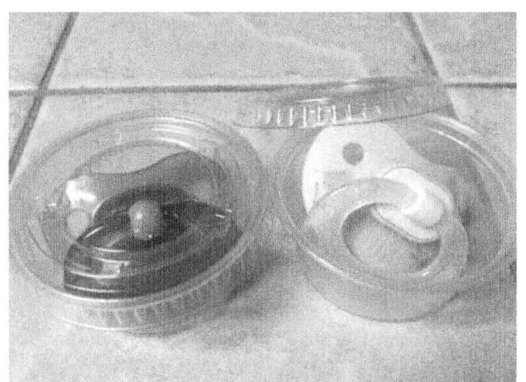

39. Use bulletin boards to stay organized.

Try a bulletin board for each kid where you can post reminders, chores for the day, or their schedule. A great place for this is the shoe area or your child's bedroom.

40. Use these cute animals to make toothbrushing fun!

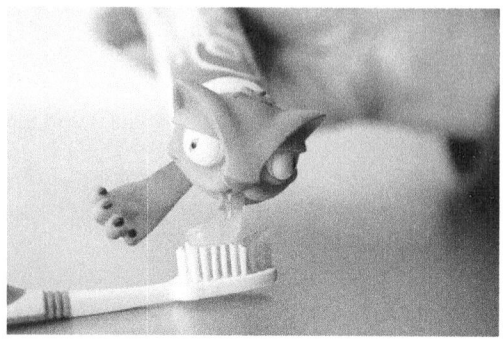

41. Allow no wandering in the parking lot with this Parking Pal sticker!

Have your kid place their hand on the Parking Pal sticker so that they won't get lost.

42. Try an Inflatable pool as a safe play area that's large enough to keep your baby busy for hours.

43.Keep the hair on dolls soft with fabric softener and water.

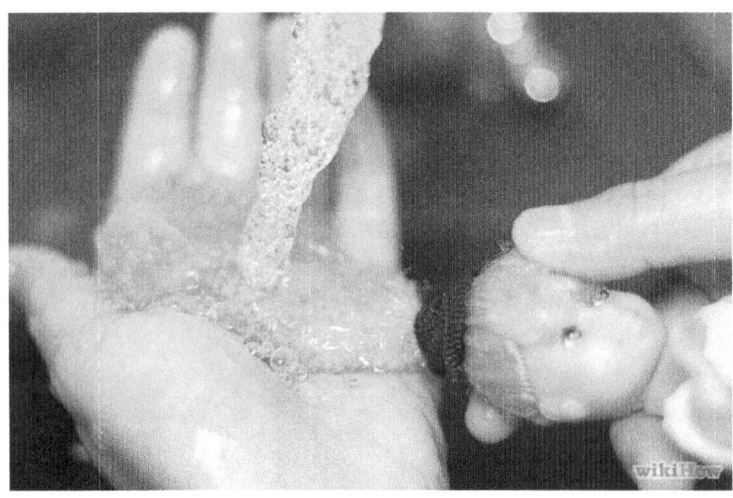

44. Make a baby tent to keep out the mosquitoes and the sun.

45. Make a batch of baby food to last for a week.

Freeze baby sized portions in an ice tray.

46. Clean shoes and toys in the dishwasher.

47. Create lawn art with a big sheet.

She Calls Me Mama Leisha

48. Make a corner shelf for the kids book with this Ikea magazine holder.

49. Make a water slide out of a plastic sheet (the kind that comes with new appliances or furniture) and a hose.

50. Hang a fort with a hoola-hoop and bed sheet.

1. If your kids are always using new cups, give them their own designated cups with magnets to stick to the fridge.

Not only does this mean less dishwashing, but cups can be kept at kid-height instead of up-high cupboards.

2. Use a Play-Doh confetti maker to make your own baby puff treats.

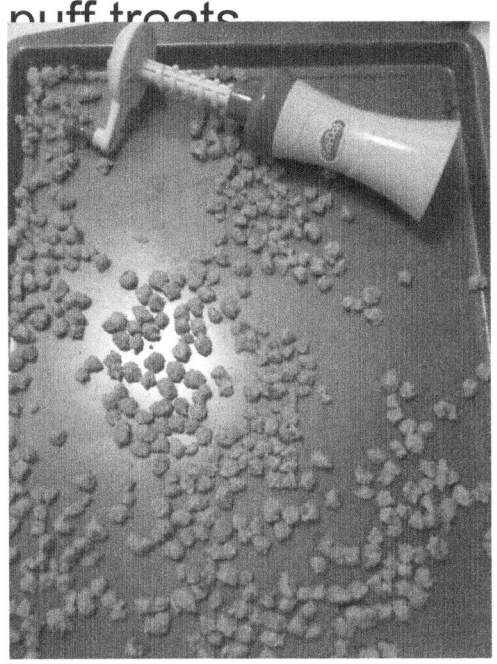

mommy-opinion.blogspot.com

You can use ingredients that are so much better than the store-bought variety. Get the directions here.

3. Cover a play table in oilcloth to create a water-resistant outdoor picnic table for the kids.

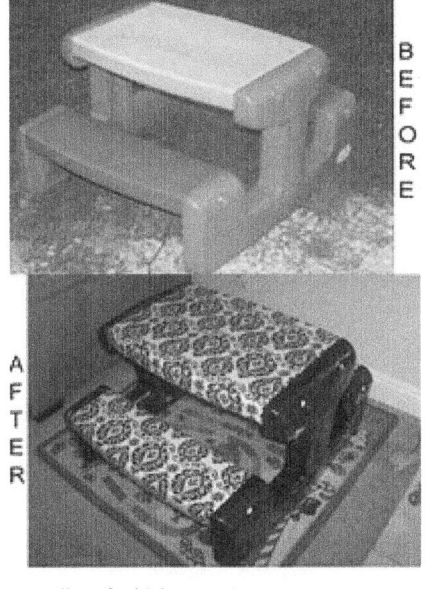

caroline-frei.blogspot.com
caroline-frei.blogspot.com

4. A Capri Sun in the freezer becomes a fun and easy slushy.

thegirlinspired.com

Just freeze for six hours, cut the top open, and scoop out with a spoon!

5. Put a sticker that has been cut in half on shoes' inner soles to show your child the correct foot for their shoes.

onecreativehousewife.com

If your child is already able to put on their shoes but still gets a little confused between right and left, this little sticker trick will help you get out the door faster.

6. Keep pacifiers clean in your bag with sauce-to-go containers, or just use a sandwich bag.

7. Dawn, hydrogen peroxide, and baking soda will get set-in baby food stains out of a onesie.

Get the recipe for this magical solution here.

8. Repurpose a large pump dispenser to fill water balloons.

finditmakeitloveit.com

9. Liquid Bandage will seal in a temporary safety tattoo on your child.

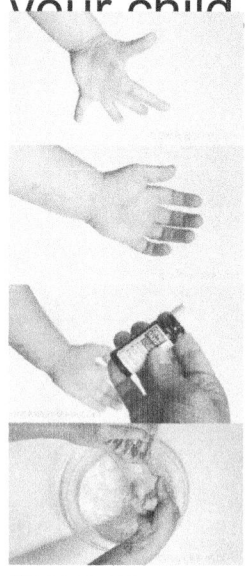

thepapermama.com

If your child gets lost at the amusement park, your phone number is emblazoned right there on their arm. Get the directions here.

10. The "You Shall Not Pass" sign provides a visual limit to how much toilet paper your child can take.

11. Easily make a Girl Scout cookie carrier out of a Tupperware tray and some duct tape.

12. A rubber band will help kids grip pencils better.

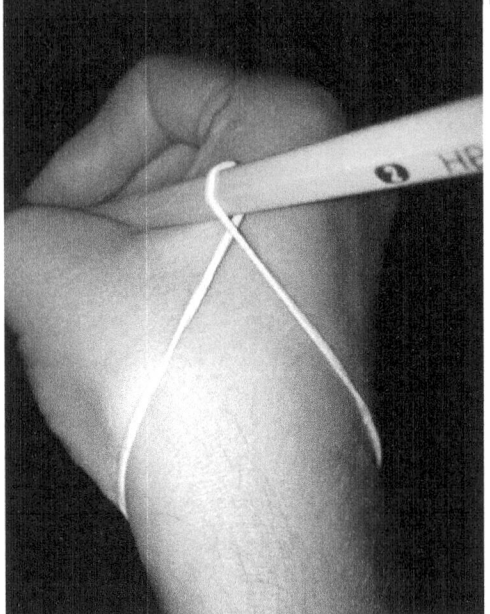

teacherlisasclass.blogspot.com

13. Helichrysum is the essential oil you need for accident-prone kids.

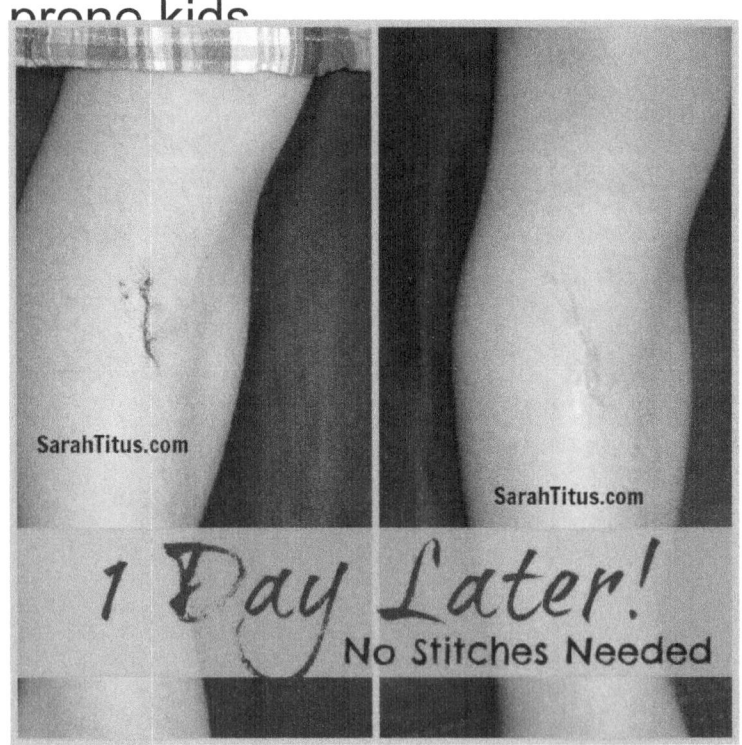

sarahtitus.com

14. Gluing pennies is a way to improvise tap dancing shoes.

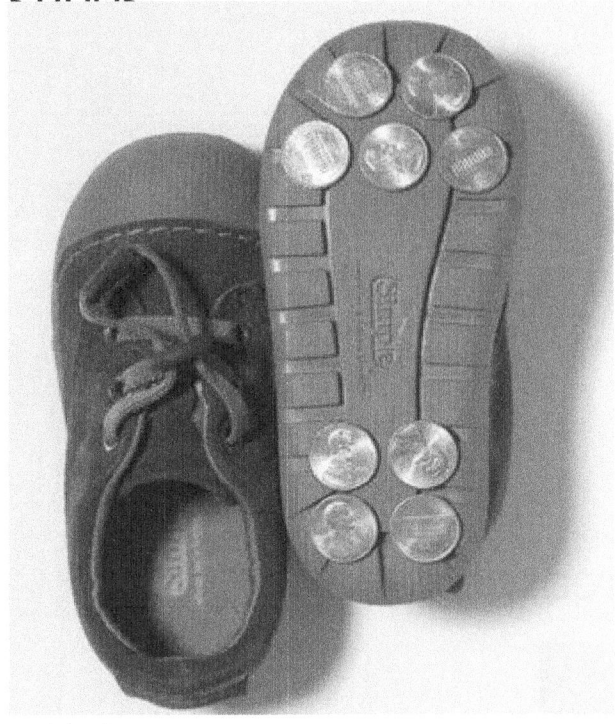

In case your child is hoping to make it to Broadway someday.

15. Put a "safety spot" sticker on your car to ensure an older child doesn't wander off while you load or unload the car.

16. A plastic cup will keep little hands safe when handling sparklers on the Fourth of July.

17. An inflatable pool makes a great safe play area for babies and toddlers.

18. A small spray bottle with 2 tablespoons of fabric softener and water = "Doll Hairspray."

19. Another use for your glue gun: Plug up those holes in your bath toys so they don't get all moldy.

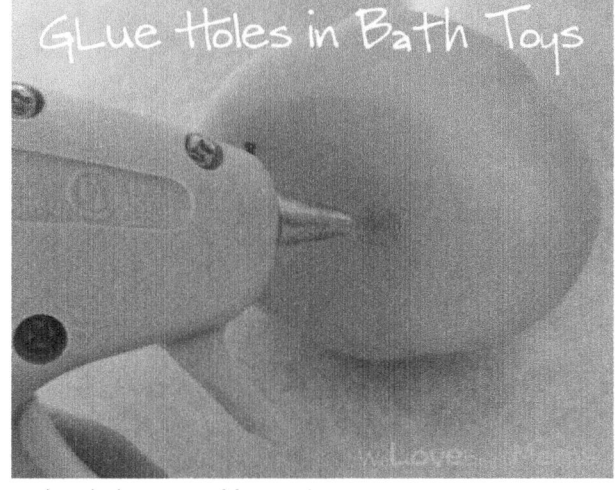

Glue Holes in Bath Toys

20. Make sidewalk chalk in deodorant dispensers for mess-free drawing.

Mess free SIDEWALK CHALK recipe

-De tout et de rien: Activités pour le Préscolaire-

Chalks are RETRACTABLE!

de-tout-et-de-rien-caroline.blogspot.ca

21. Dollar store shower caddies are great to have around for eating in the car.

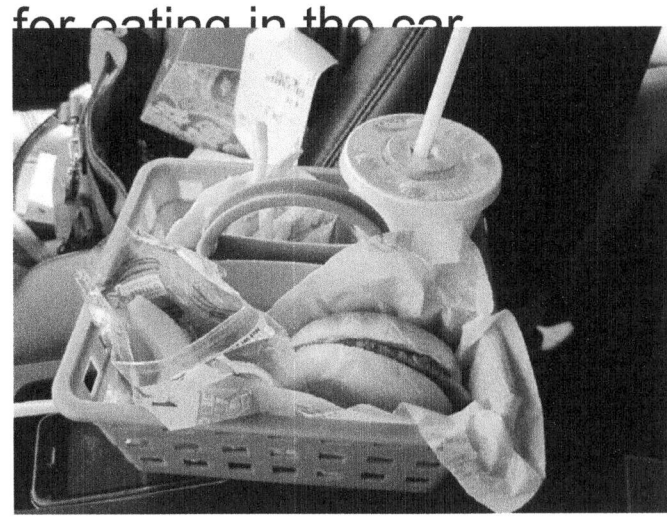

22. Cut up pieces of fleece to create a teething guard for your baby's crib.

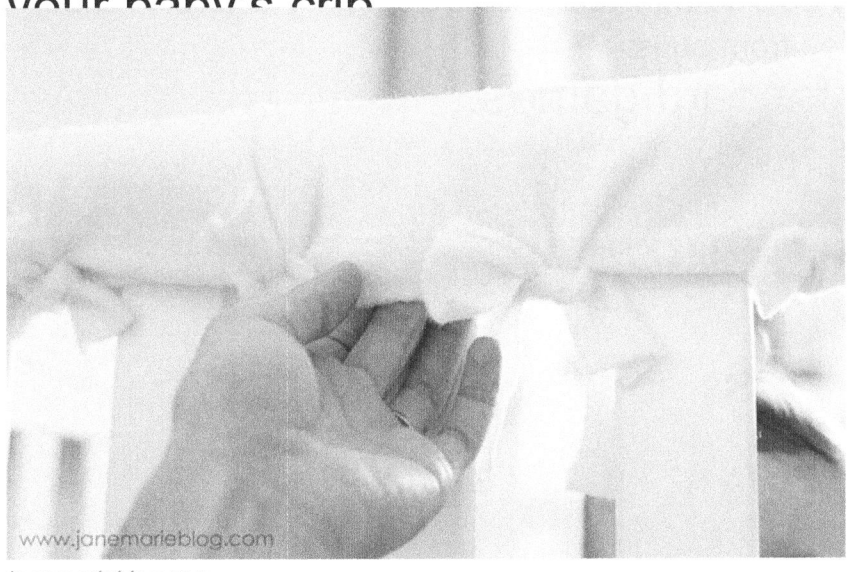

Get the full tutorial here.

23. A crib sheet will keep an outdoor baby from getting bitten up by mosquitoes.

Sometimes you want to keep baby outside with you while working in the yard. A crib sheet provides shade and protection from bugs.

24. Use an egg carton for card games.

25. Use a glue gun to prevent shoes from slipping.

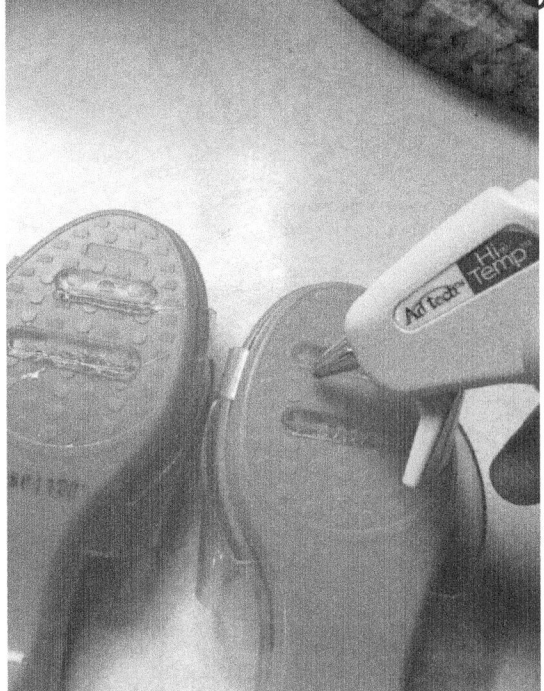

26. Catch kids trying to sneak out with this clever little hack.

LOL.

27. Have more than one child? Use the dot method to separate their clothing.

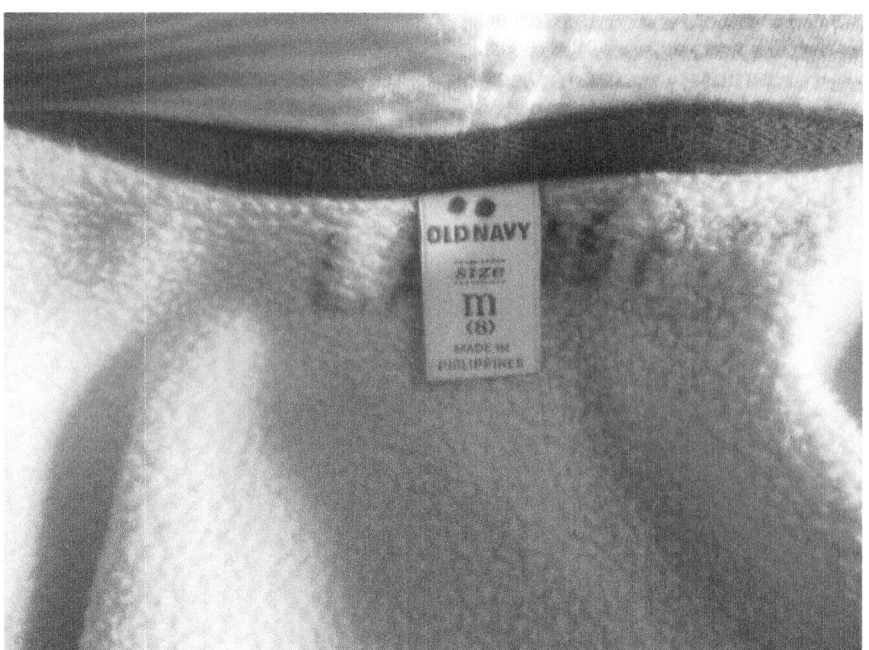

In this household, the oldest child gets one dot while the younger one gets two.

28. Make a "busy wallet" with drawing paper, fun stickers, and a pen to occupy kids while they wait for their food.

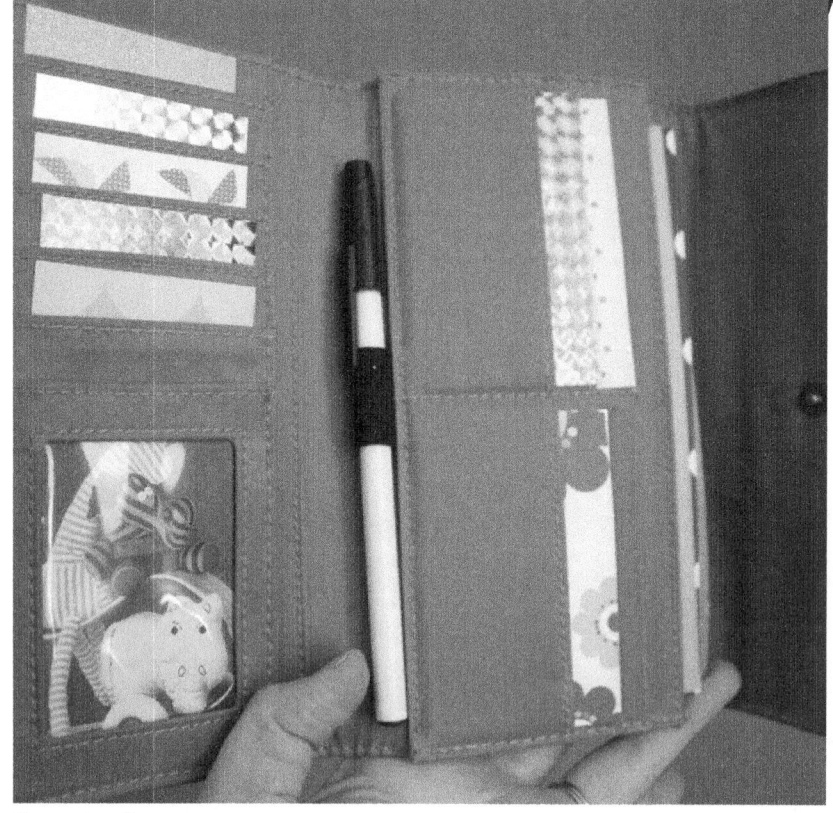

The best panacea for kids who get fidgety at restaurants.

29. Add Jell-O to your popsicles so they don't melt into a drippy mess.

Get the recipe for this slow-melt popsicle recipe here.

30. Bringing a baby bath to the beach means a baby doesn't have to miss out on splashing fun.

Mila Bridger
Photography

Just fill the tub up with beach water.

31. A $3 thrift store camera bag makes the best diaper bag ever.

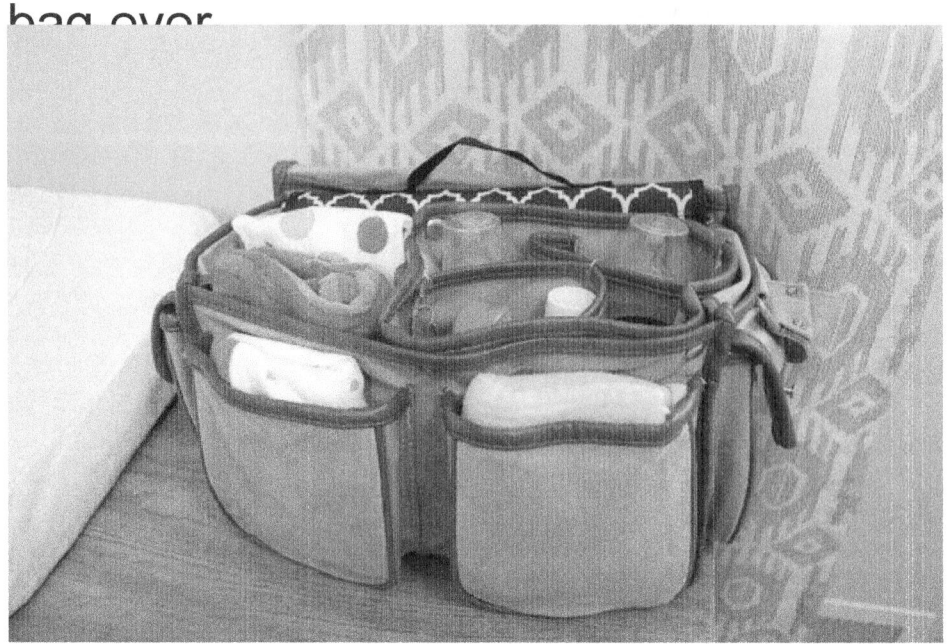

SO MANY COMPARTMENTS.

32. Put a padlock on your plugs to keep your kids from plugging in electrical appliances.

33. And finally… this solution will SAVE YOUR LIFE (and your beds) during the potty-training phase.

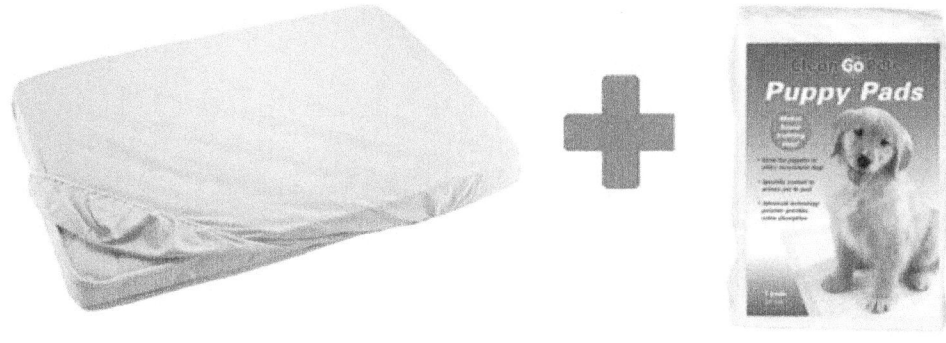

= BEST BED-WETTING SOLUTION EVER

Heather Spohr from The Spohrs Are Multiplying placed wee wee pads underneath her child's fitted sheet to protect the mattress from accidents. She actually double layers them — one layer of wee wee pads, one fitted sheet, one layer of wee wee pads, another fitted sheet — so that she could remove the top layer after bed-wetting without having to re-fit the bed. A serious time and sleep saver during a challenging time.

Toilet paper tube cars;

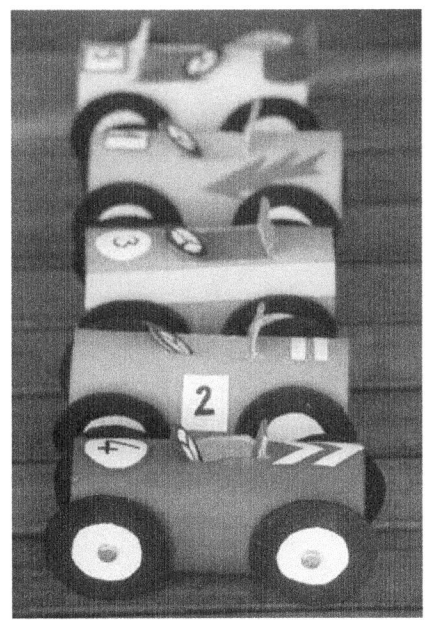

Santa's Footprints

Put shoes down and sprinkle powdered sugar around them. Kids will never stop believing in Santa again.

LifeHackable.com

Also use baby powder to stop shoes/wellies rubbing feet and legs.

If possible find a job with flexible working -

Flexi working hours makes school run slightly less stressful

Do a handprint / footprint print of your child in the centre and put various pictures, words, poem etc. around the edge;

- When potty training use something like 'urine off' to get rid of urine spills etc.

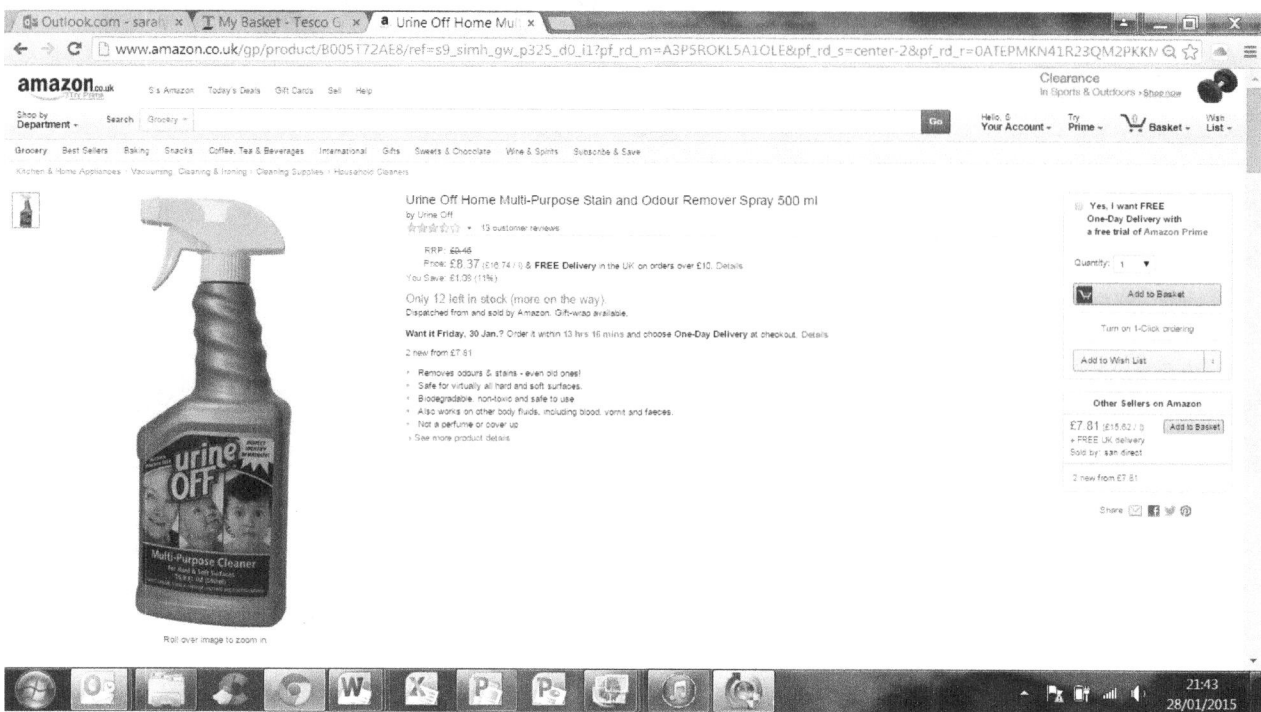

- When you take your child swimming you may want to take some bath toys for them to play with in the water.
- Sometimes they eat less, especially as they get older i.e. after a year or 2 of age when they are not growing so rapidly.
- When they are toddlers they thinks that they're the centre of the world, they are used to people running after them and getting things for them and they are discovering they are individuals and can do things independently, it will be at this age they will have temper tantrums in they don't get their own way.
- They always push the boundaries and are demanding, once they realise they can't get their own way they will be less demanding. They always test the boundaries but also need discipline and limits so let them cry for a few minutes before keep going to them when they are in bed (however do this when they are at least 9 months, before a year they need attention and not to be left to 'controlled crying').
- When reading to them, skip pages in book that maybe inappropriate, rather than not reading the whole book. You can make parts up and elaborate on the story and ask them questions in relation to it to expand their mind i.e. "that was a good dinosaur eating all his dinner, are you going to be good and eat all of your dinner, what colour was the dinosaurs jumper?"
- Nightlight – Get a small night light, ideally with a warm colour bulb to sooth them at night, and to make it easier for you to see them to check on them at night.
- Get them dressed as soon as they wake up and are sleepy so they struggle less.

- Time big events like potty training so they don't coincide with other events like moving house, otherwise it maybe too stressful for child.
- Get an a Aroma stone to burn oils at an even temperature and safely, that way if your child has a cold you can burn eucalyptus oil in their room.
- Keep a large bag in the car with extra nappies, milk cartons and spare clothes and then carry a clutch, or small bag or a pouch / makeup bag inside your handbag with your nappies, wipes, nappy sacks and cream also you may want a nursing cover up, burp cloth, changing matt water bottle or milk in carton, and a dummy in your bag. You can have a range of plastic pouches (mia tui sell these in different sizes), you can include a change of clothes and muslin in the large bag, food pouches (Ella's kitchen) with bib and spoons, in the other clear bag have nappies and wipes, bum cream and nappy sacks – you can then easily find things and grab what you need. Have bright coloured/ colour coded items to make it even easier. Or have a separate change mat with compartments in for all your nappy equipment so that you can just grab and go change, your baby. You may want a baby bag with a separate clutch for your personal item i.e. phone, purse, keys so you can 'grab and go'. I found have bottle holders were important, especially when your baby turns to a toddler and all you need is a water bottle (which you don't want leaking in your bag). I started with a large Mia Tui bag (with space or everything) and then progressed down to a smaller bag, with a drinks holder inside and space for a few nappies as my baby became a toddler. It is a good idea to keep a change of clothes/gym kit in the car, just in case they have an accident on your clothes.
- **If they bite / cut their tounge, give them a cold flannel to bite on**
- **Table cloth – are great especially for coffee tables that they want to run their cars along.**

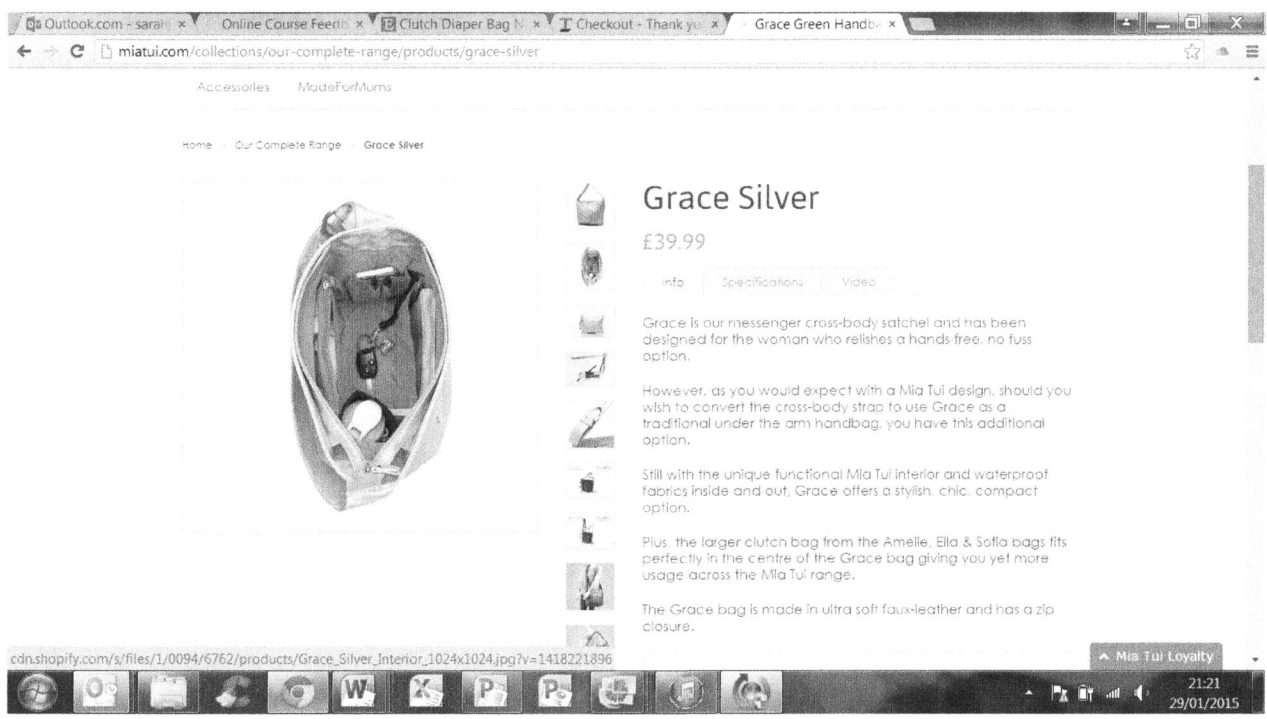

Pram clips and even yoga mat clips are also useful;

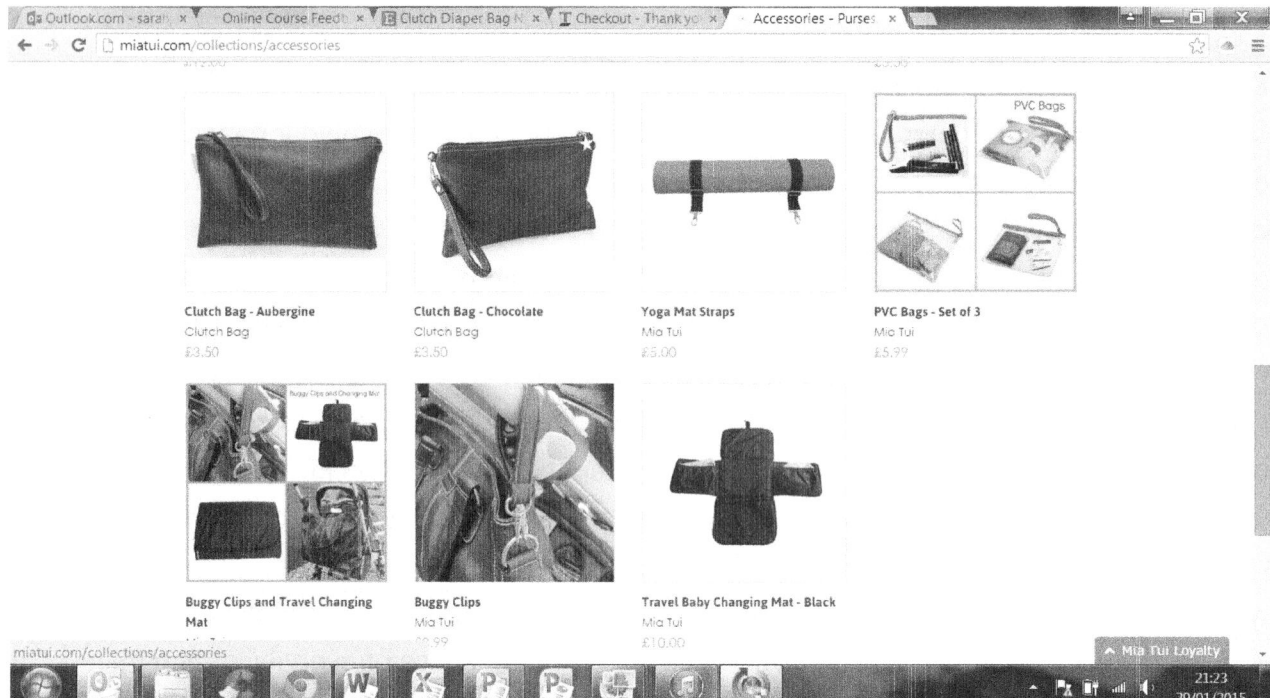

- A lockable makeup box is a good idea for when your baby becomes a toddler and starts playing with your makeup.

- In your tool kit you will need spanners to fix up the stair gate / use U tube for instructions of how to do things such as putting a stair gate up, putting your pram or cot together etc

- **Once your toddler starts the terrible 2's stage, s/he may run away and not want to get dressed; Talk to child whilst dressing / distract them get a baby doll to lay down and be changed, get them to change their baby doll, tell them how their friends get dressed, threaten to take them out in the cold if they don't get dressed, bribe them by offering incentives, be firm and consistent, try not to chase them as then they think it's a game.**

- **Give an incentive to use the potty i.e. 1 smartie each time.**

- **If you tell baby off they will turn it around by laughing, be firm and tell them it's not funny.**

- **If you cut out their day nap, to help them sleep at night they may get overtired and crash out late in afternoon, which will make it even harder for them to sleep at night, so start off by giving them a nap in the morning (so it's not too near to bed time and gradually reduce it).**

- **All babies go through bad phases; most mums forget these and remember their kids as being good, don't feel judged and remember it is normal behaviour for a kid to have tantrums etc, that said you still need to deal with it.**
- Get little toys and gifts and keep bag then if baby is ill or behaves well they can get a gift/treat
- **Tea is supposed to be okay for toddlers, don't give them anything with caffine in after lunch otherwise they won't sleep at night. Fruit tea doesn't have caffine and banana help them to sleep.**
- **Don't leave for a second, even with play water in a bowl.**
- Create a frame with child's hand/foot print in the middle and outside a photo of your child each month (going around the edge).
- Don't give them a cup of tea after midday due to caffeine (ideally try to avoid all products with caffeine for children).
- Having siblings; It's not unusual for older siblings to feel a little jealous if there's a new baby in the house. You might find your older child wants to be babied a bit as well – for example, asking to be fed when they would normally feed themselves. If you can, try and find extra time to spend one-to-one with your older child and stick to some of your old routines. This video has more advice on how to help your older child adjust to a new baby. Try and make time to play with your child every day as it's through play that children learn all about the world around them. Stacking or sorting different shape and colour blocks, filling and emptying containers of water or scribbling and painting all help your child practise skills they'll need as they grow up. Playing with your child will also teach them new words and help them learn to share.
  - **Days out;** Want to do something different with your child but stuck for ideas? Check what's on at your nearest museum. Lots of museums have child-friendly permanent or temporary exhibitions that even children as young as two and three can enjoy - and often they're free.

- Rotate nappies in the car to change them to bigger sizes, otherwise your spare stock of nappies in the car will not get used and your baby will soon outgrow them.
- As an incentive for good behaviour, if your baby is good at the end of the week you can give a reward –it can be an activity you do, something you make together i.e. Roberts from cereal box.
- Be realistic about what you can do for yourself and be happy with, when you have a baby/young child - You can take on more and succeed but you will feel guilty which is hard, it is the feeling of guilt from being away from your child which is hard, often we find it harder than them, because we worry about them more, whilst they are off having fun.
- You get things even though you feel that you won't at the time, when you look back, it always feels easier than it was. There is no such thing as the perfect child. They all go through a phase of being a pain doesn't mean there is something wrong with them.
- When cooking cut up raw vegetables for your child to eat as snack whilst waiting, for dinner, instead of snacking on biscuits.

- They need and deserve your attention, as much as possible
- School nurseries are often cleaner than private ones – if using a private nursery check how often it is cleaned, who cleans it and for what duration and what does the clean include i.e. are all toys cleaned etc
- PECS sign cards; PCS are picture communication symbols. PECS is a formalized program for using symbol supports for communication.
- It maybe a good idea to have a lockabe tool kit to keep things out of their way.
- It maybe a good idea to get a **locking tool box, so that you can safely lock away glue and sharp tools and small items etc. It is also advisable to have a lockable make up box to stop little hands getting your makeup.**

Keeping children safe from house fires

Housing safety

If you live in rented accommodation and are worried that your housing may be unsafe for you and your child, contact your housing association or your landlord

If your home catches fire, you and your child could breathe in poisonous smoke. It's especially dangerous if the fire breaks out at night while you're all asleep.

- Fit smoke alarms on every level of your home. Test the batteries every week. Change the batteries every year or, even better, get alarms that have 10-year batteries or are wired into the mains or plug into light sockets.
- At night, switch off electrical items wherever possible before going to bed and close all doors to contain a potential fire. If you smoke, ensure you put any cigarettes right out.
- Practise how you'll escape if there's a fire so you know what to do if the alarm goes off.

Your local fire and rescue service can give you the right advice for your own home and may be able to provide and fit smoke alarms free of charge.

Avoiding bath water scalds

Bath water scalds can be very serious injuries, needing prolonged treatment and care. They can kill a child. Toddlers may play with the hot tap, scalding themselves and other children sharing the bath with them.

- Never leave a child under five alone in the bath, even for a moment.
- Fit a thermostatic mixing valve to your bath's hot tap to control the temperature and stop your child being badly scalded.
- Put cold water into the bath first, then add the hot water. Always test the temperature of the water, using your elbow, before you put your baby or toddler in the bath. The water should feel neither hot nor cold.

Preventing children being burnt or scalded

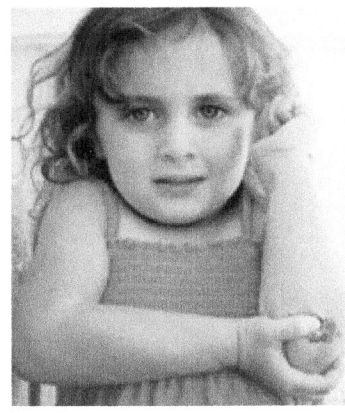

- Fit fireguards to all fires and heaters. Use a sparkguard if you have a coal or wood fire. Guards can prevent under-fives falling or reaching into fires.
- Don't leave hot drinks in easy reach of little hands. Babies and toddlers may grab at cups and mugs on low tables or on the floor and pull the contents over themselves.

Preventing child strangulation

- Make sure any cot toys have very short ribbons, and remove them when your baby goes to sleep.
- Never hang things like bags with cords or strings over the cot.
- Cut or tie up curtain or blind cords well out of your baby's or toddler's reach.

Preventing child poisoning

- Fit carbon monoxide alarms wherever there's a flame-burning appliance (such as a gas boiler) or open fire. Carbon monoxide is poisonous, but you can't see it, smell it or taste it. Make sure that your appliances are serviced regularly and that ventilation outlets in your home aren't blocked.
- Remember that child-resistant devices, such as bottle tops, strips of tablets and cigarette lighters, aren't completely childproof – some children can operate these products. Store medicines, household chemicals (including cleaning products) and lighters out of sight and out of reach, or locked away safely.

More than 1 million children a year are involved in an accident in the home. Most aren't serious, but it's sensible to make sure your first aid box contains the essentials.

Choose a waterproof, durable box that's easy to carry. It's much easier to take the box to the child than the child to the box. The box should have a childproof lock and be tall enough to carry bottles of lotion. For more information about what to include in your first aid box use the Interactive first aid kit tool.

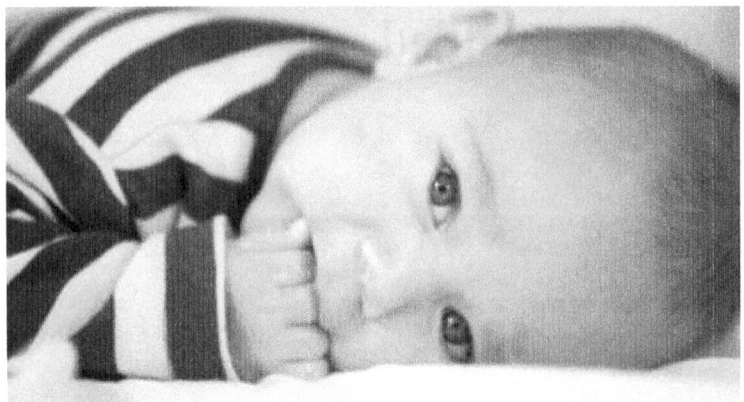

Keep the box out of the reach of children, but handy for adults. You don't want to be hunting for your first aid kit when a child is injured and frightened.

Either buy a first aid box, which is green with a white cross, or, if making up your own box, write "First Aid" on it so if you aren't around, other people know what it is. If someone else is caring for your children, let them know where the kit is kept.

First aid manual

An easy-to-use guide can help refresh your memory when panic and crying children make it hard to remember what to do. Or you could print out The Health A-Z first aid guide and keep it with your first aid box.

Painkillers and babies

Make sure you have an age-appropriate painkiller that contains paracetamol or ibuprofen, which can be used for headaches and fevers. You will also need a measuring spoon or, for younger children, a no-needle dosing syringe. Always follow the dosage instructions on the label.

Dressings for babies

- Sticking plasters. Buy them in a variety of sizes for minor cuts, blisters and sore spots.
- Adhesive tape. This can hold dressings in place and can also be applied to smaller cuts.
- Bandages. Crepe bandages are useful for support or holding a dressing in place. Tubular bandages are helpful when a child has strained a joint and needs extra support. You can also buy triangular bandages that can be used for making a sling.
- Sterile gauze dressings. These are good for covering larger sore areas and cuts.

Antiseptic cream or spray

Antiseptic cream or spray can be applied to cuts, grazes or minor burns after cleaning to help prevent infection. Some may also contain a mild local anaesthetic to numb the pain.

Antihistamine cream

This can reduce swelling and soothe insect bites and stings.

Thermometer

- Digital thermometers. Digital thermometers are quick to use, accurate and can be used under the armpit (always use the thermometer under the armpit with children under five). Hold your child's arm against his or her body and leave the thermometer in place for the time stated in the manufacturer's instructions.
- Ear (or tympanic) thermometers. Ear thermometers are put in the child's ear. They take the child's temperature in one second and do not disturb the child, but they're expensive. Ear thermometers may give low readings when not correctly placed in the ear, so read the manufacturer's instructions carefully and familiarise yourself with how the thermometer works (this applies to all thermometers).
- Strip-type thermometers. Strip-type thermometers, which you hold on your child's forehead, are not an accurate way of taking their temperature. They show the temperature of the skin, not the body.
- Mercury-in-glass thermometers. Mercury-in-glass thermometers haven't been used in hospitals for some years and are no longer available to buy. They can break, releasing small shards of glass and highly poisonous mercury. Do not use mercury thermometers. If your child is exposed to mercury, get medical advice immediately.

Calamine lotion

This can help to soothe itching irritated skin, rashes (including chicken pox) and sunburn.

Baby first aid accessories

- Small pair of scissors for cutting plasters and tape to size.
- Tweezers to remove thorns, splinters and bee stings.
- Ice packs or gel packs can be kept in the fridge and applied to bumps and bruises to relieve swelling. A packet of frozen peas is just as good, but wrap it in a clean tea towel before applying it to skin. Direct contact with ice can cause a "cold burn".
- Saline solution and an eye bath. This is useful for washing specks of dust or foreign bodies out of sore eyes.

Antiseptic wipes

Antiseptic wipes are a handy way to clean cuts and grazes and help prevent infection. To use them, take a fresh wipe and clean the wound, gently working away from the centre to remove dirt and germs.

Remember to keep your first aid box up to date. Replace items when stocks have been depleted and check use-by dates of all medicines. Throw away anything past its use-by date. You can take any out-of-date medicines to a pharmacy, which will dispose of them safely.

…………………
- Bunk beds/cabin beds are harder to clean and are a pain if your child is ill, but do give you more space in a room.
- Teach the alphabetic in phonetic form i.e. how the word sounds
- Less nightmares since out of the cot into a bed.
- Don't pick up straight away when fall
- Need quite time to play alone & develop independence - watch them discreetly
- Nosebleed are common in teenagers, especially boys, due to the changing hormone levels.
- For cradle cap – rub coconut oil in the hair and leave it in overnight if possible. However some children have allergies to nuts so it maybe best to use olive oil until your child is older and avoid almond and coconut oil, unless you are sure (grape seed oil is also less likely to cause allergies).
- To get them to learn to spell their name, get a book that uses / spells out their name i.e. lost my name book , read it to them and at the same time give them the alphabet letters to spell their own name.
- They need and deserve attention
- They may copy their friends
- Gym clothes in car/acts as a spare outfit in accident i.e. child is sick on you.
- Muslin - keep to wipe dribble off face
- Vaseline – is good to nourish skin/act as a barrier and help to prevent and soothe nappy rash, it can also be used on the face to soften and protect from dribble.
- If you child swears get them to bite on a bar of soap, to stop them doing it again.
- When stopping babies nap, reduce nap gradually.
- Keep a muslin to wipe dribble off of their face.
- Mums don't know everything straight away, being a mum you do more as you do things for your child, have to wash more muddy clothes, have more experience of illness etc so you are more aware of things, in time you then learn more and pass this on to your child. Mums know stuff but not straight away, it comes with time, you can't be expected to know everything with your first child. You don't magically know it overnight, your skills develop with time, age and patience. You also learn from others, friends and family mentors etc both good and bad techniques. Don't beat yourself up for what you don't know, just enjoy the process of learning what you do. It is a journey and the more you experience the more you learn.
- **Colds that last longer than a week are an allergy - not a cold virus**
- **If your child is over tired and is jumping up and won't sleep, you may have to hold them / restrain them and rock them to sleep. This is harder as they get older, they will cry and try to resist/fight the sleep. It seems cruel because they are crying but sometimes they need this if they are overtired.**
- **Bed in a bag for when go away (a blow up bed with built in duvet and a pump that all folds into a bag).**
- **Pack flannel when you go away**
- **Vaseline to protect face- wind burn**
- **Don't put pushchair near the edge of stairs or drops, in case they get themselves out and fall over the edge. One minute they are restrained and then before you know it they can open their pushchair buckle and get out (Ritchie could do this from 1 ½ years). My parents had him looking over a wall out to see, he undid his buckle and leaned forward, they had to grab him before he went over (in Drobrovenik)**
- **If they are whiny and you think they are sickening, get an early night in case they wake up and keep you awake all night.**
- **If have a cold and rub it in their eyes they get conjunctivitis**
- **Don't take eyes off children in play centre – you don't know who is in the tunnels there may be other adults or they may fall, get frightened or get in a fight with a kid.**
- **Break cord around neck – don't let them put things around their neck, be careful even with ribbon with a break cord safety feature because if they hold and pull the cord by that it won't open and they could strangle themselves.**

- **When going on holiday, if you don't have pets and especially if you have children with allergies, request a caravan /home that doesn't allow pets.**
- If your child makes something for you i.e. at nursery let them give it to you themselves and make a big fuss over it and display it somewhere prominently.
- Get your child a valentine's day card/gift

Inspire Children to Learn About the World. One country a month – use google to look up the flag, the capital of the country, cook a traditional dish of the country etc. put a map up pick countries and mark them off.

As an incentive to get your child to let you dress him/her, say if you get dressed nicely you can pick a sticker to wear and have a some stickers they will like to choose from.

Print and laminate pictures and make a book for your child – do a photo book of friends and family and add some text in about who is wearing what, what patterns and colours etc.
Put pictures and names up around the house ie put a picture of your child and their name on their door so they get used to saying their name.
Have lots of music and dancing and singing in the house

....
Teach them it doesn't matter if they do well but as long as they try their best. Get them to try their best at everything they do.

Don't put a label on kids, if they think they have a condition that will stop them achieving they use this as an excuse and live up to that expectation.

Startle reflex is normal

Because looks bigger people expect more & better behaviour because think he is older.

- Time goes quick when you have kids because you are so busy.
- Encourage your child - tell they can do anything. If they are scared talk through what they are scared of & reason it through with them, to show them that there is no reason to be scared, they can be brave and achive anything they want and overcome any hurdles. You could say what's the worse thing will happen, if you try x,y,z, if you never try you will never know, as long as you try your best and keep trying you will achieve success and I will still love you no matter what etc. always show them love and encouragement, kindness and treat them with respect.
- When you change their nappy change them lying down because it is more hygienic and you can check their genitals to ensure they have no infections. I used to change Ritchie standing up and sometimes he would face away and I would clean him and put his nappy on. It was hard to see him and clean so well and he got a little infection. When you change them you should check their body for rashes, marks etc. (especially because they can't tell you if they are ill).
- Give them pro-biotics if they are having anti-boitics, they need good bacteria because the anti-biotics kill the good bacteria in the gut as well as the bad bacteria.
- All kids could be slightly autistic because everyone has strange tendencies and autism is a really wide spectrum, so if you think they are doing something that is strange, get it checked out but don't over worry.
- You will form diff interests and priorities as you grow up / have children. Your priorities will be the most important thing, which is to love your children & keep them safe, make sure that this is what you do. Don't get stressed if you can't do the things you used to do, think abut the things you can the fun and love you will have now (as one door closes another one opens) - nRewrite a list of plans / goals so you still have things to look forward to but in a way that suits you now with kids. Ne aware that your requirements will change and as such you will need to make adjustments ie a bigger car maybe needed.

- Kids are impressionable & copy what they see because what they watch and what you say & do around them, also who their friends are - are they suitable?
- Once your child is out of nappies their clothes are bigger because there is no padding from the nappy filling that space (also without the padding they will feel it more when they fall on their bums).
- If you are attending a play centre - take a small over body bag to keep your valuables on you i.e. phone & purse & take a cheap bag for nappies, drink & snacks, that you can leave on the side whilst you run around with your child (you don't want to be running around after your child with a bulky handbag and equally you don't want to leave your valuables on the side), some places have lockers but they may be full and you don't always know how secure they are.
- Don't scrimp on nappies i.e. don't buy cheap nappies, even when potty training at first will need nappies at night.
- Face book and social media is a good way of asking lots of your friends in one quick go for ideas and advice i.e. for suggestions on days out, or for other tips.
- Teeth – get your child to have a go at brushing your teeth then ask them to let you brush their teeth, you could brush their teeth whilst they brush their toys teeth. Sing a song when you brush your teeth, get them to pretend to be a lion and roar and open their mouth, give them a sticker for good brushing or use a brushing app for children, where they get to play a brushing game and get rewards.
- Wash your hands regularly and teach them to wash their hands and face regularly.
- Hide delicate and valuable items, such as jewellery out of your child's reach, get a lockable box for your make up and nail polishes, also lock away chemicals and medicine. If you have a cleaner keep your child out of the way and ensure your cleaner doesn't leave chemicals lying around. I have all my cleaning products in a high level cupboard out the way (although this needs a lock adding before my son can climb up there), one day our cleaner was cleaning the floor and had left the floor cleaning product on the kitchen floor, I hadn't seen this and my son grabbed it. It's better to get your cleaner to come when your child is at nursery and then go around the house double checking, after they have left, that they haven't left anything out.
- When you start cutting the day nap your toddler may get tired early evening ad may get whinny – try to entertain him/her to stop them going to sleep then they should go down for 7;30 for 11 hours. If they don't go to bed at night, it is probably time to stop the day nap.

16/02/15 – somedays Ritchie doesn't nap now. Since Christmas he has got in the habit of going to bed late – 9.30ish, when I cut his day nap he gets tired at about 5ish and crashes but he needs to go to bed earlier so I am going to reduce his nap gradually.

- Cut nap gradually or you could try quiet time instead of a nap so that they are not burning too much energy and can keep going until bed time. Otherwise if they get over tired and then end up having a late nap they will be very late to bed.

Try getting your baby/toddler dressed straight away, as soon as they wake up, before they have their milk. Get clothes & spare nappy ready the night before.

As soon as your house bin is emptied put a blank sack in your outside bin & put it near your door so you can shove poo nappies straight in, rather than smelling your house out and of you are in a flat get a nappy bin.

Giving medicine – if your child doesn't take medicine, try not giving it to them on a syringe, try and spoon instead so that they don't know its medicine, you could hold it in an empty yoghurt pot, so that they think its yoghurt (or a suitable alternative product).

- **If you see the next size up clothes cheap in the sale - buy them.**
- **Put your childs surname on clothes, then if you have another child you can hand down the clothes and not have to put new name labels in the clothes.**
- **Don't worry if your child won't eat properly/only eats one thing, this stage will soon pass.**
- **Change nappy as soon as your baby fills it, so that your baby doesn't get nappy rash.**
- **Be wary of Velcro on change mats etc, specially if you have a silk/chiffon outfit on, I have snagged my clothes so many times this way.**

Your baby journal

Memory diary

Month 1

Your baby is called a blastocyst as it implants. The baby measures about 0.1-0.2 mm. At the end of the fourth week of pregnancy, the chorionic villi are formed. The yolk sac is helping to sustain the pregnancy until the placenta is fully formed. You might even begin to suspect you're pregnant.

Date;

Your weight;

Symptoms/moods;

Foods likes/dislikes;

What changes have you seen felt;

Space below is to write additional notes of affix a photo of the mum to be with bump...

Month 2

The second month of pregnancy is a critical month in foetal development. Your baby goes from being a blastocyst to an embryo. Early on in this month your baby's heart will begin to beat. First it beats slowly, then very rapidly, later in pregnancy the heart rate will slow a bit more.

In the beginning of this month it's hard to tell which way is up on your baby. As this month progresses it becomes very easy to tell which end is your baby's head is and which end is your baby's bottom. By the end of the month your baby's upper and lower limb buds will also appear. And the primordia of the liver, pancreas, lungs, and stomach are evident. While your baby is a girl or a boy, it is not yet apparent without genetic screening.

Your baby is now measuring between 8-11 mm from crown to rump. By the end of this month heart activity is always present on ultrasound. Toe and finger rays are present, though not quite enough for you to count yet.

Date;

Your weight;

Symptoms/moods;

Foods likes/dislikes;

What changes have you seen felt;

Month 3

During the third month of your pregnancy, your baby's bones begin to ossify or harden. Your baby is already moving spontaneously, but you usually can't feel these movements for awhile yet. Your baby's eyes are large and open. Eyelids will form later. External ears have formed.

External genitalia begin to differentiate, though it's still very difficult to tell whether your baby is a girl or a boy without genetic screening. Your baby moves from being an embryo to the fetal period, now called a fetus. S/he also loses their tail!

Your baby's head is the biggest part of their body. It is about 1/2 the size of the rest of the body. While the head is large, the brain's structure is similar to what it will be at birth. S/he weighs about 14 grams and is approximately 3.54 inches in total length. By the end of this month you should be able to hear your baby's heart beat with a Doppler. You can buy a doppler to hear it yourself but its not easy and you may panic if you can't find it.

Date;

Your weight;

Symptoms/moods;

Foods likes/dislikes;

What changes have you seen felt;

Month 4

The placenta has taken over production of the hormones needed to sustain your pregnancy. Your baby is also making some of its own insulin and bile. Your baby even urinates into the amniotic fluid in small amounts every 45 minutes or so.

Your baby's heart pumps about 25 quarts of blood a day. This will increase to be about 300 quarts by the end of your pregnancy. All of the teeth have formed and you even have a scalp hair pattern!

Your baby is about 3 ounces (85 grams) and 6.3 inches (16 cms). The gender may be detectable by ultrasound. Though gender predictions at this point are much harder to rely on.

Date;

Your weight;

Symptoms/moods;

Foods likes/dislikes;

What changes have you seen felt;

Month 5

No new organ structures are really forming at this point in pregnancy. Though the pads of the fingers and toes are forming. Your baby is also developing his or her finger prints. Your baby is also forming permanent teeth buds behind the baby teeth that are already formed. A baby girl will also begin to develop primitive eggs in her ovaries. Gender is usually visible by ultrasound, though accuracy varies.

Your baby's movements may be more apparent. Loud noises may even cause your baby to startle. It's still pretty unusual for your to be able to feel your baby move at this point unless this is not your first pregnancy. You may be aware of sleep wake cycles in your little one.

Your baby is also covered in a fine hair called lanugo and may begin to develop a lotion like substances on their skin called vernix. The weight is now up to 10 ounces (283 grams) and the baby measures about 25 cms total length, about 9.8 inches.

Date;

Your weight;

Symptoms/moods;

Foods likes/dislikes;

What changes have you seen felt;

Month 6

Eye brows are forming now and the lanugo darkens in color. Your baby is moving and practicing breathing for when he or she will be born. The practice contractions that you may or may not notice don't bother your baby one bit. Your baby may or may not be head down, because of the amniotic fluid your baby can move all around still.

Your baby is also depositing brown fat. The brown fat will help him or her regulate body temperature at birth. This brown fat will continue to be laid down until birth.

S/he weighs in at 1 lb 5 ounces (595 grams) and 30 cms or 11.8 inches total length. A few babies are born this early. They do have some chance of survival depending on many factors.

Date;

Your weight;

Symptoms/moods;

Foods likes/dislikes;

What changes have you seen felt;

Month 7

Baby's movements at this point in pregnancy have gone from wild kicks and flurries to smaller movements as the room becomes crowded in the uterus. At about week 28 babies begin to start turning head down. This is automatic in most babies and they seem to like it that way.

Your baby can sense light and dark in the uterus. This may also effect the pattern you notice of sleep and wake cycles. The uterus is also not a silent environment. While the baby can hear your heart beat, your digestive system, etc. your baby can also hear your voice as well as others close by. Think of what you can hear in a pool.

Your baby's eye lashes are developing, as subcutaneous fat is deposited. If you have a baby boy, his testes will probably begin descending. Your baby is about 13.8 inches long (35 cms) and weighs about 2 pounds 4 ounces (1 kilogram)! A baby born at this time has a good chance of survival with the help of medical technology.

Date;

Your weight;

Symptoms/moods;

Foods likes/dislikes;

What changes have you seen felt;

Month 8

Your baby is really getting ready to be born. Every day in the uterus is said to be two less days your baby would spend in the hospital at this point. Red blood cell production is done entirely by your baby's bone marrow. Amniotic fluid is still present and your baby urinates into it daily, about a half a liter of urine a day.

The baby's irises can now dilate and contract in response to light. He or she opens and closes their eyes at will. Even the finger nails reach the end of the fingers. Some babies might even need a nail trim at birth! Your baby may have a lot of hair on their head or none, both extremes are normal.

The weight gain has been fairly incredible recently. Your baby has put on about 2 pounds of weight, mostly fat and muscle tissue, since last month, bringing the total to an average of three pounds eleven ounces (1.7 kilograms), and measurements to 40 cms or 15.8 inches!

Date;

Your weight;

Symptoms/moods;

Foods likes/dislikes;

What changes have you seen felt;

Month 9

Your baby's organs have been finished forming for a long time. Now is the time for finishing touches. For example, the lungs make final preparations for birth by secreting surfactant to help them expand at birth. Your baby's kidneys are still producing lots of urine every day, helping to make up the almost two pints of amniotic fluid.

While your baby may be putting on half a pound a week up until about week 37 at which point weight gain slows drastically. The average birth weight is still about seven and a half pounds. Your baby will measure between 18-22 inches at birth.

Your due date is a guess as to when your baby may arrive. The majority of babies will show up from two weeks before this date to two weeks after this date. Labor is caused by the baby's signals to the mother's body that he or she is ready to be born. Good luck and good birth!

Date;

Your weight;

Symptoms/moods;

Foods likes/dislikes;

What changes have you seen felt;

For information please go to www.lulu.com and check out other books by Sarah Owen, in the Complete Guide series;

The Complete Guide to Events Management

The Complete Guide to Life

The Complete Guide to Setting up Your Own Business

The Complete Guide to Renting out Your Property

The Complete Guide to Investigations and Enforcement

Appendices

Baby feeding diary
Day............................ Date...

Feed/sleep/nappy change (delete as appropriate)	Time	Notes
Feed	10:10 am	From right breast, lasted 20 mins
Nappy change	11:00	Wet only

Day............................ Date...

Feed/sleep/nappy change (delete as appropriate)	Time	Notes
Feed	10:10 am	From right breast, lasted 20 mins
Nappy change	11:00	Wet only

Day............................. Date..

Feed/sleep/nappy change (delete as appropriate)	Time	Notes

Feed	10:10 am	From right breast, lasted 20 mins
Nappy change	11:00	Wet only

Baby Trouble shooting guide	
Issue	Remedy
My baby likes to be held all the time	Maybe you held your baby all the time in the past. Put baby down, gradually more often but stay nearby, pat baby and reassure you are there without picking up, gradually decrease how often you pick baby up.
S/he always cries after feeding	Ensure that you burp him/her after feeding to get all the wind out. You also need to ensure s/he has had enough food (check nappies and weight gain). Are there other symptoms like a rash? (this could indicate an allergy). Or if there are other symptoms it could indicate illness. How long has it been going on, what is the pattern? Maybe it is colic, if in doubt and it doesn't resolve you need to seek medical attention.
My baby takes a long time to feed	Is baby falling asleep whilst feeding, if so gently rub baby to wake him/her when feeding. If baby has had enough food s/he will stop sucking, so if baby moves away from breast or bottle s/he has probably had enough food (if s/he hasn't taken much try burping before feeding to ensure that babies stomach is not full from wind, remember when they are newborn they only have small stomachs). Baby maybe using the breast or bottle as a comforter, in this case you may want to introduce a dummy.
My baby is continuously hungry	Are you misreading cries for cries of hunger when baby may want something else, ensure that you burp and change baby and that you don't over stimulate him/her, equally baby may be bored and need attention and play time. Try also giving him/her a dummy. But first monitor feeds, duration of feeds and waste production to ensure baby isn't hungry. Check weight gain of baby and the amount of feed you are giving him/her. If breastfeeding ensure that you

	are not moving from one breast to the other too quickly as this could result in baby only getting watery foremilk and not thicker hind milk. Hind milk will take up to 10 mins before coming through.
My baby wakes up moody	Baby may not be getting enough sleep, or the temperature in the room could be wrong. Check the room temperature, check his/her nappy feed if s/he is due a feed and then let baby sleep for longer and see if the situation improves.
Baby is not sleeping through the night	
My baby cries all day	Look at the section on crying, also get medical advice as baby may have an infection, such as an ear infection that may not be obvious or baby could be teething (some babies teeth come through straight away). Has baby got a temperature or rash? Check the temperature of the room where baby is. Ensure baby is getting enough food and rest, has some activity but is not over stimulated.

Further notes / to do list / future plans/ appointments etc.;

i.e. get baby put on life insurance, update will, go to photo shoot

Useful links

For health advice fact sheets, look at this Australian hospital web site - http://www.rch.org.au/kidsinfo/fact_sheets/

www.gurgle.com

FSID helpline – 0207 233 2090 / www.fsid.org.uk

net mums

Useful websites

www.direct.gov.uk

www.dwp.gov.uk (Department for Work and Pensions)

www.hmrc.gov.uk/taxcredits

www.hse.gov.uk

(Health and Safety Executive)

www.equalityhumanrights.com

(Equality and Human Rights Commission)

www.adviceguide.org.uk

(Citizens Advice Bureau)

www.cmoptions.org

(Child Maintenance Options)

www.acas.org.uk (Acas)

www.direct.gov.uk/employees

www.healthystart.nhs.uk

www.workingfamilies.org.uk

www.jobcentreplus.gov.uk

www.nct.com

www.babycentre.co.uk

www.babycaretens.com **(Hire TENS machine and give NCT a donation each time).**

www.fatherhoodinstitute.org **(The National Information Centre on Fatherhood)**

www.i-c-m.org.uk **(Institute of complimentary medicine)**

www.doula.org

www.infochoice.org

www.homebirth.org

www.oaa-anaes.ac.uk

www.nice.org.uk/guidance

www.nhsbt.nhs.uk/cordblood

www.aims.org.uk

thecoupleconnection.net (relationship support)

www.nhs.uk/birthplan

Families Information Service

Your local Families Information Service (which may be called something else in your local area) can provide information about registered childcare, free early education places and other services available in your area.

You can contact them on **0800 2 346 346**. You can also search **www.childcarelink. gov.uk** for your local Families Information Service or look on your local authority's website for more details.

One Parent Families/Gingerbread

One Parent Families/Gingerbread (see page 184) is a self-help organisation for one-parent families that has a network of local groups which can offer you information and advice. They will be able to put you in touch with other mothers in a similar situation.

If money is an immediate concern, see the chapter on rights and benefits (page 156) for information on what you can claim and your employment rights. Your local Jobcentre Plus or Citizens Advice Bureau (CAB) will be able to give you more advice. If you have housing problems, contact your local CAB or your local housing advice centre. Ask your local authority at the town hall for the address.

Lone Parent Helpline

Call free on **0800 018 5026** (9am–5pm, Mon–Fri; 9am–8pm, Wed).

Breastfeeding help and support

Don't be afraid to ask for the support and information you need to make breastfeeding work for you and your baby. No problem is too small – if something is worrying you, the chances are that other mothers will have felt the same.

You can get help from a peer supporter, your midwife or health visitor. You might also want to join a local breastfeeding group. It's a great way of making new friends as well as sharing the ups and downs of looking after a new baby. Most groups usually include a mix of healthcare professionals and local trained volunteer mothers (peer supporters). These mothers have breastfed their own babies and have had some training in basic breastfeeding techniques. Some peer supporters will have had more in-depth training to help them support new mothers.

There may be specialist drop-ins in your area where you can go if you have a specific concern or difficulty.

To find out what is available in your area, talk to your midwife or health visitor, or contact the **National Breastfeeding Helpline** on 0300 100 0212 (lines are open from 9.30am to 9.30pm) or go to the website at www.nationalbreastfeedinghelpline.org.uk

You can also get information online from the **Association of Breastfeeding Mothers** (www.abm.me.uk) and the**Breastfeeding Network** (www.breastfeedingnetwork.org.uk). The Breastfeeding Network runs a Supporterline on 0300 100 0210, and also offers a helpline for speakers of Bengali/Sylheti on 0300 456 2421. Lines are open from 9.30am to 9.30pm.

NHS guidance on breastfeeding is available at www.breastfeeding.nhs.uk

The following voluntary organisations can also provide information and advice:

La Leche League 0845 120 2918 www.laleche.org.uk

NCT Breastfeeding Line 0300 330 0771 www.nct.org.uk

The **Unicef Baby Friendly** site at www.babyfriendly.org.uk provides information and links to useful resources about the benefits of breastfeeding.

The **Breastfeeding Network's Drugs in Breastmilk Helpline** can provide information about breastfeeding and medicines. Call 0844 412 4665.

All these voluntary organisations provide training for peer supporters.

The *Bump to Breastfeeding (Best Beginnings)* DVD is a useful source of information and will give you an insight into other mothers' experiences of breastfeeding. You should have been given a copy of the DVD during your pregnancy. If not, ask your health visitor or visit www.bestbeginnings.info

Action for Sick Children

Unit 6, High Lane Business Court

Rear of 32 Buxton Road

High Lane

Stockport SK6 8BH

0800 074 4519 (Mon–Fri 9am–5.30pm)

enquiries@actionforsickchildren.org www.actionforsickchildren.org

Promotes equality of healthcare services for children in hospital, at home and in the community. Gives information and support to parents and carers with a problem or query regarding their child's healthcare, from how to register your child with a GP or a dentist to what to expect when they need to go into hospital.

Action on Smoking and Health (ASH)

First Floor

144–145 Shoreditch High Street

London E1 6JE

020 7739 5902 enquiries@ash.org.ukwww.ash.org.uk

A campaigning public health charity that works to eliminate the harm caused by tobacco.

ADDISS (National Attention Deficit Disorder Information and Support Service) PO Box 340

Edgware

Middlesex HA8 9HL

020 8952 2800

Provides information and resources aboutAttention Deficit Hyperactivity Disorder to parents, sufferers, teachers and health professionals.

Advisory Centre for Education (ACE)

1C Aberdeen Studios

22 Highbury Grove

London N5 2DQ

0808 800 5793 (advice line, Mon–Fri 10am–5pm)www.ace-ed.org.uk

Provides advice and a voice for parents.

Allergy UK

3 White Oak Square

London Road

Swanley

Kent BR8 7AG

01322 619 898 (helpline)info@allergyuk.org A leading national medical charity providing up-to-date information on all aspects of allergy, food intolerance and chemical sensitivity.

Association for All Speech Impaired

Children (Afasic)

1st Floor

20 Bowling Green Lane

London EC1R 0BD

08453 55 55 77 (helpline, Mon–Fri 10.30am–2.30pm)

020 7490 9410info@afasic.org.uk www.afasic.org.uk

Represents and supports children and young people affected by the hidden disability of speech, language and communication impairments and their families.

Association for Post-Natal Illness (APNI)

145 Dawes Road

Fulham

London SW6 7EB

020 7386 0868 (Mon–Fri 10am–2pm)

0808 800 2222 (Parentline 24-hour helpline) www.apni.org

Network of telephone and postal volunteers who have experienced postnatal illness, offering information, support and encouragement.

Asthma UK

Summit House

70 Wilson Street

London EC2A 2DB

0800 121 62 44 (advice line, Mon–Fri 9am–5pm)

0800 121 62 55 (supporter and information team)info@asthma.org.ukwww.asthma.org.uk

A charity dedicated to improving the health and well-being of the 5.4 million people in the UK whose lives are affected by asthma. Works with people with asthma, health professionals and researchers to develop and share expertise to help people increase their understanding and reduce the effect of asthma on their lives.

Benefit Enquiry Line for

People with Disabilities

2nd Floor

Red Rose House

Lancaster Road

Preston PR1 1HB

0800 882 200 (Mon–Fri 8.30am–6.30pm;

Sat 9am–1pm)

0800 243 355 (textphone) Bel-Customer-Services@dwp.gsi.gov.ukwww.direct.gov.uk

Information, advice and support for parents of children with disabilities.

Bliss

9 Holyrood Street

London SE1 2EL

0500 618 140 (helpline, Mon–Fri

10am–10pm)enquiries@bliss.org.ukwww.bliss.org.uk

UK charity that cares for premature and sick babies. Dedicated to ensuring that babies survive and go on to have the best possible quality of life. Provides practical and emotional support to families so they can give the best care to their babies. Specialist study days and training support doctors and nurses to develop their skills. Funds research to improve the care of all sick and premature babies.

British Deaf Association (BDA)

10th Floor

Coventry Point

Market Way

Coventry CV1 1EA

02476 550 936

02476 550 393 (textphone) headoffice@bda.org.uk www.bda.org.uk

Provides advocacy and youth services for deaf people whose first language is British Sign Language.

Brook

421 Highgate Studios

53–79 Highgate Road

London NW5 1TL

0808 802 1234 (helpline, Mon–Fri 9am–5pm)www.brook.org.uk

Ask Brook is available free and in confidence to young people. Brook services provide free and confidential sexual health information, contraception, pregnancy testing, advice and counselling, testing and treatment for sexually transmitted infections and outreach and education work.

Challenging Behaviour Foundation

The Old Courthouse

New Road Avenue

Chatham

Kent ME4 6BE

0845 602 7885 (Mon–Fri 9am–5pm)

01634 838739 (enquiries)www.challengingbehaviour.org.uk

Provides various factsheets for individuals with severe learning disabilities who display challenging behaviour.

Child Accident Prevention Trust (CAPT)

Canterbury Court

1–3 Brixton Road

London SW9 6DE

020 7608 3828safe@capt.org.ukwww.capt.org.uk

Provides information on safety products and sources of literature. A leading charity working to reduce the number of children and young people killed, disabled or seriously injured in accidents.

Child Bereavement Charity

Aston House

High Street

West Wycombe

Buckinghamshire HP14 3AG

01494 446648 (helpline, Mon–Fri9am–5pm)enquiries@childbereavement.org.uk www.childbereavement.org.uk

Provides support to families and professionals when a child dies or when a child is bereaved of someone important in their lives.

Child Death Helpline

York House

37 Queen Square

London WC1N 3BH

0800 282 986 (helpline, Mon, Thu and Fri 10am–1pm; Tue and Wed 10am–4pm; every evening 7pm–10pm)contact@childdeathhelpline.orgwww.childdeathhelpline.org.uk

Helpline for anyone affected by the death of a child of any age, from pre-birth to adult, under any circumstances, however recently or long ago. Staffed by trained volunteers, all of whom are bereaved parents. Callers to the helpline may be parents, siblings, grandparents, other relatives and friends, and associated professionals such as teachers, emergency services and healthcare staff.

Child Growth Foundation

2 Mayfield Avenue Chiswick London W4 1PW020 8995 0257www.childgrowthfoundation.org Provides advice on problems related to pre-school stature: length, height and/or weight.

Child Maintenance Options

Selectapost 38 Sheffield S97 3FJ 0800 988 0988 (Mon–Fri 8am–8pm; Sat 9am–4pm) 0800 988 9888 (Textphone) Or visit www.cmoptions.org Impartial information about making a child maintenance arrangement, as well as directing parents to other groups that can give specialist advice.

Child Poverty Action Group

94 White Lion Street London N1 9PF

020 7837 7979

staff@cpag.org.uk www.cpag.org.uk

Campaigns for other organisations on behalf of low-income families. Provides advisers with information and advice for parents on benefits, housing, welfare rights, etc.

Coeliac UK

3rd Floor, Apollo CentreDesborough RoadHigh Wycombe Buckinghamshire HP11 2QW0870 444 8804 (helpline)01494 437 278 (admin) www.coeliac.org.uk Helps parents of children diagnosed as having the coeliac condition or dermatitis herpetiformis.

Co-ordinated Action Against Domestic Abuse (CAADA)

Maxet House28 Baldwin StreetBristol BS1 1NG 0117 317 8750 (8.30am–5.30pm)info@caada.org.uk

www.caada.org.uk

A registered charity offering accredited training for IDVAs (Independent Domestic Violence Advisers) and implementation support for MARACs (Multi-Agency Risk Assessment Conferences). MARACs are meetings that include criminal justice, local authority, health and specialist representatives that aim to share information and create a multi-agency safety

plan for high-risk victims of domestic abuse. Has recently begun training practitioners from

Family Intervention Projects.

Cry-sis

BM Cry-sis London WC1N 3XX 0845 122 8669 (helpline, 9am–10pm seven days a week) info@cry-sis.org.uk www.cry-sis.org.uk Offers non-medical, emotional support for families with excessively crying, sleepless and demanding babies.

Daycare Trust

21 St George's Road London SE1 6ES 0845 872 6251 (information line, Mon, Tue, Thu, Fri 10am–1pm and 2pm–5pm; Wed 2pm–5pm)info@daycaretrust.org.ukwww.daycaretrust.org.uk Daycare Trust is a national charity which provides information and support to parents and carers about childcare and paying for childcare.

Deaf Parenting UK

c/o Dering Employment Services 96 Park Lane Croydon CR9 2NL07789 027186 (textphone)info@deafparent.org.ukwww.deafparent.org.uk The first ever charity and small national organisation run by deaf parents for deaf parents, representing the needs of deaf parents in the UK.

Disability Alliance

Universal House 88–94 Wentworth Street London E1 7SA 020 7247 8776 (voice/text)office.da@dial.pipex.comwww.disabilityalliance.org Provides information on benefits through publications including the *Disability Rights Handbook*, and free factsheets and briefings from its website. It campaigns for improvements to the social security system.

Disabled Living Foundation (DLF)

380–384 Harrow Road London W9 2HU 0845 130 9177 (helpline, Mon–Fri 10am–4pm) 020 7432 8009 (textphone)advice@dlf.org.uk www.dlf.org.ukA national charity that provides free, impartial advice about all types of daily living equipment for disabled adults and children, older people, their carers and families.

Disabled Parents Network (DPN)

81 Melton Road West Bridgford Nottingham NG2 8EN0300 3300 639 (helpline)information@disabledparentsnetwork.org.uk www.disabledparentsnetwork.org.uk Aims to educate and increase society's acceptance of disability in parenthood.

Equality and Human Rights Commission

Freepost RRLL-GHUX-CTRXArndale HouseArndale CentreManchester M4 3AQ0845 604 6610 (Mon–Fri 9am–5pm)0845 604 6620 (textphone)info@equalityhumanrights.comwww.equalityhumanrights.com The helpline provides information and guidance on discrimination and human rights issues. All helpline staff have been specially trained to provide this service.

ERIC (Education and Resources for Improving Childhood Continence)

36 Old School House Britannia Road Kingswood Bristol BS15 8DB0845 370 8008 (helpline, Mon–Fri 10am–4pm)0117 960 3060www.eric.org.uk

Provides information and support to children and their families on potty training, bedwetting, daytime wetting and soiling.

Family Fund Trust for Families with Severely Disabled Children

Unit 4, Alpha Court Monks Cross Drive York YO32 9WN 0845 130 4542 (helpline, Mon–Fri 9am–5pm)info@familyfund.org.ukwww.familyfundtrust.org.uk Helps families with severely disabled children to have choices and the opportunity to enjoy ordinary life. Gives grants for things that make life easier and more enjoyable for the disabled child and their family, such as washing machines, driving lessons, hospital visiting costs, computers and holidays.

Home-Start UK

2 Salisbury Road Leicester LE1 7QR 0800 068 6368info@home-start.org.uk www.home-start.org.uk Volunteers offer friendship, advice and practical help for families or individuals with children under the age of five. Provides the support that local Home-Starts need to carry out their work supporting families in their communities. It also represents Home-Start at a national level. Its regional and specialist offices are located across the UK.

Hyperactive Children's Support Group (HACSG)

Dept. W 71 Whyke Lane Chichester West Sussex PO19 7PD 01243 539966 (Mon, Tue, Thu, Fri 10am–12.30pm; Wed 2.30pm–4.30pm)www.hacsg.org.uk Provides information to help with problems related to hyperactivity.

USEFUL ORGANISATIONS 183

I CAN – The Children's Communication Agency 8 Wakley Street

London EC1V 7QE

0845 225 4071info@ican.org.ukwww.ican.org.uk

Advice and information for parents of children with speech, language and communication needs.

Institute for Complementary and Natural Medicine (ICNM)

Can-Mezzanine

32–36 Loman Street

London SE1 0EH

020 7922 7980 (Mon–Fri 10am–4pm)info@icnm.org.uk www.icnm.org.uk

Can provide the public with lists of BRCP (British Register of Complementary Practitioners) members, a professional register of practitioners and therapists who have completed a recognised course and are insured. (Always check with your GP/midwife before using a complementary discipline.)

Mencap Mencap National Centre

123 Golden Lane

London EC1Y 0RT

0808 808 1111 (helpline) 020 7454 0454 help@mencap.org.uk www.mencap.org.uk

Works with people with a learning disability and their families and carers. Advice and information on local branches.

Meningitis Research Foundation

Midland Way

Thornbury

Bristol BS25 2BS

08088 00 33 44 (24-hour helpline) info@meningitis.orgwww.meningitis.org

Promotes education and awareness to reduce death and disability from meningitis and septicaemia, and supports people affected by these diseases. Funds research to prevent the diseases and improve survival rates and outcomes.

Meningitis Trust

Fern House

Bath Road

Stroud

Gloucestershire GL5 3TJ

0800 028 18 28 (24-hour, nurse-led helpline)

01453 768000info@meningitis-trust.org www.meningitis-trust.org

A registered charity set up in 1986 by families who had been affected by meningitis. The Trust is committed to increasing understanding of the disease and providing specialised services to anyone who has been affected. These services offer emotional, practical and financial support to help people rebuild their lives.

Mudiad Ysgolion Meithrin/ The National Association of Nursery Schools and Playgroups

Boulevard de St BrieucAberystwyth SY23 1PD

01970 639639post@mym.co.ukwww.mym.co.uk

Help and advice on setting up and running parent and toddler groups and playgroups. Contact with local playgroups.

Muscular Dystrophy Campaign

61 Southwark Street

London SE1 0HL

0800 652 6352 (helpline, Mon–Fri 9am–5pm)

020 7803 4800info@muscular-dystrophy.org www.muscular-dystrophy.org

Provides support, advice and information for people with muscle disease, their families and carers.

National Association of Family Information Services (NAFIS)Grosvenor Gardens House 35–37 Grosvenor GardensLondon SW1W 0BS info@familyinformationservices.org.uk www.nafis.org.uk A membership organisation consisting of over 150 Information Services across the UK. Members provide information on local services for families, in addition to helping families find suitable childcare and access appropriate benefits and financial assistance. To find your local FIS, visit the website. As the national body, NAFIS supports members via training, quality assurance and through representation of their issues to government.

National Association of Nappy Services (NANS)Unit 1, Hall FarmSouth MoretonDidcot

Oxfordshire OX11 9AH 0121 693 4949 info@changeanappy.co.uk www.changeanappy.co.uk Aims to promote the use of cotton nappies and increase public awareness of the health problems associated with disposable nappies. Provides information on local nappy services which collect soiled nappies and deliver fresh ones on a weekly basis.

National Association of Widows

48 Queens Road

Coventry CV1 3EH

0845 838 2261 (Mon–Fri 9am–5pm)info@nawidows.org.ukwww.nawidows.org.uk

A national charity offering support and friendship to widows and widowers, providing opportunities for men and women to develop a new sense of purpose as they face life on their own. It is the only national charity to serve widows and widowers of all ages. There are currently 42 branches nationwide.

National Autistic Society

393 City Road

London EC1V 1NG 0845 070 4004 (helpline, Mon–Fri 10am–4pm)

020 7833 2299www.nas.org.uk

Provides day and residential centres for the care and education of autistic children. Puts parents in touch with one another. Advice and information and local groups.

National Childbirth Trust (NCT)

Alexandra House

Oldham TerraceLondon W3 6NH0300 330 0770 (enquiry line,Mon–Fri 9am–5pm)0300 330 0772 (pregnancy and birth line,Mon–Fri 10am–8pm)0300 330 0771 (breastfeeding line, 8am–10pm seven days a week)enquiries@nct.org.ukwww.nct.org.uk

Supports 1 million mums and dads every year through helplines, courses and a network of local support. With evidence-based information on pregnancy, birth and early parenthood, it can provide support from when you first discover you are pregnant to when your baby turns 2. Visit the website for information on becoming a parent or to find your nearest NCT group.

National Deaf Children's Society (NDCS)15 Dufferin Street London EC1Y 8UR 0808 800 8880 (helpline, Mon 9.30am–7.30pm; Tue–Thu 9.30am–5pm; Fri, Sat 9.30am–12 noon)helpline@ndcs.org.uk ndcs@ndcs.org.uk www.ndcs.org.uk An organisation of families, parents and carers, providing emotional and practical support through the freephone helpline, a network of trained support workers, a wide range of other support services, publications and the website.

National Eczema Society

Hill House

Highgate Hill

London N19 5NA

0800 089 1122 (helpline, Mon–Fri 8am–8pm)info@eczema.orgwww.eczema.org

An eczema patient support organisation offering help and information to everyone affected by eczema.

National Society for Phenylketonuria (NSPKU)

PO Box 26642

London N14 4ZF

020 8364 3010 (helpline)

07983 688 664 (textphone)info@nspku.org www.nspku.org

Help and support for people with phenylketonuria, their families and carers.

Netmums124 Mildred AvenueWatford WD18 7DXcontactus@netmums.com www.netmums.comA family of local websites, each site set up around a local community, which is totally interactive, with much of the information coming from local mums. At the heart is the coffeehouse, an invaluable place members can chat and get support and advice on anything to do with being a parent.

Ofsted

Royal Exchange Buildings

St Ann's Square

Manchester M2 7LA

08456 404040enquiries@ofsted.gov.ukwww.ofsted.gov.uk

Government body responsible for the registration, inspection and investigation of childcare settings, childminders and daycare facilities.**One Parent Families/ Gingerbread**

255 Kentish Town Road

London NW5 2LX

0800 018 5026 (helpline, Mon–Fri

9am–5pm, with extended opening

to 8pm on Wed)www.gingerbread.org.uk

A national charity for single parent families. Offers a range of support services direct to single parents, including a telephone helpline, publications, training programmes and a membership scheme, and campaigns on their behalf.

ParentsCentreDepartment for Children, Schools and Families Sanctuary Buildings35 Great Smith StreetLondon SW1P 3BT 0870 000 228801928 794274 (textphone)info@dcsf.gsi.gov.uk www.parentscentre.gov.ukwww.direct.gov.uk Information and support for parents on how to help with their child's learning, including advice on choosing a school and finding childcare.

Quit

4th Floor

63 St Mary Axe

London EC3A 8AA

0800 00 22 00 (Quitline)stopsmoking@quit.org.ukinfo@quit.org.ukwww.quit.org.uk Aims to save lives by helping smokers to stop.

Restricted Growth Association (RGA)

PO Box 1024

Peterborough PE1 9GX

01733 759458 (Mon, Thu, Fri 9am–5pm; Tue 9am–5pm and 6pm–9pm; Wed 9am–1pm)office@restrictedgrowth.co.ukwww.restrictedgrowth.co.uk

A self-help organisation dealing with the social and medical consequences of restricted growth. Promotes the interests of people with restricted growth and their families.

Royal Association for Disability and Rehabilitation (RADAR)

12 City Forum

250 City Road

London EC1V 8AF

020 7250 3222

020 7250 4119 (minicom)radar@radar.org.ukwww.radar.org.uk

Conveys opinions and concerns to government and launches campaigns to promote equality for all disabled people.

Royal National Institute for Deaf People (RNID)

19–23 Featherstone Street

London EC1Y 8SL

0808 808 0123 (information line)

0808 808 9000 (textphone)informationline@rnid.org.ukwww.rnid.org.uk

Information service for deaf and hard of hearing people. Local groups.

Royal National Institute of Blind People (RNIB)

105 Judd Street London WC1H 9NE 020 7388 1266

0303 123 9999 (helpline, Mon, Tue, Thu, Fri 9am–5pm; Wed 9am–4pm)helpline@rnib.org.uk www.rnib.org.uk

Information, advice and services for blind and partially sighted people. Local branches.

Royal Society for the Prevention

of Accidents (RoSPA)

Edgbaston Park

353 Bristol Road

Birmingham B5 7ST

0121 248 2000help@rospa.comwww.rospa.com

By providing information, advice, resources and training, RoSPA is actively involved in the promotion of safety and the prevention of accidents in all areas of life – at work, in the home, on the roads, in schools, at leisure and on (or near) water.

St John Ambulance

27 St John's Lane

London EC1M 4BU www.sja.org.uk

Has developed a new range of first aid courses designed to meet the needs of home or leisure activities. Just 3–4 hours is all it takes to learn how to save a life. Courses include CPR and basic first aid.

Terrence Higgins Trust

314–320 Gray's Inn Road

London WC1X 8DP

0845 12 21 200 (helpline, Mon–Fri 10am–10pm; Sat–Sun 12 noon–6pm)

020 7812 1600 info@tht.org.uk www.tht.org.uk

Delivers health promotion campaigns, national services and local services directly to people with or affected by HIV and other sexual health issues.

WAY Foundation

Suite 35, St Loyes House

20 St Loyes Street

Bedford MK40 1ZL

0870 011 3450 (9am–8pm seven days a week)www.wayfoundation.org.uk

Self-help support for men and women widowed up to the age of 50. Welcomes people who were married or unmarried, those with children and those without. Gay men and women are also welcome to join. Runs local groups across the UK, organises weekends and holidays and offers a busy secure messageboard and online chatroom to members. Being able to talk to others who have been through a similar bereavement is helpful and comforting to anyone trying to cope with the death of a partner at a young age.

Working Families

1–3 Berry Street

London EC1V 0AA

0800 013 0313 (helpline, Mon, Tue, Thu, Fri 10am–3pm; Wed 10am–1pm)

020 7253 7243advice@workingfamilies.org.uk www.workingfamilies.org.uk

Helps working parents and carers and their employers find a better balance between responsibilities at home and work. A disability adviser is available Wed–Fri to advise parents/carers with disabled children on their rights.

Record and print out your own useful telephone numbers & links;

Your midwifes details...

Your labour ward...

Your partner/birthing partner..

Nursery rhymes;

A Wise Old Owl.

A wise old owl sat in an oak,
The more he heard, the less he spoke;
The less he spoke, the more he heard,
Why aren't we all like that wise old bird?

A Crooked Man
Children's Nursery Rhyme
John "Kinderman" Taylor

There was a crooked man,

Who walked a crooked mile.

He found a crooked sixpence

Upon a crooked stile.

He bought a crooked cat

Who caught a crooked mouse,

And they all lived together in a

Crooked little house.

Baa, baa, black sheep

Baa, baa, black sheep
Have you any wool?
Yes sir, yes sir,
Three bags full

One for my master,
One for my dame,
One for the little boy
Who lives down the lane

Baa, baa, black sheep
Have you any wool?
Yes sir, yes sir,
Three bags full

I'm a little teapot

I'm a little teapot, short and stout
Here is my handle, here is my spout
When I get all steamed up hear me shout.
Just tip me over and pour me out.

I'm a clever teapot, yes it's true
Here's an example of what I can do
I can change my handle to my spout
Just tip me over and pour me out.

I'm a little teapot, short and stout,
Here is my handle, here is my spout,
When I hear the tea-cups, hear me shout,
"Tip me up and pour me out".

List here books that you want to read and then take this list along to the library with you…………………………………………

Because you may forget things from having one baby to the next, record here your own important things that you want to remember in case you have another baby in the future, or tips you want to pass onto others…………………………………………………………………………

Here is space for you to record important moments in your child's life/log their development etc……

Children Learn What They Live.

by Dorothy Law Nolte – 1972

If a child lives with criticism he learns to condem.
If a child lives with hostility he learns to fight.
If a child lives with ridicule he learns to be shy.
If a child lives with shame he learns to feel guilty.
If a child lives with tolerance he learns to be patient.
If a child lives with encouragement he learns confidence.
If a child lives with praise he learns to appreciate.
If a child lives with fairness he learns justice.
If a child lives with security he learns to live with faith.
If a child lives with approval he learns to like himself.
If a child lives with acceptance and friendship he learns to find love in the world.

Homeopathy for mother & baby - the first year

by Bob Leckridge

Why consider homeopathy for mums and babies? There are at least three good reasons. The first is that it's safe. Although many homeopathic medicines are prepared from plants and other substances which are poisonous in their raw form, by the time they have been prepared as medicines for sale or prescription they are completely non-toxic and they be given safely to breast-feeding mums as well as to children, from the first day of life onwards. The second reason is that the remedies work by stimulating the body's own healing mechanisms. That's not to say the modern medicine is of no value. Quite the contrary. For example, the technological and scientific breakthroughs in caring for premature babies have enabled many more such children to survive those difficult first few weeks. Modern methods of care have also made death during childbearing a rarity in our country.

However, health is about more than mere survival and whilst these advances have undoubtedly been life-saving, other, more holistic approaches are needed to promote and maintain a more comprehensive well-being. This leads me to my third reason – understanding health and understanding people from a homeopathic perspective really helps us to make sense of not only our illnesses but the health and development of our children.

Let's start with mum, because when you come home with the new baby, everybody is thrilled with the baby and, sometimes, mum gets a little forgotten. In the first few days there are a couple of problems which might need attention.

Mother

Wound healing

Arnica is probably taken by many women after the baby is born as it is good for helping the body to heal areas of bruising. However, I don't recommend it routinely because often Bellis perennis (the daisy) is more effective. This has been described as the "gynaecological Arnica". It certainly seems to help better when most of the bruising is internal. Like Arnica, the bruise is painful and the person doesn't want the sore bit to be touched. In fact, they are likely to downplay the whole problem and be quite uncomplaining even though they may be feeling quite distressed about it.

Bruising, however, may not be the main problem. Sometimes a more pressing problem is a tear or a cut (an episiotomy). This is more common if there has been a forceps delivery. The wound is acutely painful and the woman will probably be feeling pretty aggrieved at having had the cut done. She will be feeling hard done by, or feeling that ahe wasn't treated well by the staff.

The homeopathic term for this is "indignation" – the feeling that "it shouldn't have happened to me. It's not fair!" This state is typical of the remedy Staphysagria and if taken over the next few days, it can promote the healing of the wound as well as begin to settle the woman's distress. Staphysagria is also a great remedy for healing clean, surgical cuts, so it is also indicated after caesarean section.

Another useful remedy to have to hand is Calendula. Often the damage to the tissues after childbirth is quite superficial. By that, I mean on the surface. There are multiple grazes and superficial lacerations. This kind of wound can be helped with Calendula. I would recommend that the homeopathic form be used and taken as tablets or powders by mouth because the local applications and creams can sometimes irritate the delicate tissues of the vagina

Breast problems

Mastitis is a common problem. When it occurs suddenly and the breast becomes red, swollen, hot and tender, then Belladonna might speed resolution of the problem, although antibiotics may still be indicated. If the inflammation isn't caught early enough, and an abscess has formed then Hepar sulph might be a better-indicated remedy. Usually once the pus has formed, the stage of Belladonna has passed.

Cracked nipples can be very painful and really make breast-feeding difficult, if not impossible. When the cracks are accompanied by sharp, shooting pains in the breast when the baby feeds, then Phytolacca may help, especially if the pains seem to shoot out from the breast to other parts of the body.

Calendula cream is a good application for cracked nipples. Stitching pain in the breast when the baby feeds in the absence of cracks around the nipples can be helped with Kali carbonicum.

Baby blues

"Baby blues" are very common around the fifth day. You might find yourself becoming very tearful and upset at that time, or, alternatively, irritable and anxious. If you find that having company at this time helps, then you may find Pulsatilla helpful. However, if you find that company and consolation actually make you feel worse, then Natrum muriaticum might be the more indicated medicine.

Postnatal depression, on the other hand, is far more serious. If your sad or upset feelings continue beyond a few days then it would be a good idea to discuss it with your health visitor, midwife, or GP. Even in the most troublesome postnatal depression, homeopathic remedies can be useful, but in such a situation it's harder to self-treat so it would be better to consult a homeopathic specialist.

Baby

Colic

This miserable condition causes enormous distress to babies and their parents. There are no good, safe drugs available, so homeopathic medicines are a great idea. There are two main remedies to consider. If the baby settles a bit when held face down with the tummy supported by the parent's hand, or if they settle when their tummy is pressed against the parent's shoulder, then there is a good chance that Colocynth will help. If these positions don't help but rubbing the tummy lightly, or holding a warm hand against the baby's tummy, helps, then Magnesium phosphoricum is more likely to help.

Teething

Teething is that other early trial which disrupts the peace of the family sleep. The most typical pattern is the baby with a bright red cheek, screaming with anger, who settles when carried around the room. This is the picture of Chamomilla.

Sleep

Sleep, or rather, lack of it, is a common problem when there is a young baby in the house. It's important to understand the place of sleep in a baby's life and not treat this issue as a disease. Initially, babies need a lot of sleep and really only wake for food or drink. They soon start to develop waking periods however and within a few short weeks are already starting to smile in response to smiles and to have periods of great alertness where they lie with eyes wide open taking in their surroundings. Babies cry for many reasons. The physical reasons include being hungry or thirsty, being physically uncomfortable and feeling insecure or unhappy.

It's always important to check and see if any of these common factors are playing a part. However, in some children, they continue to cry despite the exclusion of physical factors. Colic and teething are common explanations for sleep disturbance that won't clear up without help.

What do we do with the babies who just won't sleep? If underlying reasons of discomfort or pain have been excluded there are a couple of homeopathic remedies worth trying. Firstly, there is Jalapa. This remedy is indicated in babies who are "good all day and bad all night" particularly in those who have a tendency to diarrhoea, or just very loose stools. The other remedy to consider is Cypripedium, which is indicated in infants who are just alert and active. They wake up through the night and just want fun. They are obviously not distressed, unlike the Jalapa babies who are most distressed at night.

We can get other clues about the remedies our children might need by observing them during the night. Do they get hot and sweaty and throw off the covers, which is typical of Sulphur? Do they sweat on their heads at night, making the pillow wet, like Calcarea phosphoricum? Do they usually sleep in a particular position? (Medorrhinum children sleep on their tummies with their bottoms sticking up in the air. Pulsatilla children sleep on their backs with their arms stretched out above their heads.)

Development

All babies develop at their own rates. However, some babies definitely develop more slowly than others. The slowest ones are usually the rather chubby ones, who sit about without expressing much sense of adventure. These might be kids whose teeth are slow to come through, who are a bit sweaty, and may be constipated. These might be typically Calcarea carbonica or Baryta carbonica children. Which of the two they are is hard to tell when they are very young, but as they get a little older other personality characteristics become clearer. They are both quite fearful, the Baryta baby is shyer than the Calc baby and is more likely to have developmental delay. I think it is hard to self treat at this level but some of the child's characteristics will give the clues your homeopathic doctor needs to find the right remedy to stimulate maturational growth.

Immunisation

This is a very difficult subject for parents. It's all about trying to choose the path of least risk for you child. I think you need to consider each immunisation separately. What is the disease which we are trying to protect the child from? How serious may that disease be for the child if they catch it, and how significant is the risk of catching it? After consideration of those questions, we then ask, what are the risks associated with the immunisation? We then try to do the best for our children and choose the lowest risk. When you stop to consider this you will realise that there are no rules, no hard and fast conclusions which are applicable in all children at all times and in all places.

There isn't a homeopathic alternative vaccination programme. However, this doesn't mean that homeopathy has no role to play here. There are two approaches to consider. Firstly, when it is judged that a particular immunisation is a preferred choice, and we go ahead and vaccinate a child, sometimes there are obvious short term problems afterwards. Homeopathic medicines can help to treat, what we refer to as, ailments from vaccination. This might be anything from a local reaction at the site of the injection which may be hot, red and painful and need Belladonna, to bruising which might be helped by Arnica, to local pain and discomfort which might be helped by Ledum, which is great for puncture wounds. If there are more long-lasting problems after immunisation then a dose of Thuja might help to sort things out.

Secondly, some people advocate giving a child his or her "constitutional" remedy to boost his or her immune system. The idea of a "constitutional" remedy is one which is chosen to match the character and characteristics of the person who is going to be treated. When given, it will stimulate the body's systems of defence and repair. Think of it as a kind of tonic. If it works then the body will be in a more optimal state of health and therefore better placed to defend itself against infections.

Understanding your baby
Knowing that there is such a wide range of personalities and characteristics described in the homeopathic literature helps us to accept the uniqueness of our own children. How are they different? Begin to notice when they are most at ease and when they don't feel secure. This might be different times of day or night. It might be about the social environment, for example, how are they with mum, with dad, with brothers and sisters and with strangers. What kinds of toys do they seem to enjoy most? Are they explorers and adventurers, or do they prefer to occupy themselves with a single toy? What do they seem to be scared of? What do you do to settle them down when they are upset? Noting these kinds of things quickly gives you a sense of their unique character. But homeopathy doesn't stop there. The understanding of homeopathy is that we are unique in our whole beings and express ourselves through our whole beings. It really is a holistic understanding. So, noticing the physical features of your baby will help in finding the best remedies for them too. Are they hot children or chilly children? Are they sweaty? What is their normal sleep pattern and what position are they in when you check them in their cots at night? What foodstuffs do they refuse and which, if any, upset them? Do they like to drink, and, if so, what do they like to drink? As you build up the picture of your baby you'll be struck by how different he or she is from your other children and from other people's children. That uniqueness is a great thing.

If you are going to use any of the medicines mentioned, unless a specific dose is recommended by your homeopathic doctor, use a 30c strength and repeat the doses as often as is necessary. For babies crush one pillule between two spoons, add to a small amount of mineral or distilled water and give one teaspoon for a dose. The rule in homeopathy is to take a dose, experience the improvement, then if the improvement starts to decline, repeat the remedy. If a dose does not produce any improvement, then there is no point in repeating that particular remedy.

Bob Leckridge MBChB FFHom graduated from Edinburgh University in 1978 and worked as a GP until 1995 since when he has worked full-time as a Specialist in Homeopathic Medicine at Glasgow Homoeopathic Hospital. He teaches homeopathy internationally and is the author of Homeopathy in Primary Care. He became President of the Faculty of Homeopathy in 1998.

Positive Parenting lessons;

- **Encourage and praise effort rather than achievement** i.e. it is the taking part not the winning that counts, although it is good to encourage some healthy competition and encourage achievement, it is good to teach your child that as long as they put in 100% effort that is good enough.

- Teach them even if they don't success at first try, try, try again. They will eventually be able to do anything if they put their mind to it.

- Don't reward bad behaviour by paying attention to it; think of different ways to react.

- **Reward positive behaviour with attention.** If you give your child enough attention and attention to good behaviour they won't need to misbehave in order to get your attention. Try and give your child as much positive attention as you can when they are not demanding it.

- Reward positive behaviour. Play with your child and talk through what they are doing. Let your child lead the play and join in by imitating them, give them smiles and warm touches.

- **Be consistent** in discipline, give warnings and tell them what the consequences are in a controlled manner (don't just suddenly explode).

- Children will keep asking to go to the toilet if they are bored, they will also revert back to a baby if there are other babies and they are fighting for attention.

- Children need to be **set limits** so they know where they stand, they will try and push the boundaries in order to learn where the limits are.

- **Listen and pay attention to your child.**

- **Encourage your child to express their feelings.** Be honest with your children. Don't block things from them in order to shield the truth. Instead talk and explain, don't hide your feelings.

- Deal with things straight away – otherwise younger children will forget and don't say to child I will need to speak to you later, otherwise they will worry about it. The worrying/anticipation is always worse than the telling off.

- Don't take sides when your children are arguing; you may only see ½ of what has happened. One child may have been winding the other child up, causing that child to lash out.

- Don't call your child naughty. If children are given a label they will act upto that label.

- Have a joint approach and be consistent.

- Know when there is an issue and when you child is acting up for attention.

- Don't give empty threats, always follow through with any threats otherwise they will not take you seriously.

- Try and be positive and don't criticism you child. Constant criticism can undermine your child's confidence.

- Cuddle your child and listen to him/her a lot, stroke and touch your child and be a positive person so that you give off positive vibes to your child. In the first year of life, children's mos basic task is to develop a sense of security and trust. This is done partly by meeting their needs, but also through positive communication and human closeness, the touching, the talking, the singing, that goes along with meeting their needs.

- Notice any little contributions, efforts or improvements that they make. Reward them for making an effort and for improving, rather than on success.

- It is also a good idea to use comments that let children learn and form their own opinions. For instance by giving detailed and constructive feedback such as "I like the way you used yellow in that picture to make it brighter" (that also shows that you are paying attention), rather than "I like that picture".

- Children need to experience limits, correction and some guidance for responsibility. Help them grow gradually in responsibility. Children become more responsible when they are given responsibility so do not do for children what they can do for themselves. Instead take time to encourage them, ask questions and help them work out their own solutions. For your baby, instead of picking up a ball and handing it to your baby, encourage him/her to crawl to it. But don't push your child too hard and don't push them before they show readiness or interest because this can be very detrimental to them. The worst time for giving instruction o guidance is when we are under pressure, tired or our baby has just made a mistake. Instead it is important to set some quiet time aside for helping your child learn. Even occasional encouraging remarks are useful.

- Children pick up on how you are so it is important to be happy and relaxed. My book The Complete guide to Life on www.lulu.com/authourspotlightsarahjaneowen has some great tips on happiness. They say that happiness is to be grateful, and appreciative.

- Make time to slow down and pay your child positive attention when they are not expecting it. Also take time out for your own wellbeing so that you are happier and more relaxed around your child. Think positive thoughts and encourage yourself too.

- It is also important to look after and develop relationships around you, and encourage your child to develop their family relationships. Good support and relationships will help you and will also teach your child positive communication and social skills.

- Pay attention and listen to your child. Get down on the floor or lift them up so that you are at eye level with them. It is important to allow your child to feel safe and secure enough to except their feelings and express them freely. Even if your baby can't talk you can pick up clues from the noise, body language, eyes, face and hands. The more time you spend with your child and observe their behaviour the more you will recognise the clues and know how they are feeling. When you notice how they are feeling try and name it, this will help them to learn to understand and express their feelings. It is important to bring feelings out in the open so that they can be talked about and dealt with, rather than building up and being acted upon as outbursts.

- Sometimes children need to cry as crying releases the upset feelings, just hug them and say "there there" when they are upset rather than telling them that they mustn't cry. Instead say understand things. They may not know why they are upset and may fight with everyone, have a tantrum, push you away etc. just hold your child and after a short while the tears will come out. At first they may be unreasonable and blame unimportant things or blame you, don't argue with them and let the tears come. They may then explain what is wrong, if they don't try not to ask too many questions and just hold him/her loosely but firmly. If something is wrong they will tell you in their own time, or you could say 'teddy is sad, why is teddy sad' and coax it out of them. There may actually be nothing wrong they may just be tired. This is the same when your baby is tired, s/he will push you away, will try and sit up and get out of your arms, will then cry and will then fall asleep in your arms. You may also find that when you leave your child at nursery s/he may cry as you go but will then play fine, s/he may then cry when you come back and blame you and call you a bad mum. This will make you feel bad, this may just be his/her frustrations at being left (even though s/he was fine at nursery whilst you were gone and may have even enjoyed it. Once s/he gets used to being left and knowing you will come back and also gets used to the nursery, this frustration and upset will soon pass. Try and be strong and not take it too personally, it is just a process they have to go through. Children have to learn to deal with some stress; you can't stay at home with them and never leave them and protect them from everything. It's all part of the learning process, they will learn and develop and this is important for later on being able to deal with stress, interact with others and make decisions for themselves etc. if they always get their own way and live a protected life they will not be able to deal with their emotions or make decisions for themselves in later life. Sometimes you have to be cruel to be kind, like letting them cry and night, disciplining them and putting them to bed early. If you don't they will not sleep and will be grumpy and will find it hard to learn and develop. It is often harder for you than them, you just need to focus on why you are doing what you're doing and be strong. Eventually the child will release the tears and tell you what's wrong, then they will calm down and you can help them deal with their issues. This may take a while but it will be worth it in the long run, it will save hours, stress and more tantrums down the line. It is important to be sensitive to what is going on and make it safer and easier for your child to cry, do this by staying with them and give them good attention in the form of a hug, don't speak until the tears come so that you don't interrupt the crying, instead say soothing words and look at your child. The crying may get worst and may even turn into screaming as the child lets it all out, then your child will be calmer afterwards.

- Try play listening; This is where you join in and give them attention whilst they are playing, but be careful not to ask too many questions that may interrupt their play.

It is important to be respectful to your child and to positively communicate and listen to them. Here are some ways of listening;

1. **PAYING ATTENTION** Children can sense when your attention is genuine. Stop what you are doing occasionally and take time out to *notice* your child and to pay attention to what she is doing or saying – especially when she is not demanding attention. If children only get attention when misbehaving, you can expect more misbehaviour!

2. **EYE-LISTENING** Your eyes are usually more important than your ears for listening. It helps to get down to the same eye-level and see what your child is feeling. How do you feel when someone listens to you without looking at you?

3. **TOUCH-LISTENING** A parent touching, cuddling, or hugging him will often help a young child to express feelings more fully, including fears, affection, anger, tears, and lots of other feelings he can't put into words.

4. **PLAY-LISTENING** A child thrives on good attention – not just when she is upset. Play-listening means giving her good attention and a sense of being 'noticed,' partly by silently watching her play, and partly by saying what you see her doing: *"Mm, you've put the doll sitting up there."/ "Ah, you found the right place..."/ "Mm, you've used three of them now..."*

5. **SILENCE** You may have to bite your tongue in order not to argue or reason with an upset child. An upset child usually doesn't want to hear explanations, however reasonable – he may just want to be unreasonable, to scream and rage and say how unfair everything is! Only when he gets all that off his chest will he be open to listening to you.

6. **SINGLE WORDS** Sometimes, one or two words may be enough to give your child a sense that you are listening and that you understand. *"Mm..." "Oh..." "Really?..." "I see..." "Oh, no!..."* But a child will know if you are just going through the motions and not really listening.

7. **REPEATING** Repeating a few of your child's words, or summing up what she said, perhaps after a pause, can also let her know that you are paying attention and you understand. *"Oh, dear! Your lovely tricycle!..."/ "So that's what you're going to do today..."* That may encourage her to say more.

8. **REFLECTING FEELINGS** Noticing what your child is feeling and checking that out with him, can help him to become aware of his feelings, trust you, and become freer in himself: *"So you're **sad** it's broken..."/ "You're **angry** I won't let you do that..."/ "You sound **pleased** that granny's coming..."*

- You need to be calm and positive so that you can deal with your child in a calm and positive way and give off good vibes to them, in order to help them develop in a calm way.

reathe in and out slowly in order to relax breath in on the count of 4 and then out on the count of 4. you are relaxed and think positive thoughts you will act more positively, everything will feel easier and lmer, you will be in control, make less mistakes and appear calm and positive to those around you – they ill be more likely to react in a positive way to you. Your baby/child will be happier etc.

ou might like to think about what one thing would you like your child to learn from you, to be kind to others, be happy in life and how will you teach that?

- Teach children to be assertive and talk through their problems rather than hit back or tell tales.
- Talking to your children helps them to feel loved and secure and also helps them develop language skills.
- When speaking to your child try and use open statements and say things, such as, I wonder…
- 'I' messages such as, 'I feel sad when you behave like that' takes the accusations away from children and helps them develop empathy.
- Children naturally have personality traits, you can't change their personality but can encourage certain behavious and traits.
- If giving instructions you may need to break them down in order to simplify them. Rather than say tidy your room you may break it down into pick your clothes up, put your toys in the toy box etc.
- If you say something in an aggressive tone it makes you feel more aggressive. If you say things in a positive tone you are more likely to feel more positive.
- You may feel inpatient with your partner but remember men can't multi task and they may not have learnt yet how to look after the baby alone.
- The tone and level of your voice can have an impact. If you normally talk quietly when you do take your voice up a level you are more likely to get noticed where as if you always shout people around you will switch off and won't pay much attention. Therefore it is important not to nag or shout all the time and just do it when it is really needed in order to have more of an impact.
- There are many tools to be an effective parent. It is important to ignore some misbehaviours (not anything dangerous or really bad), avoid unnecessary confrontation, be encouraging, listen to your child, make time for guidance, allow a child to express themselves, give 'I' messages and speak in a positive manner and give positive focused attention to your child. You also need to provide disapline and set limits and give controlled choices as well as giving affection.

Disapline;

- Allowing children to make choices (within limits) and to live with the consequences is a respectful, effective method of disapline. For instance if your child doesn't want to tidy up say its your choice if you don't tidy up you can't have a story at bed time, then if your child doesn't tidy up don't give a story. You then need to follow through on this and put them to bed without a story. That way they will learn that their actions have consequences. This will then make them become more responsible.

- Children may struggle to find the limits and may push matters, if they hear an apologetic tone in your voice they may make further demands as they try to push the limit. You need to be firm but also speak positively without aggression.

- If you give consequences try to make these flow naturally out of the situation i.e. if you get up early then you need to go to bed early that night etc.

- 'Time out' can be useful but shouldn't be over used and should ony be used for more serious situations.

- It is a good idea to 'talk out' forms of disapline with children so that yiu are not reacting on the spot and they know what will happen in advance, they can adjust to the limits and know what the consequences of their actions will be. If you then follow them up they will know next time what not to do.

- Take time to prepare children for an activity is a good way to get their co-operation for instance have wind down time before bed, give a 5 minute warning before dinner or tidying up time so that they can ease themselves out of one activity and prepare for the next.

- Think ahead and prepare your child for the next activity but also be prepared yourself, for instance if you are going to the doctors, take toys to distract your child whilst s/he is in the waiting room.

- Disaplining children is about helping them to learn to become self disaplined, therefore you need to be self-disaplined and be in control of your temper, be prepared and organised and follow through on limits that you have set. You also need to be consistent so that your children know the boundries and don't get confused.

- By offering choices you can be flexible. For instance 'if you throw your bread on the floor I will take your food off you'. If your toddler then throws the bread on the floor and you take the meal away you can then say 'if you pick the bread up and put it in the bin you can have your meal back.'

Quality time;

- Sometimes you get so caught up in tidying up, doing chores etc. for your baby/child, you feel like you are on the go all the time and spend little time with them. They need your attention and will feel demanding. You need to let other things go and take time out to give your child quality time, full of positive attention. 'Relaxed' noticing time and playing together is important for developing and bonding. It will make you feel better to spend quality time with your child rather than being run ragged doing chores. Work out what is important and what can be left, be organised and have a set time for doing things and time for your child, be flexible as children may need extra time if they are unwell or feeling low etc.

- Children need you to give them hugs and attention and play with them.

- Set aside 'special time' to do what you child wants and play the games that they want to play.

- It is also important to look after yourself and have quality time for yourself and your partner.

Talking with your child;

- If your child is angry and says I hate you say well I love you, or do you want a hug.

- If you feel stressed or angry when they cry, think how they feel, they are being like that because they are upset and can't express themselves.

- Children who don't talk out feelings act out feelings

- Questions can interrupt children, they may find them pressurising, especially if they have been answering questions at school all day. They may need space to think so that they can sort things out in their own mind. If you give them space they will talk to you when they are ready to.
  Instead of asking "why don't you like that?" you could say "I wonder why you don't like x,y,z anymore." However sometimes you may need to ask questions such as "what do you think that you should do?" or "what do you want to do?".
  Let them deal with things and make their own decision, they have to learn how to do things for themselves, don't push your opinions or feelings onto them.

- Don't blow things up, if it's been dealt with at school, leave it there and don't interfere or keep going over it, let it be and don't get involved. If you weren't there you don't know the full story. You should also never fall out with parents, children will squabble and then be friends the next minute, so it's not worth you falling out as this will just make things worse.

- Don't use the words you in an aggressive tone instead use 'I' messages and take responsibility, i.e. "I'm sorry I feel cross but I have had a bad day and I feel upset when you argue". When you are upset you need to cool down before you can talk.

- Be respectful when you talk to children, small children can not understand or cope with raw adult emotions; they may feel scared and upset about your moods, when you are annoyed or impatient. If you dismiss them, they may feel rejected and may not trust you again. Threats like giving their teddy away are really scary for them and are not fair.

'I' messages are good because they attack the behaviour rather than the person. To use 'I' messages;
1. You say what you feel i.e. "I feel annoyed or upset that you kicked the ball at the window or I like it when you play nicely"
2. Or you say what you need "I need you to play quietly, because I need to rest"
3. Or you say what your position is "I want you to eat with a spoon/I can't allow you to do that".

- Be honest with your children, tell them the truth of what is going on and talk openly and share your emotions.

- Be positive and respectful when communicating with your child. Even messages that correct can be encouraging if you put something positive on the end, "I'm disappointed because you didn't tidy your toys today, I know that you can tidy them you did a great job of tidying them yesterday" or "I don't want you to play roughly with baby as it hurts her, although I know that you love her and don't mean to hurt her".

- As well as talking respectfully to children it's very important to talk to them, in a positive way, a lot.

Even a baby who can't understand words is remarkable sensitive to open and positive communication from a parent. Your baby does not need to understand the words s/he can sense your moods. Messages of love can have a calming, reassuring affect on a baby.

As children get older they still need the same positive attention, they need to be told how much we love them. Children go through so many stages in their tiny lives, learning to adjust to school etc. Childhood can be confusing and stressful so they need lots of love and reassurance to help them deal with it. They need chat, stories and positive attention. They like eye contact and stories. You could stop and ask them what they think part way through a story, in order to make it interactive. Children also love to hear what you were like at that age, it gives them a sense of their own roots.

It is important to talk to your children to help them form values and develop a sense of right and wrong. You have more influence on your children than anyone else and they take in more than you think, they will watch and copy you when you are not expecting it and if they see you smoking or swearing they will think that its okay to do that, even if you tell them it isn't. You therefore need to lead by example and not just talk the talk but also walk the walk.

If you argue in front of your children they may feel guilty. Try and take the guilt away and say "as you know we are different people and everyone argues, just like you argue with your brother/sister/friend, we still love each other sometimes we disagree; it's not your fault we argued before you were born too." My nephews used to get very upset when I argued with my sister; they told me off for upsetting their mummy. Until I pointed out that she was not just their mummy and she was my sister even before being their mummy. I pointed out that they argued with each other, that's what brothers and sisters do, but they still love each other and if someone else argued with their brother they would stick up for him. I explained that me and my sister were the same and even though we sometimes disagreed we loved each other very much and that are arguments were between us and were normal sister arguments. Not involving anyone else, once I explained this it made sense to them and they never minded if we argue again.

- If you have to be bossy/give your child an order at least justify why. If they understand why they need to do something, they will be more likely to do it i.e. you need to put your bike inside otherwise it will get rusty in the rain, then it will break and you won't have a bike because I can't afford to buy a new one.

Problem solving;

If your child is having trouble learning to do something i.e. tying a shoe lace;

- Be patient and set time aside when you are both not tired in order to guide your child.

- Be encouraging and tell your child to keep trying but try not to pressure him/her.

- Get a toy that your child can practise on when s/he isn't being watched, in his/her own time without any pressure.

If something is frightening your child;

- Smile and be reassuring, don't pull a face or show fear yourself.

- If your child is really small s/he may want cuddles, if s/he is older you may want to talk it through and reationalise the fear.

- If your child is misbehaving don't just scold them, say something like "I really love you but your behaviour is upsetting me" or "you are making me feel sad because you are doing x,y,z".

If you are struggling to get your child dressed in time for school;

- Give your child a clock and say get dressed by this time. Reward them if they are dressed early, say if you are dressed by this time we can have 10 mins cuddles or playtime before school.

Other things that you may find useful;

- Give your child a set cupboard in the kitchen with their plastic plates and cups that they can get out themselves without doing any damage. You can also put a basket with toy groceries that they can put away whilst you unpack your groceries.

- Don't just interrupt your child's play or bathtime instead give a 5 minute warning so that they can wind down first i.e. we are going to stop playing and put the toys away in 5 mins.

- **If your child is upset and they won't say why (they may not know why or may not know how to express it), get them to draw a picture of how their day was or how they are feeling etc. you can then use the picture to talk and to get a view of how they are feeling. For instance if they draw themselves far away from everyone it may indicate they felt left out at school etc.**

- **Let your child make choices but give them options i.e. instead of letting them pick what to wear and picking a jumper on a sunny day you could give them a choice between 3 T-shirts. That way they are making the decision but within your parameters.**

- Give your child chance to run around and expel their energy. Especially energetic boys, they need some 'run time' each day. Take them to the park, garden or soft play area. My son is 7 months old and I find if he has 20 mins in his jumperoo mid morning that is enough to calm him down before his mid morning nap.

- If your child is struggling to eat his/her dinner, rather than saying that they have to eat all their dinner say eat x amount more spoonfuls and then you can have your pudding.

- Swap bad words for silly words and then laugh at those silly words to take attention away from the 'bad' words and to stop your child using them.

- When buying a bike check where the pedals are, if they are too far forward your child may need longer legs to stretch to them.

- If children are fighting, try separating them or try and teach them to deal with it themselves i.e. if you can't agree on a TV channel the TV is going off.

- Try and ignore mis behaviour where you can and instead give positive attention, however children need dispaline too. Use the naughty step or chair but don't over use it because it gives attention and can be a bad thing if it is over used.

- **Each child is different and different things work, they also go through different stages and they react to your moods too. If something isn't working, walk away and calm down, think about what you are doing and try doing it a different way (always try and avoid engaging in an argument).** For instance with my son he usually crys for attention when I put him in his cot, if I leave him to cry for 5 mins he usually falls asleep, although sometimes I have to soothe him after 5 mins and put his dummy back in, then he falls asleep. One night when this wasn't working and his screaming was getting worse, rather than calmer I knew something wasn't right. He wouldn't settle so the controlled crying wasn't working. **I took a deep breath and thought things through and formulated an action plan in my mind.** I checked his nappy. I then decided to make him a bottle, in the meantime I would cuddle and rock him, if he fell asleep great, if not I would give him his bottle, if that didn't work I would give him a drop of water in case he was constipated and if that still didn't work I would give him gripe water. I also checked his room tempreture was okay. In the end he fell asleep in my arms. He was unsettled because we had been out all day and he didn't have a nap and was overtired. This slightly threw him out as he didn't want his milk the next morning so I mixed his milk in his Weetabix instead and tried to get his naps and his normal routine established as much as normal. **Sometimes you have to go through a process of elimination to find out whats wrong and what works. Often it is good to have a plan in your head of what you will do and in what order, that was when one thing doesn't work you won't get so frustrated and flustered because you will have already decided what you are doing next and can just focus on doing that.** *You will always find that you will feel calmer and more in control if you have a plan and know what you are doing.*

- **Sometimes you need to be flexible in your approach and follow your instinct, what normally works may not work one night. Your child may be uspset, or ill or going through a phase and may need cuddles or a different approach, you can't always follow the rule book to the letter.**

- Watch your body language because they pick up on your stress. When you are ignoring your child's bad behaviour they may see you watching them and see you are tense so pick up a book and pretend to read that.

- If there is a particular time that they find stressful i.e. meal time or bed time they may pick up on your stress of the anticipation to come and may play up. Therefore it maybe worth doing something fun and relaxing beforehand to get them in a better mood and to take the focus off what is about to happen.

- It is not always about what it's about – sometimes there is a deeper meaning. Someone may say something is a problem and may get upset over it but that may not be the real issue, there may be a deeper issue. Make sure that you have the right issue before you try fixing it. This is true when a child has tantrums, they may blame it on something trival. You need to get to the bottom of what the real issue is, understand the child and work out why they are feeling the way that they feel so that you can help them through it.

- Children copy you and exaggerate
- Behaviour breeds behaviour. Be respectful to your child in order to gain respect.
- Be positive and use positive language; reframe things to look on the positive side and avoid getting into a negative spiral.
- When children are tired they may play up more.
- Use positive language to say yes instead of no. Instead of no you can't play until you have tidied up say yes you can play as soon as you tidy up. Although it is important to say no when it is needed and not always give into children otherwise they will be spoilt and have tatrums etc.
- Avoid power struggles; give choices but follow through on conciquencs (threats). Don't et drawn into an argument, instead offer limited choices. Use cnciquences that you can carry out and don't don't give too far in the future otherwise theywill forget/won't understand.
- Think about what you tell them, how they say it and when. You need to protect children but not scare them i.e. bath incident.
- They lean from you so make sure that you are a good role model – do what you say and don't ask them to do anything that you wouldn't do.
- Life gets in the way no matter how good your intentions are you can't be perfect all the time, its okay to let your children see you disagree as long as you make up and they see this and you explain to them and reassure that you still love each other.
- Its important to keep communicating to your baby. Even if your baby can't speak or understand often they can understand words before they speak them and can undertand more than we think. It is also how they learn so the more we talk the better they will be at learing how to speak.
- Even new borns tell them when you are about to do something rather than just pick them up.
- Go over their teeth once they have cleaned them to make sure that they are clean enough.
- Step back and be objective
- Practise relaxing
- Children's centre – drop in days, support service and phone up advice and health visior.
- Practise relaxing- the less stressed you are the better you will handle child's tantrums. Think calmly – find relaxing techniques that work for you.
- Tantrums can be good – they let your baby get I out. Your child/baby will get fustratd because s/he can't yet deal with their emotions (they need to learn to which is why it is good if you can be in control of yours and be a good role model to show them – although this is not always possible). Just hold your child loosely, they may get worse, just let them get it out, then then they will be calm.
- If you are going to try introducing something new, doing a new technique such as controlled crying or gradual withdrawal it can be stressful so perhaps try it when your calm and have nothing else on i.e. not a week when you have a big meeting at work or during school holidays etc.

utting your child to bed;

- How you put your child to sleep in the day for naps is how they want to be put to sleep at night, this makes everything familiar and consistent, which is what babies and children need.

- Try to put them to sleep where you want them to sleep i.e. in their cot otherwise if they fall asleep in one place and then wake up elsewhere they may feel disorientated. Although sometimes it is necessary to move them into their cot from another place where they have fallen asleep (I would never wake a sleeping child unless absoloutely necessary).

- At bed time get your child settled in bed and then give him/her a story. If your child is old enough take some water up and say, no getting up after your story. If they keep getting up early tell them, and put them to bed early the next night. They will soon learn the conciquences of their actions. Let them know that you are there, go upstairs to reassure them and stand in the door way but try to avoid keep picking them up. You may need to try gradual withdraw techniques; this should be done gradually over a week.

<u>Notes from The secret of happy children – Steve Biddulph; adapted into my version with my own thoughts and ideas added in.</u>

Using certain patterns of speech we may reach the unconscious minds of our children, similar to hypnosis. Be aware of 'unconscious hypnosis' what you say may influence your child. Children ask questions, they want to know who they are, to identify themselves in the world. By saying 'You....' You are influencing them so if you keep using negative phrases and saying "you are lazy" they may be influenced by this and believe that they are lazy and then not bother trying. i.e. If you say 'you are clumsy' the child might get nervous and become clumsy. If you say 'you are a pest' the child may feel rejected and start pestering you for attention. Because you are the adult they will assume that you are right, they will believe what you say and it will affect them in later life. Therefore it is important to give good positive messages and reassurance. Be careful not to confuse them, it is not just the words that you say it is how you say them, the non verbal factors carry more weight.

Research shows that everything every sight, smell, etc. is stored in your brain, you might not recall it but it is there, stored in the brain, unconsciously influencing you. It can also be argued that perhaps the earliest memories are the most influential.

There are also 2 parts to our hearing our conscious hearing and our unconscious hearing. As well as the conscious things that you are listening to your brain also filters every other noise that is in ear shot. It picks out key words, such as your name. This is why you may notice someone in the background talking about you, also mums can hear their baby cry, even when they are asleep but sleep through much louder noises. Bear this in mind with your child, s/he is probably taking in more than you realise, perhaps even in his/her sleep. So think about what you say and how it might effect your child. Children may know more than you think they do but keep it to themselves, they maybe more affected by things going on than you realise.

Positive hearing is good for healing. You can say positive things to your child either directly or indirectly, these positive messages should help them with the healing process.

It's important to tell them how much you care, even as they get older. If they get embarrassed with you telling them directly then you can be indirect, tell other people within their earshot.

Anchoring – scientists have discovered that messages are taken in deeper in a persons mind if they are accompanied by other signals that reinforce it i.e. tone of voice and body language and how you make a person feel will anchor the message. If you use a cross voice and intimidating body language it will have a negative effect, even if you are giving a positive message. Therefore it is not just important to think about what you say, but how you say it.

Babies and children need 'love' to survive and thrive as much as they need food and water.

- frequent skin to skin contact from 2 or 3 special people.
- Movement of a gentle but robust kind, such as carrying around, bouncing on the knee etc.
- Eye contact, smiling and a colourful, lively environment, sounds such as singing, talking, cooing etc.

Music and dance, nature and fun etc. are all important for children but so is hope. Be encouraging and have a positive outlook on life so that they can have hope.

Throughout life we still need love and affection, often the amount we get will rise and fall, from falling after bottle or breast feeding stops, to falling more during teenage years. It is important to remember that even as children get older and become young adults, or even adults they still need love and affection from their parents. Love and affection helps keep us feeling safe and lets our brain develop, it leads to well adjusted happy individuals who can love others, to keep up the positive cycle.

Human brains have to have something interesting to do to keep them occupied and happy. This also helps the brain grow and develop. Without this they will start misbehaving.

Talking and communication is important – explain things to them and tell them everything you are doing. This will help with their intelligence levels.

Children will do anything for attention, even if it is negative attention i.e. being told off. This is because any stimulation or excitement is better than none, even if it's somewhat painful.

Some tantrums are natural and can be because they are testing the boundaries (children need limits), because they are frustrated and can't communicate what they want or because they want attention;

- give positive attention to reduce the likelihood of tantrums
- don't give attention to tantrums
- teach your child to communicate and how to express their needs
- Except that some tantrums are inevitable and can't be avoided, try to relax and don't worry about them staring, they have all had tantrums themselves when they were young and its their ignorance if they are going to stare.

When my baby (at 14 months has his, they last approx 30 sec to a minute so I just look a way and then give him a hug, or help him with his toy, once he has stopped).

Children play up because;

- they are bored
- they feel unwanted
- because it gets them noticed
- and when they are older, to fit in with their peers and be accepted in certain groups (humans are social creatures and like to belong to groups and feel that they have a place in the world). If you help to give them meaning, purpose and direction in their life – give them affection but also give them purpose for themselves outside the family i.e. by going to scouts, playing a music instrument, take up sport, do volunteering etc. they will be less likely to be influenced by negative peer pressure. Teach them to be strong, to know what's right from wrong and to stand up for themselves against negative influences etc.

Take time out to spend with your kids doing fun things and ensure that they get lots of positive attention. Do things with your kids that you feel relaxed about and don't actually expect to achieve anything i.e. a walk may take longer as your child gets side tracked and wants to explore. Set some time aside to go on a walk and not get stressed, let your child explore etc. Its not the destination but the journey that counts.

Actively listen to your child, show an interest and ask questions and help children to be able to talk to you and work through problems so that you can find out what the real issue actually is and assist them to come up with their own remedies. Being able to think for themselves and problem solve, rather than just telling them what to do will really help them in later life, its an important skill.

Dealing with children's issues and emotions

Emotions are important, as long as they don't get out of control. We need a certain amount of all of our emotions but need to be able to deal with them, otherwise they may take over.

- Anger keeps us freer (otherwise we would let people walk all over us)
- Fear keeps us safe
- Sadness keeps us in contact with people and the world

Children may try it on and fake/imitate emotions to get attention psychotherapists refer to this as 'racket' feelings. These are as follows;

Anger: tantrum

Sadness; Sulking

Fear; Shyness

Shyness	Make your child introduce themselves and say hello and make eye contact, then move on but don't push the issue if your child really doesn't want to. Don't make an issue out of their shyness and don't draw attention to it, otherwise they may use it as a way of attention seeking and then may become shyer as it then becomes a habit.
Anger	Teach your child to use words instead of actions to express anger. Let them know that their feelings are heard and accepted but this may not change things. Teach them that direct hitting is not acceptable. Help children to say what they do want in a positive way, rather than whining about what they don't want. Show them by leading by example.
Fear	It is natural to feel fearful and some fear is good but it shouldn't take over. 3 and 4 year old children often think about the world around them and start to get concerns (the fearful 4s). Teach them that its good to be fearful of strangers etc. but reassure them that the chance of some realistic fears happening are remote. If the fear is unrealistic i.e. monsters under the bed tell them they needn't worry. Talk through the fears and if there are lots of fears there maybe an underlying issue so discuss the fears with your child and try to get to the bottom of them. It might be a good idea to get to them professional support, such as; KIDSCAPE personal safety training.
Tantrums	1. calm yourself 2. help your child; sit or stand close to them, if you can hold or comfort them, don't yell or smack them as this will make it worse.

	3. you may find it a good idea to take them into a quiet corner or room etc. 4. don't give in, this will only lead to more tantrums in the future. 5. talk it through with them once they have calmed down. 6. prevention is better than cure – tantrums may occur when you are both overloaded ie hungry, tired etc. your child can't keep up the pace and cope with the stress that we put ourselves under. Try to recognise the signs and deal with them before they result in a tantrum ie slow down, listen to your child, get them something to eat etc. There maybe something a child has to do to be secure i.e. fasten their own seat belt (this is ok if you then check it), they may need a set bedtime and routine and lack of this may lead to tantrums.
Sulks	This is often to get attention and is usually when they need attention because they are sad about something. Don't give attention to the sulk instead get them to identify the problem and then give them positive attention by trying to deal with it together i.e. say to them I care about you and want to help, have a think about what is upsetting you or what you think you want and then come and let me know (when they let you know you can give a hug, say well done and then discuss what they can have or how the problem can be resolved – this helps problem solving skills).
Whining	Use direct eye contact and ask them to use a normal voice. Demonstrate a more positive voice and every time they whine ask them to speak in a more positive voice.

When kids are pushing you to the limit don't get stressed, just relax and softly say no.

Keep energy levels high by eating foods with slow release energy ie not high sugars and eat before you need it ie have a big breakfast and healthy snacks throughout the day.

Keeping children out of crime;

Young males seem to get into trouble more mainly due to boredom and showing off to their peers. This tends to be the case in single parent families, where there is no male role model / father figure. Youth interventions such as youth clubs help. A lot of it is also down to peer pressure and is part of growing and finding their way. Youths are easily influenced and this makes them vulnerable to become exploited into joining in with crime and also they may be vulnerable to drug pushers. Especially if they have low self esteem and don't have a solid support network at home. It is therefore important to provide a secure home with love and disapline and to find them posititve activites to do so that they don't get bored and get into a 'bad crowd'.

The office of national statistics (using home office figures states); *'As with victims of overall violent crime, offenders were most likely to be male and aged between 16 and 24.'* Nationally youth crime is an issue that needs to be addressed. Young men are obviously very vulnerable to becoming victims of crime, or offenders of crime.

'At the individual level, risk factors for offending and victimization include biological and personal factors that may lead to early aggressive behaviour or serious substance abuse, for example. Risk factors connected with relationships include family characteristics such as harsh or erratic parenting, family conflict and violence and abuse, family circumstances such as poverty and isolation, and relationships with friends and peers that can lead to risk-taking and law breaking.' - Handbook on the crime prevention guidelines by United Nations Office on Drugs and Crime.

'The minimum age of criminal responsibility in England and Wales is 10. The UK has high rates of youth crime and more young people in custody than any other European country (besides Turkey).1 The number of recorded offences committed by those under 18 in 2007/8 was 277,986.2 The past 15 years have seen more young people drawn into the youth justice system, however, the year to November 2009 saw a 21.6% reduction in first time entrants to the criminal justice system3. According to the MoJ the proven rate of reoffending for juvenile offenders within a year of sentencing is 37%.4 Its statistics show that reoffending rates range widely between prisons and that those who have served a short-term sentence reoffend at a higher rate. The cost of keeping a young person in a young offenders institution was £34,000 in 2008/9.5 The cost of dealing with young offenders to the criminal justice services 2008/9 was £4 billion a year.6 Poverty and social disadvantage are closely related to offending.7 They are strongly related to whether young people become entangled in the criminal justice system and to getting caught. Once warned or charged young people are more likely to be arrested again than those who commit similar offences, but were unknown to the police.8 25% of boys and 40% of girls in custody say they have experienced violence at home.9 Of prisoners aged 16-20, around 85% show signs of a personality disorder, 10% of a psychotic illness. In 2007, there were over 1,000 self-harm incidents among 15 to 17 year olds.10 Boys in prison aged 15-17 are 18 times more likely to kill themselves than in the community: 30 children have died in custody since 1990.11

1 Independent Commission on Youth Crime and Antisocial Behaviour. Responding to Youth Crime and Antisocial Behaviour, Key Trends. 2010.
2 Youth Justice Annual Workload Data 2007/08. YJB 2009.
3 Independent Commission on Youth Crime and Antisocial Behaviour. Op cit.
4 MoJ, Compendium of reoffending statistics and analysis. MoJ 2010.
5 Hansard, 2 March 2010.
6 Independent Commission on Youth Crime and Antisocial Behaviour. Op cit.

7 Rutter, M. 'Causes of Offending and Antisocial Behaviour.' In D.J. Smith (ed.) A New Response to Youth Crime: Willan 2010.
8 Independent Commission on Youth Crime and Antisocial Behaviour. Op cit.
9 Cites the Youth Justice Board. http://www.madeleinemoonmp.com/53610db7-61b1-4b14-6524-5244d482ac88
10 Centre for Social Justice, Breakthrough Britain: Youth Justice. CSJ 2007.
11 Ibid '

Taken from 'User Voice' charity publication - Your voice, whats your story; Young offenders' insights into tackLing
- youth crime and its causes

Years ago there was a big sense of community and everyone would help raise children. Often now with both parents working not all children get the necessary attention. Although some parents that work will have a good support network with grandparents helping out. There is often, in some areas, less of a sense of community with people renting property and the population is more transient. This means people don't look out for each other in the way they used to, there may be less role models in the area etc. If people are moving around with their family then they do not integrate into the community and will miss building connections within the community and meeting good role models.

Once someone offends that are more likely to re-offend. They may be taken away from their family/support network, especially if they are in custody and they will be more vulnerable and will be at the same time exposed to other criminals who may try and recruit them into their criminal activities.

There is some overlap between youth crime and anti social behaviour and those who commit anti social behaviour are likely to go on and commit youth crime.

Youths are more at risk of anti social behaviour (both of becoming victims and offenders). They are also more vulnerable if they have mental illness. According to the study text there is an increase in poor mental health in children and young people over the last 30 years, particularly among the socially disadvantaged.

Those youths who are socially excluded are also more at risk (10% more likely to become a victim of crime).

According to the study text the following risk factors make a youth more likely to commit anti social behaviour;

- Family issues i.e. parent criminality, poor parent supervision and lack of discipline, family conflict, low family income/social isolation.

- School issues i.e. lack of commitment to school (truancy and exclusion), disruptive behaviour, bullying, low achievement, school disorganisation.

- Individual/peer; lack of social network, early involvement in problem behaviour, peer involvement in bad behaviour i.e. getting involved in a 'bad crowd' who may influence that person (also in groups people encourage each other to do things that they would not normally do on their own). Also a high proportion of unsupervised time spent with peers.

- Early adulthood; lack of skills or qualifications, unemployment or low income, homelessness.

- Community; community disorganisation, availability of drugs, opportunity for crime, high percentage of children in the community

The following chart shows risk factors that make a youth more likely to commit anti social behaviour (taken from the study house manual);

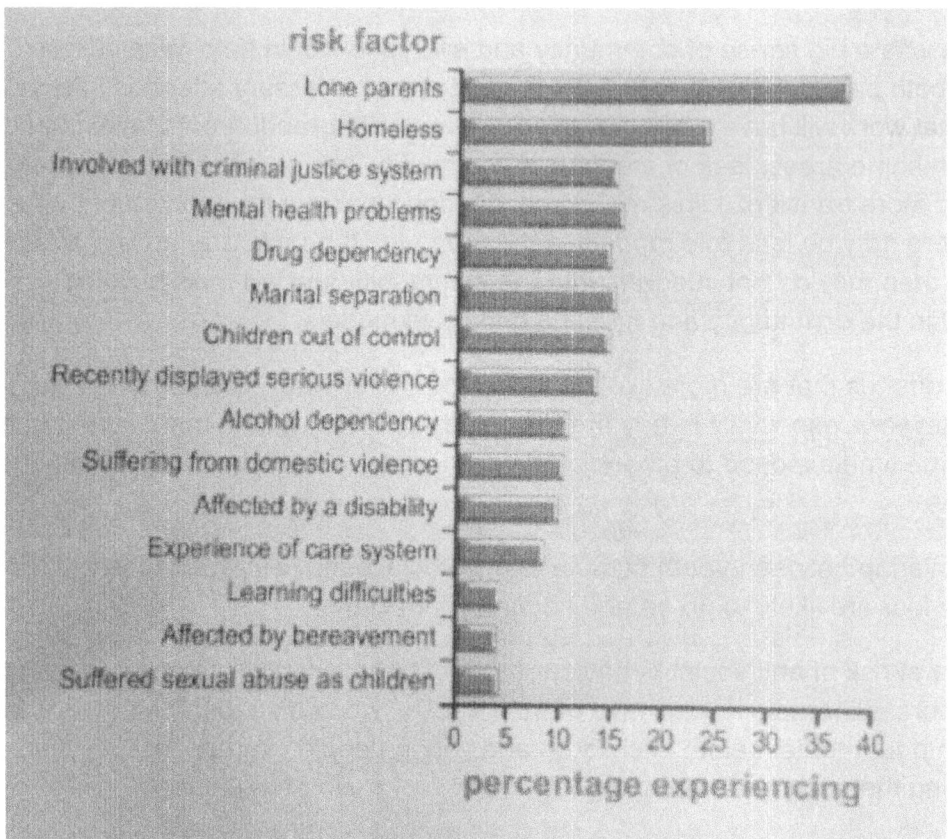

As you can see from this the biggest risk factor in youths committing anti-social behaviour (and possibly going on to commit more serious crime) is lone parenting.

Also in the aforementioned report 'User Voice charity publication - Your voice, what's your story; Young offenders' insights into tackling' one of the offenders interviewed sited his reasons for offending as; being bullied at school, no father/role model, no-one to talk to / social exclusion.

School exclusion, lack of employment and qualifications and drugs and alcohol misuse seem to be high factors. Poor neighbourhoods have a high number of problems that are drugs and alcohol related.

The United Nations Office on Drugs and Crime in the Handbook on the crime prevention guidelines, Making them work identified risk factors in crime/offending in general (irrespective of age) as follows;

These underlying or causal factors are often termed risk factors.[8] They include global changes and trends that affect the social and economic conditions of regions and countries; factors affecting individual countries and local environments and communities; those relating to the family and close relationships; and those that affect individuals. Figure I illustrates the multifaceted nature of the factors influencing crime and violence:

Figure I. Factors influencing the risks of crime and violence[a]

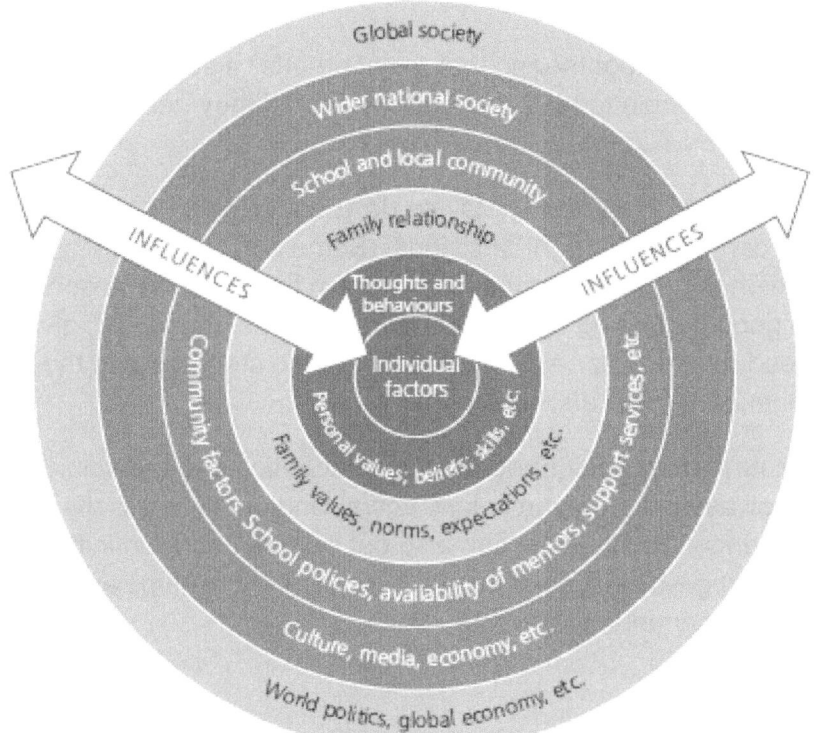

[a]Adapted from Ann Masten and Jenifer Powell, "A resiliency framework for research, policy and practice:" in *Resilience and Vulnerability: Adaptation in the Context of Childhood Adversities*, Suniya Luthar, ed. (Cambridge, Cambridge University Press, 2003), pp. 1-29. The World Health Organization ecological model for understanding violence similarly stresses societal, community, relationship and individual factors (see Etienne G. Krug and others, eds., *World Report on Violence and Health* (Geneva, World Health Organization, 2002), p. 12).

[8]"Risk factors" is a term used especially in the area of developmental prevention, to refer to characteristics affecting individuals or crime patterns. It is used here in a wider sense.

It is important that children have love and security at home, someone to talk to but also they need discipline. They need a secure home. They need someone that they can talk to and discuss concerns with. They need a 'suitable guardian' (as identified in Routine Activity Theory (RAT) developed by criminologists Lawrence Cohen and Marcus Felson, states that for a predatory crime to occur, one factor is the lack of a suitable guardian to prevent the crime from happening).

It is important that if they do not have a role model/suitable guardian at home that someone from within their community can step in and fulfil that role. Everyone in the community has a responsibility to help people in the community around them.

If you see a child is not being cared for you need to report this and if you see a crime you need to report this too, so that the authorities can step in and put measures in place to offer support where it is needed. It is important to report crime so that it is recorded and therefore initiatives to deal with the crime can be instigated.

You may also be able to support neighbouring parents, who may need some help, to take the strain off of them and support them in sorting their lives out so that they can offer the care and support that their children need.

It is a good idea for parents to get together so that they can offer a support network for each other. It is also important for people to take responsibility and if they need help, to seek out that help.

Schools and teachers also have a big part to play as do youth groups. A good education is important so that youths can make the right decisions. Some sort of education around drugs, alcohol and crime, in my opinion should take place in the schools. A good education will also give children a good grounding and help them aim towards a career, giving them a sense of purpose. A good role models i.e. youth leaders etc to steer them in the right direction / positively influence them is also important.

It is important for neighbours to help neighbours but also charities and the voluntary sector have a role to play, as well as landlords particularly social landlords (especially because they deal with vulnerable residents). Businesses can also get involved and run initiatives to help youths in their area by offering work experience, jobs and apprenticeships and also be setting up/getting involved in community projects.

The nature - nurture debate

The nature nurture debate is all about are we born a certain way with certain skills and personalities i.e. a tendency towards violent or unkind behaviour (nature), or is it nurture i.e. the way we are brought up, the environment we are in and the experiences that we are exposed to i.e. how much of our skills, ability and personality is innate and how much has to be learnt.

The phrase "nature and nurture" in its modern sense was coined by the English Victorian polymath Francis Galton in discussion of the influence of heredity and environment on social advancement, although the terms had been used previously, for example by Shakespeare and others. *English Men of Science: Their Nature and Nurture - Sir Francis Galton - Google Boeken*. Books.google.com. Retrieved 2013-12-23. His nature/nurture debate concerns the extent to which particular aspects of behaviour are a product of either inherited (i.e. genetic) or acquired (i.e. learned) characteristics.

It is a known fact that certain physical characteristics are biologically determined by genetic inheritance. These are usually physical factors. In terms of personality and characteristic it is still unclear what is inherited and what is learnt, hence the nature - nurture debate continues.

Babies are born with several innate reflexes, including the rooting reflex and the moro reflex. Binns (1965) demonstrated that certain characteristics are innate. He studied babies less than 5 days old and found clear difference in babies' reactions to suddenly being disturbed. - 'Psychology' study house text April 2012 edition 2012/01 p183.

Twin studies of very helpful in this debate, since identical twins have the same DNA, or genetic makeup. It is therefore interesting to see if they are raised the same and have similar or different personalities or if they are raised differently and have similar or different personalities. However despite many studies being conducted, the debate still remains.

Examples of research on both sides of the debate are as follows;

'An extreme nature positions in psychology include Bowlby's (1969) theory of attachment, which views the bond between mother and child as being an innate process that ensures survival. Likewise, Chomsky (1965) proposed language is gained through the use of an innate language acquisition device. Another example of nature is Freud's theory of aggression as being an innate drive (called thanatos).
In contrast Bandura's (1977) social learning theory states that aggression is a learnt from the environment through observation and imitation. This is seen in his famous bobo doll experiment (Bandura, 1961). Also Skinner (1957) believed that language is learnt from other people via behavior shaping techniques.
In practice hardly anyone today accepts either of the extreme positions. There are simply too many "facts" on both sides of the argument which are inconsistent with an "all or nothing" view. So instead of asking whether child development is down to nature or nurture the question has been reformulated as "How much?" That is to say, given that heredity and environment both influence the person we become, which is the more important?
This question was first framed by Francis Galton in the late 19th century. Galton (himself a relative of Charles Darwin) was convinced that intellectual ability was largely inherited and that the tendency for "genius" to run in families was the outcome of a natural superiority.

This view has cropped up time and again in the history of psychology and has stimulated much of the research into intelligence testing (particularly on separated twins and adopted children). A modern proponent is the American psychologist Arthur Jenson. Finding that the average I.Q. scores of black Americans were significantly lower than whites he went on to argue that genetic factors were mainly responsible – even going so far as to suggest that intelligence is 80% inherited.

The storm of controversy that developed around Jenson's claims was not mainly due to logical and empirical weaknesses in his argument. It was more to do with the social and political implications that are often drawn from research that claims to demonstrate natural inequalities between social groups.

Galton himself in 1883 suggested that human society could be improved by "better breeding". In the 1920's the American Eugenics Society campaigned for the sterilization of men and women in psychiatric hospitals. Today in Britain many believe that the immigration policies are designed to discriminate against Black and Asian ethnic groups. However the most chilling of all implications drawn from this view of the natural superiority of one race over another took place in the concentration camps of Nazi Germany.

For many environmentalists there is a barely disguised right wing agenda behind the work of the behavioral geneticists. In their view part of the difference in the I.Q. scores of different ethnic groups is due to in built biases in the methods of testing. More fundamentally they believe that differences in intellectual ability are a product of social inequalities in access to material resources and opportunities. To put it simply children brought up in the ghetto tend to score lower on tests because they are denied the same life chances as more privileged members of society.

Now we can see why the nature-nurture debate has become such a hotly contested issue. What begins as an attempt to understand the causes of behavioral differences often develops into a politically motivated dispute about distributive justice and power in society. What's more this doesn't only apply to the debate over I.Q. It is equally relevant to the psychology of sex and gender where the question of how much of the (alleged) differences in male and female behavior is due to biology and how much to culture is just as controversial.

However in recent years there has been a growing realization that the question of "how much" behavior is due to heredity and "how much" to environment may itself be the wrong question. Take intelligence as an example. Like almost all types of human behavior it is a complex, many-sided phenomenon which reveals itself (or not!) in a great variety of ways. The "how much" question assumes that the variables can all be expressed numerically and that the issue can be resolved in a quantitative manner. The reality is that nature and culture interact in a host of qualitatively different ways.

This realization is especially important given the recent advances in genetics. The Human Genome Project for example has stimulated enormous interest in tracing types of behavior to particular strands of DNA located on specific chromosomes. Newspaper reports announce that scientists are on the verge of discovering (or have already discovered) the gene for criminality, for alcoholism or the "gay gene".

If these advances are not to be abused then there will need to be a more general understanding of the fact that biology interacts with both the cultural context and the personal choices that people make about how they want to live their lives. There is no neat and simple way of unraveling these qualitatively different and reciprocal influences on human behavior.'

- http://www.simplypsychology.org/naturevsnurture.html 5th September 2012.

I believe that certain personality traits are inherited i.e. a tendency to be a certain way but they are shaped by our environment, our up brining, our experiences and our peers. Someone may for instance have an addictive personality and a tendency to try new things but with a stable upbringing and good social environment may not ever experience substance misuse. But in order for someone to become addicted to substances they must have an innate inbuilt tendency to be easily led and to be influenced to trying the drugs in the first place. The reason I believe this is that you may have 2 people with bad experiences yet one person will let this get them down and may turn to drugs and crime, where as another person may very determined to succeed and will turn their life around, despite their previous experiences, a lot of this is to do with their innate personality. I do however believe that our up bring, social circle, experiences and learning has the most influence on us. In my experience people tend to be influenced by their peers and youngsters are often influenced by the 'bad crowd' they are in. For my work and my criminology course and crime statistics it is apparent that people who commit violent crimes are often those that have been exposed to violence themselves in the past. I think with a good role model young people can be influenced to act in a positive way. This is something that I have seen firsthand from my own experience as army cadet instructor.

The diagram below shows the different approaches tof psychology and how they relate to nature vs nurture.

- http://www.simplypsychology.org/naturevsnurture.html 5th September 2014.

How a baby forms relationships and how the attachment with the mother influences a baby

A baby learns that if it behaves a certain way it gets a response from the outside world, mainly from its mother. There is therefore a mutual exchange of interactions, often referred to as reciprocal behaviour.

Infants learn from their parents how to socially interact. One of the first ways in which infants initiate social interaction is by smiling.

From reciprocal behaviour infants develop attachments to their parents/care-givers, these attachments are their early form of relationships, and they learn how to socialise and form relationships with others as they grow up, based on these early attachments, because reciprocal behaviour and attachments to care givers are their earliest form of / first experiences of 'socialisation'. It form the basis for them to build social skills on and is their base for building later relationships on (as per transfer learning).

'Researchers Rudolph Schaffer and Peggy Emerson analyzed the number of attachment relationships that infants form in a longitudinal study with 60 infants. The infants were observed every four weeks during the first year of life, and then once again at 18 months. Based upon their observations, Schaffer and Emerson outlined four distinct phases of attachment.

1. *Pre-attachment Stage: From birth to three months, infants do not show any particular attachment to a specific caregiver. The infant's signals such as crying and fussing naturally attract the attention of the caregiver, and the baby's positive responses encourage the caregiver to remain close.*
2. *Indiscriminate Attachment: From around six weeks of age to seven months, infants begin to show preferences for primary and secondary caregivers. During this phase, infants begin to develop a feeling of trust that the caregiver will respond to their needs. While they will still accept care from other people, they become much better at distinguishing between familiar and unfamiliar people as they approach seven months of age. They also respond more positively to the primary caregiver.*
3. *Discriminate Attachment: At this point, from about seven to eleven months of age, infants show a strong attachment and preference for one specific individual. They will protest when separated from the primary attachment figure (separation anxiety), and begin to display anxiety around strangers (stranger anxiety).*
4. *Multiple Attachments: After approximately nine months of age, children begin to form strong emotional bonds with other caregivers beyond the primary attachment figure. This often includes the father, older siblings, and grandparents.*

While this process may seem straightforward, there are a number of different factors that can influence how and when attachments develop. First is the opportunity for attachment. Children that do not have a primary care figure, such as those raised in orphanages, may fail to develop the sense of trust needed to form an attachment. Second, the quality of care-giving is a vital factor. When caregivers respond quickly and consistently, children learn that they can depend on the people who are responsible for their care, which is the essential foundation for attachment.

Problems with Attachment

What happens to children who do not form secure attachments? Research suggests that failure to form secure attachments early in life can have a negative impact on behavior in later childhood and throughout the life. Children diagnosed with oppositional-defiant disorder (ODD), conduct disorder (CD) or post-traumatic stress disorder (PTSD) frequently display attachment problems, possibly due to early abuse, neglect or trauma. Clinicians suggest that children adopted after the age of six months have a higher risk of attachment problems.

While attachment styles displayed in adulthood are not necessarily the same as those seen in infancy, research indicates that early attachments can have a serious impact on later relationships. For example, those who are securely attached in childhood tend to have good self-esteem, strong romantic relationships and the ability to self-disclose to others. As adults, they tend to have healthy, happy and lasting relationships. For more information, see this article on attachment styles.'

- http://psychology.about.com/od/loveandattraction/a/attachment01.htm (5 September 2014), Ainsworth, M. D. S., Blehar, M. C., Waters, E., & Wall, S. (1978). *Patterns of attachment: A psychological study of the strange situation.* Hillsdale, NJ: Erlbaum. / Bowlby J. (1969). *Attachment. Attachment and loss: Vol. 1. Loss.* New York: Basic Books. / Schaffer, H. R. & Emerson, P. E. (1964). The development of social attachments in infancy. *Monographs of the Society for Research in Child Development, 29,* 94.

'Researchers have found that attachment patterns established early in life can lead to a number of outcomes. For example, children who are securely attached as infants tend to develop stronger self-esteem and better self-reliance as they grow older. These children also tend to be more independent, perform better in school, have successful social relationships, and experience less depression and anxiety.'

- http://psychology.about.com/od/loveandattraction/a/attachment01.htm 5th September 2014.

The change in infants social behaviour is related to their development of specific attachments (this seems to be the case the world over).

'According to psychologist Albert Bandura, reciprocal determinism is a model composed of three factors that influence behavior: the environment, the individual, and the behavior itself. Essentially, Bandura believes that an individual's behavior influences and is influenced by both the social world and personal characteristics.

The environmental component is made up of the physical surroundings around the individual that contain potentially reinforcing stimuli, including people who are present (or absent). The environment influences the intensity and frequency of the behavior, just as the behavior itself can have an impact on the environment.

The individual component includes all the characteristics that have been rewarded in the past. Personality and cognitive factors play an important part in how a person behaves, including all of the individual's expectations, beliefs, and unique personality characteristics.

And finally, the behavior itself is something that may or may not be reinforced at any given time or situation'. - By Kendra Cherry, About.com Guide

'Research indicates that the development of a child's behavior is strongly influenced by how well his or her family functions. It is during this time that children are dependent upon adults to meet their needs that their concept of the importance of family develops.' - Family Influences on the Development of a Child's Behavior, Kwalombota Mahalihali
The Master's College (http://www.kon.org/urc/v5/mahalihali.html 5 September 2014)

'Research has suggested that socialization is not a unidirectional phenomenon. In reciprocal socialization parents socialize children and children in turn socialize parents. Children act as socializing agents to parents in a most basic sense as parents must be socialized to the parent role—infants demand certain care and have fundamental needs of their parents. In addition, various outside influences act on children in ways that affect parents and change their behaviors as well. For example, schooling may affect parental behaviors by placing increasing demands on children which parents must accommodate. In addition, increasing peer influences may require parents to modify strategies and behaviors in interacting with their child. Individual characteristics of children, such as their levels of attractiveness and temperaments, may also be factors in the socialization of parents. Newly arrived immigrant families provide a clear example of reciprocal socialization. Parents in these families may learn much of the new country's language and culture from their children as the children have more opportunities to learn (e.g., in school) and are more able to learn new expected roles. In this way, children socialize parents to new roles, and parents socialize children in basic behaviors the parent and other agents of socialization, schools and media included.*'*

- http://www.simplypsychology.org/naturevsnurture.html 5th September 2014.

Harlow and his collegues showed through their experiments with monkeys that not just food and care was needed but also comfort and that mokeys who were separated from their mothers, but allowed to play with their peers (other monkeys of the same age) grew up more normally than those who didn't have the same social interaction.

Bowlby, in his report to The World Health Organisation in 1951 stated that maternal separation has adverse affects on a child and that 'women going to work with children under three, or even five years put them at serious risk. Bowlby concluded that a mothers love in infancy and childhood is as important for mental health as vitamins and proteins are for physical health. He also found that long periods of sepeaton from a mother (i.e. for 6 months at a time, within the first 5 years of life) leads to delinquency. Yarrow in 1961 confirmed that there is a strong relationship between broken homes and delinquency. Bowlby also emphasised the importance of continuity in relationships.

In 1974 Tizard and Rees found that children who are not often talked to read to and are not given a variety of stimulation tend to be retarded whatever the social setting.

Rheingold and Samuels (1963) found that children in hospital, with their mothers present fretted less if they also had toys.

Source; 'Psychology' study house text April 2012 edition 2012/01

<u>**Learning influences on a baby/child**</u>

What is meant by latent learning?

'Latent learning is a form of <u>learning</u> that is not immediately expressed in an overt response; it occurs without any obvious reinforcement of the behaviour or associations that are learned. Interest in latent learning arose largely because the phenomenon seemed to conflict with the widely held view that reinforcement was necessary for learning to occur.' - Psychology In Perspective (2nd ed. ed.). New York: Longman. <u>ISBN</u> <u>0-673-98314-5</u>.

This means that the learning is present and capable of being activated, although not currently visible. Imitative behaviour may not show up straight away but may have a delayed effect on the subject For instance we may see a violent film and not go out and act violently at that given moment however at a later point, in a situation which bears some resemblance, we may be more inclined to behave in a violent manner.

'In a classic study by <u>Edward C. Tolman</u>, three groups of rats were placed in <u>mazes</u> and their <u>behavior</u> observed each day for more than two weeks. The rats in Group 1 always found food at the end of the maze; the rats in Group 2 never found food; and the rats in Group 3 found no food for 10 days, but then received food on the eleventh. The Group 1 rats quickly learned to rush to the end of the maze; Group 2 rats wandered in the maze but did not preferentially go to the end. Group 3 acted the same as the Group 2 rats until food was introduced on Day 11; then they quickly learned to run to the end of the maze and did as well as the Group 1 rats by the next day. This showed that the Group 3 rats had learned about the organisation of the maze, but without the reinforcement of food. Until this study, it was largely believed that reinforcement was necessary for animals to learn such tasks.' - Tolman, E.C.; C.H. Honzik (1930). ""Insight" in Rats". *University of California Publications in Psychology*.

It was concluded that although the rats may have not been making progress in days 1-10, they were actually storing information, and their 'latent learning' gave them a head start later on. From this Tolman (1932) developed the idea of cognitive maps (rough models that humans and animals hold in their minds).

What is meant by transfer learning?

Transfer learning occurs when we build on old learning experiences. The old learning gives us a head start when we have to learn something new / solve a new problem, it may even help us with apparently unrelated tasks (this is all positive transfer). However equally, as well as past experience helping us (positive transfer) the past learning may get in the way and hinder us (negative transfer).

What is meant by insight learning?

Imitation and latent learning are examples of cognitive forms of learning i.e. they require remembering and thinking, rather than just linking a stimulus to a response (such as classical conditioning operant conditioning, which are examples of basic linking learning).

Insight learning is another form of cognitive learning, which involves us learning by making a sudden discovery of its underlying principals i.e. a 'Eureka' moment.

A good example of this is Kohler's ape experiment. Wolfgang Kohler was a German psychologist, who was studying the behaviour of apes in the 1920.

'In his experiment, Kohler hung a piece of fruit just out of the reach of each chimp. He then provided the chimps with either two sticks or three boxes, then waited and watched. Kohler noticed that after the chimps realized they could not simply reach or jump up to retrieve the fruit, they stopped, had a seat, and thought about how they might solve the problem. Then after a few moments, the chimps stood up and proceeded to solve the problem. In the first scenario, the problem was solved by placing the smaller stick into the longer stick to create one very long stick which could be used to knock the hanging fruit down. In the second scenario, the chimps would solve the problem by stacking the boxes on top of each other, which allowed them to climb to the top of the stack of boxes and reach the fruit. Kohler called this newly observed type of learning insight learning. Based on these observations, Kohler's theory of insight learning became an early argument for the involvement of cognition, or thinking, in the process of learning.' - http://education-portal.com/academy/lesson/insight-learning-wolfgang-kohler-theory-definition-examples.html#lesson 4th September 2014.

From this Kholer developed the theory of insight learning.

'Insight learning is the abrupt realization of a problem's solution. Insight learning is not the result of trial and error, responding to an environmental stimulus, or the result of observing someone else attempt the problem. It is a completely cognitive experience, which requires the ability to visualize the problem and the solution internally, in the mind's eye so to speak, before initialing a behavioral response.

Insight learning is considered a type of learning because it results in a long-lasting change. Following the occurrence of insight, the realization of how to solve the problem can be repeated in future similar situations. - 'http://education-portal.com/academy/lesson/insight-learning-wolfgang-kohler-theory-definition-examples.html#lesson 4th September 2014.

What significance may the above 3 mentioned types of learning have on everyday life?

We will use different types of learning every day, learning occurs in a variety of ways. Depending on what our situation is and what we are trying to achieve. Everyone learns differently and some people respond better to some learning styles than others. Sometimes it is the result of direct observation, other times it is the result of experience through personal interactions with the environment. By understanding how we learn and develop teachers can be more efficient in getting students to learn and individuals can help themselves to learn new skills. By understanding different learning methods and how effective they are, we can choose the best approach to a given situation. For instance young children are unlikely to use insight learning, but may respond well to operant conditioning in the form of star charts/reward charts.

Different approaches will be more effective than others depending on the circumstance - who you are dealing with and what you want to achieve. You will therefore need to adapt your approach accordingly.

Operant conditioning may be great for children, or those with learning difficulties yet in other situations you want people to understand something well enough to think for themselves and 'insight learning' is crucial for development of new products so that we can move forward and continue to evolve.

'Inventions and innovations alike are oftentimes the result of insight learning. Insight learning is often at the root of creative, out of the box, thinking'. http://education-portal.com/academy/lesson/insight-learning-wolfgang-kohler-theory-definition-examples.html#lesson *4th September 2014.*

Transfer learning is also important in everyday life. A teacher will need to be aware of what his/her students already know so that knowledge can be built upon. S/he will also need to check prior learning to ensure what has previously been learnt is correct, in order that s/he has a good basis to build on and is not hindered by misconceptions in the first place.

Past learning may affect us learning something new for instance if we can ride a bike and you go to a circus where you try to ride a bike where the handle bars have to be turned the other way, this may create confusion and may make it harder for you to ride the bike, than someone who has never ridden a bike before.

It is also very important that we consider latent learning in everyday life, especially when it comes to children who are much more impressionable. We need to think about what we expose our children to and what affect this will have on them in the future. From my criminology course, and from my experience at work; children who are exposed to a violent home life i.e. they see their fathers being abusive to their mothers; often go on to become violent themselves. We need to reduce the violence that our children are exposed to. There has been a lot of debate over violent computer games and also violent films. It is therefore important to adhere to the age restrictions on films and computer games.

The theory of attachment & The theory of deprivation

Attachment;

Towards the end of the first year of an infant's life it can clearly distinguish between known and unknown people and will begin to start to form attachments to certain individuals.

'Researchers Rudolph Schaffer and Peggy Emerson analyzed the number of attachment relationships that infants form in a longitudinal study with 60 infants. The infants were observed every four weeks during the first year of life, and then once again at 18 months. Based upon their observations, Schaffer and Emerson outlined four distinct phases of attachment.

5. *Pre-attachment Stage: From birth to three months, infants do not show any particular attachment to a specific caregiver. The infant's signals such as*

crying and fussing naturally attract the attention of the caregiver, and the baby's positive responses encourage the caregiver to remain close.

6. *Indiscriminate Attachment: From around six weeks of age to seven months, infants begin to show preferences for primary and secondary caregivers. During this phase, infants begin to develop a feeling of trust that the caregiver will respond to their needs. While they will still accept care from other people, they become much better at distinguishing between familiar and unfamiliar people as they approach seven months of age. They also respond more positively to the primary caregiver.*

7. *Discriminate Attachment: At this point, from about seven to eleven months of age, infants show a strong attachment and preference for one specific individual. They will protest when separated from the primary attachment figure (separation anxiety), and begin to display anxiety around strangers (stranger anxiety).*

8. *Multiple Attachments: After approximately nine months of age, children begin to form strong emotional bonds with other caregivers beyond the primary attachment figure. This often includes the father, older siblings, and grandparents.*

While this process may seem straightforward, there are a number of different factors that can influence how and when attachments develop. First is the opportunity for attachment. Children that do not have a primary care figure, such as those raised in orphanages, may fail to develop the sense of trust needed to form an attachment. Second, the quality of care-giving is a vital factor. When caregivers respond quickly and consistently, children learn that they can depend on the people who are responsible for their care, which is the essential foundation for attachment.

'Researchers have found that attachment patterns established early in life can lead to a number of outcomes. For example, children who are securely attached as infants tend to develop stronger self-esteem and better self-reliance as they grow older. These children also tend to be more independent, perform better in school, have successful social relationships, and experience less depression and anxiety.'

- http://psychology.about.com/od/loveandattraction/a/attachment01.htm 5th September 2014.

Macfarlane found that infants could recognise their mothers by smell alone, at 2 days old they would turn their heads towards a strangers breast pads, as often as they would to their mother but by 10 days old they showed a definite preference for their mother. This demonstrates that babies form preferential attachments, as young as 10 days old. The attachment they form is linked to their development. Babies/children learn and develop from their relationships (which we have already established in assignment 4 when examining reciprocal behaviour).
Source; 'Psychology' study house text April 2012 edition 2012/01 p184

Schafer and Callender; demonstrated that just the ability to recognise a mother is apparently not enough to constitute the formation of attachment. In their study babies did not protest at being separated from their mothers until approximately 7 months of age.   Source; 'Psychology' study house text April 2012 edition 2012/01 p191.

'Separation protests tend to start occurring at approximately the same time as the enfant acquires the ability of object conservation. It appears that the child realises that the person to whom it seeks proximity has a separate existence and thus separation protests occur when the attachment figure is no longer with the child'......'**Schaffer and Emerson (1964**), in their study following 60 Scottish infants, found that at the age of 7 months specific attachments emerged which became more intense during the following 3 or 4 months.' Source; 'Psychology' study house text April 2012 edition 2012/01 p192 & 193.

I think that from this it doesn't mean that they don't have an attachment/bond with their mother until 7 months, but merely that they don't notice their mum as separate to them before 7 months. I wonder what this means for children who are left when their mothers go back to work, when they are only a few months old.

Ainsworth distinguished between infants who are securely attached and those who are not with the main differences being that of sensitivity. Attachment is dependent upon sensitivity i.e. the extent to which the mother can detect her infants signals, interpret them correctly and respond promptly and appropriately. Source; 'Psychology' study house text April 2012 edition 2012/01 p193.

This demonstrates the importance of the mother being attentive to her baby, picking it up when it cries and giving it what it requires, this is in stark contrast to some of the baby books that suggest you should let your baby cry, in order that it learns to self-soothe.

In my experience it's important to pick your baby up when s/he cries to avoid unnecessary distress to your baby. It is also good to cuddle your baby a lot, it helps you baby to bond. So what if your baby is then clingy and wants to be rocked, they are only small babies for a while and if they know you are there and feel loved and also get taken out and get to meet other babies and be social they won't turn into clingy children because they will feel secure and be independent, thus becoming less 'clingy' in the long run.

'**Schaffer and Emerson (1964**), in their study also noted differences with attachment with the children that they studied with one enfant displaying attachment behaviour at 22 weeks and as 2 others didn't exhibit this until after their first birthday. They examined the variables and they too, like Ainswoth found that it was dependent on how willing the mother was to pick the baby up and attend to it right away. They also noted that the amount of time and attention that the mother gave her infant besides the routine caretaking activities, was an important factor. ' Source; 'Psychology' study house text April 2012 edition 2012/01 p193 & 194.

Ainsworth distinguished that attachment was cross cultural (no cultural differences in the mother/baby attachment). She also noted crying and attempts to follow the mother from as young as 15 weeks. Source; 'Psychology' study house text April 2012 edition 2012/01 p 194.

Schaffer and Emerson (1964) also noted that it was not necessary for a person to be involved in the infants routine caretaking in order for them to become attachment figures, this shows that the infants attachment to the mother is much more than because she is a source of food/care, it is concerned with emotions that run much deeper. **Harlow** in his studies of monkeys, also came to a similar conclusion, that the bond is much more than 'cupboard love.' Source; 'Psychology' study house text April 2012 edition 2012/01 p195.

Deprivation;

'Maternal deprivation' is used to describe a whole range of situations where an infant is deprived of its relationship with its mother.

Bowlby, in his report to The World Health Organisation in 1951 stated that maternal separation has adverse effects on a child and that 'women going to work with children under three, or even five years put them at serious risk. Bowlby concluded that a mothers love in infancy and childhood is as important for mental health as vitamins and proteins are for physical health. He also found that long periods of separation from a mother (i.e. for 6 months at a time, within the first 5 years of life) leads to delinquency. **Yarrow** in 1961 confirmed that there is a strong relationship between broken homes and delinquency. Bowlby also emphasised the importance of continuity in relationships.

Source; 'Psychology' study house text April 2012 edition 2012/01

Problems with Attachment

What happens to children who do not form secure attachments? Research suggests that failure to form secure attachments early in life can have a negative impact on behavior in later childhood and throughout the life. Children diagnosed with oppositional-defiant disorder (ODD), conduct disorder (CD) or post-traumatic stress disorder (PTSD) frequently display attachment problems, possibly due to early abuse, neglect or trauma. Clinicians suggest that children adopted after the age of six months have a higher risk of attachment problems.

While attachment styles displayed in adulthood are not necessarily the same as those seen in infancy, research indicates that early attachments can have a serious impact on later relationships. For example, those who are securely attached in childhood tend to have good self-esteem, strong romantic relationships and the ability to self-disclose to others. As adults, they tend to have healthy, happy and lasting relationships. For more information, see this article on attachment styles.'

- http://psychology.about.com/od/loveandattraction/a/attachment01.htm (5 September 2014), Ainsworth, M. D. S., Blehar, M. C., Waters, E., & Wall, S. (1978). *Patterns of attachment: A psychological study of the strange situation.* Hillsdale, NJ: Erlbaum. / Bowlby J. (1969). *Attachment. Attachment and loss: Vol. 1. Loss.* New York: Basic Books. / Schaffer, H. R. & Emerson, P. E. (1964). The development of social attachments in infancy. *Monographs of the Society for Research in Child Development, 29,* 94.

'Spitz (1945) *found that children who had been separated from their mothers frequently showed apathy, slow development and general depression.' - Source;* 'Psychology' study house text April 2012 edition 2012/01 p200.

Attachment theory & deprivation theory can be applied in everyday situations by.....

It demonstrates how important it is for a child to have key care givers in their life, and to have strong bonds with these care givers. This is normally the mother or father, but may also be grandparents or other guardians. It is important to note that, for whatever reason, the mother may not be around. It has been demonstrated that children can still form attachments with someone who isn't the biological mother....

*'**Rutter** (1972) suggests that the chief bond is especially important because of its greater strength, but that most children develop bonds with several people and these are basically similar to the main one. He also states that the chief bond need not be a biological parent, or the child's chief caretaker and it also need not be with a female.'* – Source; 'Psychology' study house text April 2012 edition 2012/01 p203.

*'**Schaffer and Emerson (1964)** found that a substantial minority of their subjects formed several attachments, with the father being an important one of these, also siblings'* Source; 'Psychology' study house text April 2012 edition 2012/01 p192.

I would agree with this because my son who is now 23 months, as well as having a very strong bond with me he has a very strong relationship with my husband (his father) but also with his grandparents and also with his cousin, which I would describe as being equal to his bond with me, his mother.

This is important to note in cases of adoption/fostering. The emphasis is on the importance for the child to have consistency and love, rather than on the person giving it. This is an important distinction and supports the fostering/adoption process. I have a colleague at work who has adopted 2 young girls and they have thrived and become so much more confidents since being in her care.

It is also important for health professions to recognise the importance of key attachments so that they can offer support to parents and educate them to spend as much time with their children as possible. They can also offer support to them but as well as offering support to parents they need to recognise and offer support to grandparents, especially with the rise in both parents working and grandparents taking on the caretaking role whilst the parents are at work. Most children's centre now offer stay and play for fathers and also grandparents and child support sessions for parents, grandparents and other guardian to attend. My local children's centre even offers stay and play sessions for child minders.

It is also important for businesses and politicians to recognise the importance of the mother/key caretaker; it shows the importance of giving support and time off to both mothers and fathers, as well as the importance of offering support to others who are the primary care giver to young children, such as grandparents who may still be working and may need time off, in order to support the child.

At least the law has changed to offer fathers the chance to take longer paternity leave. Although I think it is a shame that if the mother is taking maternity leave the father only has a legal right to 2 weeks unpaid leave. It is my personal opinion that the law should change to allow for both parents to have longer maternity/paternity leave. Especially at the beginning of a child's life, it would be nice for the mother and father to both have at least a month off together to care for the child. The first month is very hard, and at the very least the mum needs support. With extra time off the father can help the mother and also bond with their child. It is also important to offer support to grandparents, who maybe working (as the pensionable age in on the increase, this may become more of an issue in the future) because it is important for grandparents to spend time bonding with their grandchildren too.

Bowlby considered that children whose mothers returned to work suffered a type of partial separation – Source; 'Psychology' study house text April 2012 edition 2012/01 p196.

I think that maternity leave should be longer and maternity pay should be better. Many other European countries such as Germany, offer mothers much longer maternity leave. In Germany a mother is able to take 3 years off and still go back to her job.

Bowlby's report to The World Health Organisation in 1951 that looked at attachments and maternal separation and stated that it has adverse affects on a child and his work that looked at the adverse affects of children in hospital led to a complete reconsideration of the care provided for children being reared in institutions or experiencing hospitalisation. This is a great example of how deprivation theory can be applied to everyday life.

Source; 'Psychology' study house text April 2012 edition 2012/01

Up to the age of 5 is when a child goes through their most significant development, and is in most need of their mother (or other caretaker). 'Observation of children admitted to hospital, and separated from their parents, shows most of the emotional stress was most apparent in ages 6 months – 4 year' (Source; 'Psychology' study house text April 2012 edition 2012/01 p203). Maybe this shows the need for the mother/caretaker to be around up to the age of 4. However it is not always practicable for a mother to be around until the child goes to school, especially as most mothers have to work. I think the first year is the most significant and if you can take a year's maternity leave (which the law allows now) that is great (unfortunately not everyone can afford to do this).

As a mother I find **Bowlbys**, research and report to The World Health Organisation quite disturbing because it suggests by leaving your child to go to work, that you will be causing emotional damage to your child, this places more guilt onto working mums. I think where as it is good to be at home with your child, I think if they have secure relationships with whoever is looking after them / they are in a good nursery where they are happy and have good friends and consistency of care that they will not be emotionally damaged. It is important to note that while Bowlby's research may be valid, it is not necessarily directly applicable to working mums. One of the reasons is that Bowlby conducted his study in orphanages, so this is a different setting to children who have their mums in the morning and evening and have somewhere else to go in the day. The impact of the child may depend on many factors such as how long the child is away from the parents for, who they are with in the meantime, if in nursery what provisions are in the nursery and what quality time they spend with their parents at the weekends. I think more research into this subject is needed.

I work full time and have a 2 year old. I am lucky that my parents assist in looking after him. Although I have less time with him he bonds well with them. When I do have time off I also spend it with him. Luckily so far he seems very well adjusted and I have had lots of positive comments about him and his behaviour. I think that it helps that he has very strong bonds with his grandparents, who care for him and I think that having so many strong relationships has allowed him to develop socially and emotionally. He also attends nursery, which seems to have also really helped with his social skills. Had he not been spending so much time building such relationships, his social skills may have not been so strong. Although I do think it will be more beneficial for me and him to spend more time together and should I be in a position to, I would like to reduce my hours at work, in order to spend more time with my son.

As we have seen there is a need for consistency in relationships. This is something that most childcare providers have addressed. At nursery they also pair the children with key workers so there is consistency with the care givers at the nursery. A lot of nursery's tend to do this and I think it is important that they have recognised the need for consistency in relationships.

Furthermore '**Klaus and Kennell** (1976) found that if a separate occurs during the first 4 hours following deliver, the mother may fail to establish a bond with her baby.

This demonstrates how important it is that a mother has time with her baby, in hospital. In hospital they encourage skin to skin contact with mother and baby as soon as the baby is born, this is something that they also heavily advocate at antenatal classes, and this protocol has come from such studies. It is great to see that there are studies that are being carried out and that advice is being taken from this and steps are actually being put into place, in childcare situations to help develop bonds with the baby and help to improve the baby care.

Privation is....

In the dictionary Privation is the absence or lack of basic necessities ("The Free Dictionary - Privation), (In a philosophical context, it can also mean, where vital qualities are absent).

In psychology the term privation refers to a lack of relationships. An example of this is when *'a child has no opportunity to form a relationship with a parent figure, or when such relationship is distorted, due to their treatment'* (Russell, Julia; Jarvis, Matt (2003). *Angles on Applied Psychology*. Nelson Thornes. p. 219. ISBN 978-0-7487-7259-9.). *It is different to deprivation, which occurs when an established relationship is severed* (Brain, Christine; Mukherji, Penny (7 June 2005). *Understanding child psychology* (New edition ed.). Nelson Thornes. pp. 44–45. ISBN 978-0-7487-9084-5).

Privation to be discussed here is when the child has not been allowed to form at affection bond at all with its mother.

How can privation be applied to an everyday situation

Privation can be applied to everyday life in a similar way that deprivation theory can be applied………i.e. the lack of bond with the mother, or other appropriate care giver can lead to emotional issues and can mean that when the child grows up s/he may be unable to form bonds with others and may be subject to delinquency/ be involved in crime.

Bowlby states those suffering maternal deprivation are unable to form true affectionate bonds with others (affectionless psychopathy).

Rutter (1972) states that; 'It is quite likely that distress arises when a child's relationship with the mother is disrupted but the affectionless psychopath probably arises because firm bonds fail to develop – that is the child suffers maternal privation rather than deprivation.

- 'Psychology' study house text April 2012 edition 2012/01 p200

This can be applied in everyday life in terms of offering high quality substitute maternal care, for instance this can be applied to adoption. Where children are being neglected and denied of maternal loving relationships i.e. they are suffering from maternal privation, they can be placed into secure loving homes. There has been a move away from institutions for care and a move to fostering, so that children can be placed in loving homes, whilst they await adoption. The issue here is that they may form a bond with their foster carers and then will ultimately move on, meaning that they are then deprived of that relationship, which for someone who already has emotional issues, can be, in my opinion, very detrimental.

Gender identity

Gender identity refers to the child's adoption of either a typically masculine or typically feminine sex-role. Adults often treat girls and boys differently, although this is not always done consciously. Each culture has certain approved ways in which males and females are expected to behave and often the way people see themselves and the way they act and develop their gender identity is often based upon cultural and social influences, as I will discuss below;

Parents have a huge influence on their children and their attitudes to each other and their children will influence the child's view of masculine and feminine roles.

The following research shows the importance of cultural/social influences of the development of gender identity.

- **Kobasigawa, Arakaki and Awiguni (1966)**

They conducted an experiment where they gave school boys on a n individual basis the choice to play with attractive looking female toys or unattractive neutral toys. They found the boys avoided the female toy, if an adult was present they avoided the female toys more but if another child played with the female toys the avoidance was less.

- **Margaret Mead (1935)**

Conducted research on men and women in three different tribes;

'After a field trip to Nebraska in 1930 to study the Omaha Native Americans, she and her husband, Reo Fortune, next headed to the Sepik region of Papua New Guinea for two years. While there Mead did pioneering work on gender consciousness. She sought to discover to what extent temperamental differences between the sexes were culturally determined rather than innate. She described her findings in Sex and Temperament in Three Primitive Societies *(1935) and explored the subject more deeply in the next decade with* Male and Female*(1949).*
Mead found a different pattern of male and female behavior in each of the cultures she studied, all different from gender role expectations in the United States at that time. She found among the Arapesh *a temperament for both males and females that was gentle, responsive, and cooperative. Among the* Mundugumor *(now Biwat), both males and females were violent and aggressive, seeking power and position. For the* Tchambuli *(now Chambri), male and female temperaments were distinct from each other, the woman being dominant, impersonal, and managerial and the male less responsible and more emotionally dependent. While Mead's contribution in separating biologically-based sex from socially-constructed gender was groundbreaking, she was criticized for reporting findings that seemed custom-made for her theory. For Mead, each culture represented a different type within her theory, and she downplayed or disregarded information that may have made her simple classifications untenable.'* - http://www.loc.gov/exhibits/mead/field-sepik.html (09/09/14).

- **Goldberg and Lewis (1969)** also studied this, please see **task 65** below.

- Source; 'Psychology' study house text April 2012 edition 2012/01 (section 17).

Further findings on the influences on gender identity;

'Observations made in the home of preschool children have found that parents reward their daughters for dressing up, dancing, playing with dolls, or simply following them around but criticize them for manipulating objects, running, climbing and jumping. In contrast, parents reward their sons for playing with blocks but criticize them for playing with dolls, asking for help, or even volunteering to be helpful (Fagot, 1978). Parents tend to demand more independence of boys and to have higher expectations of them. They also respond less quickly to boys' request for help and focus less on the interpersonal aspects of a task. And finally, parents punishes boys both verbally and physically more often than girls' (Maccoby et Jacklin, 1974). – Hilgard's introduction to psychology (12th edition) by Rita L. and Richard C. Atkinson, Edward E. Smith, Daryl J. Bem and Susan Nolen- Hoeksema, (1996, USA).

'Adults viewing newborn infants through the window of an hospital nursery believe they can detect sex differences. Infants thought to be boys are described as robust, strong and large featured; identical looking infants thought to be girls are described as delicate, fine featured and "soft" (Luria et Rubin, 1974). In one study, college students viewed a videotape of a 9-month-old infant showing a strong but ambiguous emotional reaction to a jack-in-the-box. The reaction was more often labeled as "anger" when the child was thought to be a boy, and "fear" when the same infant was thought to be a girl (Condry et Condry, 1976). When an infant was called David in another study, "he" was actually treated more roughly by subjects than when the same infant was called Lisa (Bern, Martina et Watson, 1976).

Fathers appear to be more concerned with sex-typed behaviors than mothers, particularly with their sons. They tend to react more negatively than mothers (interfering with the child's play or expressing disapproval) when their sons play with "feminine" toys. Fathers are less concerned when their daughters engage in "masculine" play, but they still show more disapproval than mothers do (Langlois et Downs, 1980). But if parents and other adults treat children in sex-stereotyped ways, children themselves are the real "sexists". Peers enforce sex-stereotyping much more severely than parents. Indeed, parents who consciously seek to raise their children without the traditional sex-role stereotypes - by encouraging the child to engage in a wide range of activities without labeling any activity as masculine or feminine or by playing nontraditional roles within the home - are often dismayed to find their efforts undermined by peer pressure. Boys, in particular, criticize other boys when they see them engaged in "girls" activities. They are quick to call another boy a sissy if he plays with dolls, cries when he's hurt, or shows tender concern toward another child in distress. In contrast, girls seem not to object to other girls playing with "boys" toys or engaging in masculine activities (Longlois et Down, 1980).

This points up a general phenomenon: the taboos in our culture against feminine behavior for boys are stronger than those against masculine behavior in girls. Four and five years old boys are more likely to experiment with feminine toys and activities (such as dolls, a lipstick and mirror, hair ribbons) when no one is watching than when an adult or another boy is present (Kobasigawa, Arakaki et Awiguni, 1966; Hartup et Moore, 1963)....Some more recent research in France in the University of Rennes and Burgundy, have tried to understand why girls do less scientific and technical studies. Together with other studies of the American book quoted above, they show that conditioning seems to be involved here too.

They use hidden cameras to show that teachers behave differently towards boys and girls. Science teachers devote in average 20% more time to boys. Girls are less questioned and are more frequently interrupted. Teachers encourage girls for their good behavior and the cleanliness of their copy, and boys for the relevance of their arguments[4]. Marie Duru-Bellat (1995) calls it a "hidden curriculum".

Other observations, reported by Aebischer in 1991[5], performed in schools, shows that teachers are asking for more participation to boys than girls (Guibert, 1987; Valabrègue, 1989), rely more on them in science and technology (Marques, 1990), talk more to them (Milner, 1989) and show more interest in what they do, "I was the only girl in a class of boys. In industrial design, the teacher has never looked at my work, except at the end of the year when he got to know that I had very good scores in mathematics", said a young woman who is an engineer today and studied at Polytechnique, one of the most prestigious engineer schools in France, while a seminar for principals of high school, organized by the Directorate of Amiens, France, in May 1991.

A survey made by the French association "Femmes et Mathématiques" (Women and Mathematics) in 1990 over 50 high schools shows that parents believe that most important parameter of their children's happiness is: professional success as much as the family happiness for their sons, while the family happiness was regarded to be three times more important than the professional success for their daughters. Regarding parents' wishes for their children, 70% want their sons to study sciences or economy in high school, but only 45% wish that their daughters do the same.

A school psychologist and counselor, Mrs. Tréreffe, observes how parents are encouraging their children and says: "With the crisis, parents are looking for safety. Many understand that there is a future in scientific professions. But I'm upset to see that, during my consultations, girls are encouraged to avoid the most challenging engineering schools, and encouraged to do short courses, while boys are still encouraged to go to the most prestigious engineering schools. Parents think "Why throw the girls in such a hard challenge while unemployment is probably waiting for them, and they will probably also miss the opportunity to find a husband". They take into account the balance between family and career for girls, but not for boys"

"Femmes et Mathématiques" raises also the problem that meet women who persist in a scientific project and start a civil engineer training, "Those who have been in these classes will remember that they were challenge on nervous and physical resistance to a big charge of work and stress, aggression and competition, as much as the expertise in mathematics. Girls must also challenge specific difficulties: lodgings are usually only for boys, and they are often the victims of sexist jokes". The idea that a woman is not in the right place when she succeeds excellent scientific studies is visible on all levels. Aebischer report in 1988 conversations between students and female engineer who came in conferences in high schools in Paris. After they have listened to the women's story, they asked about their ability to manage a family or to have other interests than their profession. While they didn't question women's work, they were not fully convinced that these women were completely lucky.'

 - Hilgard's introduction to psychology (12th edition) by Rita L. and Richard C. Atkinson, Edward E. Smith, Daryl J. Bem and Susan Nolen- Hoeksema, (1996, USA).

In contrast **John Money** conducted research to look at how much gender roles are influenced by biology (rather than cultural/social). He found that girls who were subjected to high levels of the male sex hormone (androgens), whilst they were in the womb, were born with male appearing genitals but also showed higher levels of tomboyish behaviour.

Money also studied hermaphrodites and found that sex-identity depended on how they were raised. By age 3 sex-role identity has been established.

Source; 'Psychology' study house text April 2012 edition 2012/01 p219.

From a young age I have tried to provide my son with both male and female toys, he however straight away preferred sensory toys i.e. toys that were noisy and moved. He has always had a tendency towards balls and cars (typically male toys) and less towards dolls (although I have encouraged him to play with dolls).

In conclusion the research has shown that the influences on gender identity are some part biological (nature) and some part nurture / influenced by social/cultural aspects. In my experience I would say that this is true and that the extent that children are influenced by social/cultural aspects will depend on how strong the social/cultural aspects are and what the child's natural personality/tendency is.

However from Money's study on hermaphrodites his final conclusion was that although biological and social/cultural influences have a big part to play the. Cultural/social influences had the biggest impact on gender-identity.

Bryden identified that men and women's brains work differently and therefore this would indicate that some sex differences are innate.

Psychologists Susan Goldberg and Michael Lewis in 1969, conducted a study to observe mums and their babies (32 girls and 32 boys). They asked mothers to bring their 6-month-old infants into their laboratory and told them that the study was to observe the infants' development. The study was however to observed the mothers as well as the children. They found that the mothers kept their daughters closer to them. They also touched their daughters more and spoke to them more frequently than they did to their sons. They then re conducted the study when the children were 13 months old. By the time the children were 13 months old, the girls stayed closer to their mothers during play, and they returned to their mothers sooner and more often than the boys did. When Goldberg and Lewis set up a barrier to separate the children from their mothers, who were holding toys, the girls were more likely to cry and motion for help; the boys, to try to climb over the barrier.

As far as the behaviour of the mums went Goldberg and Lewis concluded that mothers subconsciously reward daughters for being passive and dependent, and sons for being active and independent.

- Source; 'Psychology' study house text April 2012 edition 2012/01 p217 & http://www.sociologyguide.com/socio-short-notes/gender-socialization.php (09/09/2014).

They observed in terms of the children themselves that the girls chose cuddly toys or toys needing fine manipulative movements, whereas the boys preferred bigger nosier toys and enjoyed banging and exploring non- toys such as doorknobs.

I can certainly agree with this as my son loves banging furniture and jumping off things as much, if not more than, playing with his toys (something my dad, who is used to 2 girls, found it took a bit of adjusting too. He often tells me how me and my sister were never as noisy and destructive as the grandchildren, who all happen to be boys). I guess there is a reason the term boisterous sounds like boys.

On the basis of our sex, we are given different kinds of toys. Boys are more likely to get guns and "action figures" that destroy enemies. Girls are more likely to get dolls and jewellery. This re-enforces the gender-identity. Once children show a preference to certain toys, this is then re-enforced and therefore the preference to be a certain way develops.

CHILD BEHAVIOUR

Foreword

According to popular belief children's behaviour isn't what it used to be; invariably, the media especially, will claim it's getting worse. Really? Is that true? After watching UK television on an average week a visiting alien might conclude children's behaviour must at least be a matter of national concern. Images of alarming scenes, parents at the end of their tether asking, in some cases desperate, for a professional nanny to show them how to turn a chaotic home with unruly children into a tranquil oasis of order and harmony.

It doesn't stop at media reports. Primary school teachers have joined in the debate citing examples of young children entering the classroom so apparently disruptive they're at risk of exclusion before their school career has even begun. There is a powerful argument for suggesting starting school at the age of four-years is too young, certainly compared with the mainland Europe, Scandinavia and the majority of the rest of the world. Some children at least are simply not ready to conform to the expectation of sitting down still and quietly for long periods of time in an often overcrowded noisy and over-stimulating environment.

However there is evidence to strongly suggest a direct link with behavioural problems and learning differences (Rogers, 2011), sometimes quite severe behavioural issues, especially in older primary school children. Similarly, when secondary school children exhibit very challenging behaviour it can often be traced back to behavioural difficulties expressed in their early years (McNamara & Moreton, 1996). This is one of the reasons why effective liaison between a child's pre-school, primary and secondary schools is vital even if it is just in the form of detailed reports that 'travel' with the child. It enables teachers to build up a holistic picture of a child's profile, progress and where applicable issues they may have.

Frustration experienced in trying, especially if it's in vain, to access learning activities within the school environment which as indicated can be a very stressful place for some children, can lead to behavioural problems. Children with innate specific learning difficulties and even learning *differences* are particularly susceptible to behaviour that doesn't conform to the norm. Add to that the possibility of poor social and language skills, difficulty accessing literacy and a limited ability to concentrate or pay attention for long periods of time and it is little wonder that these children are very likely to develop behavioural problems.

Learning difficulties aren't the only issues that may precipitate behavioural worries; some children's behaviour will be a reaction to environmental stresses, for example their home life. Sometimes stress will be relatively transient rather than a long-term or even permanent concern. Similarly, some challenging behaviour will emerge as a direct result of a child's developmental stage and therefore considered a normal part of their overall growing up. Often it will be people's perceptions of what constitutes bad behaviour sometimes based on their own upbringing which has influenced their expectations and opinions. School can present the trigger for a child being labelled as a difficult child. It's not uncommon for parents to claim "but she's fine at home, I don't know what all the fuss is about". Here, there may be differences between the expectations and values at home where rules may be relaxed and relatively carefree or even absent. School may be the first time the child has encountered a more rigid rule-bound environment where suddenly they are expected to conform to certain standards.

Social Construction

The point here is that the replies you've given, whatever they happen to be and they will be individual to you, are a reflection of your unique personal construct system. Constructs are as individual as we are, influenced by the kind of society we grew up in. Constructs are fluid; they change according to our own particular experiences and the lives we've lived. They're like a lens to view the world through and the people within it. For example, what is your opinion of people who choose to eat with just a fork rather than a knife and fork? Whilst your answer won't depend on your upbringing it's likely to at least be influenced by it. Not all cultures of course use forks. In the not so distant past in Britain certain families would have found eating with just a fork in one hand ill-mannered. In the USA using a knife to firstly cut food and then leaving it to rest on the plate whilst picking up the fork to eat the pieces is relatively commonplace and therefore considered totally acceptable. This may seem like an inconsequential example, and how we eat is of no great importance after all, however it does serve to illustrate nonetheless that ideas concerning right or wrong and good or bad are constructed, that is made up according to social norms. When we were born, where we were born and how we were brought up may not determine our world view but it will be an influence on perception, expectations and opinions.

Attitudes to children's discipline or punishment, and there is weight of difference in those two words, vary enormously. Historically children were subjected to harsh forms of punishment which by today's standards would be considered not only cruel and harmful but thankfully also illegal. Beatings, being confined to small spaces for long periods of time and the denial of food were not uncommon. 'Spare the rod and spoil the child' and 'Children should be seen and not heard' both popular English phrases that were used as parenting guidance mantras! Compare that with similar prevailing attitudes from different parts of the world: 'A tree should be bent while it is still young' (a South African proverb). 'The egg should not be smarter than the duck' (a Vietnamese proverb).

Sayings and proverbs like these can carry very powerful messages about a society's views and expectations, and in so doing influence the way people think and behave. If we think deeply about how language can shape people's thinking it can be regarded as very powerful in the potential for influencing behaviour. When we think of *constructs* and its meaning, it refers to terms that have been constructed, that is literally created or made up and arbitrary in their evolution. Although 'spare the rod and *spoil* the child' was not heard unless perhaps in parody in the second half of the twentieth century in Britain, even up until the 1970s corporal punishment in schools in the form of the cane or the slipper was regarded as a necessary means to ensure children were sufficiently reprimanded for misbehaviour. Now of course corporal punishment has been outlawed but it isn't uncommon to hear older people say "I was hit and it never did me any harm", or actually did it? Is it sometimes easier to deny hurt than face up to an uncomfortable truth, particularly if the said punishments were administered by a nonetheless loved parent.

Do constructs, as arbitrary as they are, serve any purpose? Are they harmless or potentially quite damaging? Some constructs can be useful to us in a psychological sense as they help us to departmentalise people, however incorrect assumptions can be, and make predictions about people's likely behaviour. Sorting friends from foe in earlier and more hostile times was very useful as a skill. Some psychologists argue the ability to categorise people is instinctive, going so far as to claim that we can evaluate a stranger even within the first few seconds of meeting him or her. By labelling children, for example, 'good boy', 'naughty child', 'little angel', 'nightmare kid', we can feel on some deeper level that the world makes more sense; we tend to feel somehow safer as a result of 'knowing' who someone is and what we might expect of them. Of course we can be completely wrong in our evaluation. In fact often our summation of other people is nothing more than a stereotype which may even lead us to become prejudiced in our thinking. 'White van drivers' have become demonised in popular mythology in recent times. Just as a result of the choice of vehicle which is driven for work purposes and happens to be white in colour. Really, are drivers of blue or red vans any better or worse? No one said anything about the existence of any logic behind constructs! When people's perception becomes compromised in this way we might then only see others' behaviour in terms of a blinkered view. "Well he would say that wouldn't he?", 'What did you expect?' or "That's typical of her".

Environmental Influences

In psychology when we think of the many and conflicting influences on behaviour it is useful to start off with the nature versus nurture dichotomy and debate which side might be more significant. In reality humans, like all organisms, are the result or product of inherited influences *and* their environment. Consequently in normal circumstances usually the conclusion reached is that behaviour is the result of a combination of both factors. For example, our *genotype* refers to the group of genes we've inherited, whereas our *phenotype* is the resulting behaviour.

An example of the differences is to think of two identical twins with the same cognitive potential but adopted into very different homes: one encouraged and expected to achieve well at school and beyond, and the other neglected and ignored. Our genotype predisposes us to certain developmental outcomes but our phenotype determines the actual outcome. When it comes to children's behaviour no more so is this argument apparent. Even in the case of some conditions, for example, Attention Deficit Hyperactivity Disorder (ADHD) the environment in which a child affected is exposed to is thought to at least contribute to the physiological symptoms.

So what are aspects of the child's environment are psychologists interested in when they discuss nurture? One of the areas is the child's parents' 'parenting style', in other words *how* they parent, for example, are they punitive and controlling, relaxed and carefree or uncaring and uninvolved? Let's look at some psychological theory in the area of child-rearing or parenting styles. Erikson (1963) put forward the idea that parents ideally need to demonstrate two important abilities: warmth and control.

Warmth is needed for the child's sense of self-esteem and emotional development, and control, or discipline, is required for the child's developing sense of self-control. When children are impulsive, and act out spontaneously without thinking they're lacking the ability to regulate their own behaviour.

Hoffman (1970) investigated styles of discipline used, dividing his research findings into three categories:

- Love withdrawal
- Power assertion
- Induction

Threatening a child with statements like 'I won't love you anymore if you…' creates a sense of anxiety and a fear of abandonment that may leave deep-seated emotional scars. Power assertion includes any style that may cause hostility, fear, resentment or anger, contributing to issues like anger management in adulthood. By contrast the induction type of parenting is associated with positive behaviour; this involves explaining why certain behaviour is wrong alongside its consequences and how to repair any damage. When children show a lack of self-restraint or engage in high risk behaviours this may be due in part to having received insufficient firm guidance whilst growing up.

Baumrind (1971) cited in Flanagan (1999) conducted researched with pre-school children and their parents, concluding that parents' parenting fell into categories:

- Authoritarian
- Authoritative
- Permissive
- Uninvolved

The 'authoritarian' parent asserts rules, often relying on punishment as a means to achieve obedience and may use power assertion or love withdrawal. These parents tend to see things from their own point of view.

The 'authoritative' parent is more flexible in their approach giving some freedom but within set boundaries. Most importantly these parents use reason and firm guidance to achieve obedience. This is called 'inductive discipline'. Authoritarian parents tend to see things from the child's point of view.

'Permissive' parents are unlikely to exert any kind of control or discipline but are nonetheless warm and responsive to their child's point of view. The child can make their own choices without limits. The 'uninvolved' parents are a different case all together; these are the kind of parents who neglect or even reject their child, who are un-controlling, overly-permissive, emotionally detached.

	Supportive Parent is accepting and child-centered	**Unsupportive** Parent is rejecting and parent-centered
Demanding Parent expects much of child	**Authoritative Parenting** Relationship is reciprocal, responsive; high in bidirectional communication	**Authoritarian Parenting** Relationship is controlling, power-assertive; high in unidirectional communication
Undemanding Parent expects little of child	**Permissive Parenting** Relationship is indulgent; low in control attempts	**Rejecting-Neglecting Parenting** Relationship is rejecting or neglecting; uninvolved

It's useful to examine the effects of parenting on a child's potential behavioural response, especially in terms of understanding the causes of challenging behaviour and subsequently supporting a distressed child:

Parenting Style:	*Behavioural Profile in the Child:*
Authoritarian	Vulnerable to stress, fearful, aimless, emotional, anxious, unfriendly, passively hostile, prejudiced, responsive to commands = **'Conflicted-irritable'**
Authoritative	Self-controlled, self-reliant, co-operative, well-balanced, high self-esteem, curious, cheerful, purposeful = **'Energetic-friendly'**
Permissive	Rebellious, domineering, aimless, low-achievers, low in self-reliance, low in vitality, low in self-control = **'Impulsive-aggressive'**
Uninvolved	Hostile and rebellious, anti-social behaviour, addictive personalities (e.g. with alcohol and/or drug abuse) = **'Adolescent profile'**

Innate Influences

Not all challenging behaviour is the result of environmental influences like parenting, some behaviour can be considered as 'typical' according to age and stage of development. The pro-social, or moral, cognitive development theory suggests that children's attitudes to right and wrong are linked to biological maturity. That is, each child passes through a series of stages on their way to adulthood that is dependent on their readiness to think and reason. Let's have a look at what that means in terms of a child's age. According to cognitive psychologists the pre-school child is unable to understand rules. Over the next four years the child enters a stage in which rules are learned in such a rigid way they are regarded as unchangeable. For example, the seriousness of wrong-doing is judged by the consequences rather than the intentions. If the consequences are 'big' then by this level of reasoning punishment should fit the consequences.

A child in the 'moral realism or objectivism' stage of cognitive development is likely to judge a 'crime' in terms of the consequences. If ten glasses get broken this must be far more serious than just four however it happened. In Billy's (A) case the wind accidently blew the glasses over, this was not his fault even though it happened when he was doing something he shouldn't – sneaking a biscuit. Jessica, (B) on the other hand, knew the tray of glasses was dangerously close to the door which she pushed hard on purpose in her hurry to pass through. She was secretly pleased that the resulting chaos would slow down her rivals in the game. A child in the 'moral relativism' stage of cognitive development is more likely to look behind the 'size of the consequences' that is how much damage was done, and consider instead the 'intentions' that led to the 'crime'. Simply, was the crime caused by accident or was it intentional? At this stage the consequences are irrelevant. This is the reason that young children's challenging behaviour such as lying, cheating, stealing for example can be very difficult to rationalise. When they lack the ability to fully appreciate intentions rather than results it can be extremely hard to explain why as a parent you're so mad about these kinds of acts even if the crime seemed really small to the child.

mumslittleone.com

Pre-moral	Rules difficult to understand; reasoning ability limited
Moral realism/objectivism	Rules understood as unchangeable; actions are evaluated by their consequences: *'punishment should fit the consequences'*
Moral relativism	Actions are judged by a person's intentions; rules are decided independently: *'the punishment should fit the crime'*

⊠ **Referencing**

Erikson, E. (1977): *Childhood and Society.* London: Paladin

Flanagan, C. (1999): *Applying Psychology to Early Child Development.* London: Hodder & Stoughton

McNamara, S. & Moreton, G. (1996): *Changing Behaviour.* London: David Fulton

Rogers, B. (2006): *How to Manage Children's Challenging Behaviour.* London: Paul Chapman

⊠ **Further Reading & Sources of Support**

Childrenareunbeatable.org.uk

Cullen, K. (2011): *Introducing Child Psychology: A Practical Guide*, London: Icon Books

Familylives.org.uk

Hayes, N. & Orrell, S. (1993): *An Introduction To Child Psychology*, Harlow: Longman

Kidsbehaviour.co.uk

Kidsdevelopment.co.uk

Margaretmahler.org

Netmums.com

Nidirect.gov.uk/sure-start-services

Parenting.co.uk

Parent-link.co.uk

Parentscentre.gov.uk

Schaffer, R. (2004): *Introducing Child Psychology*, Oxford: Blackwell Publishing

Surestart.gov.uk

⊠ WELL-BEING, SELF-ESTEEM AND EMOTIONAL INTELLIGENCE

The Learning Outcomes for this assignment are:

Element	Learning Outcome
1	Understand the importance of well-being and self-esteem
2	Awareness of the impact of emotional intelligence and literacy on self-control

Where does our sense of well-being – inner contentment and fulfilment, or 'happiness' come from? Are we born with a certain genetically inherited amount or quota that could sustain us throughout life no matter what it throws at us? Or is it something that arises from interaction with our environment and therefore we might acquire more or less compared with others? If so, is it possible to 'learn' how to have a good sense of well-being or does it develop naturally as we age? Is it a matter of luck rather than circumstances? What part, if any, does a person's schooling have on their inner sense of self? Whose responsibility is happiness? These questions pose some interesting food for thought as we explore our way through three different but related aspects of a child's emotional development, and ponder how the adult is shaped by early experiences but in particular address what impact each aspect may have on children's behaviour.

Well-being

Can you recall having seen news coverage or photos of lottery winners with the ubiquitous exploding bottle of champagne and their accompanying big grins whilst holding a cardboard cheque? How ecstatically happy they appear to seem? However when independently questioned Lottery winners apparently don't report being any happier following their windfall once the initial excitement and elation has worn away. If money doesn't make us content then what does? Psychological research tends to suggest that it takes quite significant and often serious life events for a person's fundamental well-being to be seriously affected; for example, falling victim to a life threatening illness. Therefore it would seem that just considering a person's circumstances alone isn't enough to explain or predict happiness levels.

Seligman, a psychologist who has written widely on happiness and well-being, asked parents a) what they wanted most for their children's future lives and using just one or two words b) what schools seem to convey in both what was being taught and what the general ethos of their child's school seemed to be conveying. The responses were:

What they most wanted for their children's future lives:

- Happiness and confidence
- Contentment and fulfilment
- Kindness and the ability to be civilised
- Good health
- Good life balance, satisfaction, and,
- Love

What schools seem to be promoting:

- Achievement and success

- Thinking skills, literacy and maths
- Conformity, work, test taking, and,
- Discipline

Adapted from Seligman (2011)

There would seem to be quite a disparity between the two lists; whilst one might be more concerned with emotional development and attaining positive life balance, the other appears to be focused on cognitive development, achievement and behaviour balance.

The questions are interesting as primary schools in recent years have adopted strategies for promoting happiness and well-being through specific lessons. 'SEAL', which stands for social and emotional learning, aims to foster emotional contentment through the exploration of values and morals through carefully chosen strategies such as particular stories and the promotion of emotional intelligence. The belief that the more a child feels inner contentment and experiences happiness he/she can concentrate and in effect learn more ably.

A happy child is also a well-balanced child, less likely to engage in poor behaviour. A by-product of this approach is that behaviour tends to be better. Strategies to enhance well-being used in the classroom include stories that include values, happy and healthy friendships, individual 'happy booklets (like the famous Mr Men books), feelings cards to help children express their feelings and become more emotional literate.

Secondary school children tend to have lessons devoted to 'PSHE': personal, social and health education during which they may even be encouraged to discuss feelings and contentment in more depth, sometimes in ways that get closer to the promotion of mental health rather than just well-being. As young adults they can be encouraged to explore their own individual uniqueness, finding fulfilment and personal happiness, controlling anxiety and depression and the impact it can have on their lives and those of others. It is thought that by analysing what makes them happy and learning to appreciate success no matter how small and their individual surroundings mental health issues like depression may be avoided.

a. What impact do you think a child's sense of well-being has on their behaviour?
b. Can school actually be bad for some children's developing sense of well-being?

Should happiness, if not taught exactly, at least be effectively fostered within the school environment? Again it raises the question of just whose responsibility children's happiness is. Not everyone agrees that schools have a responsibility to promote much less teach well-being. It could be argued that as soon as something as intimately personal and subjective as an inner sense of well-being becomes institutionalised through state interference it immediately loses its quality and value.

It's only in relatively recent years that the state has been concerned with nurturing the whole child and taking an holistic view of childhood, including 'spiritual', 'social' and 'emotional' guidance in its remit.

The psychological research on well-being and happiness suggests it's all about one thing – attitude. This is good news because it means people, and children are no exception, can be taught in theory to change their attitudes. One secondary school in America tested this approach on 14-15-year-olds. The 'positive psychology' programme encouraged students to reflect on and think about the positive things that had occurred and to decide how they could make those very things happen again. The combination of the memory and decision-making make this a cognitive exercise; by engaging the mind the ideas and the experience generally will tend to resonate in a stronger way.

Cognitive Behaviour Therapy, or 'CBT' works in the same manner, and is a successful treatment for some individuals experiencing a variety of mental health issues, for example, depression and it can also have tremendous success with phobias. It encourages patients to literally re-think their response to certain events or triggers, allowing them to react instead in a more balanced rather than negative way. Working on a person's perception or interpretation of an event means their reaction can mean all the difference to their behaviour.

In the school exercise Seligman and his team asked the young students to discover what their 'signature strengths' were, in other words the character traits unique to them through which they could continue to achieve positive outcomes in all aspects of their lives. For example, 'I am patient, friendly, positive and kind', therefore by continuing to approach others and situations that I may meet in my life with these attributes 'I can expect good things to happen to me'.

The results demonstrated evidence for a reduction in challenging behaviour, better empathy for others and a higher degree of curiosity in lessons. It would seem that the idea of being able to influence or even control events by taking some sort of deliberate action empowers the teenagers to feel greater satisfaction and a better sense of well-being.

According to the United Nations a world 'fit for children' is one which should: "…promote the physical, psychological, spiritual, social, emotional, cognitive and cultural development of children as a matter of national and global priority" (2002: 5).

These may seem perhaps like rather lofty ideals, desirable and only attainable in certain economic climates and luxurious societies free from any other more pressing threats or concerns such as war or famine. Large-scale global issues aside, chronic poverty still remains the single largest hurdle to meeting children's needs adequately in order for their development to be appropriately nurtured. Of course there will be not only macro but micro problems impacting on certain parents' ability to effectively nurture their children which need to be taken into consideration. For example, parents' mental health issues, learning difficulties, substance abuse, poor housing, hostile communities and lack of appropriate support. Some factors may simply be outside a parent's control, whilst others could be mitigated or even removed if societal circumstances allowed.

The United Nations has stated that poverty remains the biggest hurdle to ensuring children are nurtured sufficiently to promote well-being. Poverty may be relative but few would argue that expectations of what constitutes a 'basic must-have 'possession have increased over the last three decades. To not have a mobile phone these days for example could, in the eyes of children's peers, be enough to place them as 'different' or maybe even as an outsider. The research findings described below suggest there are a number of factors which influence a sense of satisfaction with childhood, and if absent, make a powerful contribution to a feeling of dissatisfaction.

According to the Children's Society, recent research suggests a significant minority of children in the UK now have such low levels of well-being there are serious concerns being raised at government level not only for children's immediate childhoods but also their future life chances.

The research, based on surveys in which children were asked to express their opinions, highlighted a number of external factors influencing children's sense of life satisfaction. They included a number of factors such as:

- positive relationships with family and friends
- a suitable home within a safe local area
- opportunities to participate in positive activities
- favourable conditions to learn and develop, and
- access to "enough of what matters in order to fit in with peers".

Children talked about a range of issues with regards to the last point, including:

- having a similar amount of pocket money as their friends
- access to a garden or outdoor space
- clothes to fit in with their friends, and
- at least one monthly trip out with their family.

The participating children's responses have been compared with a ten-point 'deprivation index'; a score of five or less correlates with low levels of well-being (childrenssociety.org.uk; 16/6/14).

We can compare these indicators of well-being with those below Scottish government's conclusions:

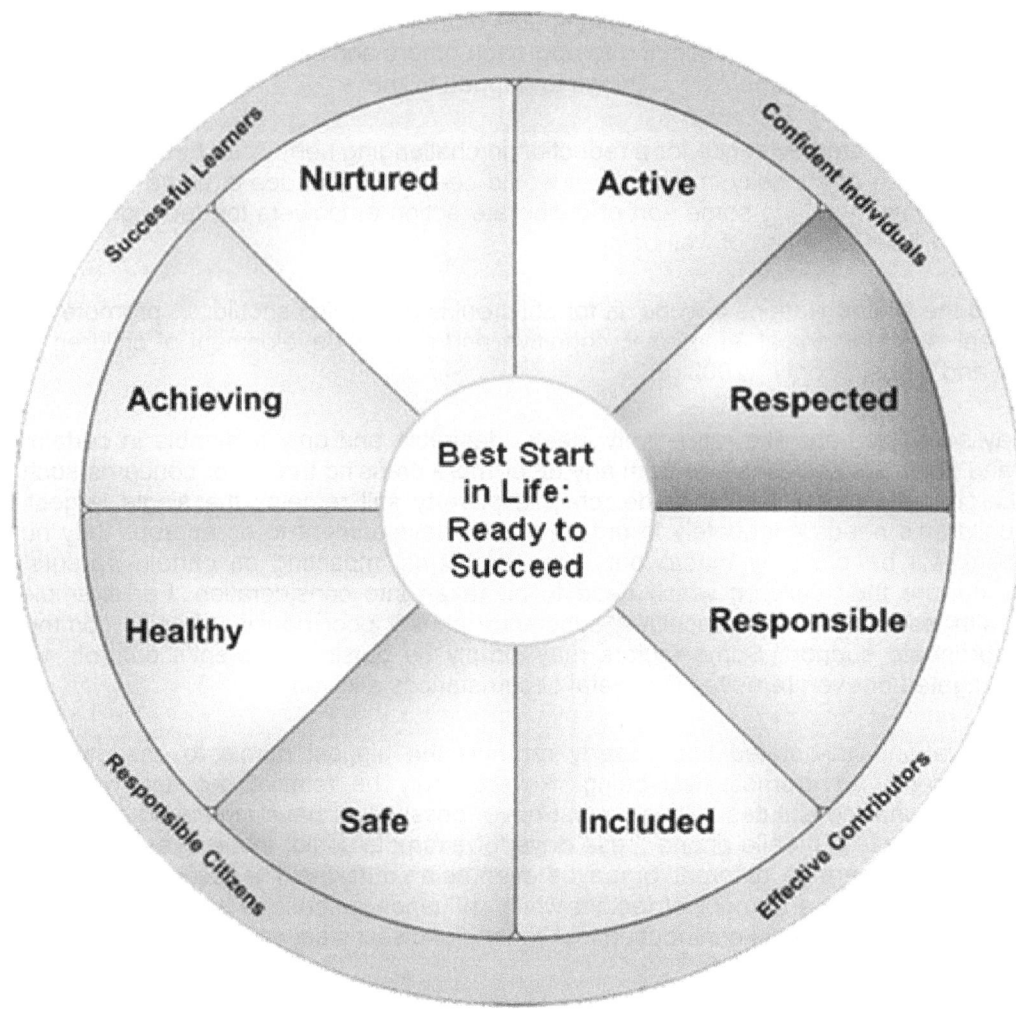

Well-being Indicators

Scottish Government (2010: 14)

Unicef commissioned a study in 2007 which subsequently placed the UK at the bottom of the children's league table for well-being among developed countries across the world. As a consequence well-being has increasingly been at the top of the political agenda. One particular concern raised by Unicef was the degree to which the UK's children feel trapped within a 'materialistic culture' and don't spend enough time with their families (unicef.org.uk, 2011; 17/6/14). A point shared and also raised by Sue Palmer in her 2007 seminal book 'Toxic Childhood'.

Unicef has argued the true measure of a nation's standing is how well it attends to its children, their health and safety, security, education and socialisation and their sense of being loved, valued and included in the families and societies into which they were born (Unicef, 2007).

Self-esteem

Self-esteem can be defined as an attitude regarding ourselves based on an evaluation which may be positive, negative or neutral. Although subject to change, it is believed that our fundamental concept tends to remain relatively stable. Self-esteem is a vital psychological component of what is considered to be good mental health, and makes a significant contribution to becoming a well-balanced and even-tempered adult later in life. Psychological research indicates that children who have had the benefit of warm and affectionate, and especially 'predictable' relationships with their parents or significant carers generally tend to have high self-esteem.

Children with good levels of self-esteem are more likely to have a positive outlook on life, be more independent, assertive and secure, and enjoy better social adjustment.

Children whose self-esteem is low tend to need reassurance, lacking a sense of self-belief in their own abilities and a somewhat negative or pessimistic outlook. With a tendency to overreact to failure, be objective about constructive criticism, there is sometimes a need to exert superiority over others which may manifest itself in bullying behaviour, either physical or verbal or both.

As a general test of self-esteem the following questions might be posed to objectively assess level – that is, high or low. Do bear in mind however the need for consistency; everyone will have their off-days but generally psychologists will be interested in establishing the stable norm for individuals. For instance, a test of any kind would not be valid following unusually distressful events or difficult circumstances, times when behaviour may not be expected to conform to what might otherwise be expected.

With regard to a child's general profile:

1. **Confidence:** secure, self-assured friendly disposition or vulnerable and dependent on approval/attention/reassurance?

2. **Self-efficacy:** high or low expectations of own ability to achieve?

3. **Independence:** willing and eager to try new activities or reluctant to engage in the unfamiliar preferring to be dependent on others' choices?

4. **Peer influence:** easily influenced by peers or self-willed?

5. **Proximity:** remains physically close to key adults or happy to explore without constant reassurance?

6. **Popularity:** able to form friendships easily? Active participant or an observer in group situations?

7. **Self-acceptance:** eager and assertive in expressing own opinions and preferences or self-conscious and passive?

8. **Disappointments:** bounces back from setbacks well or is badly affected?

9. **Non-routine:** motivated, adaptable and flexible response to out of the ordinary opportunities or anxious and rigid?

10. **Creativity:** can engage well in imaginative process driven tasks or become stressed when the end-product isn't defined for them?

11. **Concentration:** is the level of attention good and are tasks completed – is the child 'in the moment' or pre-occupied and disengaged?

12. **Bullying:** victim or perpetrator of excessive teasing or bullying; verbally or physically aggressive?

Non-verbal communication can be a very good indication of a child's sense of self but again it's very important to know what could be considered to be their typical pattern of behaviour before making any possible assumptions. For example:

- **Posture:** generally relaxed and at ease or tense and nervous?

- **Movements:** animated or rigid?

- **Anxiety:** exhibit frequent and multiple anxious gestures, such as: thumb sucking, fingernail biting, clothes picking, hair sucking?

- **Facial expression:** are a range of emotions demonstrated – smiling, sadness, surprise, joy, laughter, boredom... 'flat effect' when no emotional range is evident via the face at all can be a sign of having shut off the emotions.

An interesting indicator of self-esteem generally is observing what happens when in receipt of a compliment – is it accepted or brushed off or minimised in some way. For example: "You're looking great today, is that a new dress/shirt?" Reply: "oh, this old thing, I've had it for ages, nothing special", rather than "Thanks very much ...". Acknowledging a compliment, receiving a verbal 'stroke' and taking it at face value can be subject to cultural differences and attitudes towards modesty and so it isn't always representative of self-esteem per se. Otherwise it can be quite revealing. Try it for yourself.

Personality Development in Childhood

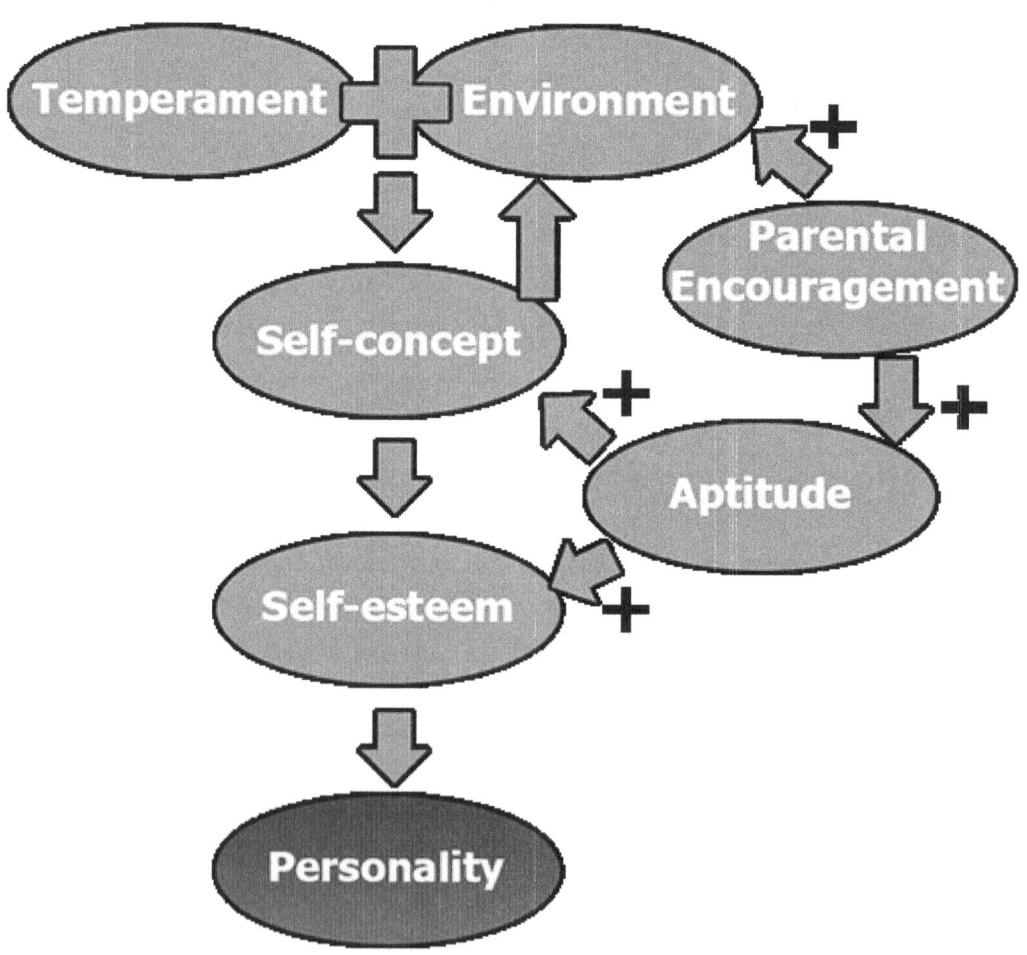

theatlantic.com

A well-known psychological study of self-esteem, conducted by Coopersmith (1968), found evidence to suggest that the type of parenting a child has experienced influences his/her degree of self-esteem and their behaviour.

The children who had been exposed to a 'firm but fair' set of clear boundaries concerning what they could and could not do tended to be self-regulating and less impulsive or rebellious. Compared with children exposed to an authoritarian or permissive style pf parenting, who were more inclined respectively to be aimless and lack self-control. High self-esteem affects levels of confidence.

In the experiment Coopersmith asked pre-adolescent boys to throw a bean bag at a choice of targets separated by range. The further away the target the higher the score. The boys were asked to name their target before throwing and to state the ideal score they expected to achieve.

The boys who had been rated as having high self-esteem demonstrated high rates of 'self-efficacy': a 'can do' attitude; they had higher goals and were actually more successful at attaining their aims. The boys with low-self-esteem conversely had lower expectations of their self-efficacy, they were unsure of themselves, their ability and unsurprisingly achieved lower results.

Maslow, a famous American psychologist, wrote a seminal book entitled 'Toward a Psychology of Being' (1962) in which he speculated what the highest level of psychological development was. He asserted that 'self-actualisation' represented the pinnacle of human achievement likely to be reached by a comparative minority of people. In order to become self-fulfilled at this level he believed it was first necessary to ascend a number of stages of personal needs. Maslow's 'hierarchy of needs' states that children, like people generally, have different levels of need and the most basic ones need to be met before the higher level needs can be reached.

For example, firstly, **physical needs** such as hunger, thirst, sleep and shelter. These needs may seem like pretty taken for granted areas for someone who has been used to the comparative luxury of never having been without food, shelter or suffered any threat to their life and the lives of their families but take a few moments to think of the many images you will have seen via the media of children spending their daily lives without the comfort of a stable roof over their heads and clean water to drink and something to eat each day. It is possible to imagine how life might be consumed by the all-encompassing fight for survival which dominates everything else.

Secondly, building on from the first layer, the need for **security**; to feel safe and out of danger. A person may have enough to eat but if he/she lives in a constant state of fear the ability to concentrate and pay attention, the necessary precursors for learning, will be impaired. Thirdly, the need for **love**; a person may be free from danger or the threat of harm but this is not the same as feeling a sense of belonging and approval.

Fourthly, a need for **esteem**; a feeling of being a worthwhile individual and having a value in the eyes of others. Only once all of these needs are satisfied and realised can a person achieve the pinnacle: self-actualisation; a state of having reached one's potential. Education, through developing skills and abilities, aims to fulfil this state but if Maslow's model is correct, teachers cannot possibly make maximum progress if children's more fundamental needs are not being met. A child who has not been given breakfast is unlikely to be able to fully concentrate and engage in the classroom. If a child who doesn't feel safe enough to trust adults won't tend to do as well as the children who can interact with their teachers with ease. Happy children are effective learners, and tend to be high achievers. A child's behaviour rather like their capacity to learn and thrive cannot be separated from their well-being, it is part of it.

SELF-
ACTUALIZA-
TION
morality, creativity,
spontaneity, acceptance,
experience purpose, meaning
and inner potential

SELF-ESTEEM
confidence, achievement, respect of others,
the need to be a unique individual

LOVE AND BELONGING
friendship, family, intimacy, sense of connection

SAFETY AND SECURITY
health, employment, property, family and social abilty

PHYSIOLOGICAL NEEDS
breathing, food, water, shelter, clothing, sleep

Aside from reaching self-actualisation significant though that may be, self-esteem is a vital psychological component of what is considered to be good mental health. Research has found that up to 15 per cent of pupils in every classroom (on average about three) have mental health issues that are undiagnosed conditions which may lead to an increased risk of developing more serious difficulties in later life (Lawrence, 2006).

Government guidance created by the Department for Education in consultation with the Department for Health has promised that teachers will receivehelp in identifying mental health problems to distinguish behavioural symptoms from bullying or trouble-making behaviour. The advice will gradually be made available to all schools in a bid to ensure un-well children receive help earlier than at present. The guidance is designed to ensure teachers are confident in locating help for at-risk pupils. The guidance also outlines strategies for dealing with disruptive and bullying behaviour, stating that schools should have policies in place, be prepared to work with parents and carers and establish mentoring programmes where older pupils support younger children. Schools should also have links with the Child and Adolescent Mental Health Services (CAMHS), an organisation run in conjunction with the NHS offering assessment and treatment for children and adolescents experiencing emotional, behavioural and mental health issues, for those pupils already identified as at risk.

Some schools already take their mental health support further by teaching pupils that mental health is as important as physical health. As already outlined earlier when discussing how some secondary schools' provision incorporates mental health 'training', it is hoped that by reducing the chances of any associated stigmatisation, that attitudes towards mental ill-health will become more accepting. It would seem that this message and the collective efforts are all worthwhile; the mental health charity 'Young Minds' declared that young people are increasingly "under enormous pressure" (2014) from bullying, social media, exam stress, sexual pressures and worries about future employment.

The psychologist Daniel Goleman (1996) defines emotional intelligence as: knowing one's feelings and using them to make good decisions in life; being able to manage moods and control impulses and being motivated and effectively overcoming setbacks in working towards goals.

For children this will mean the ability to understand their own feelings, recognise the emotion and, according to their age and stage of development, be able to name the feeling. This is where emotional 'literacy' comes in. Having the breadth of language to be able to identify an emotion. For example, knowing the difference between being angry and being upset, and being 'allowed' to be angry which traditionally has not been something children could legitimately feel.

Schools have introduced ways to encourage children to identify the diversity of feelings through such means as feelings cards and posters depicting a series of facial expressions with the appropriate label. The vocabulary work helps with another stage of literacy and that is the ability to empathise with others' feelings.

Usually, if a child has developed typically, an awareness of others' emotions will be demonstrated as young as 18-months. This is a period emotional sensitivity when children can perceive others' hurt and pain.

For example, if children of this age are playing together and one begins to cry it isn't uncommon for another child to experience distress too. It's as if hearing the crying triggers a deep-seated recognition of and connection with another person. Psychologists refer to this phenomenon as 'global empathy'.

The concept of intelligence has long been considered a controversial one in psychology circles, not least because it appears to imply a set of skills that may be genetic and as such unchangeable. Testing or measuring intelligence is even more prone to debate with suggestions that at best all it can reliably achieve is a gauge of how well an individual performs on a given day and time. Can we say with any degree of accuracy that intelligence is fixed at the moment of conception or can it develop alongside gaining life experiences and nurturing? To add to the arguments there is another school of thought in psychology that suggests there is no such thing as 'intelligence' per se, rather multiple intelligences exist, and yes, you've guessed it, we are all intelligent in various ways that may or may not coincide with what our society regards as valuable.

Not everyone is literate for instance but they may demonstrate their cognitive prowess in a number of other ways. I personally know of a very wealthy and accomplished house builder who can barely read or write (he's profoundly dyslexic) and merely has to look at a piece of land to be able to envision the end result whilst pricing up the total cost of resources required. What do you value in a person if you think of them as 'intelligent'? It can be a very subjective concept and difficult to pin down.

Different ideas regarding what constitutes intelligence aside for a moment, researchers have also begun to speculate whether another skill could be subject to the same level of difference of opinion; namely, our ability to monitor emotions; both our own and other people's feelings. This means being able to readily differentiate between emotions, and use the information to guide our thinking and behaviour as a result: a kind of 'social intelligence'; relying on social awareness, self-control, empathy and the ability perhaps most importantly of all to manage relationships.

Of course there are times when everyone at some point will lose control and behave erratically or impulsively, perhaps out of character, this is normal and to be expected. It's a person's consistent pattern of behaviour that psychologists focus on.

We might even take such 'social skills' for granted but it is only too obvious when we see conflict and disharmony at both societal and personal relationship levels that this is a skill that not everyone possesses.

Some children find it genuinely troublesome to relate to social situations and cope with the range of emotions. If we think of the way children can be brought up and the many differences in childrearing practices across the globe, sometimes we might get the impression there are some emotions that children aren't even supposed to feel and certainly not express. Anger or rage, jealousy and being mean.

Emotional literacy' is used to describe improving emotional intelligence.

The following checklist is used to help practitioners working with young children understand the different aspects of emotional intelligence and to highlight the areas that children may benefit from.

- Can the child talk about the way they feel?
- Does the child have a number of words they can use to describe feelings?
- Can the child recognise when other people are happy/sad/angry/scared?
- Can the child recall past memories and the way they felt then?
- Does the child enjoy and feel confident in their play?
- Can the child show friendliness and care towards others?
- Can the child control their anger and frustration?
- Can the child use words and negotiation to solve disputes?
- Can the child play co-operatively with others?
- If s/he is feeling anxious, is s/he reassured by a familiar adult or friend?
- Can the child wait just a little before his/her needs are met?
- Can the child initiate his/her own ideas and contribute in a familiar group?
- Can the child occupy him/herself when playing as well as playing with others?
- Can the child demonstrate confidence when trying something new?
- Is the child beginning to be aware of right and wrong?
- Does the child feel able to make mistakes and learn from them?

Adapted from Mortimer (2003: 9)

It can be impossible to separate self-esteem/ confidence from emotional literacy, one way to foster confidence is through experiencing success in achieving new things. Each new success acts as a boost to self-esteem and the happier we feel about ourselves the more we're inclined to think we're valued. However, without a good level of confidence in the first place children may be reluctant to try new things and therefore be denied the opportunity to flourish socially and emotionally and remain dependent on adults for longer than necessary.

Typically, a two-year-old child developing according to the norm, will demonstrate dependence on an adult, finding it relatively difficult to separate unless in a familiar situation. An older young pre-school child will tend to show signs of independence although may still relay on a 'transitional object' such as a favourite teddy or cuddly item for comfort.

simplypsychology.co.uk

Howard Gardner's (1983; 1999) multiple intelligences theory which was developed as a result of his dissatisfaction with the idea of intelligence as something that could be measured and in particular represented by an IQ score. Instead Gardner stove to work on creating an exploration of *how everyone is intelligent* in different ways. A view opposed to the traditional concept of intelligence that suggests *how much* is more significant. He wasn't concerned with which intelligences were present, rather the idea that everyone has a mix of certain strengths and weaknesses. Intelligence according to Gardner results from individual backgrounds, experiences and cultural opportunities to develop; in Western culture literacy and numeracy are highly rated, however in other parts of the world the practical ability to do, make and mend things is favoured above reading and writing ability.

Gardner (1999: 218-9) wrote:

"Every time we are exposed to a new individual – in person or in spirit – our own horizons broaden… Because our genes and our experiences are unique and because our brains must figure out meanings, no two selves, no two consciousnesses, no two minds are exactly alike. Each of us is therefore situated to make a unique contribution to the world."

- **Interpersonal:** interactions with others
- **Intrapersonal:** understanding of self

Interpersonal intelligence refers to the ability to interact effectively with others, intrapersonal intelligence focuses on the ability to reflect on ourselves.

⟫ References

Childrenssociety.org.uk; 16/6/14

Coopersmith, S. (1968): Studies in Self-esteem. *Scientific American*, 218 (2), 96-106

Gardner, H. (1999): *Intelligence Reframed*, London: Basic Books

Goleman, D. (1996): *Emotional Intelligence*, London: Bantam Books

Maslow, A. (1970): *Motivation and Personality*, New York: Harper & Row

Mortimer, H. (2003): *Emotional Literacy and Mental Health in the Early Years*, London: QEd

Lawrence, D. (2006): *Self-esteem Enhancement in the Classroom*, London: Sage

Scottish Government (2010): *A Guide to Implementing The Getting It Right for Every Child: Messages from Pathfinders and Learning Partners*, Edinburgh: Scottish Executive

Seligman, M. (2011): *Flourish: a new understanding of happiness and well-being*, New York: Vintage Books

United Nations report (2002): 'A World Fit for Children' – unicef.org/specialsession/wffc/ accessed 30/6/14

Unicef (2007): *Child Poverty in Perspective: An Overview of Child Well-being in Rich Countries*, Florence: Unicef

Youngminds.org.uk; 21/6/14

≫ Further Reading and Sources of Support

Argyle, M. (1978): *The Psychology of Interpersonal Behaviour*, Middlesex: Penguin

Goswami, H. (2011): *Social Relationships and Children's Subjective Well-being*, London: Springer

Growingkids.co.uk/DevelopingSelfEsteem.html

Kidshealth.org

Office for National Statistics

Palmer, S. (2007): *Toxic Childhood: How the Modern World is Damaging Our Children and What We Can Do About It*, London: Orion

Steiner, C. (1999): *Achieving Emotional Literacy*, London: Bloomsbury Books

The Nuffield Foundation

The Learning Outcomes for this assignment are:

Element	Learning Outcome
1	Understand the impact a child's temperament has on their response to external events
2	Awareness of how attachment disorder can contribute to children's stress
3	Knowledge of the range of impulsive behavioural responses

Temperament

Temperament can be described as a characteristic mode of behaviour or the typical reaction a person will tend to exhibit. In so far as the nature nurture debate, when psychologists use the term temperament they tend to be referring to an individual's genetic disposition. Whereas if the term 'personality' is used it suggests they are at least open to the idea a person's environment has exerted an influence and shaped behaviour. Here, we'll be equally open to both sides of influence.

Research has suggested there are quite strong connections between a difficult temperament at 4/5-years of age and behavioural problems in later childhood. Occasionally it's difficult to draw the line between a personality problem and an actual behavioural disorder. Psychologists tend to agree that a difficult or 'irritable' temperament in younger life can indicate vulnerability and/or a risk of later issues, such as:

- Violence
- Relationship difficulties (especially in boys)

One of the issues that psychologists see is a particularly worrying related characteristic of a difficult temperament, especially in children, is 'fearlessness'. When a child is literally fearless their capacity to get into trouble knows no bounds. A fearless child is a disturbed child, and this is a significant line when discussing behaviour as either a problem or a disorder.

a.

A mother's emotional state during pregnancy may affect a developing foetus; anxiety or distress can lead to the over-production of adrenalin which can in turn have a negative effect. The babies are more likely as a result to have a difficult temperamental profile. Associated problems are:

- Hyperactivity
- Irritability
- Irregular feeding
- Poor sleeping

Research conducted by Field et al (1985) found evidence to suggest that mothers who were stressed and anxious before the birth for whatever reason, for example, housing issues, relationship difficulties, or an unplanned pregnancy, will normally continue to have those problems after the birth, possibly to the extent the baby's arrival has made the situation worse. Therefore, this kind of mother tends to be more emotionally distant, sometimes resentful, with some resorting to punitive means of controlling the child in her frustration to control her wider circumstances.

Psychologists use the term 'goodness of fit' to describe the reciprocal interaction between a natural birth mother and her child. Sometimes this will also take into account a child's wider environment when his/her attachments to other adults are just as influential.

Let's now have a look at how the interaction of the child characteristics and the environmental variables can produce disturbed behaviour:

Temperament:	Environment:	Outcome:	Behaviour Risk:
Easy	Favourable	'Dream child'	Low
Easy	Adverse	'Resilient child'	Low
Difficult	Favourable	Hard to care for child'	High
Difficult	Adverse	'Vulnerable child'	High

Key:

- 'Easy' child: presents no major difficulties – eats, sleeps well and is easily soothed;
- 'Difficult' child: may not be as responsive to care-giving – fretful, irritable and demanding;
- 'Favourable' environment: 'good fit' between caregiver and child; and,
- 'Adverse' environment: antagonistic fit between caregiver and child

Adapted from Ding & Littleton (2005)

There are though a number of mitigating circumstances that can serve to 'protect' children from otherwise adverse or risk factors. For example, while some children remain relatively vulnerable to behavioural disorders, others may be more resilient.

Resilience as a topic is increasingly becoming a focus of research for psychologists interested in investigating 'positive psychology', in other words what makes those people who are well-balanced, well-adjusted and for want of a better word 'successful' in life just so. It may seem quite obvious when we put it like that but for decades the angle taken was exactly the opposite. Psychologists instead chose to study atypical individuals with problems to formulate their theories.

For example, **intelligence**; not all children who are exposed to adverse environments show disturbed behaviour. Even children exposed to high-risk of maladjustment can adjust well – why? Studies have demonstrated that high IQ can mediate circumstances – again why should intelligence make such a strong difference? One idea put forward is that a high IQ enables an individual to cope better with adversity and/or find alternative solutions to the problems they encounter.

What do psychologists mean when they refer to 'risk factors' associated with children's challenging behaviour?

Although there are often multiple risk factors associated with problem behaviour, five in particular were identified in a major study conducted by the Dunedin research – a multi-disciplinary Health and Development study, one of the largest longitudinal studies of development which concluded that approximately 17% of children over the age of 11-years showed significant signs of a behavioural disorder. Longitudinal studies tend to carry more credence as the data has been obtained over a long period of time, rather than a snapshot, and so is considered more reliable and valid as evidence.

The most common disorders found were:

- Attention-deficit disorders (problems associated with staying on-task)

- Conduct-oppositional disorders (defiance, confrontational and challenging behaviour)

- Separation anxiety disorders (distress and anxiety of separation)

- The least prevalent were depression and social phobias.

The five main risk factors were:

1. **Social background**: children from low social status families were found to be more likely to exhibit antisocial behaviour)

2. **Parental attitudes**: parental ambivalence to children's discipline was found to be a significant predictor of antisocial behaviour in adolescence

3. **Mother's mental state**: children whose mothers have psychiatric symptoms have higher levels of anxiety and depression as adolescents

4. **Father's behaviour:** antisocial behaviour of the father is associated with conduct problems in the children

5. **Marital relationship:** poor marital relations poses risk for behavioural difficulties

Ding & Littleton (2005)

Attachment

What is attachment? Kagan et al (1978), cited in Gross, 1998: 328, have defined attachment as:

"an intense emotional relationship that is specific to two people, that endures over time, and in which prolonged separation from the partner is accompanied by stress and sorrow."

The above definition could apply to any attachment formed at any point during life but it is the first attachment that is of major importance; the first attachment acts as a prototype for later relationships, affecting future expectations and the ability to trust others which is a major facet of any relationship. Berne (1964) referred to the prototype relationship as a 'life script'; one in which we are subconsciously motivated to repeat throughout life.

Attachment theory argues that children develop a style of relating to attachment figures who are important in their lives. This is a form of coping and adapting to the environment, a kind of survival mechanism for ensuring the best possible outcome under the circumstances. There are some children however whose challenging behaviour is very resistant to change. When children present a difficult temperament their behaviour may be out of control; exhibiting anger, aggression, volatility, impulsiveness and, if accompanied by fearlessness, they can be at high risk of disturbed behaviour to the point of receiving a behaviour disorder diagnosis. Where there is the additional difficulty of an attachment issue, especially a rejecting mother/carer the situation may not be conducive to change. However with a sensitive, warm and responsive caregiver can make a positive difference even in the most maladjusted child.

A significant factor in determining children's temperament and behaviour is the quality of their attachment to their parent or carer. We've already discussed the 'goodness of fit' concept and the idea that if the parent's personality and the child's temperament don't match too well then the interaction might be impaired.

In 1978 a female psychologist, Mary Ainsworth and her team, designed an experimental situation called the 'Strange Situation Test' to gauge the quality of the mother child bond. In it a number of carefully controlled sequences of separations and reunions occurred between the child, mother/caregiver and a stranger. The way the child responds determines whether the attachment is classified as either 'secure' or 'insecure'. The latter is further sub-divided into 'avoidant' or 'ambivalent'.

The sequences involved seven 3-minute episodes:

1. Parent and infant enter the room
2. Stranger joins parent and infant
3. Parent leaves
4. Parent returns, stranger leaves
5. Parent leaves
6. Stanger returns
7. Parent returns, stranger leaves

The most significant aspect of the experiment is how the child responds when the parent/carer leaves the room and when they return.

The resulting behaviour exhibited by the child is subsequently recorded as:

Type:	Classification:	Description:
A	Anxious-avoidant	No protest when the parent leaves; IGNORES parent's return
B	Secure	Mild protest when the parent leaves; on return SEEKS parent and is easily comforted
C	Anxious-resistant	Seriously distressed when parent leaves; on return alternately CLINGS/REJECTS

The findings of the original experiment indicated:

Type:	%:
A: Anxious-avoidant	10
B: Secure	70
C: Anxious-resistant	20

Flanagan (1999)

Securely attached children have been found to be more socially outgoing, independent, co-operative, responsive, curious and eager to learn/try new things, resilient and able to cope with stress. When attachment is secure it is likely that the child's earliest needs were reliably and consistently met, thus establishing predictability which studies have repeatedly confirmed is very significant for security.

If a parent is sensitive to the child's needs confidence, self-esteem and independence tend to be the resulting characteristics of the growing child, and later the adult's personality. If the parent is unresponsive, ambivalent or even rejecting the child may need to develop independence before they are really emotionally equipped to be ready. This represents an 'anxious-avoidant' style of attachment. As a way of avoiding being let down and hurt the child, in turn, behaves in exactly the same way he/she is being treated.

If a parent is inconsistent in their responses, perhaps arising from depression, illness, addiction, or frequent absences, a pattern of controlling attachment may arise in which the child learns a way of maintaining some predictability over their parent. It is important to note here that in order to become a good parent parents themselves ideally will have had the benefit of good parenting. A good foundation, or 'secure base' allows a blueprint from which to provide nurture and care to others. A parent who has suffered trauma, loss or abuse may demonstrate a disorganised inconsistent style of parenting that produces a form of insecure attachment with their own children.

Secure attachment is associated with positive development and outcomes for later life. A parenting style most closely linked to a securely attached child is that of sensitivity to the child's needs, an ability to interpret needs especially in the early stages following birth which are then consistently and predictably met thus ensuring the child learns to trust and become optimistic.

This idea of a positive outlook being built on early patterns of upbringing isn't new; a psychologist called Erikson (1963) developed a theory of psychosocial stages of development. He argued that it's in the first year of life when infants learn their basic sense of trust. If their needs have been reliably met the infant is likely to have a positive outlook, leading to an optimistic personality in later life.

On the other hand if their needs have been dismissed or ignored or only met sporadically rather than consistently it's probable that he/she has a more negative outlook leading to pessimism and mistrust.

Erikson's Stages of Psychosocial Development

Approximate Age	Psycho Social Crisis
Infant - 18 months	Trust vs. Mistrust
18 months - 3 years	Autonomy vs. Shame & Doubt
3 - 5 years	Initiative vs. Guilt
5 -13 years	Industry vs. Inferiority
13 -21 years	Identity vs. Role Confusion
21- 39 years	Intimacy vs. Isolation
40 - 65 years	Generativity vs. Stagnation
65 and older	Ego Integrity vs. Despair

(C) The Psychology Notes Headquarter - http://www.PsychologyNotesHQ.com

nurseryworld.co.uk

The Mental Health Foundation and Advisory Group on emotional and behavioural difficulties has provided guidance on how to identify children who might be a cause for concern in terms of challenging or disturbed behaviour. Firstly if we can have a look at the ideal characteristics a well-balanced child might be expected to exhibit:

- develop psychologically, emotionally, intellectually and spiritually according to the norms expected for his/her age and stage of development;

- use and enjoy solitude;

- become aware of the feelings of others and empathise with them;

- play spontaneously without direction and learn from experience;

- develop a sense of right and wrong; and,

- face up to and resolve setbacks and learn from them.

Conversely, mental health problems experienced by children and young people which have a direct bearing on problem behaviour include:

- attachment disorders
- conduct disorders
- emotional and behavioural difficulties

Young people who have experienced the above are not only considered to be more 'at risk' behavioural problems but also mental health issues. The two combined are generally considered to be indicative of emotional and behavioural disorder (EBD). However, as previously discussed, the degree to which an individual possesses 'resilience' is a mitigating factor as is maternal attachment.

Attachment Disorder

Attachment disorder' is the name given to a syndrome that children who have had little or no early experience of attachments can exhibit. Children who have invariably been adopted after the age of six months, having previously experienced multiple foster homes or care institutions, when offered the chance to develop an enduring relationship, it comes too late.

George was 18 months old when he was adopted. The couple who became his adoptive parents knew that his biological mother had not wanted him, had rarely touched him and that already in his short life he had twice been fostered. George's last foster family had taken care of him for a period of five months and then had suddenly handed him back to Social Services, claiming they could not handle him. George had experienced no less than three rejections by the age of 18 months. The adoptive couple realised he would need a great deal of affection and care to counter his early deprivation, however, they were unprepared for the next ten years, which in the adoptive father's words were an "almost unremitting hell and anguish". The adoptive mother had always wanted a large family but had been unable to conceive; she and her husband had already adopted two children and after George they adopted another, a handicapped, child.

George appeared to be a child suffering from shock – a pale emotionless face, not capable of either smiling or crying, his behaviour was seriously disturbed. Whilst still in primary school George would issue his adoptive parents with 'death threats', he would hide knives, take things from the house and break them, regularly swore and reacted with wild rages to anything that did not agree with him. The adoptive parents claimed their lives were geared around trying not to upset George: "I realised I was intimidated by him. I also realised he was in terrible turmoil. He had dreadful fears and seemed to be full of dark terrors, but there was no way we could get close to him."

George's (his name has been changed) behaviour is not uncommon; there are a number of adopted children on record who behave in the same way. Their behaviour is characterised mainly by the often enormous amount of rage and anger they feel at having been deserted. Children with Attachment disorder also appear not to have developed a conscience which may be due to the fact they have been unable to 'identify' with their adoptive parent figure in the same way a child would ordinarily with their biological parent. Therapy for these confused and hurt children, and also for their adoptive parents and siblings, involves working on allowing the child to express their overwhelming feelings of anger towards those who have 'abandoned' (whether real or imagined) them, accepting their previous challenging behaviour as a manifestation of that repressed rage and working through it which could take many years.

Adapted from: Flanagan (1999: 167-8)

In terms of parenting style there's a lot of psychological interest in the idea that the way parents were themselves nurtured as children influences their own parenting if and when they go on to have their own children. This is referred to as 'attachment history' which can include unresolved issues deriving from early relationships that resurface in later life. The simple fact is not everyone, despite what we're presented in in the media, has their emotional needs recognised let alone met. Professional therapists using the 'Adult Attachment Interview' can divide the responses into one of three categories of relationships. Often it's not the actual answers people give but the way they are given that is most revealing. For example, a short dismissive brusque reply might indicate a more distant relationship.

- Distant – dismissive
- Indulgent – over-involved
- Functional – autonomous

The last, the most desirable in terms of healthy relationships, is characterised by a 'balanced' approach. Consistency is repeatedly hailed as the key ingredient to what constitutes good parenting, most likely to lead to well-balanced and well-behaved children. If we think about parenting as an interaction of 'giving' and 'receiving' balance is important for the development of trust. Think of apparent who might be termed 'inconsistent' who might jump from being warm to rejecting, approving and critical, overly controlling to permissive. The child learns that they are unpredictable and unreliable and this may lead to resentment, frustration and possibly aggressive tendencies, and thus behavioural problems.

Let's be specific, from a psychological and emotional point of view what – ideally – would all children receive from their parents or carers:

- Attention (the positive variety)
- Approval
- Nurturing
- Security
- Warmth
- Discipline of the firm but fair kind (for balanced and self-regulated behaviour)

Children of inconsistent parents grow up with feelings of insecurity and anxiety, leading to low self-confidence, lack of an ability to trust others and difficulties with controlling their behaviour.

Impulsive Behaviour

What are the reasons why a child might behave in an impulsive way? If parenting has been too authoritarian, characterised by being too directive, disapproving and harsh, the child's behavioural style may reflect a tendency to be antagonistic towards authority figures like teachers for instance which may lead to lashing out either physically or verbally. Similarly is parenting has been too over-protective, characterised by being too interfering and intrusive; the child's behavioural style may reflect a tendency to be smothered. Their need to assert their own independence might manifest in emotional explosiveness.

A parenting style referred to earlier is that of 'distant' parenting; characterised by an attitude of parenting as merely a responsibility. Children with distant parents may feel that there is nothing they can do receive attention other than to misbehave. Neglectful parenting refers to those parents unable to provide care. Children who have suffered neglect and extreme privation grow up with quite severe lack of even basic needs for reason such as food, clothing and adequate housing. The reasons can range from economic, psychological and emotional damage arising from childhood, mental illness, learning difficulties and addiction. The psychological effects can be extremely serious.

Children can react by shutting off their emotional response to the extent they no longer experience empathy for others. Sometimes this impaired emotionality manifests in a child growing up to mistrust and shun contact with others, preferring their own company, again as a means to unconsciously avoid being hurt again.

Resilient Behaviour

Securely attached children tend to exhibit by contrast the ability to regulate their own response showing self-control and the capacity to think before behaving. Why, where does this ability come from? One of the aspects of balanced parenting, or authoritative parenting, that contributes to resilience is the role of discipline: setting firm boundaries and limits. Another is warmth and approval: allowing independence and choice, giving praise and encouragement and being reasonable.

This kind of treatment when not constant but consistent tends to support children's development, leading to energetic, well-adjusted and stable behaviour with a resilient outlook. Resilient children can take disappointments, sudden changes in routine and difficult circumstances and bounce back. Instead of being trapped in the moment, impulsively reacting to provocation and showing a lack of empathy, resilient children exhibit 'delayed gratification' – the ability to think of the bigger picture and future consequences.

This is key to problem behaviour and behaviour control. When children can be mindful of the consequences of their actions, any temptation to act impulsively is likely to be curbed, particularly if they have developed the ability to be empathetic.

⌖ AGGRESSION AND VIOLENCE

The Learning Outcomes for this assignment are:

Element	Learning Outcome
1	Understand the influence of modelling
2	Knowledge of how frustration can manifest into different types of aggressive behaviour
3	Awareness of relevant psychological theory

There has been and continues to be a great deal of speculation in psychology as to the influence of the media in children's lives. In the media itself you'll often read reports about how violence in games and on the television has a negative influence, some going so far as to suggest it causes children to become violent. Really? Can children in effect copy aggressive acts they may have seen without engaging their filter for what is right and wrong? If we think of the media as widely as possible the debate can become even more complicated to pin down. Written material – newspapers, magazines; the spoken word – pop songs, radio; visual multimedia – films, video, computer games, TV are just some of the potential influences – for good or ill – that the majority of children will come across sometimes on a daily basis.

Psychologists have debated the effects on young children's development of seeing, hearing and even interacting with content that can be too advanced for their level of maturity. And that's without going into the arguments for the 'electronic babysitter' and the reduced opportunities for human interaction that the electronic stimulation prevents.

The main issue with aggression and violence and whether it can be encouraged by media influence is that we already know how powerful TV is for example for altering people's opinions and attitudes, and behaviour. One convincing example of this is the amount of money that's spent on advertising – it works! When was the last time you found yourself buying a certain product out of a choice available to you on the supermarket shelves because you thought it was better than an alternative?

Where did you get that information from to affect your opinion enough to influence even change your buying behaviour? Of course there's a huge amount of psychological research behind the advertising industry in order to create images that not only people can remember but also respond to. That means having an effect on attitudes and behaviour.

One very popular and recurring theme in TV adverts regardless of the product, service or message for sale is affective dissonance. This is a technique used by advertisers and sales people too to make us more likely to connect with the product at a deeper level. An emotion rousing reaction, whether it's guilt, laughter, shame, any feeling really that's jerked as a result of a scenario that deliberately puts us in an uncomfortable state. For example, we might be exposed to a character who feels embarrassed because he/she hasn't bought a particular product and is consequently made to look silly or somehow inferior compared with his more cool friends (who have). These character types are often based on stereotypes that manipulate the tendency to scapegoat, when we make ourselves feel better by putting others down.

Projecting our own insecurities or fears onto others allows us to identify with them from a safe distance. So adverts in this way can resonate with us very successfully; therefore if we buy this product we can avoid looking like the loser, or alternatively we can become more like the popular cool guy if we have things that he owns. It works it different ways but when you start to look for the advertising techniques it can be quite satisfying to recognise the processes, usually repeated time and time again but in more modern versions – just don't fall for them!

So, back to children, what's their role in advertising? Well they might not having the spending power but they certainly have a pestering power, and of course a massive ability to exert guilt on their parents, even if they aren't directly causing the guilt. Advertisers can make parents feel guilty that if they're not treating their children to certain products just by the comparison association. Adverts are aimed directly at children though and this is where the debate can become very heated. Is it fair that impressionable young children can become the manipulated victims of a multi-million pound profit oriented industry?

Adults it could be said at least have a choice. Children's opinions, attitudes and stereotypes are developing and so in this sense they can be deemed to be extremely vulnerable. When children are learning about the world, the real world and not the celluloid version, their ideas are being shaped.

The argument from psychologists centres here on the belief that children are more inclined to copy behaviours, sometimes directly, and when characters are particularly appealing or attractive their influence is even potentially greater. Psychologists

therefore have set up experiments to test whether this is a valid argument and if so if there are certain circumstances that are more likely to be influential than others. Before we look at these in any more detail have a think about what these circumstances could be.

One of the questions psychologists have been interested in testing is does the amount of violence in the media increase levels of aggression? In other words can watching violent acts cause an aggressive response? This raises a fundamental question about the origins of aggression – is it innate or learned? If we believe strongly in the influence of the media in creating or at least contributing to aggression then we're on the side of nurture or experience. If on the other hand we think the level of aggression is acquired through nature then we won't be too concerned about media representations of violence. Is it that simple though?

There is another approach in psychology which suggests a blend of the two approaches. Instead of nature or nurture, the 'interactionist' angle explores the contribution of both sides, a sort of fifty-fifty.

Modelling

Let's now look at one particular psychological experiment to help you make your mind up on the issues raised so far. A psychologist named Bandura and colleagues in the early sixties in America devised an artificial situation to test the influence, if any, of being exposed to aggressive acts on children as young as three-years of age. The children were exposed to an adult 'model' who acted aggressively: shouting and hitting a 'Bobo' doll – a life-sized doll that if hit could bounce back in an upright position.

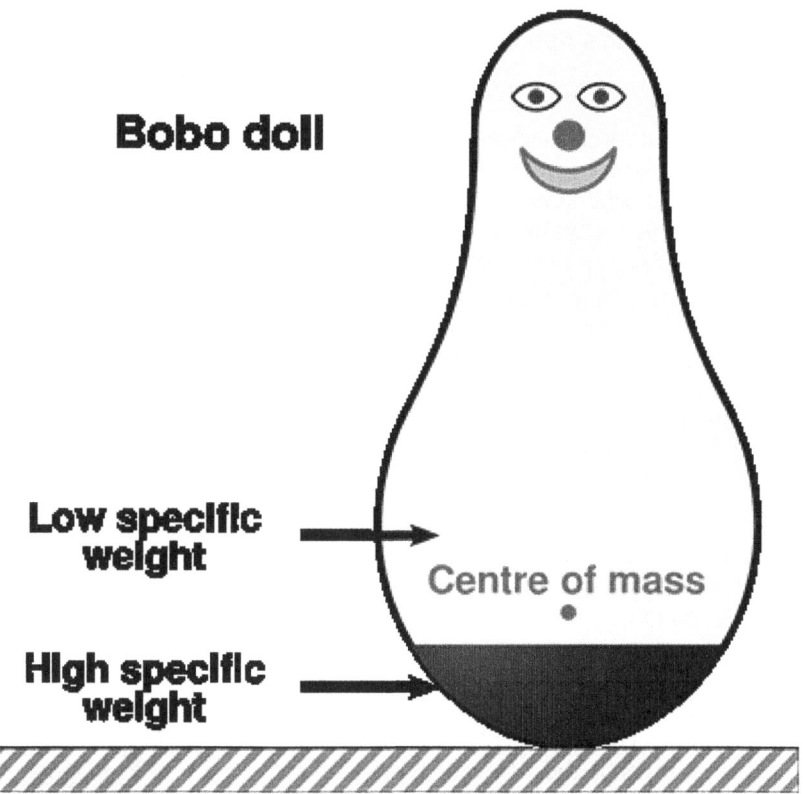

Bobo doll

Low specific weight

Centre of mass

High specific weight

Boundless.com

The conclusions drawn indicated that exposure increased levels of general aggression in the children. In addition it also led to the children imitating specific acts of aggression they had witnessed. We know that children will act out things they've seen, this is an entirely normal part of development and thought to be the result of a child trying to process information, that is understand it at a deeper level.

In adapted versions of the original experiment Bandura exposed children to filmed cartoon models to see if changing from a real life event taking place in real time to one that had been recorded involving 'pretend' characters. This was done to replicate the effects of children watching violence on TV or films. The results of the latter experiment showed that although these models were still influential they were less significant than the live models.

In the last activity you reflected on whether circumstances would make a difference to a child being more easily influenced, for example, having limited experiences or living in an isolated location. Another variable that interested Bandura and his team was the children's personality characteristics. Low self-esteem was found to be significant; it led to greater rates of imitation.

As we have discussed previously in an earlier module, high self-esteem is an important determinant of being self-directed. The other interesting variation employed was changing the status of the model. High status characters are more influential and seemingly worthy of imitation when compared with low status models. This is very interesting when we consider the way the media manipulates the use of characters in advertising aimed at children.

Bandura showed that children could actually learn aggression vicariously, that is, through others and modelling which is also sometimes referred to as 'social learning'. So this seems pretty good evidence for negative influence. Can it be used in reverse though, for positive influence? However if the model was seen to be punished for their acts of aggression the children were found to be less likely to imitate their acts.

Subsequent psychological investigations into the links between television violence and aggressive behaviour have been conducted over the years with varying conclusions reached. Whilst a causal link is difficult to announce categorically because there are so many diverse contributing factors to take into account, for example, a child's upbringing, temperament, intelligence, gender and so forth, some studies have come close.

Comstock (1991) explored research evidence from almost 200 separate studies, concluding that there is a relationship between violence on TV and copied aggression. However this may be the result of innate characteristics; people who have a natural tendency to be more aggressive than others will perhaps find violent films more enjoyable to watch.

Another study found that very young nursery children, who were rated as having above average rates of aggression when observed over a three week period, were subsequently influenced much more by violent cartoons. An aggressive temperament could be described as a cause rather than an effect of watching violent programmes or films, and in turn, their nature increases the likelihood that they will imitate what they've watched.

Frustration

Psychologists believe that frustration can be a precursor to aggression, and in turn, aggression is the precursor to violence. Some people, children included, may experience higher levels of aggressive feelings because of the amount of frustrations they encounter in their lives. Let's just picture a scene: small child displaying natural curiosity and the need to explore their environment. This will involve picking things up, feeling them; perhaps holding the objects close to their mouths and maybe throwing them down again once satisfied of their shape, texture and function.

All's well, up to the point when the big tall adult person comes along and stops the fun. "Don't do that", "What do you think you're doing", "NOooooo". Why do you seem so angry when I'm only doing what comes naturally? Disappointment and confusion all round. This can lead to children feeling resentful and frustrated. And it doesn't end there as the child grows up and their desire to explore increases, along with their growing confidence and need for adventure. In fact it just gets worse with mobility, independence and a growing imagination. (Image from Talktotoddler.com)

Controlling the urge, natural and all part of normal development, to hit out either verbally, physically in some way or both when an impulse is thwarted, comes with maturation. Temper tantrums can be quite awesome in range, noise level, inconvenience and effect.

Everyone has been witness at some time or other to the sprawled out child along the supermarket floor limbs flayed and tonsils roaring. At the age of two-years these are not uncommon, in fact quite prevalent and typical as the growing child begins to test out boundaries and release the pent up feelings associated with frustration as they exercise their need for independence against what passes for acceptability in their own particular upbringing.

Depending on the type of behaviour that accompanies the verbal outcries these temper tantrums can seem quite aggressive in nature, especially with an older child.

As the child grows and become solder their need for independence and a sense of separateness from their care takers gains momentum. They need to become an individual in their own right. If parenting is sensitive, responsive and respectful the transition is likely to be relatively smooth and tension-free but if parenting is over-involved, intrusive and over-bearing it may increase feeling of being smothered, resentment and frustration in the child leading inevitably to problem behaviour in the teenage years especially.

Frustration as a trigger for aggression is well documented, fuelled by adrenalin; when roused adrenalin surges automatically leaving little time for rational thought. We tend instead to respond to its signal in predictable and really quite limited ways, usually tried and tested means that are all too often counter-productive.

The evolutionary response to a rapid rise in adrenalin is the so-called fight-flight response, or abject fear causing temporary paralysis. When we react aggressively, whatever our age and stage of development, we're in fight mode. Flight is a more constructive mode if it means aggression, and certainly violence, is to be avoided.

Choosing to avoid confrontations takes maturity and an ability to be 'self-regulating, a theme we've visited before. Choosing one path of action over another may come from learned behaviour that has become habitual. But, psychology teaches us that whatever can be learned can be unlearned.

Aggression takes on many different forms though and not all are immediately obvious. Some forms can be subjective. What's your opinion of the following: shouting, swearing, spitting, and biting? Depends on the circumstances? Who's committing the acts? What about culture, societal expectations and the decade? Attitudes are fluid and not fixed, rather they are influenced by outside factors. When children display 'aggressive' behaviour, the response they receive can make all the difference to whether it's repeated or not. If negative attention is the only response the child is likely to get then the behaviour is almost certain to continue. There's a weight of psychological evidence to support the idea that a balanced consistent approach towards anti-social behaviour can work in improving an even eradicating the unwanted behaviour.

Take the following scenario as an example of this technique in action:

Scenario:

Tom and Debbie have been trying to encourage their daughter Maisie, a naturally boisterous three-year-old, to play in a more friendly way with other children instead of her tendency to snatch toys from them, push them over and shout and scream when things didn't go her own way.

Things have taken on a greater urgency now that Maisie has started to bite other children if they don't release toys she wants to play with immediately. The staff at Maisie's nursery have told Debbie that she may be turned away unless the behaviour stops as they can't allow the other children to get hurt.

Tom seems to think Maisie will grow out of it but Debbie just wants to be able to feel less embarrassed about her daughter's behaviour and have the freedom to let her mix with other children without the other mums talking about her. It's causing a lot of tension at home. The nursery practitioners have realised Debbie seems to be at the end of her tether. One of the girls who works there has talked to Debbie about a behaviour management approach she is currently studying on her college course. It involves ignoring 'minor' unwanted behaviour, and a system of rewards for behaviour that is to be encouraged.

The behaviour mentioned above may seem daunting but nursery staff and those who work with young children, teachers included, report incidents of children's behaviour that could be perceived as much worse.

Very difficult behaviours include:

- hitting other children, and adults
- kicking
- biting
- acting dangerously without regard for themselves or others' safety
- setting fires
- torturing animals
- running off
- spitting at people
- destroying possessions

(adapted from Jenner, 1999)

One technique for dealing with the kind of behaviour mentioned above which is suitable for young and older children alike especially is the giving of positive attention. It involves finding the times when the child is behaving in more desirable ways, noticing them and deliberately engaging with them. By rewarding their good behaviour the bad should be extinguished. All children desire attention, and they'll take the bad if the good isn't available just as well.

Of course that can be easier said than done but there are ways to exercise the 'good attention' approach in a systematic manner that can become as automatic as the otherwise angry reaction approach, it just takes enormous effort initially, determination and patience. Similarly 'time out' can be very effective if it's used properly and consistently. Consistence is the key here, it creates associations and predictability.

Time out has been found to be a particularly effective means of controlling the extent of behaviour like tantrums in young children (Klein, 1996). It's often be said that to break any habit it takes three weeks for the new pattern of response to become totally established.

Unfortunately parents can give in all too soon or fail to remain consistent in the new way of dealing with unwanted behaviour and report 'it doesn't work' before sticking with it long enough for the effects to be felt.

Psychological Theories of Aggression

The manner in which problem behaviour is responded to is considered extremely important. Psychological theory supports the notion that a vicious cycle of cause and effect can exist where behaviour is fuelled and continually reinforced by a feedback loop. One such example that can be linked to children's behaviour is the link between parental style and aggressive behaviour in children. In one particularly strong study parents of aggressive children were found to use punitive discipline responses, that is, they were likely to be harsh and strict but above all use some form of physical punishment method. However, these parents at the same time they were also found to be permissive.

In this sense these parents gave no clear guidance or response on what appropriate behaviour might otherwise be. How can that be, it doesn't seem on the face of it to be particularly likely to go together does it? The study in question pointed to a confusing contrast between the parents being punishing and distant and uninvolved, swinging from one extreme response to the other with no rational reason. This is very significant. There have been a huge number of psychological studies that have supported the idea that when children are exposed to contradiction and especially unpredictable patterns of response it can be very damaging.

Without consistency in their lives there is an unsettled anxious and on edge waiting, waiting for what could happen next. This has been found to be a common factor in violent individuals' childhoods. The stress hormone cortisol is naturally aroused under stress; if continually present research indicates it can have serious consequences for the brain's physical development. And that's without considering also the psychological effects of frustration no doubt felt when receiving severe punishment.

Punishment has been found to actually stimulate aggressive behaviour in some circumstances, leading to negative short-term and, in some cases, also long-term consequences with implications for later adult life (Gershoff, 2002).

These effects have been found to include:

- Increased aggression
- Decreased mental health
- Decreased quality of relationships with others, and
- Increased likelihood for anti-social behaviour and criminal behaviour

A very interesting in-depth study on the effects of punishment was carried out in 1991 (Patterson and his colleagues) who involved over 200 families. They compared families with at least one very aggressive son with other families matched for size and socio-economic level who didn't have any problem children. The assessments also involved surveys with the children's teachers, parents, peers, the children themselves as well as home observations. This study was therefore not only unusual in its depth and scope but also very revealing. The research team found evidence in the families with at least one aggressive boy of 'coercive home environments', by that they meant:

- Families where little affection is present or demonstrated;
- Families constantly bickering, shouting and using aggressive means to cope;
- Parents rarely use approval or positive reinforcement as a means of controlling behaviour; instead:
- Use nagging, teasing and physical punishment

The team discovered that the aggressive children from the coercive homes were typically manipulative and the parents would report they were difficult to control. Once the study had been completed the team came to the following conclusion that aggressiveness can be 'created' or provoked in several ways:

- Harsh discipline: disrupts parental bonding and respect
- Lack of adequate supervision: interferes with the identification process between parent and child
- Nagging: resentment
- Teasing: stress and frustration
- Marital quarrelling: stress and frustration
- No clear alternative methods for dealing disputes: learn through imitation how to respond
- Resistant to punishment: de-sensitised so become in turn harder to control
- Rejected by peers: join deviant peer groups and to fail in school and beyond

Adapted from Patterson (1991)

Patterson suggested ideally families if identified by social services or other agencies should be offered remedial training in anger management, involving conflict resolution, and help in bonding with their children. To avoid rejection and a potential spiral of failure at school, children could be offered social skills training. Rather than singling out certain children mainstream schools tend to take this into account during personal, health, social and emotional (PHSE) lessons. One of the problems with punishment, the more obvious reasons aside, is that it only teaches a child what not to do. If we're interested in *changing* children's behaviour they also need to learn alternative responses that are more appropriate. These new responses then need to be reinforced positively.

Again this is a process that takes time dedication and repeated consistent (there's *that* word again!) patterns of response. If the parents are at a loss how to deal with conflict themselves this is where there's a need for schools to intervene.

It's not always that straight-forward, psychologists do differ in their interpretations and explanations of behaviour. The different schools, or perspectives, in psychology tend to offer approaches according to their general explanations of human behaviour. Biological psychologists for instance suggest that genetic influences contribute to an explanation of aggression.

The evidence they cite for this argument lies in the fact that most violent acts are committed by men. Males have a far greater volume of the hormone testosterone which has been linked to aggression. By contrast, cognitive psychologists are interested in the role of mental processes in explaining behaviour. The way we think, perceive and interpret events will shape the way we then respond. If we see behaviour as threatening for example, our response is likely to match, whereas the behaviour may – objectively – be quite neutral.

This is referred to as 'selective attention', things we may regard as provocative may not be. Social psychologists on the other hand emphasise the role of the wider social situation and a person's culture. Standing up for yourself, responding to threats or insults physically can be regarded as the norm, a kind of honourable response, whereas not responding might be seen as weak in social identities.

⧁ References

Comstock, G. (1991): *TN and the American Child*, London: Academic Press

Gershoff, E. (2002): 'Parental corporal punishment and associated child behaviors and experiences: a meta-analytic and theoretical review', *Psychological Bulletin*, vol. 128, pp. 539-79

Jenner, S. (1999): *The Parent/Child Game*, London: Bloomsbury

Klein, S. (1996): *Learning: Principles and Applications*, New York: McGraw Hill

Patterson, G. (1991): "Family, school and behavioural antecedents to early adolescent involvement with antisocial peers", *Developmental Psychology,* vol. 27, pp. 172-180

Pound, L. (2005): *How Children Learn*, London: Step Forward Publishing

⊠ PSYCHOLOGICAL DISABILITIES

The Learning Outcomes for this assignment are:

Element	Learning Outcome
1	Understand how particular disorders can affect behavioural responses
2	Knowledge of behavioural symptoms and the potential causes

Psychological Disorders

The importance of mental health has continued to be stressed in government, health, education and media circles over the course of the last two decades when previously it was something that had been somewhat brushed under the carpet. A sort of taboo subject, for example, not a topic for easy conversation and neither freely admitted to if someone had experienced ill-health. In recent years in Britain we have seen public information advertisements alerting us to the need to talk about mental health and more directly mental ill-health as a part of illness generally.

Consequently illnesses like depression for instance are perceived in exactly the same light getting the flu or suffering from migraine, just one of those things that can affect us and can be dealt with, thank you. However the situation with children and their mental health is perhaps not so readily admitted to if they become affected. Children are meant to be happy aren't they? What have they got to worry about or feel sad about? Well quite a lot actually in some circumstances.

If mental health, with an emphasis on children's needs, can be defined as the ability to:

- Develop 'normally', that is, psychologically, emotionally, intellectually and spiritually
- Initiate, develop and sustain mutually satisfying personal relationships
- Use and enjoy solitude
- Become aware of others and empathise with them
- Play and learn
- Develop a sense of right and wrong
- Resolve/face problems and setbacks and learn from them

Mortimer (2003: 5)

The 'Every Child Matters'(ECM) framework was established by the former government to promote a multi-agency approach towards the well-being and safety of children following the highly documented widespread horror that resulted from one of the worst examples of child abuse ever recorded in England and Wales, the Victoria Climbie case.

The government vowed to make sweeping radical changes to children's services in order to prevent such a catastrophic failing of communication between different agencies from ever occurring again. Sadly we have seen other similar cases of horrific neglect and violence committed towards children since then. The one small consequence for good that has happened is at least abuse is now much more out in the open as an issue to be raised and dealt with.

The ECM, now disbanded by the coalition government, promoted five key areas of welfare, well-being and emotional health as not only a reminder for those that come into professional contact with children to be aware of their needs but also as an assessment checklist to ensure those needs are being addressed and met. Its ethos lives on however and many practitioners who come into contact with children professionally are still influenced by the essence of the underlying message and values it set out to foster in children's development. Those values were/are: staying healthy; being safe; achieving economically; contributing positively to society; and, enjoying and achieving.

The Child Adolescent Mental Health Services (CAHMS) has a mission to improve the emotional health and well-being of children and young adults, and to that as an organisation it offers assessment and treatment for emotional, behavioural and mental health difficulties/disorders. Referrals can be made by GPs who will often take on board information passed to them from children's teachers who have become concerned about the child's behaviour. CAHMS offer help and support with the behavioural consequences of emotional disturbances, usually referred to collectively as 'EBD', or emotional, and behavioural disorder.

The symptoms can vary enormously for example: violent/angry behaviour, difficulties with eating (not enough or too much), low self-esteem, self-harming, bullying (either perpetrator or victim) and abuse (victim or abuser). EBD is highly complex and takes dedicated specialist intervention to treat and specialist non-mainstream schooling is strongly advised.

The intervention and treatment for children experiencing mental health disorders varies according to the individual and the disorder. The aim is always to manage behaviour, the outward symptom, whilst supporting psychological well-being. Generally speaking techniques will tend to focus on building up and maintaining the child's personal, social and emotional development before attempting anything more specific.

For example, if a child is to feel secure enough to behave reasonably, they must first have trust in the adults around them. In a pre-school or school environment, whether mainstream or special needs, and this includes EBD units, trust and security is built around two significant aspects: 1) routine, and 2) consistency. Psychologically these are vital ingredients for the setting to become a 'secure base'.

This is especially essential for children whose home lives have not offered secure attachments; here the school for example becomes a substitute, a sort of surrogate 'attachment figure'.

Adjustment Disorder

Ainsworth, a psychologist who has been continually associated with studies of attachment and the effects of separation on young children since the 1970s, has concluded that children who experience separation from their parents for at least a month during their early years have an above average risk of later psychological disturbance. However it's less likely to be the direct result she commented of the short separation but more likely to arise from factors that may be related to the absence. For example: problems in the home, inadequate parenting, insecure relationships, poor housing, hospitalisation and so on. It's very important to consider risk factors and not to take one single event as a cause. Similarly a child's age and stage of development, temperamental differences and the existence or absence of other support networks can contribute or mitigate circumstances. And of course some children will be more temperamentally resilient and better able to cope with emotional hurt than others, however the risks associated with disrupted bonds and insecure attachments are well documented and supported by research.

buzzle.com

Children without the benefit of a secure attachment or a secure base substitute can experience difficulties with adjustment to a change in their circumstances. Transitional periods are often very difficult to cope with and can cause a great deal of stress, for example, moving from a familiar pre-school environment to an unknown school.

Of course most settings will take positive steps to ensure all children are eased in to their new environments by organising visits but for children with serious emotional disturbances this may only serve to increase their anxiety levels even further. The impact of stress, anxiety and change will not tend to improve behaviour; rather problems will tend to escalate. One intervention technique developed by a psychologist interested in supporting children affected by adjustment issues, was the 'nurture group' approach.

The groups were established to create a form of family life often absent from the children's lives. The technique used is to demonstrate dedicated and committed interest in the child. One way to achieve this is through intense interactive play time that is totally child-centred. For example if the child decides s/he wants to do some drawing the assistant engages in the same activity allowing him/herself to be 'led' by the child. The accompanying conversation serves to give the child as much positive reinforcement as possible. "I really like the way you're drawing some spots on the dog William", "Great, he's running after his ball".

Typically using any form of questioning with the child is not encouraged as it represents a form, however neutral the question might be, of 'demand', instead the upbeat commentary provides encouragement and undivided attention. For children who have only previously experienced ambivalent or detached parenting it could represent a rare time of feeling valued. Of course it's not meant to be an isolated experience; nurture groups are designed to be part of and fit in with pre-school or school life.

That said, parents are often encouraged to participate where possible, for example being invited to 'come along for coffee', sometimes as a way of helping them to interact with their children by modelling appropriate skills.

 **Children's learning is understood developmentally including knowledge of key 'attachments.'**

 **The classroom offers a safe base where they have fun.**

 **Nurture is essential for the self-esteem of children.**

 **Adults act as , "Human Bridges" helping children to 'cross over' their difficulties with support.**

cope-yp.blogspot.com

Another interventionist strategy similar in aims and somewhat in scope to that of nurture groups is the 'Sure Start' initiative. Although it isn't found to be practised on the same scale it was during the last government's administration, centres do still operate where funding is available. Aimed at children specifically under the age of three-years along with their families, this approach had at its heart the notion that children and their families should be considered as a unit, therefore any intervention needs to be targeted at addressing holistic needs.

There are parallels here with the nurture group philosophy but whereas bring in parents to group and encouraging interaction was recommended, with Sure Start it was more actively fostered. The centres were as a result set up in geographical areas of social and economic disadvantage, where resources and services were most at need. Also, from a practical perspective, where 'preventative 'provision for families could be concentrated in order to achieve a one-stop shop approach.

One of the criticisms that had been laid at the door of services like social services and health care prior to the Sure Start initiative was the disconnected nature of different agencies and support groups; the most common complaint received was the lack of joined up thinking and in particular effective inter-communication.

Consequently, Sure Start aimed to involve all aspects children's lives and those of their families as much as possible, like health care, education, support services, recreational facilities and social contact, with the intention of breaking down barriers such as communication between the different agencies. Seamless provision is the ultimate goal whether organisations are voluntary, statutory or private.

From a psychological perspective the Nurture Group and Sure Start initiatives are founded on research findings on children's early emotional development and the significance of secure attachment. Hence, concentrating on practical intervention, targeted directly at those most at need and risk, is a proactive step towards preventing and protecting children in adverse circumstances. Of course the cynical might suggest that from an economic angle, spending resources in preventative ways is a cost saving exercise for the future, well yes it may well be but the psychological benefits and advantages of having children raised in supportive communities doesn't just bring positive outcomes for the vulnerable individuals themselves but also for society as a whole.

Anxiety Disorder

Anxiety is a perfectly normal and advantageous response, in fact without it we wouldn't be able to function normally. Adrenaline serves an extremely important and worthwhile purpose in maintaining ordinary bodily functions not to mention the energy required for emergency situations like fight or flight. However when we're discussing anxiety in a purely psychological sense rather than a biological one, we 're usually alluding to the idea that in some cases it can be detrimental to normal functioning to the extent it can even interfere with leading an enjoyable life. Anxiety can adversely affect up to 10% of young people, getting in the way of their lives causing problems with things we take for granted.

Examples of the kind of interference are an inability to engage with others, go out, and participate in social interaction which could affect participation in schooling and the ability to make friends. Specific examples of the kind of disorders associated with anxiety are: GAD – generalised anxiety disorder, the most common; separation anxiety, although to be expected at certain sensitive periods of development this can prove to be dysfunctional at others; social and specific phobias; and, PTSD – post-traumatic stress disorder. Although a state of arousal is necessary for normal everyday living in some cases too much or too little can prove to be disadvantageous.

Children experiencing forms of anxiety show signs of cognitive impairment; their ability to pay attention, concentrate and learn can be severely adversely affected. Studies demonstrate children with low self-esteem are even more likely to be susceptible to learning impairment, and this is exacerbated when the learning environment is less structured. Anxious children tend to require environments with a high degree of routine, predictability, consistency and expected boundaries. Why? All of these things impart a sense of reassurance, stability and security, good antidotes to anxiety. A high state of arousal can also affect behavioural response; too much can in certain circumstances, for example, performance related, lead to freezing like 'stage fright' referred to above. High arousal, as a physiological determinant, can contribute to impulsivity, a significant antecedent of challenging behaviour and acting before thinking, a classic example of the fight-flight response. Poor behaviour in children can be observed and examined in three ways in order to try and determine what might be fuelling or contributing to the behaviour.

For example:

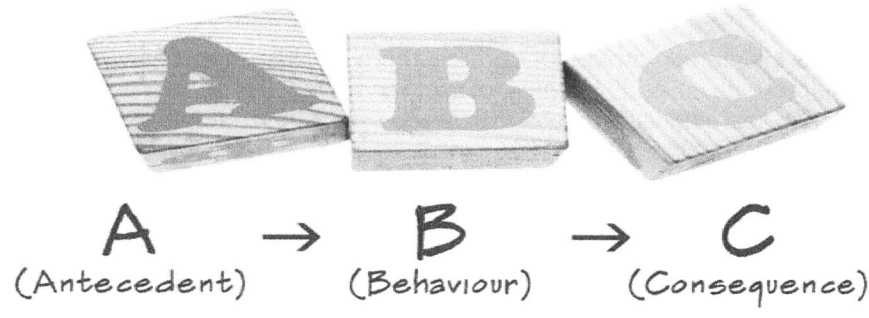

johnnyholland.org

Determinant:	Analysis:	Explanation:
A	Antecedents	Discovering what happens directly *before* incidents have occurred
B	Behaviour	Focussing on the *type* of behaviour A has produced
C	Consequences	Finding out if the response to B is inadvertently *reinforcing* its repeat

Depressive Disorder

Depression, whether experienced by an adult or a child, is generally characterised by certain symptoms in order for a clinical diagnosis to be made. These are: a persistent low mood, a feeling of overwhelming sadness, disturbances or impairment of typical (for the individual concerned) sleep, appetite, concentration and memory, and an inability to enjoy normally pleasurable activities. It has also been described more specifically in a psychological sense as: holding attitudes and feelings relating not just to ourselves in a general sense but also with our environment and our future (Beck, 1976). When we're thinking about children's experiences of depression there are several angles to take. Firstly, children suffering with depression. Secondly, children who experience the effects of depression indirectly through a parent or a carer's illness. Add into that mix the different types of depression and it can become a complex issue. Children though have an addition vulnerability connected with depression and that is related to their cognitive understanding.

Children's understanding of illness generally is something that is strongly linked to their age and stage of development. Children between 5-7-years don't seem to differentiate between physical and mental illness, while older children between 9-11-years are able to clearly differentiate between the two. Children develop their understanding of mental illness as their experiences grow. In studies concerned with the different stages of children's development and their ability to comprehend illnesses, it's been found that whilst only 13% of 5-7-year-olds relate to depression as requiring 'help and support', 50% of 7-9-year-olds do (Buchanan-Barrow & Barrett, 2005). The 5-7-year-olds studied reported that depression is something that's caught, like a cold. Whereas the older children questioned thought depression was something to do with how someone feels and thinks.

Cognitive psychologists would explain the difference in response to the level of cognitive development the different groups of children were at the time they were questioned. 'Pre-operational' children, under the age of approximately seven years tend to use intuition or guessing when they don't know the real answer to a difficult question. 'Operational' children, over the age of seven years will on the other hand tend to use logic and rational thought processes as is evident from the different explanations they give to a complex question like 'what is depression' and 'how do people become depressed'.

Studies demonstrate that certain groups of children seem more susceptible to depression than others. For example, children with special learning difficulties appear to be more prone than the general population. One such learning difficulty, or 'difference' as some people prefer to address it as, is dyslexia. Goldstein and his colleagues (1985) used an inventory to objectively assess children with dyslexia. They found that 26% were severely depressed.

In a typical sample of children selected generally the comparative figure would have expected to be 10%. Other studies seem to support the finding that children with special learning difficulties are over-represented in depression rates. Why should this be the case? When people have been asked to respond to questions like 'what is success?' and 'what would make you think you'd been successful, they respond by attributing success to their abilities.

Failure by contrast, and as a test measure in the same questionnaires/surveys, tends to be attributed to external factors outside their own control. We can then perhaps start to appreciate why children with special learning difficulties become depressed if despite their efforts they may appear to lack ability in others' eyes. It's therefore extremely important that children with disabilities are encouraged to feel good about themselves as a whole person and not just in response to things like academic ability.

We've already addressed separation from the main caregiver earlier in previous modules and when we looked at adjustment disorder, separation features highly too in depression. For example, in a well-known study of children admitted to hospital carried out just after the second world war, concluded that even children apparently unaffected by trauma (this was very prevalent at the time due to having lived through the war, particularly with children who had lived in London) experienced ill-effects of separation. A condition known as anaclitic depression describes children's reaction to the separation as: 'quiet, apathetic and sad' (Spitz & Wolf, 1946). Long periods of hospitalisation for children suffering from tuberculosis continued throughout the forties and fifties in Britain, sometimes for months at a time.

The prevailing attitude at the time – and this seems really strange if not cruel even in our more modern eyes – was that it would be better for the children not to see their parents when they visited them because it would only upset them. Consequently parents would creep into the hospital wards after the children were asleep to peer at them and presumably satisfy themselves they were OK. The children though didn't know that and must have felt they had been abandoned. How times change, it's very common now if not standard practice for one parent to sleep over with their sick child in hospital even if the child is staying for a relatively short period of time. This is one benefit of psychological research because Spitz and Wolf's findings, and that of the other researchers who came along to also test the notion of the effects of deprivation and separation, convinced hospital mangers to decades later allow, even encourage, parents to stay with their children. Hurrah for psychology! But let's turn our attention back to the children in the original version of the classic study. They didn't have the benefit of our more enlightened approach sadly.

Spitz and Wolf found that children who had effectively been deprived of their parents for three months and longer suffered long term emotional damage. There was a strong link between hospitalisation and a greater risk of difficult behaviour particularly in adolescence. These findings have been supported by subsequent similar studies, although it is difficult to isolate other variables that may also have an influence. For example, the style of parent-child attachment that was present in the first place. A problem which blights psychology research! Because we're dealing with human beings, a notoriously awkward bunch pf subjects, we can never be too scientific in our subsequent analysis of studies, not like those pesky science scientists like chemists and biologists. Their subject matter can be kept under constant fixed circumstances. And so the study does bring to bear the secure versus insecure dilemma we have broached before.

The behavioural symptoms of depression in children relates highly to maternal sensitivity, their mother's response to the child in early infancy. The mother's own depression is a very significant factor in shaping their ability to respond and interact with the child. One study found evidence to suggest much higher rates of insecure attachment. Murray (1992) found that children of depressed mothers were also more likely to have:

- Temper tantrums
- Eating difficulties sleep disturbances
- Be overly clingy and dependent
- Difficult behaviour

In turn children who have grown up with depressive behaviour are more likely to develop ways of responding and interacting with others that closely resembles the patterns of behaviour that they are familiar with. A high percentage of children with mothers with depression experience less warmth and harsher discipline styles associated with aggressive behaviour.

>> **References**

Beck, A. (1976): Cognitive Therapy and the Emotional Disorders, New York: International Universities Press

Buchanan-Barrow, E. & Barrett, M. (2005): 'The development of children's conceptions of mental illness', available from esrc.ac.uk (accessed 16/6/14)

Goldstein, P. (1985): 'Depression and achievement in subgroups of children with learning disabilities', *Journal of Applied Developmental Psychology*, vol. 6, pp. 263-75

Mortimer, H. (2003): Emotional Literacy and mental Health in the Early Years, Staffs: QEd

Spitz R. & Wolf, K. (1946): "Anaclitic Depression", *Psychoanalytic Study of the Child*, vol. 2, pp. 313-342

⟫ Further Reading and Support

⊠ FOCUS ON BULLYING

The Learning Outcomes for this assignment are:

Element	Learning Outcome
1	Understand the causes of bullying
2	Awareness of the effects of bullying

Bullying

Kidscape, the UK's leading charity founded in 1985, to prevent bullying and child sexual abuse believes that:

"All children should be able to grow up in a world free from bullying and abuse, and that all adults should keep children safe and help them to reach their full potential"

Kidscape.org.uk (8/8/14)

The values that Kidscape promote are:

- All children have the right to lead their lives free from bullying and abuse;

- All adults have a responsibility to support, nurture and care for children in order for them to reach their full potential;

- All children should have the opportunity and confidence to report bullying and abuse;

- Bullying and abuse in all forms are not acceptable and should not be tolerated; and,

- Children, confidence and trust are at the heart of all we do

Ibid (8/8/14)

guardianlv.com

The archetypal image of the bully tends to be associated with school days; children who hold some sort of malevolent power over other children causing them to fear and loathe them in return. As a society we have become increasingly intolerant of bullying behaviour and are now much more likely to take an active stand against it in all its forms. More recently the idea of adult bullying has come to the fore especially in relation to the workplace. Definitions of bullying use terms such as intimidation, teasing, persecution, oppression, terrorising relating to both physical and moral. In an old English dictionary the definition reads:

Bully: "A blustering, overbearing fellow; a cowardly tyrant; a bravo; a swashbuckler"

Baker (1932: 136)

So, bullying is defined as deliberately hurtful behaviour, where it is difficult for those being bullied to defend themselves. As an adult it would almost be worth receiving a bit of bullying just to be able to retort with " Sir, I regard you as a blustering, overbearing fellow ....." Seriously though The Elton Report on discipline (1989) concluded that bullying in school was serious and widespread arguing that teachers have a should take an active part in addressing it. Identifying the prevalence of bullying is always going to be difficult due to the lack of legislation and could otherwise define how it may be appear categorically in practice.

We all have a very good idea of course what bullying is but to criminalise it for example could be tricky. Victims of bullying are often reluctant to come forward. All schools, indeed all educational institutions, are require to have anti-bullying policies in place that have to conform to the Equality Act 2006. The Act makes some forms of bullying subject to prosecution, for example, sexual orientation or religious beliefs.

The main types of bullying are:

- physical (hitting, kicking, theft)
- verbal (name calling)
- indirect (spreading rumours, excluding someone from social groups)
- cyber (via internet or mobile phones)
- sexual (unwanted physical contact, sexually abusive comments)
- homophobic (because of, or focusing on the issue of sexuality)
- racist (racial taunts, graffiti, gestures)
- religious (because of, or focusing on religion)
- extortion (demanding money/goods with threats)

In extreme cases bullying is responsible for pupils attempting or committing suicide. Help and support is available for children in the form of on-line organisations such as Kidscape, Childline, Bullying UK and a government web site 'Don't Suffer in Silence' , each of which endorse and encourage victims to report incidents

The increase in technological forms of 24-hour communication various forms of cyberbullying have developed and these are very difficult to prevent. Malicious texting, so-called 'happy slapping' in which perpetrators attack their victims whilst recording it and then post it on-line for others to see. This is relatively new way of taking bullying to new levels of humiliation and despair. Where bullying incidents might once have been small-scale cyber bullying allows many other children to witness a victim's distress compounding their misery.

Bullying behaviours can be divided into direct forms, such as: physical violence, mental and verbal abuse or blackmail, and indirect forms which can include: non-overt aggression, for example in the form of threatening behaviour which can be quite subtle, and social exclusion. Whilst there may be some debate about exactly what constitutes bullying, and to some extent it's the victim's prerogative to decide for themselves, the following is an interesting example of one way to differentiate between behaviours.

According to the psychologist Minton (2012) bullying can be defined as:

- Aggressive (verbally, psychologically or physically)
- Deliberate
- Unprovoked
- Repeated or systematic in nature
- Imbalanced of power (e.g. physical size/strength, social popularity and the ability to manipulate friendship groups in order to exclude, technological power)

Minton (2012: 100)

Minton argues that it's much more relevant to think of bullies as the perpetrators and 'victims' as 'targets'; the word victim carries with it notions of helplessness, whereas target is a more neutral and potentially reactive term. Bullying behaviour can only thrive in an atmosphere of silence. When children are too afraid to tell someone it can escalate which ids precisely why active anti-bullying campaigns and interventionist strategies are so vitally important in putting forward the message that bullying is not acceptable.

The effects of bullying on children's sense of self are varied and can be serious. When someone has a poor self-concept as the result of being the target of bullies psychological evidence suggests they will do anything to defend their label; that is idea of themselves. The tendency is to avoid anything else that could possibly make them feel any worse. A common reaction therefore is to retreat inside and cut off from outside contact. With some victims of bullying this can go to extremes, such as elective mutism – refusing to speak.

One of the earliest psychologists whilst contemplating self-concept wrote:

"with no attempt there can be no failure, with no failure no humiliation"

James (1890), cited in McNamara & Moreton (1996: 14

The alternative to withdrawal, or the 'flight' response, as a coping technique and a defence mechanism is the 'fight'; displaying anger, rage, aggression and violence. Sometimes we hear people say the latter is 'attention seeking', well if we take behaviour as a sign of underlying problems then it may well be, a cry for help – notice me please, something is wrong. Violence is perhaps sometimes easier to understand as a reaction, it's after all a more close resemblance to the aggression of the bullying, like for like, for even when bullying isn't violent it still represents hostility.

Children who are bullied may suffer from loss of self-esteem for the rest of their lives; such can be the extent of the affects. One survey suggested that as many as between 5 – 10% of school pupils have experienced being bullied at some point (Yates & Smith, 1989). A link has been suggested by a longitudinal piece of research which followed children in later life, finding many experienced continued relationship difficulties. This finding led other researchers to question whether in some cases children who become targets for bullies lack social skills.

However the bully can also experience long lasting consequences. One study found evidence of former school bullies being four times more likely to have three or four more court convictions by the age of twenty-four (Olweus, 1989). Psychologists who take a behaviourist approach to their explanations of human behaviour would suggest the role of reinforcement is key in explaining the continuing trouble making.

Even if reinforcement takes the negative form it's still attention and this is what may be motivating the bully's behaviour. It still doesn't however explain why bullies bully. One suggestion is they too have been bullied and their bullying is simply a transference of what happened to them being applied to someone else. A kind of distant re-living of the experiences, perhaps a way albeit unconscious of re-living it as a means to come to terms with the experiences.

As a means of treating the problem of bullying from the perpetrator's perspective psychology offers a number of approaches. One is the therapeutic angle which tends to take a person's background as the starting point to understanding behaviour. What has happened to the individual to influence their current behaviour is one fundamental question.

Taking a regression approach, here the therapist/interventionist tries to ascertain what has happened or what is happening in the perpetrator's life usually starting in early childhood. Bullying as a behaviour form could be described as negative, hostile and malevolent; what has caused those responses? Aggression according to this position is caused by underlying hurt and anger that is manifesting itself in the form of hurting others.

One of the prevailing questions that have been raised concerning bullying is why; when it does occur in front of others don't they intervene to stop it. When other people become aware of bullying behaviour why does it tend to be ignored, dismissed or even colluded with? It's seems that the somehow the sense of fear pervades not only the target but also the witnesses. Why is that?

One theory that's been put forward to explain this at first glance unlikely phenomenon is bystander intervention. Why do bystanders sometimes fail to act?

The key event which led to psychologists becoming a) aware and b) interested in investigated the occurrence was a horrific murder of a young woman in residential New York in 1964. She was murdered by a stranger who had followed her home in the early hours of the morning.

The newspaper reported that she had been stabbed and raped, and that incredibly, thirty-eight people had either heard her cries for help or even witnessed her attack as it was taking place. They were all bystanders to the event and yet none had intervened least of all come to her rescue.

This became the catalyst for a whole string of psychological investigations to investigate the appalling lack of altruism and absence of human response. What could possibly explain this apparent loss of humanity? In the aftermath many people were angry, appalled but also incredulous that people could be so callous. Most people assumed that New Yorkers had become so hardened and de-sensitised by hearing about multiple murders and crime in general that they had somehow become apathetic and indifferent.

Two psychologists, Darley and Latané (1968), were not influenced by the popular conclusion and decided therefore to conduct their own research into the phenomenon of 'bystander apathy' to find if a more reasoned and less judgemental explanation could be found. They pointed out that when people are witnesses to an event that raises our level of adrenalin, such as an emergency or we see something shocking or frightening happening, we have a tendency to get lost in our own genuine confusion. This may seem like a human frailty and we might like to think 'well *I* for one wouldn't behave like that, *I'd* do something'.

In fact we'd probably all like to *think* we would be heroes and save the day. However, Darley & Latané argued that in an event we are pulled in opposite directions by a) our wanting to help but b) our fears about what might happen to us if we do. OK, this becomes understandable and now we can start to relate to the explanation.

Is there more to it? Yes, it turns out there's a big difference in whether we're alone or with others when a startling event occurs. The findings of their research suggest:

Condition:	Result:
In a group	Diffusion of Responsibility
Alone	Individual Accountability

The researchers concluded that when several people witness an event each individual feels less responsible for taking action than if they were the only person available to help. The responsibility is therefore diffused; the responsibility is being spread across the number of people witnessing the act, so no individual feels it's up to them to intervene.

The pictures below show stills from a set up depicting someone who's fallen over and has apparently passed out or worse. It's actually an actor but the scene is real in that it was filmed on a street, actually demonstrates 'bystander intervention' in general, which we have discussed describes the situation when people in a group/in public fail to act but when alone we take responsibility for alerting help.

Furthermore Darley and Latané argued not only is responsibility diffused across all the bystanders (or 'rubberneckers' as they tend to be referred to when an incident occurs on the motorway) but there's a diffusion of blame.

Where several people have been questioned following an incident where blame for failing to act can be applied, such as neglecting to come to aid a woman who was being slowly murdered, each person tends to say things along the lines of 'it wasn't up to me to help, I thought someone else was going to/already had'.

This is especially true when we can't see the responses of other bystanders, and this was the situation during the murder – people were in their apartments looking out of their windows. To an extent this is also true if we're driving past an accident on the motorway, we don't know if other people have telephoned for the emergency services for example.

However, what about incidents in much more public places that are relatively much more personal, like the street or the shopping mall? We can actually see what other people are doing there. The studies suggest that, unfortunately, it's less likely that we'll *do* anything the more people there are beside ourselves observing the same event.

The researchers tested this theory further by creating events, such as re-creating epileptic fits, smoke suggesting a fire, or the sound of someone falling in an accident and crying out in pain for help so, in other words, proper emergency scenarios. Unbelievably perhaps or maybe not by now because you're already anticipating what we're about to talk about next … yes, you guessed it, not a lot!

The answers people give when questioned later typically, almost word for word, are: "I didn't want to get involved". Before we condemn these 'other people' because *we*wouldn't behave like that, would *we*? Well, yes, *we* probably would actually if this powerful research evidence is anything to go by. Unless we knew about the study in which case it will change our response – thanks psychology!

The conclusions from tittle tattlers and the media might suggest these findings demonstrate society has gone to the dogs, no one has any morals anymore, and we've all become dehumanised. Sociologists call this 'alienation' when we become separate from the norms of human interaction as a result of living in over-crowded urban environments. A bit like when we're walking down a pleasant country lane we're much more generally inclined to speak to strangers, say hello and make eye contact, maybe even have a brief. THAT doesn't happen on the tube though does it? Need we say more on that subject, no not really.

So, one suggestion that's been put forward is what is happening is that the normal rules or norms of human engagement and interaction, empathy for others, breaks down in certain circumstances. 'Anomie' describes such a situation when human beings behave in unnatural sometimes inhuman ways as a result of disturbing environmental change. This state does require some degree of arousal though, a surge of adrenalin in response to for example, shock or fear. For example, looting following urban rioting following someone in the community getting shot by the police. We can suddenly, out of character and totally opposite to how we would normally react, become part of the crowd which renders us anonymous and temporarily irresponsible.

Psychologists address this as 'situational forces' determining the outcome. When we're alone the pressure is on us to respond, we can't hide or use the excuse 'I thought someone else had responded'. The process of 'deindividuation' or 'social loafing' which is untypical of any of the group members when alone is the opposite of altruism - 'behaviour that benefits other individuals even when there is a cost involved to the altruist'.

Witnessing bullying as a member of a group and not intervening to help the victim can be described as a form of diffusion of responsibility.

⊠ **References**

Baker, E. [Ed] (1932): *New English Dictionary*, London: Oldham's Press

Darley, J. & Latané, B. (1968): 'Bystander intervention in emergencies: Diffusion of Responsibility', *Journal of Personality and Social Psychology*, vol. 3, no. 4, pp. 3777-83

Kidscape.org.uk (8/8/14)

McNamara, S. & Moreton, G. (1996): *Changing Behaviour*, London: David Fulton

Minton, S. (2012): *Using Psychology in the Classroom*, London: Sage

E. & Munthe, E. *(eds). Bullying: An International Perspective*, London: David Fulton

Olweus, D. (1989): "Bully/victim problems among schoolchildren: basic facts and effects of a school-based intervention program", In Rubin, K. & Pepler, D. *(eds) The Development and Treatment of Childhood Aggression*, Hillsdale, N.J.: Erlbaum

Yates, C. & Smith, P. (1989): *Bullying in two English comprehensive schools*, In Roland

≫ Further Reading/Support

Anti-bullyingalliance.org.uk

⊠ FOCUS ON ADHD

The Learning Outcomes for this assignment are:

Element	Learning Outcome
1	Knowledge of the impact of ADHD on children's behaviour
2	Understand the psychological approaches to coping with ADHD

It isn't uncommon for many young children to be overactive, sometimes they will be labelled 'hyperactive' whether this is warranted or not. The label can simply mean those who are responsible for looking after the child are finding him or her a bit of a handful. These children may just be finding sitting still and remaining quiet naturally difficult. In Britain attending formal schooling, shortly before the child's fifth birthday, is to be expected and a norm of society. However in most developed parts of the world this is unheard of and would be considered far too young.

In most of Europe and Scandinavia for example children don't start formal school until they reach the age of six or even years. Until that age they're still happily developing and learning through playing in kindergartens or nurseries. In Britain we're expecting children to start reading and writing which usually requires that they sit relatively still and quiet, a tall order when your natural tendency at that age is to run around and explore. So any child who doesn't conform to perhaps these unrealistic expectations might be wrongly labelled as 'hyper' when what they really are is pretty normal!

A DHD, or 'attention-deficit hyperactivity disorder' is generally characterised by exhibiting inappropriate behavioural responses like inattention, impulsiveness and an excess of motor activity. It is essentially a mental disorder of childhood that is a life-long condition. The cause is loosely linked with the brain's arousal mechanism; either as a result of over or under-arousal. Over-arousal leads to constant switching of attention from one thing to another with very short gaps if any at all

in between. This behaviour version is a kind of extreme restlessness which can appear quite frantic that can be very exhausting to watch. Under-arousal on the other hand is characterised by the inability to maintain attention. Although a relatively quieter version of the disorder, not nearly as frantic or restless, the effects are just as worrying from the point of view of potential for learning for example.

The child may begin to pay attention and show signs of concentration only to 'switch off' and drift away. In the past these children would have been inclined to have been instantly labelled as 'daydreamers'.

These children tend to respond very well to stimulants which raise the arousal levels sufficiently to increase concentration time.

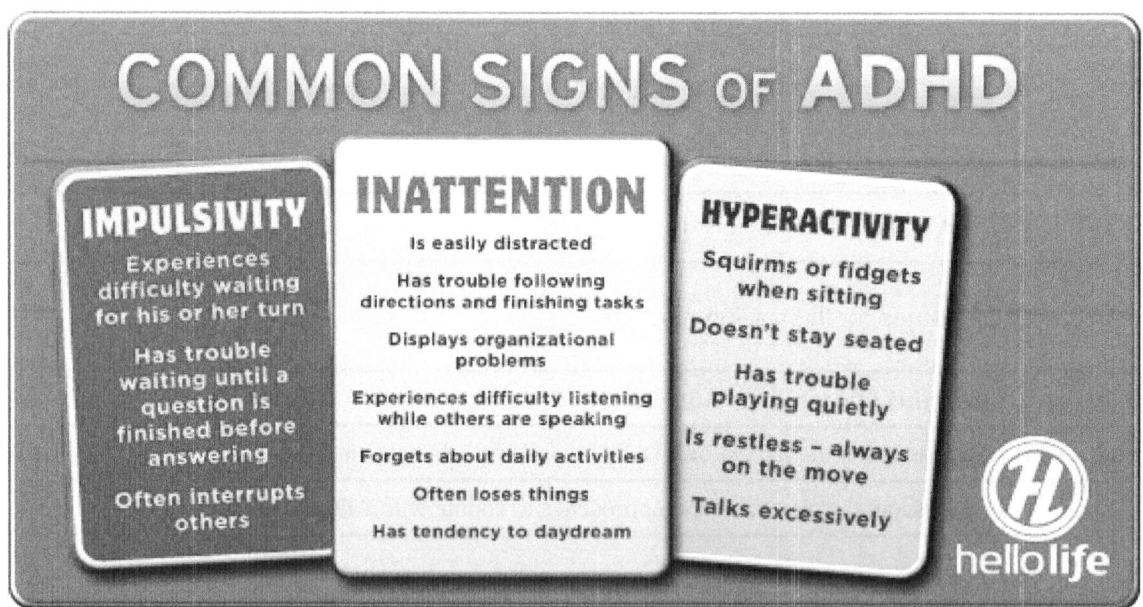

hellolife.net

Children with ADHD can't be cured nor will they 'grow out of it' but for the vast majority of children affected they will grow accustomed to their symptoms and most will be able to gradually cope better with the effect it has on their energy levels and behavioural characteristics. It has been estimated that ADHD affects between 2-10% of school-age children. It's at least three times more common in boys than in girls.

ADHD is characterised by:

- Persistent inattention
- Hyperactivity
- Impulsivity

Most children affected will receive an official medical diagnosis before the age of seven years. Frequently diagnoses are made considerably earlier. The signs will certainly tend to be noticed before the age of 7 but depending on how these signs are then interpreted and regarded a diagnosis might be delayed or made faster. A great deal depends on the child's parents or carers. A child's attendance at pre-school regardless of whether it's a playgroup or a nursery, will also make a huge amount of difference to the disorder being identified.

All qualified early years practitioners will have had some training in order to obtain their qualification on special needs, including the signs and symptoms of ADHD. Quite often their observation records will help a GP get a better understanding and general picture of the child's behaviour and can help considerably with decision-making regarding the child's overall behavioural profile. Certainly the child's behaviour will usually tend to have been highlighted as a source of concern by teachers by the time he or she enters school.

The behavioural characteristics of ADHD usually interfere significantly with ordinary functioning and that can affect any aspect of normal everyday life, from going to school, participating in leisure activities and just normal social interaction.

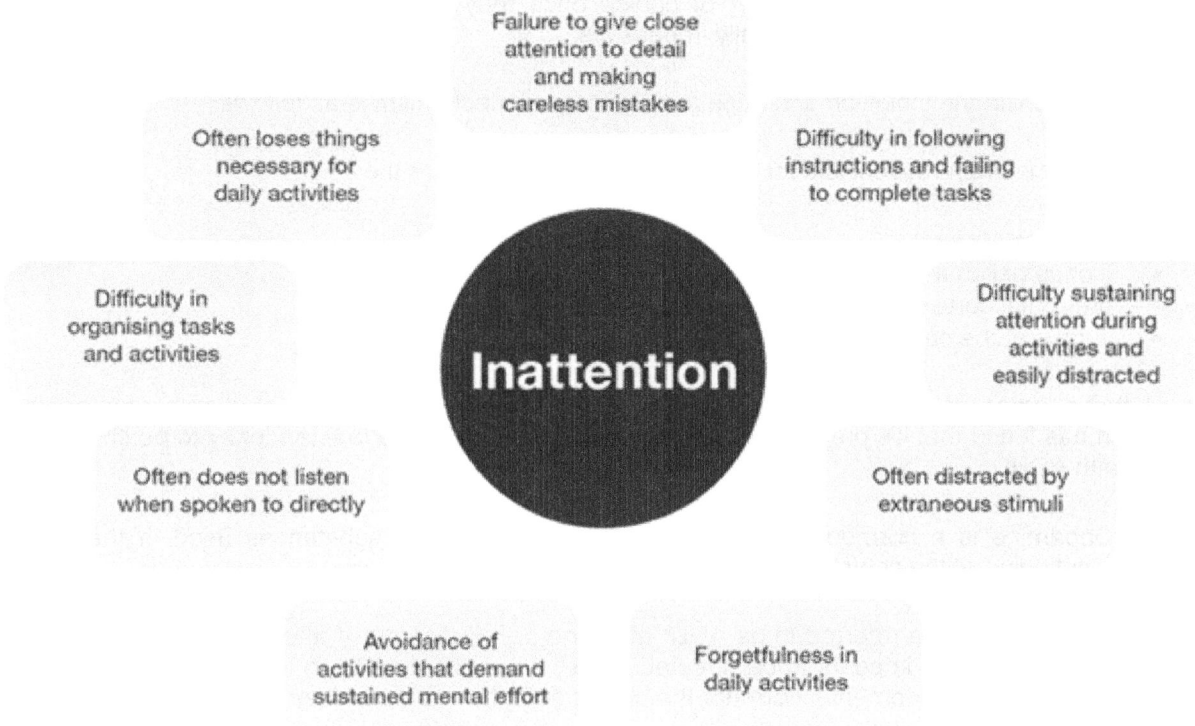

adhd-institute.com

There are considerable differences however between individuals with ADHD. We need to be reminded that just as ordinary individuals are unique so too are children, and adults too for that matter, with special needs no matter what the type. There is a danger that a label representing a category can take on an identity of its own; the individual behind it can get lost as people choose to see the condition and not the person. There will be considerable individual differences between children with the disorder in terms of the level of severity of the symptoms and the breadth of symptoms. For example some children with ADHD display almost continual hyperactivity, demonstrating constant movement and an inability to stay still for hardly any length of time except when they're asleep. Other children with ADHD don't have an issue with hyperactivity but do show signs of a disturbing impulsivity; a tendency to act before thinking, sometimes getting into very dangerous risk-taking behaviours that are harmful to themselves and occasionally others too.

When diagnosing ADHD it will tend to be classified according to the different type or 'manifestation'.

Types of ADHD can differ according to the main or predominate 'subtype'; for example:

1. Inattentive subtype
2. Hyperactive-impulsive subtype
3. Combined subtype

ADHD isn't, as was once and still is commonly believed, a disorder of attention as such but rather a developmental problem in the areas of the brain that are responsible for the inhibition and self-control. Normally in ordinary development children will quite quickly learn to respond to the body's natural tendency to shut down when faced with danger. In order to prevent us from getting into harm, the, for want of a better description, self-preservation signal will alert us to put the brakes on. Fear is a normal response in such situations. However in children with ADHD their brain isn't functioning in quite the same way as described.

The problem lies with the impaired, insufficient or lack of the inhibitory signal that would normally tell us to 'stop' isn't working. Without that self –control is not possible; in order to be able to control our behaviour we need first to have the ability to do so. We can now start to understand how for children with ADHD self-control is not a matter of choice once they are developed enough to be able to exercise it independently it can be literally impossible.

The biology behind the inhibition and impaired self-control mechanism is as follows:

The areas of the brain responsible for inhibition and self-control are the –

- Caudate nucleus
- globus pallidus
- prefrontal cortex
- vermis of the cerebellum

All of these areas use dopamine* in order to communicate and send signals with one another. Research has found that it's precisely these areas of the brain that have a tendency to be shrunken in people with ADHD.

- Dopamine is a hormone and one of the neurotransmitter substances used in the normal functioning of the central nervous system.

The disorder can also be referred to as ADD: attention-deficit disorder if attention is the main aspect of child's behaviour that appears to be affected. Here, if the attention-span is particularly short when compared with the developmental norm for the child's age, the separate diagnosis may be made.

a.

The aetiology of ADHD concerns the possible causes or origins of the disorder. It isn't without controversy and debate. As we have already mentioned for child to be diagnosed with ADHD a medical diagnosis needs to be made and this will usually require a GP's intervention. Occasionally further information and evidence from other professionals who come into contact with the child will be taken into consideration. For example as we've said earlier if the child attends pre-school the observation findings as a form of documentary supporting evidence may be used as a source of additional information.

The standard medical approach is to prescribe a drug named Ritalin (Methylphenidate), a derivative of cocaine, as a means to alleviate some of the hyper symptoms, if appropriate in order to calm and quieten the child and reduce hyperactivity. The rationale behind this form of essentially sedation is that once relatively still and calm the child can then concentrate in order to learn and thrive. Ritalin is a stimulant commonly prescribed; its effect works in a way on ADHD that is opposite to its true effect in people who don't have the disorder. As a stimulant it would cause most people to be more hyperactive but in ADHD sufferers it has the reverse effect.

In America in particular the use of this drug has become incredibly and perhaps horrifyingly widespread, and in Britain too its take up rate has caused some medics to be alarmed. The long term side-effects of continual use have yet to be fully realised. However, as a relatively cheap and effective means of reducing motor activity and improving concentration and attention levels its use isn't likely to be halted any time soon.

The arousal problems may be aroused by the genetically inherited neurological differences, however there has also been some controversial speculation regarding the role of the environment, such as diet. An enormous amount of research has been dedicated to the question of whether children's diet can contribute or even cause ADHD. This question has been responsible in turn for causing a great deal of distress for some parents who have previously felt under besiege for being somehow to blame for their children's disorder in the eyes of the popular media and in some cases widespread public opinion.

The focus of such dietary concern has at different points shifted from artificial food colours particularly those used in fruit cordials, to flavourings used to enhance taste perception, as well as specific foods like wheat, milk and chocolate. In some cases there was actually a lot of hope being pinned on diet being the blame because cutting out those offending foods or substances would have proven to be far easier to not only provide a definitive answer but also use as a 'cure'.

If anything the research and speculation only proved false hope for many parents and the children alike. The fact is there remains no hard factual evidence that a food allergy or any other kind of allergy is responsible for causing the differences in brain development which are attributable for the disorder. However we can fully appreciate why many families have clung on to the idea of dietary control and in some cases still do, some parents will insist that changes they have made to their children's diet actually do make a significant difference.

If the dietary changes have made a difference it's probably because of a placebo effect. Changing the diet and avoiding certain foods or food substances gives people something to practical to do which gives back a feeling of being in control. There is no doubt that ADHD makes people, parents in particular, feel out of control and helpless.

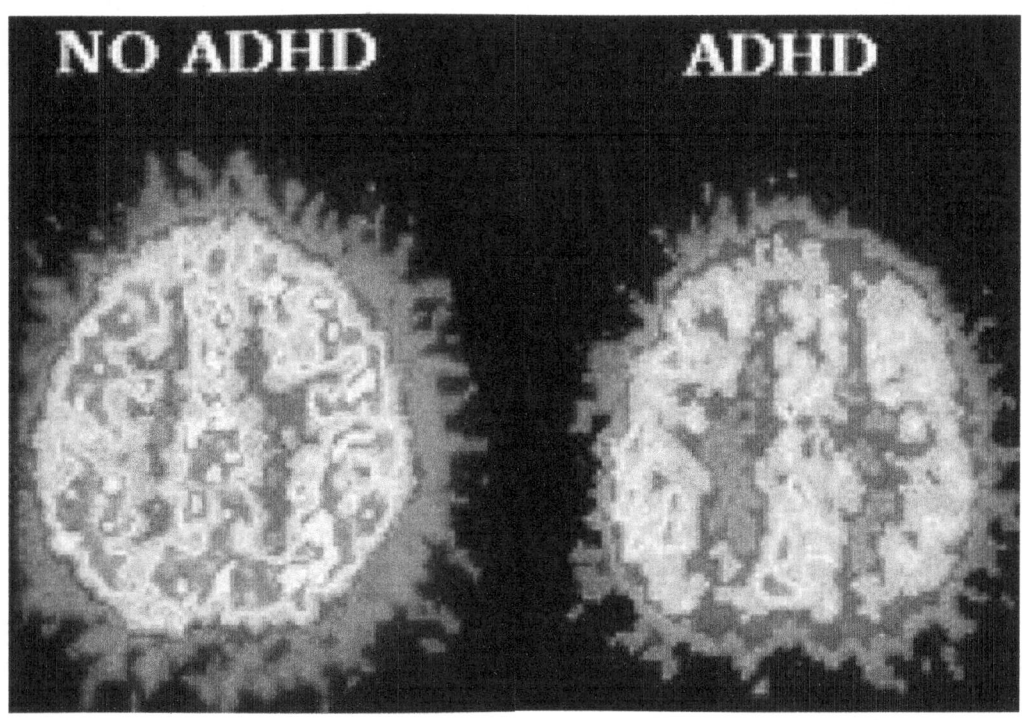

mythreeaspies.com

Aside from the medical and physiological causes and treatment methods, psychology offers a quite different opinion and approach. Whilst there is little disagreement concerning what happens inside the brain to either the over or under-arousal mechanism, psychologists have argued that environmental factors can significantly contribute to how the disorder is managed. In some instances psychologists have gone so far as to state that some parenting styles can actually exacerbate the symptoms, and by the same token, alleviate some of the more extreme behavioural characteristics. The psychological theories tend to emphasise the role of reinforcement as a means of either encouraging and promoting better behaviour (positive reinforcement) or inadvertently perhaps fostering poorer behaviour (negative reinforcement).

This may seem harsh and very accusatory, whilst it's quite obvious that no parent would want to make their child's behaviour any worse, it's also difficult to imagine that if it were that relatively simple why wouldn't all parents of children with ADHD be able to control their child's behaviour through their parenting? Behaviour modification isn't that well known as a technique though and unless parents have been made aware of its existence, use and of course how to precede then it might be unlikely that they would use it without intervention.

Behaviour modification aims to teach parents how to give their child attention for positive rather than negative reasons, and if necessary and certainly at the beginning of any programme, to find reasons to give positive attention.

The 'time out' method is used alongside as a means of trying to eliminate at best or at least alleviate the king of behaviour that is causing the most distress. The psychology behind the time out approach is it's designed to deliberately break the cycle of positive reinforcement – the system of rewards which the child wants, in order to eliminate the behaviour that's causing the problems. So, unacceptable behaviour is met with 'time'; time away from the more pleasurable reinforcing activities or rewards in temporary isolation until such a time when the child calms down.

That's the principle and practice of time out in its essence; the problem arises though when people think 'of that sounds simple and straight- forward, no problem I could do that'. Well, yes and no. The psychological approach driving from the behaviourist school is very systematic, ordered and planned down to the number of minutes a child is recommended to stay in isolation, as well as precisely how a programme should be followed. For example, the manner of 'isolation' can vary according to the child's age and the circumstances – whether it's to be followed at home, in the child care setting or at school.

The most common advice is the time spent in time out should mirror the child's age in minutes; so if a four-year-old is subject to isolation she or he shouldn't spend more than four minutes precisely away from normal interaction. Some parents for example of taken the idea of time out and 'isolation' to mean exactly that isolation and placed the child literally away, for example in a room or a space alone. This is obviously not only potentially dangerous it's totally unacceptable.

A more considered and recommended approach is the 'naughty step', 'naughty chair' or facing the wall. The ethos behind the approach is that the child is given time to not only cool down but more importantly to think about what they've previously been doing or how they've been behaving in order to begin to see it as a cause and consequence sequence. For a behaviour modification programme to be successful it's vitally important that the time spent out is regarded as negative reinforcement by the child; they need to genuinely prefer the alternative compared to the punishment so to speak. That's why sending most modern children to their lavishly kitted out bedrooms doesn't work!

Another way that ill-considered time out can fail is that those administering it can fail to ensure the child is given positive reinforcement initially every time they're engaging in behaviour that resembles the desired response. All too often people can forget that part whilst they're busy concentrating on the time out or negative side of reinforcement. The child has got to want the alternative, that is, to behave well. Behaviour modification as a technique is not without its critics though. Some psychologists have questioned the role of motivation and how it is being manipulated by the approach. Pointing to the difference between intrinsic and external motivation, they cite the point concerning external rewards can ruin intrinsic motivation.

The widespread use of rewarding primary school children with stickers for example, which can be given out sometimes for very superficial reasons, can render them redundant. If on the other hand they're given out sparingly with real meaning their value can be extremely worthwhile. Some commentators have made the point that children can learn to do something or behave in a certain way just to get the reward. A bit like a dog that has learned to associate sitting on the edge of the kerb with a tasty treat and not for its own sake. Consequently he refuses to play ball without the reward. The real objective of course with behaviour modification whether we're applying it to animal behaviour training or human beings is that the subject really has to value a) the reward system, and b) genuinely prefers behaving in the way that's wanted. Generally it is of course netter for children to learn to develop their own internal sense of control and motivation rather than learn to do things just for the outcome. This is the main criticism that's applied to behaviour modification, however in its defence time out is only meant, if it's being used properly, to be relatively short time measure and not a long term strategy.

Beliefs about parenting as the either the cause or a contributory factor in exacerbating the symptoms of ADHD reflect the behaviourist perspective in psychology, suggesting that behaviour is largely acquired and so is totally opposite to the physiological approach. Parents of aggressive children for example have been found to use punitive discipline strategies whilst also being unpredictably permissive. This creates confusion, contradiction and a very unsettling environment for a child to be brought up in. A cause and effect stance was taken by a researcher in America who investigated a group of boys between the ages of 7 and 10-years with problems of restlessness, short attention spans and impulsivity. The children had previously met the criteria for a diagnosis of ADHD. The boys were filmed whilst interacting with their mothers and observed throughout engaging in a set programme of activities:

- 4-minute mother and child free play

- 3-minute period of mother busy completing a questionnaire while their sons sat in a chair waiting for her to finish

- A paper and pen period when the mothers told the sons to work on either a maths or a handwriting task

- A cleaning-up period when mothers instructed the sons to tidy up the things that had been used during the session

The behaviour of both the mothers and the sons meanwhile were coded by the research team. They used the following dimensions of variability in response:

- Authoritative control
- Sensitivity of control
- Responsiveness
- Positive affect
- Acceptance of the child
- Involvement with the child
- No control

The children's behaviour issues: restlessness, lack of attention and impulsivity were found to be directly related to the mothers' responsiveness.

a.

⊠ CONDUCT DISORDER (CD) AND OPPOSITIONAL DEFIANT DISORDER (ODD)

The Learning Outcomes for this assignment are:

Element	Learning Outcome
1	Understand the differences between CD & ODD
2	Knowledge of the behavioural challenges associated with the two disorders
3	Awareness of psychological intervention techniques

Conduct Disorder (CD) is a particular category of disruptive behaviour so called because it's an example of repetitive and persistent transgression of the social norms, for example, the rights of others, rules in general and social norms. Examples of the kind of behaviour that separates conduct disorder from 'normal' challenging behaviour are:

* Bullying
* Aggression
* Threatening behaviour
* Property destruction
* Deceitfulness
* Theft
* Fighting

The one key characteristic of conduct disorder is *persistence.* To some lesser extent all of the behaviours listed above might be committed by an ordinary child exhibiting problem behaviour but when that kind of behaviour is a regular occurrence the seriousness has another level. The behaviour is likely to cause significant impairment for example in the child's normal functioning and their ability to lead an ordinary life. The disruption is likely to impact on their social relationships, their ability to learn and thrive, and, if the problems stretch into adolescence, their occupational chances. At which point the label 'delinquent' might be applied. Very extreme individuals may suffer from a more antisocial personality disorder such as sociopath or even psychopath. Both of these types of disorder are strongly thought to arise from a genetic dis-function; they're associated with serious crimes that exhibit a lack of empathy. Certain upbringings though are thought to interact very negatively with sociopath's vulnerability to being conditioned. Certain backgrounds can be linked with aggression and lack of social responsibility, and if discipline is too harsh or too permissive there may be further problems. This can be especially true if the child has also failed to form a bond with the mother or substitute carer.

There are a number of risk factors associated with children's challenging behaviour. Five factors in particular have been singled out as being of significant interest. These are:

* Social background
* Parental attitudes
* Mother's mental state
* Father's behaviour
* Marital relationship

(Liu et al, 1999)

Conduct Disorder

Young people with conduct disorder usually have little concern for others and repeatedly violate the basic rights of others and the rules of society. Conduct disorder causes children and adolescents to act out their feelings or impulses in destructive ways

Feels:

- Angry
- Irritable,
- Frustrated
- Hostile

Acts:

- Bullies and threatens
- Fights
- Steals
- Lies
- Runs away
- Destroys property

slidespeech.com

Children who tend to engage in antisocial behaviour have been found to be more likely to come from families with socio-economic challenges to deal with. Whilst it's difficult to determine exactly what it is about having less money than members of the average population that seems to be a contributory factor in children's poor behaviour, it's a finding that nonetheless has been replicated many times. Commentators have put forward suggestions however citing a number of possibilities. For example, the pressure and stress of having to cope with little money, housing issues associated with low income like overcrowding and lower social status.

Parental attitudes and behaviour towards children has been found to be a significant factor in increasing the chances of children displaying problem behaviour. In so far as actually being a predictor of poor behaviour. Parental disagreement, inconsistency and permissiveness have been found to seriously disturb children's chances to predict the outcome for antisocial behaviour.

Conversely when parents 'sing from the same hymn sheet' and there is consistency in their approach the children tend to learn to accept their discipline. This is particularly true when the home is subject to firm but fair boundaries. Similarly when reasoning is used as a communication method, the discipline 'fits the deed' and, most importantly, discipline is favoured over punishment.

The mother's mental state has been found to be significant in a number of studies. Children whose mothers have psychiatric problems have higher levels of both anxiety and depressive symptoms in their teenage years. The father's behaviour is also a predictor of children's problem behaviour. Fathers' antisocial behaviour in particular is associated with conduct problems in children.

Children's parents and their relationship are also indicated in studies of challenging behaviour in children. As a risk factor and a predictor of future problems, poor relationships for example have been found to be twelve times more likely to develop behavioural difficulties. An additional complication arises when mothers going through separation or divorce restrict the contact between the child and his/her father leading to frustration, anger and ultimately resentment.

Herbert (1991: 131) has argued that:

"Childhood signs of psychological abnormality are, by and large, manifestations of behavioural, cognitive and emotional responses common to all children. Their quality of being dysfunctional lies in their inappropriate intensity, frequency and persistence."

He's making the very valid point here that whenever children's behaviour is labelled as a 'problem' it begins to be perceived in that way. This process then makes any rational and objective thinking more difficult as a result of the frame already in place. How can we then make reasoned judgements on what constitutes typical and atypical behaviour is the starting point is already biased? Plus, we've got the additional problems of deciding what is typical for different age group, not to mention what is to be expected for an individual child with his or her own personality and upbringing.

In clinical psychological practice parental questionnaires are used as a means of ascertaining children's behavioural problems. Parents are asked to state according to a three-point scale whether statements are: not true [0], sometimes true [1] or often true [3]. The following extract from a rating scale will give you a good idea of how assessments of typical/atypical behaviour are used as an impartial measure of children's behaviour:

- Can't sit still, restless or hyperactive
- Destroys things belonging to his/her family or others
- Disobedient at home
- Fears going to school
- Nervous, highly strung or tense
- Not liked by other children
- Steals outside the home
- Underactive, slow moving or lacks energy

(Adapted from Achenbach, 1991)

Oppositional defiant disorder is characterised by reoccurring defiance, disobedience and hostile negative behaviour towards authority figures. It includes signs such as:

- Arguing with adults
- Temper tantrums (beyond those associated with the typical developmental stages)
- Defying rules
- Deliberate antagonistic behaviour
- Unfairly blaming others for own misbehaviour
- Extreme sensitivity
- Very highly strung
- Anger
- Rage
- Resentment
- Spiteful malicious behaviour
- Vindictiveness

All of the above symptoms are likely to lead to severe interruption of normal everyday life, and interference with academic progress and social relationships.

There is some evidence that there is a genetic component to ODD; an overactive 'behavioural activation system' (BAS) leads to the energy required for extreme behaviour associated with the disorder and an underactive inhibition system (BIS) explains the lack of self-control in be able to prevent outbursts of excessive hostile behaviour. Together this makes for quite a phenomenal potential for extreme, excessive, persistent and frequent rigid children. However there has also been some speculative mainly but not without its supporters evidence that in some cases at least birth complications have contributed to the disorder.

For example mothers who have consumed toxic substances including alcohol, recreational drugs and having suffered from lead poisoning can also cause damage to the developing foetus. The evidence is not particularly strong when compared with BAS and BIS though' one reason for this is the relatively small number of cases who have been medically investigated.

Intervention techniques tend to focus on the behaviourist approach which emphasises positive reinforcement but much more is required in addition to the standard approaches when behavioural challenges are extreme. Consistency, routine, boundaries, predictability and firm but fair treatment is vitally important for the children to establish a framework of acceptable and unacceptable behaviour expectations.

Modelling the behaviour to be replicated is also vital. It's important for carers to remember that behaviour is combination of a response to an immediate stimulus and learned behaviour. If we can teach new approaches, new ways to meet incidents that we know are likely to trigger outbursts, then there is hope in learning to control uncontrollable urges.

DO:	DON'T:
Be clear about what you expect	Be controlling
Focus on positive behaviour	Focus on punishment
Have high but achievable expectations	Set children up for failure
Maintain eye contact	Stand with your back to children
Model the right behaviour	Be hypocritical
Establish rules and stick to them	Be flexible in rule breaking
Have rules that start with 'do' not 'don't'	Start with 'don't do this/that' use 'do'
Give reminders before a reprimand	Jump on discretions
Provide incentives and rewards	Fail to pay attention to positive behaviour
Focus on what you want the child to do	Focus on what they are doing wrong
Be authoritative	Be authoritarian
Smile and be friendly	Scowl and be hostile
Be interested in the child	Be indifferent
Actively listen	Passively listen
Acknowledge strengths	Ignore good qualities
Be light-hearted a lot of the time	Be serious *all* the time
Use praise	Use put downs
Use a soft tone of voice	Shout
Refer to the behaviour as unacceptable	Refer to the child as unacceptable
Aim for win-win solutions to problems	Present a no-win situation for the child
Provide a structured predictable routine	Present a chaotic permissive spontaneous home

There is strong evidence to suggest that children with ODD experience a higher degree of egocentrism than the typical population of children long after the stage of cognitive development when we would expect it to have subsided.

In normal development this would be about 7-years-old. Egocentrism is characterised by an inability to see things from others' perspective. It includes a visual element 'out of sight is out of mind' generally under the age of seven. It also includes an emotional element however suggestive of empathy. This makes sense when we think of children behaving in hostile aggressive and vindictive ways towards family members and strangers alike.

Another feature of dysfunctional development concerns cognitive distortion. This involves faulty interpretation of people's intentions whether from their verbal communication, non-verbal body language or their actual behaviour. Reading signals as hostile, offensive or threatening when they are entirely neutral is a real problem.

To be permanently on the defensive, looking for trouble where none exists explains why children with ODD are constantly on edge with a short fuse. Added to that their highly strung sensitivity and we can start to appreciate how volatile and explosive being around children with ODD cab get.

As a means of addressing cognitive distortion, psychologists have advocated using behavioural therapy relying mainly on the positive reinforcement approach. However cognitive behavioural therapy (CBT) can also be used as a means of preventing problematic thoughts and establishing new behavioural patterns. It involves addressing thought and speech patterns for common phrases that an individual has a tendency to use a lot. These can be very indicative of a person's mind set.

The way we think often dictates how we behave. Children with ODD can get 'stuck' in a mode of behaviour that becomes a habitual pattern that's hard to break.

CBT aims to train individuals to adopt new more constructive ways of behaving.

" ...reflection can slowly bring us wisdom. We can come to see we are falling again and again into fixed repetitive patterns, and to begin to long to get out of them. We may, of course, fall back into them, again and again, but slowly we can emerge from them and change. "

(*Adapted from* Rinpoche, 2002: 31)

Rinpoche, S. (2002): *The Tibetan Book of Living and Dying*, London: Rider; *adapted US to UK, my emphasis*

▷ References

Achenbach, T. (1991): *Manual for the Child Behaviour Checklist 4-18 and 1991 Profile*, Burlington, University of Vermont, Department of Psychiatry

Liu, X. et al (1999): 'Risk factors for psychopathology among Chinese children', *Psychiatry and Clinical Neurosciences*, vol. 53, pp. 497-503

Rinpoche, S. (2002): *The Tibetan Book of Living and Dying,* London: Rider

⊠ TECHNIQUES FOR MANAGING CHALLENGING BEHAVIOUR

The Learning Outcomes for this assignment are:

Element	Learning Outcome
1	Understand the differences in psychological techniques for managing children's challenging behaviour
2	Knowledge of the diverse maladaptive behaviour management techniques

Psychological techniques for understanding, managing or changing behaviour vary considerably according to the different perspectives, or schools in psychology. The way different psychologists and researchers approach behaviour is a reflection on how they perceive the subject of psychology as a whole.

To give us an idea of the differences that exist let's have a look at the five most predominant perspectives which are:

- Physiological
- Behaviourist
- Psychoanalytic
- Cognitive
- Humanist

The physiological perspective ignores external factors in favour of the internal biological influences on behaviour. Psycho-biologists concentrate on genetic inheritance mainly but other biological influences like the role of hormones in determining cognitive processes, emotions and behaviour are also of interest. The role of the brain in determining abilities and its influence on behaviour is studied.

The behaviourist perspective ignores internal factors in favour of cause and effect influences on behaviour. Behaviourists concentrate on behaviour; what conditions are associated with certain behaviour, what happens after the behaviour, and how the antecedents and the consequences of behaviour influence that behaviour. They are particularly interested in the external role of the environment in shaping acquired or learned behaviour. The role of negative and positive reinforcement and imitation and the effects they have on behaviour are studied.

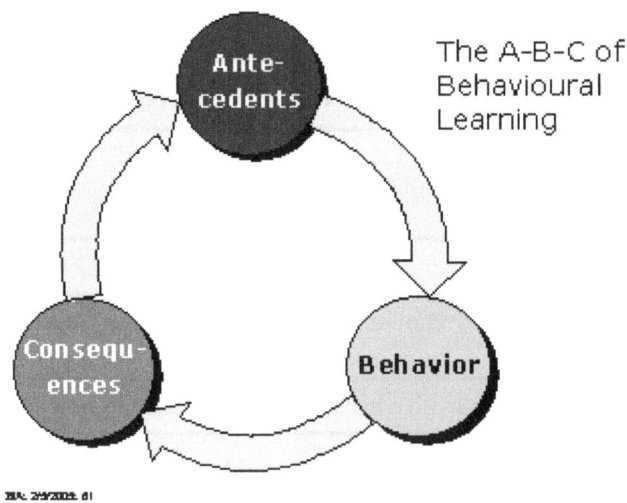

The A-B-C of
Behavioural
Learning

learningandteaching.info

The psychoanalytic perspective ignores the role of innate and environmental actors in favour of early childhood influences. Psychoanalysts concentrate on the effects of unconscious influences on behaviour. They are particularly interested in investigating the origins of irrational sometimes self-destructive behaviours as an insight into how a person feels and ultimately behaves. Events occurring in early childhood and the bearing they have on later development are studied.

The cognitivist perspective ignores both the biological influences and events and behaviour itself in favour of stressing the importance of rational processes. Cognitivists concentrate on reasoning as an internal influence on behaviour. They are especially interested in how a person thinks and their attitudes and beliefs influence their outlook on life. Internal processes such as learning, memory, logic and problem solving, motivation and language and the effect on behaviour are studied.

The humanist perspective tends to ignore any influences as mentioned above as starting points for studying human behaviour. Instead humanists are in favour of studying individuals as unique individuals who can interpret their own behaviour. They are interested in fulfilment and reaching our full potential. Internal and external factors may be of interest if they seem to be significant to the individual.

Here's a brief summary:

Perspectives:	Influence:	Treatment examples:
Physiological	Internal: genetic	Medical
Behaviourist	External: experience	Positive reinforcement
Psychoanalytic	Internal: early childhood	Play therapy
Cognitive	Internal: attitudes	Cognitive behavioural therapy
Humanist	Unique nature of individuals	Counselling

Physiology

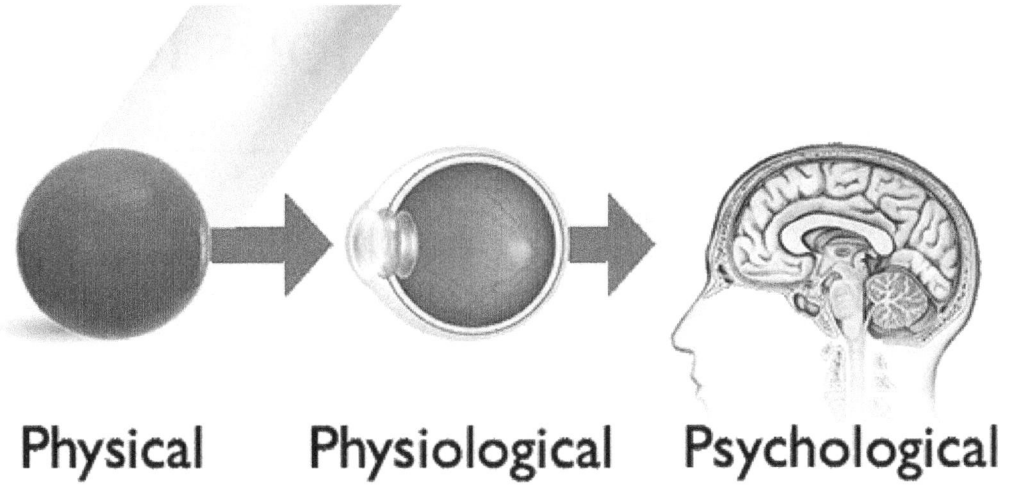

dot.color.com

Lisa may have a predisposition to be fearful and a general tendency to be anxious.

This could develop further into a specific phobia or she may just have an above average capacity for a tendency to be anxious (generalised anxiety disorder – GAD). If it interfered with her normal day to day life her GP might consider giving her anti-anxiety medication.

Behaviourism

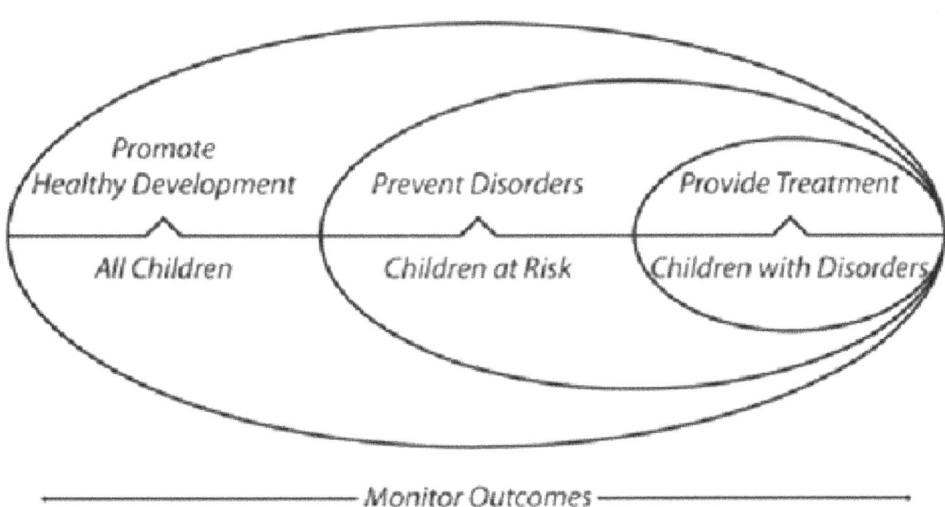

[8]

Lisa may have acquired her fear of spiders from imitating a scared reaction towards them that she has seen someone else show. She has learned somehow to associate fear with spiders and this had developed into a cause and effect relationship. She is also getting quite a lot of attention as a result. The family need to be aware that they may be inadvertently rewarding her 'fear'. If she does go on to develop a phobia though this could be treated by a 'de-sensitisation' technique; learning to relax whilst gradually beginning to cope in the presence of spiders.

Psychoanalytic

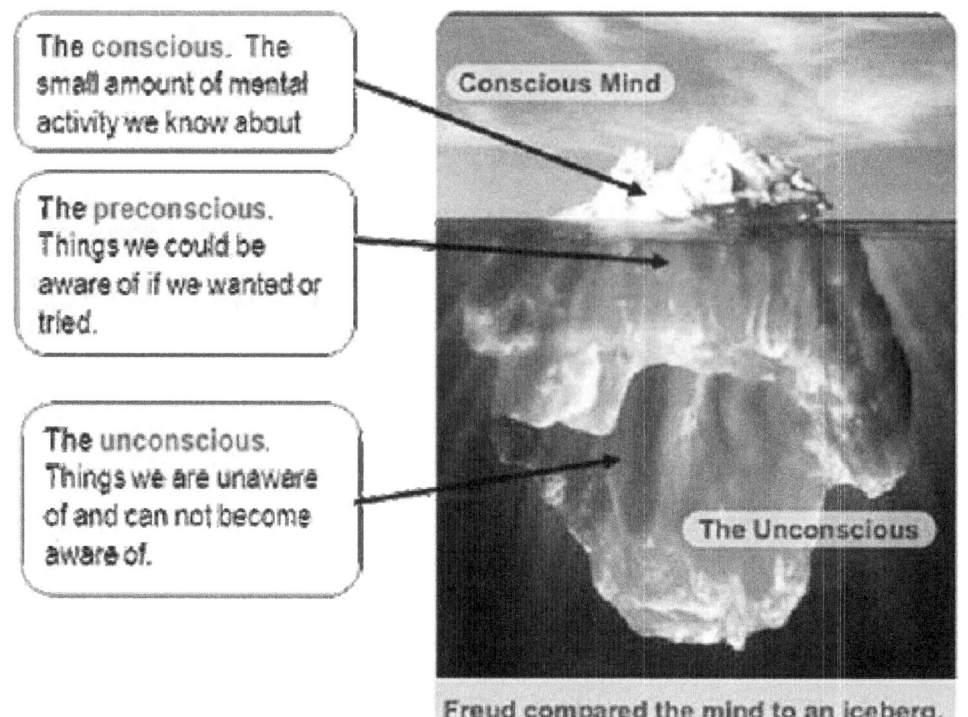

The Unconscious Mind

The conscious. The small amount of mental activity we know about

The preconscious. Things we could be aware of if we wanted or tried.

The unconscious. Things we are unaware of and can not become aware of.

Conscious Mind

The Unconscious

Freud compared the mind to an iceberg.

Thoughts
Perceptions

Memories
Stored knowledge

Fears
Unacceptable sexual desires
Violent motives
Irrational wishes
Immoral urges
Selfish needs
Shameful experiences
Traumatic experience

simplypsychology.org

Lisa may be projecting a more general sense of fear onto spiders which is a safer option; the real object of her fears may be too difficult for her to deal with. Spiders may be acting as a substitute. If the fear of spiders continued she could have some hypnosis when she got older.

Cognitive

Lisa has developed a belief that spiders are scary; her behaviour is congruent with the typical behaviour for fear. Essentially the problem is internal, in her head. She could be re-trained using cognitive behavioural therapy (CBT) to think differently along rational lines: 'the vast majority of spiders are not harmful therefore there is nothing to be afraid of'.

Humanist

traditional perspective

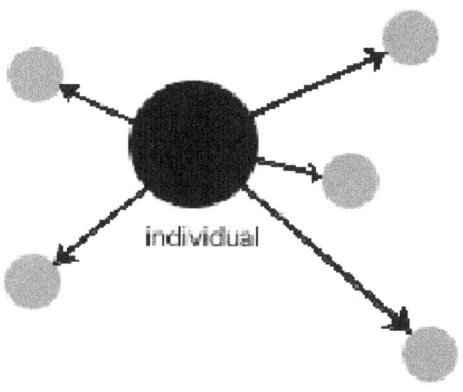

blogschmog.net

Lisa would need to explain in her own words and in her own way why she thinks/feels she may have an issue with her behaviour towards spiders. For her it may not present a problem. If she does however then talking about it using counselling could help her to understand her fear and also how she could control it.

Hopefully the above has served two purposes by giving us an idea of how different psychologists approach behaviour according to their beliefs about 'where' behaviour comes from, either internally or externally, the influences and how also it can be managed.

The illustration used was quite general, that is fear to get us started thinking like psychologists. If we were to try and explain children's challenging or maladaptive behaviour could we still use the five approaches. Let's try again:

It makes perfect sense that one particular perspective that we've examined is more closely associated with children's challenging b*ehaviour* than the other schools. Yes, you've guessed it – behaviourism. That wasn't too hard was it! One technique that's used is the ABC approach. This involves observing a child to discover what tends to happen immediately *before* an incident of unwanted behaviour occurs, what happens *during* the behaviour itself, and, what happens directly *after* the behaviour.

A: Antecedents

B: Behaviour

C: Consequences

As we saw with Lisa earlier her fearful response to spiders – the crying, screaming and running away whenever she came into contact with spiders met with attention. What do you think might happen to her behaviour if the family members reacted instead by ignoring her outbursts and just carried on normally with whatever they were doing at the time? It would be interesting to see whether Lisa received positive attention from her older brother and mum in equal measure when she was being calm.

Positive parenting involves imparting an environment from which children can learn through example of how to behave. It involves giving children positive quality attention whilst they are being well-behaved and providing a general atmosphere based on the following below to promote good behaviour:

- encouragement

- builds confidence
- values the child
- teaches perseverance
- promotes independence and achievement
- attitude towards attainment
- is interested in the child
- shows respect
- is authoritative but not authoritarian
- has a rapport with the child
- trusts the child
- sticks to firm boundaries of discipline, using reasoning
- is fair and kind

Poor parenting tends to produce children who are more likely to exhibit challenging behaviour and is characterised by: *Power-orientated actions*: the exercise of power (authority) in a dominant manner, such as using coercion, threats, intimidation, reprimands and punishments.

Inductive reasoning parents by contrast are:

1) Human, accessible, reliable and consistent; 2) Respectful of their children and sensitive to their needs; and, 3) Positive and enthusiastic most but not all the time.

Behaviourists advocate using a technique based on rewarding desirable behaviour. This is referred to as 'positive reinforcement'. Unwanted behaviour can either be ignored or sanctioned which is referred to as 'negative reinforcement'. The idea behind ignoring, or withdrawing, is that all children ultimately want attention; by taking it away we're removing their motivation for misbehaviour. Negative reinforcement in the form of sanctions involves taking away privileges or treats until such a time when the desired behaviour is re-established.

Below is an example of a behaviour modification programme:

BEHAVIOUR MODIFICATION PROGRAMME

1. Observe

The exact nature of the behaviour problem. Make a record of how long the behaviour goes on and how often it occurs. What are the antecedents? Keep records so that you have feedback as to how the programme is working.

2. Select Reinforcers

Primary:

Fulfil an immediate need, e.g. a pleasurable activity

Secondary:

    i.   The 'Token Economy' – tokens, e.g. stickers or pebbles in a jar that can be exchanged for other reinforcers, e.g. a treat or a trip;

    ii.   Social reinforcers – praise and positive attention which should be given alongside the tangible reinforcer

3. Time Out?

It is important NOT to give attention for unwanted behaviour. Even unpleasant attention can be reinforcing. Time Out is usually reserved for particularly poor behaviour; the number of minutes corresponding with the age, in years, of the child.

4. **The Goal**

State the goal precisely. Decide which 'successive approximations' (steps that resemble the desired behaviour) to the goal you will reinforce – remembering to make it very easy for the child to succeed in the beginning. Then, as the child improves, gradually raise the standard needed to get the reward; this is referred to as *'shaping'* the behaviour. Decide the exact way the reinforcement will be given. Discuss the programme with everyone involved with the child in order that s/he receives the same treatment from everyone.

5. **Ending the Programme**

This stage can cause a relapse. Try to avoid this by changing over from *constant* reinforcement to *partial* reinforcement when the goal is reached; continue to give the secondary reinforcers – praise and positive attention; try to ensure that the changed behaviour brings its own reward.

Child Psychology

I recently came across an interesting article on the tendancy of unhappiness in intelligence people. The author (a sociologist) claims that unhappiness develops in childhood, primarily because of Western cultures lack of esteem for intellectual values.

Children develop along four streams: intellectual, physical, emotional (psychological) and social. In classrooms, the smartest kids tend to be left out of more activities by other children than they are included in. They are "odd," they are the geeks, they are social outsiders. In other words, they do not develop socially as well as they may develop intellectually or even physically where opportunities may exist for more progress.

Their emotional development, characterized by their ability to cope with risky or stressful situations, especially over long periods of time, also lags behind that of the average person.

Adults tend to believe that intelligent kids can deal with anything because they are intellectually superior. This inevitably includes situations where the intelligent kids have neither knowledge nor skills to support their experience. They go through the tough times alone. Adults don't understand that they need help and other kids don't want to associate with kids the social leaders say are outsiders.

Don't assume your child can deal with something.

Also more intelligent people have higher goals, want to achieve more and are always striving to better themselves and achieve the next goal, they are not so easily satisfied and aren't happy with what they have because once they have achieved one thing they are looking for something to do next and therefore tend never to complete their goals.

Child Psychology

Compared to adults, children have a different outlook on life in many ways. To understand how a child sees the world makes you more competent and more effective when it comes to responding to the many trials that a child encounters on the road to adulthood.

Being involved with children is a big responsibility, because our interactions have a lasting effect on their future. As adults we can help children grow in knowledge and self confidence. With the insights we get from child psychology, they can begin to take their place as citizens of the world, free from paralysing constraints that warp and stunt.

James Mark Baldwin, an American early developmental theorist saw development as a fabric woven from threads of heredity and environment. He believed that children continually adjust their view of the world while they learn through observation and mime and are influenced by their social surroundings.

Freud;

Perhaps the best-known theorist in history is Sigmund Freud. Freud suggested there were three parts to the personality: The *id* is the largest part of the mind and represents the basic needs of the person, like sucking, sexual desire and safety; the *ego* is the moderator, finding effective ways for the id and superego to be satisfied; the *superego*, or conscience, is the understanding of the values of society.

Id: I want the toy that child is playing with.
Ego response: Grab the toy from the child using it.
Superego: It is not acceptable to simply grab the toy.
Ego's new response: Ask the child if you may take a turn playing with the toy. (A socially acceptable way of getting the toy.)

…..

It is becoming more accepted that genetics (nature) and environment (nurture) are inextricably interwoven and that children interact with and influence their environment while simultaneously being shaped by the influence their environment has on them.

……………

Changing from being a pregnant mother to the mother of a tiny baby can be overwhelming. It's also a life-changing experience for the father too. One day you're both looking forward to the birth, although with some trepidation (will our baby be healthy and strong?), the next there is this little person in your arms who you're responsible for. No matter how many books you read or ante-natal classes you attend, preparing for the dependency your baby will have on you is a challenge.

If it's your first baby you may wonder how you'll know how to change their nappy, stop them crying or know if they're ill. Even with the second or third child you may still feel unsure about certain aspects of their care and development. And as the child grows you wonder how to deal with each exciting stage of their life, from learning to eat solid food, to walking and talking. This module guides you through the main changes in a baby's life, from newborn to two years old, and addresses how to deal with someof the main challenges.

DEVELOPMENT AND MILESTONES

There are four main stages in a baby's development, based on their age. Each is measured in terms of the changes they undergo.

- 0-3 months
- 3-6 months
- 6-12 months
- 1-2 years

Something to consider is that every baby is different, and will develop at its own pace.

0-3 MONTHS

From the moment a baby is born it starts to develop. It leaves the comfort and security of its mother's womb and enters a new world of light, sound, taste and touch. A new baby can't focus further than about 45cm yet so sees a lot of blurry moving objects. In the womb it could hear its mother's voice and heartbeat. It could even hear the music she listened to. Now it can hear these things with greater clarity. It needs to learn to feed, yet can only cry when it's hungry. And suddenly people are cuddling it and rocking it, when previously it's only known the gently movements of its mother's body. No wonder babies cry! One of the first things midwives recommend as soon as a baby is born is putting it to the mother's breast. It may not feed straight away, but it will have the natural suckling instinct and will soon be feeding. It is believed this procedure is invaluable in helping the mother and baby to bond. There may be circumstances, such as a Caesarean section, or the mother's decision not to breastfeed, where a baby is bottle fed soon after the birth. This is a personal choice. Babies need stimulation from the moment they are born. For the first few days they may spend a lot of time sleeping. Then, as each day passes they will become more aware of their surroundings. Newborns don't need lots of toys. Grandma may think the teddy she's bought is wonderful, but actually it may be frightening to a young baby. Effective stimulants for a baby of this age are large black and white toys or pictures. This is because young babies can identify contrasts, as opposed to small coloured patterns. Gentle sound is also good. A musical mobile above the cot may help relax a baby. Also, playing the music a mother listened to while the baby was in her womb is said to calm a baby, as they may remember the familiar sounds.

3-6 MONTHS

During the second three months of its life a baby changes a lot. It starts to form a personality, and as each day and week passes parents will notice the changes. One of the most miraculous things a baby does at this stage is smile at its parents. 'Ooh, he's got wind', many people will say! But, these first smiles are true recognition of those that care for him. The baby will start to put on weight now and become 'chubby'. This baby fat will eventually disappear, once the baby becomes more active. It will start to become fascinated by its own hands and stare at them for periods of time. It will also begin to grab large objects, although may not be able to hold on to them for any length of time.

Another major development stage between 3-6 months is when a baby rolls over for the first time. It's starting to get stronger and stronger, and may also start to push itself up on its arms when put on its front. This is also when the 'baby babble' starts. Although it may sound ridiculous to the rest of the world, cooing and gooing at a baby helps it learn different sounds, and eventually speech.

Depending on the parents' preference, solid foods can be introduced between 4 and 6 months. If a baby is waking in the night more often than usual it may be a sign that it's hungry and ready to start on solids, such as baby rice.

For lucky parents a baby may start to sleep through the night at around 4 months. However, there is no standard rule for this, and some are still waking in the night at 3 years old!

6-12 MONTHS

From 6 months onwards a baby really starts to change and become more of a 'little person'. Some people think this stage is more fun than when a baby is tiny, as it's now much more responsive.

A baby will now start to sit up, at first supported by cushions. Then they start to crawl. After that comes the stage of pulling themselves up whilst holding items of furniture. Then slowly moving around (known as cruising) whilst taking the weight on their legs, which is preparation for walking.

Some babies never learn to crawl, they go straight from sitting to standing and walking. When they sit they manoeuvre themselves by shuffling on their bottom.

Ah, Babies! Module 2 Page 5

When a baby takes its first steps it's a sure sign that they're on their way to toddlerhood. This is such a momentous occasion, both for the baby and the parent.

This moving stage is also a tense time for parents. Now the expression 'eyes in the back of your head' comes into its own, as the baby attempts to climb and grab everything in sight!

At around 1 year a baby will start to say its first understandable words, which unfortunately for mothers is usually 'dada'. Of course, this isn't because they prefer their father! The 'd' sound is much easier to pronounce than 'm'.

For the first 3 months of its life a baby can only grasp things put into its hands and doesn't unfurl its fingers often. Look at a sleeping baby at this age and notice how its tiny fists will be clenched tightly. This is because it hasn't yet developed the reflex to unfurl its fingers. From 3-6 months a baby can grasp objects put into its hands, but can't keep hold of them for long.

At 6 months it starts to use a pincer movement with its thumb and forefinger, to pick up small objects. This is the time when a baby may start to put things in its mouth.

Teeth usually appear at about 6 months. The initial joy a parent feels when they discover the first tiny tooth coming through may be short lived when their baby cries for hours because it's teething.

A sign of teething is the baby feeling generally unwell, having a temperature, red cheeks and dribbling a lot. Babies also go off their food sometimes when teething.

1-2 YEARS

The changes from newborn to 2 years are amazing. In such a short space of time the baby has learnt to walk and talk, and is now officially a toddler. As each day passes the toddler learns new skills and will be ready to start trying things on their own.

Feeding themselves with a knife, fork and spoon is an important part of this stage. They may not use the utensils correctly, and most of the food may not end up in their mouth, but they will grasp the concept if allowed to practise. A toddler will also drink from a cup, rather than a bottle now.

The vocabulary will now start to expand and slowly the toddler will pick up more and more words. As time progresses they will then start to put two words together, then three, and before you know it a whole sentence. Words may not be in the right order at first, or grammatically correct, for example 'my want to', instead of 'I want to'.

Ah, Babies! Module 2 Page 7

It's important that parents and carers don't imitate this baby talk, which leads the toddler to believe it's correct. Just saying the sentence correctly, without making the child think they've done something wrong is enough at this stage. They will soon copy and pick up correct expressions. In addition, nothing is more satisfying to a parent than when a child starts to understand what you're saying to them (although they may not do what you ask!)

Play is an important part of this developmental stage. The toddler will start to play alone or with toys and towards the end of the second year will start to demonstrate imaginative play. This is also a stage when toddlers start to develop friendships and play with others.

The toddler that is cared for by a nursery or childminder, family or friend may now start to become clingy and not want to be left. It's important to explain that you will be coming back, however, in most cases the tears have stopped 5 minutes after the parent has left.

This desire not to be separated can become a habit, which is more upsetting for the parent than the child. It is important to be firm and hand the child over to the carer with authority. A quick kiss and hug goodbye is enough, and then leave. Hanging around and going back to see if the child is ok will upset them further and start the whole process again.

A baby usually shows its needs by crying. At such a young age it has no other way to communicate if it is:

- Hungry
- Unwell
- Too cold or too hot
- Tired
- Bored

These needs are soon recognised by parents and experienced carers. However, sometimes it seems impossible to know what the baby wants, and no amount of soothing, feeding or attention will calm them.

This may be the time to ask for help. Often, a baby just needs a change of scenery or person to distract it, and tired and frustrated parents may not be able to see this and worry unnecessarily.

Some babies cry more than others. Some are content whilst others require constant attention. Each should be treated as an individual.

Babies also need stimulation, even when they are tiny. Short periods of play with toys can assist the baby's development and bond with its parents. This also teaches the baby about the world around it.

Ah, Babies! Module 2 Page 9

A great way to stimulate a young baby is a baby gym, which encourages it to reach and grab for hanging toys. As a baby gets older a play mat, in bright colours is a safe place to put it, and it gives the baby a different view of the world.

Once a baby can sit up a static play gym is invaluable, the sort where the baby sits in the middle and can play with the fixed toys. There are many other baby toys on the market, specifically designed to aid development and amuse a baby in the first years of its life.

A daily walk in the fresh air is also very good for a baby (and its parents or carers!) It may seem an effort to get out of the house sometimes, with all the equipment a baby needs, but a trip out is worth the effort.

SOOTHING

Knowing how to calm and soothe a baby is instinct to some people, but not all. At 3.00am when a baby is screaming it can be hard to know what the right thing to do is. Parents faced with this situation should remember they're not alone – there will be plenty of others going through exactly the same thing.

An important issue is that of sharing the care of a baby. It may not always be possible for both parents to be up in the middle of the night, so an agreement should be made, where turns are taken, depending on what suits both parents.

Ways to soothe a baby:

- Cuddling – the baby may be feeling insecure
- Rocking – to comfort
- Being in a baby carrier – the sort that fits to the parent
- A trip out in the pram or buggy
- Singing – many babies love music
- A bath – to relax
- Massage – baby massage is a wonderful thing
- Swaddling – can recreate the security of being in the womb

INFANT STATES

As a tiny baby grows, its periods of sleeping, waking and feeding will start to form a pattern.

Often the pressures of day to day life mean a routine is essential. There may be other children in the family to take to school, feed and bath, do homework with and read a bedtime story to. With a first baby it's much easier to have a more flexible routine than if there are other children to care for.

There are many arguments for and against a strict routine, and it's up to the parents how much of a routine they wish to implement.

A baby needs periods of both stimulation and inactivity.

- Stimulation can include playing, singing or playing music and trips out.
- Inactivity is when a baby just needs to sit in its baby chair or pram and watch the world or its parents.

Sleeping is also a major part of a baby's inactivity. A tiny baby will spend approximately 16 hours a day sleeping, which will be broken up into chunks. This sounds fantastic for a new mother, but unfortunately most of this time is spent catching up on housework and chores. However, it's important for a new mother to get all the rest she can, which is why all offers of help should be accepted.

Ah, Babies! Module 2 Page 11

As a baby gets older it will spend less time sleeping and more time taking in its surroundings. This is fine as long as its wakeful periods are not in the middle of the night!.

EXERCISE 2.3

Do you think a baby should have a regular sleep at the same time each day, or should it be allowed to fall asleep when it wishes, including at night?

Suggested answers can be found at the end of the module

THE TERRIBLE TWOS

Anyone who's experienced the 'terrible twos' knows they don't just happen at age 2. This expression should be re-named 'The terrible toddler stage'.

Suddenly a cute little baby turns into a walking, talking nightmare. They refuse to put on their coat and shoes, throw tantrums in the supermarket, shout and hit, touch things when they're told not to, snatch toys and even kick and bite. Plus, their favourite word is 'no!'

It's important to remember that this stage won't last, and the toddler is going through a developmental stage. Suddenly they are discovering they can make their own choices, whether it's which toy they want to play with or what they'd like to eat.

However, rules have to be set or the toddler will become very confused.

Ah, Babies! Module 2 Page 12

A solution to try and minimise tantrums is to limit choices. For example, saying to a young child 'would you like cereal or toast for your breakfast?' is much easier for them to understand than 'what would you like for your breakfast?'

It's hard to always be patient and follow all the good advice about explaining why they have to clean their teeth or sit nicely at the table.

However, if you get cross, it shows the toddler they are rising to the bait, and won't resolve anything.

Ignoring a tantrum can help calm the toddler down. People often feel embarrassed if a child decides to cause a scene in a public place, however, many observers will have been through the same thing. The important thing is to ensure the child is safe and show them the tantrum isn't going to allow them to get their own way.

1. You understand the major developments and milestones in a baby's life, from newborn to two years. Each stage brings a new and miraculous change in the baby.

2. You've learnt the main infant needs and why babies cry. Every baby is an individual and has its own needs.

3. There are many ways to soothe a baby, and only trying each will show which works.

4. Infants have several different states, and don't always need to be stimulated.

5. The terrible twos are hard work, but many parents suffer this period and it doesn't last forever. This is a developmental stage, not the child being deliberately difficult.

THE EFFECT OF PRAISE AND CRITICISM

The effects of overprotection and criticism can be equally bad for a child's emotional health. Overly indulged children are often spoiled, selfish, inconsiderate and demanding. Early research indicates that high permissiveness and low punishment in homes make children antisocial and aggressive, paving the way for criminal activity in adulthood.

A parent who watches over their child constantly, protects them from the slightest risk, overly clothes and medicates them, and make up their mind for them at every opportunity, is doing more harm than good to the child.

Closely related to overprotection is restrictiveness. In this case, parents enforce rigid rules and standards of conduct and give the child very little autonomy or personal freedom.

Placing unrealistic demands on the child is also counterproductive. For instance, some parents place high expectations in terms of academic performance from their children. Where the child is naturally gifted, things may work out fine. But, if the child is unable to live up to their parents' expectations, the result can be disastrous for the child's self esteem and confidence.

In addition, inconsistent discipline makes it very hard for the child to establish stable values for guiding their behaviour. Since punishment is self-devaluing, it is considered important for a parent to make it clear to the child that in disapproving the child's behaviour they are not condemning or rejecting the child themselves, but merely disapproving of the offending behaviour.

BED-WETTING

Nocturnal bed-wetting may be considered 'normal' in a 3-year-old, but not in a 9-year-old. Bed-wetting, baby talk or thumb sucking in older children are signs of distress, anxiety and continued dependence. Although bed-wetting is common in both boys and girls under the age of 5, by 11, almost twice as many boys as girls continue to wet their bed, for reasons that are not clear to child psychologists.

For over four decades, the standard treatment for nocturnal bedwetting was the use of a urine alarm or bell-and-pad procedure. This is an alarm system that gets activated whenever a child wets the bed and is awakened. Studies show that over 75% children respond to this treatment.

Children prone to wetting the bed should also be taken to the toilet before they go to bed, and again 'lifted' or woken up to go to the toilet later in the night. Sometimes it is just a case of breaking the habit of bed-wetting.

Sight;

Vision is the least developed sense in a newborn baby. Cells in the retina are much less densely packed than they are in adulthood or even in youth. The optic nerve takes several years to become fully developed. The muscles of the lens are underdeveloped too, so focus is blurred and depth perception is minimal.

Focus becomes fairly developed in the first two months or so and the infants' original 20-600 vision normally becomes 20-20 vision in about six months.

Like any new task, infants learn how to effectively use the tools they were given and begin to understand what their eyes are doing. As they do, they test out their new skills to become more adept at identifying depth, pattern and object perception.

WATCH WHERE YOU'RE GOING

Crawling is very important in the development of depth perception, and perhaps the reverse is true as well. Children learn to anticipate dangerous situations by experiencing the depth cues as they move through their environment. Each time a new method of movement is used (crawling, walking, running), they must learn the new cues to avoid danger.

One very famous experiment is the "visual cliff" designed by Eleanor Gibson and Richard Walk in 1960. It is made with a Plexiglas-covered table that has a platform in the middle, a shallow side, and a 'deep side' that is several feet below the glass. The shallow and deep sides have matching checkerboard patterns.

Researchers found that children had no concerns about travelling across the shallow side, but, as they approached the platform and what they perceived as the edge of the table, they became afraid. The research conducted with this tool revealed the innate link between crawling and avoiding falling down. This fear of falling does not seem to be directly related to the development of depth or pattern perception, though.

....

Signs of speech or language delays may include:

- Lack of response to sound or vocalizing
- Difficulty sucking or prolonged feeding times
- Failure to use gestures by 12 months
- Preference for gestures to vocalizations after 12 months
- Trouble imitating sounds after 18 months

Help your child develop vital speech and language skills by:

- Spending time communicating
- Reading to your child
- Using everyday situations to reinforce language skills

Read to your child from 6 months old;

Up to about two years of age, children begin to recognise the proper pronunciations of words and start speaking. At this age their vocabulary can grow to hundreds of words and they will start using strings of two or three words. As this develops, they begin to apply grammar and engage in conversations that involve taking turns talking. Between three and five years of age, children's phonological awareness increases and their pronunciation improves. They might create words to replace those that they haven't yet mastered. Grammatical structure complexity develops and they begin to master conversation. They start to understand the illocutionary force of words: that is, the intent of the statement (e.g. to warn, to enquire, to promise). They will start asking for clarification and telling chronologically ordered stories. Through ages six to about 10 years of age, children master syllable stresses and phonemes (sounds that will change the meaning of a word, such as in the case of pad, tad, sad). As they begin school they will have a vocabulary of around 10,000 words and understand that there can be multiple definitions for them. They're in constant refinement

of grammar and pragmatics as they build a command of language as a tool.
From 11 years to adulthood, people continue to improve their mastery of language and understand subtle and non-literal meanings used in sarcasm and irony.

BILINGUALISM

There was a period when it was widely believed that bilingualism in young children led to dissociation from society and hindered linguistic, social and cognitive development. This is to the contrary, as it was recently proven that bilingualism leads to more adaptive concept formation and cognitive flexibility.
Simply, this means a bilingual child, through integration and immersion in a second or third language, is likely to have flexible language skills. Processing the different formations, sounds and pronunciation of a non-native language is a skill that, once mastered at an early age, can be used throughout life.

DO APES USE LANGUAGE?

While it's true that apes are capable of learning to communicate their needs through sign language, their ability to use language to converse is debated.
Certain chimpanzees are adept at sign language and one, Kanzi, is believed to have learnt sign language and learned to understand hundreds of English words by watching caregivers talk to his mother through sign language. He could act out unusual commands that he'd

never heard before, like "Put the toy in the box."
While his ability to understand was quite advanced for an animal, it's not widely believed he could hold a conversation. He could string together two or three words, like, "You carry Kanzi," but it seemed to be only to get what he wanted, not to engage in a transfer of information. His comprehension does not appear to have exceeded that of a two-year-old. Since he lacks language centres in the brain and has no real language model to learn from, it's unlikely he could progress much further.

It is now widely accepted that, while there are important influences on IQ that are innate, ideal conditions of child rearing (healthy lifestyle, access to education, variety of activities, loving parents, enough time with family and enough autonomous time – the influences go on and on) result in children with higher IQs and rates of personal success.

Some researchers believe that unpredictable one-time events – a strong connection to a teacher, a summer of love, the sudden death of a mentor – are of the greatest influence on mental development.

Recently, the back-and-forth argument about the intelligence of children who have been breast-fed has swung toward the side of nursing. It is currently the belief that there is a component of mother's milk that enhances a child's ability to learn. It might be a coincidence that the same types of studies used to say that formula feeding was advantageous. It is probably safe to say that the interaction between mother and child is of greater influence.

HOW DO WE KNOW WHAT CHILDREN THINK?

Children take a relatively long time to develop to full mental maturity. Humans, as a species, are unusual in that our babies are unable to fend for themselves when born. Many other mammals can stand and walk within minutes of birth, but because humans have a very large head, relative to the size of our bodies and the birth canal, a human baby is born with a brain that is not yet fully developed.
Our mental capacity comes at the cost of an extended development phase after we are born. Many months of learning must pass before a human baby can do the things that a lamb or calf can do almost immediately after birth.

It is important to expose your child to rich, sensory experiences.

Adults focus on one area, like a spot light, whereas children take in everything and don't focus on one area, because they are still learning. They therefore find it hard to focus where as we may miss things when we are too focused on one area. When we are in a new situation we open our minds to take more in, are brains are more stimulated and see more of what is going on around and take the detail in around us, because we are more open minded we notice things that we wouldn't normally see. The same is true when we take time out away from work, our focus is less on work so we can see whats going on around us more and notice our family etc. Children aren't bad at paying attention, they are just bad at blocking other things out.

LEARNING BY TALKING

One of the most important abstract maps that a child learns to use is that of language. Language is a symbolic representation of the world, in that the word 'apple' is not an apple, it is a symbol that represents an apple.
When the child learns to use the symbol, it can communicate its needs to a parent or carer.

Children learn in lots of ways, from the people they spend time with, the books they read and the programmes they watch on television. As adults it's important we monitor this learning process and ensure children are not exposed to learning material or situations beyond their years. It's also important we influence them by helping them to learn.

UPBRINGING

There are many arguments for and against children being conditioned by their upbringing.
Some people believe that a child with a warm loving family will be a better person than a child who is not cared for well and left to entertain themselves. However, there is no real evidence to suggest this is the case, and a child who comes from a broken home can be as caring, affectionate and intelligent as one who has the most protected of upbringings. The important thing to consider is the personality of a child, and how they are influenced by the people around them and how they deal with individual experiences.

WHO DO CHILDREN LEARN FROM?

The behaviour of others and the life experiences a child encounters have a major effect on how and what they learn. Children copy and as they grow from babies to young adults they learn the rights and wrongs of the world.

CONFIDENCE

A confident child is a happy child. Giving praise to a child who has done something right, such as sharing a toy or getting dressed without being asked, is much more effective than telling them off. A child

needs to feel secure and know they are doing the right thing.
Praising a child also helps them develop their social skills. An example
of this would be telling them they are right when they are polite to
adults and other children.

Communication is also an important aspect of growing and securing
confidence. A child may have a temper tantrum because they are frustrated
and can't express themselves. Leaving them to calm down and
then addressing the problem will give better results than punishing
them for getting cross.

CONCENTRATION

Concentration is an important factor of the learning process for a
child. A child learns to concentrate at school and both the teacher and
the other pupils in the class can influence the art of concentration.
A child that can concentrate well and focus on the task they are doing
is likely to get more satisfaction than the child who is unable to concentrate
and behaves badly.

Being able to concentrate is also important at home. If children have
to do homework or read they need to be able to concentrate. A parent
can help to teach this skill by giving the child a quiet area of their own
to do the tasks they need to.

BEHAVIOUR

How do children learn to behave well? It takes time, and a major influencing
factor is the behaviour of the adults around them,
particularly their parents and carers. One of the classic mistakes a parent
makes is to yell at a child 'will you stop shouting/screaming!' At
times of stress it's hard not to do this, but it has a very bad effect on
the child's learning.

Children are also influenced by their friends' and siblings' behaviour.
How many times do we hear 'but he did it so I thought it was ok'.
When this happens it's up to the parent or carer to decide if the child
is telling the truth, and if they have a sufficient level of maturity to
understand they shouldn't copy bad behaviour.

ENVIRONMENT

Children are constantly learning from the environment around them.
This includes:

- books and magazines
- the internet
- television
- signs on roads and in shops
- experiences on days out
- games and play
- rules within the home and at school

Most children go through a phase of asking 'why':

- Why doesn't that man have any hair?
- Why do I have to go to bed at 8.00pm?
- Why do I have to eat my vegetables?

This list could be endless and the questions are irrelevant. What's important is that a child is inquisitive, keen to learn and wants to understand the reasoning behind things.

To help the child learn their questions should always be answered. If they ask at an inconvenient time (which they often do!) it's important to spend time with them later on, explaining the answers to their questions.

SPEECH AND LANGUAGE

Children learn to speak by copying the sounds they hear around them. As a toddler grows they start to string sentences together until there's no stopping them talking. It's said that children are like sponges – they absorb language, then repeat what they've learnt.

Besides learning from hearing others speak, children also learn from hearing people talk on the television and radio, and from songs and nursery rhymes. Often toddlers will suddenly start to sing a song that their mother has sung to them over and over again, or one that is played on the car stereo often.

As their language develops children may test the boundaries by swearing or repeating bad words they've heard on television or in the playground. Adults should explain that these words are wrong and not nice to hear. It doesn't matter who informs the child that they are breaking the rules by using bad language. The important thing is the bad language doesn't continue.

You need to sensor as much as you can for children. However you can't protect them from everything. They will always be exposed to some things, for instance older children playing with toy guns etc. and even if you could take them away and shelter them from all bad influnces, this wouldn't do them any favours when they are older because they would be less street wise and less able to deal with negative influences. All you can do is shelter them where appropriate but mainly teach them morals and how to make good choices, so that they can have confidence and sense to make good choices, when they have the appropriate levels of independence.

HOW CAN WE HELP CHILDREN ATTAIN THEIR GOALS?

Learning for a child isn't just about having the best education. Of course this helps, but of greater significance is that their education is monitored and they are given the greatest opportunities available to them. These can include:

- playing sport
- learning a language
- playing a musical instrument
- being given books to read

If a child shows an interest in something, from cooking to drawing to

playing football or dancing, if possible they should be allowed to learn
and experience these activities. It's not always possible to pay for expensive
after-school clubs, but there are other ways a child can learn,
such as from the internet (monitored) or from their parents or carers.
With help and guidance a child will learn and grow and receive a
depth of knowledge on subjects they are interested in.

those theories developed and how you can apply them practically.

WHAT IS PERSONALITY?

You probably instinctively know what 'personality' is, but perhaps
find it harder to define. Even the ancient Greeks tried to define personality
traits and introduce some objectivity to personality definition.
We could say that a person's personality is their unique combination
of perceptions, attitudes and behaviours:

- Perception – How they experience the world and outside events
- Attitude – How they think and feel based on those events
- Behaviour – What they do based on those thoughts and feelings

You will have already read, in earlier modules of this course, that a
child must learn their basic perceptions and process the information
that they receive constantly from the outside world in order to make
sense of and organise it.

If you think back to a child's mental development stages, the child
first learns to understand their sensory experience and behaviour, then
they learn to attach symbols to those experiences, then they learn to
manipulate the outside world, then they finally learn to manipulate the
symbols themselves.

All of these stages add something to a child's 'personality' which adds
weight to the argument that a child's personality is not an innate quality
that it is born with. It is a learned response to the outside world and
is therefore largely shaped by parents and siblings.

Parallel play – they play next to each other. Collaborative play – they paly together to
work towards a common goal.

Understanding different personality traits;
https://www.youtube.com/watch?v=0Y12OySgaCA&src_vid=iN9VkGbU9v8&featur
e=iv&annotation_id=annotation_356529

TEMPERAMENT CHARACTERISTICS

In 1977, Doctors Chess and Thomas developed a personality theory
with 9 traits, based on the work of Dr Herbert Birch.
1. Activity Level: Is the child constantly active or can they be quiet
and still for extended periods of time?
2. Distractibility: Can the child concentrate or are they easily distracted?
3. Intensity: Does the child react mildly or strongly to stimulus?
4. Regularity: Does the child naturally follow a regular pattern of

behaviour and physiological needs?

5. Sensory Threshold: Does the child need a high or low level of stimulus to get a response?

6. Approach/Withdrawal: Does the child react openly to new people and experiences or withdraw from them?

7. Adaptability: Does the child respond well to changes in routine or behaviour?

8. Persistence: Is the child persistent in achieving its goals?

9. Mood: Does the child generally focus on positive or negative experiences?

It's important that you remember that any theory is not 'true' in itself, it is merely an explanation that helps us to categorise our observations. Therefore, the above traits are not 'true' and there are many other explanations for those aspects of a child's behaviour.

Understand your child's personality so that you can guide them in areas that suit them and find activities that suit their personality but also encourage them to do activities that they would naturally shy away from, so that they can develop in that area. Steer them towards a career path that would suit their personality.

No personality is bad, it all has good areas, bring out the strengths in your child i.e. determined not stubborn, teach them to negotiate etc.

Under 3 it is too hard to classify their personality

https://www.youtube.com/watch?v=0Y12OySgaCA&src_vid=iN9VkGbU9v8&feature=iv&annotation_id=annotation_356529

A tendency towards a particular response is not always helpful, it is important to be flexible and adaptable to change, to be able to thrive in different environments. It is good to teach your child activities to come up with some practical ways to increase their flexibility. You can structure activities and experiences for a child that give them opportunities to learn new perceptions, new attitudes and hence new behaviours so that they can continue to grow, develop and succeed in life.

Children See, Children Do, make your influences positive.

Kohlberg identified the following six stages of moral development in children:

- Stage 1 - Children avoid breaking rules. They avoid punishment and are ready to blindly submit themselves to authority.
- Stage 2 - Children follow rules, if only to serve their own interests. A high degree of individualism and inability to delay gratification are other characteristics of this stage of development.
- Stage 3 - Children live up to what is expected. Rule obedience is noticeable at this stage.

■ Stage 4 - A rudimentary development of conscience; obeying social norms and laws begins to emerge. Children begin making greater contribution to society and their social group.

■ Stage 5 - There is greater awareness of social behaviour, others' values and desire for ensuring the common good of a group.

■ Stage 6 - An evolving awareness of universal norms, ethical principles and non-relative values, such as the right to life and freedom exists.

In Kohlberg's understanding, each of these levels shows an increase in the child's ability to reason rationally. At Stage 1 and 2, children operate mainly at hedonistic levels. For this child any action that avoids

punishment is moral. They submit to authority only because the authority has the power to punish them. Therefore they obey not out of love, respect or reasoning, but because they fear punishment or rejection.

At stages 3 and 4, the child gradually begins to interpret morality as a rule-based conduct. They begin to act in ways that are conforming and preserving of social order.

In the final stages 5 and 6, when children become young adults, they become more tolerant of others' values, while developing their own opinions on justice, equality, and freedom.

PSYCHOLOGICAL, MORAL AND ETHICAL EGOISM

Our behaviour is a balance of egoism and morality. For some a human being has just one ultimate aim - to further their self interest. Thus if A does something for B, it must be because this serves A's selfinterest in some tangible or intangible manner. Perhaps it makes A feel better; it wins them the love and praise of society etc. This line of reasoning is called psychological egoism.

Moral egoism dictates that our action should further the other person's (rather than our own) self-interest. Fitting examples of "moral egoism" are revolutionaries who give up their lives fighting for others' freedom.

Ethical egoism falls somewhere in between. It claims that if an action is "morally" right, it is fine to maximise one's self-interest. So if A

and B decide to go to a football match together, it's because both enjoy a game of football.

These forms of egoism appear in the youngest of children. A young child probably doesn't understand which form of egoism they are displaying, but it doesn't take them long to learn how to use them.

For example;

■ A child gets a biscuit for everyone in the family, including one for them; this is psychological egoism, because they have benefited from their kindness to others.

■ A child fetches his brother or sister a drink without them asking,

yet they don't have a drink; this is moral egoism, because they
have done so of their own accord.

■ Two children play together on a see-saw; this is ethical egoism,
because both are enjoying the activity.

We often have to take other people's wishes into consideration. Imagine
the implications of a scenario where everybody lives solely for
themselves! How would the world run, and who would undertake social
roles, such as nurses, teachers or army officers?

How can 'Moral Benchmarking' be Applied to Children?

The primary responsibility of children's morals lies with parents and
significant others in a child's life. Here are some tips on how to
achieve this and guide children to learn what is right and wrong:

■ Talk early and often to a child - Establish and maintain an open
line of communication. Get into the habit of talking with a child
from a young age every day. This will make it easier for you to
have conversations about serious subjects when necessary.

■ Get involved - Talking with a child about their activities opens up
an opportunity for you to share both your interests and values.

■ Be a role model - Think about what you say and how you act in
front of a child. Your own actions are the most powerful indicator
to children of what is appropriate and acceptable.

■ Monitor a child's activities - Know where children are and get
acquainted with their friends. Unsupervised children have more
opportunities to experiment with risky behaviours, including the
use of alcohol, tobacco, and illegal drugs, and they may start substance
abuse at earlier ages.

■ Set ground rules - Make clear, sensible rules for a child and enforce
them with consistency and appropriate consequences. Tell
children what the law is, what your rules are, and what behaviour
you expect. For example, "Alcohol is for adults. Smoking is dangerous
for your health. Our family follows the law."

■ Be consistent - Be sure children understand that the rules are
maintained at all times, and that they are obeyed in public and at
other people's houses.

■ Follow your own rules - Set an example.

Be reasonable - Don't change the rules in mid-stream or add new
consequences without talking to children.

■ Avoid unrealistic threats - Negative punishments don't work as
well as positive ones do.

■ Reward good behaviour - Always let children know how pleased
you are when they respect the rules.

■ Put it into practice - Write out your most important rules and post
them clearly, where they will be seen by everyone. Then review
the rules regularly with children.

GUNS FOR JAMES, DOLLS FOR JANE

Children show clear gender-based behaviour differences by the age of one-and-a-half.

At three years, they show strong leanings for gender-based toys. For example, Mary will consistently prefer not to play with guns or trucks, and Jason will avoid dolls.

Also by the age of three, children are very aware of 'male' and 'female', even though they may not have the vocabulary to express it. In a way, it's a limitation of language development, not a limitation of gender-role understanding.

In describing the differences between men and women, kids will commonly refer to physical features like haircuts, e.g., "Daddy has short hair, and Mummy has long."

SOCIAL LEARNING THEORY

The Social Learning Theory is that all behaviour is based on a set of 'learning principles'. The three principles that this theory discusses are:

1. Observation
2. Reinforcement
3. Imitation

In their understanding of gender, Social Learning theorists argue that children learn by all these three methods. They first observe certain gender-specific behaviour (Daddy shaving, Mummy cooking), then have it reinforced through their parents' attitudes and example (Mummy calling out, "Jon, you go and help Daddy in the garden. Jane, you follow me in the kitchen,") until the child imitates that pattern and gradually begins to imitate it. This completes the socialisation process.

Meanwhile, various cultural forces also influence the establishment of a gender role identity with the use of reward or punishment. As a result, Jon develops an active interest in motor racing games and Jane in painting and artwork. These differences may be more pronounced in some cultures than in others.

Children and aggression;

Long ago, Sigmund Freud in *Civilization and Its Discontents* wrote, "Men are not gentle creatures, who want to be loved, who at the most can defend themselves if they are attacked; they are, on the contrary, creatures among whose instinctual endowments is to be reckoned a powerful share of aggressiveness..."

Whether or not we agree with Freud's negative view of man's basic nature, there is a growing body of research that suggests that aggression is not so much in-born as in-bred in children. This can be due to external influences, such as media or peers. However, aggression can also be due to hormones.

Whatever the reason, children need support from adults to help them control and channel their aggression.

Films are given age ratings for a very good reason. They have been carefully reviewed and giving a rating according to their suitability for children of certain ages. This is also why the 'watershed' is set for television programmes.

The only way to ensure children watch films and television programmes suitable for their age is to monitor their viewing. It's too easy to let one programme finish and another start without realising what is being watched, or a child to select their own viewing, when as busy parents and carers we need the 'quiet time', or so does the child. However, setting rules will ensure children know what they are allowed to watch and what is forbidden.

Younger children don't have the ability to separate reality from fiction, and may not understand the depth or intensity of what they see on screen. Older children may be influenced by the violent scenes they see in the media and be tempted to imitate them, with severe consequences. It's said that by the time an average American child leaves primary school, they will have seen more than 8,000 murders and more than 100,000 other assorted acts of violence (e.g., assaults) on television! There are currently no similar UK figures available. However, it is also likely children in the UK will view many acts of media violence during their early years.

LEARNING BY IMITATION

Children learn some forms of development by copying behaviour they see around them. If a child sees or experiences violence they are likely to think this is acceptable behaviour, and so act in an aggressive way towards others.

Imitation of aggression and violence can be a result of:

- physical or emotional abuse from parents or carers
- living in a family where shouting is the norm
- copying aggression seen on television and in computer games or on the internet
- mixing with other children who are aggressive
- trying to replicate the behaviour of peers who children admire
- bullying
  - children standing up for themselves if they have aggressive siblings

Therefore, aggression is often learnt as a result of a situation a child is exposed to, rather than them being born naturally aggressive.

If a child is displaying aggressive behaviour the source should be found and dealt with. It may be the child doesn't know how to express their anger or can't see that imitating others is wrong.

One way to deal with aggression is to talk to the child and help them channel their aggression into other activities.

This will depend on the child's level of maturity, but all children should be taught that aggression is not appropriate behaviour.

BULLYING

The problem of bullying is common throughout the world. Parents and carers may encounter bullying if their child is bullied or becomes a bully.

Both situations need careful handling and won't be resolved overnight. But with dedication, and commitment to finding the source of the problem and resolving it bullying can be overcome.

https://www.youtube.com/watch?v=bH22z3jl5Bo

http://fosterparent.dshs.wa.gov

Low self esteem can lead to anger
New situations – fight of flight may cause anger
Teach coping mechanisms ie deep breathing – to control and stop breathing i.e. so tummy goes up and down

CHILDREN WHO ARE BULLIED

If a child is being bullied it may not be evident at first. Common signs of bullying are withdrawal, or not wanting to go to school or play with friends. If you suspect a child is being bullied you should address the problem immediately, whether it is your own child or someone else's. Bullying can lead to depression in children, have long term psychological effects and even, in extreme cases cause suicide.

If a child is being bullied they should be encouraged to talk about the problem. Find out where it happens, why they think it happens and how they react.

Fighting back is not the answer, but there is a balance, because if a bully sees a weakness they will exploit it.

Children being bullied should be encouraged to walk away from the situation and not show they are upset. It is helpful for them to have a key figure they can go to when the bullying starts, such as an older child or a teacher.

Bullying that takes place at school should be discussed with the school and a plan of action should be agreed. The child being bullied should be involved in the discussions, so they are aware action is being taken to help them. This will encourage them to open up and face the problem, as they know they have support. Sometimes, this is all it takes for the bullying to stop, as the bullies know they are being monitored.

CHILDREN WHO BECOME BULLIES

Children become bullies for a number of reasons:

- copying peers
- wanting to impress within their social group
- feeling unloved
- like to dominate others
- enjoy the feeling of power
- are bullied at home
- used to getting their own way

A child who is bullying should be given time and attention to explore why this behaviour is happening. They must be told that it is wrong (although clearly they should know this) to hurt others, either emotionally or physically.

Bullying often takes place in pairs or in a group. The bullies tend to encourage each other. Splitting the group and asking them individually why they are bullying may help stop it. Often one child bullies because they are told by the leaders of the group they are not part of the 'in crowd' if they don't join in. They may actually want to break free, but not know how to.

Stopping bullying takes patience and time. As a parent or carer any support you can get from school, professionals or other parents will help you and your child feel you are not alone in dealing with this problem.

HOW CAN WE HELP CHILDREN REDUCE THEIR AGGRESSION?

Children can control their aggression by learning to channel their excess energy and anger into activities that don't harm others.

Rough and tumble play is a very good way for boys (and some girls) to let off steam. There should be certain rules to this kind of play, as it can quickly turn into fighting and hurting, sometimes accidental and sometimes on purpose.

The rules:

- no one should get hurt
- everyone should enjoy the play
- everyone should stay safe
- take care with small children

Girls are less likely to play like this, but can still learn to release their aggression by running and jumping, tickling and playing outdoor games.

Sports are an excellent way for both boys and girls to utilise the excess amounts of energy that most children seem to have.

However, if outdoor activities are not available there are other ways to help a child control their aggression. If they are indoors or in the close confines of others (such as in the classroom) an idea is to have a secret code. When they feel angry either you, or if you're not there, the child, should repeat the secret code over and over again as they walk away.

The code should be a secret between the parent or carer and the child. So when they feel the need to use it they know the other person is with them in mind, if not physically.

INTRODUCTION

Play is important for a child's social development. It encourages them to learn about the world around them, how to interact with others and how to expand their creativity and imagination.

Play also helps a child grow its levels of maturity, by encouraging skills associated with mental and physical growth. As a child plays alone or with others it learns to copy and ask why. It gathers information and by processing this information into play gains knowledge without realising it.

THE IMPORTANCE OF PLAY

A child is influenced by the world around them. From the moment they are born a child learns how to express its wants and needs and how to amuse itself with objects.

A young baby doesn't need many toys. A small baby is given all sorts of gifts, but initially they will be most fascinated with their fingers and toes!

As babies grow they become more and more interested in the physical objects that surround them, and slowly become more aware of toys and what they can do. For example soft toys that contain a bell or squeak, or have a mirror will give endless satisfaction.

As a child enters the toddler stage they start to understand what toys can do and how they can entertain. A child's development is often monitored by what they do with toys and how they react to objects they are given.

Important developmental stages can be monitored by assessing if a child can:

- put things into containers, and remove them
- do simple jigsaw puzzles
- throw a ball
- hold a pen or pencil
- sort shapes
- turn the pages of a book

As a child gets older they will start imaginary play. Nothing is more fascinating than watching a child play alone or with friends, talking and giving toys or objects roles. This can be seen in a boy that plays with cars or trains and makes 'vroom vroom' noises, or a girl who gives dolls and teddies a tea party and puts them to bed. Of course, we shouldn't be too gender specific, girls can play with cars and boys can play with dolls, there are no rules.

Some children have an imaginary friend, who has to go everywhere with them. This 'friend' can be extremely useful if the child has a tantrum or gets upset, as the parent or carer can bring the 'friend' into the situation and use them as an example.

Imaginary friends are no cause for concern as long as a child is happy and socially interactive. They can be a great playmate and confident when secrets are shared.

What do Children Learn Through Play?

Playing allows a child to develop their imagination and learn how the world works. A child that plays in the kitchen with their mother will learn how food is important and how meals are prepared. The simple action of baking a cake with a child shows them not all cakes are bought off a supermarket shelf; they are put together with ingredients and undergo a process to make the final product.

Similarly, a child that plays with blocks and bricks will learn that those objects can make some of the most useful items for them to play with, such as a garage, house or furniture.

As a child grows it learns that this type of toy can be used to make whatever they want, although without guidance there can sometimes be frustration. It's not uncommon to see a child throw their Lego across the room because the race track or doll's house they want to make seems impossible. This is when parent or carer interaction is required.

Role Play

Role play is an important part of play. Children love to dress up, which teaches them about the world of 'pretend', and how they can become whoever they want: a pirate, a princess, a king or queen, Batman or Superman, or Barbie.

You don't need to buy expensive dressing up clothes for the child that loves to role play. Use your imagination, and that of the child, to see what household objects you can use to create a dressing up box.

For example, scarves, belts, old clothes, jewellery, wigs, sheets, feathers, beads, bags and shoes.

This form of play also teaches good behaviour, and what is socially acceptable. The child that enjoys dressing up as a soldier should be taught that it is fine to imitate the character, but guns and killing are not the norm.

Equally, pretend games where children love to copy adult roles, such as teacher and pupil, mother or father and child, doctor or nurse and patient or shop keeper and customer can all teach valuable social skills. These situations can demonstrate that both roles can display different forms of good behaviour.

For example, through play a child can be taught that a teacher needs respect by the pupil showing good behaviour. This theory can be further backed up by demonstrating rewards, such as a teacher giving stars for good work.

CREATIVE PLAY

Creativity is an important part of play. Through learning to make things and paint and draw a child expresses their thoughts. Children love to cut and stick, glitter and glue and generally make a mess! This is an important part of a child's development, as they learn to hold a pencil or crayon, and form shapes and letters.

A child's first drawing of its family is one of the most precious gifts they can give a parent, and this gift should be treasured and kept in the 'memory box'.

It is a good idea to keep a 'make and do' box, and fill it with scraps of coloured paper and card, string, wool, buttons and any other bits and pieces that can be turned into a creative master piece.

NURSERY PLAY

Nursery play gives a structured form of development for a child. Most children's nurseries follow a pre-school curriculum, preparing them for the formalities of school.

Although this may sound rather harsh for a young child, it's done in such a way that a child doesn't realise they are being taught through play.

Nursery play can teach:

- how to interact with other children
- how to share
- how to play games
- how to express feelings
- how to listen

In the UK children's nurseries are OFSTED (The Office for Standards in Education) checked to ensure they reach the minimum standards required to care and educate children. OFSTED is also the main school inspectorate.

In the US the equivalent inspecting bodies are different in each state.

An approved nursery aims to meet the following criteria, whilst concentrating on learning through play:

- activities are structured and planned
- the children play in a safe and inspiring environment
- progress is monitored and reported to parents and carers
- toys and play equipment are motivational and aid learning

For more information on OFSTED visit www.ofsted.gov.uk.

PLAY THERAPY

Play therapy is an important way to help a child learn good behaviour without them realising they are learning. It can be useful for a wellbehaved child's development or to help improve a badly behaved child's behaviour.

Play therapy takes a lot of patience and some time to see results. However, the rewards of achieving the objective of seeing a child learn through play are immense.

Some examples of play therapy are:
- Teaching a child not to interrupt when adults are speaking (unless there is a dangerous situation occurring).This can be done through role play, such as playing teachers and pupils or parent and child.
- Encouraging a shy child to join in with a group. A shy child can slowly be introduced to group play by gradually increasing the number of children they play with. This can be done by inviting one or two friends to play at home, where the child feels safe, meeting a small group in the park and then visiting other peoples' houses or play places with larger groups.
- When a child has a particular fear of something, such as animals, loud noises, riding a bike or water the fear can often be gradually overcome through play.

Depending on the level of the fear and the type, a programme should be established for gradually facing the fear. For example, if a child is afraid of dogs they could be bought a toy dog or be shown books and TV programmes about dogs, to help them get over the fear.

ways play therapy could be used to overcome a fear include:
1. Fear of the dark – give a nightlight shaped as a person and tell the child it is a friend to watch over them.
2. Fear of insects – look at books, internet pictures, visit animal parks and buy imitation insects to play with.
3. Large characters (the sort dressed up as Mickey Mouse that come up to you in the shopping centre!) – tell the child it is only a person dressed up, look at pictures of the character and talk about the fear and buy the child a toy sized character

Unstructured play is positive i.e. play eye spy whilst emptying the dishwasher.

Family roles;

A child's link with their family can affect them throughout the whole of their life. These links include a child's interaction not only with immediate family such as parents and brothers and sisters, but also their relationship with grandparents, aunts and uncles and cousins.
A stable family life is core to a child's security. Sadly, not all families stay together as a unit, for various reasons, and if a family splits a child should be given reassurance that they will always be loved and cared for.
It is said that whatever happens to us in our childhood, the way we are treated and influenced, affects us throughout our lives. But is this theory true? Does a child with a stable family background really turn out

to be calm, well behaved, and 'normal'? Or are those the children that rebel against society? And does the child with an unstable upbringing and family difficulties turn into a teenage monster? Or do they learn from their family experiences?

up in the night, who will change nappies and who will rise early in the morning to tend to the baby's needs. A simple agreement will avoid many arguments and disputes.

It is also important parents agree on who, within the family, will care for children in the absence of the parents.

For example, if a mother or mother-in-law wishes to help with childcare, both parents should be happy about the situation.

ADULT BEHAVIOUR AND ITS EFFECT ON CHILDREN

Children are influenced by adult behaviour. From an early age children mimic adults, and what they say and do. This behaviour begins when a child starts to copy what its mother does around the house.

Children also like to dress like their mother and father, particularly in their work roles.

When children copy good adult behaviour it is a bonus. They learn to:

- talk and communicate with others
- be polite and have good manners

A negative aspect of children imitating adults is when they copy antisocial behaviour, such as shouting or aggression.

This observational behaviour can also be seen when children imitate the behaviour of adults they see in films and computer games. If a toddler watches a thriller on TV they may imitate the use of guns or state 'I'm going to kill you'.

Very young children are unlikely to understand their behaviour is incorrect, which is why monitoring the television programmes a child watches or the games they play is so important.

PARENTING STYLES

It's important for parents to agree on how they intend to bring up their children, in terms of:

- discipline
- care and affection
- communication
- maturity

Differing parenting styles can affect a child's behaviour. If a child is treated and disciplined in different ways by their parents they are likely to become confused.

It's also important that external carers of a child know what styles parents use and they follow them.

For example if a child is naughty and is sent to sit alone to calm down the same discipline should be used when they are cared for by others.

Children learn by routine and example, and differences just confuse them.

They may also use the different styles to their advantage, by playing one parent against the other.

DISCIPLINE

Levels of punishment can vary greatly within a family. Disciplining a child may range from telling off, withdrawing a privilege, or isolating the child to a designated 'naughty' area.

The important thing is that family rules are established so a child and both parents know when the boundaries are being broken. For example, if a child throws a toy at a friend or sibling the rule is 'we don't throw things'. The child should be told why this rule exists (it will hurt someone else or precious things will get broken).

Consequently the punishment should match the level of bad behaviour, and both parents should agree on what this should be.

CARE AND AFFECTION

Caring for a child means having concern for their well-being. Parents may adopt different styles of care which show they interact with the child.

One parent may enjoy playing games, colouring, baking and reading to the child, while the other may prefer watching TV or chatting with the child. Each differing style shows caring in a different way, and no matter how many times we hear 'you don't care about me', from a child displaying a tantrum, it's unlikely they mean it.

Some parents may be naturally more affectionate than others and give physical hugs and kisses to the child. As long as the child feels safe and secure and understands both parents love them equally there should not be an issue with this. If you are the kind of person who finds it hard to show physical affection, try saying what you feel instead, and vice versa.

COMMUNICATION

Communication between members of the family is essential so that everyone understands the rules that help the family function. Without communication it's impossible for a child to understand where the boundaries lie.

To ensure communication is maintained parents should try and make the time once a week or month to talk to each other about various family issues. Once parents agree on things it is a good idea to hold a regular family meeting, where everyone, no matter how old or young, can have their say.

MATURITY

Expected levels of maturity of a child can differ between parents, which can be the cause of arguments. For example, would you expect a three year old to sit through a three course dinner without leaving the table? Probably not, but at what stage do you let them leave? This is where both parents should agree on how long the child is expected to sit at the table.

WORKING MOTHERS

Sometimes a mother has no choice but to return to work when her children are young, to assist family finances. Other mothers may wish to continue with their career, and not want to stay at home to look after the children. There is no right and wrong answer to this situation, as the needs of every family are different.

Children often go to a nursery or childminder from a young age (about 4 – 6 months), right through until when they start school. The benefit of this is they will be used to mixing with others and will learn the basics of good behaviour.

A mother that stays at home is likely to also teach her child these things, but they will learn in a less structured way. If grandparents live nearby they may be able to assist with childcare, although this can be a big responsibility for older grandparents.

As long as the mother knows the child is happy with their carer she shouldn't feel guilty at leaving them. It's a good idea to give consistency of childcare, as children like familiarity and to know they will be with the same person every day.

It isn't easy to be a working mother, and sometimes the mother can experience incredible feelings of guilt. However, if the mother allocates quality time with the child each day and weekend, when tasks are done and she isn't tired, the situation can work.

This can be as simple as a regular bedtime story, the child helping prepare the dinner or just sitting and talking for five minutes each day.

Consider how short five minutes is, to spend time devoted to the child, and it will soon become routine.

ABSENT FATHERS

Sometimes the father isn't always there to help with child care. They may have to work away, be separated or divorced from the mother or simply not enjoy the responsibility fatherhood brings.

If an absent father makes up for being away by assisting with nappy changing, taking the children out and spending time with them, meal preparation and the general roles and responsibilities that come with child-rearing, it's likely the children will settle into the routine of the father being away.

However, expensive gifts and treats to make up for a father not being there on a regular basis will possibly cause conflict within the family. These gifts will delight the child, but for how long? No amount of money can buy the love a child needs from both parents.

Absent fathers can cause a lot of stress within the family. The child may look to them as the 'favourite' parent, as the mother is left to discipline and take care of the daily routines.

Alternatively, a child may see the mother as the core of their world, and reject the father for not being there when they need them.

BROTHERS AND SISTERS

Love them or hate them, many children have one or more brothers and sisters. As we grow up we often argue with our siblings and disagree on every little thing, from which toy to play with, to who's going to have the last biscuit, to who bashed who first. This sibling rivalry can extend into adulthood, with children continuing to compete against each other.

On the other hand, having a brother, sister or both can be one of the most rewarding things in a person's life. Some siblings are close, and as they grow up get closer. Brothers and sisters can be great play mates, help with homework and sort out disputes with friends.

Spacing between the ages of children is another issue. Some parents plan right down to the moment of conception, to get what they see as the 'perfect gap' between siblings. Others don't have this choice, and may find it hard conceiving, or conceive by accident.

Children with a small age gap between them can be the best of friends, and even similar to twins, or they can fight like cat and dog throughout their childhood. There's no magic formula for the perfect age gap, parents just have to get on with it and handle whatever situation they are blessed with as best they can.

The school setting;

children
to enjoy learning. In their first years of school, children are subjected to new structure, new people, and probably a lot of new rules. They are encouraged to try new things and talk to new people. A lot of effort is dedicated to ensuring this is a positive time for youngsters. It is, in particular, a time to develop a trust in and respect for the teachers.

As they mature, they are urged to learn more of the traditional content. They are able to understand that learning is not all exploration; it is a transfer of information, too. But it's that initial exploration and freedom in educational development that sets the foundation for children to succeed against national and international standards.

For children, life is about accepting change and learning how to work within new rules and social groups. The transition from the loose structure of playing at home to the structured environment of school is daunting for anyone.

A child starting school encounters all these feelings, but they don't always understand why. Everything they know and love suddenly changes. They move from the safety and routine of home to an environment where they are expected to sit still, eat and play at certain times and have to share the teacher's attention with the others in the class.

Children who have never been in such an environment might be a little apprehensive about being "on their own" in school. They might resist going and, once there, might be very clingy toward the teacher or even become very introverted and withdraw from the social element of school.

In contrast, children who have spent time in nursery or other such structured groups tend to make an easier transition to going to school. Furthermore, children who have had positive social relationships tend to make friends quickly and bond with their teachers. This leads to better academic achievement.

Parents can enhance the transition to school by teaching strong, positive social skills to their children and by sending them to a preschool group.

Most preschools will encourage the parents to visit the facility with the child a couple of times to get them used to the environment without the stress of being left behind by their caregiver.

Plus, teachers are trained to deal with very young children and how they react to starting school. They often put friends together in classes so that there is a level of familiarity in the classroom. A good teacher will have the skills to educate a young child whilst making learning seem like fun.

TRANSITIONS – ADOLESCENT YEARS

You might think the transition to secondary school is just a matter of changing buildings. But it is a brand new social structure, and very different to what children experience in primary school. They used to be the big fish in a small, caring, supportive pond.

brings new freedom, and often a more impersonal relationship with teachers.

Going to secondary school also brings new methods of study. A child now has to cope with changing classrooms for lessons and remember to take the right books with them. These things are another development stage that teaches a child responsibility and independence.

Enhanced support from family and friends, particularly early on, can help adolescents through these changing times. However, there is a common theme evident in most situations involving development: the many years of trust and confidence built in early childhood will have the greatest positive effect on an adolescent's ability to adapt.

PEER GROUPS

Watch children playing in a playground and you will see them assemble in small groups of peers. These groups form a collective of shared values and standards of behaviour. They even exhibit a social structure with leaders and followers.

These peer groups tend to get shuffled a bit due to classroom changes and shifts in loyalty within the group. Often, groups that don't get physically separated tend to last from year to year.

Peer groups are different from simple friendships. Friendships are built on trust and intimacy. Peer groups develop group activity skills like cooperation, leadership and following. They develop a loyalty to a common goal. They are, in a way, a broader social state than 'simple' friendships.

The leaders are usually quite ruthless 'Alphas' that control and exclude followers. But, the need for group belonging is very strong in middle-childhood. A child who is ousted from a peer group will often attempt to be included in another group as soon as possible.

Peer pressure seems to be most prevalent in day-to-day decisions – what to wear, choice of friends and which music to listen to. A confident child with a supportive background is less likely to bow to peer pressure.

CLIQUES AND CROWDS

As they enter their early teens, peer groups become much more tightly organised around cliques, usually numbering about five to seven members. Cliques are made up of friends and tend to have common lifestyles and backgrounds.

Often several cliques will become loosely grouped into a crowd. This group is less about friendship or common goals and more about social position and reputation. Cliques and crowds can affect a child's beliefs and behaviours.

Membership of a clique provides a child with a sense of belonging and a more tangible identity.

Eventually, children will become interested in dating and boys' and girls' cliques will start to come together. This offers an opportunity for them to learn to interact and approach the opposite gender. The larger groups will divide into couples that will hang out with other couples. This goes on until boys and girls feel comfortable enough to approach each other outside of the group. Then, the crowds and cliques tend to dissipate.

Every interaction becomes an exercise in social development. With positive reinforcement and success in a crowd, a child will become more confident and develop strong communication and social skills.

As they grow up, children will deal with a number of school transitions that may add to the complexity of their social skills development. Enhanced support from parents and teachers is necessary to help ease the stress.

Whether the child is physically changing schools due to a move or if they're moving to secondary school or college, the child will have to deal with a number of emotions. The success of these transitions can impact their social development.

STAGES OF LEARNING

Jean Piaget, a Swiss cognitive theorist, had a very significant impact on early childhood and middle childhood education. Piaget suggested there are a predictable series of steps in cognitive development, and children pass through four basic stages:

The sensorimotor stage is the core skills development and involves learning about the permanence of objects, learning how to interact with others, and other categorising and organisational skills.

The preoperational stage spans from ages two to seven. This stage is marked by the extraordinary increase in mental representation. This is children's ability to express their understanding of their world by make-believe playing, by painting and drawing, by playing musical instruments and by their experimentation and mastery of language. Preschool and nursery encourage exploration of these types of play to promote an interest in learning.

At this stage, children are egocentric (only focusing on their own point of view). They also have an inability to conserve, meaning, for example, they do not understand that just because an object appears to have changed shape does not mean the mass of the object has changed.

Ages seven to 11 years are considered the concrete operational stage. Thought becomes remarkably more logical, flexible and organised during this period of development. This is a time when children are able to think about how concepts relate to each other and apply this thinking to their environment. This is also when a child starts to interact with peers in a mature way.

The fourth stage is the formal operational stage, which covers ages 11 and up. During this stage, children develop the ability to think abstractly and scientifically.

In adolescence, young people become capable of hypotheticodeductive reasoning. This is essentially the ability to approach a problem with a general theory of the factors that can affect its outcome; and deduce from it a hypothesis or prediction of what might happen. They then go about testing the hypothesis in a logical, organised manner.

This stage is also punctuated with self-consciousness and selffocusing. Children begin to think about their beliefs and themselves in general. This helps them to develop their sense of individuality and to establish independence from their parents. At this age, children sometimes develop the belief that they know everything. We know they don't, but this is a normal stage of development.

Adolescents also, through abstract thinking, can explore idealism and criticism. No longer bound by the tangibility of their environment, they are free to look for hypothetical situations and further define their moral systems. Their decision making, though more advanced than in previous stages, still lacks discipline and, to some degree, rationality. This is a time of upheaval as adolescents reach puberty and go through many physical and mental changes. This is often a time when an adolescent wants to be treated as a grown up, but is still a child inside.

EDUCATIONAL PRINCIPLES

Piaget's theories have led to three educational principles that still are taught widely to teachers and used in classroom practices. You may wish to evaluate the environment at your next parent-teacher meeting by keeping these principles in mind.

The first is discovery learning. In a Piagetian classroom, children are encouraged to investigate and explore their environment. Teachers supply building blocks, dressing-up clothes, books, measuring tools, musical instruments and similar learning objects, to give children a variety of ways to measure, test, and experience. There is little or no prepared verbal lecturing that would involve passive learning.

The second is sensitivity to children's readiness to learn. A Piagetian classroom would not engage children in a learning timeline. Rather, children would build upon their current knowledge, meaning, once they are (or feel they are) ready to learn more, they will. The thought is that, if they're not comfortable with the current concept children will only gain an acceptance of future teaching ("if you say so,") rather than a true understanding.

The third principle is acceptance of individual differences. Piaget's theory is that all people go through the same stages of learning, but at different rates. The classroom planning would involve many smaller groups and even individuals rather than teaching to the class as a whole. Children are measured against their own individual development rather than against same-age peers.

Piaget's impact on this field of research cannot be overstated. His findings have been the inspiration for virtually every contemporary line of research. Piaget's stages of development have been criticised for not taking into account significant influences by verbal teaching and correction techniques. It is also widely believed that learning is not entirely self-generated, as he suggests.

INFORMATION-PROCESSING PERSPECTIVE

Contemporary theories follow the idea that there is a standard order of development. However, it is believed that thought processes are the same at all ages but that elements of these processes are more or less prominent at different ages and periods of development. This approach is known as the information-processing perspective.

There are numerous theories on the ways we gather, store and retrieve information. In general, though, information processing involves three milestones:

1. From about two to five years of age, children exhibit processing skills like attention, recognition, recall and reconstruction. Attention becomes more focused while knowledge expands and becomes better organised and more elaborate.

2. From about ages six to 10 years, the overall capacity of the system continues to increase. Cognitive abilities improve allowing for better association between concepts and better strategy development. Knowledge of the impact of strategies and knowledge increases.

3. From 11 years to adulthood, the capacity of the system tends to increase, however, much more slowly. Knowledge and cognitive abilities continue to improve.

The impact of external influences on children's ability to learn can be great. For instance, living in an aggressive or abusive environment may lead to underachievement in both academic and social pursuits. Context of language and information is another factor. Gender, nationality, personal experience; these are all factors that can affect children's self image and confidence. A lack of self-confidence is often linked to a deficiency in learning.

FEAR OF GOING TO SCHOOL

Many children, at one time or another, will express a fear of attending school. In situations of high stress (e.g., bullying, exams, a new school) it's normal for a child to try to avoid going to school. Parents sometimes inadvertently encourage such behaviour by giving more attention to the child. As the fear is reinforced, it can actually grow into Didaskaleinophobia, the irrational fear of going to school. This is a form of separation anxiety and is most prevalent in ages seven to 10 years.

HOW CHILDREN LEARN

Aside from formal education, children learn by watching, listening and copying. They observe anyone that they come into contact with. They experiment by emulating what they have observed and they notice the results that they get.

If the result is that their parents are pleased, they discover that the behaviour is valuable and they repeat it.

If the result is that their parents are angry, they discover that the behaviour gets attention and they repeat it. They probably do it even more, depending on how they think they may benefit from their parents' anger.

A child tends not to differentiate between 'good' and 'bad' attention, so the child gains either way. 'Bad' attention also usually lasts longer, and can even end with a reward for a promise not to do it again, or a reward to appease the parents' feelings of guilt.

Fundamentally, children learn in order to have more independence, because independence gives them control, and everyone has a need to have control over their environment.

When you ensure that boundaries are appropriate to the age and abilities of the child, you respect the child's independence and individuality, and their need to rebel is minimised.

SETTING A BOUNDARY

When you set a boundary, make it

- clear
- concise
- fair
- appropriate

CLEAR

Make the boundary easy to understand and state it clearly and in a steady, unemotional tone of voice. If you shout, that's usually a clear signal to the child that you are not in control.

You need to address the child's behaviour, not vent your anger. The fact that you love and care for the child should never be in any doubt.

☑ No hitting

☒ Mummy doesn't like it when you hit her

CONCISE

Make sure that the child remembers the boundary and that there's no room for ifs and buts.

☑ Bath then bed

☒ You have a bath before bed unless you went swimming today or if it's the weekend or if we've been out all day and we've come in late

FAIR

Make sure that the child understands why the boundary is appropriate for them.

☑ Bedtime is 8:00 for Sarah (age 9) and 7:00 for Jake (age 7)

☒ Bedtime is 7:00 because I say so

APPROPRIATE

Make sure the boundary takes into account the child's age, knowledge and environment, and continue to revise the boundary as the child and its environment change.

☑ Always wear your cycling helmet when you ride your bike

☒ You are not allowed to ride your bike by yourself (the child is 15!)

CONSISTENCY

Consistency means that the boundary is always enforced in the same way. It isn't enforced one day and not the next, or enforced by you but not by your partner.

You can't make other people uphold your boundaries, you can only ensure that your own boundaries are consistently maintained in the environment that you control.

When you are consistent with your boundaries, the child will feel safer and more secure. Because they know in advance what the boundaries are, they can make decisions for themselves and know that they are the right decisions, and so they become more independent.

PUSHING BOUNDARIES

If boundaries are in place to keep a child safe, why do they push them?

Firstly, let's look at how children push boundaries:

- Blatantly do the thing that they are told not to do
- Almost doing the thing that they are told not to do
- Playing one parent off against another
- Sulking or crying when the boundary is enforced
- Blaming a sibling
- 'Playing up' when the parent is likely to be embarrassed
- Waiting until the parents are in a good mood
- Waiting until the parents aren't watching

It's how they learn what the rules are

- They don't have the same sense of risk as their parents do
- They are unable to communicate their needs effectively
- To get attention
- As a response to a change in their environment
- To cover up or distract from other problems
- To hide issues of bullying or low self-esteem

Prevention is always better than cure, so it is easier to pre-empt and manage 'difficult' behaviour before it arises.

For example, if you have told your child that they can't have any chocolate because it's nearly tea time, what do you do when you see them hovering around the sweet cupboard?

- Do you have no idea what they're doing?
- Do you know what they're doing but hope they're not?
- Do you tell them that you know what they're about to do?
- Do you distract them?
- Do you get distracted yourself and not notice them taking it?

Often, parents are distracted for many different reasons, so the child gets their own way, and then if the parent does find out, the child is punished as a knee-jerk reaction, which does more harm than good in terms of reinforcing boundaries because the parent is responding out of anger, not out of consistency.

CONSEQUENCES

A boundary in itself is fine, but sooner or later your implicit authority is not enough, and a child will want to know what happens if they don't comply. This is why we have consequences.

For example, if you have told your child that they can't have any chocolate because it's nearly tea time, what do you do when you see them hovering around the sweet cupboard?

- Do you have no idea what they're doing?
- Do you know what they're doing but hope they're not?
- Do you tell them that you know what they're about to do?
- Do you distract them?
- Do you get distracted yourself and not notice them taking it?

Often, parents are distracted for many different reasons, so the child gets their own way, and then if the parent does find out, the child is punished as a knee-jerk reaction, which does more harm than good in terms of reinforcing boundaries because the parent is responding out of anger, not out of consistency.

CONSEQUENCES

A boundary in itself is fine, but sooner or later your implicit authority is not enough, and a child will want to know what happens if they don't comply. This is why we have consequences.

Consequences must therefore be realistic, otherwise you won't be able to enforce them and you risk losing your credibility and authority. There are two kinds of consequences:

1. Natural Consequences - Natural consequences are a direct result of the behaviour that you want to manage.
For example, if a child is jumping on the furniture, a natural consequence is that they will fall and hurt themselves, and that will discourage them from jumping on the furniture.
Sometimes, you can allow a child to experience a natural consequence, but when that would compromise the child's safety, it is not acceptable.
2. Logical Consequences - Logical consequences don't automatically follow the behaviour that you want to manage. You need to intervene in order for a logical consequence to take place.

SETTING AN EXAMPLE

Often, parents fail to enforce boundaries because their own behaviour is exactly the opposite of what they expect from the child.

- DON'T SHOUT! (shouted by the parent!)

Tell the truth (when the child contradicts the parent's lie!)

- Don't interrupt (when the parent interrupts to say it)
- Don't speak with your mouth full (as the parent sprays food)
- Don't *%$@#* swear at me!

Therefore, always be prepared to either comply with the boundary yourself or explain the reasons why the boundary is fair.

IMPLEMENTING CONSEQUENCES

It is better to observe a child and pre-empt any potential problems, because that reinforces the boundary and makes it easier to enforce all boundaries.

If you don't, you risk losing credibility and control, and that makes it more likely that the child will push other boundaries. How would you feel if, as a result of you failing to enforce one boundary, a child ignored the rule about crossing the road by themselves?

You can't be everywhere, and you can't pre-empt every possibility, and children are endlessly creative when it comes to getting what they want, especially when that involves chocolate or attention.

Engaging the child in any kind of discussion is giving it attention. The child might lose the battle over bed time but win the war for attention. The longer you spend on 'punishment', the more the child gains and the more you undermine your own authority.

When you implement the consequence, do it quickly, decisively and consistently.

THE 'TIME OUT' AREA

The 'Time Out' area could be a particular area of the house, a step on the stairs or a mat. A mat is useful because you can take it anywhere you go; on holiday, to other people's houses, even to the shops if necessary. A carpet sample is ideal for the purpose.

The 'Time Out' mat gives you a Logical Consequence that can be used for enforcing almost any boundary.

Probably the only times you wouldn't use it is when there is a more obvious Natural Consequence or if it's bed time, because time on the mat is time not in bed, and that's exactly what the child wants!

Usually, the mat is used immediately the child breaks the rule, because you need to make a clear connection between the behaviour and the consequence.

Use of the mat is very simple, you just tell the child to sit on the mat for one minute per year of their age, and consider their behaviour.

Explain clearly that the child is there as a result of their specific behaviour and remind them that the agreed consequence is time on the mat.

At the end of the time, an apology and explanation from the child ensures that the child knows exactly why they were on the mat in the first place.

After the apology, make no further reference to the behaviour or the consequence. The child is more than smart enough to work out what's going on.

For example, if a girl hits her brother, she spends 8 minutes on the mat because she is 8 years old.

You might say, "Sarah, I told you not to hit your brother, and you know that hitting your brother is wrong, so that means you have to sit on the mat for 8 minutes".

At the end of that time, you would prompt her to apologise, perhaps expecting, "I'm sorry for hitting Jake". If she says, "I'm sorry that I accidentally pushed Jake", or "I'm sorry that Jake that was horrible to me and made me hit him" then clearly she is trying to avoid responsibility for her actions which immediately gets another 8 minutes on the mat.

GIFTED AND TALENTED CHILDREN

In the past, the words 'gifted' and 'talented' were used informally to refer to children with notable abilities. Today, the term 'Gifted and Talented' refers specifically to children who have been identified with an ability to develop ahead of their year group in two areas:

- 'Gifted' refers to children in the top 5% of ability in academic subjects, such as mathematics or English.
- 'Talented' refers to children in the top 5% of ability in non-academic subjects such as sport, music, design, creative arts or performing arts.

A child's Special Educational Needs are assessed into one of five categories:

1. Profound and multiple learning, physical or sensory difficulties
2. Severe communication, sensory or physical difficulties
3. Severe emotional difficulties or significant sensory or physical difficulties
4. Severe developmental or sensory difficulties, or moderate physical difficulties
5. Other learning difficulties or disabilities

More info is available at;
http://nationalstrategies.standards.dcsf.gov.uk/giftedandtalented
http://www.literacytrust.org.uk/database/able.html

You don't have to have lots of money to have fun with your child, just lots of imagination;

Play is the universal language of children. Play enables me to work, live and be with others.

When playing your child will:

- Develop imagination
- Extend their language and understanding
- Increase their self-awareness, self-esteem, and self-respect
- Improve and maintain their physical and mental health
- Give them the opportunity to mix with other children
- Allow them to increase their confidence through developing new skills
- Promote their imagination, independence and creativity
- Offer opportunities for children of all abilities and backgrounds to play together
- Provide opportunities for developing social skills and learning
- Build resilience through risk taking and challenge, problem solving, and dealing with new and novel situations
- Provide opportunities to learn about their environment and the wider communityHaving time and space to play gives children the opportunity to meet and socialise with their friends, keeps them physically active, and gives the freedom to choose what they want to do.

Junk modelling with a friend

Invite a friend over, set out a variety of cereal boxes, paper towel rolls, paper plates/cups, string, straws, old CD's, fabric pieces etc. Provide glue, tape, staples and string. Encourage the children to create whatever they like or are interested in.

Mummy, daddy and me

Your two year old will be a curious and impulsive explorer of his/her environment and will now want to be as independent as possible.

Encourage this natural curiosity by taking walks together, touch and feel plants, flowers, notice the weather.
Play seasonal games, such as conker and acorn hunts in the autumn or finding daisies in the spring.

Building block for development

 "My brain grows better when you respond to me!"

Sit next to your child or sit them on your lap. Model making funny faces and new or interesting sounds with your child.

Then wait and watch and see if they copy or make new ones. Copy what the child does and encourage them to make up new ones.

Play = 'All I need for learning'

Sharing, taking turns, getting along with others, following and giving directions and being a part of a group are all skills that we need as adults in the work place. Playing gives children time to practice, rehearse and try out their developing skills.

Make and do

- Make and fly a kite with your child!

How to Make a Kite Out of a Plastic Bag

1.

Find a plastic shopping bag. It doesn't have to be huge - one that's standard size works.

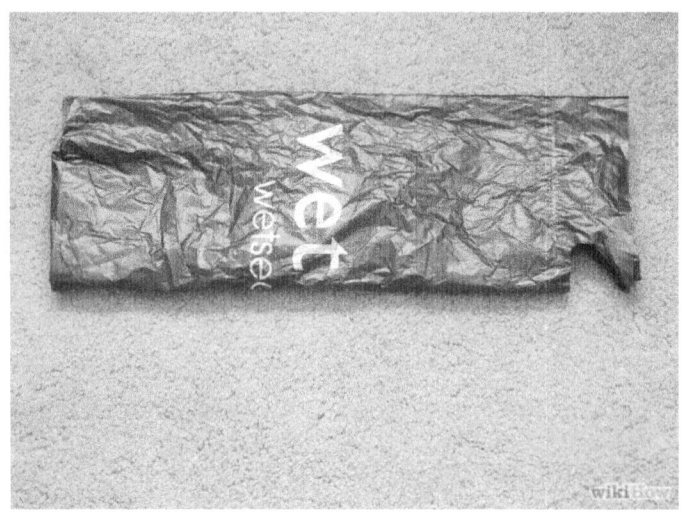

2

Fold the plastic bag in half vertically. Be sure it is flat, and even.

2.

3

Cut out the kite shape. Here are the cuts you need for your kite:

- Cut off the bottom of the bag. Position your scissors 2 or 3 inches (5 or 7.5 cm) up from the bottom, and cut so that all the air is removed.

- Cut the bag in the middle, from the base straight up to the center of the bag.

- Make a cut from the center of the bag back out to the fold, at about a 45-degree angle.

3.

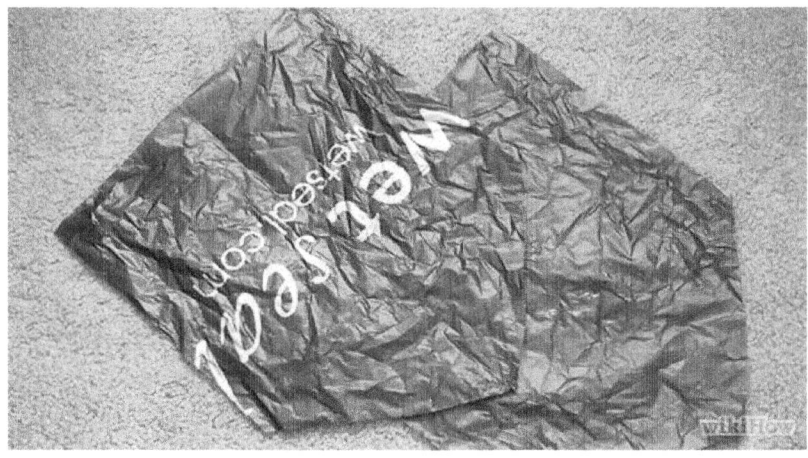

4

Save the section that includes most of the fold and set aside the rest of the

bag. Lay the pieces out flat. You should have 2 irregular pentagons.

4.

5

Cut two sticks. One stick should be as long as the length of the kite, from top to bottom. The other stick should be just a bit longer than the width of the kite, from right to left.

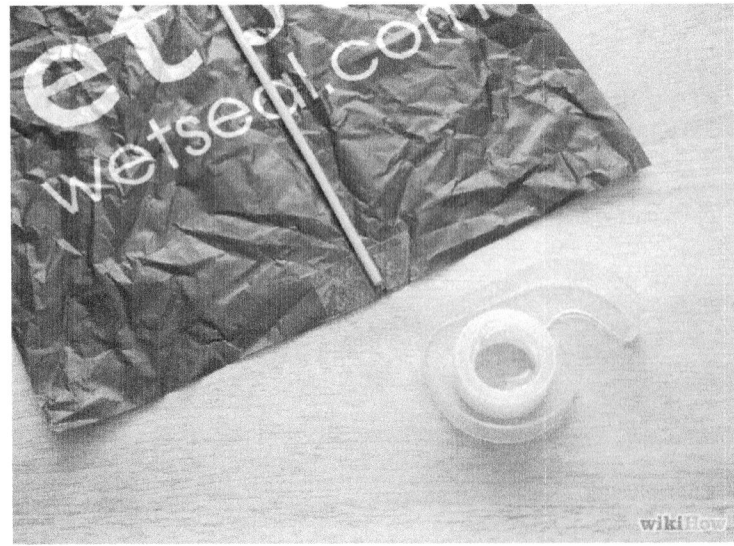

5.

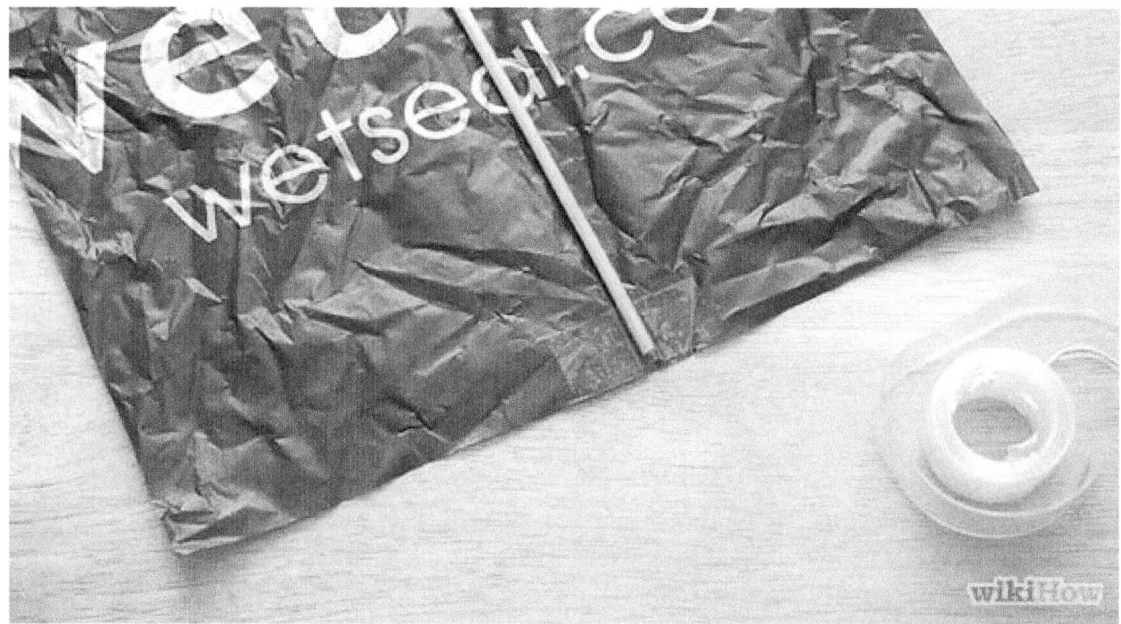

6Tape the longer stick to the vertical center of the kite. Tape the top end (at the

tip of the kite) first. Before you tape the bottom part, stretch the plastic a little and

then tape the stick onto the bottom.

6.

7

Tape the one end of the shorter stick to the left corner of the kite.

7.

8

Bow the horizontal stick. That is, bend it slightly toward the top corner of the kite so that it curves as it moves from left to right. Tape the right corner.

8.

9

Tape the two sticks together. Where the sticks cross, use a bit of tape to attach the

bowed section to the vertical stick.

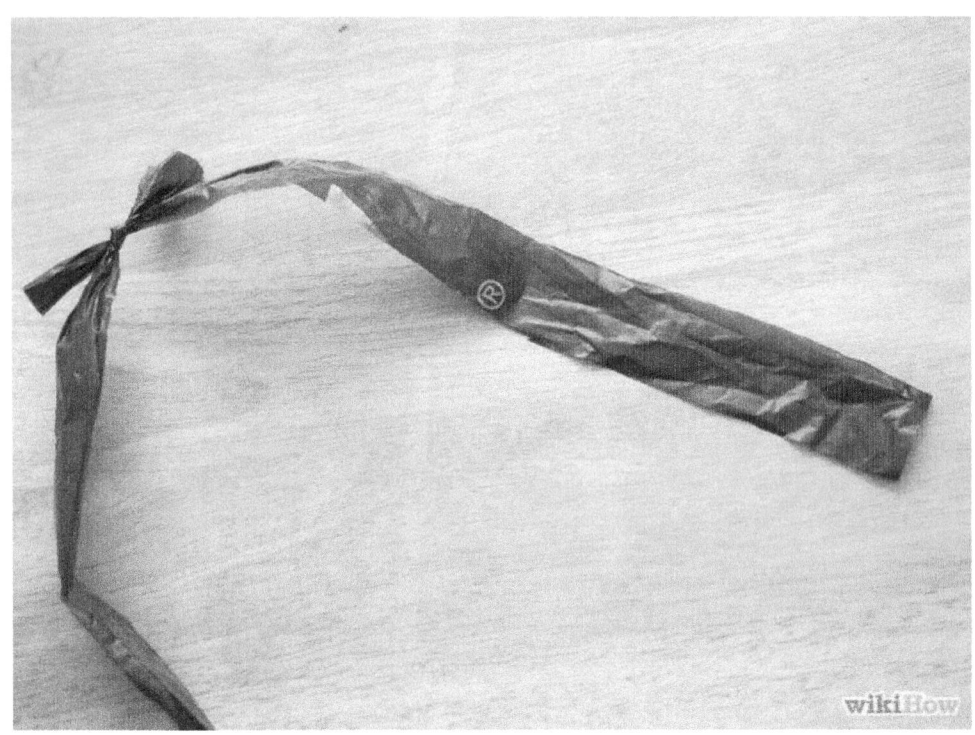

9.

10

Cut the extra plastic into strips and tie together. This will be the tail of your kite, and it should end up being a few feet long (or a meter, give or take a bit). You could use different colors to add more flair to your tail.

10.

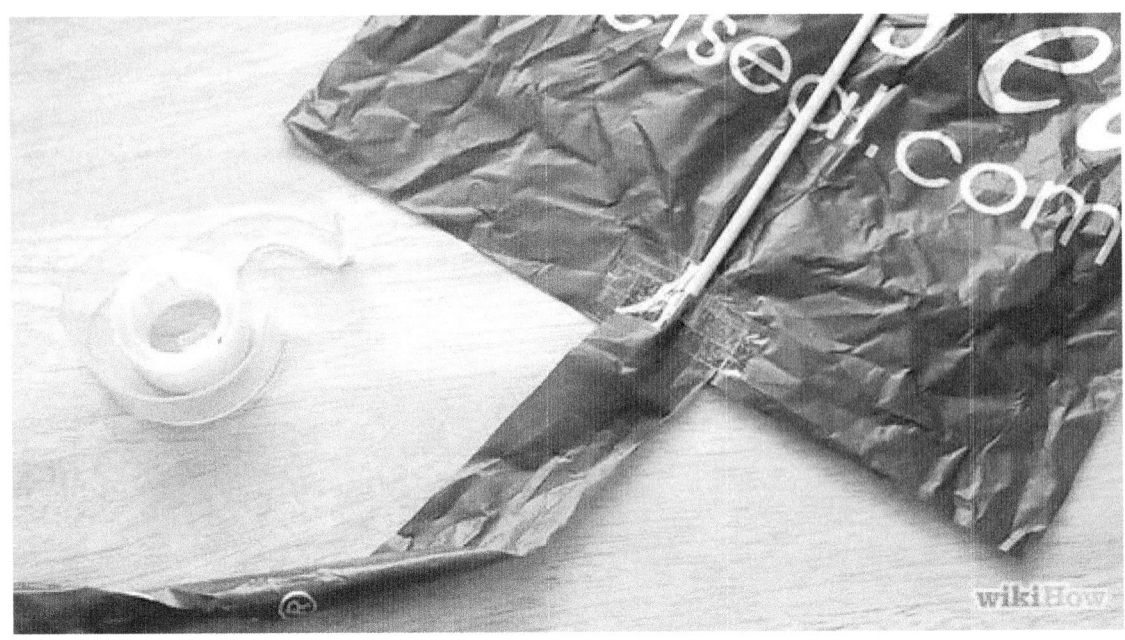

11

Tape one end of the tail to the bottom of the kite.

11.

12Cut two small holes in the plastic. Use a pointed item to make a hole at the intersection where the two sticks meet, as well as at the bottom.

12.

Cut a piece of string 1 foot (30cm) in length. Push one end of the string to the intersecting sticks at the other side of the plastic. Tie firmly. Do the same with the other end. Now you have the "bridle".

13.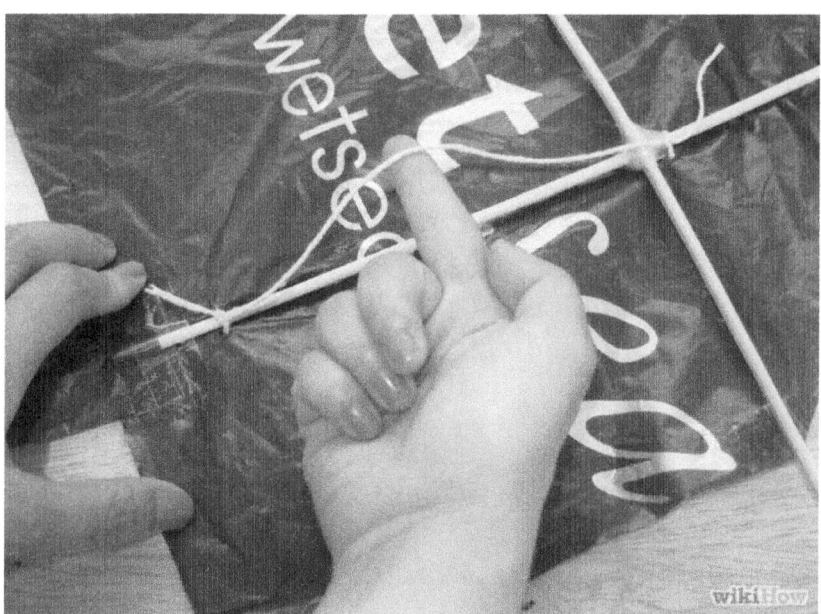

14

Decide where to tie a loop into the bridle line. When you are outside, hold the bridle string between your thumb and finger, so that the kite tries to fly from your hand. Start in the middle of the bridle and gradually move your fingers up toward the intersection. At one point, the angle of attack will be right and the kite will fly best, so this is where you want to tie a loop into the bridle line. This loop needs to move up or down depending on the wind speed, so you have to adjust the location for each flying session.

14.

15

Cut more string (up to 20 feet, or 6 m, long) and tie it to the bridle.

15.

16

Fly the kite. To fly, simply throw the kite and pull the string as if you are fishing. Extend the string while doing this. You may need to give it some help to get into the air by running a little. If so, check that the ground ahead is free of obstacles as you are likely to be looking up as you do this and not concentrating on the ground.

Get active

All children should be physically active for at least one hour a day. You can help by encouraging your child to find activities they enjoy, and by building physical activity into family life.

Take your child to the park or playground at least twice a week this month!

One reason why physical activity in childhood is so important is because it helps your child to maintain a healthy weight through life.

Rich play can be had with items that cost no money.

Making a collage'

- Collect old cards, magazines, catalogues and printed images available for cutting up.
- Provide a large piece of paper, glue, scissors, markers. Encourage the children to create a large poster with pictures they have selected and designs they choose.

Mummy, daddy and me

By 2½, children's vision and understanding is sufficient for them to recognise familiar people and places in photographs. They can identify even small details in picture books.

Share family photographs with your child, talking about the people and places you can see. Have fun playing games such as "Where's Mummy?".

Building block for development

 "My brain grows better when you cuddle with me!"

Rhyming games. Play 'Round and Round the garden' with your baby or toddler. Encourage your child to do it back to you.

Repeat this as many times as your child is interested in doing it.

Play = 'All I need for learning'

The cost of toys is not what is important. It is being with playmates - other children or adults; that makes the play important and meaningful to children.

Make and do

- Make and sail a boat with your child!

Get active

Physical activity is a part of the way children discover the world and themselves. It helps to build strong muscles and healthy bones, as well as to improve self-confidence.

Walk or cycle to and from school with the kids as often as possible

Play has also frequently been described as 'what children and young people do when they are not being told what to do by adults'.

Play is a process that is freely chosen, personally directed and intrinsically motivated. That is, children and young people determine and control the content and intent of their play, by following their own instincts, ideas and interests, in their own way for their own reasons.

Natural material play

Gather a variety of safe objects from your garage, kitchen, bedrooms and garden

Like:

- tubes
- pipes
- guttering
- wool
- fabric
- bangles
- shower curtain hooks
- bowls
- wooden spoons
- reels
- beads
- hangers etc.

Place in a big space in your home and allow your children to create whatever they choose with these items. Talk with them about what they have made, observe it, take pictures of their creations and create a story log together!

Mummy, daddy and me

Most two year olds have developed a strong sense of sounds and can readily distinguish one sound from another. Your two year old will delight in music and simple musical instruments. They will love joining in with signing and rhymes.

If you don't have any instruments, you can make these very easily by filling empty containers and bottles with different objects, such as pasta, rice, beads etc to make shakers.

Building blocks for development

 "My brain grows better when you relax with me!'

Make a small den with your child somewhere in your home. Find a puppet or a favourite stuffed animal and tell a story to your child inside a 'hide away den'. You could re-create a known story or make one up yourself.

Keep this den up for a while so the child can bring his/her own activities into the space.

# Play = All I need for learning

Rough and tumble play is vital for development.

- Children learn best when they are active, moving and using their senses - it helps them to remember and recall.
- When we are using both sides of the brain, physical and thinking; optimal learning occurs.

# Make and do

Make a blanket fort with your child!

Get active

Children love using their bodies to crawl, walk, run, jump and climb. The more opportunities you give them to burn off energy, the happier they'll be.

Visit a National Park this month with your children

Play = imagination, creating, problem-solving

'When playing, I'm always right'

Creating your own home learning environment

All children and young people need to play. The impulse to play is innate. Play is a biological, psychological and social necessity, and is fundamental to the healthy development and well being of individuals and communities.

Box play

- Gather a number of empty boxes of all sizes.
- Provide paint, fabric, books, dress up clothes etc.
- Watch what your children do with these resources and observe the games they begin to play. Join in and play alongside them.

You might be called on to take on the role of princess, knight or superhero? Enjoy!

Mummy, daddy and me

Four year olds happily develop their own early literacy skills, when allowed to practice and try

out their reading and writing skills as   part of their natural daily play and not as a separate sit at the table and lean activity - and with no need for pressure.

Your child will still love to be involved in your daily chores, so take advantage of these to develop reading and writing. Let them write their own shopping lists or leave messages for family members.

Provide old birthday cards or calendars. Look for writing together when out and about - use

- road signs
- food packages etc.

and see if your child can find letters from their name. It is especially important for your child to see you reading and writing too!

Building block for development

"My Brain Grows better when you play with me!"

 **Playing in the Puddles**

Buy some cheap wellies and paint images all over them. Go out and splash in the puddles with your children and observe what happens to the paint.

Gather various items from your home, some that float and some that sink. Take them out to the puddles and play 'sailing' games with your child.

Play = 'All I need for Learning'

Play is a key opportunity for children to think creatively and flexibly, solve problems and link ideas. Establish the enabling conditions for rich play:

- space
- time
- flexible resources
- choice, control
- warm and supportive relationships

Challenges are essentially problems that the children have to work together to solve.

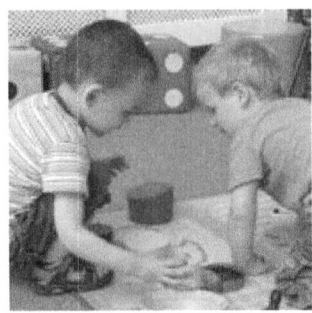 # Make and do

Make and fly a parachute with your child!

Get active

Being active should be encouraged from birth. Before your baby begins to crawl, encourage them to be physically active by reaching and grasping, pulling and pushing, and moving their head, body and limbs during daily routines, and during supervised floor play, including tummy time.

Lay your baby down so that they can kick their legs.
Once your baby has started crawling, let them crawl around the floor. First, make sure it's safe .

Get messy - Touch, feel, see, smell and learn.

Creating your own home Learning Environment

Young children need to move, to learn and remember things, to take experiences in through their senses as they move. Sitting still for too long can disrupt learning.

Go on an Insect hut

Get a large Tupperware container from your cupboards. Fill it with moss, grass, stones and leaves. Go through your garden and hunt and collect insects and place them in their new home!

Set up an insect picnic for them and share lunch together.

Mummy, daddy and me

4 year olds are very open to possibilities and have an enthusiasm for using ideas and materials in lots of different ways. For example, a saucepan can be a spaceman's helmet.

Support your child's growing creativity and imagination by providing simple props for their pretend play. A box of hats and bags can provide hours of fun and enjoyment, and you will be helping your child express their own individual ideas and thoughts as they pretend to be someone or something else.

Building block for development

"My brain grows better when you talk with me!"

Take you child/ren on a walk. Talk about things you see, things you hear and things you feel. Name them, share ideas about them, re-create the sounds they make and find something funny or scary or exciting about the things your child is the most interested in.

Talk about your favourite things and why. Repeat the words you've used over and over so the child can learn them.

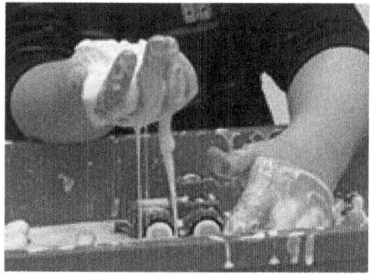

Play = 'All I need for Learning'

If I see it, feel it, hear it, I learn all about it.

When the senses are engaged, memories are made.

 Make and do!

Make and fly paper aeroplanes with your children!

Visit this web clip to find out how to make a free and easy, yet effective paper aeroplane.

Toys that your child can pick up and move around will help improve their co-ordination and develop the muscles in their arms and hands.

Play a hide and seek game!

Hide your child's favourite items around your home or garden. When they find them encourage them to create a game with their toys!

The more opportunities you give them to burn off energy, the happier they'll be.

Play is fun; but its hard work too!

Creating your own home learning environment

They may not get paid for it, but children's play is their work. It's a full-time occupation... and it's important. The early years are the time when a child's brain is developing, making connections and creating the network of skills that they need for the rest of their lives.

Salt dough play

Decide what city, fortress, play space or fantasy land you will create
Play with your child making the various models needed
Bake them when completed
Paint them and display them on a large board or tray
Add people, plants, paper or fabric to bring your scene to life

When your child has mastered using a wide range of tools, such as scissors, pencils and cutlery, they will want to to practice these regularly to develop the muscles in their wrists and hands.

Providing play-doh, jigsaws, sewing kits and craft activities will be both enjoyable and useful in supporting your child's physical development- aiding their handwriting skills later in their school life!

 # Building block for development

"From the moment I was born I needed you! I couldn't do much but everything I did, the sounds and movements I made were for you. I was asking you to respond to me so that I could live."

Play 'Simon Says' game with me.
You say and do: Simon says (action) 'touch your nose'
I copy and do the action. 'I touch my nose'

Name what I am doing as I do it so I can learn language too.

 # Play = 'All I need for learning'

We need adults who show genuine interest, offer encouragement, clarify ideas and ask open questions as they play with children, in order to support and extend children's thinking and help them to make connections in learning.

Make and do

Make sock puppets with your children!

By getting your children out and about, you'll probably find they sleep better and are more easygoing. By giving them the chance to exercise, you'll be helping their muscle development and general fitness. It also starts habits that will help them grow into fit, healthy adults.

Make a small obstacle course in your garden this month!
Use crates, planks, hoola-hoops, benches and mats and put together an obstacle course that will challenge your children!
Taking risks and learning from them is an inevitable and important part of growing up. We parents should encourage this in our children!

'I get more from play when you play with me.

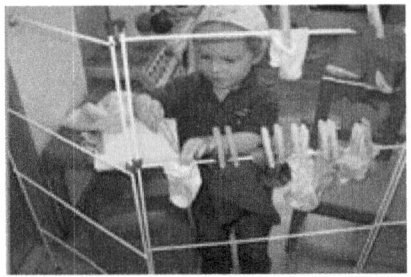

Creating your own home learning environment

Representing ideas and experiences

Children deepen their understanding as they recreate experiences or communicate their thinking in many different ways; in role-play or small world play, pictures, movements, models, and talk.

Doll play

Gather a selection of dolls, teddies, stuffed toys or action figures along with a baby bath, lotion, diapers, towels, powder, clothes, baby toys etc.

Play and recreate giving the doll a bath, modelling for your child how to complete this task in full, playing alongside them, labelling their actions and introducing new words and concepts.

Mummy, daddy and me

Children of 3 will chat to themselves as they play. They are developing their own creative use of grammar
and pronunciation. They can even make up their own new words and practice using words they have heard you saying.

By providing small world toys, such as dolls houses, farms, garages, soft toys and puppets, you can encourage your child to try out using new words and, by spending time together, they can learn all about conversations.

Building block for development

'When I am close to you my body begins to work in tune with yours.
When you feel excited or stressed your heart beasts faster and so does mine. When you feel calm your heart
beats slower, so does mine.'

Have 'Sofa Time' with your child each day for 10 minutes.

Spend time reading a favourite book or talking about an activity from the day or just chatting about whatever the child wants to talk about with you!

Play = 'All I need for learning'

From the moment children are born they are actively seeking out stimulation and

opportunity.

Their brains have extra cell connections which either grow or die, depending on the response from those around them. The way we stimulate a child shapes the brain structure.

What happens in the early years has a direct impact on the child's capacity for living, learning and relating as a social being.

The child needs adults to be:

- Sensitive
- Regularly available and reliable
- Warm
- Responsive
- Consistent

Make and do

Make a collage with your children!

Do what you can to get your children interested in Sports!

Support your kids in sports, clubs or any other activities that may interest them.

Joining a weekend club sport ensures commitment to a team and regular exercise.

When I play I learn about what makes me happy.

Creating your own home learning environment

Meeting physical and mental challenges

Working out what to do, trying hard, persevering with problems, finding out and thinking for themselves are opportunities for developing real understanding. These challenges may occur in play, or in real-life or planned activities.

Pots and pans play

Set out a variety of pots, pans, safe cooking utensils, spoons, forks, bowls; along with dried pasta, beans, rice and/ or lentils. Play cooking, pouring, filling and emptying games with your child and use language to extend their understanding of various concepts and action words.

By six months old, your baby sees and hears the world almost as well as you do. His/her communication skills are expanding rapidly too, including squeals, bubbling sounds and babbling.

Sharing books with your child comes into its own now, as s/he will enjoy looking at bright pictures and having a quiet snuggle on your lap. Reading provides an opportunity for cuddling and socialising that both you and your baby can enjoy.

As you share the pictures repeat to your baby any sounds that they make, acknowledging you are pleased with their efforts.

Building block for development

Find some of your own time to do the special things that help you relax. You have to look after yourself well if you want to look after your children well.

All I need for learning

That can we do in our setting?

A teacher's perception of a student's intelligence strongly affects the student's own view of his or her ability, and the pupil's opinions of peers are heavily influenced by such perceptions. Oxford Brookes 2000

Make sure you support children in feeling good about themselves.

Make and do

Love flowers and plants and watching them grow?

Make sure you get plenty of variety

Make a list of enjoyable activities your family like to take part in, such as dancing and climbing, cycling or bug hunting, and place them in a jar.

Pick a different activity to do each week as a family.

By varying your activities, you are less likely to get bored and lose interest.

Learning: it's not just about table work.

"All this sitting down stops me learning"

Creating your own home learning Environment

Playing - indoors and out, alone and with others, quietly or boisterously - allows children to find out about things, try out and practise ideas and skills, take risks, explore their feelings, learn from mistakes, be in control and think imaginatively. Playing is an important centre of learning for young children.

Den building

Gather a variety of objects and place in your garden or garage this month for your children to create dens from. (Chairs, mats, blankets, large sticks, large pieces of fabric, cushions, baskets, string, laundry pegs, etc)

Allow your children to create the den however they choose. You can also support them in making even more complex dens when you have time to play with them. They will learn so much from your ideas too!

Mummy, daddy and me

It is not unusual for 2 1/2 year olds to stop and start in their flow of speech.

They have to gather their thoughts and are trying to express something for which they don?t have all the words.

Your child's language benefits enormously from having your attention, patience and encouragement. Really try to show an interest in what your child is saying or asking.

This is the beginning of the 'what and why' questions and it can be exhausting, but remember, your child is only trying to find out about their world.

 ## Building block for development

Playing helps me make sense of my world. I can find out how things work and fit together. I copy what
you do and begin to find out how it feels to be a person who can do things.

Make sure you let me play on my own sometimes so I can experience this.

Place all your Tupperware and wooden spoons and other safe kitchen items on the floor and allow your child to explore and build and create with them.

Play = 'All I need for Learning'

We remember

- 10% of what we read

- 20% of what we hear
- 30% of what we see
- 50% of what we see and hear
- 70% of what we discuss with others
- 80% of what we personally experience
- 95% of what we teach others

When I am interested and challenged it helps me to love learning.

I will develop the life-long skill of a hunger for 'new learning'.

Make and do

 Make a Dinosaur land with your child.

t how to make a free and easy, yet very real dinosaur land out of a box and other junk you may have lying around.

Its perfect for make believe play with your child!

Get active try not to drive so much

We can all be more active as part of our daily lives. Walk rather than drive and encourage your kids to
cycle and walk where possible.

If you're out with the kids on the bus, why not get off a stop early and walk the rest of the way to your destination? You can also spend time talking about all you see!

Being active throughout daily life by walking and cycling is a great way for your children to achieve their daily 60 minutes of activity. Read more »

Play - Not a luxury, a necessity! 'Don't rush me, I need time to play and learn'

Creating your own home learning environment

Children deepen their understanding as they recreate experiences or communicate their thinking in many different ways; in role-play or small world play, pictures, movements, models, and talk.

Gather a variety of logs, sticks, pine cones, stones, plants and flowers, wooden planks etc and create a bug hotel.

Sit back and watch the bugs come and stay!

Perhaps you can give your children a magnifying glass, a camera, paper and pens etc so they can explore what they find and record what they see!

Four year olds are very open to possibilities and have an enthusiasm for using ideas and materials in lots of different ways.
For example, a saucepan can be a spaceman's helmet.

Support your child's growing creativity and imagination by providing simple props for their pretend play. A box of hats and bags can provide hours of fun and enjoyment, and you will be helping your child express their own individual ideas and thoughts as they pretend to be someone or something else.

Building block for development

"My brain is very active, but it still can't work on it's own. I need my brain to be linked to the brain of an adult. I need you to respond to me so that I can learn to manage my own responses?

Play 'Ready Steady Go' games each day with your child, whenever you can. Allow your child to lead the next action. (e.g. Ready, Steady, Splash the water! Ready, Steady, jump on the bed!)

Play = 'All I need for learning

A child learns through play - in all ways; a truth adults do not always understand.

'Young children learn best by playing and following their own curiosities, by solving real problems, such as how to balance a stack of blocks, or how to negotiate a zipper, put together a picture puzzle and most of all, by making mistakes and trying again.'

David Elkind, 'The Hurried Child'

Make and do

Make a book with your child.

A silly, funny or interesting personalised book all about what your child is interested in.

Be active together

Why not bond with the kids by doing some physical activity together? It's important that you set a good example - you are your child's most important role model - and the activity will always improve your own health as well!

- Go for walks or play active games
- Play a game of ball together
- Join an exercise class together
- Play physical games with family and friends (tag, Frisbee, catch, hide and seek)
- Plan a nightly jog or walk
- Go golfing as a family
- Play a game of one-on-one basketball or soccer with family

- # Creating your own home learning environment

  - There is no place for dull, repetitive activities. Laughter, fun, and enjoyment, sometimes being whimsical and nonsensical, are the best contexts for learning.

    Activities can be playful even when they are not actually play.

- # Make mud pies and petal perfume

- Gather old pots, baking trays, spoons, jugs and bowls and place them in a space in your garden where your children can make mud pies and petal perfume. Let the imagination begin!

-

Mummy, daddy and me

- Two and three year olds are very motivated to use their growing fine motor skills in everyday activities, which adults may discount as they don't see them as learning or play. Young children love joining in with real cooking, washing up, tidying and dusting.

- You may not think to involve your child, as you find these things boring and tedious, but from your child's point of view they are doing 'grown-up' tasks and putting into practice all of those physical skills they have learnt - try to find time to do things together.

Building block for development

- "Being able to use words is so important to me because it is language that makes my brain work together in an organised way.

- I love it when you listen to me too. It makes me feel like a real person who matters and it helps my brain to build patterns for communicating!"

- Take time Everyday to talk to your child, no matter how old they are! Even if they aren't using words you understand, their babble and sounds are their first words. Copy them and give them new words to learn!

Play = 'All I need for learning'

- "For children to be confident to try new activities and initiate ideas, practitioners will need to provide an environment that allows a wide range of choices and opportunities for self-initiated activity." QCA, 2000

Make and do

- Make a Puppet Theatre with your child and tell fun and silly stories together!

- Find out how to make a free and easy yet very effective Puppet Theatre.

- You can use toys, sock puppets or stuffed animals to tell your stories!

Get active

- ## Play at home

- Children need and want the freedom of real play rather than virtual entertainment and passive TV time.

- At home, parents are often 'too busy' to play with their children. Parental concern, while sometimes justified, may lead us to be over protective. Can you imagine a childhood without muddy knees or grazed palms?

- All work and no play certainly makes for a dull life. Children need real play, and adults need to set the scene so that children can lead their own play activities. If not, we are in danger of losing childhood altogether.

Final word;

Don't worry about things, often perception makes things feel worst than they actually are/will be. It does get easier as your baby gets older. I found by about 6 months I knew what I was doing. I had systems for everything and would be able to get everything packed up and get out the house much quicker and stress free than before. I also became better at interpreting what my baby wanted and he became more content in himself. He would play without demanding so much of my attention and would go for longer between meals by about 7 months. However as we left one stage and some things got easier, we would start a next stage of our journey and somethings would get harder i.e. as he was crawling about more I had to change the way I changed my sons nappy to stop him crawing away whilst I was changing him. Having him on solid foods was easier but fitting his feeds, naps and bottles in so that he was eating late enough to stay full but not too late before eating etc. was a challenge in itself. He would also put his hands in his mouth and smear food all over himself and me, the amount of stain remover I used increased rapidly (in the end I would keep a bucket in the downstairs cloackroom full of water and stin remover, all his clothes would go in there and then I would put them all in the wash every other day). Different stages bring different issues and you will need a different approach to deal with them.

It would be foolish not to listen to experts but don't let experts dictate to you or tell you how to bring up your children, this is your choice. Go with the flow/trust your instincts. Don't get too hung up on doing things. Get to know your babies cues.

Babies need independent play to learn how to play alone and they need you to play with them so that they feel loved and supported and know how to play with others and can develop social skills, the more time they have to play with other children and learn how to share etc. the better their social skills will be. Its good to hold your baby a lot, give them lots of cuddles and love and attention. This will make them secure. When they feel loved and secure they are relaxed and develop better.

Appreciate the small things - take time for your child. Don't worry about what needs to be done. Cuddle your child as soon as you get home for a minute.

It's easy to be hard on yourself. Other mums tell you that it's easy & you think why am I finding it hard. It's normal everyone finds it hard & no one is perfect.

Being a parent is hard, there is no set way and each child is different, you will worry that you are doing everything well enough. Others forget and say that they found it easy, its tough when they say they found it easy and you think well why am I finding it hard. Often they are not telling the truth or they forget or they are going through an easy stage but find it hard later on so try not to compare yourself with others/don't compare your child. There are different stages..

'One good mother is worth a hundred school masters' - Anon

Don't get too caught up in the advice & what you should do. Follow your instinct and do what's right for you. People have survived for 100s of years doing things there way and not by the book. Although new research is useful all children are different and there is no manual so trust your instincts.

<u>Important points for any parent to remember;</u>

- **Don't stress if can't breast feed**
- **Make bottles in advance**
- **Don't do baby led weaning**
- **Feed at 4 months purée**
- **Have more routine / structure - less activities & put baby down to sleep b4 over tired/falls asleep.**
- **If wingy do nappy, try sleep then feed/water or give a toy.**
- **Carry on giving cuddles - make the most of cuddles / feeds.**
- **Trust yourself.**
- **Keep calm.**
- **Don't over think / over analyse**
- **Sleep when you can**

Bibliography

Net mums

Forums and talking to friends and family

Sure start NCT sessions

Department of Health

Doublet PM, Benson CB, Nadel AS, et al. 1997. Improved birth weight table for neonates developed from gestations dated by early ultrasonography. Journal of Ultrasound Medicine 16:241

Hadlock FP, Shah YP, Kanon DJ, et al. 1992. Fetal crown rump length: Reevaluation of relation to menstrual age with high resolution real-time US. Radiology 182(2):501-5

Usher R and McLean F. 1969. Intrauterine growth of live-born Caucasian infants at sea level: Standards obtained from measurements in 7 dimensions of infants born between 25 and 44 weeks of gestation. Pediatrics 74(6):901-10

Wigglesworth JS. 1996. Perinatal Pathology. Second Edition. W.B. Saunders Company. p.24

BBC web site health pages

The guardian – science pages (article on fertility Tuesday 20th October 2009).

M Sunderland, The Science of Parenting.

Brain rules for babies: how to raise a smart child – John Medina

Lightning Source UK Ltd.
Milton Keynes UK
UKOW07f2309030116

265685UK00012B/356/P